Principles of
SHOULDER
IMAGING

Principles of
SHOULDER
IMAGING

Editor

David J. Sartoris, M.D.

Professor of Radiology
Musculoskeletal Imaging Section
Chief, Quantitative Bone Densitometry
UCSD Medical Center
University of California, San Diego

McGRAW-HILL, INC.
Health Professions Division

New York St. Louis San Francisco Auckland Bogotá
Caracas Lisbon London Madrid Mexico City Milan
Montreal New Delhi San Juan Singapore
Sydney Tokyo Toronto

PRINCIPLES OF SHOULDER IMAGING

Copyright © 1995, by McGraw-Hill, Inc. All rights reserved. Printed in the United States
of America. Except as permitted under the United States Copyright Act of 1976, no part
of this publication may be reproduced or distributed in any form or by any means, or
stored in a data base or retrieval system, without the prior written permission of the
publisher.

1234567890   KGP   KGP   987654

ISBN 0-07-054941-9

This book was set in Garamond by Ruttle, Shaw & Wetherill, Inc.
The editors were Jane Pennington and Mariapaz Ramos Englis
the production supervisor was Richard C. Ruzycka;
the cover designer was José Fonfrias;
the page layout was done by Tony Voss and Edward Goshow;
the indexer was Maria Caughlin for Ruttle, Shaw & Wetherill, Inc.
Quebecor Printing/Kingsport was printer and binder.

Library of Congress Cataloging-in-Publication Data

Principles of shoulder imaging / editor, David J. Sartoris.
     p.   cm.
  Includes bibliographical references.
  ISBN 0-07-054941-9
  1. Shoulder—Imaging.   I. Sartoris, David J.
  [DNLM: 1. Shoulder—radiography.   2. Shoulder—injuries.
3. Shoulder—pathology.   4. Shoulder Joint—radiography.   WE 810
P957 1994]
RC939.P75 1994
617.5'720754—dc20
DNLM/DLC
for Library of Congress   94-32749

TO MY PARENTS, HELEN AND CORNELIUS, WHO
TAUGHT ME THE REWARDS OF SELF-DISCIPLINE
AND HARD WORK

TO MY DEAR WIFE AND BEST FRIEND, CYD, THE
LOVE OF MY LIFE, FOR HER ENCOURAGEMENT,
SUPPORT, AND COMPANIONSHIP

TO PATIENTS SUFFERING FROM CLINICAL
DEPRESSION, MAY THIS BOOK PROVIDE HOPE
BY SERVING AS PROOF THAT THE DISEASE CAN
BE DEFEATED

CONTENTS

Contributors   ix

Preface   xi

Acknowledgments   xiii

1. Technical Aspects of Shoulder Imaging   1
  1A. Conventional Radiography and Tomography   1
    William J. Vanarthos
  1B. Technical Aspects: Fluoroscopy and Contrast Arthrography   13
    David S. Levey, Shannon M. Berry, David J. Sartoris
  1C. Technical Aspects: Computed Tomography with Normal Anatomy   33
    William E. Palmer, Susan V. Kattapuram
  1D. Technical Aspects: Magnetic Resonance Imaging with Normal Anatomy   45
    Mahvash Rafii, Hossein Firooznia
  1E. Technical Aspects: Ultrasonography of the Shoulder   65
    David J. Sartoris
  1F. Technical Aspects: Scintigraphic Techniques   75
    Penny R. Vande Streek, Robert F. Carretta, Frederick L. Weiland, David K. Shelton, Leonard Rosenthall
  1G. Technical Aspects: Interventional Procedures   103
    J. F. Naouri, L. Bellaiche, B. Hamze, J. M. Bondeville, J. M. Tubiana, J. D. Laredo

2. Normal Variants and Artifacts   117
    Bttavin Jankharia, Theodore E. Keats, David J. Sartoris

3. Congenital and Developmental Disorders of the Shoulder: Imaging Principles   141
    Joan K. Zawin, Andrew K. Poznanski

4. Imaging of Shoulder Infections   175
    Cheryl A. Petersilge

5. Imaging of Bone Tumors in the Shoulder   193
    Roger Kerr, Bruce Wollman, David J. Sartoris

6. Imaging of Soft Tissue Neoplasms in the Shoulder   227
    Philip M. Hughes, Charles S. Resnik

7. Imaging of Bone Marrow Disorders in the Shoulder   241
    Joseph S. Yu, Bor-Yau Yang, David J. Sartoris

8. Osseous Trauma to the Shoulder: Imaging Principles   263
    Ronald Hendrix, Lee F. Rogers

9. Imaging of Shoulder Instability   285
David A. Rubin, Murray K. Dalinka, Richard J. Herzog

10. Soft Tissue Injury to the Shoulder: Imaging Principles   315
Curtis W. Hayes, William E. Palmer

11. Postoperative Imaging of the Shoulder   335
Kyle C. Bryans, Leyla H. Alparslan, Barbara N. Weissman

12. Endocrine and Metabolic Disorders of the Shoulder:
Imaging Appearances and Diagnoses   353
Dennis J. Stoker

13. Rheumatic Disorders of the Shoulder:
Imaging Principles   375
Serge Sintzoff, Serge Sintzoff II

14. Imaging of Neuromuscular Disease of the Shoulder   401
Robert R. Brown, Alain Chevrot, David J. Sartoris

15. Miscellaneous Conditions of the Shoulder:
Imaging Principles   413
Mark D. Murphey

16. Imaging of the Shoulder: A Surgical Perspective   431
Joseph P. Iannotti

Index   445

CONTRIBUTORS

Leyla H. Alparslan, M.D. [11]
Fellow in Radiology
Harvard Medical School
Fellow in Radiology
Beth Israel Hospital
Boston, Massachusetts

L. Bellaiche, M.D. [1G]
Service de Radiologie osseuse
Hôpital Larisoisiere
Paris, France

Shannon M. Berry, M.D. [1B]
Research Assistant
UCSD School of Medicine
La Jolla, California

J. M. Bondeville, M.D. [1G]
Service de Radiologie
Hôpital Saint-Antoine
Paris, France

Robert B. Brown, M.D. [14]
Resident, Department of Diagnostic Radiology
The Western Pennsylvania Hospital
Pittsburgh, Pennsylvania
Research Fellow
University of California at San Diego
San Diego, California

Kyle C. Bryans, M.D. [11]
Assistant Professor of Radiology
University of Kansas
Assistant Professor of Radiology
Kansas Medical Center
Kansas City, Kansas

Robert F. Carretta, M.D. [1F]
Nuclear Medicine Director
Roseville Hospital
Roseville, California
Associate Clinical Professor of Radiology
University of California, Davis
Sacramento, California

The numbers in brackets following the contributors' names refer to the chapters written or co-written by the contributors.

Alain Chevrot, M.D. [14]
Service de Radiologie B
Hopital Cochin
Paris, France

Murray K. Dalinka, M.D. [9]
Professor of Radiology
Hospital of the University of Pennsylvania
Philadelphia, Pennsylvania

Hossein Firooznia, M.D. [1D]
Professor of Radiology
New York University School of Medicine
NYU Medical Center
New York, New York

B. Hamze, M.D. [1G]
Service de Radiologie
Hôpital Saint-Antoine
Paris, France

Curtis W. Hayes, M.D. [10]
Associate Professor of Radiology
Director of Trauma and Musculoskeletal Sections
Department of Radiology
Medical College of Virginia Hospitals
Richmond, Virginia

Ronald Hendrix, M.D. [8]
Associate Professor of Radiology
Northwestern University Medical School
Chief, Section of Musculoskeletal Radiology
Northwestern Memorial Hospital
Director of Radiology
Rehabilitation Institute of Chicago
Chicago, Illinois

Richard J. Herzog, M.D. [9]
Associate Professor of Radiology
Hospital of the University of Pennsylvania
Philadelphia, Pennsylvania

Philip M. Hughes, M.D. [6]
Consultant Radiologist
Derriford Hospital
Plymouth, England

Joseph P. Iannotti, M.D. [16]
Associate Professor
Orthopaedic Surgery
Chief of the Shoulder Service
Hospital of the University of Pennsylvania
Philadelphia, Pennsylvania

Bttavin Jankharia, M.D. [2]
Visiting Radiologist
LTMGH Hospital, Sion, Bombay
Bombay, India
Radiologist
Bombay Hospital
Bombay, India
Research Fellow
V.A. Hospital, University of California at San Diego
San Diego, California

Susan Kattapuram, M.D. [1C]
Associate Professor of Radiology
Harvard Medical School
Associate Radiologist
Massachusetts General Hospital
Boston, Massachusetts

Theodore E. Keats, M.D. [2]
Professor of Radiology
University of Virginia Health Sciences Center
Charlottesville, Virginia

Roger Kerr, M.D. [5]
Staff Radiologist
Orthopaedic Hospital
Clinical Professor of Radiology
University of California School of Medicine
Los Angeles, California

Jean-Denis Laredo, M.D. [1G]
Chief of the Radiology Department
Hôpital Larisoisiere
Paris, France

David S. Levey, M.D. [1B]
Director of Orthopedic MRI
Chief of Musculoskeletal Imaging
Spohn Hospital Systems and
Doctors' Regional Medical Center
Corpus Christi, Texas

Mark D. Murphey, M.D. [15]
Chief Musculoskeletal Radiology
Armed Forces Institute of Pathology
Washington, D.C.

J. F. Naouri, M.D. [1G]
Service de Radiologie
Hopital Saint-Antoine
Paris, France

William E. Palmer, M.D. [1C,10]
Instructor in Radiology
Harvard Medical School
Assistant in Radiology
Massachusetts General Hospital
Boston, Massachusetts

Cheryl A. Petersilge, M.D. [4]
Assistant Professor of Radiology
University Hospitals of Cleveland
Case Western Reserve University School of Medicine
Cleveland, Ohio

Andrew K. Poznanski, M.D. [3]
Professor of Radiology
Northwestern University Medical School
The Children's Memorial Hospital
Chicago, Illinois

Mahvash Rafii, M.D. [1D]
Associate Professor of Clinical Radiology
New York University School of Medicine
NYU Medical Center
New York, New York

Charles S. Resnik, M.D. [6]
Associate Professor of Radiology
University of Maryland Medical Center
Baltimore, Maryland

Lee F. Rogers, M.D. [8]
Frederick J. Bradd and William Kennedy Professor
and Chairman Department of Radiology
Northwestern University Medical School
Chicago, Illinois

Leonard Rosenthall, M.D. [1F]
Professor of Radiology
McGill University
Director, Nuclear Medicine
The Montreal General Hospital
Montreal, Canada

David A. Rubin, M.D. [9]
Assistant Professor of Radiology
Montefiore University Hospital, UPMC
Pittsburgh, Pennsylvania

David J. Sartoris, M.D. [1B,1E,2,5,7,14]
Professor of Radiology
Musculoskeletal Imaging Section
Chief, Quantitative Bone Densitometry
UCSD Medical Center
University of California, San Diego
San Diego, California

David K. Shelton, M.D. [1F]
Assistant Professor of Radiology
University of California, Davis
Sacramento, California

Serge Sintzoff, M.D. [13]
Professeur à l'Université Libre de Bruxelles
Consultant aux Cliniques Universitaires de Bruxelles
Hopital Erasme
Université Libre de Bruxelles
Brussels, Beligum

Serge Sintzoff II, M.D. [13]
Radiologist
Institut Médico-Chirurgical
Edith Cavell
Consultant aux Cliniques Universitaires de Bruxelles
Hopital Erasme
Université Libre de Bruxelles
Brussels, Belgium

Dennis J. Stoker, M.D. [12]
Director of Clinical Radiology
Royal National Orthopaedic Hospital
London, England

J. M. Tubiana, M.D. [1G]
Chief of the Radiology Department
Hôpital Saint-Antoine
Paris, France

William J. Vanarthos, M.D. [1A]
Assistant Professor of Diagnostic Radiology
Chief of Musculoskeletal and Emergency Radiology
Chandler Medical Center
University of Kentucky
Lexington, Kentucky

Penny R. Vande Streek, M.D. [1F]
Nuclear Medicine Staff
Roseville Hospital
Roseville, California
Assistant Clinical Professor of Radiology
University of California, Davis
Sacramento, California

Frederick L. Weiland, M.D. [1F]
Nuclear Medicine Staff
Roseville Hospital
Roseville, California
Assistant Clinical Professor of Radiology
University of California, Davis
Sacramento, California

Barbara N. Weissman, M.D. [11]
Professor of Radiology
Harvard Medical School
Chief of the Musculoskeletal Radiology Section
Brigham & Womens Hospital
Department of Radiology
Boston, Massachusetts

Bruce Wollman, M.D. [5]
Research Associate in Radiology
University of California at San Diego School of Medicine
San Diego, California

Bor-Yau Yang, M.D. [7]
Attending Radiologist
Chang Cung Memorial Hospital
Kaohsiung, Taiwan
Research Fellow
UCSD School of Medicine
San Diego, California

Joseph S. Yu, M.D. [7]
Assistant Professor
Ohio State University Medical Center
Department of Radiology
Columbus, Ohio

Joan K. Zawin, M.D. [3]
Assistant Professor of Radiology
Northwestern University Medical School
The Children's Memorial Hospital
Chicago, Illinois

PREFACE

The articulations of the shoulder mechanism are perhaps the most fascinating joints in the human body and afford unique functional capabilities. Peculiar anatomical aspects of the glenohumeral articulation include marked disparity between humeral head size and glenoid depth, intimate connection between the loose joint capsule and rotator cuff musculature, and the combined intra- and extra-articular course of the biceps tendons. These features permit incredible freedom of movement in virtually every possible direction.

It is thus not surprising that shoulder dysfunction results in significant patient morbidity, chiefly manifested as pain and restricted functional ability. The impact of such symptoms on the life of an individual patient can range from inability to conduct activities of personal hygiene, to loss of occupational function and possibly employment, to the end of a career in professional sports. These considerations underscore the extreme importance of accurate diagnosis in the setting of shoulder dysfunction, which relies heavily upon imaging studies.

This book has been designed with these factors in mind, as well as to fill an important void in the diagnostic imaging literature. Previous books on the subject, although excellent, have been short and focused primarily on post-traumatic abnormalities of the shoulder. From its inception, this project has attempted to improve upon previous works in several important respects.

First, the book takes a unique modality-oriented and disease-oriented approach to the subject. Second, coverage is comprehensive, with the entire spectrum of shoulder pathology discussed and illustrated. Third, I have been blessed with the opportunity of working shoulder-to-shoulder with an exceptionally knowledge-able and creative team of contributors, who have added international perspectives from England, France, Belgium, Taiwan, and India. Finally, the insight of an orthopaedic surgeon on the indications for shoulder imaging is provided, and the extremely controversial topic of glenohumeral ultrasonography is covered by a completely unbiased author (straight from the shoulder!).

This book is probably best utilized as a reference text, although individuals with particular interest in the shoulder or musculoskeletal imaging in general may benefit from a cover-to-cover reading approach. The work is also intended to be useful for trainees in diagnostic imaging, orthopaedic surgery, rheumatology, and sports or occupational medicine.

Finally, this book is a tribute to the marvels of modern imaging technology, in that all modalities are applicable to the shoulder region. Bernard of Chartres used to say that we are like dwarfs on the shoulders of giants, seeing more than they, and at a greater distance, not because we are imbued with any sharpness of sight or physical distinction, but because we are carried high and raised up by their great height.[1,2] This statement might well refer to radiologists at the dawn of the twenty-first century. In preparing this work, I have put my shoulder to the wheel in an attempt to provide the reader with enhanced understanding of the subject matter. If in the process I have seen further than my predecessors, it has only been by standing on the shoulders of these giants.[3]

1. John of Salisbury, *Metalogicon* (1159), bk. III, ch. IV.
2. R. K. Merton, *On the Shoulders of Giants* (1965).
3. Adapted from Sir Isaac Newton's letter to Robert Hooke, 5 February 1675/6.

ACKNOWLEDGMENTS

This book could not have been completed without the dedication and hard work of each and every one of its outstanding contributors. My sincere gratitude is extended to this exceptional team of physicians, with whom it has been a pleasure working.

I would also like to thank Jane Pennington, Ph.D., of McGraw-Hill, Inc., for initially approaching me about the need for such a book, as well as my irreplaceable secretary, Gale Hurley. Her incredible patience, organization, and perseverance were essential to the successful completion of this project.

Finally and most important, I would like to acknowledge my mentor, colleague, and friend, Dr. Donald Resnick, for the knowledge and inspiration behind this work. During our ten years together, I have had the opportunity and pleasure to witness firsthand the preparation of his numerous masterful textbook contributions to the medical literature. Without question, the organism that stimulates physicians to write books is contagious, and I thank Dr. Resnick for his role as the ultimate vector in my case.

Principles of
SHOULDER
IMAGING

TECHNICAL ASPECTS OF SHOULDER IMAGING

CONVENTIONAL RADIOGRAPHY AND TOMOGRAPHY

William J. Vanarthos

Routine radiographic examination of the shoulder includes the distal clavicle, the scapula, and the proximal humerus, allowing visualization and interpretation of the glenohumeral joint and, at least in part, of the acromioclavicular joint. This is of practical significance since the sternoclavicular joint and proximal clavicle, though both intimately related to the function of the shoulder, generally are not studied following shoulder trauma unless specifically requested.[1] In addition, complete radiographic evaluation of the scapula requires special views.[1]

PLAIN RADIOGRAPHY

Glenohumeral Joint

Basic radiographic examination of the glenohumeral joint includes anteroposterior (AP) radiographs with the arm in both external and internal rotation (Fig. 1A-1).[1–3] With the arm in external rotation, the greater tuberosity is viewed in profile, allowing accurate detection of avulsion injuries of this structure and calcification of the supraspinatus tendon.[2] Internal rotation of the arm projects the greater tuberosity en face over the humerus and allows visualization of the lesser tuberosity near the glenohumeral joint.[2] This position may aid in detecting subtle calcifications of the infraspinatus and teres minor tendons along the outer margin of the humerus and of the subscapularis tendon adjacent to the lesser tuberosity. Internal rotation also provides a non-weight-bearing stress to the acromioclavicular joint, which may be useful in detecting Grade III joint separations, which are discussed later (Fig. 1A-2).[4]

Though highly informative, an AP radiograph of the shoulder with the arm in internal or external rotation does not allow adequate visualization of the glenohumeral joint.[1–3] To view the glenohumeral articulation tangentially, a true AP projection of the shoulder is obtained by rotating the patient 40° in a posterior oblique position (Fig. 1A-3).[2,3] A supine patient can be supported with a wedge.

In addition to the aforementioned AP frontal radiographs, it is very helpful routinely (and is mandatory for a trauma patient) to obtain another image approximately at a right angle to the frontal view.[1–3] This can be accomplished by using one of several projections. At our institution we favor obtaining either the axillary projection (Fig. 1A-4)[1–3,5] or the West Point projection (Fig. 1A-5).[2] Either of these views, though not obtained routinely at most institutions, provides more information about the shoulder joint than any other single projection.[1] Both clearly depict the coracoid and acromion processes, making it possible to diagnose minimally displaced fractures of these structures.[1] Also, fractures of the anterior and posterior cortical surfaces of the humeral head and subtle subluxations of the joint can be detected, and position and alignment of fracture fragments of the humeral neck can be assessed.[1] The West Point technique demonstrates the anteroinferior glenoid rim to best advantage and usually includes a portion of the chest wall as well, making it possible to detect concomitant rib fractures or pneumothoraces.

The axillary view is best obtained with the patient in a supine position with the arm abducted 90° (see Fig. 1A-4), but this may be difficult to achieve in cases of severe fractures or dislocations.[1,2] Satisfactory films can be acquired with only 10° to 15° of arm abduction with the central beam directed at the apex of the axilla.[1,3]

Similar difficulty may be encountered in trying to obtain the West Point view, which traditionally is taken with the patient lying prone with the arm abducted 90° and the hand dangling over the edge of the table. In this position the central beam is angled 25° cephalad and 25° medially (see Fig. 1A-5).[2] Alternatively, the patient can be evaluated in a sitting position with the arm slightly abducted and the central beam originating at the floor or ceiling (Fig. 1A-6). The latter method is much more

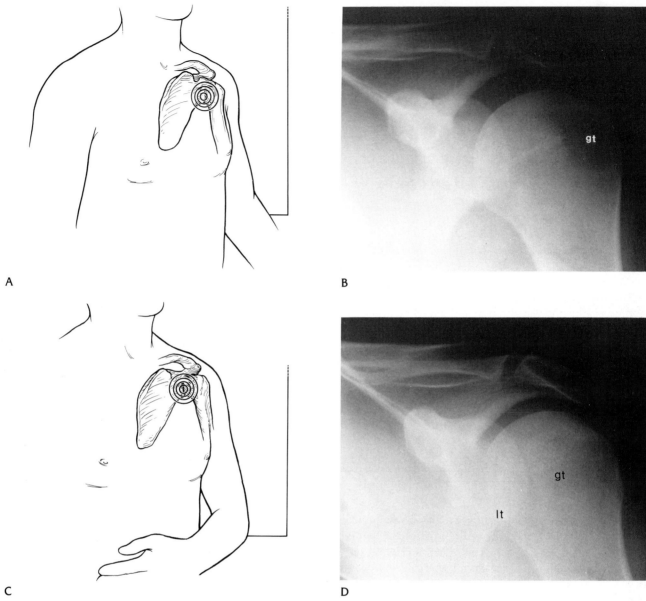

Figure 1A-1   Routine imaging of the glenohumeral joint. **A, B.** External rotation. The greater tuberosity (gt) is seen in profile. **C, D.** Internal rotation. The greater tuberosity (gt) projects over the humerus and the lesser tuberosity (lt) projects medially.

comfortable for the patient and is feasible in cases of significant shoulder trauma.

When the injury precludes evaluation of the shoulder with either an axillary or a West Point view, a true lateral projection of the scapula, or scapular Y view, can be obtained. This view is acquired with the patient in a 60° anterior oblique position (Fig. 1A-7),[2,3,6,7] either upright or recumbent, whichever is more comfortable. In this projection, the humeral head is centered over a Y configuration formed by the wing of the scapula, the scapular spine, and the coracoid process.

A multitude of other projections have been advocated

in the literature to evaluate the shoulder. In patients with a history of anterior dislocation of the glenohumeral joint or chronic shoulder instability, a variety of radiographs can be obtained, in an effort to depict a fracture of the anterior glenoid rim (bony Bankart lesion) or a compression fracture along the posterolateral aspect of the humeral head (Hill-Sachs lesion), lesions that are associated with these injuries.[2,3,6–13] Though standard views (Table 1A-1) most often are sufficient for diagnosing and analyzing these abnormalities, other projections have been described. These include Hermodsson's tangential projection,[2,14] the Didiee projection,[2,14] and, most nota-

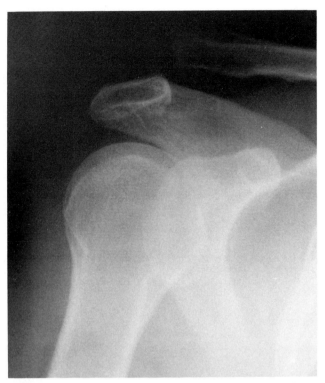

Figure 1A-2 Non-weight-bearing AP view of the glenohumeral joint with the arm in internal rotation elicits Grade III acromioclavicular joint separation.

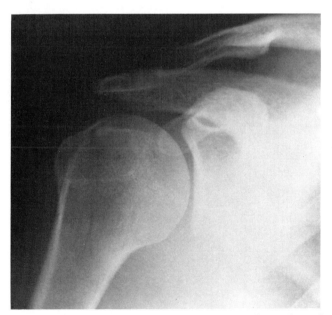

Figure 1A-3 True AP radiograph of the glenohumeral joint obtained with the patient rotated 40° posteriorly.

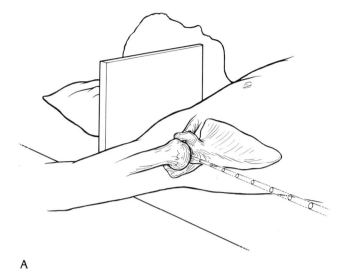

A

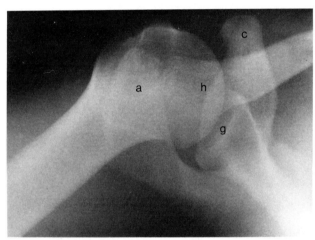

B

Figure 1A-4 Routine imaging of the glenohumeral joint: axillary views. **A, B.** Visualized structures include the coracoid process (c), acromion process (a), glenoid cavity (g), and humeral head (h).

bly, the Stryker notch projection.[2,3,14] The latter projection is acquired with the patient supine and the palm placed on top of the head with the elbow directed vertically. The central beam is angled 10° cephalad and centered on the palpable coracoid process (Fig. 1A-8).[2,3] In combination with routine AP frontal views (with the arm in, respectively, external and internal rotation) and an axillary or West Point view, the Stryker notch view is likely to reveal any significant shoulder injury.[3,14]

Another projection which has been recommended for acute shoulder trauma is the apical oblique projection.[8,11,12] To obtain this image, the patient is placed in the 45° posterior oblique position relative to the x-ray tube with the uninjured shoulder rotated away from the cassette (which is held vertical if the patient is seated and horizontal if supine).[12] The central beam is directed at an angle of 45° to the coronal plane of the patient's body and 45° caudad (Fig. 1A-9).[8,11,12] With this technique, a coronal profile of the glenohumeral joint is obtained that is ideal for detection of intraarticular fractures, dislocations, instability, glenoid injuries, and a Hill-Sachs deformity (Fig. 1A-10).[3,8,11]

Last, a view that has been used occasionally to visualize the bicipital groove is one made with the patient flexing the trunk across the examination table while holding the cassette on the forearms.[2] The central ray is directed vertically in a superoinferior direction (Fig. 1A-11).

In summary, a basic examination of the glenohumeral joint should include a frontal AP view with the patient's arm in internal rotation, a similar radiograph with the arm externally rotated, and either a West Point or an axillary view (see Table 1A-1). If owing to the patient's condition none of the three views is feasible, it is recommended that a 40° posterior oblique—or perhaps a Stryker notch—view be attempted.

Acromioclavicular Joint

Although the acromioclavicular articulation is visualized on routine views of the shoulder, it is seen to better advantage in the frontal projection with a cephalad tilt of the central beam of approximately 15° (Fig. 1A-12).[15]

Figure 1A-5 Routine imaging of the glenohumeral joint: West Point views. **A, B.** Note inclusion of a portion of the chest wall in addition to the coracoid process (c), acromion process (a), glenoid cavity (g), and humeral head (h).

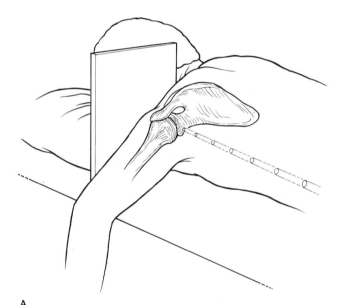

A

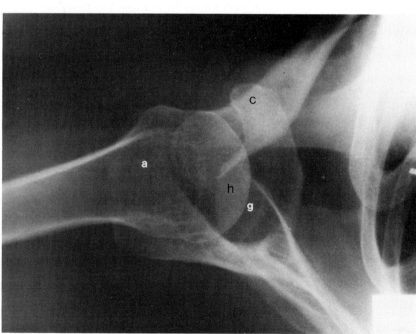

B

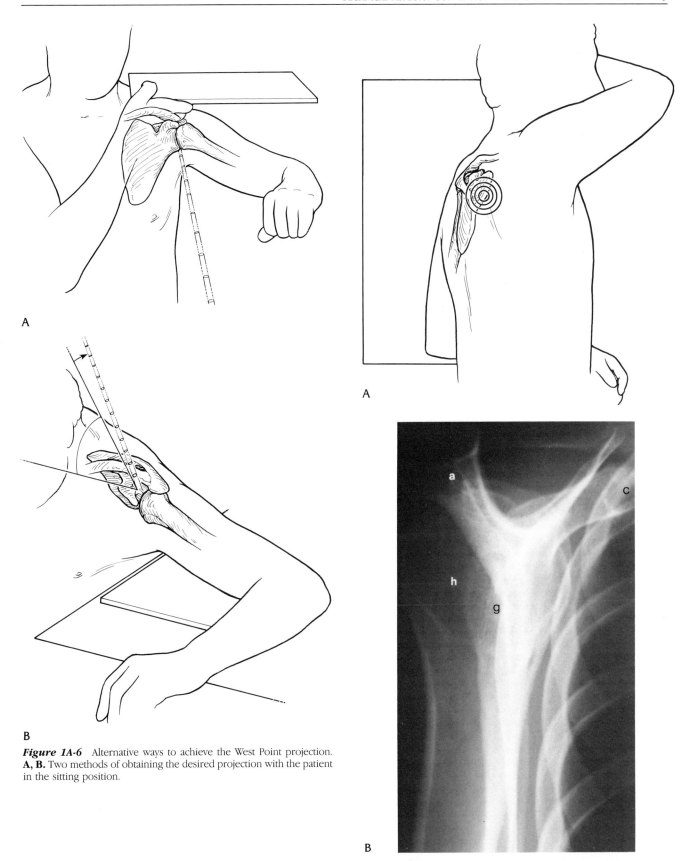

A

B

Figure 1A-6 Alternative ways to achieve the West Point projection. **A, B.** Two methods of obtaining the desired projection with the patient in the sitting position.

A

B

Figure 1A-7 Routine imaging of the glenohumeral joint. **A, B.** Anterior oblique, or scapular Y, views. The humeral head (h) is superimposed on the glenoid (g) between the coracoid process (c) anteriorly and the acromion process (a) posteriorly.

Table 1A-1   Radiographic Examination of the Glenohumeral Joint

BASIC VIEWS

AP, internal rotation
AP, external rotation
Axillary or West Point view

OPTIONAL VIEWS

40° posterior oblique
Stryker notch view
Scapular Y view
Apical oblique

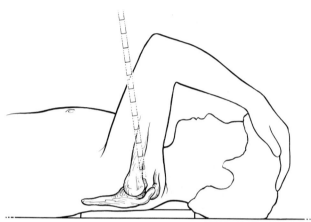

Figure 1A-8   Diagram of the Stryker notch projection. The patient's palm is placed on the head and the central beam is angled 10° cephalad.

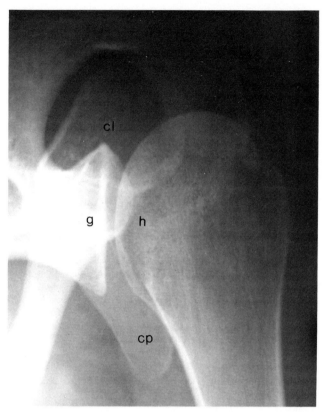

Figure 1A-10   Normal apical oblique radiograph clearly depicts the glenohumeral joint. Note also the glenoid (g), humeral head (h), clavicle (cl), and coracoid process (cp).

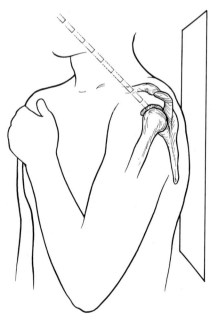

Figure 1A-9   Diagram illustrating positioning for the apical oblique view of the shoulder. The injured shoulder is placed in a 45° posterior oblique position, and the central beam is angled 45° caudad.

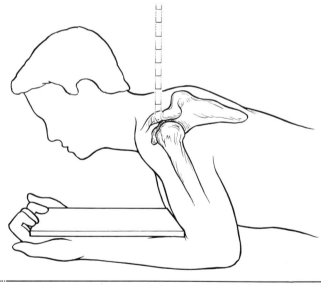

Figure 1A-11   Diagram of the bicipital groove projection. The patient flexes the trunk across the table while holding the cassette on the forearms. The central beam is oriented vertically.

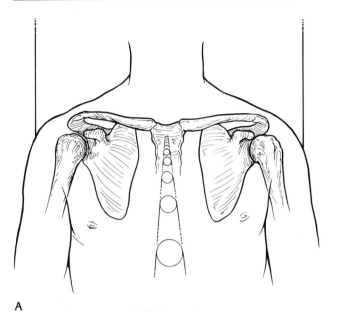

A

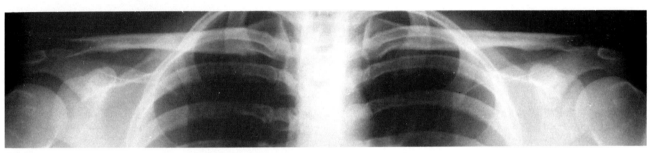

B

Figure 1A-12 Routine imaging of the acromioclavicular joint. **A, B.** Frontal projection with a cephalad tilt of the central beam of approximately 15°.

To diagnose acromioclavicular joint subluxation and dislocation an AP view with cephalad tilt, as described, is obtained of *both* shoulders, for comparison purposes. Traditionally, this is followed by a similar view made with weight-bearing stress applied to the joint in hope of eliciting a dissociation abnormality. It is best accomplished by tying weights of 5 to 15 lb (2.3 to 7 kg) from each wrist[2,16]; however, the maneuver is uncomfortable for the patient and can even be painful enough to require local anesthesia.[16] Thus, before stressing the joint with weights, we recommend that a standard AP frontal radiograph of the shoulder with the patient's arm in internal rotation first be obtained. This has proven effective in eliciting at least some Grade III acromioclavicular joint dissociations in which there is a tear of both the acromioclavicular and coracoclavicular ligaments.[4] The proposed mechanism is a force generated with internal rotation of the humerus that protracts and rotates the scapula so that the acromion levers the clavicle superiorly (Figs. 1A-2, 1A-13).[4] Though Grade I (no ligament disruption) and Grade II (acromioclavicular ligament disruption without coracoclavicular ligament disruption) injuries are not diagnosed with this method, the patient is treated conservatively in either case. Only for Grade III injuries is surgery contemplated, so recognition of this entity is most important. If a Grade III injury is not diagnosed using this standard view, a weight-bearing view of both shoulders is suggested, to confirm the absence of a Grade III dissociation and to diagnose more subtle (i.e., lesser grade) lesions. Other views, including a lateral projection, a lordotic frontal radiograph, a shoulder-forward projection, an axial projection, and a supraspinatus outlet view, have all been described,[2,3] but they are utilized less frequently.

A basic radiographic examination of the acromioclavicular joint should include an AP frontal film of both shoulders with 15° caudal angulation followed, in cases of suspected acromioclavicular joint separation, by an AP frontal radiograph of the affected side with the patient's arm internally rotated. If to this point no abnormality has

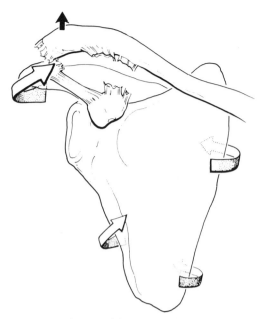

Figure 1A-13 With internal rotation of the arm (not illustrated), protraction and rotation of the scapula cause the acromion to lever the clavicle superiorly, thereby eliciting Grade III acromioclavicular joint dissociation.

been appreciated, an AP frontal weight-bearing image of both shoulders with caudal angulation similar to that of the initial film is obtained (Table 1A-2).

Sternoclavicular Joint

The sternoclavicular joint is a difficult articulation to study adequately with plain radiography. Often, conventional tomography or computed tomography (CT) must be employed to make a useful assessment.

Though frontal and oblique radiographs are frequently obtained they do not provide optimal visualization of this joint (Fig. 1A-14). Thus, a variety of special views have been advocated.[2] Hobbs's view or a lordotic view (Fig. 1A-15) may be beneficial, especially in cases of

Table 1A-2   Radiographic Examination of the Acromioclavicular Joint

BASIC VIEWS

AP, without weights (both joints)
AP, internal rotation without weights (affected joint)

OPTIONAL VIEW*

AP with weights (both joints)

* Used if AP internal rotation view of affected joint is normal or equivocal.

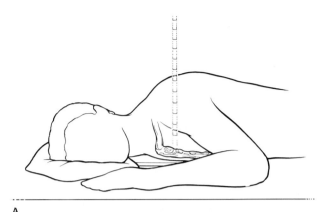

A

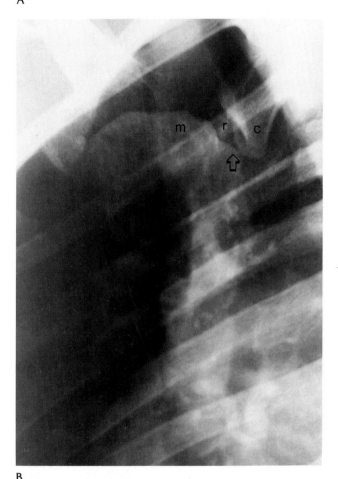

B

Figure 1A-14 Oblique projection of the sternoclavicular joint. **A, B.** Although the sternoclavicular joint can be visualized (*arrow*), it is partially obscured by an overlying rib (r). Note also the clavicle (c) and the manubrium (m).

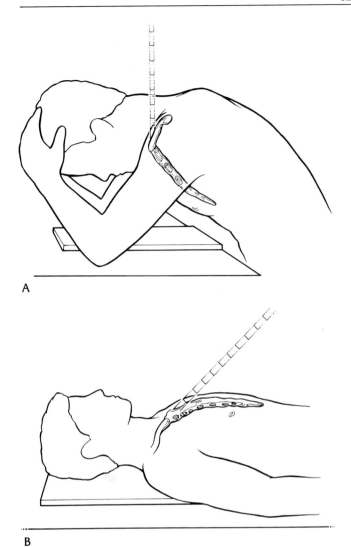

Figure 1A-15 Alternative positions for viewing the sternoclavicular joint. **A.** Hobbs's view taken with the patient bent over the table with hands on the head. **B.** Lordotic view taken with the patient supine (may be taken erect) and the central beam directed with a 40° to 50° cephalad tilt.

suspected subluxation or dislocation of the sternoclavicular joint.[2] The latter may be obtained with the patient supine or erect. Other projections, such as Heinig's view (in which the patient is recumbent with the arm closest to the tube abducted and the central ray centered at the sternoclavicular joint and directed along the axis of the clavicle) are occasionally helpful but are not commonly utilized.[2]

Trauma to the sternoclavicular joint usually is associated with sternal injury as well, mandating a properly penetrated coned lateral projection of the sternum, which can be acquired with the patient erect or recumbent. Long exposure times (on the order of 5 to 7 sec)

enhance the image since normal respiration blurs overlying rib and lung shadows.[2]

To evaluate the sternum and sternoclavicular joint one should obtain a lateral view of the sternum, and a posteroanterior image with the beam directed in a manner that minimizes confusing overlapping structures. To this end, of course, conventional tomography or CT is superb.

CONVENTIONAL TOMOGRAPHY

In general, the role of conventional tomography in the evaluation of musculoskeletal lesions has diminished significantly since the advent of advanced imaging techniques. CT and, more recently, magnetic resonance imaging (MRI) have to a large extent supplanted conventional tomography. With increasing demand for CT and MRI, however, conventional tomography may be a more expeditious approach to making a diagnosis. Furthermore, depending on the body part to be examined and the limitations on patient positioning imposed by CT or MR scanners, certain problems may be evaluated equally well, or even better, with conventional tomography.[3,17] In addition, though coronal or sagittal reconstruction is readily available with CT, key information may be lost during reformation.[17]

Conventional tomography is a technique that affords clearer visualization of specific structures that lie in a particular tissue plane by eliminating superimposed images of structures in other planes.[3,17,18] This is accomplished in most systems by blurring the unwanted structures via motion of the x-ray tube and film while the patient remains stationary.[17] In this scheme, structures that lie in the same focal plane ("slice") on the film remain focused while structures outside the focal plane are blurred.[17]

There are several important applications for conventional tomography in the assessment of bones, joints, and soft tissues: (1) identification of osteochondral defects, intraarticular and periarticular osseous bodies, and cortical disruption and sequestra in chronic osteomyelitis; (2) evaluation of fracture healing; (3) assessment of bone neoplasms; and (4) visualization of structures not seen adequately with other modalities.[17] Though conventional tomography is seldom indicated for the shoulder, it may be useful as an adjunct to routine plain films or special views in the evaluation of the sternoclavicular joint since superimposed thoracic structures usually obscure this region (Fig. 1A-16).[3,17,18]

Finally, in combination with arthrography, tomography may better delineate important ligamentous and tendinous structures outlined by contrast medium.[3,17]

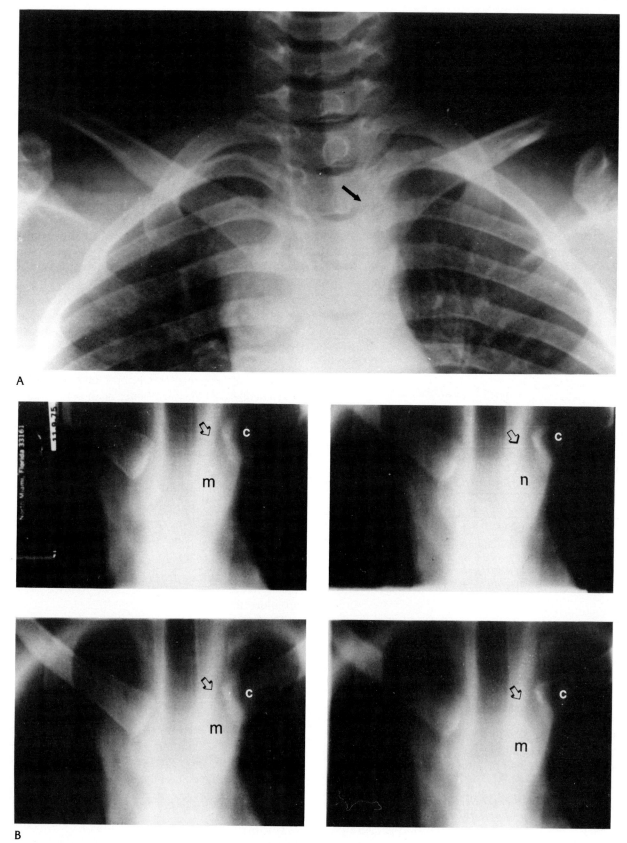

Figure 1A-16 Dislocation of the left sternoclavicular joint is better visualized with conventional tomography. **A.** AP frontal view of the sternoclavicular joints raises suspicion of left-sided dislocation (*arrow*). **B.** Tomographic slices of this region more clearly depict superior and posterior dislocation of the clavicle on the left (*arrows*). Clavicles (c), manubrium (m).

References

1. HARRIS JH, HARRIS WH, NOVELLINE RA: Shoulder, including clavicle and scapula, in Harris JH, Harris WH, Novelline RA (eds): *The Radiology of Emergency Medicine*, 3d ed, Baltimore, Williams & Wilkins, 1993, pp 283–336.
2. SARTORIS DJ, RESNICK D: Plain film radiography: Routine and specialized techniques and projections, in Resnick D, Niwayama G (eds): *Diagnosis of Bone and Joint Disorders*, 2d ed, Philadelphia, Saunders, 1988, pp 2–55.
3. BERQUIST TH: Shoulder and arm, in Berquist TH, Kricun ME (eds): *Imaging of Sports Injuries,* 1st ed, Gaithersburg, Md., Aspen, 1992, pp 221–265.
4. VANARTHOS WJ, EKMAN E, BOHRER SB: Radiographic diagnosis of acromioclavicular joint separation without weight bearing: Importance of internal rotation of the arm. *AJR* 162:120–122, 1994.
5. JONES A, WATT I: Diagnostic imaging of the shoulder joint. *Bailliere's Clin Rheumatol* 3:475–510, 1989.
6. DeSMET AA: Anterior oblique projection in radiography of the traumatized shoulder. *AJR* 134:515–518, 1980.
7. RUBIN SA, GRAY RL, GREEN WR: The scapular "Y": A diagnostic aid in shoulder trauma. *Radiology* 110:725–726, 1974.
8. KORNGUTH PJ, SALAZAR AM: The apical oblique view of the shoulder: Its usefulness in acute trauma. *AJR* 149:113–116, 1987.
9. WORKMAN TL, BURKHARD TK, RESNICK, D, et al.: Hill-Sachs lesion: Comparison of detection with MR imaging, radiography, and arthroscopy. *Radiology* 185:847–852, 1992.
10. HILL HA, SACHS MD: The grooved defect of the humeral head: A frequently unrecognized complication of dislocations of the shoulder. *Radiology* 35:690–700, 1940.
11. SLOTH C, LUNDGREN J: The apical oblique radiograph in examination of acute shoulder trauma. *Eur J Radiol* 9:147–151, 1989.
12. GARTH WP, SLAPPEY CE, OCHS CW: Roentgenographic demonstration of instability of the shoulder: The apical oblique projection. *J Bone Joint Surg* 66A:1450–1453, 1984.
13. ROKOUS JR, FEAGIN JA, ABBOTT HG: Modified axillary roentgenogram. A useful adjunct in the diagnosis of recurrent instability of the shoulder. *Clin Orthop* 82:84–86, 1972.
14. ROZING PM, DE BAKKER HM, OBERMANN WR: Radiographic views in recurrent anterior shoulder dislocation. *Acta Orthop Scand* 57:328–330, 1986.
15. PETTRONE FA, NIRSCHL RP: Acromioclavicular dislocation. *Am J Sports Med* 6:160–164, 1978.
16. KEATS TE, POPE TL: The acromioclavicular joint: Normal variation and the diagnosis of dislocation. *Skel Radiol* 17:159–162, 1988.
17. RESNICK D: Conventional tomography, in Resnick D, Niwayama G (eds): *Diagnosis of Bone and Joint Disorders*, 2d ed, Philadelphia, Saunders, 1988, pp 130–136.
18. MORAG B, SHAHIN N: The value of tomography of the sternoclavicular region. *Clin Radiol* 26:57–62, 1975.

1B

TECHNICAL ASPECTS: FLUOROSCOPY AND CONTRAST ARTHROGRAPHY

David S. Levey
Shannon M. Berry
David J. Sartoris

Fluoroscopy of the shoulder allows dynamic imaging of the glenohumeral relation, which can be observed in multiple static positions. In addition, both passive motion (achieved by the radiologist's placing the humerus in various positions about the glenoid) and active motion (by the patient directed to move the humerus) can be viewed in real time, in a rapid, noninvasive manner, relatively inexpensively. Expanding on this technology, percutaneous introduction of a small-gauge needle into the glenohumeral joint and injection of contrast medium and air, opacifies structures that would otherwise be invisible on fluoroscopy. Invaluable static and dynamic information can be obtained relating to the rotator cuff structures, articular surfaces, capsulolabral structures, and intracapsular bodies. In our discussion we combine the technical elements of fluoroscopy and shoulder arthrography with information about pathologic lesions that may be visualized with each procedure. The fluoroscopic and arthrographic investigation of shoulder problems follows a continuum from standard radiographic scout films, fluoroscopic examination of the shoulder, and needle guidance into the glenohumeral joint, to the contrast opacification and subsequent fluoroscopic and spot film examinations that represent the standard arthrographic examination of the shoulder.

FLUOROSCOPY

Physics

The fluoroscope has two main components: an x-ray source (cathode ray tube) and an image intensifier (x-ray receptor). All other parts are designed to provide appropriate protection for patients and radiologists or to facilitate the performance of the examination. The tube is equipped with an automatic x-ray collimator, cones, and magnification settings, to enhance the image representation by decreasing scatter and quantum mottle. The perceived brightness of the fluoroscope is dim, owing to the inherently small photon flux and subsequent statistical fluctuation of photon number, coupled with the rapid integration time of the retina. As a result, much effort is made by manufacturers to provide an efficient system for light amplification (i.e., the image intensifier) to improve the statistical quality of the image. Tabletop exposures should not exceed 10 R per minute,[1] and current equipment yields considerably less radiation. The fluoroscopic unit may be used alone or in combination with the arthrogram to examine shoulder structure and function. Additionally, cinefluoroscopy or videofluoroscopy can enhance a study by recording the examination, thus allowing playback for further scrutiny of subtle findings that may not be appreciated at the time of fluorographic monitoring or contrast injection. This can be important because, although the process of dark adaptation begins when the radiologist walks into a dimly lit room to begin the study, full visual adaptation, resulting from the shift from photopic to scotopic vision, may take as long as 20 minutes.[2] As the initial views may yield crucial results, a permanent record of the fluoroscopic portion of an arthrogram may be indicated, particularly when a subtle or difficult diagnosis such as a partial rotator cuff tear is being sought.

USES

Fluoroscopy is a fundamental tool that is used in many diagnostic procedures related to orthopedic and rheumatic disorders. This is readily apparent when one considers that fluoroscopy is a prerequisite to the performance of arthrography, bursography, tenography, and fluoroscopically guided biopsy procedures. Although computed tomography (CT) can monitor percutaneous biopsy procedures, many operators prefer fluoroscopy because of its lower cost and convenience. The applications of fluoroscopy in the shoulder are less well known, and some of the more common ones are described here.

The most valuable method for initial evaluation of fractures about the glenohumeral joint and proximal humerus remains conventional radiography. When initial radiographs are equivocal, additional views may be obtained. This is often time-consuming and commonly yields unsatisfactory results. Using fluoroscopy, the patient can be evaluated in multiple orientations until the optimal position is obtained, after which the findings can be recorded on spot films. The procedure is quick, information to the radiologist is immediate, and the radiation dose to the patient is minimal. In addition, if significant pain is associated with the fracture, preprocedural conscious sedation may be indicated.

Fluoroscopy, with or without injection of small volumes of positive (iodinated) or negative (air) contrast medium, represents an important method of identifying intraarticular osteochondral fragments or intracapsular bodies in the shoulder joint. Such osseous bodies may arise from idiopathic, posttraumatic, or chronic arthritic conditions. If multiple intraarticular bodies of similar size are seen, the possibility of idiopathic synovial osteochondromatosis must be considered (Fig. 1B-1).[3] Although the knee and hip are among the joints most commonly affected,[4] in multiple reports the shoulder has been similarly involved.[5–8] The degree to which these bodies can be seen by fluoroscopy is directly proportional to the degree of mineralization (calcification or ossification) in each lesion.[3]

Fluoroscopy (and contrast arthrography) can identify the precise location of these fragments and detect additional bodies not discovered by conventional radiography.[9] A typical tumbling or rolling motion of a nonadherent osseous body generally confirms the intraarticular or intrabursal site, indicating that it is not attached to the synovial lining.[10] However, since the fragment may be fixed or free within the joint, we discourage the commonly used radiographic term "loose body," unless this is clearly seen by fluoroscopic means.

The shoulder impingement syndrome is an important source of shoulder pain that occurs when the bone and soft tissue structures of the superior aspect of the shoulder encroach upon the coracoacromial arch during abduction of the arm.[11] Although many classification systems have been developed, Neer's three-stage classification for impingement is widely accepted.[12] Regardless of the classification system, shoulder impingement syndrome is a common clinical entity. Impingement is characterized as being of two types: outlet and nonoutlet impingement.[13] The more frequent outlet impingement occurs mainly between the anterior third of the acromion and the underlying tendons. It is the most common cause of rotator cuff lesions.[14] Fluoroscopic examination of the shoulder demonstrates bone contact between the greater tuberosity region of the superolateral humerus and the inferior aspect of the anterior acromion when an abduction maneuver is performed. This is particularly problematic in the presence of a subacromial enthesophyte or a Type III acromion[5] (Fig. 1B-2).[15] Less commonly, shoulder impingement may result in abduction from osteophytes that form in association with capsular hypertrophy at the inferior margin of the acromioclavicular joint. Circumduction and abduction under real time fluoroscopic visualization may yield valuable information relating to the contact between the osteoarthritic acromioclavicular joint and the humeral head.

Open reduction and internal fixation of humeral fractures, the presence of a hemiarthroplasty or total shoulder replacement, and other orthopedic appliances create diagnostic problems during conventional radiography by obscuring adjacent bone structures. Fluoroscopy enables

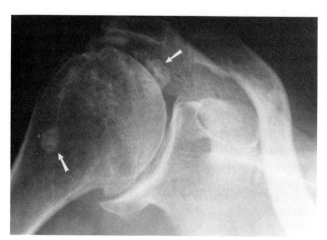

Figure 1B-1 AP radiograph of the shoulder demonstrating multiple osteochondral bodies (*arrows*) within the capsule.

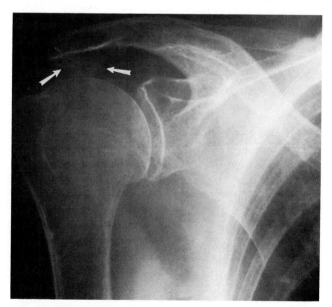

Figure 1B-2 AP radiograph of the shoulder demonstrating a Type III ("hooked") acromion (*arrows*).

the radiologist to examine the patient in a position which may more fully reveal the relationship between these appliances and the adjacent bone. This may be particularly valuable if multiple Kirschner wires, pins, or screws have been placed in the bone or if the device is suspected to have transgressed the epiphyseal cortical surface and entered the joint space. This may be difficult to appreciate when using routine radiographic positioning as opposed to dynamic, real-time fluoroscopic viewing. In addition, conventional radiography may fail to detect and localize foreign bodies in the soft tissues. Thus, fluoroscopy may be an inexpensive and immediate method of clarifying the presence and location of iatrogenic or acquired foreign bodies in soft tissue.[16]

SHOULDER ARTHROGRAPHY

Arthrography of the glenohumeral joint by percutaneous introduction of iodinated contrast material and air under fluoroscopic guidance is still a common procedure in many hospitals, across the United States and in other countries. The aggravation and disability associated with glenohumeral joint dysfunction are debilitating to millions of patients in developing countries, where access to more expensive technologies (e.g., computed tomography [CT], magnetic resonance imaging [MRI]) is extremely limited, and to those in nations where these technologies are readily available. In addition, access to the more sophisticated two- and three-dimensional imaging modalities is not uniformly available to all patients owing to cost. Thus, arthrography should be in the armamentarium of every radiologist, as it is quite accurate,[17] minimally invasive, and associated with little postprocedural morbidity, particularly when double-contrast shoulder arthrography (DCSA) is performed using nonionic contrast medium in the absence of intraarticular epinephrine.[18] In a recent survey of shoulder arthrography in both academic and private institutions, 30 percent of the respondents experienced a recent increase in these examinations and 10 percent showed a decrease. Overall, shoulder arthrography accounted for 20 percent of all arthrographic studies.[19]

Embryology

The important relationships of the bursae of the shoulder to the glenohumeral joint are well-established by approximately the sixth or seventh week of fetal development, since most of the bursae are present by this time.[20] The subacromial bursa, the largest bursa at the shoulder, does not normally communicate with the glenohumeral joint.[21] The embryonic subdeltoid bursa, which develops separately from the subacromial bursa in the fetal shoulder, unites with the subacromial bursa in most cases, achieving the "adult configuration." The subscapularis

bursa also develops separately from the shoulder joint, but usually a communication develops with it during the fourth month of embryonic development, forming the subscapularis recess.[17]

The tendon of the long head of the biceps first develops outside the joint capsule, but as fetal development progresses it becomes attached to the deep surface of the capsular synovium by a mesentery-like fold of this synovial membrane. In time this attachment breaks down, and in the final stage of development the tendon of the long head of the biceps is left unattached to the capsule, enveloped by its synovial sheath, which is a direct developmental remnant of the capsule.[22]

The glenoid labrum becomes progressively more fibrous during fetal development and demonstrates a fibrocartilaginous transitional zone between the labrum and the contiguous hyaline articular cartilage of the glenoid proper. At term, the labrum is a mix of fibrous and elastic-type fibers.[23]

Regional Anatomy of the Shoulder Joint

The glenohumeral joint lies between the shallow cavity of the glenoid fossa of the scapula and the roughly hemispheric head of the humerus. The shallow nature of this fossa, the discrepancy between the shallow glenoid region and the large humeral head, and the redundancy of the joint capsule produce an articulation which is inherently unstable. This joint therefore derives much of its support from the surrounding musculature and ligaments. Although a thorough treatment of cadaveric and radiographic anatomy is beyond the scope of this discussion, a brief discussion will be undertaken in other sections of Chapter 1. Essentially, the capsule is reinforced above by the supraspinatus tendon, below by the long head of the triceps, anteriorly by the subscapularis, and posteriorly by the infraspinatus and teres minor. The tendons of the supraspinatus, infraspinatus, teres minor, and subscapularis form an enveloping musculotendinous apparatus, which stabilizes the joint, referred to as the *rotator cuff*. Additional stabilization is imparted by the coracohumeral and superior, middle, and inferior glenohumeral ligaments, which are capsular thickenings that come to confluence, respectively, with the coracohumeral ligament, the subscapularis tendon, and the base of the labrum. These ligaments act as restraints during external rotation of the humeral head.

Radiographic Anatomy

In arthrography, preliminary scout radiographs are taken before the introduction of contrast material into the glenohumeral joint. Four standard projections may be used. Many excellent textbooks provide detailed discussions of patient positioning during radiographic examination of the shoulder girdle.[24,25] The anteroposterior (AP) view in external rotation (Fig. 1B-3) brings the greater tuberosity into view at the superolateral aspect of the proximal humerus. The radiograph is obtained with the patient's arm adducted, the hand supinated, and the elbow in extension. This view is useful for detecting calcification in the supraspinatus tendon, inspecting the greater tuberosity for fracture or erosion, and examining the glenohumeral joint for evidence of joint space narrowing or irregularity associated with osteoarthritis. At one author's (D.S.L.) institution both AP scouts are acquired with 15° to 20° of posterior oblique angulation, thus bringing the glenohumeral articulation into a nearly tangential relation to the x-ray beam. This pseudo-AP view of the scapula allows a compromise in position that enables the radiologist to get a good look at both the joint surfaces and the important humeral landmarks. In addition, we include an additional 15° to 20° caudal angulation, which artifactually widens the subacromial space[26] for better visualization of the acromiohumeral interval.

As the arm is rotated internally the greater tuberosity is projected en face over the humerus and the lesser tuberosity may overlie the glenohumeral joint. This *AP view in internal rotation* (Fig. 1B-4) is obtained with the arm adducted, the hand and forearm pronated, and the elbow extended. In this position, calcification in the infraspinatus and teres minor tendons is seen on the outer aspect of the humerus and calcification in the subscapularis tendon may be seen adjacent to the lesser tuberosity. An additional structure seen on this view is the peribursal fat plane. Anatomic studies show that a thin layer of extrasynovial fat lines the subacromial-subdeltoid bursae,[27] the superior portion of which sits immediately beneath the critical zone of the tendon supraspinatus.[28] On the internal rotation view, a 1- to 2-mm curvilinear radiodensity deep to the deltoid muscle extending laterally from the subacromial region over the greater tuberosity can be seen, especially with the aid of a high-wattage backlighting system ("hot light"). Mitchell and coworkers[27] demonstrated a peribursal fat plane in 60 percent of controls, but only 21 percent of patients with rotator cuff tears (a sensitivity rate of nearly 80

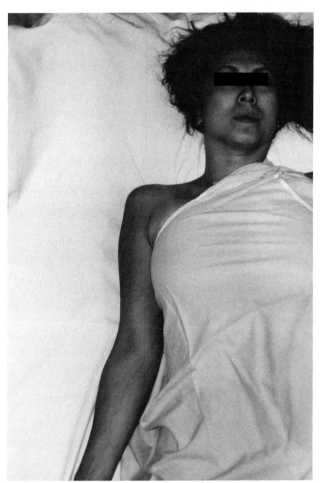

A

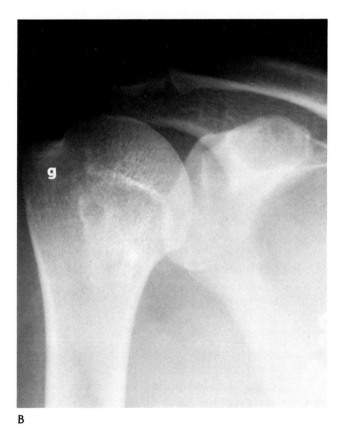

B

Figure 1B-3 **A, B.** Anteroposterior views in external rotation. (g, greater tuberosity.)

percent). In addition, focal blurring, complete obliteration, and displacement of this structure have been reported in association with rheumatoid arthritis,[29] as well as nonrheumatoid peritendinitis and bursitis.[30]

Another view, the axillary Y view (Fig. 1B-5), may be produced by employing several different projections.[31] Regardless of patient positioning, this view allows better judgment of the AP relationship of the humeral head to the glenoid, especially when a fracture or dislocation is a diagnostic consideration. The x-ray cassette is placed above the patient's shoulder, and the arm is gently abducted to 30°. Several variations have been attempted,

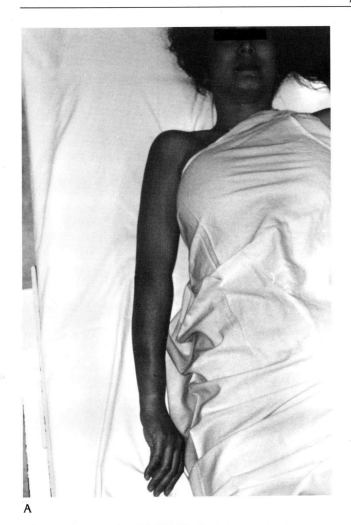

A

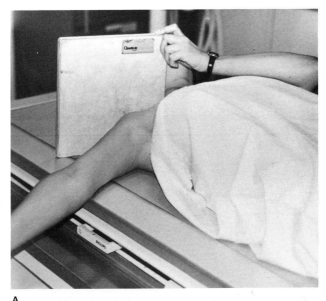

A

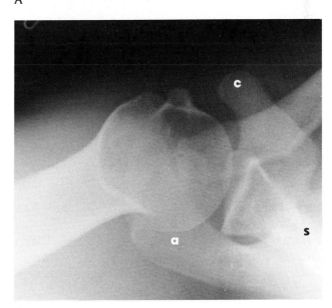

B

Figure 1B-4 **A, B.** Anteroposterior views in internal rotation (arrow, lesser tuberosity).

B

Figure 1B-5 **A, B.** Axillary Y views. Notice that the Y is made up of the acromion (a), the coracoid process (c), and the spine of the scapula (s).

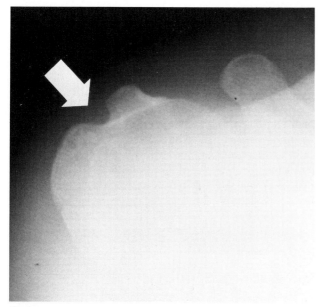

A

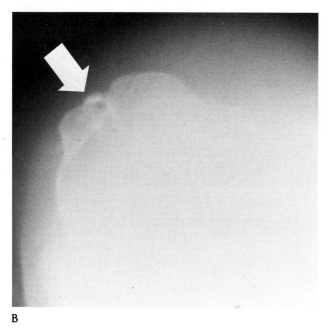

B

Figure 1B-6 **A, B.** The bicipital groove view, before and after arthrography (arrows, bicipital groove).

but best results are usually obtained using the projection that is most comfortable for the patient.

Next, the bicipital groove (Fig. 1B-6) view is taken with the patient supine on the table and the x-ray cassette on the superior aspect of the shoulder. The patient's hand is at the side, the arm abducted approximately 20°, the elbow in full extension, and the hand maximally supinated. The x-ray beam is directed along the arm toward the inferior aspect of the bicipital groove.[32] This view helps determine whether ossification of the transverse

humeral ligament or bony fragments are present over the bicipital groove. It also is valuable for comparison with the postarthrographic bicipital view, where one should see the normal filling defect of the bicipital tendon and its sheath surrounded by contrast material in the groove (see Fig. 1B-6). If a scout view is not obtained in this orientation, a calcification within the bicipital groove could be mistaken for high-density contrast material and the misdiagnosis could be bicipital tendon subluxation.

One author supports the routine use of a silicone exposure compensation filter to overcome peripheral overpenetration on scout films, allowing for equalization of beam penetration across the glenohumeral and acromiohumeral windows.

Normal Arthrographic Anatomy (Figure 1B-7)
Arthrographic Technique

No single technique, or variation on a technique, has been shown to be irrefutably superior for performing shoulder arthrography. Many excellent publications have reviewed various approaches to performing the shoulder arthrogram.[33–35]

In our institutions, the authors prefer DCSA to single-contrast shoulder arthrography (SCSA); however, the latter technique will be reviewed briefly and preparation for and performance of both techniques will be discussed.

After preliminary scout radiographs are obtained, the patient is placed supine on the radiography table with the shoulder that is to be injected at the edge of the table closest to the radiologist. With the patient's arm resting comfortably along the thigh, the hand and elbow are externally rotated, placing the entire upper extremity in full supination. The tendon of the long head of the biceps is thus kept out of the projected path of the needle. A sandbag is placed over the wrist and hand to remind the patient to maintain the external rotation throughout the exam.

In our radiology departments, we use an open paper clip under fluoroscopic guidance to find the correct position on the skin which correlates with the site of needle puncture. The paper clip is taped to the skin, with the metallic tip directly over the junction of the middle and distal thirds of the glenohumeral articulation. This point on the skin is then marked with indelible ink. In markedly obese, large-breasted, or dorsally kyphotic patients, anterior chest tissues are taped back away from the point of entry of the needle.

A standard arthrogram tray is usually employed, including a Betadine-soaked sponge that sterilizes a wide area circumscribing the proposed puncture site. A fenestrated drape is placed over the site, after which the

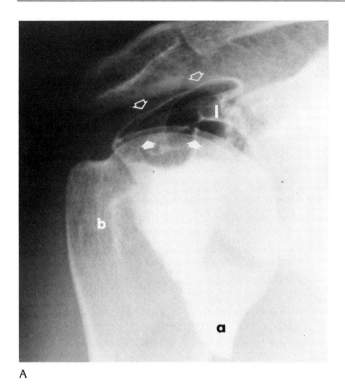

A

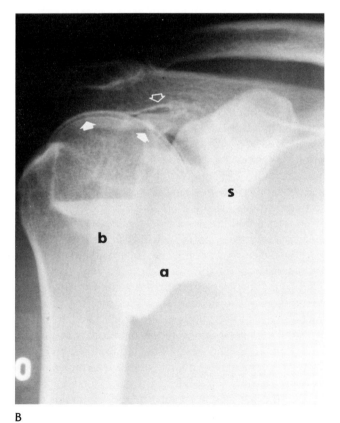

B

Figure 1B-7 Arthrographic anatomy of the normal shoulder. **A.** External rotation view. **B.** Internal rotation view. (Key: Open arrows, inferior aspect of supraspinatus tendon; closed arrows, hyaline cartilage of humeral head; l, superior glenoid labrum; a, axillary recess; b, bicipital tendon sheath; s, subscapularis or subcoracoid recess.)

skin and deep subcutaneous tissues are anesthetized with 1 percent Xylocaine without epinephrine, employing a 25-gauge, 1½-in. needle. Liberal use of lidocaine (in the absence of an allergic history) and patient reassurance promote the success and rapid completion of this procedure.

Using sterile technique, the examiner then introduces a 20-gauge, 3½-in. spinal needle in a direction perpendicular to the plane of the floor at the site of the skin mark. Choosing the length of the needle is somewhat subjective: one author (D.S.L.) has used a 1½-in. needle in a small patient with atrophic musculature and as large as an 8-in. needle for morbidly obese patients. A 22-gauge needle may be substituted, but we occasionally find that its flexibility can make directing the needle problematic. Throughout this procedure intermittent fluoroscopy can be used to follow the track of the needle, so that if it deviates from the proper path, the needle can be reoriented before it is advanced farther. The needle is advanced slowly until mild resistance is felt. When the joint space is entered, if the tip comes in contact with subarticular bone, the patient usually feels mild discomfort. At times, the extreme tip of the needle may bend slightly to conform to the joint space, and this finding on fluoroscopy is almost always a sign that the needle is clearly within the joint. To verify that the needle is actually within the joint, approximately 0.5 ml of contrast material may be introduced, which should flow freely from the tip of the needle and outline the articular cartilage of both the humeral head and the glenoid fossa. If the injected contrast medium collects at the needle tip in a cloudlike configuration, the most likely cause is extravasation due to extraarticular placement of the needle.

The choice of contrast material varies much, depending on the type of examination. In our department, diatrizoate meglumine (Hypaque 60) is used routinely in double contrast arthrography, though if the patient has a history of allergic reaction to iodinated contrast material, nonionic low-osmolarity contrast material may be used. Premedication has not been used at our institutions for injection of contrast into the glenohumeral joint, and the literature shows no studies that confirm or deny its efficacy. As clear guidelines have not been established, the decision to premedicate such patients should be individualized. Of note, magnetic resonance (MR) arthrography has been developed in our and other centers. An injection of either saline or a 1:250 solution of gadolinium and sterile saline can be used to perform MR arthrography of the shoulder joint.[36] In the event of previously documented severe reaction to iodinated contrast medium, this may be a viable alternative to DCSA. Studies in vitro[37] and in vivo[36,38] have been used to look at its efficacy. We agree with Hodler and coworkers[38] that a false positive result may occur if a baseline preinjection

MR shoulder study is not performed before MR arthrography. In practical terms this means that the patient must undergo two MR examinations, one before the saline injection and one after it, thus significantly increasing both the cost and time of the examination. Alternatively, Stoller has emphasized the use of fat-suppressed T1-weighted images used in conjunction with MR arthrography to obviate the need for preinjection MRI.[39]

Single- or double-contrast techniques may be utilized. With the SCSA, 12 to 15 ml of 60% Hypaque is injected into a joint of normal capacity. The needle is withdrawn, and as the tip leaves the skin pressure is placed over the puncture site with a gauze pad for a few moments, so that extravasation of contrast from the joint space into the extracapsular soft tissues is under tamponade. Following mildly vigorous exercise of the shoulder by repeated abduction and circumduction, AP radiographs are obtained in internal and external rotation, along with axillary and bicipital groove radiographs.

The DCSA, introduced more recently, is held by many to be a superior technique.[33,40,41] Large volumes of positive contrast material used in SCSA usually obscure detail at the site of the abnormality.[42] Advocates of the DCSA emphasize that it provides optimal coating of the torn ends of a rotator cuff and more accurate assessment of the width of a tear and that it may delineate the glenoid labrum more clearly, thus allowing documentation of the presence of a purely cartilaginous injury.[15] Conversely, DCSA is more difficult to perform and more time consuming than SCSA. Furthermore, DCSA may be more difficult to interpret, and so may require a more experienced examiner. At the authors' institutions, DCSA is used to the exclusion of SCSA to examine the shoulder joint. The one exception may be when SCSA is used for joint distention in adhesive capsulitis in conjunction with the brisement procedure.[43]

DCSA requires the injection of approximately 4 to 5 ml of Hypaque and 10 to 11 ml of air into the shoulder joint after adequate documentation of intraarticular placement of the needle. The addition of 0.2 to 0.3 ml of epinephrine to the liquid Renografin is advocated by some authors to improve the contrast coating of the cartilaginous surfaces.[44] The proposed mechanism of action of intraarticular epinephrine is vasoconstriction, which delays exchange of fluid across the synovial membrane. This vasoconstriction decreases the influx of hypotonic fluid into the joint secondary to the injection of the hyperosmolar contrast medium while decreasing the egress of contrast material from the shoulder joint into the surrounding draining veins. Infrequently, painful synovitis is a sequela of intraarticular epinephrine. This is due to an irritant effect on the synovium—either directly or secondary to prolonged contact of the contrast material with the synovium.[45] We suggest this technique be abandoned, as high-quality studies are obtainable

without it and the benefit of such an injection is outweighed by the risk of painful synovitis.

Following the injection, the needle is withdrawn and instantaneous fluoroscopic evaluation of the rotator cuff, glenohumeral articular cartilage, adjacent bursae, and capsulolabral structures is conducted. The immediate early flow of contrast medium within the articulation and over the humeral head allows visualization of focal cartilaginous lesions and identification of irregularities in the head or neck, manifested as contrast spill into the lesions. This is a unique opportunity to visualize early extravasation into the subacromial and subdeltoid bursae and to locate precisely a tear in the musculotendinous junction. Importantly, real time fluoroscopic visualization with immediate postinjection imaging while applying traction on the shoulder by gently pulling the wrist can help "liberate" contrast material into the shoulder bursae, effectively "bringing out" a partial undersurface or a small but complete tear. In addition, the humerus may be rotated, abducted, or adducted by gently twisting and pulling the forearm, which orients the humeral head in various relations to the glenoid fossa. Following these maneuvers, the patient is placed upright with the aid of a motorized fluoroscopic tilt table. The patient holds the arm in external rotation and holds a 5- to 15-lb sandbag in the ipsilateral hand. Spot films are obtained in the frontal plane, using a tube angulation of 10° to 15° caudad, which will display the rotator cuff without superimposing the acromion.[33] We find that this angulation can be produced if the patient is encouraged to assume a position in which the shoulders are forward and the neck is extended as the upper torso leans toward the fluorographic spot unit (Fig. 1B-8A, C). This is effective in visualizing a small partial articular-sided tear that would otherwise be obscured by the inferior aspect of the acromion, the superolateral humeral head, or the osseous enthesophytic bone projecting into this space secondary to underlying shoulder pathology any number of abnormal conditions of the shoulder (e.g., subacromial enthesophyte, posttraumatic callus, postoperative reparative changes, acromioclavicular osteoarthritis).

Complications of this procedure are few. They stem from faulty needle placement, the patient's response to penetration of the needle, or sequelae of the microarthrostomy. If the needle is malpositioned and a volume of positive contrast is injected, it may collect in the anterior soft tissues and obscure the region for subsequent needle placement and interpretation. Intermittent fluoroscopic visualization while placing the needle and delivering the contrast in the absence of significant resistance is beneficial. Two infrequent pitfalls in needle placement warrant mention. One is placement of the needle into the subacromial bursa, where contrast flows freely from the needle, creating a bursogram that does not communicate with the joint.[46] The other pitfall can

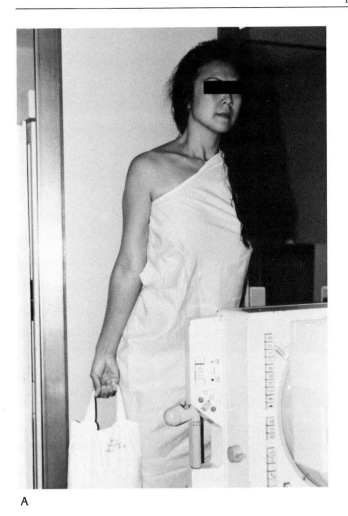

A

B

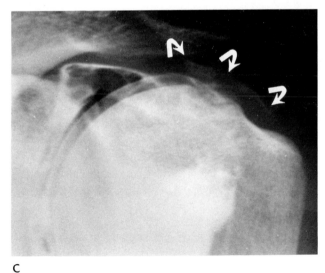

C

Figure 1B-8 Correct upright positioning of the patient for visualization of a partial rotator cuff tear by DCSA. **A.** AP view. **B.** Lateral view. **C.** Arthrogram of partial tear. Contrast material lies within the supraspinatus tendon (*arrows*) but does not opacify the subacromial-subdeltoid bursae.

be averted by placing the shoulder in external rotation while the needle is introduced, so that the biceps tendon is out of its path. This protects the biceps tendon and sheath.

As for contrast reactions, a series of 6500 procedures demonstrated no significant contrast sensitivity.[17] We

know of no reports of death from shoulder arthrography. Vasovagal syncope has been noted on several occasions, and many such responses may be predicted from the patient's preexamination affect. These reactions may be treated with comfort measures, supine or slight Trendelenburg positioning, or ammonium-based inhalants.

For persistent bradycardia, intravenous fluids and intra-muscular atropine are quite effective.

The Normal Double-Contrast Shoulder Arthrogram

After percutaneous introduction of liquid iodinated contrast material into the shoulder joint, the glenohumeral space is initially identified as a curvilinear, radiodense opacity between the glenoid surface and the humeral head. With further filling of the joint, the subscapular recess, axillary recess, and bicipital tendon sheath are identified (Fig. 1B-9). The smooth, bluntly rounded axillary pouch is seen at the medial edge of the surgical neck of the humerus, whereas the thin subcapularis recess, containing the subscapularis tendon, extends medially from the glenohumeral joint to a region beneath the coracoid process. In the position of external rotation, the subscapular recess is poorly filled; however, the axillary recess is well visualized along the inferior surface of the humeral head and adjacent portions of the scapula. In contrast, on internal rotation the subscapular recess is seen to be maximally distended. In both internal and external rotation, the bicipital tendon sheath frequently may be seen to fill with contrast material or air. Opacification of this sheath, which demonstrates the central tubular filling defect of the bicipital tendon, may extend some distance into the bicipital groove along the metaphysis of the humerus. On the axillary view, the contrast-filled or air-filled subscapularis recess and bicipital tendon sheath also may be demonstrated. In this position, the glenoid labrum, including both anterior and posterior margins, is often seen. Also well demonstrated are the cartilaginous surfaces of both the glenoid fossa and the humeral head.

The Abnormal Shoulder Arthrogram

COMPLETE TEARS OF THE ROTATOR CUFF

A complete tear of the rotator cuff is a common cause of both acute and chronic shoulder pain. One of the major indications for arthrography of the glenohumeral joint is a clinically suspected rotator cuff tear. In patients with chronic rotator cuff tears, the plain radiographic alterations that result are well-known. As seen on the scout films, they include, but are not limited to, these: (1) narrowing of the distance between the inferior surface of the acromion and the humeral head, usually to 5 mm or less[47]; (2) notching between the humeral articular surface and the greater tuberosity, as the degree of excavation appears to correspond to the severity of the tear[48]; (3) subchondral cystic changes in the upper two-thirds of the anatomical neck; and (4) sclerosis or irregularity of the greater tuberosity.[49] In the absence of other radiographic abnormalities, sclerosis of the greater tuberosity is an unreliable sign of a rotator cuff tear. These

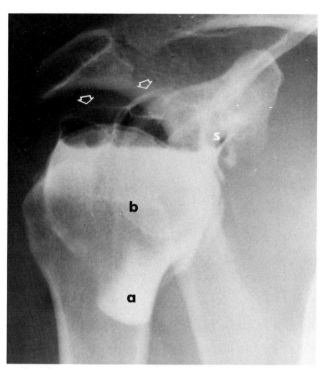

Figure 1B-9 DCSA demonstrating the subscapular recess (s), axillary recess (a), and bicipital tendon sheath (b) containing contrast. (*Arrows*, inferior aspect of supraspinatus tendon.)

findings may occasionally be seen with adhesive capsulitis.[50] Conversely, the plain radiograph of the shoulder may belie the presence of an acute disruption of the rotator cuff, as these usually are not detected by conventional radiography and additional techniques are required for diagnosis. DCSA remains the most popular of the minimally invasive accessory techniques in this regard. It is the preferred technique in this clinical situation, when the application of stress[51] or supplementary CT[52,53] will be utilized, and when intraarticular pressure determination is determined during injection of increasing volumes of contrast into the glenohumeral joint.[54]

The cornerstone of the arthrographic diagnosis in the presence of complete tear of the rotator cuff is based on identification of an abnormal communication between the glenohumeral joint cavity and the subacromial-subdeltoid bursae (Fig. 1B-10). Normally, communication between the intraarticular space proper and these bursae is prevented by the capsule, ligaments, and rotator cuff muscles, but with a full-thickness tear the introduction of positive contrast material or air, or both, into the articular cavity will lead to extravasation and identification of the subacromial-subdeltoid bursae. Liquid contrast medium entering the subacromial bursae can be recognized as an opaque collection superior to the greater tuberosity of the humerus and superior to the line of contrast-outlined articular cartilage just medial to the greater tuberosity. This abnormality is demonstrated most dramatically on the internal rotation projection. If the remaining musculature is thick and only minimal

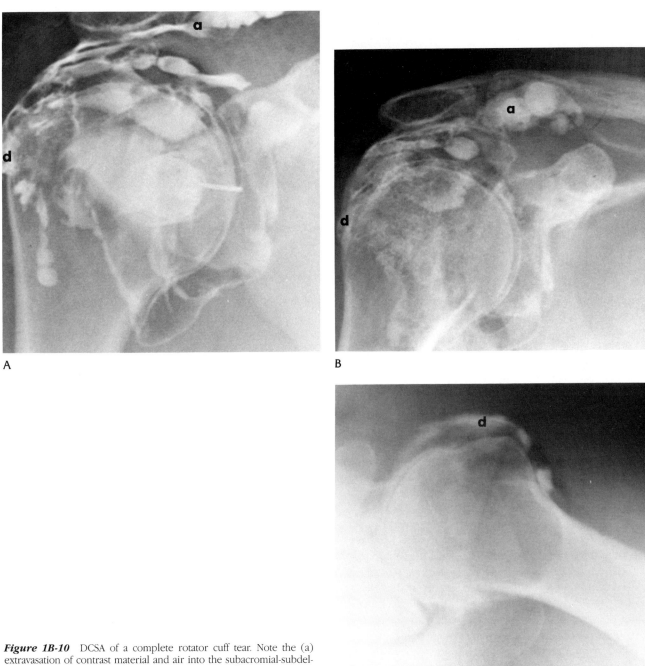

Figure 1B-10 DCSA of a complete rotator cuff tear. Note the (a) extravasation of contrast material and air into the subacromial-subdeltoid (d) bursae. **A.** External rotation view. **B.** Internal rotation view. **C.** Axillary view.

retraction of the cuff is seen, the air entering the subacromial bursae shows a prominent lucency. If the musculature is atrophic, the lucency in the cuff is diminished and the separation between the contrast material within the bursae and that within the joint may be less obvious. Regardless of the cuff status, when the spot radiograph is obtained with the external rotation projection, contrast material will be present along the outer aspect of the greater tuberosity. This finding unequivocally indicates that a rotator cuff tear is present and that abnormal extravasation into these bursae has occurred. The axillary

view may aid in the identification of a tear: contrast material appears as a "saddlebag" radiodensity across the surgical neck of the humerus.[55] Occasionally, air or contrast material that has entered the subacromial bursae escapes even farther superiorly into the acromioclavicular joint; the appearance has been referred to as the *geyser sign* (Fig. 1B-11).[56]

Although diagnosis of a complete rotator cuff tear by DSCA may be relatively straightforward, there are multiple sources of possible error: (1) Inadequate distention of the joint or distribution of positive or negative contrast

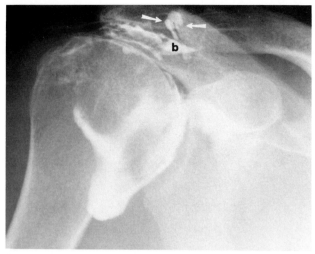

A

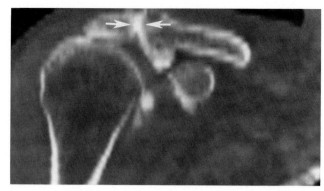

B

Figure 1B-11 The geyser sign.[53] **A.** Internal rotation radiograph. **B.** CT re-formation in coronal plane. Extravasation of contrast into the acromioclavicular joint (*arrows*) from the underlying subacromial bursa (b).

material within the joint can prevent visualization of the subacromial bursa. (2) The air- or contrast-filled biceps tendon sheath may project slightly lateral to the greater tuberosity on the external rotation projection, simulating filling of the subdeltoid bursa. (3) An adjacent bursa that does not communicate with the glenohumeral joint and surrounding capsule may inadvertently be injected. With respect to the first pitfall, the joint capacity is approximately 28 to 35 ml[34]; yet injections during DCSA using 4 ml contrast medium and 10 ml air distend the capsule to only approximately half this capacity. This volume, however, is only an approximation, based on my experience and that of others (personal communication, D. Resnick, 1992) and slow filling of the joint capsule is advised so that distention may be complete without undesirable decompression into the soft tissues. Postexercise images are usually adequate to distribute the opaque material within the joint. To avoid erroneous reading of a tear owing to the contrast-filled sheath of the biceps tendon, the reader should identify the linear tubular filling defect of the biceps tendon within its sheath and note that the opacified sheath moves medially with internal rotation, both on fluoroscopy and on the spot film. In contradistinction, when the rotator cuff allows extravasation through the torn supraspinatus tendon, an opacified subacromial subdeltoid bursa is seen superior and lateral to the greater tuberosity in all projections.[57]

In one study of DCSA, Mink and colleagues found its overall accuracy to be greater than 99 percent in 152 surgically confirmed cases.[40] The authors found a strong correlation in quantitative and qualitative assessment of the size of the rotator cuff tear and the degree of degeneration of the torn tendon. Another investigation prospectively compared DCSA with high-field MR imaging in 38 patients with suspected rotator cuff tears. Shoulder MRI and arthrography showed identical results, with 92 percent sensitivity and 100 percent specificity.[58] In this study, the accuracy of arthrography compared with that

of surgery was 94 percent for both techniques. Competing evidence for disparity in the accuracy of MRI and arthrography is given by Zlatkin et al., who reported an accuracy rate of 93 percent for MRI and of 68 percent for arthrography in 31 surgically proven cases.[59] In the setting of a complete rotator cuff tear, it is probable that DCSA and high-field MRI are similarly accurate. Associated changes in the shoulder, (joint effusion, labral abnormalities, cartilaginous surface defects, bicipital tendon dislocations, bone contusions, and the integrity of the infraspinatus, teres minor, and subscapularis tendons) are all better evaluated using MRI, however.

PARTIAL TEARS OF THE ROTATOR CUFF

The diagnosis of a partial rotator cuff tear may be accomplished by DCSA, though this finding is uncommon. The diagnosis is difficult to make, and in most instances requires adequate beam angulation to demonstrate air or contrast material entry into the articular aspect of the cuff tear. Partial tears may be small, medium, or large, and the degree to which the mildly viscous contrast material interdigitates the tear is in part dependent on the size of the abnormality. Partial tears may be of two types: (1) partial undersurface tears, which communicate with the joint space and articular capsule, and (2) dorsal-sided tears, which may communicate with the subacromial and subdeltoid spaces.

Partial undersurface rotator cuff tears are amenable to diagnosis by arthrography. When the contrast medium is placed into the joint, it may flow into the tear in the musculotendinous junction, usually in the portion of the tendon referred to as the critical zone (Fig. 1B-12).[28] Contrast arthrography fails to diagnose bursa-sided tears, which originate and communicate with the outer or superficial surface of the cuff, a portion that is inaccessible to injected contrast or air. Additionally, the diagnosis of an intrasubstance partial tear cannot be made, as it does not communicate with the joint space proper. The iden-

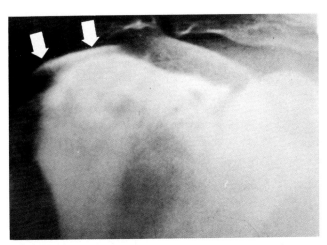

Figure 1B-12 Partial rotator cuff tear. Single-contrast arthrogram reveals opacification within the substance of the supraspinatus tendon (*arrows*), but no filling of the subacromial-subdeltoid bursa.

tification of partial bursal-surface defects and intratendinous partial-thickness tears is better accomplished by MRI may be a subsequent test if findings of DCSA are negative when the clinical suspicion for this type of rotator cuff abnormality is great.[13]

The DCSA is performed according to the normal protocol described above. In the case of a partial undersurface tear, the arthrogram may demonstrate an ulcerlike, linear or curvilinear collection of positive contrast material or air extending into a tear in the undersurface of the rotator cuff at the *critical zone*. This is a crucial area that some believe to be a hypovascular zone that may be more susceptible to degenerative change and traumatic tear than other parts of the tendon. Others do not accept this theory related to the critical hypovascular zone hy-

pothesis.[60] Regardless of its pathogenesis, a partial undersurface tear is best seen on external rotation views. Postexercise films are particularly valuable since what appeared on preexercise images to be a partial-thickness undersurface tear may be identified as a full-thickness tear on the postexercise films.[61]

ADHESIVE CAPSULITIS

For many years, adhesive capsulitis has been a clinical diagnosis and shoulder arthrography has had both a diagnostic and a therapeutic role, in combination with physical therapy, and in some cases, surgical capsular release. The patient may complain of pain and limitation of motion. Intracapsular adhesions decrease the capacity of the shoulder joint and limit mobility, particularly with internal and external rotation maneuvers or abduction.[62] The term *adhesive capsulitis* was suggested first by Neviaser, to supplant the term *frozen shoulder*. Other authors have noted that this condition may mimic clinical disorders originating from the neck, chest wall, or heart.[60]

The scout film examination is often unrewarding, showing only osteopenia or mild degenerative changes. Fluoroscopically, a decrease in rotatory motion or abduction may be seen. However, if a rotator cuff tear is superimposed on adhesive capsulitis, these chronic changes may on plain films indicate chronic rotator cuff tear with subsequent obscuration of the primary diagnosis.

The arthrographic diagnosis is based on the characteristic finding of restricted capacity and resistance to filling of the glenohumeral joint (Fig. 1B-13). Intraarticular needle placement may be more difficult in these

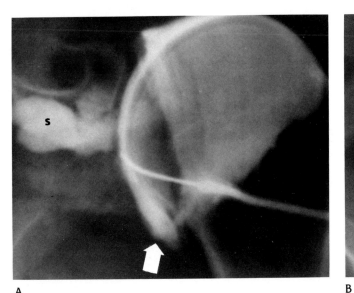

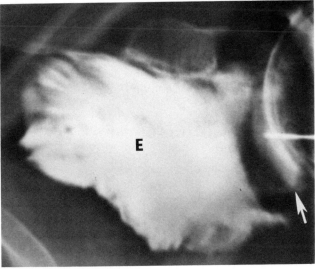

A   B

Figure 1B-13 **A.** Adhesive capsulitis. Single-contrast arthrogram reveals a small axillary recess (*arrow*) and sparse filling of the subscapularis recess(s). **B.** Following a brisement procedure, extravasation (E) of contrast beneath the pectoralis musculature is evident. Extravasation indicates capsular rupture and terminates the study. (*Arrow*, small axillary recess.)

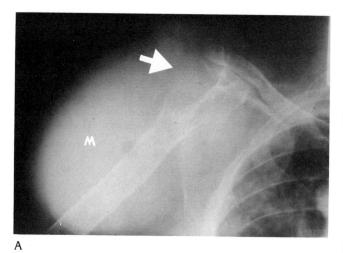
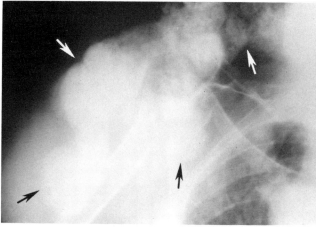

A   B

Figure 1B-14   Rheumatoid arthritis. **A.** Frontal radiograph demonstrates typical erosive alterations of the disease (*arrow*) along with a large abnormal soft tissue mass (M). **B.** Single-contrast arthrography reveals an extensive dissecting synovial cyst (*arrows*).

patients, owing to the tight joint capsule. In some cases, the decreased capacity of this articulation becomes apparent after 5 to 6 ml of contrast material have been introduced. At this point, if the radiologist releases pressure on the plunger of the syringe, retrograde filling of contrast into the syringe may occur.

Small size, narrowing, or complete obliteration of the subscapularis recess, axillary pouch, or bicipital tendon sheath may be noted.[35] Extravasation of contrast material into the surrounding tissues may be observed; however, leakage from the subscapularis recess or the biceps tendon sheath alone is not an abnormal finding.[61]

Treatment of this condition may be undertaken with arthrography (the *brisement procedure*).[43,46,63] It appears that this is efficacious in cases of mild to moderate severity after gradual joint distension is performed by arthrography. Subsequent manipulation using physical therapy immediately thereafter has met with variable success. In addition, some authors use a mixture of steroids and Marcaine together with the contrast medium for additional pain reduction both during and after the procedure.

OTHER ABNORMALITIES DIAGNOSABLE BY ARTHROGRAPHY

Other abnormalities that may be diagnosed by DCSA include lesions of the synovial lining, bicipital tendon abnormalities, and posttraumatic changes. In practical terms, however, many of the lesions may be seen to greater advantage using double-contrast computed arthrotomography or MRI of the shoulder. We will review a few of the well-known additional indications for shoulder arthrography.

The synovial cavity of the shoulder joint, as seen on arthrography, demonstrates a smooth contour which has two major compartments, the anterior capsule and the posterior capsule. The contrast medium should be uniformly and homogeneously distributed throughout the anterior and posterior joint capsule. If synovial aberrations such as rheumatoid arthritis occur, they impart an abnormal appearance, which may be represented by mottling of the contrast material or decreased density secondary to dilution of the contrast by a large joint effusion. Frank filling defects may be noted within the intracapsular contrast medium, which may be the result of projections from an inflammatory pannus (Fig. 1B-14) in rheumatoid arthritis, intracapsular bodies secondary to primary osteoarthrosis of the joint, or metaplastic nodules in the joint (Fig. 1B-15) secondary to synovial (osteo)-chondromatosis. These entities have a well-recognized, characteristic appearance on plain films, and usually

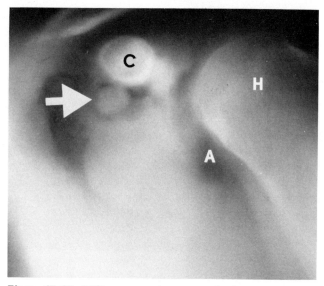

Figure 1B-15   DCSA contrast arthrotomography demonstrates an osteochondral body (*arrow*) within the subscapularis or subcoracoid recess. (A, axillary recess; C, coracoid process; H, humeral head.)

DCSA is not necessary for their diagnosis. The exception is rheumatoid arthritis, which may be manifested as markedly inflamed synovium with little or no osseous change.

Abnormalities of the biceps tendon may include bicipital tendinitis, partial or complete tears of the bicipital tendon (Fig. 1B-16), and medial or lateral subluxation or dislocation of the long head of the biceps tendon. Commonly, bicipital tendinitis may occur secondary to impingement, osteoarthritis, rheumatoid arthritis, or other inflammatory processes, but it is rare for it to occur as a primary or solitary entity. Mild swelling of this tendon is not well appreciated by contrast arthrography. Moreover, in the setting of bicipital tendon rupture, arthrographic criteria for diagnosing rupture of the bicipital tendon are lacking.[64] The tendon sheath may fail to fill in an otherwise normal arthrogram,[65] yet leakage of contrast material along the sheath may be seen secondary to simple joint distention rather than a torn tendon or sleeve,[65] which occurs in approximately 11 percent of normal shoulders.[66] Of note, rupture of the biceps tendon is perhaps easiest to recognize by physical examination on the basis of distal retraction of the muscle, and diagnostic imaging may be superfluous.[17,67]

Dislocation of the long head of the biceps from the bicipital groove is a well-recognized phenomenon first described in 1939.[68] In this condition, the DCSA bicipital groove view is the most reliable view to demonstrate that the tendon and sheath have dislocated medially. Absence of the normal filling defect in the groove, with

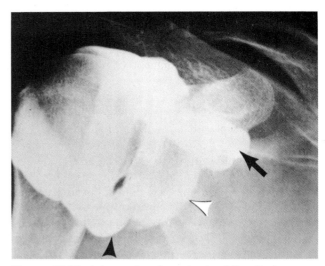

Figure 1B-16 Arthrography of anterior instability. Single-contrast study demonstrates capacious axillary (*black arrowhead*) and subscapularis (*black arrow*) recesses, as well as anterior capsular stripping (*white arrowhead*) from the glenoid.

subsequent filling of the groove with positive contrast material or air establishes the diagnosis. In the arthrographic study of previous anterior shoulder dislocation, posteromedial displacement of the biceps tendon is seen, with interposition between the humeral head and glenoid preventing reduction. As arthrography may demonstrate this lesion and indicate its position, it plays an adjunctive role in preoperative planning. This lesion requires open reduction of the shoulder if adequate reconstruction is to be achieved.[69]

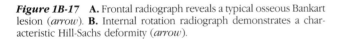

Figure 1B-17   A. Frontal radiograph reveals a typical osseous Bankart lesion (*arrow*). **B.** Internal rotation radiograph demonstrates a characteristic Hill-Sachs deformity (*arrow*).

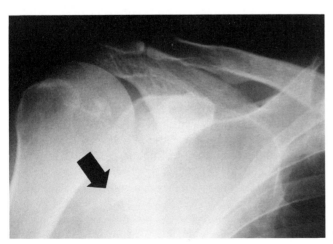

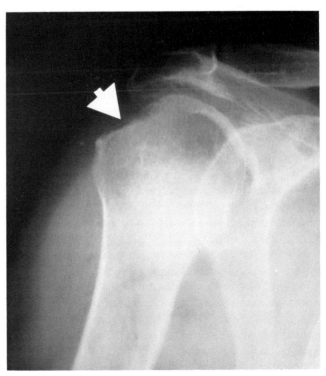

A   B

Chronic recurrent shoulder dislocations may yield a number of findings, depending on their number and severity. The most typical arthrographic finding in this case is redundancy of the anterior or posterior capsular structures, but this is not always present (see Fig. 1B-16). Infraglenoid and humeral head defects may be revealed on scout films, yielding respectively, the well-described bony Bankart and Hill-Sachs deformities (see Fig. 1B-17A, B). It appears that with anterior dislocation, anterior and inferior subluxation of the humeral head under the glenoid creates a combined injury. Impaction fracture at the superolateral margin of the humeral head is created by the inferior glenoid, which simultaneously fractures as a fragment of bone which is slightly displaced from the anteroinferior edge of the glenoid.[70,71] The Bankart lesion is demonstrated well using DCSA, but perhaps more importantly, additional information concerning the integrity of the articular cartilage and the glenoid labrum may be seen. Various authors have drawn conflicting conclusions about what is the most desirable patient position for optimal visualization of the glenoid labrum; supine, axillary[72] and prone views[73] have been suggested following DCSA. Labral abnormalities, including blunting or irregularity of the free margin of the labrum, indicate a tear. Leakage of contrast material outside the joint may occur, particularly when anterior capsular stripping is present. Other capabilities of DCSA are the detection of small Hill-Sachs deformities, secondary intracapsular osseous bodies, and rotator cuff tears that may be associated with anterior dislocations.

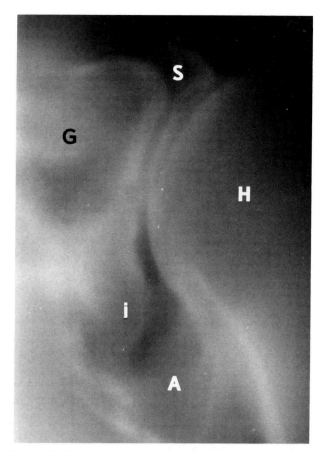

Figure 1B-18 Double-contrast arthrotomography demonstrates the superior (s) and the inferior (i) glenoid labrum. (A, axillary recess; G, glenoid; H, humeral head.)

SUMMARY

Fluoroscopy and shoulder arthrography have stood the test of time and have enjoyed wide application to many glenohumeral abnormalities of both bone and adjacent soft tissues. The examinations are readily performed, as most radiology departments have adequate equipment, and they provide a cost-effective initial investigation into abnormalities of the shoulder.

DCSA is an accurate technique that in the hands of a skilled radiologist may yield valuable information about the rotator cuff. This method may assist in nonsurgical rehabilitation of the shoulder, combining elements of physical therapy, intraarticular anesthetic or steroid injections, or other maneuvers that decrease pain and increase function. In addition, it can have a large impact on the choice of surgical approach (either open or arthroscopic) and on the accessibility of the shoulder abnormality in the case of a partial tear of the rotator cuff. The chosen approach will be on the articular or the bursal side, depending on the site of the partial-thickness lesion as revealed by DCSA or bursography. After operative repair of the torn rotator cuff, DCSA may also be undertaken to assess continued pain or decreased function. One caveat is that watertight closure is not necessarily essential for a good functional result; thus, the typical signs of extravasation of contrast material or air through the cuff may not be helpful in the investigation of failed repair.[74]

DCSA has been compared to MRI and arthroscopy. DCSA shows good sensitivity and specificity, particularly in the case of complete rotator cuff tears. Recent enthusiasm for MRI stems from its ability to demonstrate the adjacent soft tissues, capsulolabral structures, intraarticular bodies, and effusions, as well as changes in the adjacent marrow including localized edema in the setting of bone contusion or fracture. For patients unable to tolerate MRI because of shoulder pain or claustrophobia, or for those patients without access to MRI, DCSA may be the best first choice for the investigation of shoulder abnormalities. In addition, if DCSA yields a normal examination in the setting of much clinical suspicion of rotator cuff tear, the patient can be taken immediately to the CT or tomographic unit for a cross-sectional evaluation. This may yield further valuable information concerning the rotator cuff, the adjacent subacromial-subdeltoid bursae, and the labral structures (Fig. 1B-18). In addition, I feel that coronal reconstructions using both bone and soft tissue algorithm can be accomplished with no additional scan time and only minimal postprocessing image manipulation by the CT technologist.

ACKNOWLEDGMENT

We would like to express our gratitude to Dennis Carter and the Department of Radiology at Spohn Health Systems for their technical support in this endeavor.

References

1. :Fluoroscopy, in Curry TS III, Dowdey JE, Murry RC: *Christianson's Introduction to the Physics of Diagnostic Radiology*, 3d ed, Philadelphia, Lea & Febiger, 1984, pp 184–189.
2. Fluoroscopic imaging, in Kelsey CA (ed): *Essentials of Radiology Physics,* 1st ed, St. Louis, Warren H. Green, 1985, pp 243–265.
3. MADEWELL JE, SWEET DE: Tumors and tumor-like lesions in or about joints, in Resnick D, Niwayama G (eds): *Diagnosis of Bone and Joint Disorders*, 2d ed, Philadelphia, Saunders, 1988, pp 3889–3943.
4. MUSSEY RD, HENDERSON MS: Osteochondromatosis. *J Bone Joint Surg* 31A:619, 1949.
5. PAUL RG, LEACH RE: Synovial chondromatosis of the shoulder. *Clin Orthop* 68:130, 1970.
6. VARMA BP, RAMAKRISHNA YJ: Synovial chondromatosis of the shoulder. *Aust NZ J Surg* 46:44, 1976.
7. MISHRA KP: Synovial chondromatosis of the shoulder. A case report and review of the literature. *East Afr Med J* 55:130, 1978.
8. TORMES FR, HARDIN NJ, PLEDGER SR: Synovial chondromatosis of the shoulder: Case report. *Milit Med* 143:872, 1978.
9. RESNICK D: Fluoroscopy, in Resnick D, Niwayama G (eds): *Diagnosis of Bone and Joint Disorders*, 2d ed, Philadelphia, Saunders, 1988, pp 79–83.
10. HUDSON TM: Joint fluoroscopy before arthrography: Detection and evaluation of loose bodies. *Skel Radiol* 12:199, 1984.
11. CONE RO III, RESNICK D, DANZIG L: Shoulder impingement syndrome: Radiographic evaluation. *Radiology* 150:29, 1984.
12. NEER CS II: Anterior acromioplasty for the chronic impingement syndrome: A preliminary report. *J Bone Joint Surg* 54A:41, 1972.
13. CUOMO F, ZUCKERMAN JD: Magnetic resonance imaging of impingement and rotator cuff disorders. A surgical perspective. *MRI Clin North Am* 65, 1:1, 1993.
14. STOLLER DW, FRITZ, RC: Magnetic resonance of impingement and rotator cuff tears. *MRI Clin North Am* 47, 1:1, 1993.
15. BIGLIANI LU, MORRISON DS: Morphology of the acromion and its relationship to rotator cuff tears. *Orthop Trans* 10:216, 1986.
16. PUHL RW, ALTMAN MI, SETO JE, NELSON GA: The use of fluoroscopy in detection and excision of foreign bodies in the foot. *J Am Podiatry Assoc* 73:514, 1983.
17. TIRMAN RM, TIRMAN WS, NELSON CL: Arthrography of the shoulder joint: State of the art. *Crit Rev Diagn Imaging* 17:19–76, 1981.
17a. VILLER SP, MOITREL C, CHEMIN JJ: L'arthrographie de l'epaule en double contrast. *Ann Radiol* 23:599, 1980.
18. HALL FM, GOLDBERG RP, WYSHAK G, KILCOYNE RF: Shoulder arthrography: Comparison of morbidity after using various contrast media. *Radiology* 154:339–341, 1985.
19. HALL FM: Arthrography: Past, present and future. *AJR* 149:561–563, 1987.
20. GARDNER E, GREY DJ: Prenatal development of the human shoulder and acromioclavicular joints. *Am J Anat* 92:219, 1953.
21. GARDNER E: The prenatal development of the human shoulder joint. *Surg Clin North Am* 43:1465, 1963.
22. BRASCH JC, JAMIESON EB: *Cunningham's Textbook of Anatomy,* 7th ed, New York, Oxford University Press, 1937.
23. PETTERSON G: Rupture of the tendon aponeurosis of the shoulder joint in anterior inferior dislocations. *Acta Chir Scand* 87(suppl 73), 1942.
24. BALLINGER PW: The shoulder girdle, in Ballinger PW: *Merrill's Atlas of Radiographic Positioning*, 5th ed, St. Louis, Mosby, 1982, pp 153–182.
25. MESCHAN I: The upper extremity, in Meschan I: *Synopsis of Radiologic Anatomy with Computed Tomography*, Philadelphia, Saunders, 1980, pp 55–96.
26. BERENS DL, LOCKIE LM: Ossification of the coracoacromial ligament. *Radiology* 74:802–805, 1960.
27. MITCHELL MJ, CAUSEY G, BERTHOTY DP, SARTORIS DJ, RESNICK D: Peribursal fat plane of the shoulder, anatomic study and clinical experience. *Radiology* 168:699–704, 1988.
28. MOSLEY H, GOLDIE I: The arterial pattern of the rotator cuff of the shoulder. *J Bone Joint Surg* 45B:780, 1963.

29. WESTON WJ: The enlarged subdeltoid bursa in rheumatoid arthritis. *Br J Radiol* 42:481–486, 1969.

30. DEICHGÄRBER E, OLSSON B: Soft tissue and radiography in the painful shoulder. *Acta Radiol* 16:393–400, 1975.

31. DESMET AA: Axillary projection in radiography of the non-traumatized shoulder. *AJR* 134:511, 1980.

32. NEVIASER RJ, NEVIASER TJ: Major ruptures of the rotator cuff, in Watson M (ed): *Practical Shoulder Surgery*, London, Grune & Stratton, 1985, pp 169–224.

33. GHELMAN B, GOLDMAN AB: The double contrast shoulder arthrogram: Evaluation of rotator cuff tear. *Radiology* 124:251, 1977.

34. NEVIASER TJ: Arthrography of the shoulder. *Orthop Clin North Am* 11:205, 1980.

35. RESNICK D: Shoulder arthrography. *Radiol Clin North Am*, 19:243–253, 1981.

36. FLANNIGAN B, KURSUNOGLU-BRAHME S, SNIDER S, KARZEL R, DEL PIZZO W, RESNICK D: MR arthrography of the shoulder: Comparison with conventional MR imaging. *AJR* 155:829, 1990.

37. HAJEK PC, SARTORIS DJ, NEUMANN CH, ET AL.: Potential contrast agent for MR arthrography: In vitro evaluation and practical observations. *AJR* 149:97–104, 1987.

38. HODLER J, KURSUNOGLU-BRAHME S, SNIDER SJ, ET AL.: Rotator cuff disease: Assessment with MR arthrography vs standard MR imaging in 36 patients with arthroscopic confirmation. *Radiology* 182:431–436, 1992.

39. FRITZ RC, STOLLER DW: Fat-suppression MR arthrography of the shoulder (letter). *Radiology* 185:614–615, 1992.

40. MINK J, HARRIS E, RAPPAPORT M: Rotator cuff tears: Evaluation using double-contrast shoulder arthrography. *Radiology* 157:61–63, 1985.

41. GOLDMAN AB, GHELMAN B: The double-contrast shoulder arthrogram. A review of 158 studies. *Radiology* 127:655, 1978.

42. KAYE JJ, SCHNEIDER R: Positive contrast shoulder arthrography, in Frieiberger R, Kaye JJ (eds): *Arthrography*, New York, Appleton-Century-Crofts, 1979, p. 140.

43. ANDRÉN L, LUNGBERG BJ: Treatment of rigid shoulders by joint distention during arthrography. *Acta Orthop Scand* 36:45, 1965.

44. SPARTARO RF, KATZBERG RW, BURGENER FA, FISHER HW: Epinephrine enhanced knee arthrography. *Invest Radiol* 13:286–290, 1978.

45. HALL JM, ROSENTHAL DI, GOLDBURG RP, WYSHAK G: Morbidity from shoulder arthrography: Etiology incidence and prevention. *AJR* 136:59–62, 1981.

46. NAIMARK A, BAUM A: Pitfall to avoid—injection of the subcoracoid bursa: A cause of technical failure in shoulder arthrography. *J Can Assoc Rad S* 40:170–171, 1989.

47. WEINER DS, MACNAB I: Superior migration of the humeral head. A radiological aid in the diagnosis of tears of the rotator cuff. *J Bone Joint Surg* 52B:524–527, 1970.

48. COLTON RE, RIDEOUT DF: Tears in the humeral rotator cuff. A radiological and pathological necropsy survey. *J Bone Joint Surg* 46B:314–326, 1964.

49. SKINNER HA: Anatomical consideration relative to rupture of the supraspinatus tendon. *J Bone Joint Surg* 19:137–151, 1937.

50. DeSMET AA, TING YM, WEISS JJ: Shoulder arthrography in rheumatoid arthritis. *Radiology* 116:601–605, 1975.

51. GARCIA JF: Arthrographic visualization of rotator cuff tears. Optimal application of stress to the shoulder. *Radiology* 150:595, 1984.

52. BELTRAN J, GREY L, BOOLS JC, ZUELZER W, WEIS LD, UNVERFERTH LJ: Rotator lesions of the shoulder. Evaluation by direct sagittal CT arthrography. *Radiology* 160:161–165, 1986.

53. COOK JV, TAYAR R: Double-contrast computed tomographic arthrography of the shoulder joint. *Br J Radiol* 62:1043–1049, 1989.

54. RESNIK C, FRONEK J, FREY C, GERSHUNI D, RESNICK D: Intraarticular pressure determination during glenohumeral joint arthrography. Preliminary investigation. *Invest Radiol* 19:45–50, 1984.

55. RESNICK D: Arthrography, tenography, and bursography, in Resnick D, Niwayama G (eds): *Diagnosis of Bone and Joint Disorders*, 2d ed, Philadelphia, Saunders, 1988, p 346–347.

56. CRAIG EV: The geyser sign and torn rotator cuff: Clinical significance and pathomechanics. *Clin Orthop* 191:213, 1984.

57. ARNDT RD: Arthrography of the shoulder, in Arndt R, Horns JW, Gold RH (eds): *Clinical Arthrography*, Baltimore, Williams & Wilkins, 1984, p 70.

58. BURK LD, KARASICK D, KURTZ AV, MITCHELL DG, RIFKIN MD, MILLER CL, LEVY DW, FENLIN JM, BARTOLOZZI A: Rotator cuff tears: Prospective comparison of MR imaging with arthrography, sonography, and surgery. *AJR* 153:87–92, 1989.

59. ZLATKIN MB, IANOTTI JP, ESTERHAI J, DALINKA MK, KRESSEL HY: Magnetic resonance imaging of rotator cuff disease. Presented at the Society of Magnetic Resonance in Medicine, San Francisco, 1988.

60. McLAUGHLIN HL: The "frozen shoulder." *Clin Orthop* 20:126–131, 1961.

61. WEISSMAN B: The shoulder, in Weissman B (ed): *Orthopedic Radiology*, 1st ed, Philadelphia, Saunders, 1986, pp 215–278.

62. NEVIASER RJ: Adhesive capsulitis of the shoulder. *J Bone Joint Surg* 27A: 211, 1945.

63. GILULA LA, SCHOENECKER PL, MURPHY WA: Shoulder arthrography as a treatment modality. *AJR* 131:1047–1048, 1978.

64. NEVIASER RJ: Lesions of the biceps and tendonitis of the shoulder. *Orthop Clin North Am* 11:343–348, 1980.

65. KILLORAN PJ, MARCOVE RC, FREIBERGER RH: Shoulder arthrography. *AJR* 103:658–688, 1968.

66. ENNEVAARA K: Painful shoulder joint in rheumatoid arthritis: Clinical and radiological study of 200 cases with special reference to the glenohumeral joint. *Acta Rheumatol Scand* 11(suppl):11, 1967.

67. VANLEERSUM M, SCHWEITZER ME: MRI of the biceps complex. *MRI Clin North Am* 1:777–786, 1993.

68. ABBOTT LC, SANDERS LB: Acute traumatic dislocation of the tendon of the long head of the biceps brachii: Report of six cases with operative findings. *Surgery* 6:817, 1939.

69. FREELAND AE, HIGGINS RW: Anterior shoulder dislocation with posterior displacement of the long head of the biceps

tendon: Arthrographic findings, a case report. *Orthopedics* 8:468–469, 1985.

70. HILL HA, SACHS MD: The grooved defect of the humeral head: A frequently unrecognized complication of dislocations of the shoulder joint. *Radiology* 35:690–700, 1940.

71. BANKART ASV: The pathology and treatment of recurrent dislocation of the shoulder joint. *Br J Surg* 26:23–29, 1938.

72. GOLDMAN AB: Double contrast shoulder arthrography, in Freiberger RH, Kaye JJ (eds): *Arthrography*. New York, Appleton-Century-Crofts, 1979, pp 165–188.

73. MINK JH, RICHARDSON A, GRANT TT: Evaluation of the glenoid labrum by double contrast shoulder arthrography. *AJR* 133:183–887, 1979.

74. CALVERT PT, PACKER NP, STOKER DJ, BAYLEY JIL, KESSEL L: Arthrography of the shoulder after operative repair of the torn rotator cuff. *J Bone Joint Surg* 68B:147–150, 1986.

1C TECHNICAL ASPECTS: COMPUTED TOMOGRAPHY WITH NORMAL ANATOMY

William E. Palmer
Susan V. Kattapuram

The combination of computed tomography and arthrography (CTA) of the shoulder has been most valuable in evaluating the labral-ligamentous complex for suspected glenohumeral instability. Rotator cuff and bicipital tendon disorders are also identified and are best localized on images reformatted in the optimal plane.

Anterior glenohumeral instability is a disabling condition, particularly for athletes. Clinical history and physical examination findings are conclusive in patients with recurrent dislocations. Instability due to glenohumeral subluxation, however, is more common and often poses a diagnostic dilemma for the orthopedist. Other internal derangements of the joint, including rotator cuff tears, may cause similar, nonspecific symptoms and signs. As therapeutic approaches to labral and rotator cuff disorders have become more specialized, orthopedists have depended more heavily on the anatomic delineation and diagnostic accuracy of imaging studies, particularly CTA, as important tools in the preoperative evaluation of patients with suspected glenohumeral instability.

Plain radiographs and stress views may demonstrate a Hills-Sachs defect, glenoid fracture, or abnormal glenohumeral translation, but they do not show the soft tissue structures that are critical to joint stability. While conventional arthrography has been successful in diagnosing complete rotator cuff tears, this technique is limited in patients with labral-ligamentous injury and glenohumeral instability. Arthrotomography was the first tomographic technique used to delineate the labrum. Results depended greatly on patient positioning, the distribution of gas and contrast around the labrum, and the expertise of the radiologist.[1-8] Patients, especially those with shoulder pain, had difficulty maintaining the appropriate position for the duration of the study.

Since the early 1980s, CTA of the shoulder has been performed to assess the labral-ligamentous complex. Numerous reports have described the advantages of this technique over arthrotomography, including spatial resolution, patient comfort, and diagnostic accuracy.[4,9-30] All suggest it is accurate in the detection of glenoid labral abnormalities. CT images are obtained in the axial plane and are most useful for evaluating the anterior and posterior segments of the labrum (Fig. 1C-1). One report has described an innovative approach to patient positioning that permits direct multiplanar imaging.[31] Although direct CT coronal imaging improves visualization of the superior labrum as well as the critical zone of the rotator cuff, only one or two slices are obtained. By combining axial, direct coronal, and sagittal oblique scanning, CTA permits a complete evaluation of the shoulder disorder.[26]

Although CTA is generally considered to be superior to conventional magnetic resonance imaging (MRI) in evaluating the labrum, MR arthrography, which is discussed in separate chapters, has shown promise in detecting abnormalities of the labral-ligamentous complex and in identifying patients with instability. Intraarticular contrast solution offers similar advantages whether combined with MR imaging or CT.[32] Nondisplaced labral tears are more conspicuous because they fill with contrast solution, whereas detached labral fragments are separated from the glenoid rim by tension from the glenohumeral ligaments (GHLs). The GHLs can be distinguished from labral fragments because they are outlined by contrast solution and can be followed from their labral origin until they merge with the distended capsule (Fig. 1C-2–5).

TECHNIQUE

During arthrography, the patient is positioned supine on the fluoroscopy table. If scout radiographs are not already available, they are obtained at this time to detect rotator cuff calcifications that could be mistaken for contrast material. The scout radiographs are also used to detect avulsion or impaction fractures of the humeral head or glenoid rim, degenerative changes of the glenohumeral or acromioclavicular joint, calcified loose bodies, and acromial spurs.

Figure 1C-1   Normal labrum. Axial image distal to the coracoid process shows contrast outlining the anterior and posterior labrum. The anterior labrum (*small, straight arrow*) has a triangular configuration, and the posterior labrum a more rounded appearance (*open arrow*). The biceps tendon (*large, straight arrow*) is surrounded by gas in the tendon sheath. The subscapularis muscle (S) defines the anterior capsular margin, and the teres minor (T) defines the posterior.

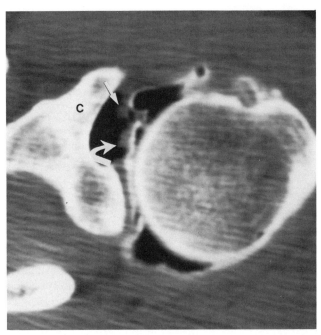

Figure 1C-3   Glenohumeral ligaments. Axial image at the midcoracoid (C) level shows the normal SGHL (*straight arrow*) and MGHL (*curved arrow*).

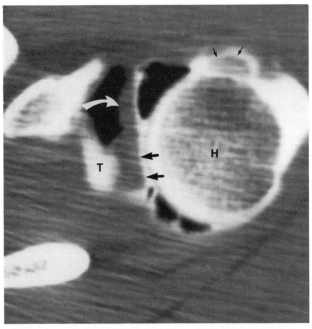

Figure 1C-2   Glenohumeral ligaments. Axial image at the level of the supraglenoid tubercle (T) shows the normal superior labrum (*straight arrows*) and the SGHL (*curved arrow*). The bicipital tendon (*small arrows*) is coursing over the humeral head (H), which should have a rounded contour at this level.

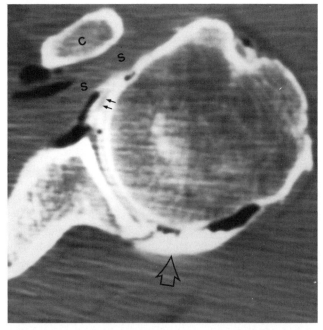

Figure 1C-4   Glenohumeral ligaments. At the inferior level of the coracoid process (C), contrast medium outlines the normal MGHL (*arrows*), which is an intraarticular structure located deep to the subscapularis tendon (S). With external rotation, the posterior capsule (*open arrow*) is redundant.

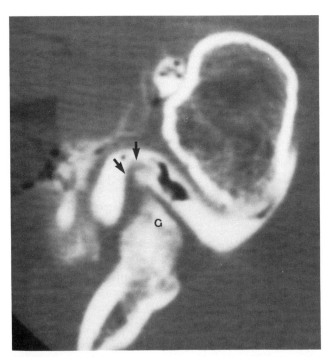

Figure 1C-5 Glenohumeral ligaments. Normal IGHL. Axial view in internal rotation at the inferior glenoid level (G) shows the lax IGHL (*arrows*).

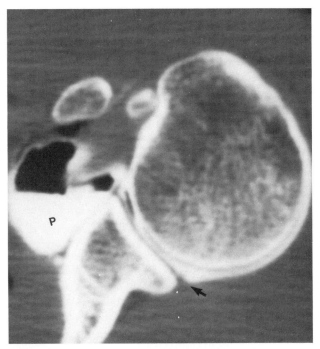

Figure 1C-6 Internal rotation axial view. Internal rotation results in redundancy of the subscapularis recess and anterior capsule (P), which becomes separated from the anterior glenoid rim and increases conspicuousness of the labrum. The posterior labrum (*arrow*) is less well visualized because the capsule is drawn close to it.

After positioning the shoulder in external rotation, fluoroscopic guidance is used to mark the desired entry point on the skin. The contrast solution is made by mixing 2 to 3 ml of iodinated contrast (Renografin M-60) with 1 ml of Xylocaine 1% and 0.3 ml of 1:1000 epinephrine. The epinephrine delays absorption of intraarticular contrast, thus allowing time for completion of the CT study. After sterile preparation and draping, a 20-gauge spinal needle is inserted into the glenohumeral joint using skin anesthesia. The contrast solution is injected with 12 ml room air (double contrast technique). Spot films are obtained before exercise with the patient supine and the shoulder positioned in internal followed by external rotation. While bending at the waist, the patient exercises the joint by making smaller and then larger circles with the arm. The intraarticular Xylocaine enables the patient to exercise with less discomfort. Upright anteroposterior spot films are obtained in internal and external rotation with the patient holding weights. These views may be repeated with the patient leaning forward at the waist to maximize the distance between the humeral head and acromion. This positioning optimizes detection of gas or contrast material in the subacromial space. Finally, an axillary view is obtained.

The fluoroscopic films are useful for detecting complete rotator cuff tears and partial tears of the inferior surface. These tears may be more difficult to identify on axial CT images. An axillary view shows glenohumeral alignment and displaced glenoid rim fractures, but it cannot be used to assess the labrum.

CT should follow arthrography immediately to minimize contrast absorption and dilution. At the Massachusetts General Hospital, the studies are performed on a GE 9800 unit at 140 kVp and 170 mas. The large body calibration file is employed, using a prospective target factor of 15 FOV and a detailed algorithm. If the shoulder is scanned by contiguous 3-mm sections, two sets of contiguous axial images are obtained, from the undersurface of the acromion process superiorly to the axillary recess inferiorly. One set is obtained with the shoulder in internal rotation, to show the anterior labrum (Fig. 1C-6), and the other in external rotation, to show the posterior labrum (see Fig. 1C-1). External rotation is achieved by elevating the elbow and apposing it to the body while the palm of the hand rests against the thigh. If 1.5-mm contiguous sections are prescribed, a single set of images is obtained with the shoulder in neutral position. Radiation exposure may be decreased using a helical scanner since the patient is scanned at 3 mm and the images are reconstructed at 1 mm. Images are filmed with both bone- and soft-tissue window settings. If thin sections are obtained, coronal oblique (parallel to the supraspinatus muscle) and sagittal oblique (perpendicular to the supraspinatus muscle) images then may be reformatted in selected cases.

ANATOMY

Rotator Cuff

The cross-sectional appearance of the humeral head varies according to the level of the axial image. Superior to the greater tuberosity, the head is essentially round and smooth in contour (see Fig. 1C-2). A posterolateral defect due to a Hill-Sachs fracture is best identified at this level. The greater tuberosity is the site of insertion of the supraspinatus, infraspinatus, and teres minor muscles. Images at this level may show degenerative sclerosis and cysts in patients with chronic tendinopathy as well as displaced or nondisplaced avulsion fractures following trauma.

The supraspinatus and infraspinatus tendons become conjoined over the greater tuberosity to form what is commonly termed the rotator cuff (Fig. 1C-7). The teres minor tendon has a separate humeral insertion site that is located posteroinferior to the infraspinatus tendon and is rarely torn, even in patients with retracted supraspinatus and infraspinatus tears. The subacromial-subdeltoid (SA-SD) space, the largest bursa in the human body, is located between the acromion and the rotator cuff and extends a variable distance under the deltoid muscle. This bursa creates gliding surfaces that lubricate the motion between the rotator cuff and the overlying acromion and the acromioclavicular joint. This space communicates with the glenohumeral joint in the presence of a full-thickness rotator cuff tear (Fig. 1C-8).

The subscapularis tendon inserts on the lesser tuberosity, which is anteromedial on the humeral head and separated from the greater tuberosity by the bicipital groove. The subscapularis bursa is a recess that communicates with the glenohumeral joint through an opening between the superior and middle glenohumeral ligaments. Just as the SA-SD bursa protects the supraspinatus tendon during motion, the subscapularis bursa

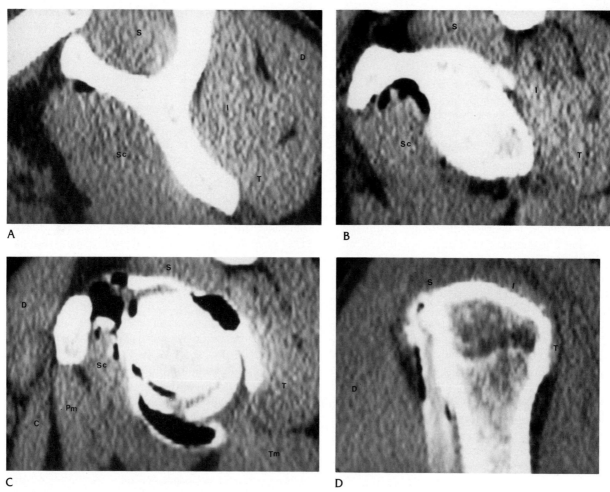

Figure 1C-7   Normal muscles. Sagittal oblique reformatted images at the level of the spine of the scapula **A**, glenoid **B**, humeral head **C**, and greater tuberosity **D**, showing the normal muscles around the shoulder joint. The supraspinatus (S), infraspinatus (I), teres minor (T), and subscapularis (Sc) muscles taper to their tendons. Also seen are the deltoid (D), teres major (Tm), coracobrachialis (Pm), and pectoralis minor (C).

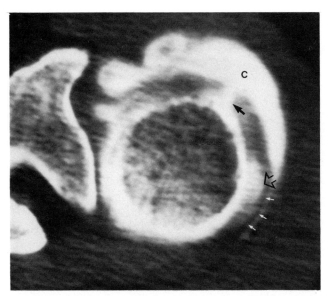

Figure 1C-8   Rotator cuff tear. Axial image at the apex of the humeral head shows loss of continuity of the distal cuff tendon (*small black arrow*) indicating a full-thickness tear through the supraspinatus. A contrast collection at the inferior surface of the infraspinatus (*open arrow*) represents a partial tear since the superior margin of the tendon (*white arrows*) remains intact. Contrast solution (C) has leaked into the SA-SD bursa.

protects the subscapularis tendon by providing a gliding mechanism adjacent to the coracoid process and the neck of the scapula. Synovitis may be intense in this bursa. It enlarges in patients with anterior instability and often collects loose bodies.

The coracoacromial arch protects the humeral head and the rotator cuff from direct trauma. This bony and ligamentous roof is formed by the coracoid process, coracoacromial ligament, acromion, and acromioclavicular joint. Axial images are suboptimal for evaluating the coracoacromial arch and its degenerative changes associated with the impingement syndrome. Reformatting in the sagittal oblique plane best shows the relationship between the rotator cuff and abnormalities of the arch, including acromial spurs and acromioclavicular joint hypertrophy.

On CTA images, a full-thickness rotator cuff tear is diagnosed if the contrast solution extends through a tendon defect into the SA-SD space (Fig. 1C-8, 9). A partial tear is diagnosed if the contrast solution penetrates the inferior surface of the tendon without reaching the SA-SD space (Fig. 1C-10). Partial cuff tears at the superior

Figure 1C-9   Rotator cuff tear. **A.** Axial, **B.** reformatted coronal, and **C.** sagittal oblique images show a vertical full-thickness tear (*arrow*) through the supraspinatus tendon. Although contrast is confined to the tear, gas has leaked into the subdeltoid bursa, best seen on the sagittal oblique image.

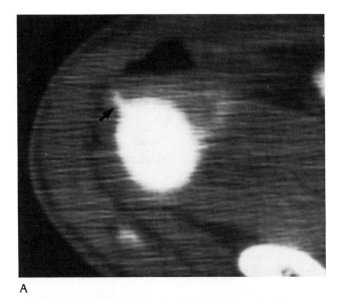

A

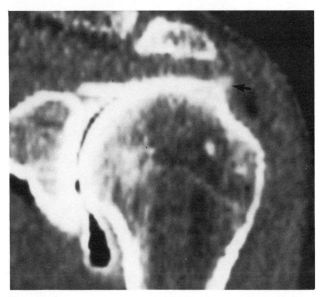

B

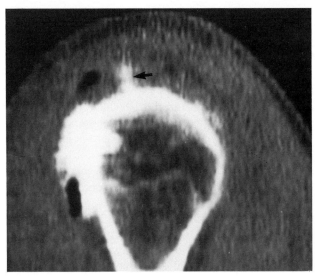

C

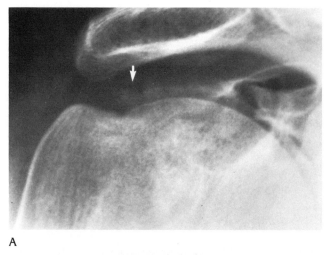

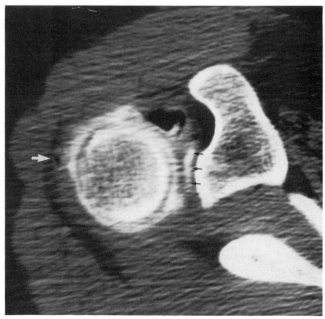

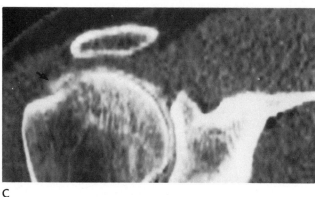

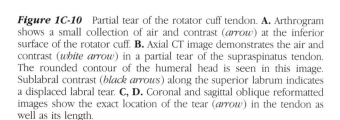

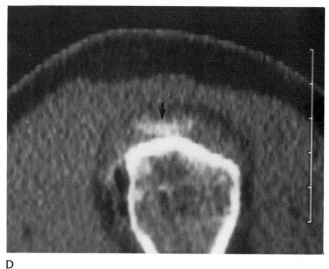

Figure 1C-10 Partial tear of the rotator cuff tendon. **A.** Arthrogram shows a small collection of air and contrast (*arrow*) at the inferior surface of the rotator cuff. **B.** Axial CT image demonstrates the air and contrast (*white arrow*) in a partial tear of the supraspinatus tendon. The rounded contour of the humeral head is seen in this image. Sublabral contrast (*black arrows*) along the superior labrum indicates a displaced labral tear. **C, D.** Coronal and sagittal oblique reformatted images show the exact location of the tear (*arrow*) in the tendon as well as its length.

tendon surface may not be visible since the contrast solution cannot fill them. Partial tears isolated to the superior surface or interstitium of the tendon are much less common than inferior surface tears.

Rotator cuff tears that are horizontally oriented begin anteriorly, in the distal supraspinatus tendon, and extend posteriorly. Thus, small horizontal tears are localized to the anterior margin of the cuff. Larger horizontal tears show retraction of the anterior cuff margin (Fig. 1C-11) with gradual tapering of the tear posteriorly. Vertical tears are more variable in location and may be confined to the junction of the supraspinatus and infraspinatus tendons (see Fig. 1C-9). Complete cuff avulsion involves both the supraspinatus and the infraspinatus tendons and may be obvious on scout radiographs obtained before

intraarticular contrast injection. Findings include superior subluxation of the humeral head and eburnation of the inferior margin of the acromion due to bony remodeling and contact with the humeral head (see Fig. 1C-11A).

Determining the location and size of a cuff tear requires the synthesis of numerous axial CT images, a process that may be difficult. Multiplanar reformation can display this information on a few selected images. Reformation in the coronal oblique plane shows the relationship between the greater tuberosity of the humerus and the critical zone of the rotator cuff (see Fig. 1C-10C, 9B). In patients with cuff tears, the degree of retraction can be assessed (see Fig. 1C-11A) and the supraspinatus muscle can be evaluated for bunching. Reformation in

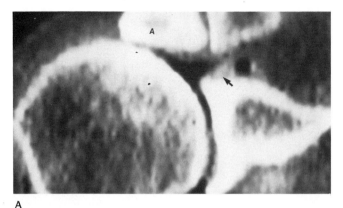
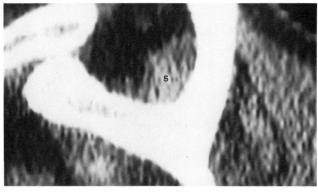

A   B

Figure 1C-11 Rotator cuff tear. **A.** Coronal reformatted image shows a torn, retracted supraspinatus tendon (*arrow*). There is a high-riding humerus with sclerosis and remodeling along the undersurface of the acromion (A), indicating a long-standing tear. **B.** In the sagittal oblique plane, atrophy of the supraspinatus muscle (S) also implies a chronic tear.

the sagittal oblique plane may help demonstrate the location of small cuff tears (see Fig. 1C-9C and 10D) and the presence of muscle atrophy (Fig. 1C-11B).

Glenoid Fossa and Labrum

The glenoid has an anterior tilt relative to the axis of the scapula. Patients with congenitally increased angle of tilt may have a predisposition to anterior instability. The glenoid fossa forms a concavity that is lined by articular cartilage, which may be thinner centrally than peripherally. On axial images, the posterior rim of the bony glenoid is more rounded than the anterior rim. The fibrocartilaginous labrum is attached to the hyaline cartilage of the glenoid rim, and it may contribute to the stability of the joint by deepening the concavity of the glenoid fossa.[29,31] In cross section, the labrum typically is triangular in shape, but it can show normal morphologic variations, including attenuation or notching of the free margin. The posterior labrum tends to be more blunted than the anterior labrum (see Fig. 1C-1).

A tear is diagnosed if the labrum is detached from the glenoid rim or if contrast material extends at least halfway through the body of the labrum or along its base at the junction with the underlying hyaline cartilage. Normal sublabral sulci may be misinterpreted as tears. These pseudotears, which become more prominent in older patients, occur at the base of either the superior labrum at its junction with the bicipital tendon or the anterosuperior labrum between the origins of the middle glenohumeral ligament (MGHL) and the inferior glenohumeral ligament (IGHL). Sublabral contrast confined to these sites should not be diagnosed as tears unless the labrum is displaced from the hyaline cartilage of the glenoid rim.

Deficiency is diagnosed if the labrum is severely truncated or absent (Fig. 1C-12). Because of the normal var-

iability in labral size and shape, a labrum that is blunted cannot with a high degree of confidence be diagnosed as deficient. Since a small labrum that is normal in contour may not be deficient, morphologic criteria may not be sufficient to distinguish between a mildly blunted deficient labrum and a small intact labrum.

GLENOHUMERAL LIGAMENTS AND BICEPS TENDON

Depending on the distribution of gas and contrast medium in the joint, the intraarticular course of each gle-

Figure 1C-12 Posterior instability of the shoulder joint. Axial image shows absence of the posterior labrum, indicating deficiency. The posterior capsule is stripped medially. There are associated degenerative changes, including sclerosis and subchondral cyst formation (*arrow*).

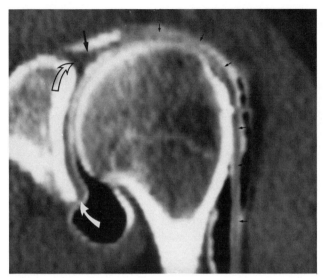

Figure 1C-13 Biceps tendon. Coronal oblique reformatted image shows the superior labrum (*curved, open arrow*), the labral-bicipital junction (*straight arrow*), and the continuation of the tendon (*small arrows*) in the distal sheath. Reformatting in this plane best shows the inferior labrum (*curved, closed arrow*).

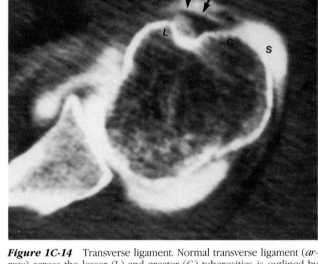

Figure 1C-14 Transverse ligament. Normal transverse ligament (*arrow*) across the lesser (L) and greater (G) tuberosities is outlined by contrast. Contrast solution is in the subdeltoid space (S) because of a rotator cuff tear.

nohumeral ligament may be visible from the glenolabral origin to the capsule. The superior glenohumeral ligament (SGHL) originates from the superior labrum (1 cm anterior to the labral-bicipital junction) and courses anteriorly parallel to the coracoid process (see Fig. 1C-2). The origin of the MGHL is conjoined with that of the SGHL, but rarely it can arise independently from the midlabrum. The MGHL takes a vertical path adjacent to

the superior margin of the subscapularis tendon and becomes imperceptible distally as it merges with the anterior capsule (see Fig. 1C-3, 4). Although the IGHL is formed by three components—the anterosuperior and posterosuperior bands and intervening axillary pouch—the anterosuperior band is most important to anterior stability. The anterosuperior band originates from the anteroinferior labrum and is thicker than the SGHL or

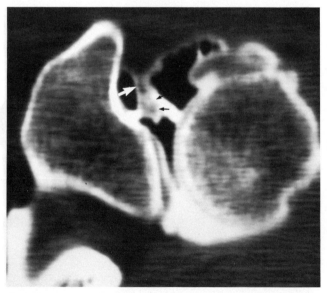

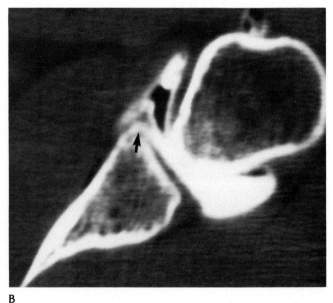

A B

Figure 1C-15 Anterior labral tear. **A.** Axial image shows the anterior labrum (*small black arrows*) displaced from the glenoid rim by the SGHL (*white arrow*). **B.** At an inferior level the tear (*arrow*) extends distally into the origin of the IGHL. At arthroscopy, this patient had anterior instability and underwent Bankart repair.

the MGHL. When the shoulder is adducted, which is the usual scanning position, the anterosuperior band is lax as it courses into the axillary pouch and curves toward the humerus (see Fig. 1C-5). The superior margin of the anterosuperior band of the IGHL arises variably from the two to the five o'clock position along the anterior labrum (mean distribution at 3 o'clock). Whereas the SGHL and MGHL show discrete labral attachment sites measuring less than 1 cm, the origin of the IGHL is broadbased and spans 1 to 3 cm.

The tendon of the long head of the biceps originates from the supraglenoid tubercle and is attached to the superior labrum. On axial images, the bicipital tendon is first identified as it emerges from its junction with the superior labrum. Its intraarticular course may be difficult to follow, resulting from volume averaging with the adjacent humeral head and subscapularis tendon. The bicipital tendon passes through the groove between the greater and lesser tuberosities (Fig. 1C-13) and is secured by the transverse humeral ligament (Fig. 1C-14). A single CTA image reformatted in the coronal oblique plane shows continuity of the bicipital tendon from the supraglenoid tubercle to the distal tendon sheath (see Fig. 1C-13). Bicipital tendon disorders include tendinitis and degeneration, both of which may lead to partial tear or complete tendon rupture. Bicipital tendon injury may occur at its origin, due to extension of a tear of the superior labrum, or in the bicipital groove, due to bony proliferation at the margins of the tuberosities. Axial images show absence of the tendon in the groove following rupture with retraction. If the tendon dislocates out of the bicipital groove, it may lie outside the joint if

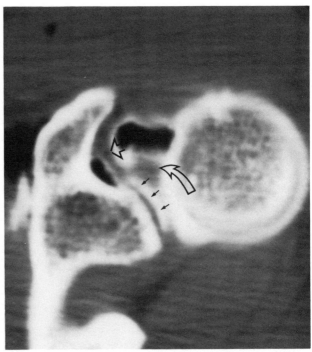

A

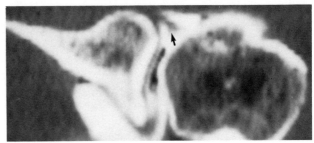

B

Figure 1C-17 Superior labral tear. **A.** SLAP lesion. The axial image shows the SGHL (*straight open, arrow*) and labral-bicipital junction (*curved, open arrow*). Contrast (*black arrows*) extends under the superior labrum. **B.** Reformatted coronal oblique image shows displacement of the superior labrum (*arrow*) from the glenoid rim. Labral tear in this location is not associated with instability.

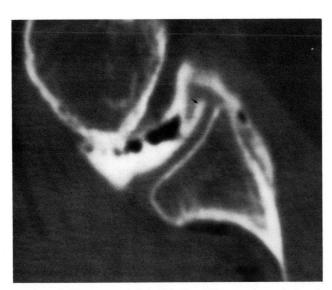

Figure 1C-16 Anterior inferior labral tear. Contrast (*arrow*) extends under the anteroinferior labrum at the origin of the IGHL. A labral tear in this site is closely correlated with anterior instability. This patient had Bankart reconstruction of the capsule.

the subscapularis tendon remains intact, or within the joint if the subscapularis tendon is completely torn. Loose bodies may collect in the bicipital tendon sheath.

FUNCTIONAL SIGNIFICANCE OF THE LABRAL ATTACHMENTS

The most common sites of labral tears correspond to the attachment sites of the GHLs and the bicipital tendon (Fig. 1C-15–17). The functional anatomy of the labral-ligamentous complex and labral-bicipital junction helps to explain this pathophysiologic relationship.

Structures that attach to the labrum create stress points that may cause labral injury. Excessive tension on the GHLs or bicipital tendon places traction on the labrum

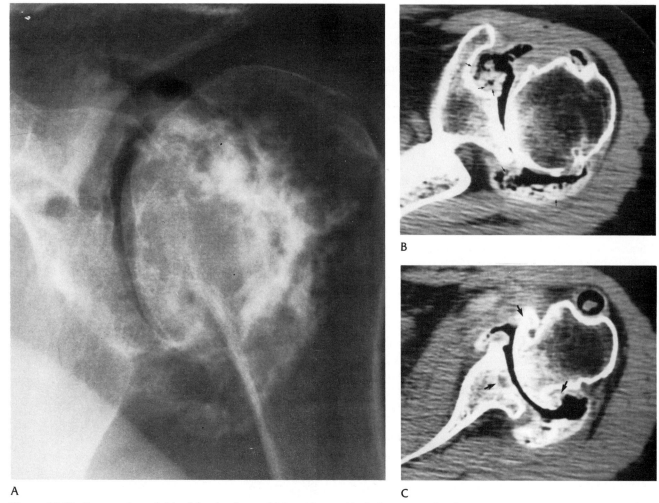

A   C

Figure 1C-18 Degenerative arthritis of the glenohumeral joint with synovitis. **A.** Anteroposterior view after contrast injection shows loss of the joint space. Note the irregular capsular filling defects due to synovitis. **B, C.** Axial views show the thickened synovial fronds (**B**, *small arrows*) projecting into the joint. There is complete loss of the articular cartilage with other degenerative changes including sclerosis, cysts, and osteophytes (**C**, *straight arrows*) of the glenohumeral joint.

and can tear it. Thus, stress on the IGHL during anterior glenohumeral subluxation or dislocation can avulse the anteroinferior labrum from the glenoid rim. This mechanism results in the classic Bankart lesion (Fig. 1C-16). Acute injury of the superior labrum often results from violent contraction of the biceps muscle, as occurs when an athlete dives to catch a ball and falls on an outstretched arm. Injury also can develop over time from the cumulative stress of repeated overhead motion (overuse syndrome) associated with pitching, serving (tennis), and swimming. When these tears are confined to the superior labrum, they are called SLAP lesions (*s*uperior *l*abrum, *a*nterior to *p*osterior; see Fig. 1C-10B, 17).

Because the labral and ligamentous collagen fibers intertwine to form a strong histologic bond, injury is more likely to occur at the glenolabral junction than at the labral-ligamentous junction. The location and length of labral tears may be described in relation to the bicipital tendon and the origins of the glenohumeral ligaments. Since a Bankart lesion can extend superiorly into the labral-bicipital junction and a SLAP lesion can extend inferiorly into the origin of the IGHL (similar to the meniscal tear of the knee that propagates longitudinally from the posterior horn into the anterior horn and develops a buckethandle configuration), it may be impossible to determine the starting point of a large tear.

GLENOHUMERAL INSTABILITY

The pathophysiologic mechanism of instability has been attributed to abnormalities of the articular surfaces, labrum, GHLs, and rotator cuff.[4,7–10,14–18,20,22–25,29,31,33] Although the anatomy of these structures is known, their functional contributions to stability remain incompletely understood. A shallow glenoid was once considered a predisposing factor in dislocation. The labrum was subsequently emphasized as a mechanical barrier that increased stability by deepening the concavity of the glenoid fossa. However, the function of the labrum as a mechanical barrier against humeral subluxation is much less important than its function as an attachment site for the GHLs. The results of kinematic and cutting experiments in the orthopedic literature suggest that the IGHL functions as a major stabilizing restraint and that the labrum is significant as the ligamentous attachment site. Labral tears at the attachment site of the IGHL may lead to ligamentous insufficiency and, therefore, to anterior instability (see Fig. 1C-15, 16). Ligamentous insufficiency is important to identify because chronic instability may result in degenerative joint disease (Fig. 1C-18), pain, and loss of shoulder function.

References

1. EL-KHOURY GY, ALBRIGHT JP, ABU YOUSEF MM, MONTGOMERY WJ, TUCK SL: Arthrotomography of the glenoid labrum. *Radiology* 131:333–337, 1979.
2. McGLYNN FJ, EL-KHOURY GY, ALBRIGHT JP: Arthrotomography of the glenoid labrum in shoulder instability. *J Bone Joint Surg* 64A:506–518, 1982.
3. BRAUNSTEIN EM, O'CONNOR G: Double-contrast arthrotomography of the shoulder. *J Bone Joint Surg* 64A:192–195, 1982.
4. DEUTSCH AL, RESNICK D, MINK JH, ET AL.: Computed and conventional arthrotomography of the glenohumeral joint: Normal anatomy and clinical experience. *Radiology* 153:603–609, 1984.
5. RESNIK CS, DEUTSCH AL, RESNICK D, ET AL.: Arthrotomography of the shoulder. *RadioGraphics* 4:963–976, 1984.
6. KLEINMAN PK, KANZARIA PK, GOSS TP, ET AL.: Axillary arthrotomography of the glenoid labrum. *AJR* 141:993–999, 1984.
7. EL-KHOURY GY, KATHOL MH, CHANDLER JB, ET AL.: Shoulder instability: Impact of glenohumeral arthrotomography on treatment. *Radiology* 160:669–673, 1986.
8. PAPPAS AM, GOSS TP, KLEINMAN PK: Symptomatic shoulder instability due to lesions of the glenoid labrum. *Am J Sports Med* 11:279–288, 1983.
9. KNEISL JS, SWEENEY HJ, PAIGE ML: Correlation of pathology observed in double-contrast arthrotomography and arthroscopy of the shoulder. *Arthroscopy* 4:21–24, 1988.
10. DANZIG L, RESNICK D, GREENWAY G: Evaluation of unstable shoulders by computed tomography. A preliminary study. *Am J Sports Med* 10:138–141, 1982.
11. TIRMAN RM, NELSON CS, TIRMAN WS: Arthrography of the shoulder joint: State of the art. *Crit Rev Diagn Imaging* 17:19–76, 1981.
12. HAYNOR DR, SHUMAN WP: Double contrast CT arthrography of the glenoid labrum and shoulder girdle. *RadioGraphics* 4:411–420, 1984.
13. DEUTSCH AL, RESNICK D, MINK JH: Computed tomography of the glenohumeral and sternoclavicular joints. *Orthop Clin North Am* 16:497–511, 1985.
14. RANDELLI M, ODELLA F, GAMBRIOLI PL: Clinical experience with double contrast medium computerized tomography (CTA) in instability of the shoulder. *Ital J Orthop Traumatol* 12:151–158, 1986.
15. RAFII M, FIROOZNIA H, GOLIMBU C, MINKOFF J, BONAMO J: CT arthrography of capsular structures of the shoulder. *AJR* 14:361–367, 1986.
16. RAFII M, FIROOZNIA H, BONAMO JJ, MINKOFF J, GOLIMBO C: Athlete shoulder injuries: CT arthrographic findings. *Radiology* 162:559–564, 1987.
17. SINGSON RO, FELDMAN F, BIGLIANI L, ROSENBERG ZS: Recurrent shoulder dislocation after surgical repair: Double-contrast CT arthrography. *Radiology* 164:425–428, 1987.
18. SINGSON RO, FELDMAN F, BIGLIANI L: CT arthrographic patterns in recurrent glenohumeral instability. *AJR* 149:749–753, 1987.
19. SHUMAN WP, KILCOYNE RF, MATSEN FA, ROGERS JV, MACK LA: Double-contrast computed tomography of the glenoid labrum. *AJR* 141:581–584, 1983.
20. KINNARD P, TRICOIRE JL, LEVESQUE R, BERGERON D: Assessment of the unstable shoulder by computed arthrography. A preliminary report. *Am J Sports Med* 11:157–159, 1983.
21. PENNES DR: Shoulder joint: Arthrographic CT appearance. *Radiology* 175:878–879, 1990.
22. RIBBANS WJ, MITCHELL R, TAYLOR GJ: Computerised arthrotomography of primary anterior dislocation of the shoulder. *J Bone Joint Surg* 72B:181–185, 1990.

23. WILSON AJ, TOTTY WG, MURPHY WA, ET AL.: Shoulder joint: Arthrographic CT and long-term follow-up, with surgical correlation. *Radiology* 173:329–333, 1989.
24. STILES RG, OTTE MT. Imaging of the shoulder. *Radiology* 188:603–613, 1993.
25. KIEFT GJ, BLOEM JL, ROZING PM, OBERMANN WR: MR imaging of recurrent anterior dislocation of the shoulder: Comparison with CT arthrography. *AJR* 150:1083–1087, 1988.
26. BELTRAN J, GRAY LA, BOOLS JC, ZUELZER W, WEIS LD, UNVERFERTH LJ: Rotator cuff lesions of the shoulder: Evaluation by direct sagittal CT arthrography. *Radiology* 160:161–165, 1986.
27. McNIESH LM, CALLAGHAN JJ: CT Arthrography of the shoulder: Variations of the glenoid labrum. *AJR* 149:963–966, 1987.
28. PENNES DR, JONSSON K, BUCKWALTER K, ET AL.: Computed arthrotomography of the shoulder: Comparison of examinations made with internal and external rotation of the humerus. *AJR* 153:1017–1019, 1989.
29. COUMAS JM, WAITE RJ, GOSS TP, ET AL.: CT and MR evaluation of the labral capsular ligamentous complex of the shoulder. *AJR* 58:591–597, 1992.
30. HUNTER JC, BLATZ DJ, ESCOBEDO EM: SLAP lesions of the glenoid labrum: CT arthrographic and arthroscopic correlation. *Radiology* 184:513–518, 1992.
31. BLUM A, BOYER B, REGENT D, SIMON JM, ET AL.: Direct coronal view of the shoulder with arthrographic CT. *Radiology* 188:677–681, 1993.
32. ZLATKIN MB, BJORKENGREN AG, GYLYS-MORIN V, RESNICK D, SARTORIS DJ: Cross-sectional imaging of the capsular mechanism of the glenohumeral joint. *AJR* 150:151–158, 1988.
33. ROTHMAN RH, MARVEL JP Jr., HEPPENSTALL RB: Anatomic considerations in the glenohumeral joint. *Orthop Clin North Am* 6:341–352, 1975.

1D TECHNICAL ASPECTS: MAGNETIC RESONANCE IMAGING WITH NORMAL ANATOMY

Mahvash Rafii
Hossein Firooznia

Magnetic resonance imaging (MRI), the newest and most sophisticated imaging modality, has revolutionized diagnostic imaging. It has had an impact on musculoskeletal imaging not paralleled by any other imaging modality, owing to its exquisite resolution of soft tissue structures and its multiplanar capability. Perhaps the most significant improvement achieved by MRI is in imaging articular disorders. For many diagnostic applications MRI has replaced arthrography, and this noninvasive modality has proved to be more accurate. Furthermore, MRI has expanded the horizon of diagnosis to a variety of other articular and intrinsic soft tissue disorders that cannot be visualized by other imaging modalities.

Optimal MRI of the shoulder joint was achieved with some difficulty, owing to the anatomic characteristics of this joint. Technical advances such as off-center zoom technique, oblique plane imaging capabilities, and the development of dedicated surface coils were essential to improving image quality and to appropriately displaying rotator cuff and capsulolabral anatomy.[1-5] Nevertheless, high accuracy rates have been achieved in evaluating pathologic changes of the rotator cuff and the capsulolabral complex and other disorders in and around the glenohumeral joint.[6-20] MRI, a noninvasive modality, provides the most detailed and comprehensive imaging for evaluation of shoulder joint disorders.

IMAGING TECHNIQUE

Pulse Sequences

CONVENTIONAL SPIN-ECHO SEQUENCE

The majority of the criteria developed for the diagnosis of rotator cuff and glenohumeral lesions have been based on conventional spin-echo pulse sequences. Although newer pulse sequences have since been introduced for shoulder imaging, the spin-echo sequences continue to be widely utilized owing to their established efficacy and to radiologists' widespread familiarity with their contrast

scale and imaging parameters.[21] A combination of T1-weighted, proton-density and T2-weighted or a double-echo T2-weighted sequence is most often used for shoulder imaging.

T1-weighted images provide excellent osseous and soft tissue anatomic detail in the least imaging time. They are specifically useful for depiction of periarticular fat planes and for assessing the bone marrow. Imaging parameters include repetition time (TR) of 500 to 800 msec, echo time (TE) of 12 to 30 msec, and two to four excitations.

Proton-density images display the highest signal-to-noise ratio, improving depiction of anatomic detail and increasing sensitivity in detection of intrinsic signal alterations of the rotator cuff and capsulolabral structures. T2-weighted images characteristically have a low signal-to-noise ratio, owing to longer TE (80 to 100 msec); however, these images, by virtue of higher signal intensity of fluid collections and soft tissue edema, are essential for characterization of signal alterations within and around the rotator cuff and capsulolabral complex. The long TR (2000 msec) in proton-density and T2-weighted sequences prolongs imaging time and may increase the likelihood of involuntary patient motion and degradation of images. Other imaging parameters include 3- to 4-mm slice thickness, 128 by 256 to 192 by 256 imaging matrix, and a field of view of 14 to 16 cm.

FAST SPIN-ECHO SEQUENCES

Fast spin-echo (FSE) sequence is based on the rapid acquisition relaxation enhanced sequence.[22] This method employs a single 90° excitation pulse followed by a series (train) of 180° radiofrequency refocusing pulses. Each pulse generates spin echoes that are separately phase encoded. The imaging time is reduced by the number of echoes per excitation. The time saving can be used to improve image quality and resolution; tissue contrast equivalent to that of conventional spin-echo images is generally achieved.[21,23,24] The major differences in tissue contrast include increased signal intensity of fat on T2-weighted FSE images and reduced sensitivity to susceptibility effects related to blood breakdown products.[21] Other characteristics of FSE sequence include image blurring with the use of short TE or long echo train and reduced image quality with use of a low-resolution imaging matrix.[21] Because signal characteristics in FSE sequences may reduce the conspicuousness of some lesions,[25] we have not used this sequence routinely for musculoskeletal and shoulder imaging.

GRADIENT-ECHO IMAGING

In gradient-echo (GRE) imaging the 180° refocusing pulse is replaced by reversal of gradients. GRE sequences also employ relatively short TR and TE, and reduced flip angles. The imaging time is thus shorter than with spin-echo sequences. Tissue contrast on GRE images is different from that of spin-echo images: generally signal intensity from muscle is higher and that from bone marrow is lower (susceptibility artifact). Tissue contrast in GRE sequences is dependent on TR, TE, and flip angle values; reducing flip angle or increasing TE results in increased T2 weighting on these images.

Contrast in GRE sequence also depends on whether the transverse magnetization from the previous excitation is allowed to persist (steady state: GRASS, FISP) or destroyed through the application of spoiler gradients (spoiled: FLASH, SPOILED GRASS). Steady state sequences can generate T2*/T1-weighted tissue contrast, whereas FLASH and Spoiled GRASS sequences result in T1 weighting.[21]

The use of GRE sequence for rotator cuff imaging has been reported[26]; however, the data are insufficient and the accuracy of these sequences, as compared with spin-echo sequence, has not been determined. It is our impression that the generally higher signal intensity of soft tissue elements on GRE images (again, compared with spin-echo images) may result in false positive readings.

Visualization of the glenoid labrum is enhanced on GRE sequences owing to high signal intensity of the articular cartilage, resulting in an arthrographic effect.[27] Another characteristic feature of GRE images is the low signal intensity of the marrow space. Magnetic susceptibility artifacts[28] are also more prominent on these images, owing to the absence of a 180° radiofrequency refocusing pulse.[21] GRE sequences may be used to obtain three-dimensional images. Three-dimensional images with thin slice and no interslice gap take longer to acquire; however, reformatting may be performed in any plane.

FAT-SUPPRESSION IMAGING

The use of fat-suppression sequences has been advocated to improve visualization of bone marrow abnormalities and rotator cuff lesions.[28–32] In addition to improved visualization of fluid on fat-suppressed T2-weighted images, the advantages of this sequence include reduced artifacts related to respiratory motion and elimination of chemical shift misregistration artifacts.[21,31] These sequences are not universally available, and several technical disadvantages preclude their routine use for shoulder imaging.

Patient Positioning

MR examination of the shoulder is performed with the patient supine and the arm in neutral rotation; the palm is placed against the thigh and is wrapped to the trunk for immobilization. This position maintains the oblique coronal orientation of the supraspinatus tendon and reduces partial volume averaging with surrounding fat. Additionally, in this position the anterior and the posterior components of the joint capsule are equally relaxed. Axial imaging in both internal and external rotation of the humerus have been advocated for optimal visualization of the capsulolabral lesions.[33] Routine employment of this technique is time consuming, though it may be used selectively in appropriate clinical settings. The patient's arm and forearm should be supported, if necessary, to prevent involuntary motion. Utilization of a dedicated shoulder surface coil is mandatory in order to obtain high-resolution images.[5,11]

Imaging Planes

Complete MR examination of the shoulder requires imaging in axial, oblique coronal, and oblique sagittal planes.

AXIAL PLANE

First, a series of coronal scout images is obtained. Axial images are obtained from the acromion process to below the glenoid margin using the scout coronal image of the glenohumeral joint as the localizer (Fig. 1D-1). A T1-weighted or intermediate (long-TR, short-TE) spin-echo sequence provides adequate information about the glenoid labrum and the glenohumeral joint. When shoulder instability and a labrum tear are suspected, and routinely in younger persons, a double-echo T2-weighted sequence is utilized.[15–17] The density-weighted images of this series portray the morphology and signal alterations of the capsulolabral complex to the best advantage, while the long-TR and long-TE images, because they highlight areas of fluid collection, add to the specificity of MRI findings.

OBLIQUE CORONAL PLANE

The oblique coronal images are obtained in an orientation parallel to the main axis of the supraspinatus and span the joint from the tip of the coracoid process anteriorly to the scapular spine posteriorly. The axial image of the supraspinatus is used as a localizer (Fig. 1D-2). A double-echo T2-weighted sequence is most suited for imaging in this plane. The anatomy of the rotator cuff is

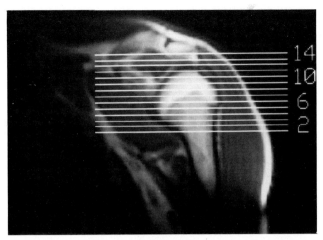

Figure 1D-1 Coronal scout "plan scan" for axial plane imaging sequence.

best displayed on proton-density images, whereas a T2-weighted sequence is essential for accurate evaluation and differentiation of cuff lesions.[6–14] An additional T1-weighted sequence for evaluation of the subacromial peribursal fat is useful but not essential.[14,33]

OBLIQUE SAGITTAL PLANE

Oblique sagittal plane images are acquired perpendicular to the long axis of the supraspinatus or oblique coronal images (Fig. 1D-3). They display the sectional anatomy of the coracoacromial arch and the rotator cuff in the sagittal plane of the shoulder. A double-echo T2-weighted sequence is preferred for imaging in this plane.

MR-Arthrography

MRI of the shoulder enhanced by intraarticular paramagnetic contrast solution or saline has been advocated for improved visualization of some partial or small full-thick-

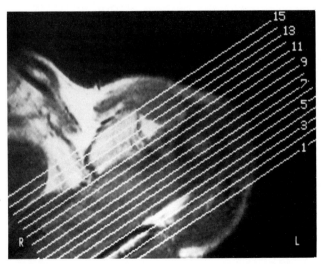

Figure 1D-2 "Plan scan" for oblique coronal imaging. Image selected from the axial sequence.

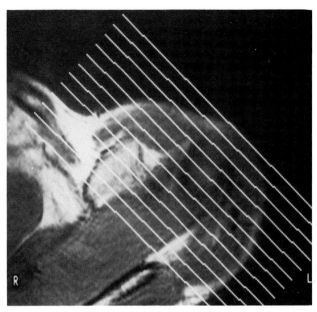

Figure 1D-3 "Plan scan" for oblique sagittal imaging sequence.

ness rotation cuff and labrum tears.[34–36] Disadvantages of MR arthrography include invasiveness, added expense, and decreased sensitivity for detection of intratendinous or bursal surface tears unless T2-weighted imaging is also performed. In addition the bright appearance of the subacromial-subdeltoid peribursal fat on T1-weighted images simulating contrast agent in the bursa necessitates the use of a fat suppression technique for oblique coronal imaging.[30,31,37] In our opinion, the high accuracy rates reported in the MRI diagnosis of rotator cuff and labrum tears precludes the routine use of MR-arthrography for routine shoulder MR imaging. MR-arthrography may selectively be utilized when conventional MR imaging has failed in clearly identifying or excluding an expected lesion.[38]

MR-arthrography uses either a diluted solution of paramagnetic contrast material or normal saline as the contrast agent.[35,38,39] Gadopentetate dimeglumine (Magnevist) in a concentration of 469.01 mg/ml has been used in variable dilutions ranging from one ml gadopentetate dimeglumine in 150 to 250 ml normal saline. Using the standard arthrographic technique and under fluoroscopic guidance a 20 gauge spinal needle is placed in the shoulder joint at the junction of the middle and the distal third of the anterior glenohumeral joint. The intraarticular position of the needle tip is confirmed by injection of 0.5 ml iodinated contrast agent. Diluted gadopentetate solution or saline, 12 to 18 ml, is injected into the joint with caution, to avoid overdistending the joint capsule or introducing air bubbles. The intraarticular use of paramagnetic contrast has not yet been approved by the U.S. Food and Drug Administration, so it is necessary to obtain institutional approval and informed consent to perform this procedure. Experimental and

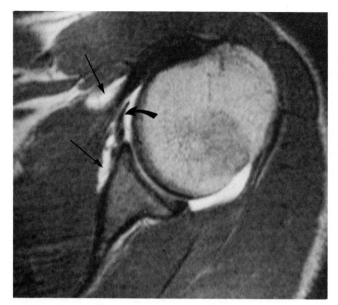
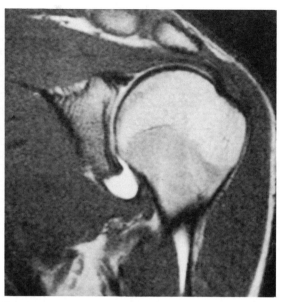

A   B

Figure 1D-4 MR arthrogram of the left shoulder. **A.** Axial T1-weighted (560/29) image at the superior margin of the subscapularis tendon. The midglenohumeral ligament *(curved arrow)* is attached to the anterior labrum. Normal extension of the subscapularis bursa over the scapular cortex and at the ventral aspect of the subscapularis tendon is visualized *(straight arrows)*. **B.** Oblique coronal T1-weighted image. Contrast material defines the articular surfaces. The axillary pouch and the bicipital tendon sheath are also an opacified subscapularis bursa.

clinical studies demonstrate no adverse effect on the synovial lining and articular cartilage as a result of intraarticular administration of such contrast agents.[35,36,40]

The imaging sequence used in MR arthrography varies with the contrast agent. Originally a T1-weighted sequence was used with paramagnetic contrast agents (Fig. 1D-4).[35] Owing to difficulty in differentiating the normally bright subacromial subdeltoid peribursal fat from paramagnetic contrast agent extravasated through a cuff defect, a fat-suppression sequence is necessary for oblique coronal imaging.[30,31,37] With saline as contrast agent T2-weighted or fat-suppressed imaging is utilized.

NORMAL ANATOMY

The shoulder girdle consists of four separate articulations: the glenohumeral, the scapulothoracic, the acromioclavicular, and the sternoclavicular joint. Supported by several groups of strong muscles, each of these joints plays an important role in the coordinated movement of the arm.

The glenohumeral joint is a complex yet highly mobile joint. Its range of motion and stability are provided and supported by a redundant fibrous joint capsule[41] and by four strategically situated groups of muscles (Table 1D-1).[42] The osseous anatomy of this joint is notable in that it consists of a relatively flat glenoid fossa and a considerably larger, and round, humeral head (Fig. 1D-5).[43] At the peripheral margin of the humeral head articular surface a slight indentation forms the anatomic neck of the

humerus, which is the lateral site of attachment of the joint capsule. The greater and the lesser humeral tuberosities are situated peripheral (lateral) to the anatomic neck. The greater tuberosity is the site of attachment of the supraspinatus, infraspinatus, and teres minor tendons. The lesser tuberosity, situated anteriorly, is the site of attachment of the subscapularis tendon.

Between the humeral tuberosities the intertubercular, or bicipital, groove is formed. The transverse humeral ligament extends between the two tuberosities, forming the roof of the bicipital groove. The long tendon of the biceps brachii muscle passes through the intertubercular groove. Certain variations in the depth or the shape of the groove may make the biceps tendon vulnerable to

Table 1D-1   Anatomy of the Shoulder Muscles

Scapulohumeral group	Axioscapular group
Supraspinatus	Trapezius
Infraspinatus	Rhomboids
Teres minor	Serratus anterior
Subscapularis	Levator scapula
Deltoid	Axiohumeral
Teres major	Pectoralis major
Scapula to forearm	Pectoralis minor
Biceps	Latissimus dorsi
Triceps	

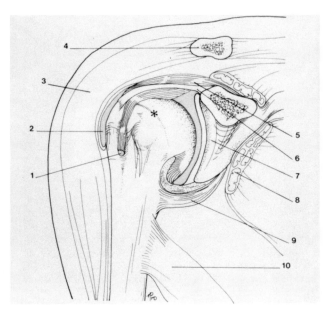

Figure 1D-5 Glenohumeral joint, anterior view. (Key: 1, biceps tendon, long head; 2, subdeltoid bursa; 3, deltoid; 4, acromion; 5, coracohumeral ligament; 6, joint capsule; 7, glenoid; 8, subscapularis; 9, joint capsule [axillary pouch]; 10, teres major.) Anterior, neck of the humerus. (Rafii M: Shoulder, in Firooznia H, et al. (eds): *MRI and CT of Musculoskeletal System,* St. Louis, Mosby–Year Book, 1992, p. 465.)

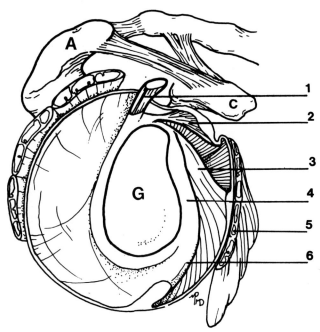

Figure 1D-6 Capsular mechanism. (Key: 1, biceps tendon, long head; 2, superior glenohumeral ligament; 3, middle glenohumeral ligament; 4, glenoid labrum; 5, subscapularis; 6, inferior fold of inferior glenohumeral ligament. G, glenoid fossa; A, acromion; C, coracoid.) (Rafii M: Shoulder, in Firooznia H, et al. (eds): *MRI and CT of Musculoskeletal System,* St. Louis, Mosby–Year Book, 1992, p. 465.)

impingement.[44] The surgical neck of the humerus is the segment immediately below the humeral head and the tuberosities. The attachments of the latissimus dorsi and teres major tendons are seen in this region anteriorly, and the attachment of the pectoralis major tendon laterally. Additional muscle attachments to the proximal humerus include the deltoid tendon, which is inserted on the deltoid tuberosity in the lateral aspect of the midshaft, and the coracobrachialis muscle, which is inserted medially at the same level.

The glenoid fossa is a shallow concavity that is wider and round in its inferior aspect and relatively pointed superiorly. Overall, it has the appearance of an inverted comma (Fig. 1D-6).[45] The hyaline articular cartilage covering the surface of the glenoid is slightly thinner in its center, adding to the concavity of the articular surface. Also adding to the concavity of the glenoid articular surface is the glenoid labrum, which is attached to the peripheral margin of the glenoid fossa.

The capsular mechanism of the glenohumeral joint (see Fig. 1D-6) consists of the fibrous joint capsule and the capsular ligaments, the synovial recesses, the glenoid labrum, and the rotator cuff tendons.[41] The long tendon of the biceps brachii superiorly and the long head of the triceps inferiorly designate the division of the capsular mechanism into the anterior and posterior components.

The fibrous joint capsule is a lax and redundant structure whose surface is twice as large as the articular surface of the humeral head.[41] Anteriorly, the joint capsule

is reinforced by three capsular ligaments: the superior glenohumeral ligament (SGHL), the middle (MGHL), and the inferior one (IGHL) (see Figs. 1D-6, 1D-7).[41,43] These ligaments are variably thickened fibrous bands formed within the capsule whose primary function is limiting external rotation of the humeral head.[41] The SGHL and the joint capsule extend medially to the glenoid margin with attachments to the base of the coracoid process and the supraglenoid tubercle. The glenoid insertion of the MGHL extends from that of the superior ligament to the junction of the middle and the inferior third of the glenoid rim. The glenoid insertion of the MGHL is variable from near the labrum to the scapular neck, based on anatomic variations of this ligament and the synovial recesses.[45,46] Laterally, the SGHL and the MGHL are attached to the anterior aspect of the anatomic neck of the humerus adjacent to the lesser tuberosity. The MGHL is quite variable and may be absent or ill defined in up to 30 percent of the population.[41,45] The capsular bursa that is almost always present, the superior subscapularis, is formed through an opening in the capsule between the SGHL and the MGHL.[41,45]

The IGHL exhibits less normal variation in structure. Functionally the most important of the glenohumeral ligaments in providing joint stability, it is a broad ligament with two major anterior and posterior components having attachments to the anterior, inferior, and posterior glenoid margin, nearby or contiguous with the inferior glenoid labrum.[47]

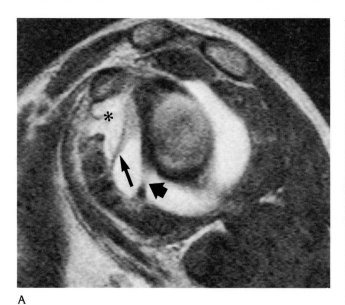
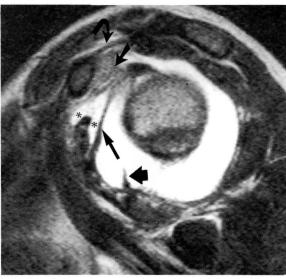

A   B

***Figure 1D*-7   A, B.** T2-weighted (1800/80) oblique sagittal images of right shoulder distended with joint effusion. The superior (*slanted arrow*), middle (*thin arrow*) and the anterior band of the inferior (*thick arrow*) glenohumeral ligaments are visualized. The subscapularis bursa (*asterisks*) and the coracohumeral ligament (**B,** *curved arrow*) are also visualized.

The glenoid insertion of the joint capsule anteriorly below the subscapularis bursa forms a smooth reflection over the scapular cortex and is adherent to the scapular periosteum.[48] Three types of anterior capsular insertions are recognized. In Type I the capsule and/or the glenohumeral ligament insertion is near or directly onto the glenoid labrum; in Type II it is medial to the labrum; and in Type III it is near or at the scapular neck.[41,49] The posterior capsular insertion is always adjacent to the glenoid labrum.[41,48]

The glenoid labrum (see Fig. 1D-6) is a capsular fold and is composed mostly of dense fibrous tissue.[41] A small amount of fibrocartilage is often found at its base, where it is attached on the glenoid margin. The base of the glenoid labrum otherwise overlies the glenoid articular cartilage. It is usually more triangular in outline anteriorly and more rounded posteriorly. Peripherally, its nonarticulating surface is parallel with the joint capsule and it may be covered by a layer of synovial tissue.

An additional capsular ligament, the coracohumeral ligament, is recognized at the outer aspect of the anterosuperior joint capsule extending between the lateral margin of the coracoid process and the greater tuberosity of the humerus (Figs. 1D-5, 1D-7B). This superficial thickening of the capsule is situated in the rotator interval capsule, between the anterior margin of the supraspinatus tendon and the superior margin of the subscapularis.[49,50] The coracohumeral ligament restrains external rotation of the humerus[51] and, in conjunction with the supraspinatus muscle, supports the dependent arm[50] and provides support for the long head of the biceps tendon.[18]

The coracoacromial arch includes the acromion and

coracoid processes and the coracoacromial ligament between them (see Fig. 1D-6). The acromion process is the flat termination of the scapular spine, which extends anteriorly and forms an articulation with the distal end of the clavicle. The coracoacromial ligament is a broad and triangular ligament. It originates along the lateral margin of the coracoid process and is inserted on the anteromedial and anteroinferior surfaces of the acromion. The coracoacromial arch provides stability for the glenohumeral joint superiorly. The subacromial space (Fig. 1D-8) is the area between the coracoacromial arch and the glenohumeral joint. The entire supraspinatus tendon and the upper segments of the subscapularis tendon anteriorly and the infraspinatus tendon posteriorly cross the subacromial space to their insertions on the humeral tuberosities.

The acromioclavicular joint is a relatively flat one that is variously oriented from vertically to horizontally.[52] The articular surfaces are covered by fibrocartilage and are separated by a fibrocartilaginous disc which is incomplete or more pronounced superiorly (see Fig. 1D-8).[53]

The subacromial-subdeltoid bursa (see Fig. 1D-8) is a synovium-lined cavity which forms a gliding mechanism between the rotator cuff tendons and the coracoacromial arch. A structure that is always present, this bursa extends laterally between the greater tuberosity and the deltoid muscle, facilitating the movement of the latter over the former. The floor of the subacromial bursa is firmly adherent to the greater tuberosity and the musculotendinous cuff. Its roof is adherent to the undersurface of the acromion and the coracoacromial ligament. Its lateral wall extends loosely downward under the deltoid mus-

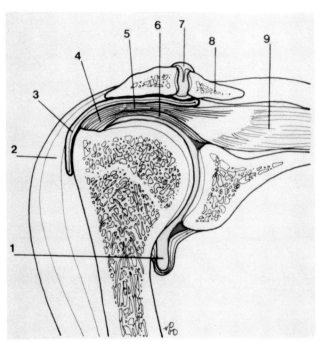

Figure 1D-8 Coronal view of the subacromial space and glenohumeral joint. (Key: 1, axillary pouch of joint capsule; 2, deltoid; 3, subdeltoid bursa; 4, combined capsule and supraspinatus tendon; 5, supraspinatus tendon; 6, superior joint capsule; 7, AC joint capsule and articular disk; 8, clavicle; 9, supraspinatus.) (Rafii M: Shoulder, in Firooznia H, et al. (eds): *MRI and CT of Musculoskeletal System,* St. Louis, Mosby–Year Book, 1992, p. 465.)

cle, backward and outward under the acromion, and medially under the coracoid process.[45] A layer of fat 1- to 2-mm wide covers the outer (extra) aspect of the synovial lining of the bursa.[54]

The rotator cuff is a group of four muscles which arise from the scapula and form tendinous insertions on the humeral tuberosities: from anterior to posterior, the subscapularis, supraspinatus, infraspinatus, and teres minor. They hold the humerus against the glenoid and assist in internal and external rotation of the arm.

The subscapularis (Fig. 1D-9A) originates from the medial two-thirds of the costal surface of the scapula. It has multiple tendons that cross the glenohumeral joint anteriorly and are inserted onto the lesser tuberosity. The combination of tendinous components forms a broad tendon which is fused with the anterior joint capsule. The subscapularis bursa is formed along its superior margin, and as a result a portion of the tendon forms a free margin and assumes an intraarticular position.[46] The subscapularis muscle is an adductor and internal rotator of the humerus.

The supraspinatus (see Figs. 1D-8, 1D-9B) originates in the supraspinatus fossa of the scapula and extends laterally over the humeral head to insert on the superior facet of the greater tuberosity. The supraspinatus tendon is formed within the muscle belly with muscle fibers surrounding it and converging into it. This central tendon gradually assumes a more anterior position and forms

the prominent anterior component of the supraspinatus tendon.[55] Inferiorly, the supraspinatus tendon is confluent with the joint capsule. The gap between the anterior margin of the supraspinatus and the superior margin of the subscapularis is bridged by the rotator interval capsule. The major function of the supraspinatus is to initiate abduction.

The infraspinatus (Fig. 1D-9C) muscle arises from the infraspinatus fossa of the scapula and crosses the joint posterosuperiorly to insert onto the middle facet of the greater tuberosity. This muscle is formed from several components, and its tendons unite to form the most prominent tendinous structure of the rotator cuff.[55] The uppermost aspect of the infraspinatus tendon crosses under the posterior acromion process and over the humeral head, merging with the posterior margin of the supraspinatus tendon. In this region the supraspinatus tendon is comparatively thinner than its anterior component. The two tendons overlap just before their insertion on the greater tuberosity.[56] According to Skinner, from childhood to adult life there occurs progressive transformation of muscle to tendon at the supraspinatus musculotendinous junction and progressive incorporation of the tendon and the joint capsule, and the connective tissue interface between these tendons becomes gradually more fibrous with advancing age.[57] The infraspinatus is a lateral rotator that also holds the humeral head in the glenoid cavity.

The supraspinatus and infraspinatus muscles are innervated by the suprascapular nerve (C5 and C6 roots). This branch of the brachial plexus passes through the suprascapular notch at the base of the coracoid process and then through the spinoglenoid notch to extend down at the dorsal surface of the scapula.

The teres minor (see Fig. 1D-9C) is a narrow muscle which originates from the lateral border of the scapula. It extends upward and inserts onto the lower facet of the greater tuberosity and the surgical neck of the humerus. It is intermittently associated with—and at times inseparable from—the infraspinatus. It acts as an external rotator and adductor of the arm.

Two other muscles extend from the scapula to the humerus. Teres major arises from the lateral border of the scapula near the inferior angle and forms a tendinous insertion onto the crest of the lesser tuberosity (see Fig. 1D-9C). It is an adductor, medial rotator, and extensor of the arm. The deltoid is a triangular muscle which arises from the lateral third of the clavicle, the lateral border of the acromion, and the adjacent scapular spine. It inserts on the deltoid tuberosity of the humerus. This muscle is the principal abductor of the humerus, with the supraspinatus participating with it up to 90° of abduction.

Other muscles identified with the shoulder include the biceps brachii, coracobrachialis, triceps brachii, pectoralis major and minor, and latissimus dorsi.

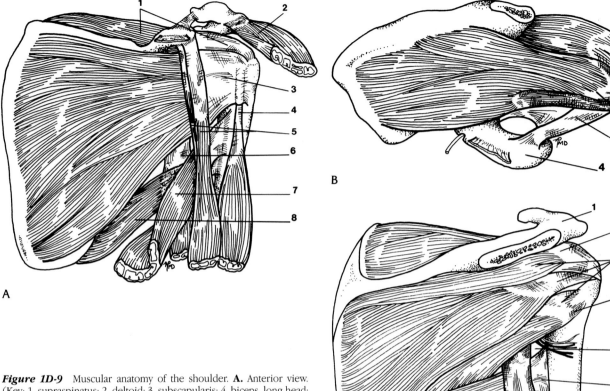

Figure 1D-9 Muscular anatomy of the shoulder. **A.** Anterior view. (Key: 1, supraspinatus; 2, deltoid; 3, subscapularis; 4, biceps, long head; 5, coracobrachialis and biceps, short head; 6, triceps, long head; 7, latissimus dorsi; 8, teres major.) **B.** Superior view. (Key: 1, infraspinatus; 2, supraspinatus; 3, coracohumeral ligament; 4, coracoid.) **C.** Posterior view. (Key: 1, acromion; 2, supraspinatus; 3, infraspinatus; 4, teres minor; 5, quadrangular space and circumflex vessels; 6, teres major; 7, triceps, long head.) (Rafii M: Shoulder, in Firooznia H, et al. (eds): *MRI and CT of Musculoskeletal System,* St. Louis, Mosby–Year Book, 1992, p. 465.)

Biceps brachii (see Figs. 1D-5, 1D-6, 1D-9A) is the most prominent muscle in the anterior aspect of the arm. The long tendon of this muscle originates from the supraglenoid tubercle of the scapula, extends anterior to the humeral head beneath the rotator interval capsule, and exits the glenohumeral joint through an opening in the capsule above the bicipital groove. Within the groove the biceps tendon is secured in place by the rigid transverse humeral ligament, which bridges the humeral tuberosities at the upper aspect of the groove. A synovial sheath covers the long head of the biceps tendon from its origin and extends into the bicipital groove, forming the synovial sleeve of this tendon. The short head of the biceps brachii arises from the tip of the coracoid process conjoined with the tendon of the coracobrachialis. The two muscles extend along the ventral surface of the subscapularis. The coracobrachialis muscle inserts into the medial surface of the humerus, proximal to its midportion.

Triceps brachii (see Fig. 1D-9A, C) is formed by three separate heads and occupies the entire posterior aspect of the arm. The long head of the muscle arises by a broad tendon from the infraglenoid tubercle of the scapula and descends between the teres minor and teres major muscles. The lateral and the medial heads of this muscle originate from the humerus. Its distal tendon inserts onto the olecranon process.

Latissimus dorsi (see Fig. 1D-9A) is a large triangular muscle with a flat tendon which inserts to the floor of the bicipital groove ventral to the insertion of the teres major.

NORMAL PLANAR MR ANATOMY

Axial Plane

The glenohumeral joint, the capsulolabral complex, and the anterior and posterior aspects of the rotator cuff are best visualized on axial images (Fig. 1D-10). At the superior aspect of the joint and immediately below the acromion process and the acromioclavicular joint, the supraspinatus and the upper aspect of the infraspinatus muscle and tendons are visualized (see Fig. 1D-10A, B).

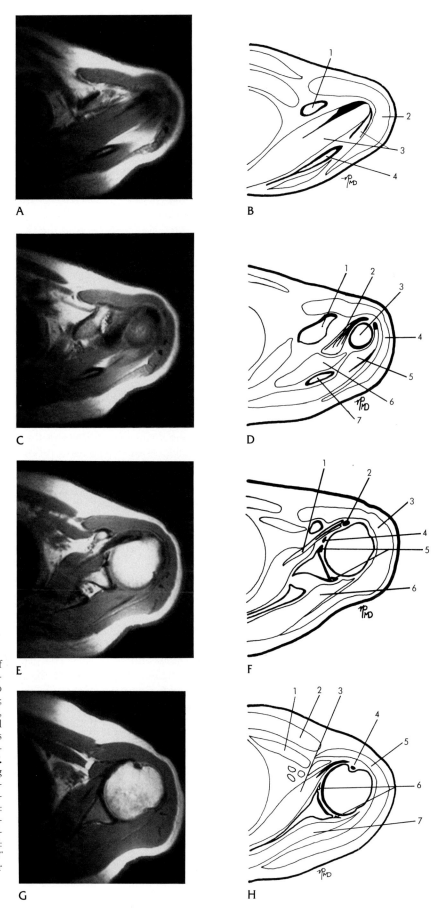

Figure 1D-10 Normal MRI planar anatomy of the left shoulder in the axial plane. Proton-density–weighted (900/30) images. **A, B.** Superior to the glenohumeral joint. (Key: 1, coracoid process; 2, deltoid; 3, supraspinatus and infraspinatus; 4, scapular spine.) **C, D.** Superior glenohumeral joint. (Key: 1, coracoid; 2, long head of biceps tendon; 3, humeral head; 4, deltoid; 5, infraspinatus; 6, supraspinatus; 7, scapular spine.) **E, F.** Below the coracoid. (Key: 1, subscapularis; 2, long head of biceps tendon; 3, humeral head; 4, glenohumeral ligament; 5, anterior and posterior labrum; 6, infraspinatus.) **G, H.** Midglenoid. (Key: 1, pectoralis minor; 2, pectoralis major; 3, subscapularis; 4, long head of biceps tendon; 5, deltoid; 6, glenoid labrum; 7, infraspinatus.) (Rafii M: Shoulder, in Firooznia H, et al. (eds): *MRI and CT of Musculoskeletal System*, St. Louis, Mosby—Year Book, 1992, p. 465.)

The signal-void central tendon of the supraspinatus is displayed forming the anterior free margin of this tendon. The upper aspect of the infraspinatus is identified at the same level as the supraspinatus, posterior and lateral to the scapular spine. The forward orientation of the infraspinatus tendon over the posterior aspect of the humeral head and its confluence or overlap with the supraspinatus tendon is often well visualized.

Immediately below the supraspinatus tendon (see Fig. 1D-10C, D), the intracapsular segment of the long tendon of the biceps and the superior glenoid labrum are often visualized at the level of the base of the coracoid process. A nondistended subscapularis bursa beneath the coracoid process is visualized by the high signal intensity of peribursal fatty connective tissue in this region. The coracohumeral ligament may be identified at this level as a low-signal band extending between the tip of the coracoid process and the humeral head.

The broad signal-void tendon of the subscapularis is visualized anteriorly beginning at the level of the tip of the coracoid process (see Fig. 1D-10E–H). It forms the musculotendinous junction at the level of the glenohumeral joint. The posterior aspect of the rotator cuff is more muscular. Except for the upper portion of the tendon, the infraspinatus and teres minor tendons are less conspicuous and form within the immediate vicinity of the insertion site on the posterior aspect of the greater tuberosity. The deltoid muscle drapes around the shoulder, covering the rotator cuff anteriorly and posteriorly and the humerus laterally. The articular capsule is identified as a low-signal band against the medium–signal intensity rotator cuff muscles. The glenoid insertion of the articular capsule can best be characterized as the confluence of the equally low-signal capsule and the glenoid cortical bone separated by a small layer of fatty tissue from the overlying rotator cuff (see Fig. 1D-10G, H). The glenohumeral ligaments are variably visualized. The middle glenohumeral ligament is most frequently observed on axial images at midglenoid level as a low-signal band against the joint capsule and parallel to or aligned with the peripheral surface of the glenoid labrum (see Fig. 1D-10E, F). The inferior glenohumeral ligament may similarly be visualized. The glenoid labrum is visualized as a signal-void structure. The anterior labrum is more often triangular, though the anterosuperior labrum could be rounded or smaller in contour. The outline of the posterior labrum is also more often round. The peripheral aspect of the glenoid articular cartilage appears as a fine line of medium signal intensity intervening between the base of the labrum and the glenoid articular cortex (see Fig. 1D-10G, H).

Oblique Coronal Plane (Figure 1D-11)

Oblique coronal images anterior to the glenohumeral joint (see Fig. 1D-11A, B) display the subscapularis ex-

tending immediately beneath the coracoid process with its tendinous insertion on the lesser tuberosity. The coracohumeral and the coracoclavicular ligament are constant findings on these images, while the coracoacromial ligament is variable. When distended with fluid the subscapularis bursa occupies space at the base of the coracoid process above the subscapularis tendon and may expand ventral to the subscapularis tendon. Otherwise, the region of the bursa is identified with high signal intensity of fatty connective tissue. The long tendon of the biceps brachii is visualized on one or two consecutive images at the anterior aspect of the joint based on the degree of rotation of the humeral head. The tendon within the bicipital groove is visualized immediately lateral to the lesser tuberosity insertion of the subscapularis tendon.

The oblique coronal images at the anterior aspect of the joint (see Fig. 1D-11C, D) display the low-signal anterior component of the supraspinatus tendon. With its characteristic graduated musculotendinous junction, this tendon originates medial to the AC joint. On anterior images the greater tuberosity insertion of the supraspinatus tendon is first visualized immediately lateral to the long tendon of biceps brachii within the uppermost aspect of the bicipital groove. Posterior to the main tendinous component, the supraspinatus and the upper aspect of the infraspinatus tendons form a musculotendinous junction above the center of the humeral head or about the peripheral margin of the acromion process (see Fig. 1D-11E–H). The infraspinatus tendon is identified on sections at the posterior aspect of the glenohumeral joint (see Fig. 1D-11G, H). Often on one posterior image from medial to lateral the supraspinatus, the scapular spine, and the infraspinatus muscle and tendon are visualized. Lateral to the scapular spine the infraspinatus and the supraspinatus muscles are separated by fatty connective tissue; the gradual confluence of the two tendons is visualized on adjacent images. The junction of the two tendons may be identified by medium–signal intensity tissue on T1-weighted and proton-density images. The greater tuberosity insertions of both tendons begin at the anatomic neck and cover the entire surface of the tuberosity.

The superior surface of the cuff is separated from the undersurface of the acromion process and the deltoid muscle by the high-signal subacromial-subdeltoid peribursal fat, which continues medially beneath the trapezius and laterally under the deltoid. The inferior surface of the cuff is covered by the low-signal articular capsule. The acromion process, the acromioclavicular joint, and the distal clavicle are visualized on coronal images from posterior to anterior.

Oblique coronal plane images also display the glenohumeral joint, the superior and the inferior glenoid labrum, and the axillary pouch. Due to oblique orientation of the intraarticular segment of the long tendon of the

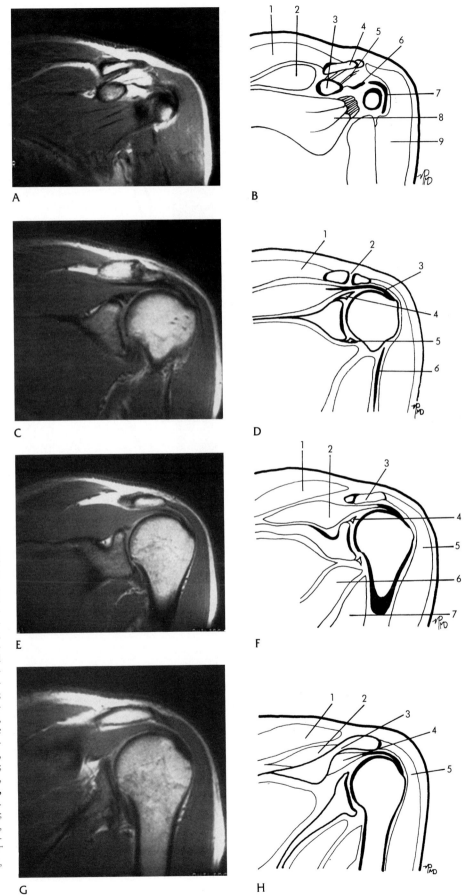

Figure 1D-11 Normal MRI planar anatomy of the left shoulder in the oblique coronal plane. All images proton-density (2100/30). **A, B.** Anterior to the glenohumeral joint. (Key: 1, trapezius; 2, supraspinatus; 3, coracoid and coracoclavicular ligament; 4, clavicle; 5, coracoacromial ligament; 6, coracohumeral ligament; 7, long head of the biceps tendon; 8, subscapularis; 9, deltoid.) **C, D.** Anterior glenohumeral joint. (Key: 1, trapezius; 2, acromioclavicular joint; 3, supraspinatus; 4, superior labrum; 5, inferior labrum; 6, long head of the biceps tendon.) **E, F.** Midglenohumeral joint. (Key: 1, trapezius; 2, supraspinatus; 3, acromion process; 4, superior labrum; 5, deltoid; 6, teres major; 7, latissimus dorsi.) **G, H.** Posterior glenohumeral joint. (Key: 1, trapezius; 2, supraspinatus; 3, scapular spine; 4, infraspinatus; 5, deltoid.) (Rafii M: Shoulder, in Firooznia H, et al. (eds): *MRI and CT of Musculoskeletal System*, St. Louis, Mosby—Year Book, 1992, p. 465.)

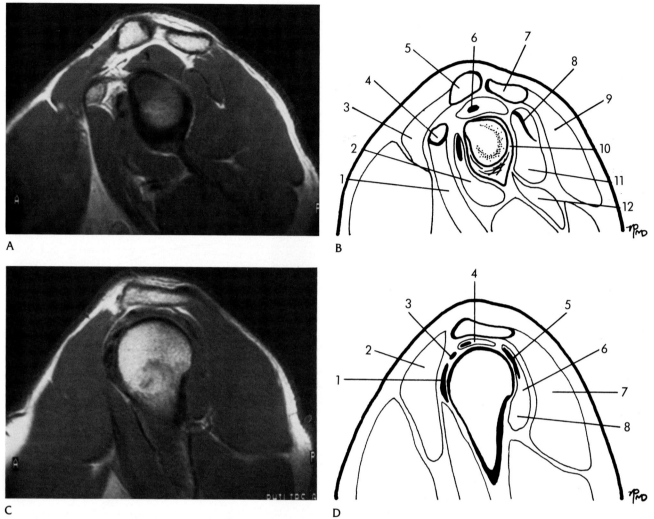

Figure 1D-12 Normal MRI planar anatomy, oblique sagittal plane, left shoulder. All images proton-density–weighted (1800/30). **A, B.** Level of the glenohumeral joint. (Key: 1, coracobrachialis; 2, subscapularis; 3, deltoid; 4, coracoid process; 5, clavicle; 6, supraspinatus; 7, acromion process; 8, infraspinatus; 9, deltoid; 10, labrum and capsule; 11, teres minor; 12, triceps, long head.) **C, D.** Lateral to **A**, midhumeral head. (Key: 1, subscapularis tendon; 2, deltoid; 3, long head of the biceps tendon; 4, supraspinatus tendon; 5, infraspinatus tendon; 6, teres minor; 7, deltoid; 8, teres major.) (Rafii M: Shoulder, in Firooznia H, et al. (eds): *MRI and CT of Musculoskeletal System*, St. Louis, Mosby—Year Book, 1992, p. 465.)

biceps to the plane of imaging, the superior labrum-biceps combination on anterior images appear elongated and larger than the posterosuperior segment. The inferior glenoid labrum may not be as clearly outlined owing to anatomic contiguity with the joint capsule and the inferior glenohumeral ligament.

Oblique Sagittal Plane (Figure 1D-12)

In this plane the coracoacromial arch and the cross section of the rotator cuff surrounding the glenohumeral joint are displayed. The coracoacromial ligament is variable in thickness and, owing to its oblique orientation to the plane of imaging, it is visualized in parts on two or three consecutive images. The cross section of the

rotator cuff on these images optimally displays the heterogeneity of these tendons. The prominent anterior component of the supraspinatus tendon is visualized below the anterior margin of the acromion process. The remainder of the supraspinatus tendon is thinner, and lateral extension of muscle fibers is demonstrated. The short head of the biceps brachii tendon and the coracobrachialis are visualized anterior to the subscapularis muscle.

Oblique sagittal images at the level of the glenoid (see Fig. 1D-12A, B) optimally display the comma-shaped configuration of the glenoid fossa and the low-signal glenoid labrum at its peripheral margin. The axillary pouch is usually well visualized on sections lateral to the glenoid fossa. The lateral insertion of the axillary pouch to the surgical neck of the humerus may also be identified. The region of the subscapularis bursa in a nondistended joint is characterized by fatty connective tissue at the base of the coracoid process and along the superior margin of the subscapularis.

On oblique sagittal images the structures within and in the vicinity of the rotator interval capsule are identified between the free margins of the supraspinatus and subscapularis tendons (Fig. 1D-13). The coracohumeral ligament extends as a low-signal band from the superior margin of the coracoid process to the inferior margin of the supraspinatus. Below this ligament the capsule forms the superior glenohumeral ligament. Also visualized in this region is the cross section of the intracapsular component of the long tendon of the biceps immediately beneath the anterior margin of the supraspinatus and the rotator interval capsule.

ANATOMIC VARIATIONS AND PITFALLS

Rotator Cuff

The criteria for diagnosis of a rotator cuff disorder are based on variations in signal intensity and morphology of these tendons. Although the rotator cuff tendons are usually hypointense, the signal intensity of the supraspinatus tendon may vary somewhat even in the absence of correlative pathology. Peripheral extension of supraspinatus muscle fibers often observed in young persons results in a variable degree of increased signal intensity of the supraspinatus tendon between the major component of the tendon anteriorly and the upper aspect of the infraspinatus tendon posteriorly.[32,58,59] This normal variation is recognized by the isointense nature of the increased signal region with the supraspinatus muscle (Fig. 1D-14). The junction of the supraspinatus and the infraspinatus tendon may also appear as an oblique line of medium signal intensity on posterior coronal oblique images. Occasionally this line is prominent and may mimic a lesion.[14-33] However, with interposed "muscle fibers," this junctional line is hypointense on T2-weighted images. Overlap between the infraspinatus and supraspinatus is usually accentuated when the patient is imaged with the arm in internal rotation. In this position the infraspinatus tendon is visualized superior and lateral to the infraspinatus. This may result in apparent discontinuity of the supraspinatus tendon.[59]

Another variation of signal intensity in the supraspinatus tendon involves the anterior aspect of the tendon approximately 1 cm from the greater tuberosity.[21,60-63] In this region which constitutes the critical zone of supraspinatus, a round or oval area of high signal intensity is

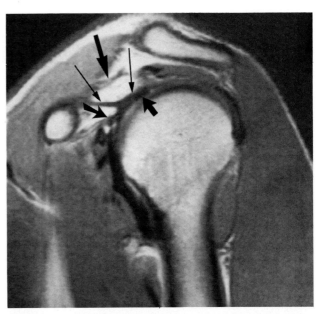

Figure 1D-13 Proton-density oblique sagittal image. At this level the articular capsule and the coracohumeral ligament (*long, thin arrows*), the superior glenohumeral ligament (*slanted arrow*), and the medial fibers of the coracoacromial ligament (*thick, long arrow*) are visualized. The long head of the biceps tendon (*thick, short arrow*) is seen between the capsule and the humeral head.

occasionally observed on T1-weighted and proton density images. This focal area of increased signal intensity when present is more prominent on images acquired with fat suppression or gradient-echo sequences.[21,60] No increase in signal intensity, however, is observed on T2-

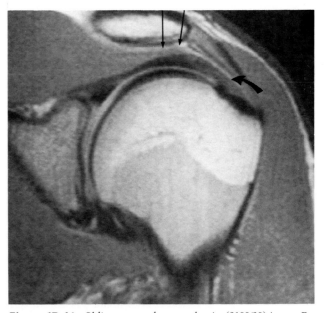

Figure 1D-14 Oblique coronal proton-density (2100/30) image. Extension of muscle fibers superior to supraspinatus tendon (*thin arrows*) and increase in signal intensity of the distal segment of the tendon (*curved arrow*) are demonstrated in this 18-year-old who has no symptoms referable to the rotator cuff.

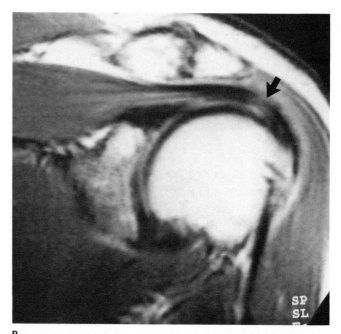

A

B

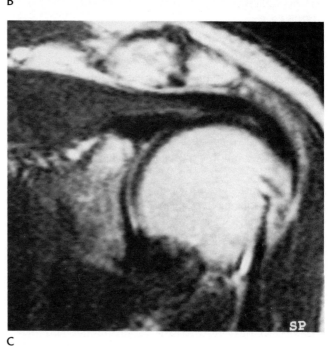

Figure 1D-15 Oblique coronal gradient-echo (810/26/30) **A,** and proton-density and T2-weighted (2000/29/80) images, **B, C.** There is focal high signal intensity in the critical zone of the supraspinatus on gradient-echo and proton-density images (*arrow*, **A, B**) and no increased signal on T2-weighted image, **C.** This signal variation is similar to that of the muscle.

C

weighted images and the focus appears isointense with skeletal muscle on all sequences (Fig. 1D-15). Two explanations have been offered for this finding. One is the aberrant vascularity of the critical zone or the presence of subclinical tendon degeneration.[21] This hypothesis is supported by the fact that the hypovascular critical zone of the supraspinatus is the predominant site for development of pathologic changes in impingement syndrome. Another explanation is based on the "magic angle" theory.[64] Based on this theory, artifactual increased signal intensity of tendons may be observed when the

tendon fibers are oriented at 55° to the main magnetic field. This phenomenon may contribute to increased signal intensity of the anterior supraspinatus tendon because the tendon deviates anteriorly at or near this position.[21]

Based on the orientation of the oblique coronal images, partial volume averaging of the anterior margin of the supraspinatus with the connective tissue of the rotator interval capsule may result in increased signal intensity and simulate a lesion.[58] Also, the anterior margin of the supraspinatus musculotendinous junction may develop a concave configuration as a result of advanced muscle atrophy which on oblique coronal images may appear as a defect. Both these pitfalls can be recognized by the low-signal appearance on T2-weighted images as well as by correlation with oblique sagittal images that optimally visualize the anterior margin of the supraspinatus. Another cause for partial volume averaging of the anterior supraspinatus is fluid in the bicipital tendon sheath, particularly when the shoulder is examined in external rotation.[59] Again, correlation with T2-weighted oblique sagittal images is helpful for avoiding this pitfall. Occasionally the high–signal intensity hyaline articular cartilage overlying the humeral head may be mistaken for increased signal intensity within the supraspinatus tendon, which may suggest the misdiagnosis of tendinitis.[58]

Variations may exist in the position of the supraspinatus musculotendinous junction. Ordinarily the junction overlies the center of the humeral head at the peripheral margin of the acromion process. Some medial extension of the junction may be seen without existing pathology; however, this does not normally exceed more than 15° medial to the 12 o'clock position.[61] When the muscle fibers extend peripherally a distinct musculotendinous junction may not be visualized; rather, there is a gradual transition from muscle to tendon.

In addition to specific causes listed above, focal or generalized increased signal intensity of the rotator cuff has been described in asymptomatic persons.[60,61,63,65] Although some variation in signal intensity could be due to technical factors, age-related tendon degeneration cannot be excluded as the underlying factor. Increased signal intensity is limited to T1-weighted or proton-density images. Increased signal intensity on T2-weighted images reflects a pathologic change of the tendon such as a tear. Tendinitis may also be manifested as a relative increase in signal intensity on short TE images, and it may not be possible to distinguish it from tendon degeneration, or in some instances from regions of partial tear.[14]

Subacromial-Subdeltoid Bursa

Alterations in the subacromial-subdeltoid peribursal fat signal have been observed in rotator cuff tears and in tendinitis.[14] Abnormalities of the peribursal fat are due to fluid accumulation, inflammation, or formation of granulation tissue within the bursa; however, partial obliteration or absence of the peribursal fat has been observed in asymptomatic subjects.[32,60,61,65] Apparent absence of the peribursal fat plane, which is most frequently observed anterolaterally, may be due to limitations in spatial resolution.[32] There is a greater tendency for younger and more muscular persons to exhibit partial absence of the peribursal fat. A small amount of fluid within the subacromial-subdeltoid bursa may also be

seen in normal subjects, most frequently on fat-suppressed T2-weighted images.[32,62] Any loculation of fluid, however, should be considered abnormal, although bursal fluid collections are not specific for rotator cuff tear and may also be observed with rotator cuff tendinitis.

Acromion Process

Variations in shape and configuration of the acromion process may be visualized by MRI. From radiographic studies three types of acromion process have been described.[66] A type I acromion process is straight; a Type II has a curved contour; and a Type III process is hook-shaped (Fig. 1D-16). On MRI a hook-shaped acromion is an uncommon observation. The reported prevalence of hooked acromion associated with impingement syndrome is more likely to be due to secondary degenerative processes and enthesopathy.[67] Variations in acromial arch and its shape are important factors in the development of acromion spurs.[68] Based on visualization on oblique coronal MR images a low-lying acromion process has been identified with a greater frequency in patients with a rotator cuff lesion (Fig. 1D-17).[8] Hypertrophic changes of the acromion process may appear as true osteophytes and are characterized by presence of high–signal intensity bone marrow within them. Also fibrocartilaginous thickening of the undersurface of the acromion process may develop which exhibits low signal intensity similar to that of the acromion cortex. The insertion of the inferior tendon slip of the deltoid muscle may simulate a spur.[60] Differentiation is based on continuity of the deltoid insertion beyond the margin of the acromion on oblique coronal images. A similar finding may be seen on oblique sagittal images at the site of insertion of the coracoacromial ligament onto the ante-

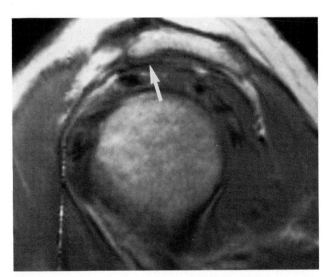

Figure 1D-16 Oblique sagittal proton-density image. The hook-shaped configuration of the anterior aspect of the acromion process is observed (***arrow***).

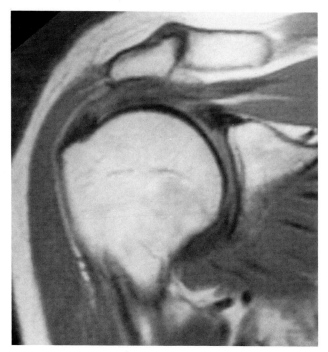

Figure 1D-17 Oblique coronal proton density image. A "low-lying" acromion is observed in a patient with rotator cuff tendinitis.

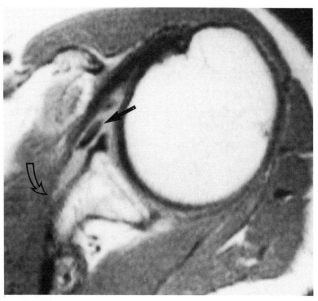

Figure 1D-19 T1-weighted axial image (983/29) at midglenohumeral joint level. The middle glenohumeral ligament is well visualized (*solid arrow*). Both the ligament and the labrum are clearly outlined, owing to the presence of a small amount of joint effusion. At this level the lower aspect of a normal subscapularis bursa which extends to the scapular neck is demonstrated and should not be mistaken for a normal Type III or an abnormally stripped capsule (*open arrow*). The posterior labrum is small and rounded.

rior and inferior margins of the acromion process (Fig. 1D-18).

Capsulolabral Complex

The signal intensity, size, and morphology of the glenoid labrum are subject to variations. The normal glenoid labrum is signal void. Morphologically the labrum is usually triangular anteriorly and rounded posteriorly.[44,46,48] The anterior labrum is also usually larger

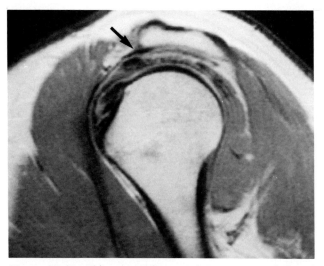

Figure 1D-18 Oblique sagittal proton density image. A thickened acromial insertion of the coracoacromial ligament is observed (*arrow*).

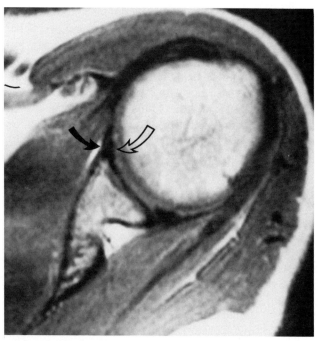

Figure 1D-20 T1-weighted axial image at midglenoid level. The anterior capsule (middle glenohumeral ligament) has a near labral insertion (*solid arrow*). The notched configuration of the labrum is most likely due to proximity of the superior glenohumeral ligament (*open arrow*). The posterior labrum is slightly larger and triangular in shape.

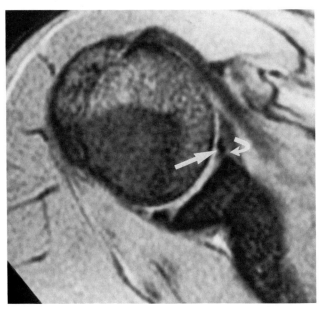

Figure 1D-21   MPGR axial image (400/15/25) at the junction of the superior and the midglenoid level in asymptomatic subject. A linear high-signal band is present between the glenohumeral ligament and the relatively flat anterosuperior labrum (*straight arrow*). The labrum also appears separated from the glenoid margin (*curved arrow*). Note normal extension of high-signal articular cartilage beneath the posterior glenoid labrum.

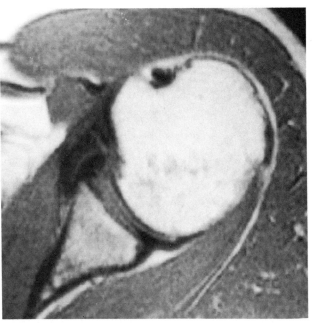

Figure 1D-23   Axial proton-density image (1100/29) below the glenoid notch level. The anterior labrum is prominent and rounded. In addition, a notched configuration is present.

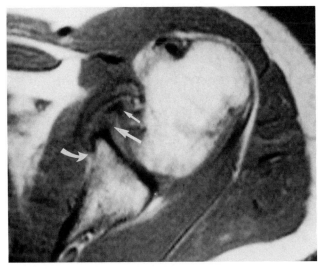

Figure 1D-22   Axial T1-weighted image at the level of the inferior glenoid margin in the patient shown in Figure 1D-19. At this level the low-signal inferior glenohumeral ligament (*small arrow*) blends with the labrum, which is ill-defined and shows medium signal intensity (*large arrow*). A normal capsular attachment is visualized near the glenoid margin (*curved arrow*).

than the posterior labrum.[60] Variations in morphology and size are most often observed involving the anterior labrum; the labrum may be round, flat, notched, cleaved, or may demonstrate a cleft.[27,69,70] The posterior labrum may occasionally be larger than the anterior one, or it may have a triangular contour. The morphologic varia-

tions of the anterior labrum are characteristically observed at midglenoid level or anterosuperiorly. Most likely these reflect the developmental variations of the labrum and the capsular ligaments.[33,45,71] The middle glenohumeral ligament when well developed appears as a low-signal band parallel to the peripheral surface of the labrum (Fig. 1D-19). The middle and the superior glenohumeral ligaments, however, may have a direct labral or near labral attachment, which consequently alters the morphology of the labrum (Fig. 1D-20). A high-signal band traversing both surfaces of the labrum has been regarded as a sign of a labrum tear.[72] Such a finding has also been reported as a normal variant in asymptomatic subjects.[27] Proximity of the middle and superior glenohumeral ligaments to the labrum may result in a high-signal band which may simulate a tear through both surfaces of the labrum (Fig. 1D-21). These variations are less frequent along the anteroinferior quadrant of the glenoid, where specific lesions of glenohumeral instability, i.e., labrum detachment or tearing are observed.

The inferior glenoid labrum is usually less well-defined as it becomes confluent with the anterior band of the inferior glenohumeral ligament (Fig. 1D-22).[17,71] Variations in the size of the glenoid labrum have been observed (Fig. 1D-23).[27,69,70] A large or elongated labrum may be seen on axial images as a result of direct labral insertion of the glenohumeral ligaments. Normal variations that have been reported are flattening, attenuation, and even absence of the labrum (Fig. 1D-24).[70] Absence of the labrum may be present in long-standing shoulder

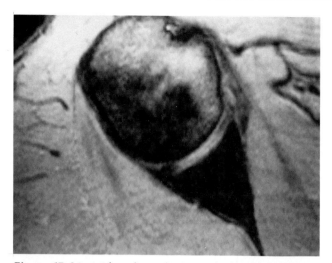

Figure 1D-24   Axial gradient-echo image (594/18/40) below mid-glenoid level. The anterior labrum is diminutive and shows high signal intensity. This 30-year-old man had no clinical findings relevant to glenohumeral joint dysfunction, labral tear, or instability, but he was a serious recreational athlete, and the labrum morphology and signal intensity probably reflect the development of labrum degeneration owing to repeated microtrauma.

instability, and it has been reported as a specific sign of labrum pathology.[17,27]

Increased signal intensity of the glenoid labrum has been observed in asymptomatic persons, presumably owing to a degenerative process.[27,65,70] The signal intensity of the glenoid hyaline articular cartilage undercutting the glenoid labrum is a potential pitfall and may mimic labrum detachment.[27,60,72] Differentiation is based on termination of the high-signal smooth band of normal articular cartilage at the glenoid margin, whereas abnormal signal intensity in a detached labrum extends beyond the glenoid margin beneath the peripheral aspect of the glenoid labrum.[17] Detachment of the anterosuperior labrum, however, may be observed without correlative clinical findings.[17–73] Gradual separation of the labrum, particularly the superior segment, is also known to be due to aging.[45,48] Morphologic and signal variations of the glenoid labrum are more pronounced on gradient-echo images (Fig. 1D-25). This results in increased sensitivity but reduced specificity of MRI findings. A combination of T1-weighted or proton-density plus T2-weighted pulse sequences increases the specificity of MRI findings.

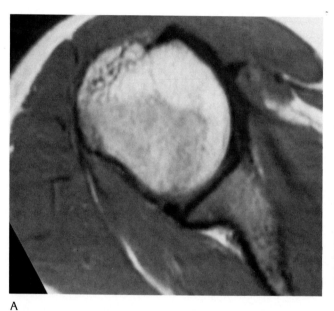
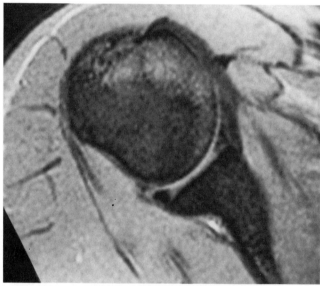

A   B

Figure 1D-25   Axial gradient-echo, **A,** and proton-density (2000/17), **B,** images at the same location at the midglenoid level. The high signal intensity of the glenoid articular cartilage and notched configuration of the anterior labrum are more pronounced on the gradient-echo image. (**A**).

References

1. HUBER DJ, SAUTER RS, MULLER E, ET AL.: MR imaging of the normal shoulder. *Radiology* 158:405, 1986.

2. MIDDLETON WD, KNEELAND JB, CARRERA GF: High resolution MR imaging of the normal rotator cuff. *AJR* 148:559, 1987.

3. KIEFT GJ, BLOEM JL, OBERMAN WR: Normal shoulder: MR imaging. *Radiology* 159:741, 1986.

4. SEEGER LL, RUSZKOWSKI JT, BASSETT LW, ET AL.: MR imaging of the normal shoulder: Anatomic correlation. *AJR* 148:83, 1987.

5. KNEELAND JB, CARRERA GF, MIDDLETON WD, ET AL.: Rotator cuff tears: Preliminary application of high-resolution MR imaging with counter-rotating current loop-gap resonators. *Radiology* 160:695, 1986.

6. KNEELAND BJ, MIDDLETON WD, CARRERA GF, ET AL.: MR imaging of the shoulder: Diagnosis of rotator cuff tears. *AJR* 149:333, 1987.

7. ZLATKIN MB, REICHER MA, KELLERHOUSE LE, ET AL.: The painful shoulder: MR imaging of the glenohumeral joint. *J Comput Assist Tomogr* 12:995, 1988.

8. SEEGER LL, GOLD RH, BASSETT LW, ELLMAN H: Shoulder impingement syndrome. MR findings in 53 shoulders. *AJR* 150:343, 1988.

9. EVANCHO AM, STILES RG, FAJMAN WA, ET AL.: MR imaging diagnosis of rotator cuff tears. *AJR* 151:751, 1988.

10. KIEFT GJ, BLOEM JL, ROZING PM, ET AL.: Rotator cuff impingement syndrome: MR imaging. *Radiology* 166:211, 1988.

11. ZLATKIN MB, DALINKA MK, KRESSEL H: Magnetic resonance imaging of the shoulder. *Magn Reson Q* 5:3, 1989.

12. ZLATKIN MB, IONNATTI JP, ROBERTS MC, ET AL.: Rotator cuff tears: Diagnostic performance of MR imaging. *Radiology* 172:223, 1989.

13. BURK DL, KARASICK DK, KURTZ AB, ET AL.: Rotator cuff tears: Prospective comparison of MR imaging with arthrography, sonography, and surgery. *AJR* 153:87, 1989.

14. RAFII M, FIROOZNIA H, SHERMAN O, ET AL.: Rotator cuff lesions: Signal pattern at MR imaging. *Radiology* 177:817, 1990.

15. SEEGER LL, GOLD RH, BASSETT LW: Shoulder instability: Evaluation with MR imaging. *Radiology* 168:695, 1988.

16. IANNOTTI JP, ZLATKIN MB, ESTERHAI JL, ET AL.: Magnetic resonance imaging of the shoulder. Sensitivity, specificity and predictive value. *J Bone Surg* 73A:17, 1991.

17. RAFII M, FIROOZNIA H, GOLIMBU C, WEINREB J: Magnetic resonance imaging of glenohumeral instability. *MRI Clin North Am* 1:87, 1993.

18. ERICKSON SJ, FITZGERALD SW, QUINN SF, ET AL.: Long bicipital tendon of the shoulder: Normal anatomy and path-

ologic findings on MR imaging. *Am J Roentgenol* 158:1091, 1992.

19. CHAN TW, DALINKA MK, KNEELAND JB, ET AL.: Biceps tendon dislocation: Evaluation with MR imaging. *Radiology* 179:649, 1991.

20. CARTLAND JP, CRUES JVI, STAUFFER A, ET AL.: MR imaging in the evaluation of SLAP injuries of the shoulder: Findings in 10 patients. *Am J Radiol* 159:787, 1992.

21. MIROWITZ SA: Imaging techniques, normal variations and diagnostic pitfalls in shoulder magnetic resonance imaging. *MRI Clin North Am* 1:19, 1993.

22. HENNIG J, NAURETH A, FRIEDBURG H: RARE imaging: A fast imaging method for clinical MR. *Magn Reson Med* 3:823, 1986.

23. JONES KM, MULKERN RV, SCHWARTZ RB, ET AL.: Fast spin-echo MR imaging of the brain and spine: Current concepts. *Am J Roentgenol* 158:1313, 1992.

24. SMITH RC, REINHOLD C, LANG RC, ET AL.: Fast spin-echo MR imaging of the female pelvis. Part I. Use of a whole-volume coil. *Radiology* 184:665, 1992.

25. CATASCA J, MIROWITZ SA: Fast spin echo T2-weighted MR imaging of the abdomen. *Radiology* 185:234, 1992.

26. RESENDES M, HELMS CA, EDDY R, ET AL.: Double-echo MPGR imaging of the rotator cuff. *J Comput Assist Tomogr* 15:1077, 1991.

27. McCAULEY TR, POPE CF, JOKL P: Normal and abnormal glenoid labrum: Assessment with multiplanar gradient-echo MR imaging. *Radiology* 183:35, 1992.

28. HARNED EM, MITCHELL DG, BURK DL JR, ET AL.: Bone marrow findings on magnetic resonance images of the knee: Accentuation by fat suppression. *Magn Reson Imaging* 8:27, 1990.

29. MIROWITZ SA, REINUS W: Relative conspicuity of bone marrow lesions on MR: Comparison of conventional and fat suppressed spin echo and inversion recovery pulse sequences. *J Magn Reson Imaging* 2:47, 1992.

30. MIROWITZ SA, SHADY K, REINUS WR: Diagnostic performance of fat suppression MR imaging for detection of rotator cuff pathology. *Radiology* 181:247, 1991.

31. TRAUGHBER PD, GOODWIN TE: Shoulder MRI: Arthroscopic correlation with emphasis on partial tears. *J Comput Assist Tomogr* 16:129, 1992.

32. MIROWITZ SA: Normal rotator cuff: MR imaging with conventional and fat-suppression techniques. *Radiology* 180:735, 1991.

33. RAFII M: Shoulder, in Firoaznia et al. (eds): *MRI and CT of Musculoskeletal System*, St. Louis, Mosby–Year Book, 1992, p 465.

34. HAJEK PC, BAKER LL, SARTORIS DJ, ET AL.: MR arthrog-

raphy: Anatomic-pathologic investigation. *Radiology* 163:141, 1987.

35. FLANNIGAN B, KURSUNOGLU-BRAHME S, SYNDER S, ET AL.: MR arthrography of the shoulder: Comparison with conventional MR imaging. *Am J Roentgenol* 155:829, 1990.

36. HODLER J, KURSUNOGLU-BRAHME S, SNYDER SJ, ET AL.: Rotator cuff disease: Assessment with MR arthrography versus standard MR imaging in 36 patients with arthroscopic confirmation. *Radiology* 182:431, 1992.

37. PALMER WE, BROWN JH, ROSENTHAL DI: Rotator cuff: Evaluation with fat-suppressed MR arthrography. *Radiology* 188:683, 1993.

38. TIRMAN PFJ, APPLEGATE GR, FLANNIGAN BD, ET AL.: Magnetic resonance arthrography of the shoulder. *MRI Clin North Am* 1:125, 1993.

39. BIEZE J: Saline injection enhances shoulder defect diagnosis. *Diagn Imaging* 14:13, 1992.

40. HAJEK PC, SARTORIS DJ, GRYLYS-MORIN VM, ET AL.: The effect of intraarticular gadolinium-DTPA on synovial membrane and cartilage. *Invest Radiol* 25:179, 1990.

41. MOSELEY HF, OVERGAARD B: The anterior capsular mechanism in recurrent anterior dislocation of shoulder. Morphological and clinical studies with special reference to the glenoid labrum and the glenohumeral ligaments. *J Bone Joint Surg* 44B:913, 1962.

42. BLAND JH, MERRIT JA, BOUSHEY DR: The painful shoulder. *Semin Arthritis Rheum* 7:21, 1977.

43. WARWICK R, WILLIAMS PL: *Gray's Anatomy*, 36th ed, Philadelphia, Saunders, 1989, p 456.

44. AHOVUO J: Radiographic anatomy of the intertubercular groove of the humerus. *Eur J Radiol* 5:83, 1985.

45. DEPALMA AF: Regional variational and surgical anatomy, in DePalma AF (ed): *Surgery of the Shoulder*, 3d ed, Philadelphia, Lippincott, 1983.

46. PETERSILGE CA, WITTE DH, SEWELL BO: Normal regional anatomy of the shoulder. *MRI Clin North Am* 1:1, 1993.

47. TURKEL SJ, PANIO MW, MARSHAL JL, GIRGIS FG: Stabilizing mechanisms preventing anterior dislocation of the glenohumeral joint. *J Bone Joint Surg* 63A:1208, 1981.

48. RAFII M, FIROOZNIA H, GOLIMBU C, ET AL.: CT arthrography of capsular structures of the shoulder. *AJR* 146:361, 1986.

49. EDELSON JG, TAITZ C, GRISHKAN A: The coracohumeral ligament: Anatomy of a substantial but neglected structure. *J Bone Joint Surg* 73B:150, 1991.

50. FERRARI DA: Capsular ligaments of the shoulder: Anatomical and functional study of the anterior superior capsule. *Am J Sports Med* 18:20, 1990.

51. NEER CS II, SATTERLEE CC, DALSEY RM, ET AL.: The anatomy and potential effects of contracture of the coracohumeral ligament. *Clin Orthop* 280:182, 1992.

52. NEVIASER RJ: Anatomic considerations and examination of the shoulder. *Orthop Clin North Am* 11:187, 1980.

53. SALTER EG, NASCA RJ, SHELLEY BS: Anatomical observations on the acromioclavicular joint and supporting ligaments. *Am J Sports Med* 15:199, 1987.

54. MITCHELL MJ, CAMSEY G, BERTHOTY PD, ET AL.: Peribursal fat plane of the shoulder. Anatomic study and clinical experience. *Radiology* 168:699, 1988.

55. MIDDLETON WD, KNEELAND JB, CARRERA GF, ET AL.: High-resolution MR imaging of the normal rotator cuff. *AJR* 148:559, 1987.

56. NEER CS II: Anterior acromioplasty for chronic impingement syndrome in the shoulder: A preliminary report. *J Bone Joint Surg* 54A:41, 1972.

57. SKINNER HA: Anatomical considerations relative to rupture of the supraspinatus tendon. *J Bone Joint Surg* 19:137, 1937.

58. TSAI JC, ZLATKIN MB: Magnetic resonance imaging of the shoulder. *Radiol Clin North Am* 28:279, 1990.

59. DAVIS SJ, TERESI LM, BRADLEY WG, ET AL.: Effect of arm rotation on MR imaging of the rotator cuff. *Radiology* 181:265, 1991.

60. KAPLAN PA, BRYANS KC, DAVICK JP, ET AL.: MR imaging of the normal shoulder: Variants and pitfalls. *Radiology* 184:519, 1992.

61. NEUMANN CH, HOLT RG, STEINBACH LS, ET AL.: MR imaging of the shoulder: Appearance of the supraspinatus tendon in asymptomatic volunteers. *Am J Roentgenol* 158:1281, 1992.

62. VAHLENSIECK M, POLLACK M, LANG P, ET AL.: Two segments of supraspinatus muscle: Cause of high signal intensity at MR imaging? *Radiology* 186:449, 1993.

63. LIOU JT, WILSON AJ, TOTTY WG, BROWN JJ. The normal shoulder: Common variations that simulate pathologic conditions at MR imaging. *Radiology* 186:435, 1993.

64. ERICKSON SJ, COX IH, HYDE JS, ET AL.: Effect of tendon orientation on MR imaging signal intensity: A manifestation of the "magic angle" phenomenon. *Radiology* 181:389, 1991.

65. CHANDNANI V, HO C, GERHARTER J, ET AL.: MR findings in asymptomatic shoulders: A blind analysis using symptomatic shoulders as controls. *Clin Imaging* 16:25, 1992.

66. BIGLIANI LU, MORRISON DS: The morphology of the acromion and its relationship to rotator cuff tears. *Orthop Trans* 10:228, 1986.

67. EPSTEIN R, SCHWEITZ ME, FENLIN J: Hooked acromion: Prevalence on MR images of painful shoulder. *Radiology* 187:479, 1993.

68. EDELSON JG, TAITZ C: Anatomy of the coracoacromial arch. Relation to degeneration of the acromion. *J Bone Joint Surg* 74B:589, 1992.

69. McNIESH LM, CALLAGHAN JJ: CT arthrography of the shoulder: Variations of the glenoid labrum. *AJR* 149:963, 1987.

70. NEUMANN CH, PETERSEN SA, JAHNKE AH: MR imaging of the labral-capsular complex: Normal variations. *Am J Roentgenol* 157:1015, 1991.

71. ZLATKIN MB, BJORKENGREN AG, GYLYS-MORIN V, ET AL.: Cross-sectional imaging of the capsular mechanism of the glenohumeral joint. *AJR* 150:151, 1988.

72. LEGAN JM, BURKHARD TK, GOFF WB II, ET AL.: Tears of the glenoid labrum: MR imaging of 88 arthroscopically confirmed cases. *Radiology* 179:241, 1991.

73. COOPER DE, ARMOCZKY SP, O'BRIEN SJ, ET AL.: Anatomy, histology and vascularity of the glenoid labrum. *J Bone Joint Surg* 74A:46, 1992.

1E TECHNICAL ASPECTS: ULTRASONOGRAPHY OF THE SHOULDER

David J. Sartoris

Shoulder pain is a common clinical problem. Findings on physical examination often are nonspecific, and arthrography is normally used to investigate the most frequent cause of shoulder pain, noncalcific tendinitis secondary to impingement.

Ultrasonography (US) has recently shown itself to be of value in the diagnosis of rotator cuff tears.[1] In addition, sonography can demonstrate abnormalities within the intact rotator cuff tendon, including changes in echogenicity and thickness. The patterns of abnormality demonstrated correlate with pathologic changes associated with tendinitis.[2]

The estimated frequency of rotator cuff tears in people more than 60 years old is approximately 30 percent. With such a large potential group of patients, some radiologists prefer US over more invasive, expensive, and time-consuming methods such as arthrography, arthroscopy, and magnetic resonance imaging (MRI). The cost effectiveness of the technique and its noninvasive character are strong factors favoring US as a screening method.[3]

US examination may be indicated when a patient has chronic shoulder symptoms, normal radiographs, and clinical findings suggestive of rotator cuff disease (painful arc, positive impingement test, positive supraspinatus test, or limited abduction). Arthrography or arthroscopy would then be limited to patients with normal radiographs and sonograms but unequivocal findings on clinical examination. Approximately 3 percent of patients referred for US of the rotator cuff fall into this category.[3]

On rare occasions, further investigation is necessary after a negative arthrogram. Superficial tears of the rotator cuff can be shown by injection of the subacromial-subdeltoid bursa, which can be performed under sonographic or fluoroscopic guidance.[4]

TECHNIQUE

The technique for US of the rotator cuff has been well described with reference to the normal anatomy of the region. US of the shoulder easily and rapidly displays normal rotator cuff anatomy.[5]

High-frequency linear-array transducers (5, 7.5, 10 MHz) are essential for evaluation of the rotator cuff. Linear-array transducers provide the wide field of view required superficially, whereas radial arrays and sector scanners are less desirable.[6] The wedge-shaped image produced by sector scanners severely limits the width of the visualized superficial tissue.[3]

The long head of the biceps tendon is considered the most important landmark in shoulder sonography. Identification of this tendon helps distinguish the subscapularis muscle and tendon from the supraspinatus tendon. The anteriorly positioned supraspinatus tendon is most often affected by rotator cuff tear secondary to impingement.[3]

Ideally, the patient is positioned on a rotating chair, with the examiner facing the lateral side of the shoulder. The long head of the biceps tendon is first identified within the bicipital groove on the anterior humeral surface with the shoulder in neutral position. The biceps tendon has a circular shape in the transverse plane. Medial to the biceps tendon, the subscapularis muscle covers the anterior surface of the humeral head, and its tendon inserts on the lesser tuberosity with some fibers continuing across the bicipital groove to form the transverse humeral ligament. The most distal extent of the subscapularis tendon is rarely torn, whereas biceps tendon dislocation usually follows proximal separation of the subscapularis fibers from the lesser tuberosity while fibers of the transverse ligament remain intact. The biceps tendon is thus located posterior to the subscapularis muscle in most dislocations.[3]

More laterally, the supraspinatus tendon is identified adjacent to the lateral edge of the acromion. Scanning with simultaneous palpation of the acromial edge prevents the examiner from imaging below the supraspinatus insertion, resulting in a false positive result. The supraspinatus tendon extends only a few centimeters inferior to the lateral acromial edge. It is thus important to move the transducer medially to confirm absence of cuff material. With the transducer ideally positioned immediately beneath the lateral border of the acromion, the shoulder is moved into internal rotation to uncover more of the supraspinatus tendon. Sonography is capable of screening about 95 percent of the rotator cuff substance, but the acromion covers the remaining 5 percent. Two percent of rotator cuff tears are thus missed by sonography because they are obscured from view by the acromion.[3]

The normal supraspinatus tendon lies deep to the deltoid muscle and is slightly more reflective (Fig. 1E-1). In older persons, the supraspinatus tendon can be hypoechoic, resulting in reflectivity less than or equivalent to that of the deltoid muscle. The normal tendon has a homogeneous appearance and any inhomogeneity should prompt suspicion of rotator cuff injury or an artifact. True lesions can be distinguished from artifact by rotating the transducer 90° in an attempt to confirm the abnormality in the coronal plane. A focal area of hypo- or hyperreflectivity observed in only one plane represents anisotropy. The supraspinatus tendon, which appears as a curvilinear band on transverse images, is a triangular structure on coronal images. An imaginary line between the acromion and the humeral head forms the base of the triangle, and the apex is the insertion of the supraspinatus on the greater tuberosity.[3]

The posterior portion of the cuff is next evaluated in the transverse plane, and this approach is most sensitive for detecting small effusions. The transducer is placed over the posterior aspect of the shoulder at the midglenohumeral level. The infraspinatus muscle and tendon are triangular, whereas the posterior labrum appears as

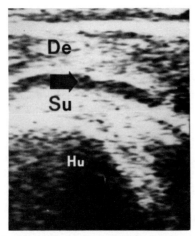

Figure 1E-1 Transverse image of normal rotator cuff. (Key: De, deltoid muscle; Hu, humeral head; Su, supraspinatus tendon; *arrow*, subdeltoid fat.) *(Reproduced in modified form with permission from VAN HOLSBEECK M, INTROCASO JH (eds):* Musculoskeletal Ultrasound, *St. Louis, Mosby, 1992.)*

a hyperechoic triangle separating the infraspinatus tendon from the glenoid. The teres minor is visualized 2 to 3 cm farther inferiorly and has a more rectangular appearance. The posterior portion of the cuff is torn only in the most advanced cases.[3]

SHOULDER PATHOLOGY

In an important imaging–anatomic pathology correlative study, 26 shoulder joints from 10 male and three female cadavers, ranging in age from 40 to 89 years (mean 65.9), were examined with a linear-array real-time US scanner provided with a 7.5-MHz transducer. Arthrotomy and histologic preparations were made after US. Thinning and discontinuity of echogenic homogeneity of the rotator cuff tendons were the most reliable signs of complete tear. Focal hyper- and hypoechogenic foci within the tendons were unreliable criteria. Partial tears of the rotator cuff were difficult to detect on static scans. US readily revealed discontinuity of the biceps tendon as a sign of rupture, which was commonly associated with rotator cuff tear.[7]

A method of shoulder sonography that uses lateral and anterior elevation of the arm has been demonstrated to be effective in cases of suspected impingement syndrome. The technique is able to demonstrate fluid collections in the subacromial-subdeltoid bursa as gradual distension of the bursa and lateral pooling of fluid in the subdeltoid portion with arm elevation. In 102 of 381 patients studied, surgical diagnosis was available for correlation. Among this group there were seven false negative and three false positive sonographic findings. A comparison of sonographic and surgical findings demonstrated sensitivity of 81 percent and specificity of 95 percent in the early stages (I and II) of impingement syndrome.[8]

Rotator cuff tears (Table 1E-1) and rotator cuff calcifications both cause inhomogeneity in the sonographic architecture of the cuff. Punctate echogenic foci, with or without acoustic shadowing, are consistent with calcification.[6] Only a minority of rotator cuff tears are hyperechogenic, and they tend to be more linear than calcifications. It is important to distinguish between definite and suggestive sonographic signs of rotator cuff tear.[6,9]

Large rotator cuff tears are manifested sonographically as complete absence of the supraspinatus tendon; only the deltoid muscle is visible adjacent to the acromion (see Fig. 10-11). In chronic disease the acromiohumeral space is markedly decreased, a phenomenon best demonstrated on coronal images. The supraspinatus tendon may be replaced by hypoechoic fluid, and often fluid is present in the subacromial-subdeltoid bursa (Fig. 1E-2). Fluid is easily distinguished from a hypoechoic tendon by its deformability with compression.[3]

Table 1E-1 Diagnostic and Suggestive Signs for Rotator Cuff Tear[3]

DIAGNOSTIC SIGNS

Complete absence of the tendon
Focal atrophy of the tendon
Hypoechoic cleft in the tendon
Distended subdeltoid bursa
 with joint communication

SUGGESTIVE SIGNS

Inhomogeneous areas in the cuff
 (hypoechoic or hyperechoic)
Increased amount of fluid in the
 biceps tendon sheath and
 subacromial-subdeltoid bursa
Small joint effusion

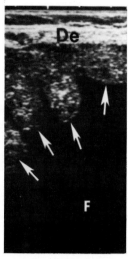

Figure 1E-3 Coronal image of subacromial-subdeltoid bursitis with thickened inflammatory synovium (*arrows*) in rheumatoid arthritis. (Key: De, deltoid muscle; F, bursal fluid.) *(Reproduced in modified form with permission from VAN HOLSBEECK M, INTROCASO JH (eds): Musculoskeletal Ultrasound, St. Louis, Mosby, 1992.)*

Large tears in patients with arthritides such as rheumatoid and septic arthritis are often associated with significant distension of the subacromial-subdeltoid bursa. The synovium of the bursa is very irregular, and its lumen is filled with echogenic material (Fig. 1E-3). US-guided aspiration is indicated for effusions if infection is suspected clinically.[3]

Tears no larger than 1 cm are much more difficult to diagnose (see Fig. 10-12). If fluid is present within the tear, the lesion appears hypoechoic (Fig. 1E-4), whereas in the absence of fluid the lesion is seen as a linear echogenic band (Fig. 1E-5). The diagnosis of an echogenic band as a complete rotator cuff tear can be made only when it extends through the entire thickness of the cuff. Small tears may also be manifested as focal atrophy of the cuff (Fig. 1E-6), whereas indentations in the normally smooth curvilinear contour of the supraspinatus tendon are indicative of partial rotator cuff tear (Fig. 1E-7).[3]

Many controversial reports in the literature discuss the clinical utility of shoulder sonography.[10,11] In general, results are highly dependent on technique and the examiner's experience. In addition to the use of proper equipment, real time dynamic evaluation is important in obtaining reliable results. Movement of the shoulder into full extension and internal and external rotation demonstrates the greatest possible percentage of cuff tissue and

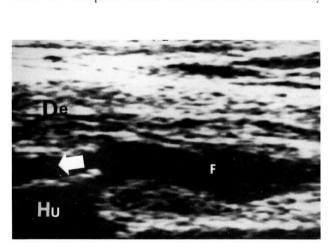

Figure 1E-2 Coronal image of large rotator cuff tear with retraction (*arrow*). (Key: De, deltoid muscle; F, fluid in subdeltoid bursa; Hu, humeral head.) *(Reproduced in modified form with permission from VAN HOLSBEECK M, INTROCASO JH (eds): Musculoskeletal Ultrasound, St. Louis, Mosby, 1992.)*

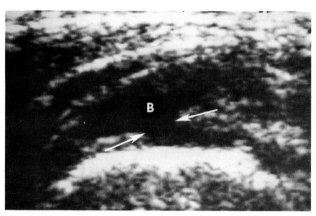

Figure 1E-4 Transverse image of full-thickness rotator cuff tear (*arrows*) with fluid in the subacromial-subdeltoid bursa (B). *(Reproduced in modified form with permission from VAN HOLSBEECK M, INTROCASO JH (eds): Musculoskeletal Ultrasound, St. Louis, Mosby, 1992.)*

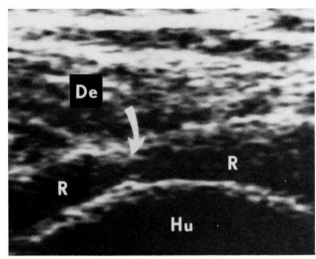

Figure 1E-5 Transverse image of hyperechoic cleft (*arrow*) in the rotator cuff (R) indicative of a tear. (Key: De, deltoid muscle; Hu, humeral head.) *(Reproduced in modified form with permission from VAN HOLSBEECK M, INTROCASO JH (eds):* Musculoskeletal Ultrasound, *St. Louis, Mosby, 1992.)*

minimizes the portion obscured by bony structures. Failure to identify artifacts encountered when imaging a sphere and anisotropy of tendons lead to misdiagnosis, particularly problematic detection of hyperechoic rotator cuff tears. Abnormalities should be confirmed in two imaging planes if there is any question of imaging artifact.[3]

Tears of the surrounding muscles, including the deltoid, pectoral, brachial, and biceps muscles, can also be observed by shoulder sonography. Sonographic screening of these muscles is performed quickly and easily as part of the routine rotator cuff examinations.[3]

Biceps tendon lesions are common in shoulder impingement syndrome (Fig. 1E-8). Characteristic findings include fluid in the tendon sheath and edema of the tendon, resulting in a hypoechoic appearance. Fluid in the biceps tendon sheath may represent tendinitis (Fig. 1E-9) or may be secondary to intra-articular pathology,

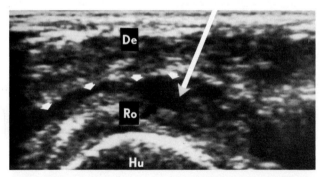

Figure 1E-6 Transverse image of small rotator cuff tear (*long arrow*) with fluid present in the subacromial-subdeltoid bursa (*short arrows*). (Key: De, deltoid muscle; Hu, humeral head; Ro, rotator cuff.) *(Reproduced in modified form with permission from VAN HOLSBEECK M, INTROCASO JH (eds):* Musculoskeletal Ultrasound, *St. Louis, Mosby, 1992.)*

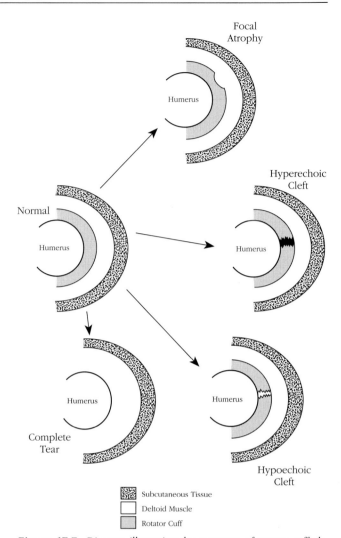

Figure 1E-7 Diagram illustrating the spectrum of rotator cuff abnormalities amenable to diagnosis by US. *(Reproduced in modified form with permission from VAN HOLSBEECK M, INTROCASO JH (eds):* Musculoskeletal Ultrasound, *St. Louis, Mosby, 1992.)*

which usually manifests itself as fluid elsewhere in the joint.[3]

High-resolution real time sonography of the biceps tendon was performed on 80 patients referred for shoulder arthrography in one investigation. The arthrograms and sonograms were compared at the levels of the biceps tendon groove and distal tendon. Sonography and arthrography were equivalent in the demonstration of the configuration of the bicipital tendon groove, but sonography provided superior depiction of the biceps tendon within the groove. In 16 patients, bicipital tendon sheath effusions were detected by sonography, and 15 of these subjects had an associated shoulder lesion. Arthrography did not demonstrate a bicipital tendon or sheath abnormality in any of these patients.[12]

Rotator cuff tears may cause fluid to accumulate within the subacromial-subdeltoid bursa, though this may occur

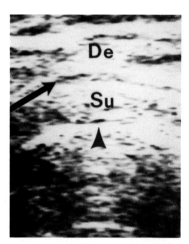

Figure 1E-8 Transverse image of shoulder impingement syndrome. The subdeltoid fat is sparse (*arrow*), with the supraspinatus tendon (Su) occupying most of the space between the deltoid muscle (De) and the humeral cortex (*arrowhead*). *(Reproduced in modified form with permission from VAN HOLSBEECK M, INTROCASO JH (eds): Musculoskeletal Ultrasound, St. Louis, Mosby, 1992.)*

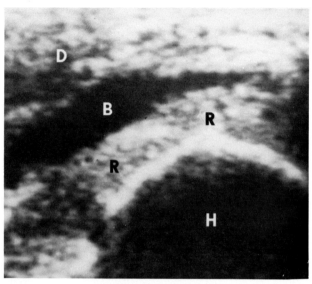

Figure 1E-10 Transverse image of subacromial-subdeltoid fluid in bursitis (B). (Key: D, deltoid muscle; H, humeral head; R, rotator cuff.) *(Reproduced in modified form with permission from VAN HOLSBEECK M, INTROCASO JH (eds): Musculoskeletal Ultrasound, St. Louis, Mosby, 1992.)*

as a primary inflammatory phenomenon (Fig. 1E-10). Arthritis of any cause is often associated with fluid in all the synovial recesses of the shoulder. The most sonographically accessible recess of the glenohumeral joint lies posteriorly, and more than 2 mm displacement of the infraspinatus tendon from the posterior glenoid labrum is a definite sign of effusion. When the cause of a fluid collection cannot be established, US-guided aspiration for culture can be performed to exclude infection (Fig. 1E-11).[3]

Size, location, transducer frequency, and focal zone are the most significant factors in providing an acoustic shadow in the setting of calcification (Fig. 1E-12).[3] US may supplement conventional radiography when osteochondral bodies occur in sites such as the subscapularis recess.

The value of dynamic sonography for adhesive capsulitis of the joint has been studied in patients suspected on clinical grounds to have frozen shoulder. The sonographic criterion of adhesive capsulitis was continuous limitation of the sliding movement of the supraspinatus

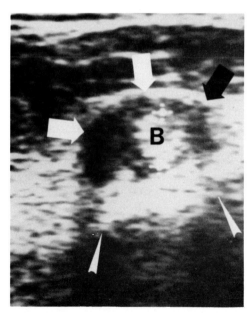

Figure 1E-9 Transverse image of bicipital tendinitis with distension of the bicipital sheath by fluid (*arrows*). (Key: B, biceps tendon; *arrowheads*, bicipital groove of humerus.) *(Reproduced in modified form with permission from VAN HOLSBEECK M, INTROCASO JH (eds): Musculoskeletal Ultrasound, St. Louis, Mosby, 1992.)*

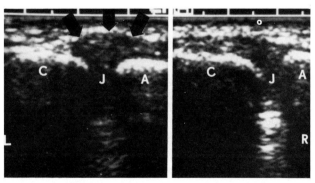

Figure 1E-11 Coronal image of septic arthritis involving the left acromioclavicular joint. Soft tissue swelling of mixed echogenicity (*arrows*) is centered over the joint space (J). (Key: A, acromion; C, clavicle; L, left; R, right.) *(Reproduced in modified form with permission from VAN HOLSBEECK M, INTROCASO JH (eds): Musculoskeletal Ultrasound, St. Louis, Mosby, 1992.)*

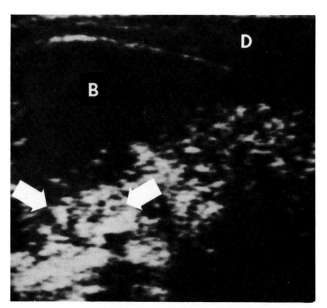

Figure 1E-12   Coronal image of subdeltoid bursitis (B) with calcific deposits (*arrows*). (Key: D, deltoid muscle.) *(Reproduced in modified form with permission from VAN HOLSBEECK M, INTROCASO JH (eds): Musculoskeletal Ultrasound, St. Louis, Mosby, 1992.)*

tendon against the acromion of the scapula. Arthrography was regarded as the gold standard in the diagnosis of adhesive capsulitis against which the sonographic results were evaluated. Among 23 patients with arthrographically documented adhesive capsulitis, sonographic examination showed limitation of movement of the supraspinatus tendon in 21. This sonographic sign thus had sensitivity of 91 percent, specificity of 100 percent, and accuracy of 92 percent for detecting adhesive capsulitis.[13]

US frequently is also valuable in evaluating acute trauma to the shoulder. The technique can demonstrate Hill-Sachs defects following anterior shoulder dislocation and rotator cuff tears following greater tuberosity fractures. Isolated biceps tendon dislocation is uncommon, but this lesion may be associated with large rotator cuff tears. Intermittent dislocations may not be demonstrated by MRI. Sonography in neutral position and external rotation optimally demonstrates an empty bicipital groove and dislocated biceps tendon.[3]

In a retrospective study, the sonographic appearance of humeral greater tuberosity fracture was evaluated in 17 men and 14 women aged 20 to 69 years with acute, subacute, or "remote" shoulder trauma. Clinical data, radiologic reports, sonograms, and initial plain radiographs of the shoulder were analyzed and clinical follow-up information was available for 22 patients. Sonography showed discontinuity and irregularity of the humeral cortex in all patients. In 25 patients (81 percent) displaced fracture fragments could be seen. Sonographic findings were suggestive of, but not specific for, fracture. Cortical abnormalities of the humerus were identified

without modification of standard scanning protocols. Humeral fracture was confirmed by radiography in 24 patients, and the lesion had been missed initially on plain radiographs in 10 of these.[14]

Experience with rotator cuff sonography in 106 patients has been analyzed to identify the causes of scan misinterpretation. Interpretive errors may be caused by unfamiliarity with sonographic anatomy, soft tissue or bone abnormalities, or technical limitations of the study. Errors in recognition of normal anatomy are easily overcome by experience and comparison to the normal contralateral rotator cuff. Errors resulting from soft tissue abnormalities were seen in two patients with calcific tendinitis simulating rotator cuff tear. Problems in interpretation resulting from fractures in two patients and inferior glenohumeral subluxation in two others could have been avoided by reviewing the radiographs before performing sonography. The major technical limitation involves inability to image the rotator cuff beneath the acromion; however, rotator cuff tears rarely are isolated in this site, and passive maneuvers often allow otherwise hidden parts of the cuff to be visualized.[15]

POSTOPERATIVE SHOULDER

In one investigation, 53 patients with 60 symptomatic shoulders underwent shoulder sonography for recurrent postoperative symptoms after either acromioplasty (10 shoulders) or repair of a full-thickness rotator cuff tear in addition to acromioplasty (50 shoulders). After acromioplasty, the characteristic sharp margin of the acromion was replaced by a less distinct, irregular surface. After repair of a cuff tear, characteristic sonographic appearances included visualization of a reimplantation trough and loss of the echogenic subdeltoid bursa. When the cuff was intact after surgery, echogenicity was abnormal in all 17 cases. Sonography accurately diagnosed recurrent cuff tears in all 26 shoulders for which surgical proof was available and confirmed intactness of the cuff in 10 of 11 cases. In one shoulder, a cuff hematoma was misinterpreted as a full-thickness tear. Because surgery distorts landmarks, an understanding of the surgical procedures and their characteristic sonographic appearance is essential.[16]

In another study, 40 patients were studied sonographically at 1 week to 6 years after rotator cuff repair. The postoperative rotator cuff is abnormally echogenic and can look very similar to a small unrepaired rotator cuff tear. Soft tissue planes about the tendon are distorted or absent. Criteria for diagnosis of retear are different from those used in detecting new tears in a nonoperated cuff. Postoperative echogenicity is normal, but the finding of a defect or gap within the rotator cuff tendon is the only accurate sign of a recurrent rotator cuff tear.[17]

COMPARISON TO OTHER MODALITIES

In one investigation, 38 patients with suspected rotator cuff tear were examined at 1.5 T by using a loop-gap resonator surface coil. The MRI findings were compared prospectively in a blinded fashion with the results from double-contrast arthrography in 38 patients, high-resolution sonography in 23 patients, and surgery in 16 patients. In the total group of 38 patients, MRI detected 22 of 22 tears and 14 of 16 intact cuffs as determined by arthrography. In the 16 surgically proven cases, MRI and arthrography had identical results: 92 percent sensitivity in the diagnosis of 12 tears and 100 percent specificity in the confirmation of four intact cuffs. In a subgroup of 23 patients, sonography detected nine of 15 tears and seven of eight intact cuffs as determined by comparison with arthrography. In 10 surgically proven cases, sonography was 63 percent sensitive in the diagnosis of eight rotator cuff tears and 50 percent specific in the diagnosis of two intact cuffs. In this study, sonography was not as accurate as the other two techniques in the diagnosis of rotator cuff tear.[18]

In another series, 39 consecutive patients referred for shoulder arthrography underwent sonography to determine its ability to detect rotator cuff tear. Fifteen patients had arthrographically proven rotator cuff tears. Of these, 14 were detected by sonography (sensitivity 93 percent). The three sonographic criteria indicative of rotator cuff tear were (1) discontinuity in the normal homogeneous echogenicity of the rotator cuff, (2) replacement of the normal homogeneous echogenicity by a central echogenic band, and (3) nonvisualization of the cuff. Twenty patients had normal sonographic examinations, 19 of whom were proved normal by arthrography. Therefore, the predictive value of a negative sonogram was 95 percent.[19]

Another investigation involved 81 patients, and the standards of comparison were arthrography in 79 cases and surgery in two. The sonograhic technique used was based on literature review and experience gained by scanning normal subjects. The sonographic criteria for diagnosis of complete rotator cuff tear were a focal defect in the cuff or complete absence or nonvisualization of the cuff. All sonograms were interpreted prospectively without knowledge of arthrographic or surgical results. With arthrography as the standard of comparison for the diagnosis of rotator cuff tear, sonographic results included 15 true positives, 52 true negatives, eight false negatives, and four false positives. With surgery as the standard of comparison, the results were one true positive and one true negative sonogram. The sensitivity of sonography in detecting rotator cuff tear was 67 percent, specificity 93 percent, and accuracy 85 percent.[20]

In another study, US was performed in 88 patients,

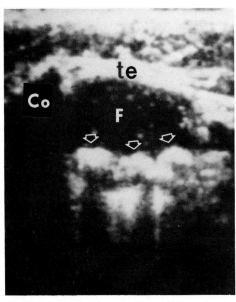

Figure 1E-13 Longitudinal image of multiple osteochondral bodies (*arrows*) in the subscapularis recess, which is distended by fluid (F). (Key: Co, coracoid process; te, subscapularis tendon.) *(Reproduced in modified form with permission from VAN HOLSBEECK M, INTROCASO JH (eds): Musculoskeletal Ultrasound, St. Louis, Mosby, 1992.)*

15 of whom were referred for surgery. A real time linear-array scanner provided with a 7.5-MHz transducer was used. Subsequently, all patients underwent single-contrast arthrography of the shoulder. As compared to arthrographic findings, US yielded 21 true positive results, three false positives, 57 true negatives, and seven false negative diagnoses of full-thickness rotator cuff tear. Small tears (2 cm or less in diameter) were the most difficult to assess. The technique reliably demonstrated bicipital tendinitis and rupture of the biceps tendon, as well as fluid in the subacromial-subdeltoid bursa (Fig. 1E-13).[21]

In another investigation, 98 patients suspected of having rotator cuff tears underwent sonography of both shoulders. Sixty-two patients underwent double-contrast arthrography performed on the same day as sonography, and 38 patients underwent surgery after sonography. A comparison of the results from US and arthrography using published diagnostic criteria demonstrated sensitivity of 75 percent and specificity of 43 percent for rotator cuff tears. Use of more restricted criteria, a subset of published criteria, yielded sensitivity of 68 percent and a specificity of 90 percent. A comparison of sonography with surgery, using restricted criteria, demonstrated sensitivity of 32 percent and specificity of 76 percent.[22]

Seventy-five patients underwent both sonography and arthrography in another study. Major sonographic diagnostic criteria included (1) well-defined discontinuity usually visible as a hypoechoic focus within the cuff, (2) nonvisualization of the cuff, and (3) an echogenic focus within the cuff. Compared with arthrography alone, US afforded detection of 92 percent of rotator cuff tears (24 of 26 tears), with a specificity of 84 percent and a negative predictive value of 95 percent. In 30 surgical cases, the sensitivity of sonography for detection of a tear was 93 percent, with specificity of 73 percent, whereas for arthrography sensitivity was 87 percent and specificity 100 percent.[23]

In another study, the diagnostic value of US and MRI in 24 shoulders with suspected rotator cuff tear was evaluated using arthrography as gold standard. Sonography demonstrated 14 of 15 and MRI 10 of 15 rotator cuff tears. Sonography diagnosed seven of nine intact rotator cuffs correctly; MRI documented eight of nine. The authors concluded that, owing to cost and patient compliance, sonography should be the initial test for suspected rotator cuff tear if it can be performed by an experienced sonographer, but that MRI is superior in depicting more extensive lesions and is less operator dependent.[24]

In another series, 406 patients with shoulder pain underwent bilateral shoulder US, and a rotator cuff lesion was diagnosed in 197 patients. There was good correlation between sonographic and arthrographic findings as well as surgical results, with a sensitivity of 91 percent for each examination technique. Rotator cuff tears larger

Table 1E-2   Cost-Effective Diagnostic Algorithm for Shoulder Pain

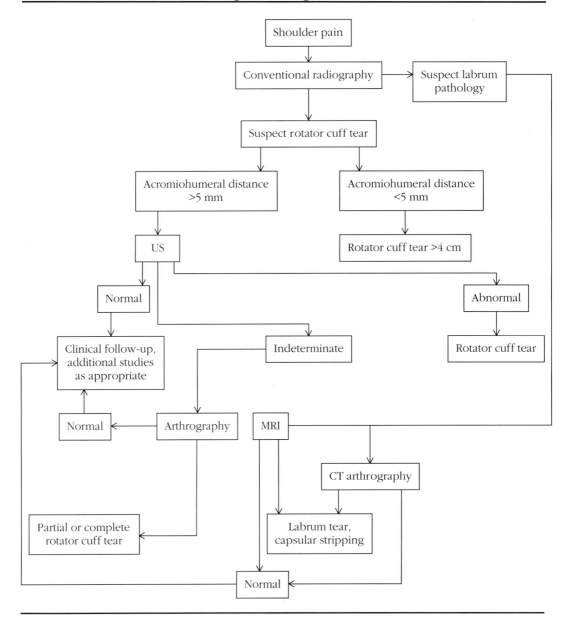

than 1 cm were commonly documented by US. Thirty-six postoperative patients were studied sonographically, all of whom exhibited some degree of increase in rotator cuff echogenicity. The degree of scar formation at the reinsertion of the tendon was adequately documented by US. An indeterminate or negative US finding for a "clinically suspicious" shoulder was deemed the only indication for arthrography.[25]

US of the rotator cuff has been shown to be of value in diagnosing rotator cuff tears in a series of 500 patients in one investigation. All subjects were examined with the hyperextended internal rotation view using commercially available high-resolution real time US equipment. Rotator cuff tear was diagnosed if a focal echogenic lesion or a defect in the rotator cuff was identified. Accuracy, sensitivity, and specificity all exceeded 90 percent, and results correlated with surgical findings. The results were superior to those of arthrography in the same patient population.[26]

In another study, high-resolution, real time US of the rotator cuff was performed in 51 shoulders, and the results were correlated with findings obtained during subsequent surgery. Prospective sensitivity of US in detecting a tear was 100 percent, specificity 75 percent, and accuracy 92 percent. Retrospective estimation of tear size on sonograms correlated well with the intraoperative measurements for small and moderate-sized lesions. The size of large lesions was often underestimated sonographically. Retrospectively, partial tears were diagnosed

correctly in seven patients, and bursal thickening was recognized in 17 patients.[27]

In another investigation, bilateral rotator cuff sonography was performed on 57 shoulders referred for arthrography to detect rotator cuff tear. Twenty-seven shoulders had rotator cuff tears shown on arthrography, 15 of which were detected by US. Eleven were false negative by sonography, and one was indeterminate. Of the 30 shoulders with negative arthrograms, 28 had normal sonograms with two false positives. Sensitivity was 58 percent, specificity 93 percent, and overall accuracy 77 percent. The positive and negative predictive values were 88 percent and 72 percent. These results suggested that sonography has limited value for screening patients for rotator cuff tears and that a positive sonographic reading is more reliable than a negative one.[28]

CONCLUSION

In experienced hands, sonography can be a useful technique for the evaluation of shoulder lesions. It is important to note that rotator cuff sonography is characterized by a significant "learning curve",[1] and novices are encouraged to begin performing the technique immediately after single-contrast arthrography. As a screening tool for rotator cuff disorders US has advantages, including its noninvasive nature, relatively low cost, and potential availability at the time of clinical consultation (Table 1E-2).[29,30]

References

1. MACK LA, MATSEN FA III, KILCOYNE RF, DAVIES PK, SICKLER ME: US evaluation of the rotator cuff. *Radiology* 157:205–209, 1985.
2. CRASS JR, CRAIG EV, FEINBERG SB: Clinical significance of sonographic findings in the abnormal but intact rotator cuff: A preliminary report. *J Clin Ultrasound* 16:625–634, 1988.
3. VAN HOLSBEECK M, INTROCASO JH: Sonography of the shoulder, in van Holsbeeck M, Introcaso JH (eds): *Musculoskeletal Ultrasound*, St. Louis, Mosby, 1991, pp 265–284.
4. VAN HOLSBEECK M, INTROCASO J: Sonography of the postoperative shoulder. *AJR* 152:202, 1989.
5. MIDDLETON WD, EDELSTEIN F, REINUS WR, MELSON GL, MURPHY WA: Ultrasonography of the rotator cuff: Technique and normal anatomy. *J Ultrasound Med* 3:549–551, 1984.
6. MACK LA: Sonographic evaluation of the rotator cuff. *Radiol Clin North Am* 26:161–177, 1988.
7. AHOVUO J, PAAVOLAINEN P, HOMSTROM T: Ultrasonography of the tendons of the shoulder. *Eur J Radiol* 9:17–21, 1989.
8. FARIN PU, JAROMA H, HARJU A, SOIMAKALLIO S: Shoulder impingement syndrome: Sonographic evaluation. *Radiology* 176:845–849, 1990.

9. CRASS JR, CRAIG EV, FEINBERG SB: The hyperextended internal rotation view in rotator cuff ultrasonography. *J Clin Ultrasound* 15:416–420, 1987.

10. HALL FM: Sonography of the shoulder. *Radiology* 173:310, 1989.

11. MIDDLETON WD: Status of rotator cuff sonography. *Radiology* 173:307–309, 1989.

12. MIDDLETON WD, REINUS WR, TOTTY WG, MELSON GL, MURPHY WA: US of the biceps tendon apparatus. *Radiology* 157:211–215, 1985.

13. RYU KN, LEE SW, RHEE YG, ET AL.: Adhesive capsulitis of the shoulder joint: Usefulness of dynamic sonography. *J Ultrasound Med* 12:445–449, 1993.

14. PATTEN RM, MACK LA, WANG KY, LINGEL J: Nondisplaced fractures of the greatest tuberosity of the humerus: Sonographic detection. *Radiology* 182:201–204, 1992.

15. MIDDLETON WD, REINUS WR, MELSON GL, ET AL.: Pitfalls of rotator cuff sonography. *AJR* 146:555–560, 1986.

16. MACK LA, NYBERG DA, MATSEN FR III, KILCOYNE RF, HARVEY D: Sonography of the postoperative shoulder. *AJR* 150:1089–1093, 1988.

17. CRASS JR, CRAIG EV, FEINBERG SB: Sonography of the postoperative rotator cuff. *AJR* 146:561–564, 1986.

18. BURK DL JR, KARASICK D, KURTZ AB, MITCHELL DG, RIFKIN MD, MILLER CL, LEVY DW, FENLIN JM, BARTOLOZZI AR: Rotator cuff tears: Prospective comparison of MR imaging with arthrography, sonography and surgery. *AJR* 153:87–92, 1989.

19. MIDDLETON WD, EDELSTEIN G, REINUS WR, MELSON GL, TOTTY WG, MURPHY WA: Sonographic detection of rotator cuff tears. *AJR* 144:349–353, 1985.

20. VICK CW, BELL SA: Rotator cuff tears: Diagnosis with sonography. *AJR* 154:121–123, 1990.

21. AHOVUO J, PAAVOLAINEN P, BJORKENHEIM JM: Ultrasonography in lesions of the rotator cuff and biceps tendon. *Acta Radiol* 30:253, 1989.

22. BRANDT TD, CARDONE BW, GRANT TH, POST M, WEISS CA: Rotator cuff sonography: A reassessment. *Radiology* 173:323–327, 1989.

23. SOBLE MG, KAYE AD, GUAY RC: Rotator cuff tear: clinical experience with sonographic detection. *Radiology* 173:319–321, 1989.

24. HODLER J, TERRIER B, VON SCHULTHESS GK, FUCHS WA: MRI and sonography of the shoulder. *Clin Radiol* 43:323–327, 1991.

25. FURTSCHEGGER A, RESCH H: Value of ultrasonography in preoperative diagnosis of rotator cuff tears and postoperative follow-up. *Eur J Radiol* 8:69–75, 1988.

26. CRASS JR, CRAIG EV, FEINBERG SB: Ultrasonography of rotator cuff tears: A review of 500 diagnostic studies. *J Clin Ultrasound* 16:313–327, 1988.

27. HODLER J, FRETZ CJ, TERRIOR F, GERBER C: Rotator cuff tears: Correlation of sonographic and surgical findings. *Radiology* 169:791–794, 1988.

28. MILLER CL, KARASICK D, KURTZ AB, FENLIN JM JR: Limited sensitivity of ultrasound for the detection of rotator cuff tears. *Skel Radiol* 18:179–183, 1989.

29. MIDDLETON WD: Ultrasonography of the shoulder. *Radiol Clin North Am* 30:927, 1992.

30. CRASS JR, CRAIG EV, BRETZKE C, FEINBERG SB: Ultrasonography of the rotator cuff. *Radiographics* 5:941–953, 1985.

1F TECHNICAL ASPECTS: SCINTIGRAPHIC TECHNIQUES

Penny R. Vande Streek
Robert F. Carretta
Frederick L. Weiland
David K. Shelton
Leonard Rosenthall

NUCLEAR MEDICINE

Plain film radiographs, contrast arthrograms, and magnetic resonance imaging (MRI) are the modalities most frequently used to evaluate the shoulder. Bone scintigraphy complements these studies by providing whole-body imaging, perfusion studies, and evaluation of osteoblastic activity. Scintigraphic imaging of the bone marrow can be used to evaluate marrow activity or infarctions or to detect tumor. Bone imaging should be considered for patients whose other examinations are nondiagnostic, and it serves as a sensitive, noninvasive, and relatively inexpensive test for the detection of skeletal lesions. The bone scan is utilized to ascertain the significance of incidental signal abnormalities from marrow seen on MRI. Scintigraphy is applicable for the detection of benign and malignant disorders of bone, and occasionally for muscle and soft tissue disease. Bone scan is more sensitive than plain film radiography, which cannot detect a bone lesion until it is at least 30 percent demineralized. The presence of increased or decreased uptake in a bone lesion, though not specific, adds significantly to correlative imaging diagnosis.

The four standard techniques utilized in nuclear skeletal imaging are the site-specific limited scan, three-phase bone scintigraphy, whole-body imaging, and single-photon emission computed tomography (SPECT). Three-phase bone scanning allows the physician to evaluate perfusion, blood pool distribution, and skeletal uptake. Gilday and coworkers[1] Majd and Frankel[2] were leaders in the use of blood pool imaging to evaluate osteomyelitis. Radionuclide angiograms and blood pool imaging have since been investigated in many disorders.[3-6] The scan is divided into three phases: (1) radionuclide angiogram, or "flow" phase; (2) the blood pool image (reflecting extravascular and soft tissue activity); and (3) delayed static images for skeletal uptake bound to hydroxyapatite crystals.

The use of whole-body imaging or multiple spot views which encompass the skeletal system is particularly applicable to disease states which involve numerous sites (i.e., tumor, stress injuries, metabolic bone disease, infarction, trauma, arthritides). Finally, SPECT imaging improves localization, anatomic correlation, and definition of the lesion's extent. This technique is particularly useful in evaluating the cervical spine since shoulder pain may be referred from spinal pathology.

MECHANISM OF LOCALIZATION

New bone is produced when osteoblasts form osteoid matrix, which is composed of 90 to 95 percent collagen. The osteoid matrix becomes mineralized with hydroxyapatite crystals, amorphous calcium phosphate, and other minerals to become an osteon.[7] As osteogenesis occurs, bone-imaging agents are incorporated by chemisorption, binding to the hydroxyapatite crystal. Increased bone turnover and blood supply are the key factors in bone-seeking radiotracer localization.[8] Technetium 99m–hydroxyethylidene diphosphonate (^{99m}Tc-HEDP), Tc-hydroxymethylene diphosphonate (^{99m}Tc-HMDP), and ^{99m}Tc-methylene diphosphonate (^{99m}Tc-MDP) are the bone imaging agents used most frequently. They characteristically localize in the bone with excellent target-to-background ratios. The biodistribution of the radiopharmaceutical may be affected by factors such as kit preparation, renal function, and medications the patient is taking.

Two patterns of abnormal bone flow and labeling may occur: increased localization ("hot spots") and diminished uptake ("cold spots" or photopenia). These abnormal regions vary in extent, intensity, and configuration. Altered flow can result in cold defects (photopenia) on skeletal images. Compromise of the vascular supply to bone may be secondary to marrow infiltration, trauma, infarction, postradiation vascular changes, or early osteomyelitis. Of note, aggressive bone lesions such as rapidly progressive tumors may be photopenic on delayed static images. The tumor destruction outpaces the ability of the bone to repair as the lesion progresses.

Increased skeletal uptake occurs when there is an imbalance in osteogenesis with more bone formation than resorption. Elevated radiotracer uptake is seen with recent fractures, infections, and many benign and malignant bone tumors. Myositis ossificans, calcifying hematomas, and calcific tendinitis are additional causes of abnormal focal activity.[9] Another cause of increased radiopharmaceutical activity is secondary to the "hyperemic" phenomenon which occurs when there is altered sympathetic control of the microvasculature which allows blood to flow through normally constricted vessels. The three-phase bone scan may demonstrate this response in disorders such as infection, trauma, and reflex sympathetic dystrophy.

INDICATIONS

The clinical indications for bone scintigraphy in the shoulder run the gamut of skeletal disease. As for the majority of bone scans, referrals for evaluation of the shoulder arise from bone pain or bone lesions detected by other imaging modalities. Additional indications for bone scintigraphy are postoperative evaluation of orthopedic hardware or bone graft revascularization, vascular compromise, infarction, osteomyelitis, bone tumors, muscle injury, metabolic bone disease, and arthritides.

TECHNIQUE AND ANALYSIS

The interpretation of bone scintigraphy is dependent on three fundamental concepts. The first is the routine performance of quality control studies of the cameras, collimators, and radiopharmaceuticals. Early detection of technical or radiopharmaceutical problems will avoid the introduction of artifacts or the misfortune of later having to image the patient again. With the advent of SPECT, additional quality control measures, such as high count extrinsic floods for uniformity, routine center of rotation evaluations, and detector alignment (for multihead systems), are imperative to the reconstruction of the data.

The imaging techniques are the second key to a successful study. The use of a bolus technique for three-phase scintigraphy of an adult requires rapid injection of the ^{99m}Tc-diphosphonate, typically using 20 mCi (740 MBq) with simultaneous acquisition of the radionuclide angiogram (2 to 3 seconds per frame). Care should be taken to position the extremities symmetrically within the field of view of the camera, and the site of injection should be distant from the area of interest. The tourniquet effect results in a reactive hyperemia of the distal extremity when the tourniquet is released. To avoid this, it has been recommended to wait 3 to 5 minutes between removal of the tourniquet used in obtaining intravenous access and injection of the radiopharmaceutical.[10,11]

Upon completion of the radionuclide angiogram a 300,000 to 500,000 count blood pool scan is acquired. Delayed images of the shoulder with 750,000 counts are obtained 3 hours after the injection. Typically, a low-energy, all-purpose collimator is used, and the area of interest is viewed with orthogonal images. Pinhole, or low-energy, high-resolution collimators may alternatively be used; then count acquisition is increased to 1,000,000.[12] Information obtained from the patient—before or during imaging—about a history of trauma, surgery, radiation, chemotherapy, bone pain, and known medical disorders greatly enhances interpretation of the study.

SPECT imaging utilizes the same radiopharmaceutical dose, but the images are three-dimensional representations of data reconstructed and displayed in transverse, coronal, and sagittal views. This technique separates activity that may overlie or underlie an abnormality on a two-dimensional planar view. The typical acquisition employs 64 projections (for about 20 seconds per projection) over a 360° orbit.[12] The camera is positioned as close to the patient as is safely possible and either a circular or elliptical orbit is used. The reconstruction filters should be tailored to the camera system and to the data acquired. SPECT bone scanning can improve sensitivity[13,14] and serves to complement other imaging modalities (CT, MRI) by giving functional information and better anatomic correlation concerning a lesion.[15]

The final component to interpretation of a bone scan is a systematic approach that ensures careful review of the entire scan. Focusing on the region of interest will lead to errors. The scan should be evaluated for the detection of focal increased or decreased skeletal activity, presence of asymmetry, focal or generalized increased soft tissue activity, and abnormalities in the kidneys and bladder. Within the shoulder, areas of increased physiologic uptake are commonly seen in the glenoid, the coracoid process, the tip of the scapula,[16] and muscular insertions (Fig. 1F-1).

The epiphyseal plates of children older than 1 year have intense radiotracer accumulation in a transverse band. Children younger than 15 months may show increased epiphyseal-metaphyseal region activity as compared to the diaphyseal uptake.[17] The intensity of the scintigram should be adjusted to allow proper evaluation of the bone adjacent to the epiphyseal plates, as the metaphyses are frequent sites of neoplasms and infections in children.

In pediatric imaging proper positioning of the patient is also imperative. The increased physiologic activity in the growth plates should appear as transverse, linear

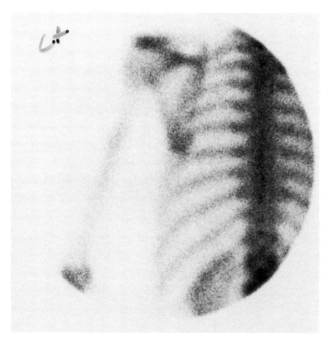

Figure 1F-1 Posterior delayed view of the left humerus demonstrates mildly increased uptake at the deltoid tuberosity, a normal variant.

bands that are symmetric (Fig. 1F-2). To obtain excellent images, the child must be placed so that the extremities are aligned and straight. With younger children rolled linens and tape often help achieve and maintain a desired position. The need for sedation depends on the patient's age and ability to cooperate. In patients with severe bone pain the referring physician can be of much assistance

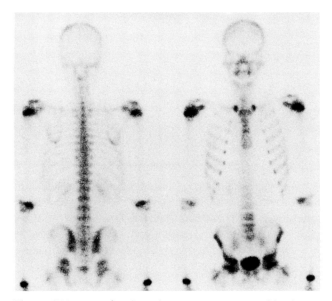

Figure 1F-2 Normal pediatric bone scan in a 13-year-old girl. Anterior and posterior views demonstrate the increased radiotracer uptake typically seen in the epiphyses.

by providing analgesics before the study. The quality of the image depends on minimizing motion.

The degree of radiotracer uptake, extent of uptake, anatomic site, and pattern are important features in determining the diagnosis. Correlation of the bone scan findings with available studies provides invaluable aid in trying to tailor a differential diagnosis. Plain film radiographs are essential for characterizing the bone lesion. CT is used to better demonstrate anatomic features, calcifications, and cortical or trabecular alterations of the bone. MRI can be used to evaluate marrow, soft tissue, and vascular structures and to define the extent of a tumor.

IMAGING: GALLIUM 67 AND INDIUM 111–LABELED LEUKOCYTES

Indium-111 leukocytes and Gallium-67 (Ga-67) citrate are used as adjuncts to three-phase scintigraphy for the evaluation of skeletal infection. The preparation, biodistribution, and characteristics of these agents may be reviewed in the literature.[18–20] The localization of ^{111}In-labeled leukocytes in sites of infection and inflammation is most frequently used when investigating acute osteomyelitis. The patient is given 0.5 mCi (18.5 MBq) of ^{111}In labeled to his or her own white blood cells. Imaging is typically performed 14 to 24 hours after the reinjection of the ^{111}In-labeled leukocytes to allow the white cells to migrate to the site of infection.

Gallium-67 is an iron analogue which concentrates in inflamed, infected, and neoplastic lesions. Hoffer[21] offered these mechanisms as the route for gallium localization: direct bacterial incorporation mediated through siderophores,[22,23] local binding to tissue lactoferrin (which is increased at the site of infection),[24] and neutrophil deposition.[25,26] Capillary permeability[27] and localization within tumor lysosomes[28] have been proposed as well. Gallium-67 citrate (Ga-67) is injected intravenously in an average dose of 5 to 8 mCi (185 to 296 MBq). The dose may be increased to 10 mCi (370 MBq) for performing SPECT. Images are typically acquired following a 48- to 72-hour delay. Lesions suspected of abnormal gallium accumulation often benefit from additional delayed images to evaluate for increasing target-to-background activity. A medium-energy collimator is used to acquire images that make use of the 172- and 247-keV photons from ^{111}In and the 93-, 184-, 296-, and 388-keV gamma emissions of [67]Ga. Spot images are acquired for 300,000 to 500,000 counts.

BONE MARROW IMAGING

Bone marrow imaging may complement bone scintigraphy in cases of avascular necrosis or possible bone

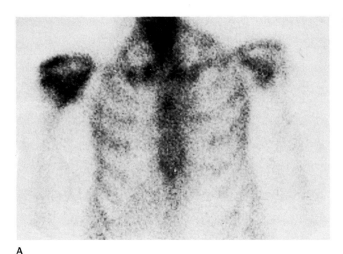

A

B

Figure 1F-3 **A.** A spot view of the shoulders in patient with right shoulder and bilateral hip pain. Increased ^{99m}Tc-MDP uptake in the right humeral head was secondary to avascular necrosis. **B.** An anterior whole-body view demonstrates increased uptake in the shoulders and hips from multiple sites of avascular necrosis in a patient taking steroids.

marrow metastases. Technetium 99m small-particle sulfur colloid is administered, and images are acquired of regions that contain reticuloendothelial cells, such as the proximal humerus. In avascular necrosis, a localized area of photopenia on ^{99m}Tc-sulfur colloid scan is correlated with the bone scan findings, which may demonstrate photopenia acutely or increased uptake (reparative phase) on ^{99m}Tc-MDP imaging (Fig. 1F-3). Photopenia on the bone marrow scan may also be seen with cortical bone infarctions, marrow metastases, or in the presence of orthopedic hardware.

TRAUMA

Trauma is a major cause of shoulder pain. An understanding of the traumatic event assists in the evaluation of the patient and the tailoring of special approaches (e.g., selected views, three-phase scintigraphy). The recent start of a vigorous exercise program may explain intense localization of radiotracer in the muscles of the arms or shoulders (Fig. 1F-4).

In children, a suspicious history or one that does not fit a given type of injury may prompt evaluation for child

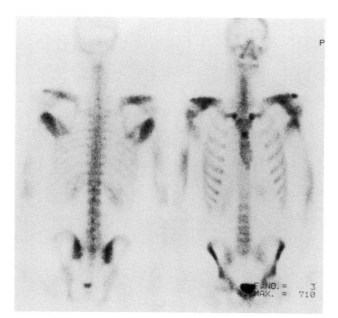

Figure 1F-4 Anterior and posterior views of a bone scan in a male following strenuous exercise show increased uptake in the muscles of the shoulders and upper arms.

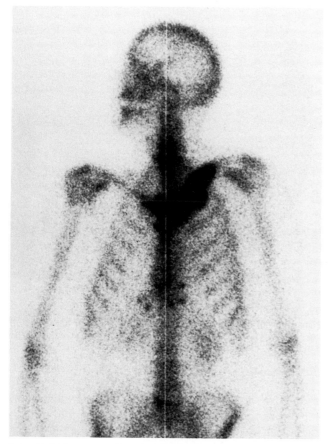

Figure 1F-5 Anterior bone scan in a patient with multiple fractures of ribs, sternum, and clavicles sustained in a motor vehicle accident.

abuse and consideration of whole-body imaging. Though bone scanning should not replace skeletal surveys in the evaluation of child abuse, scintigraphy is useful in identifying additional lesions or periosteal injury.[29,30]

Evaluation for possible occult or multiple fractures is a frequent indication for bone scanning, particularly in elderly patients whose history may be difficult to obtain (Fig. 1F-5). Bone scintigraphy is an excellent tool for detecting fractures which may not be evident on plain radiographs. In nonosteoporotic patients aged 65 years or younger, 95 percent of closed fractures are detected within 24 hours after injury.[31] In older patients 95 percent of scintigrams are positive by 72 hours after injury. An important feature of bone healing and scintigraphy is the interval to normalization. In long bone fractures, radiotracer uptake normalizes within a year in 64 percent of patients, in 2 years in 91 percent, and in 3 years in 95 percent.[31,33] Persistent bone uptake may occur within chronic bone remodeling (Fig. 1F-6) or posttraumatic degenerative changes.

Stress fractures represent the bone's response to repeated mechanical stress. Though the vast majority of stress fractures occur in the lower extremities, there are case reports in the literature of stress injuries to the scapula, clavicle, and humerus.[32] A history of activity is a vital clue to understanding abnormal tracer localization in these cases. Bone scans may also detect insufficiency or pathologic fractures secondary to osteoporosis, metabolic bone disease, Paget's disease, fibrous dysplasia, metastatic disease, rheumatoid disease, steroid use, and primary bone tumors.

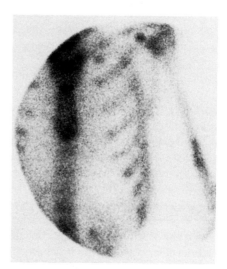

Figure 1F-6 Anterior spot view from a bone scan with increased uptake in the left humerus secondary to a fracture that occurred 24 years before the study.

NONUNION

Nonunion or incomplete healing of a fracture 6 to 8 months after injury has been described relative to the osteoblastic activity seen. *Atrophic nonunion* presents as mild or absent uptake of the ^{99m}Tc-MDP at the fracture site.[33] The absence of uptake may be secondary to compromised vascular supply, pseudoarthrosis, or infection. In contrast, *reactive nonunion* demonstrates increased tracer activity, which peaks at about 4 weeks and is sustained for an additional 4 to 5 months. *Delayed union* (excessively slow healing) is indistinguishable scintigraphically from reactive nonunion.

The combined use of three-phase scintigraphy and ^{67}Ga or ^{111}In leukocyte imaging may be useful in the further evaluation of nonunion (Fig. 1F-7).[33] The work of Seabold and colleagues[34] found the use of ^{99m}Tc-MDP and ^{111}In-leukocyte scans to have a sensitivity of 84 percent and specificity of 72 percent in the evaluation of fracture nonunion with suspected infection.

GRAFTS

Bone grafting is used to correct congenital and traumatic defects, repair limbs following tumor resection, and achieve spinal fusion. Smith and coworkers[35] evaluated patients undergoing resection for bone tumor with allograft reconstruction. During long-term follow-up they utilized radiographs, bone scans, and clinical examination to detect tumor recurrence or fracture at the site. Uptake of the radiotracer in the allograft was increased at the host-graft junction, decreased in the grafted cortical bone, and variable at the periphery. These scintigraphic findings correlate with "creeping substitution," the mechanism of bone healing in which the allograft serves as a matrix for new bone formation.

In the evaluation of vascularized grafts, the studies are performed within the first postoperative week to assess for blood flow through the anastomoses.[36] The uptake associated with creeping substitution occurs after the first postoperative week.[37] Conventional tomography and CT are used to follow up graft procedures to assess bone density. Bone scintigraphy can be performed to evaluate the degree and location of uptake within the graft. Successful interpretation of the scintigraphic uptake requires correlation to the type of graft and the time of surgery.

REFLEX SYMPATHETIC DYSTROPHY

Presenting with a spectrum of complaints, including pain, swelling, tenderness, vasomotor instability, and dystrophic skin changes, the patient with reflex sympathetic dystrophy (RSD) may be a diagnostic challenge.[38] The shoulder-hand syndrome (Fig. 1F-8) is associated with shoulder pain and decreased range of motion. In slightly

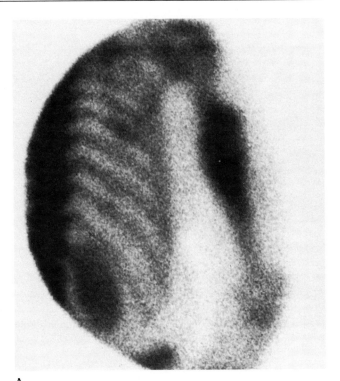

A

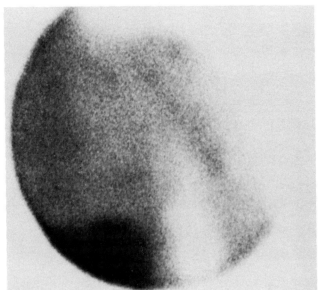

B

Figure 1F-7 **A.** Bone scan with posterior spot view of the right humerus with intense uptake proximal and distal to a linear area of relative decreased uptake in a patient with fracture nonunion. **B.** The Gallium-67 citrate scan demonstrates only mildly increased uptake in the region of the increased bone turnover. This finding is inconsistent with osteomyelitis.

more than a third of patients there is no clear explanation for the occurrence of this syndrome. Plain film radiography may demonstrate patchy demineralization (osteoporosis) of cancellous bone. There may be associated soft tissue swelling. Juxtaarticular and subchondral bone lysis may be seen. The three-phase bone scan is the

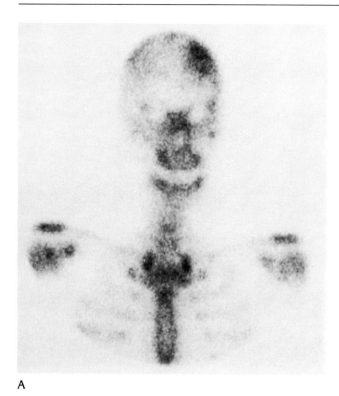

A

B

Figure 1F-8 **A.** Anterior bone scan spot view in a patient with left-sided cerebral infarction with shoulder-hand syndrome. Note the increased uptake in the cerebral infarction and the right shoulder. **B.** Palmar views of the hands of the same patient demonstrate increased periarticular and carpal uptake.

technique of choice for evaluating these patients. The radionuclide angiogram and blood pool images are made of the hands, and delayed static images of the entire upper extremities are obtained. The "positive" scintigram is described as demonstrating increased periarticular uptake in multiple joints of the affected hand with sensitivity and specificity of 60 and 92 percent, respectively, as compared with 69 and 79 percent for radiography.[38–40] The demonstration of asymmetric blood flow to the affected limb is a useful adjunct. The flow is typically increased, but it may be decreased in the presence of vasomotor spasm.

OSTEOMYELITIS

Osteomyelitis may occur in children or adults, and it is one of the indications for emergency bone scan. The physical findings (bone pain, swelling, tenderness, and altered range of motion) may or may not be present. The infection may invade the bone via a traumatic wound hematogenous seeding, or contiguous spread. The major concern with the hematogenous route is that multiple sites may be involved. The most common site for osteomyelitis in young persons is in rapidly growing bone; thus the metaphyseal region of the humerus is susceptible to infection.[41] *Staphylococcus aureus* is the most common bacterial pathogen. In immunocompromised persons other unusual pathogens must be considered. Findings of three-phase bone scintigraphy may be abnormal early in the course of the infection and can lead to rapid diagnosis and initiation of therapy (Fig. 1F-9). In osteomyelitis the bone scan is usually positive within 72 hours after onset of symptoms but it can be positive within 24 hours.[1] Early (less than 48 hours) osteomyelitis may demonstrate either photopenia or focal increased uptake of the radiotracer. Scintigraphy can demonstrate both bacterial and fungal osteomyelitis (Fig. 1F-10). MRI may also be used to evaluate suspected osteomyelitis[42–44]; it has a sensitivity rate of about 95 percent and specificity of 88 percent.[45] The limitations of MRI are false positive findings associated with infiltrative bone marrow processes or increased tissue water (secondary to surgery or fracture).[45] MRI is also limited by its inability to inexpensively "survey" for multiple foci of infection.

The reported sensitivity of three-phase scintigraphy for osteomyelitis in intact bone is 90 to 100 percent and its specificity is about 70 to 80 percent[3,46,47] Nelson and Taylor[48] reported sensitivity of 95 percent and specificity of 92 percent whereas for radiography the figures were 32 and 89 percent, respectively, in the diagnosis of osteomyelitis in older children. The limitations to the use of bone scintigraphy for suspected skeletal infection is intense radionuclide uptake in neuropathic joints,[49] sites of previous trauma (fracture or surgery),[50] certain bone tumors,[51] Paget's disease,[52] and arthritides,[53] which re-

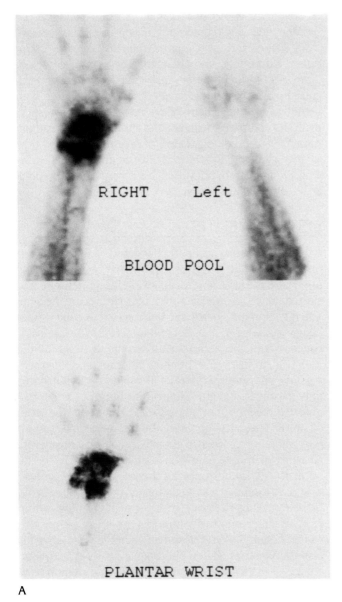

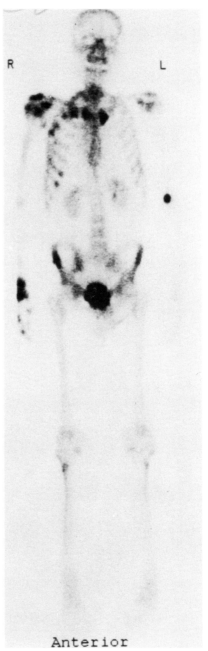

Figure 1F-9 **A.** Blood pool (*top*) and delayed static (*bottom*) images of the hands and wrists of a patient with osteomyelitis in the right carpal bones, distal radius, and ulna. **B.** Whole-body anterior image demonstrates the ability to survey for multiple sites of involvement.

sults in false positive interpretations (Fig. 1F-11). Furthermore, a very aggressive infection may not allow new bone formation to occur, resulting in a false negative reading.[54-56] Subperiosteal abscess in a child with osteomyelitis may be visualized as a photopenic defect.[57] In addition, antecedent initiation of antibiotic therapy may produce false negative findings.

Differentiating septic arthritis, cellulitis, and osteomyelitis often requires three-phase scintigraphy to better define the characteristics of bone flow and uptake. Cellulitis results in diffusely increased soft tissue activity on the blood pool image with minimally increased bone uptake on delayed views. The presence of a soft tissue infection

may cause increased perfusion to the shoulder but results in diffuse radiotracer localization on blood pool and static images. Septic arthritis may be suspected when there is increased blood pool activity in the joint space with increased periarticular activity. Delayed images may show uptake on one or both sides of the joint in the juxtaarticular bone. The pattern seen most frequently in osteomyelitis is a matched focus of increased flow, blood pool activity, and intense focal bone uptake. Septic arthritis, transient synovitis, and early osteomyelitis have been associated with photopenic defects which may be due to altered blood supply.[1,17]

Gallium-67 citrate (Ga-67) or ^{111}In-labeled leukocyte

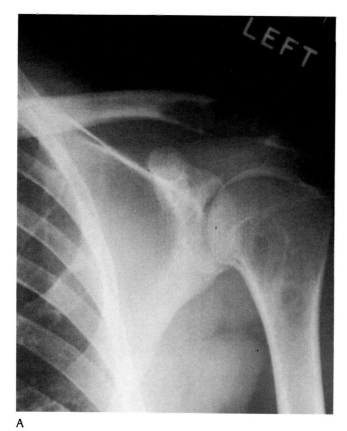

A

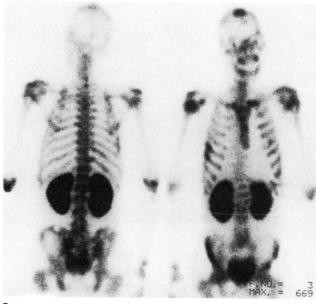

B

Figure 1F-10 **A.** Radiograph of the left shoulder demonstrates lytic lesions in the distal left clavicle and proximal left humerus. **B.** Anterior and posterior bone scan demonstrates multiple sites of increased uptake, including the lytic regions seen on radiograph, which were secondary to coccidioidomycosis. Note the increased renal uptake related to amphotericin therapy.

scans may be used (1) when there is strong clinical suspicion of infection but no diagnostic bone scan or radiographic findings, (2) in the evaluation of chronic or complicated bone injury, and (3) to differentiate osteomyelitis from bone infarction in a child with sickle cell disease. Gallium 67 uptake equal to or greater than bone

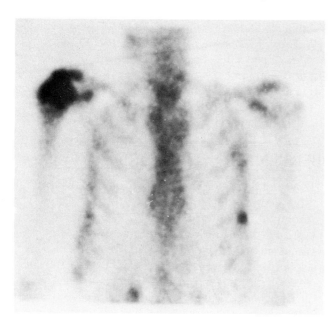

Figure 1F-11 Increased intense uptake in the right shoulder following repair of a rotator cuff tear. Indium 111 scan was negative for evidence of infection.

scan activity is more likely to be osteomyelitis than bone infarction.[58] Sequential 67 Ga scans can be useful in assessing patients with osteomyelitis for response to antibiotic therapy. Sequential scans should reveal diminution or resolution of the activity that was seen on the initial scan, whereas the bone scan demonstrates increased uptake much longer.[59]

In acute osteomyelitis ^{111}In-leukocyte scans have reported sensitivities ranging from 80 to 100 percent and specificity of about 80 to 95 percent.[60–62] The sensitivity of this technique, however, decreases to 50 to 60 percent for chronic osteomyelitis.[61,63] Schauwecker found that the sensitivity of ^{111}In-leukocyte scans for chronic osteomyelitis depended on the site of the lesion. For central lesions (marrow-containing axial regions) ^{111}In-leukocyte scans had a 53 percent sensitivity rate, but lesions between the distal extremities and the central region (termed *middle* locations) were detected with 80 percent sensitivity. Indium 111 is used in conjunction with three-phase scintigraphy to evaluate complications of orthopedic hardware (Fig. 1F-12).

Gallium 67 has also been useful in the evaluation of acute and chronic osteomyelitis and joint infections. Sensitivity ranges from 48 to 100 percent and specificity from 67 to 86 percent for gallium citrate (Ga 67).[60,64,65] Gallium-67 citrate (Ga-67) scans may be more sensitive to chronic infections, though this remains controversial. In a trial of bone scintigraphy, ^{111}In-leukocytes, and ^{67}Ga performed by Al-Sheikh and coworkers both ^{111}In leu-

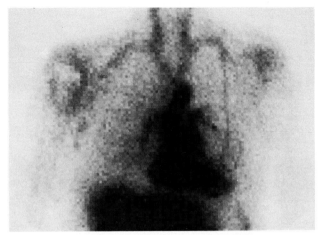

A

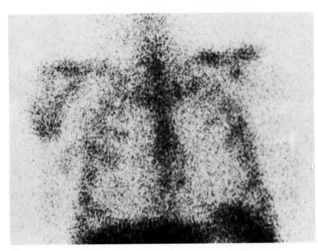

C

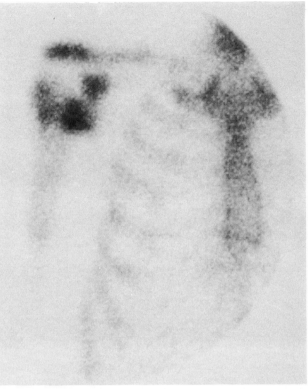

B

Figure 1F-12 **A.** Anterior blood pool image demonstrates increased tissue activity in the right shoulder. **B.** Anterior static bone image with increased focal activity around the site of the orthopedic hardware. **C.** Anterior view from ^{111}In-leukocyte scan with increased activity that correlates to site of bone scan abnormality. At surgery the patient had an infected prosthesis in the right humerus.

kocytes and ^{67}Ga exhibited similar sensitivity (80 percent) and specificity (80 percent) for chronic or subacute osteomyelitis.[65]

The differentiation of radiotracer uptake due to infection from uptake due to surgery or trauma has been evaluated by Lisbona and Rosenthall and by Tumeh.[66,67] In their work, the presence of ^{67}Ga activity, which demonstrates greater intensity or extends beyond the activity (discordant) seen on bone scintigraphy, was reported to be accurate for osteomyelitis in traumatized bone. Gallium 67 activity which is increased but less so than that of ^{99m}Tc-labeled bone agents may represent localization of the ^{67}Ga secondary to new bone formation and heterotopic bone formation.

Several newer approaches are being taken in the evaluation of infections, including white blood cell labeling with ^{99m}Tc-hexamethylpropyleneamine oxime (HMPAO) and polyclonal immunoglobulin imaging. The use of leukocytes for labeling remains laborious, and the ^{99m}Tc-HMPAO leukocytes produce uptake patterns similar to those of ^{111}In-leukocyte scans. The advantages of ^{99m}Tc-HMPAO leukocyte scans include radiation dosimetry, which would favor its use in pediatric cases, and ready availability. Work by Oyen and coworkers with ^{111}In-labeled nonspecific polyclonal human immunoglobulin identified acute osteomyelitis (four of four patients), chronic osteomyelitis or low-grade infection (18 of 18 patients), and infectious arthritis (five of five patients). In cases of noninfectious bone disease, five of seven cases were negative with ^{111}In-immunoglobulin. As new agents and techniques become available, delineation of infection and inflammatory bone disease will improve.

BENIGN BONE TUMORS

The use of three-phase scintigraphy in the evaluation of suspected bone tumors has been reported[52,72]; it may be useful to evaluate the vascularity of the tumor mass and associated bone involvement. Tumors which may demonstrate increased blood flow and blood pool activity include fibrous dysplasia, osteoblastoma, chondroblastoma, osteoid osteoma, giant cell tumors, sarcomas, and soft tissue neoplasms.[73,74] Leukemia has also been reported to display increased flow, blood pool, and delayed static activity.[75] The appearance may be a flame-shaped area of increased radiotracer uptake.

Bone scintigraphy is used in the evaluation of primary bone lesions to determine the presence and degree of osteoblastic activity and to determine if the lesion is solitary or multiple.

Bone Cyst

UNICAMERAL (SIMPLE) BONE CYSTS

Unicameral bone cysts are usually found in the proximal humerus or proximal femur. Typically they are not associated with pain unless a pathologic fracture occurs. The bone cyst typically does not show increased uptake on bone scintigraphy unless the lesion is enlarging or a fracture is present (Fig. 1F-13).

ANEURYSMAL BONE CYSTS

Aneurysmal bone cysts may be seen in any bone and typically are associated with pain. The majority of these lesions are seen in the first two decades of life. The bone scan may demonstrate moderate to intense increased uptake, depending on the vascularity of the lesion.

Nonossifying Fibroma

Nonossifying fibromas are commonly detected as incidental findings on plain radiographs. The lesions are seen in the first two decades of life and regress over time by undergoing sclerosis or remodeling. They are typically asymptomatic and are found in the metaphyseal region of the long bones. A nonossifying fibroma has normal to minimally increased bone radiotracer uptake. With active involution of the fibroma, osteoblastic activity will result in increased activity in the lesion on bone scan. The activity decreases when the lesion becomes dormant.

Osteochondroma

Osteochondroma, or osteocartilaginous exostosis, typically is seen in persons younger than 30 years. It presents as a mass. Commonly a lesion of the metaphyses of long bones, it is frequently located near the proximal humerus. The lesion shows increased radiotracer uptake when it is actively growing but may show only mild to moderate uptake when stable. If there is malignant degeneration in an osteochondroma, the scintigram will demonstrate a "hot" lesion, but the intense uptake is similar to the uptake within an enlarging benign lesion.

In multiple osteocartilaginous exostosis syndrome the shoulder is also a common site of involvement (Fig. 1F-14). The patient with multiple exostoses Ps is also at increased risk for malignant transformation. Again, they may show intense uptake when enlarging, but this alone cannot serve to distinguish malignant degeneration. Serial bone scintigraphy can be used for periodic follow-up in children with multiple exostoses. A lesion which

has been quiescent and now demonstrates increased uptake and pain warrants further evaluation.

Osteoid Osteoma

Osteoid osteoma is a relatively common benign bone tumor most often seen in the tibia or femur. In persons with shoulder pain, however, osteoid osteoma occasionally may be related, either because of humeral involvement or secondary to a cervical spine lesion with nerve root irritation.[76] The lesion occurs most commonly in adolescent and young adult males. The pain may be severe and frequently is worse at night. Aspirin typically relieves the discomfort.

The lesion which is composed of osteoid and woven bone within loose fibrovascular tissue[77] has variable degrees of calcification. The plain film radiographs may demonstrate a nidus, which is either a radiolucent or a radiopaque lesion surrounded by sclerotic bone. In three-phase bone scintigraphy there is intense radiotracer localization on the blood pool study and on the delayed static images.[78–80] The *double-density sign* described by Helms is an intense focus of activity within a larger focus of less intense activity.[81] The primary differential diagnoses are osteoid osteoma, stress fractures, bone island, and Brodie's abscess. Bone islands typically demonstrate normal radiotracer uptake, and stress fractures typically are linear.

Bone scans may be helpful in localizing the bone lesion for further evaluation with CT for identification of the nidus. In addition, bone scintigraphy has been applied to the intraoperative evaluation of bone resection to ensure that the lesion's nidus has been completely resected.[82] The surgical site is evaluated using count rates to help localize the very intense radiotracer uptake in the nidus, which must be resected for successful therapy.

Eosinophilic Granuloma

Eosinophilic granuloma belongs to a group of diseases known as histiocytosis X or Langerhaus cell disease. The lesions may be single or multiple. The most frequent sites are the skull, ribs, pelvis, spine, and long bones. The lesion typically demonstrates moderately increased uptake on bone scintigraphy. Bone scans can be helpful in identifying the sites of disease, but may be less reliable than radiographic skeletal survey.

Myositis Ossificans

Following trauma, heterotopic bone may form within the injured soft tissues. These lesions demonstrate increased activity on bone scintigraphy and are most mature and well defined peripherally. Heterotopic bone formation can be followed serially to assess for quiescence. In postsurgical patients comparison with plain film radiographs may help delineate heterotopic bone from persistent bone uptake associated with infection.

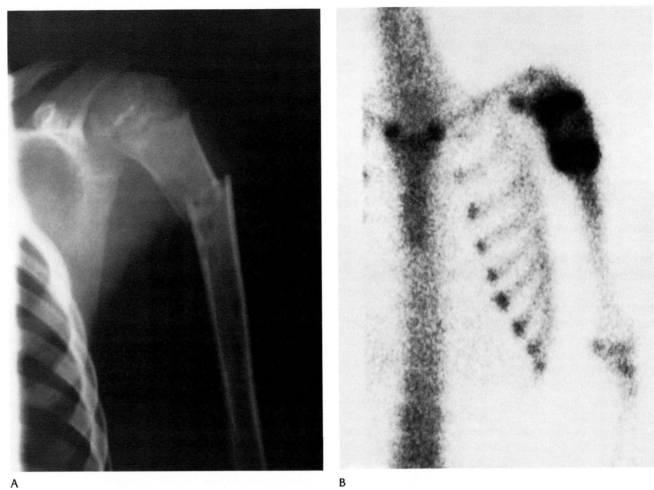

A   B

Figure 1F-13 **A.** Pathologic fracture at the site of a bone cyst in the left humerus of a child is demonstrated on x-ray. **B.** Anterior spot view with increased bone radiotracer uptake at the site of the fracture and within the normal epiphyses.

Enchondroma

Enchondromas, frequent incidental findings on radiographs, are typically painless until a pathologic fracture occurs. The lesions show increased uptake on bone scintigraphy. The major element of the differential diagnosis for these lesions is bone infarct, which may demonstrate decreased blood pool activity on three-phase scintigraphy.

Fibrous Dysplasia

Fibrous dysplasia is a vascular bone lesion in which osteoblasts fail to differentiate normally and mature. It may be monostotic or polyostotic. Polyostotic fibrous dysplasia differs in distribution from the monostotic form, which is typically in the femur, tibia, and ribs. The polyostotic form involves one side of the body in 90 percent of cases. The areas affected are the pelvis, long bones, skull, and ribs. The articular ends of the long bone usually are spared. The scintigram typically demonstrates increased uptake on the blood pool and on the

delayed images, a feature that makes it indistinguishable from tumor[83] or fracture; correlation with plain film studies is required.

Hemangioma

Hemangiomas are relatively uncommon in the humerus and scapula. These vascular lesions may be present as regions of normal or even decreased radiotracer uptake owing to the decreased cortical bone mass. Technetium 99m–tagged red blood cells have been used to study hemangiomas of the soft tissue such as those seen in Maffucci's syndrome.[84]

Condensing Osteitis

Condensing osteitis was first described by Brower and colleagues[85] and is a rare, benign lesion that typically presents in middle-aged women who report a history of heavy lifting. The patient develops shoulder pain, particularly with abduction. Pain and swelling of the medial

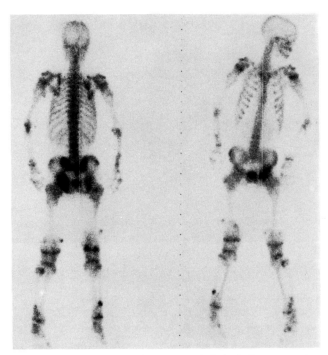

Figure 1F-14 Anterior and posterior whole-body bone scans in a patient evaluated for left hip trauma who has a history of multiple exostoses. These lesions demonstrate mild to moderately increased uptake and are seen in the upper and lower extremities.

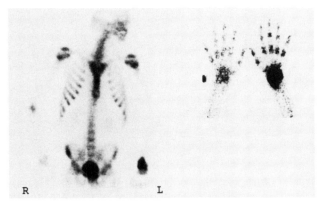

Figure 1F-15 Delayed static images of the torso and hands. (Note marker on right for hand view.) There is intense uptake within the left distal radius secondary to a giant cell tumor. The asymmetric increased uptake in the proximal left humerus is secondary to prior resection of a giant cell tumor.

clavicle may be evident on physical examination. There is sclerosis and enlargement of the medial clavicle on plain film radiographs. The bone scan demonstrates increased radiotracer uptake within the medial clavicle of the affected bone. The key elements of the differential diagnosis are osteomyelitis, osteoarthritis, osteoid osteoma, Tietze's syndrome, sternocostoclavicular hyperostosis, Paget's disease, and Friedrich's disease.[86] Another rare disorder, combined clavicular hyperostosis and acne, results in diffuse increased uptake in the clavicles. This disorder may cause thoracic outlet syndrome, which may be treated with indomethacin.[87]

Giant Cell Tumor

Relatively uncommon in the proximal humerus, these lesions are most often discovered during the third decade of life.[88] The lesion is epiphyseal in location, and in the vast majority of patients it presents as a tender, palpable mass. The scintigraphic appearance typically involves increased uptake of the tracer at the periphery of the tumor, which has been described as a doughnut pattern.[89,90] The very intense uptake may cause a "blooming" appearance, which can cause the size of the lesion to be overestimated (Fig. 1F-15).

PAGET'S DISEASE

Paget's disease of bone is characterized by accelerated bone turnover. Rapid resorption and production of bone

results in disorganized, weakened bone structure. The three-phase bone scan may show intermediate to intense blood flow and increased radiotracer on blood pool images. The delayed static images also show increased activity during the lytic and mixed lytic and blastic phases of these lesions.[33,52] As the disease burns itself out and the bone becomes sclerotic, the radionuclide uptake decreases. This pattern may make this entity difficult to distinguish from osteomyelitis based on scintigraphic features alone. Paget's disease may also be monostotic or polyostotic (Fig. 1F-16). The most common areas of involvement are the skull, ribs, vertebrae and/or pelvis.

PRIMARY MALIGNANT BONE TUMORS

The most common primary bone tumors of childhood are Ewing's sarcoma and osteosarcoma. Scintigraphy is often prompted by a referral for the evaluation of bone pain or a mass. Scintigraphy is also employed to identify metastatic lesions. The bone scan cannot be used to determine the extent of the lesion, as vascularity and reaction of bone can cause overestimation of tumor size.

Osteosarcoma is most frequently identified in the metaphyses of the distal femur, proximal tibia, and proximal humerus (Fig. 1F-17).[91] Parosteal osteosarcomas are rare lesions that originate in the periosteum. Both the classical and the parosteal osteosarcomas demonstrate increased radiotracer uptake. CT and MRI delineate local tumor extent and provide invaluable morphologic information. The role of scintigraphy is again related to the detection of metastatic disease. The incidence of metastatic disease at the time of diagnosis with osteosarcoma ranges from 3 to 20 percent; most commonly it involves bones and lungs.[91,92]

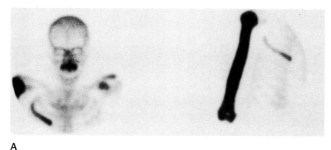

A

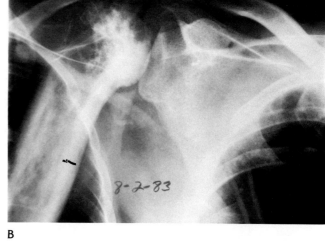

B

Figure 1F-16 **A.** Spot views of a bone scan demonstrate intense uptake in the maxilla, right humerus, and ribs secondary to polyostotic Paget's disease. **B.** Correlative radiograph of the right humerus corresponding to the site of the bone scan abnormality is consistent with Paget's disease.

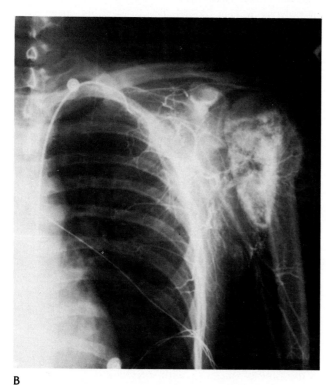

A

B

Figure 1F-17 **A.** Intense uptake in proximal left humerus shown on the anterior and posterior delayed static views of a patient with osteosarcoma. **B.** Angiogram of the osteosarcoma in the left humerus.

Ewing's sarcoma involves the diaphyseal portion of the bone *most frequently* (Fig. 1F-18). In addition, half of all patients present with lesions in the extremities. Metastatic disease is seen in about 18 percent of patients at the time of presentation, usually in lung, bone, and bone marrow.[93] The staging of Ewing's sarcoma may include chest CT, bone scan, and bone marrow biopsy. Abnormalities on bone scan are further evaluated to confirm or rule out metastatic disease, which has implications for patient management and prognosis.

Chondrosarcoma, which usually develops later in life than the entities described earlier, occurs in the proximal humerus, among other sites. These lesions can arise as malignant transformation from an osteochondroma. On bone scintigraphy there is increased radiotracer uptake. The work of Hudson and colleagues demonstrated 100 percent sensitivity for the 18 cases of chondrosarcoma studied.[94]

METASTATIC SKELETAL DISEASE

The utility of bone scintigraphy is illustrated in the work of O'Mara,[95] who related that 30 percent of patients with known neoplastic disease, bone pain, and normal radiographs were found to have skeletal metastases on bone scans. The controversy surrounds the precise implementation of bone scintigraphy. There is little disagreement in cases of advanced breast, lung, and prostate carcinoma, that bone scintigraphy is a useful screening tool.[73] Furthermore, bone scanning is indicated in the evaluation of patients with pain and advanced disease secondary to cervical, endometrial, bladder, and gastrointestinal tumors. The use of a baseline bone scan also offers the advantage of detecting benign bone disease, which may be identified on the first examination and used for comparison later. The bone scan is typically used in periodic follow-up, particularly when the patient shows evidence

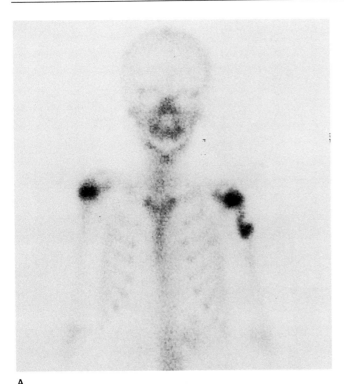

A

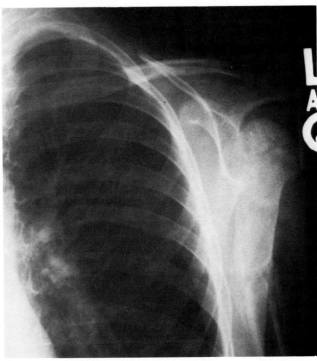

B

Figure 1F-18   Increased uptake in the proximal left humerus on scintigram, **A,** correlated to the x-ray abnormality, **B,** in a patient with Ewing's sarcoma.

of disease progression via biochemical markers (Fig. 1F-19), local recurrence, or new bone pain (Fig. 1F-20).

Renal cell carcinoma is noted for its predilection to demonstrate osteoblastic or osteolytic activity, or a mixture of the two. Bone scintigraphy may therefore demonstrate lesions that have increased or photopenic activity (Fig. 1F-21). Plain film radiography and bone scan are essential to the evaluation of these patients. Other lesions which may demonstrate a lack of radiotracer uptake are anaplastic tumors, leukemia, and thyroid carcinoma. Multiple myeloma (a primary bone tumor) also demonstrates variable uptake on bone scintigraphy (Fig. 1F-22, p. 92). Scintigraphy can be useful as a complementary tool to plain film radiographs, particularly in symptomatic patients.

The sensitivity of bone scintigraphy is greater than that of radiography, serum alkaline phosphatase, or bone marrow biopsy in identifying bone lesions secondary to lymphoma. Hodgkin's disease and histiocytic lymphoma are more likely to be detected than lymphocytic lymphoma.[96] Lymphoma and leukemia have a "reversed" distribution of malignant lesions from the typical axial pattern seen with most metastic disease. In this case, the appendicular skeleton shows as many or more than the axial skeleton. These lesions are predominantly in the diaphyses of the long bones.[97] The appendicular skeleton shows as many or more lesions, which are predominantly in the diaphyses of the long bones.[97] Bone scans typically are used in cases of lymphoma and leukemia when there

is bone pain or for correlation with a plain film finding.

The importance of evaluating the entire scintigram cannot be understated. There is often important anatomic information, such as a solitary kidney (see Fig. 1F-21) or a previous amputation (Fig. 1F-23, p. 92), which should be noted in the report. Soft tissue evaluation is imperative when evaluating a bone scan. The localization of radiotracer has been noted in primary tumors such as breast cancer, neuroblastomas, sarcomas, and melanomas (Fig. 1F-24, p. 92). Occasionally, radiotracer may be taken up into abnormal lymph nodes (Fig. 1F-25, p. 92). Lymphedema, seen most frequently in mastectomy patients, is another cause of increased regional soft tissue uptake (Fig. 1F-26, p. 93). Finally, referred shoulder pain may arise from occult rib metastases or pleural effusions (Fig. 1F-27, p. 93).

THERAPY

An important adjunct to the care of patients with painful metastatic bone disease is strontium 89. A palliative for bone pain, it is administered intravenously in an average dose of 30 to 40 μCi/kg. Skeletal metastatic disease is first documented by bone scintigraphy, and a complete blood count is evaluated for adequate leukocyte and platelet counts. The patient may have a transient decrease in these hematologic parameters following therapy. In a

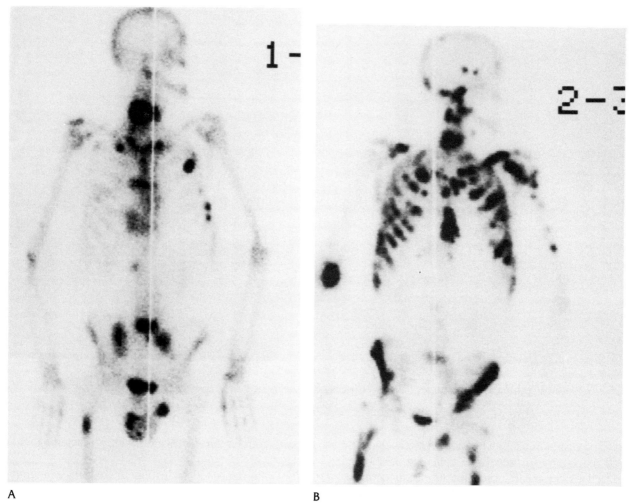

A   B

Figure 1F-19   **A.** Anterior whole-body bone scan of a patient with prostate carcinoma and multiple regions of increased uptake consistent with metastatic disease. **B.** Anterior whole-body scan made approximately 1 year later shows increased uptake in numerous lesions, with no soft tissue or renal activity. These findings are consistent with a superscan secondary to prostate carcinoma.

series of patients treated with 40 μCi/kg, 20 percent had no hematologic change and the remaining 80 percent had an average decrease in platelet and leukocyte counts of 15 to 20 percent.[98] If there is a favorable response, the patient may be re-treated at intervals of no less than 3 months.

RADIATION NECROSIS

With radiotherapy, bone scans may show relative photopenia, particularly if the exposure was greater than 2000 rad.[99] In the first several months following treatment there may be an initial increase in bone uptake within the radiation port. Typically, photopenia is seen about 4 to 6 months after therapy. Radiation necrosis, which results from compromise of the vascular supply, most commonly occurs within 1 to 5 years after radio-

therapy. Utilizing a three-phase bone scan the physician would note decreased uptake in the necrotic bone.

ARTHRITIDES

The evaluation of arthritis centers on the extent, distribution, and intensity of uptake in the lesions. Of the many arthritides known to affect the shoulder, those in which nuclear imaging has a diagnostic role are rheumatoid, secondary (posttraumatic) osteoarthritis, and infectious, plus systemic lupus erythematosus. In pyogenic and nonpyogenic forms of infectious arthritis the infectious agent can enter the synovial fluid either by direct penetration or by hematogenous spread to cause inflammation.[68] Bone scintigraphy demonstrates increased radionuclide uptake at infection sites.[69] These findings can

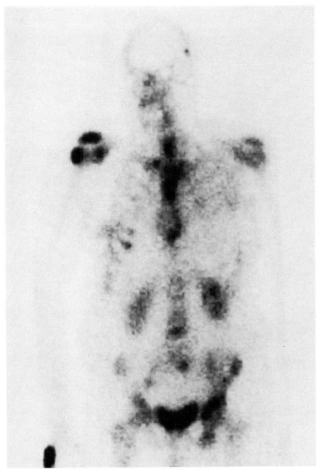

Figure 1F-20 Anterior whole-body bone scan with multiple sites of increased uptake in a patient with breast carcinoma and right shoulder pain. Note also activity in the sternum, which is often a site for skeletal metastatic disease in these patients.

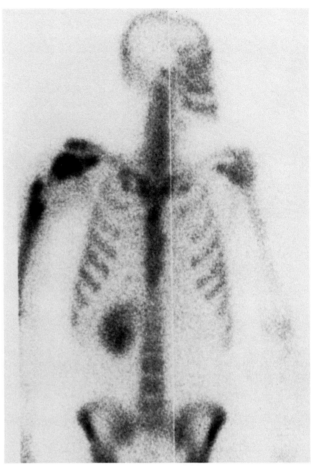

Figure 1F-21 Increased uptake proximal and distal to a photopenic region in the right humerus on this anterior bone scan. Note the absent left kidney in this patient with renal cell carcinoma and metastasis with pathologic fracture in the right humerus.

be correlated with ^{67}Ga imaging, which can then be used to sequentially evaluate response to treatment.

Systemic lupus erythematosus has been associated with cystic bone lesions,[70] arthritis, and extraosseous calcifications. Patients treated with steroids are at increased risk for osteonecrosis (hips, knees, shoulders) and septic arthritis, which may result in monarticular arthritis. Bone scintigraphy can be used to evaluate the arthritis and the extraosseous calcifications.

In proliferative, inflamed synovium, as seen in rheumatoid disease (Fig. 1F-28, p. 94), increased blood flow results in increased activity on the perfusion and blood pool portions of the three-phase bone scan. Localization of the radiotracer in the delayed images has been ascribed to the increased osteoblastic activity in response to the periarticular and subchondral bone erosions (symmetric involvement seen in the hands).[71] If the shoulder is involved, there may be joint space narrowing, osteoporosis, and articular erosions. Rotator cuff tears and

resorption of the distal end of the clavicle may also be seen. Noninflammatory arthritis typically involves the glenohumeral and acromioclavicular portions of the shoulder with increased uptake of variable intensity.

Cervical spine evaluation is included in this section since arthritic disease may cause pain and dysfunction of the upper extremity. Imaging to evaluate for the presence of increased uptake related to arthritis, compression fractures, and bone tumors may lead to the appropriate diagnosis. SPECT can be helpful in separating overlying tissues and provide improved radiotracer localization within the spine (Fig. 1F-29, p. 94). Pancoast's tumor and thoracic outlet syndrome may also present with shoulder pain. Bone scintigraphy may demonstrate destruction of bone secondary to Pancoast's tumor. Flow studies are used to evaluate for thoracic outlet syndrome while the arm is in the position that reproduces the symptoms.

For purposes of radionuclide imaging, the arthritides can be grouped into two categories: those that are pri-

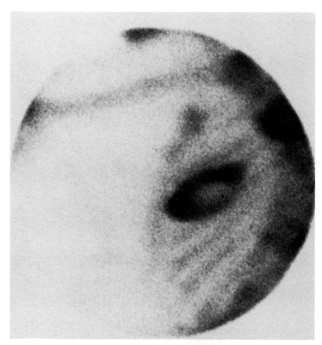

Figure 1F-22   Spot view of the thorax in a patient referred for bone scan due to left chest and shoulder pain. The intense doughnut-shaped increased uptake is within a plasmacytoma of the rib.

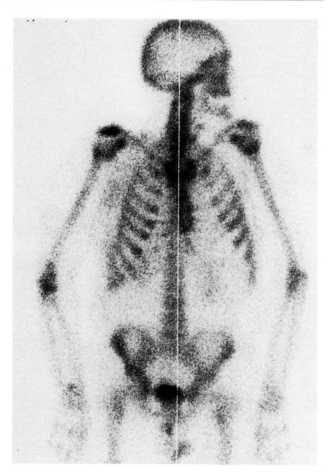

Figure 1F-24   Anterior spot view of a patient with a right chest wall melanoma. Note the soft tissue uptake of the bone radiotracer in the primary tumor.

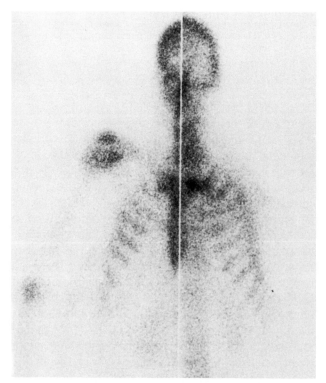

Figure 1F-23   Anterior spot view from bone scan of a patient who has undergone forequarter amputation. Care must be taken to fully assess images for artifactual (as opposed to clinical) findings.

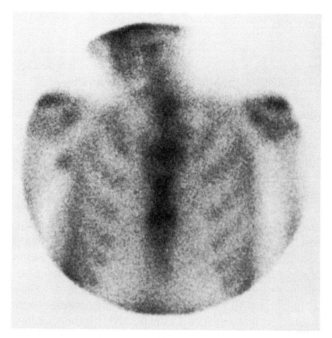

Figure 1F-25   Anterior view of patient with bone agent uptake in a node in the right axilla. Biopsy demonstrated histiocytic lymphoma.

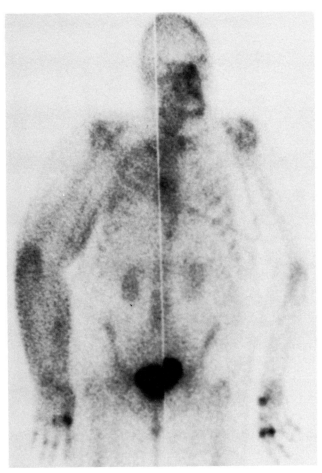

Figure 1F-26 Anterior bone scan of patient with a history of breast carcinoma and surgical resection demonstrates diffuse increased soft tissue activity in the right arm secondary to lymphedema.

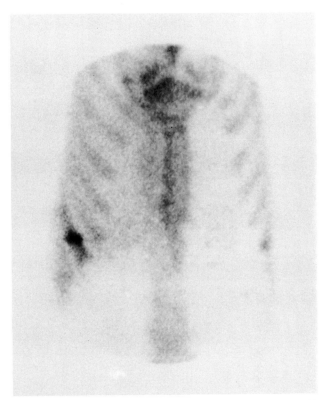

Figure 1F-27 Anterior bone scan view of the thorax in a patient with shoulder pain. The diffuse uptake in the right hemithorax is secondary to a malignant pleural effusion. The focal activity in the rib was a metastatic lesion from a primary lung carcinoma.

marily of synovial origin and those subsequent to primary bone disease. This distinction is not rigid, as there can be erosive bone disease with primary synovial inflammation and synovial inflammation secondary to the bone disorder. The entities most frequently encountered in primary synovitis are rheumatoid arthritis, ankylosing spondylitis, Reiter's syndrome, psoriasis, gout, systemic lupus erythematosus, and infection. Osteoarthritis is the most common noninflammatory condition, followed by trauma, mechanical abnormalities, neuroarthropathy, and reflex sympathetic dystrophy, among others.

Application of radionuclides to the study of synovial permeability began in the early 1950s using sodium 24 as the test agent. It was instilled into the normal knee joint space, and its rate of disappearance, which was exponential, was monitored externally by a Geiger counter.[100] In rheumatoid arthritis the clearance of ^{24}Na was also exponential, and its rate constant varied with the severity of the synovitis. Intraarticular hydrocortisone reduced the clearance rate to values approaching normal.[101] Iodine 131–labeled albumin and globulin clear-

ance rates were also studied in normal and abnormal knees. The normal synovium was found to be equally permeable to albumin and globulin, and this permeability was enhanced in synovitis.[102,103] To obviate recirculation of ^{24}Na into the joint which would render ostensibly lower clearance rates, intracavitary instillation of xenon 133 gas in saline solution was proposed. This was based on the fact that there is almost complete removal of the xenon gas in circulation on the first pass through the lungs by exhalation. Synovial blood flow can be quantified from the joint half disappearance time of ^{133}Xe by the relation $69.3P/T_{1/2}$, where the unit of flow is milliliters per 100 milliliters synovial tissue per minute, P denotes the partition coefficient between synovial tissue and blood, and $T_{1/2}$ is the time in minutes to half disappearance. This technique demonstrated a clear distinction between normal knees and those involved with rheumatoid arthritis. It was also shown that, in patients with rheumatoid arthritis who have clinically and radiographically normal knees, a large percentage of the knees had increased synovial blood flow, indicating subclinical involvement.[104,105] Presumably, this would hold true for other apparently normal joints, but the knee was the only site tested in these early investigations because it was

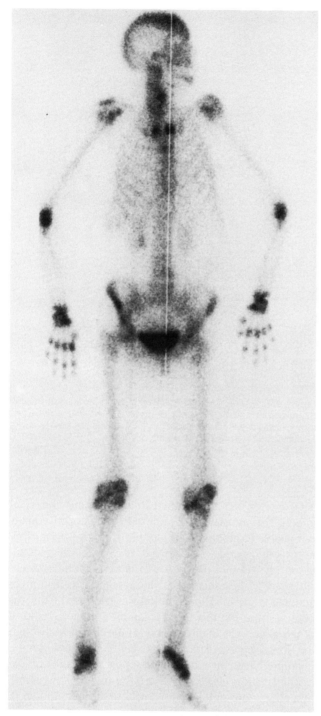

Figure 1F-28 Anterior bone scan in a patient with rheumatoid arthritis. Note the multiple symmetric joint involvement, particularly in the hands.

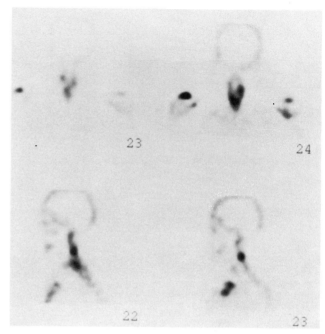

Figure 1F-29 SPECT images of a patient with pain radiating from the neck to the right shoulder. There is increased uptake within the cervical spine on the coronal (*top row*) and sagittal (*bottom row*) images and right shoulder consistent with degenerative arthritis.

large and manageable. The technique of intracavitary instillation of a radioactive tracer to monitor clearance rates as an indicator of synovial integrity has merit as a quantitative research tool, but it is time-consuming and impractical to apply to patients with polyarticular disease and does not qualify as a screening device for patients who have diffuse joint symptoms.

The advent of intravenous delivery of radiopharmaceuticals that have either active or passive tropism for the synovium or adjacent bone (which may be affected by synovial and regional hyperemia) has made patient screening feasible and improved its clinical utility. Iodine 131-albumin was the first of these agents, and as a vascular compartment marker it revealed the expanded blood pool of the inflamed synovium. The intravenous route also facilitated total body joint surveys with a single administration.[106] Over the years other radioactive test agents were introduced with varying degrees of success and popularity. These may be grouped into three categories:

Inflammatory Site Compartment: ^{67}Ga-citrate,[107] ^{111}In- and ^{99m}Tc leukocytes,[108,109] ^{99m}Tc liposomes,[110] ^{99m}Tc-albumin nanocolloids,[111] ^{111}In-chloride,[112] ^{99m}Tc-polyclonal immunoglobulin G,[113] ^{99m}Tc-monoclonal antibodies to granulocytes,[114] ^{99m}Tc-CD4 specific antibody.[115]

Bone Compartment: ^{85}Sr,[116] ^{87m}Sp, ^{18}F,[117] ^{99m}Tc-phosphate complexes.[118]

Vascular Compartment: ^{131}I-albumin, ^{99m}TcO$_4$ (pertechnetate),[119] ^{99m}Tc-albumin,[120] ^{113m}In,[121] ^{99m}Tc-DTPA,[122] ^{99m}Tc erythrocytes.

There are varying degrees of increased blood flow, enlargement of the vascular pool, and interstitial edema in synovitis, whether noninfectious or infectious. Vascular compartment markers reflect these properties by increased transit on first-pass intravenous radionuclide angiography and, at equilibrium, as a higher concentration in the synovium relative to surrounding tissues because of the expanded blood pool and interstitial extravasation. Anastomoses between the synovium and juxtaarticular bone enable the bone to be involved in the hyperemia of synovitis. This results in diffuse increased accumulation of the bone-seeking test agents, such as ^{99m}Tc-phosphate complexes, on both sides of the joint. Regional hyperemia may give a similar pattern. If there is subchondral bone destruction, the local accretion of radiophosphate represents the normal bone reaction to an insult, and the degree of uptake is a function of bone remodeling, and in particular of osteoblastic activity.

The mechanism of indium and gallium concentration in the inflamed synovium is still debated, but it is probably related to their behavioral similarity to iron. Synovial iron and transferrin receptors are increased in rheumatoid synovitis, and a correlation between the inflammatory infiltrate and synovial ferritin content has been reported.[123] Both indium and gallium are iron analogues, and as such they will bind to intravascular transferrin and then fix onto transferrin receptors in the inflamed synovium, or bind directly to the transferrin located at the site, following intravenous injection.

Radiolabeled leukocytes migrate to sites of infection and are very efficient at disclosing septic synovitis. Leukocytes are also present in relatively smaller numbers in rheumatoid arthritis, and involved joints can be visualized on routine imaging with either the ^{99m}Tc or ^{111}In label. Thus, the distinction between sepsis and absence of sepsis may not always be made with this test agent. In general, acute sepsis exhibits an intense accretion of radioactivity, whereas aseptic synovitis is low grade. Granulocytes labeled with monoclonal ^{99m}Tc antigranulocyte antibody behave as the other leukocytes. Its main attribute is that granulocytes are labeled in vivo with a simple intravenous injection of the antibody, whereas the labeling of leukocytes with ^{99m}Tc or ^{111}In is a laborious, time-consuming in vitro procedure that requires care and expertise.

The mechanism of ^{99m}Tc-liposome uptake in synovitis, and perhaps in the adjacent tendon sheaths, is believed to be phagocytosis by the resident macrophages. The number of macrophages increases with the severity of inflammation, so the level of radioactive uptake is an index of the inflammatory activity.[110] Accretion of albumin colloid of nanometer size may be partly due to phagocytosis, but some authors postulate that these inert particles pass into the pericapillary spaces through loose basement membrane junctions induced by the inflammatory processes.[111]

There remains no adequate explanation for the mechanism by which radiolabeled human polyclonal immunoglobulin G (IgG) accumulates at inflammation sites.

One theory states that there is exudation of the tracer, along with other plasma proteins, through a leaking capillary bed, after which the IgG binds to the FC receptor located on inflammatory cells (i.e., neutrophils, lymphocytes, and macrophages).

CD4-bearing T cells play a predominant role in the development of rheumatoid arthritis. Pharmacologic doses of monoclonal antibodies to these cells have been used, with some success, to treat rheumatoid arthritis. When these antibodies were labeled with ^{99m}Tc they were seen to concentrate in the diseased joint by external imaging, and in other areas rich in CD4-bearing T cells (spleen, bone marrow, lymph nodes).[124]

Synovitis

With synovitis there are alterations in the terminal arterioles, capillaries, and venules that result in increased blood flow, expanded blood pool volume, and vascular permeability. As a consequence there is increased transit of ^{99m}Tc-labeled agents on first pass and a relatively higher concentration on the equilibrium blood pool images immediately thereafter. Anastomoses between the inflamed synovium and periarticular bone are responsible for the increased concentration of ^{99m}Tc-phosphate on the delayed images (made 2 hours or more after injection). This increased periarticular uptake can also be seen in hyperemia from causes other than synovitis (e.g., reflex sympathetic dystrophy; Figs. 1F-30 through 1F-32). Cellular changes of rheumatoid arthritis and related disorders promote the concentration of other radiolabeled test agents. In the acute phase there is accumulation of polymorphonuclear leukocytes that are located primarily in the synovial fluid. The onset of the chronic phase features infiltration of lymphocytes, macrophages, and plasma cells into the interstitium, whereas the polymorphonuclear leukocytes remain in the fluid. This cellular infiltration probably explains the low-grade migration of ^{99m}Tc- or ^{111}In-labeled leukocytes to the site and the concentration of monoclonal antibody to CD4-bearing T cells, the helper-inducer subset of T lymphocytes.

Figure 1F-30 Active rheumatoid arthritis in multiple joints. Increased periarticular concentrations of ^{99m}Tc-MDP are depicted in the left shoulder, left elbow, right shoulder, both wrists, and scattered joints in the hands.

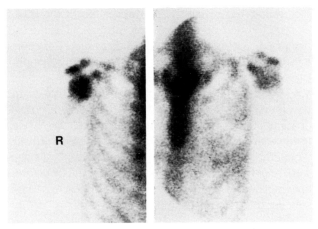

Figure 1F-31 A 41-year-old woman who experienced spontaneous onset of adhesive capsulitis in the right (*R*) shoulder complained of pain and progressively limited range of motion. The ^{99m}Tc-MDP bone scan shows diffuse increased uptake in the right humeral head, coracoid, and acromioclavicular area. The pattern is nonspecific and probably develops from regional hyperemia, with or without the low-grade synovitis that may occur in adhesive capsulitis.

The normal synovium is not depicted by scintigraphy with the various blood compartment markers, because their concentration does not exceed that of the surrounding soft tissue. It rises above background when inflammation intervenes. The test agents, such as ^{99m}TcO$_4$ and ^{99m}Tc-albumin, were shown to be largely concentrated in the inflamed synovium with very little in the joint fluid.[119] The distribution of ^{99m}TcO$_4$ and ^{99m}Tc-phosphate was determined in a rabbit model of arthritis induced by intraarticular injection of ovalbumin into sensitized animals. The two agents were found in both soft tissue and bone, but uptake of ^{99m}TcO$_4$ was maximal in the synovium, whereas ^{99m}Tc-phosphate was predominant in bone.[125] A similar study in the rabbit model of zymosan-induced arthritis demonstrated a high concentration of ^{67}Ga in the inflamed synovium, but there was also accretion in the fat pad, patella, meniscus, and adjacent tendons. No ^{67}Ga was present in the juxtaarticular bone.

Blood compartment markers or radiopharmaceuticals that are concentrated directly in the abnormal synovium are theoretically preferable to radiophosphate. The periarticular concentration of radiophosphate in synovitis is secondary to the synovial hyperemia, but it may occur in other conditions such as osteoarthritis, metabolic bone disease, tumor, trauma, and reflex sympathetic dystrophy, (i.e., it is not specific). Few false positive results occur with the blood compartment markers, and these are usually caused by overlying cellulitis and edema. A major disadvantage is the low target-to-background ratios that are often observed in peripheral joints. This is due to the shift of ^{99m}TcO$_4$ and ^{99m}Tc-albumin from the intravascular space to the extravascular space of the back-

ground tissues during the time it takes to complete a total body joint survey (Fig. 1F-33). This shift is overcome, for the most part, with ^{99m}Tc erythrocytes; it remains less sensitive than ^{99m}Tc-phosphate, but more specific.

Gallium citrate (Ga 67) is allegedly more closely associated with the cellular components of the inflammatory process than the blood compartment markers, and this is a desirable attribute. The drawbacks are the delay of at least 24 hours before imaging, which requires two patient visits, and the low count rates obtained with the permissible doses. These low count rates necessitate long imaging times for each joint for adequate resolution, and the time required for a total body study is impracticably long. It is more appropriate to limit the use of ^{67}Ga to the study of specific joints, and perhaps to monitoring the effects of treatment, as in septic arthritis (Figs. 1F-34, 1F-35).

An extensive clinical evaluation of ^{111}In-chloride, ^{99m}Tc- or ^{111}In-labeled IgG, ^{99m}Tc-albumin nanocolloid, ^{99m}Tc-liposomes, and ^{99m}Tc-CD4 antibody has yet to be done, as these radiopharmaceuticals are either under investigation, not readily available because of regulatory restrictions, or both. The indium-labeled tracers, such as ^{67}Ga, require at least 24 hours' delay before imaging, and in some reported studies as much as 72 hours. Indium is normally concentrated in the red marrow, and low-grade uptake in the humeral head with any of the ^{111}In tracers can be misread as synovitis of the glenohumeral joint. As with ^{67}Ga, the procedure does not lend itself to total body joint surveys, owing to the low count rates obtained for the permissible doses. This limitation is avoided with the ^{99m}Tc label, because its physical properties permit larger diagnostic doses that result in higher count rates, better resolution and imaging within a few hours of administration.

A limited crossover study comparing ^{99m}Tc-IgG, ^{99m}Tc-leukocytes, and ^{99m}Tc-albumin nanocolloid in imaging rheumatoid arthritis of the hands, wrists, knees, ankles, and feet was reported. It showed that ^{99m}Tc-IgG and ^{99m}Tc-albumin nanocolloid were equally sensitive and superior to ^{99m}Tc-leukocytes. None of these recent tracers has been adequately assessed for efficacy in the glenohumeral joint. An important clinical criterion of acute synovitis is discernible joint swelling by physical examination. The overlying muscle mass at the shoulder (and hip) makes the detection of an edematous joint very difficult. This underestimates the incidence of clinical synovitis in correlative studies with any of the radiopharmaceuticals. In one report of 60 joint groups, in which the clinical diagnosis was compared to findings of ^{99m}Tc-IgG imaging, swelling was detectable in 19 shoulders and was ostensibly absent in 41. Corresponding specificity and positive predictive value of ^{99m}Tc-IgG joint imaging were both only 39 percent.[126] Perhaps the number of false positive results was overestimated because of the

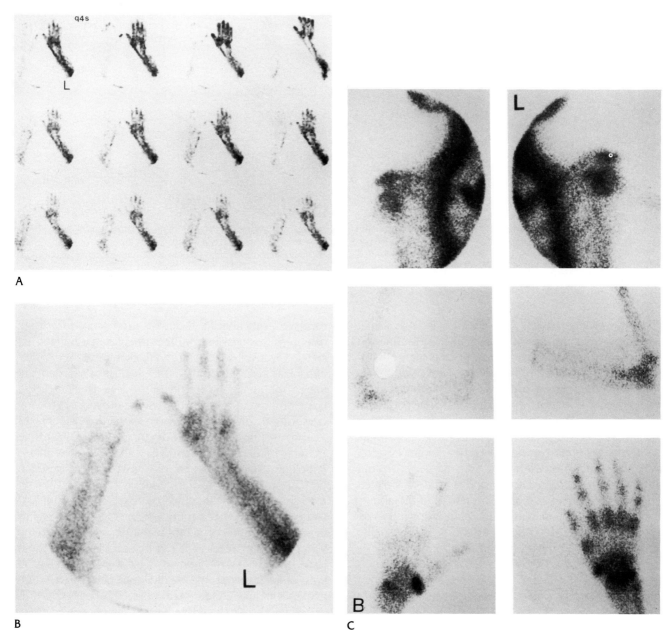

Figure 1F-32 Shoulder-hand syndrome on the left side in a 48-year-old woman with multiple sclerosis. **A.** On the perfusion study the left forearm, wrist, and hand demonstrate increased transit. **B.** Blood pool image obtained about 1 minute after the perfusion study exhibits a similar disparity between the left (*L*) and right sides. **C.** Delayed views show increased uptake of ^{99m}Tc-MDP at the shoulder, elbow, wrist, and hand. The diaphyses exhibit less activity. This is a typical pattern of the first phase of reflex sympathetic dystrophy.

clinical difficulty in determining whether glenohumeral joint swelling exists. Many radionuclide correlative studies often omit the shoulder for this reason. Short of synovial biopsy as the gold standard, which gathers essential information on cellularity and vascularity, or perhaps MRI and US, doubt about the status of the shoulder joint for purposes of correlation will prevail. Interpretation of ^{99m}Tc-phosphate scans of the glenohumeral

joint can be hampered by the variable and normal accretion in the periarticular region. Avid symmetric, and especially asymmetric, increased uptake due to synovial hyperemia is easy to diagnose, but small or moderate symmetric increases may not be visually appreciated, and so contribute to false negative interpretations. The intensity of the ^{99m}Tc-phosphate activity subsides to normal with successful treatment if the inflammation is limited

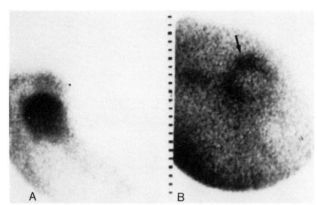

Figure 1F-33 Rheumatoid arthritis. **A.** There is enhanced uptake of ^{99m}Tc-phosphate in the humeral head owing to hyperemia. **B.** Radiopertechnetate (^{99m}TcO$_4$) blood pool study defines the increased synovial blood pool directly (*arrow*). The high background is due to a shift of some of the radiopertechnetate from the intravascular to the extravascular space.

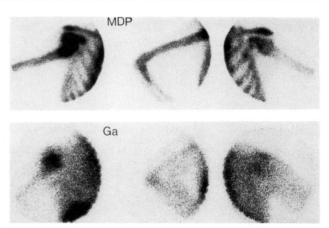

Figure 1F-35 Osteomyelitis of the head of the humerus. The ^{99m}Tc-MDP images demonstrate intense, nonspecific regional uptake in the right shoulder, with extension down the humeral shaft secondary to local hyperemia. The major concentration of ^{67}Ga-citrate is localized to the humeral head, the site of the infection.

to the synovium; however, low-grade uptake may signal persistent subclinical synovitis. When it is complicated by bone erosions the bone uptake persists after clinical remission. In one study involving 387 joints with newly developed rheumatoid arthritis and followed for 24 months, only the joints that exhibited avid, persistent uptake of ^{99m}Tc-phosphate were prone to develop erosions demonstrable by conventional radiography. Joints that were consistently normal on scans did not develop erosions within the 24-month time frame.[127] In the chronic phase of rheumatoid arthritis with established radiographic evidence of erosions, not all of the abnormal joints exhibited increased uptake. Presumably those erosions that failed to concentrate the ^{99m}Tc-phosphate were stable in size and metabolically inactive.[128]

Osteoarthritis

Whether osteoarthritis develops initially in the subchondral bone or in cartilage is still a matter of debate, but as the disease progresses there is degeneration of the

cartilage, subchondral sclerosis and cyst formation, osteophyte extension from the articular margin, and increased synovial cellularity and thickening.[129] The ^{99m}Tc-phosphate response to the bone changes varies, depending on the metabolic activity of the lesions (Fig. 1F-36). Generally, osteophytes that are in the process of growing demonstrate high uptake, whereas mature osteophytes tend to manifest low-grade or normal uptake. A prime example of this occurs in patients with established diffuse idiopathic skeletal hyperostosis (DISH), whose accretion of ^{99m}Tc-phosphate in the vertebral column is not remarkable. The lumbar spine–soft tissue and sacrum–soft tissue ratios have been found, on average, to be higher than those for the normal spine but not significant to the 0.05 probability level.[130] It can be speculated that these large osteophytes and bony bridges were mature at the time of radiography but would have been seen scintigraphically during the growth phase. There is other evidence for this. Radiography and ^{99m}Tc-phosphate bone scanning were performed in 14 patients who had generalized nodal arthritis of the hands and wrists and who

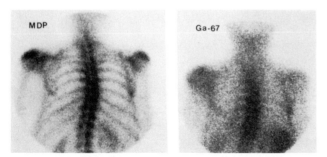

Figure 1F-34 Septic arthritis of the left shoulder in a 72-year-old woman. The low-grade uptake of ^{99m}Tc-MDP in the shoulder region indicates hyperemia, but the ^{67}Ga-citrate concentration is far more striking and covers the area diffusely.

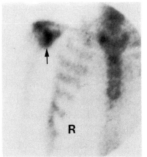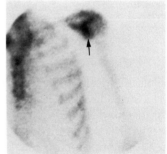

Figure 1F-36 Bilateral osteoarthritis of the glenohumeral joint (*arrows*). There is no regional hyperemia, and the ^{99m}Tc-MDP uptake is limited to the subchondral region of the glenoid. *R*, right.

were then followed for 3 to 5 years. The joint scan abnormality appeared to antedate the development of radiographic signs, and the joints that had increased uptake of ^{99m}Tc-phosphate showed the most progressive radiographic change. The radiographically abnormal joints that appeared normal on scans did not exhibit additional deterioration (i.e., they were stable).[131]

CONCLUSION

Bone scintigraphy can be used as a sensitive tool for the evaluation of shoulder pain. As a complementary aid to other imaging modalities this technique can provide invaluable information on perfusion and osteoblastic activity. The limitation of this technique, its nonspecificity, underscores the importance of obtaining relevant historical data and available correlative studies.

ACKNOWLEDGMENT

The authors gratefully acknowledge the assistance of Dr. Nancy Zefo for her expertise. We appreciate the help and support of Ralph Evans, Betty Heyl, Nancy Brown, John Crane, Aileen Kingdon-Vogeler, and the technologist of Roseville Hospital, University of California-Davis Medical Center, and Wilford Hall Medical Center. Finally, we would like to gratefully acknowledge the support and patience of our families in the preparation of this work.

References

1. GILDAY DL, PAUL DJ, PATERSON J: Diagnosis of osteomyelitis in children by combined blood pool and bone imaging. *Radiology* 117:331–335, 1975.

2. MAJD M, FRANKEL RS: Radionuclide imaging in skeletal inflammatory and ischemic disease in children. *Am J Roentgenol* 126:832–841, 1976.

3. MAURER AH, CHEN DC, CAMARGO EE, ET AL.: Utility of three-phase skeletal scintigraphy in suspected osteomyelitis: Concise communication. *J Nucl Med* 22:941–949, 1981.

4. GREYSON ND: Radionuclide bone and joint imaging in rheumatology. *Bull Rheum Dis* 30:1034–1039, 1980.

5. RUPANI HD, HOLDER LE, ESPINOLA DA, ET AL.: Three-phase radionuclide bone imaging in sports medicine. *Radiology* 156:187–196, 1985.

6. KOZIN F, JAGMEET SS, RYAN LM, ET AL.: Bone scintigraphy in the reflex dystrophy syndrome. *Radiology* 138:437–443, 1981.

7. MATIN P: Bone scanning of trauma and benign conditions, in Freeman LM, Weissman HS (eds): *Nuclear Medicine Annual,* New York, Raven, 1982, pp 81–118.

8. CHARKES ND: Mechanisms of skeletal tracer uptake. *J Nucl Med* 20:794–795, 1979.

9. HECK LL: Gamuts: Extraosseous localization of phosphate bone agents. *Semin Nucl Med* 10:311–312, 1980.

10. LECKLITNER ML, DOUGLAS KP: Increased extremity uptake on three-phase bone scans caused by peripherally induced ischemia prior to injection. *J Nucl Med* 28:108–111, 1987.

11. DESAI A, INTENZO C: The "tourniquet effect." *J Nucl Med* 25:697–699, 1984.

12. THAKUR S, COLLIER BD: Bonescan: A useful test for evaluating bone and joint pain. *Appl Radiol* 20:19–26, 1991.

13. COLLIER BD, JOHNSON RP, CARRERA GF, ET AL.: Painful spondylolysis or spondylolisthesis studied by radiography and single-photon emission computed tomography. *Radiology* 154:207–211, 1985.

14. BLINDER RA, JASZCZAK RJ, COLEMAN RE: Single-photon emission computed tomography: Survey of current clinical applications, in Freeman LM, Weissman HS (eds): *Nuclear Medicine Annual 1986,* New York, Raven, 1986, pp 19–56.

15. MURRAY IP, DIXON J: The role of single photon emission computed tomography in bone scintigraphy. *Skel Radiol* 18:493–505, 1989.

16. CHAUDHURI TK, CHAUDHURI TK: The "hot" spot in bone imaging. *Semin Nucl Med* 13:75–77, 1983.

17. Bone scintigraphy, in Treves ST (ed): *Pediatric Nuclear Medicine,* New York, Springer-Verlag, 1985, pp 1–25.

18. HOFFER PB, NEUMANN RD: Gallium and infection, in Gottschalk A, Hoffer PB, Potchen EJ (eds): *Golden's Diagnostic Nuclear Medicine,* 2d ed, Baltimore, Williams & Wilkins, 1988, pp 1111–1124.

19. JOHNSON DG, COLEMAN RE: Detection of inflammatory

disease using radiolabeled cells, in Gottschalk A, Hoffer PB, Potchen EJ (eds): *Golden's Diagnostic Nuclear Medicine,* 2d ed, vol 2, Baltimore, Williams & Wilkins, 1988, pp 1125–1136.

20. Tumor and abscess imaging, in Mettler FA Jr, Guiberteau MJ (eds): *Essentials of Nuclear Medicine Imaging,* 2d ed, Orlando, Grune and Stratton, 1986, pp 302–322.

21. HOFFER PB: The utility of gallium-67 in tumor imaging: A comment on the final reports of the Cooperative Study Group. *J Nucl Med* 19:1082–1084, 1978.

22. MENON S, WAGNER HN JR, TSAN M-F: Studies on gallium accumulation in inflammatory lesions: II. Uptake by *Staphylococcus aureus:* Concise communication. *J Nucl Med* 19:44–47, 1978.

23. EMERY T: Role of ferrichrome as a ferric ionophore in *Ustilago sphaerogena. Biochemistry* 10:1483–1488, 1971.

24. HOFFER PB, HUBERTY JP, KHAYAM-BASHI H: The association of Ga-67 and lactoferrin. *J Nucl Med* 18:713–717, 1977.

25. TSAN M-F, CHEN WY, SCHEFFEL U, ET AL.: Studies on gallium accumulation in inflammatory lesions: I. Gallium uptake by human polymorphonuclear leukocytes. *J Nucl Med* 19:36–43, 1978.

26. BURLESON RI, JOHNSON MC, HEAD H: Scintigraphic demonstration of abscesses with intravenous ^{67}Ga citrate and ^{67}Ga-labeled leukocytes. *Ann Surg* 178:446–452, 1973.

27. LARSON SM, RASEY JS, ALLEN DR, ET AL. A transferrin-mediated uptake of gallium-67 by EMT-6 sarcoma. I. Studies in tissue culture. *J Nucl Med* 20:837–842, 1979.

28. BERRY JP, ESCAIG F, POUPON MF, ET AL.: Localization of gallium in tumor cells. Electron microscopy, electron probe microanalysis and analytical ion microscopy. *Int J Nucl Med Biol* 10:199, 1983.

29. STY JR, STARSHAK RJ: The role of bone scintigraphy in the evaluation of the suspected abused child. *Radiology* 146:369–375, 1983.

30. HAASE GM, ORTIZ VN, SFAKIANAKIS GN, ET AL.: The value of radionuclide bone scanning in the early recognition of deliberate child abuse. *J Trauma* 20:873–875, 1980.

31. MATIN P: Appearance of bone scans following fractures; including immediate and long-term studies. *J Nucl Med* 20:1227–1231, 1979.

32. FINK-BENNETT DM, BENSON MT: Unusual exercise-related stress fractures: Two case reports. *Clin Nucl Med* 9:431–434, 1984.

33. ROSENTHALL L, LISBONA R: Role of radionuclide imaging in benign bone and joint diseases of orthopedic interest, in Freeman LM, Weissmann HS (eds): *Nuclear Medicine Annual,* vol 1, New York, Raven, 1980.

34. SEABOLD JE, NEPOLA JV, CONRAD GR, ET AL.: Detection of osteomyelitis at fracture nonunion sites: Comparison of two scintigraphic methods. *AJR* 152:1021–1027, 1989.

35. SMITH JT, SMITH LM, RINSKY L, ET AL.: Long-term scintigraphic appearance of extremities following bone tumor resection and allograft reconstruction. *Clin Nucl Med* 16:907–909, 1991.

36. MOSKOWITZ GW, LUKASH F: Evaluation of bone graft viability. *Semin Nucl Med* 18:246–254, 1988.

37. SHAFFER JW, FIELD GA, WILBER RG, ET AL.: Experimental vascularized bone grafts: Histopathologic correlations with postoperative bone scan: The risk of false-positive results. *J Orthop Res* 5:311–319, 1987.

38. KOSIN F, SOIN JS, RYAN LM, ET AL.: Bone scintigraphy in the reflex sympathetic dystrophy syndrome. *Radiology* 138:437–443, 1981.

39. BEKERMAN C, GENANT HK, HOFFER PB, ET AL.: Radionuclide imaging of the bones and joints of the hand. *Radiology* 118:653–659, 1976.

40. GENANT HK, KOZIN F, BEKERMAN C, ET AL.: The reflex sympathetic dystrophy syndrome. A comprehensive analysis using fine-detail radiography, photon absorptiometry, and bone and joint scintigraphy. *Radiology* 117:21–32, 1975.

41. GUPTA NC, PREZIO JA: Radionuclide imaging in osteomyelitis. *Semin Nucl Med* 28:287–299, 1988.

42. UNGER E, MOLDOFSKY P, GATENBY R, ET AL: Diagnosis of osteomyelitis by MR imaging. *AJR* 150:605–610, 1987.

43. BELTRAN J, NOTO AM, McGHEE RB, ET AL.: Infections of the musculoskeletal system: High–field strength MR imaging. *Radiology* 164:449–454, 1987.

44. MODIC MT, PFLANZE W, FEIGLIN DHI, ET AL.: Magnetic resonance imaging of musculoskeletal infections. *Radiol Clin North Am* 24:247–258, 1986.

45. SCHAUWECKER DS: The scintigraphic diagnosis of osteomyelitis. *AJR* 158:9–18, 1992.

46. SELDIN DW, HEIKEN JP, FELDMAN F, ET AL.: Effect of soft tissue pathology in detection of pedal osteomyelitis in diabetics. *J Nucl Med* 26:988–993, 1985.

47. ALAZRAKI N, DRIES DJ, DATZ F, ET AL.: Value of a 24-hour image (four phase bone scan) in assessing osteomyelitis in patients with peripheral vascular disease. *J Nucl Med* 26:711–717, 1985.

48. NELSON HT, TAYLOR A: Bone scanning in the diagnosis of acute osteomyelitis. *Eur J Nucl Med* 5:267–269, 1980.

49. MITCHELL ML, LALLY JF, ACKERMAN LV, ET AL.: Case report 697. *Skel Radiol* 20:550–554, 1991.

50. FELDMAN F: The radiology of total shoulder prostheses. *Semin Roentgenol* 221:47–65, 1986.

51. DELBEKE D, HABIBIAN MR: Noninflammatory entities and the differential diagnosis of positive three-phase bone imaging. *Clin Nucl Med* 13:844–850, 1988.

52. SHAFER RB, EDEBURN GF: Can the three-phase bone scan differentiate osteomyelitis from metabolic bone disease? *Clin Nucl Med* 9:373–377, 1984.

53. HANTZSCHEL H, BIRD HA, SEIDEL W, ET AL.: Polymyalgia rheumatica and rheumatoid arthritis of the elderly: A clinical, laboratory, and scintigraphic comparison. *Ann Rheum Dis* 50:619–622, 1991.

54. ASH JM, GILDAY DL: The futility of bone scanning in neonatal osteomyelitis: Concise communication. *J Nucl Med* 21:417–420, 1980.

55. MOK PM, REILLY BJ, ASH JM: Osteomyelitis in the neonate: Clinical aspects and the role of radiography and scintigraphy in diagnosis and management. *Radiology* 145:677–682, 1982.

56. SULLIVAN DC, ROSENFIELD NS, OGDEN J, ET AL.: Problems in the scintigraphic detection of osteomyelitis in children. *Radiology* 135:731–736, 1980.

57. ALLWRIGHT SJ, MILLER JH, GILSANZ V: Subperiosteal ab-

scess in children: Scintigraphic appearance. *Radiology* 179:725–729, 1991.

58. SUMMERVILLE DA, TREVES ST: Pediatric applications of radionuclide bone imaging, in Mettler FA (ed): *Radionuclide Bone Imaging and Densitometry,* New York, Churchill Livingstone, 1988, pp 161–195.

59. ALAZRAKI N, FIERER J, RESNICK D: Chronic osteomyelitis: Monitoring by [99m]Phosphate and ^{67}Ga citrate imaging. *AJR* 145:767–771, 1985.

60. MERKEL KD, BROWN ML, DEWANJEE MK, ET AL.: Comparison of indium-labeled leukocyte imaging with sequential technetium-gallium scanning in the diagnosis of low-grade musculoskeletal sepsis. *Amer J Bone Joint Surg* 67:465–476, 1985.

61. SCHAUWECKER DS, PARK HM, MOCK BH, ET AL.: Evaluation of complicating osteomyelitis with Tc-99m MDP, In-111 granulocytes, and Ga-67 citrate. *J Nucl Med* 25:849–853, 1984.

62. SCHAUWECKER DS: Osteomyelitis: Diagnosis with In-111-labeled leukocytes. *Radiology* 171:141–146, 1989.

63. COLEMAN RE, WELCH DM, BAKER WJ, ET AL.: Clinical experience using Indium-111 labeled leukocytes, in Thakur ML, Gottschalk A (eds): *Indium-111 Labeled Neutrophils, Platelets, and Lymphocytes,* New York, Trivirium, 1981, pp 103–118.

64. HANDMAKER H, GIAMMONA ST: Improved early diagnosis of acute inflammatory skeletal articular diseases in children: A two-radiopharmaceutical approach. *Pediatrics* 73:661–669, 1984.

65. AL-SHEIKH W, SFAKIANAKIS GN, MNAYMNEH W, ET AL.: Subacute and chronic bone infections: Diagnosis using In-111, Ga-67, and Tc-99m MDP bone scintigraphy and radiography. *Radiology* 155:501–506, 1985.

66. LISBONA R, ROSENTHALL L: Observations on the sequential use of 99m-Tc phosphate complex and ^{67}Ga imaging in osteomyelitis, cellulitis and septic arthritis. *Radiology* 123:123–129, 1977.

67. TUMEH SS, ALIABADI P, WEISSMAN BN, ET AL.: Tc-99m-MDP/Ga-67 scan patterns associated with active disease. *Radiology* 158:658–688, 1986.

68. Infectious arthritis, in Rodnan GP, Schumacher HR (eds): *Primer on the Rheumatic Diseases,* 8th ed, Atlanta, Arthritis Foundation, 1983.

69. MORENO AJ, WEISMAN IM, RODRIQUEZ AA, ET AL.: Nuclear medicine imaging in coccidioidal osteomyelitis. *Clin Nucl Med* 8:604–609, 1987.

70. LESKINEN RH, SKRIFVARS BV, LAASONEN LS, ET AL.: Bone lesions in systemic lupus erythematosus. *Radiology* 153:349–352, 1984.

71. PARK HM, TERMAN SA, RIDOLFO AS, ET AL.: A quantitative evaluation of rheumatoid arthritic activity with Tc-99m HEDP. *J Nucl Med* 18:973–976, 1977.

72. McLEAN RG, MURRAY IPC: Three-phase skeletal scintigraphy for suspected bone tumors. *Clin Nucl Med* 9:378–382, 1984.

73. HOLDER LE: Clinical radionuclide bone imaging. *Radiology* 176:607–614, 1990.

74. GREYSON ND, NOYEK AM: Clinical otolaryngology, in Maisey MM, Britton KE, Gilday DL (eds): *Clinical Nuclear Medicine,* London, Chapman and Hall, 1983, pp 371–380.

75. GINSBERG HN, SWAYNE LC: Three-phase bone scanning in chronic myelogenous leukemia. *Clin Nucl Med* 12:823–824, 1987.

76. WELLS RG, MILLER JH, STY JR: Scintigraphic patterns in osteoid osteoma and spondylolysis. *Clin Nucl Med* 12:39–44, 1987.

77. KRANSDORF MJ, STULL MA, GILKEY FW, ET AL.: Osteoid osteoma. *RadioGraphics* 11:671–696, 1991.

78. SWEE RG, McLEOD RA, BEABOUT JW: Osteoid osteoma: Detection, diagnosis, and localization. *Radiology* 130:117–123, 1979.

79. SMITH FW, GILDAY DL: Scintigraphic appearance of osteoid osteoma. *Radiology* 137:191–195, 1980.

80. LISBONA R, ROSENTHALL L: Role of radionuclide bone imaging in osteoid osteoma. *AJR* 132:77–80, 1979.

81. HELMS CA: Osteoid osteoma: The double density sign. *Clin Orthop* 222:167–173, 1987.

82. KLONECKE AS, LICHO R, McDOUGALL IR: A technique for intraoperative bone scintigraphy: A report of 17 cases. *Clin Nucl Med* 16:482–486, 1991.

83. JONES DN, MARION M: Polyostotic fibrous dysplasia as a mimic of bony metastatic disease. *Clin Nucl Med* 16:54–56, 1991.

84. TUPLER RH, TURBINER EH: Tc-99m labeled RBC scan in Maffucci's syndrome. *Clin Nucl Med* 16:872–873, 1991.

85. BROWER AC, SWEET DE, KEATS TE: Condensing osteitis of the clavicle: A new entity. *Am J Roentgenol Radium Ther Nucl Med* 121:17–21, 1974.

86. STEWART CA, SIEGEL ME, KING D, ET AL.: Radionuclide and radiographic demonstration of condensing osteitis of the clavicle. *Clin Nucl Med* 13:177–178, 1988.

87. JIRIK FR, STEIN HB, CHALMERS A: Clavicular hyperostosis with enthesopathy, hypergammaglobulinemia, and thoracic outlet syndrome. *Ann Intern Med* 97:48–49, 1982.

88. OSBORNE RL: The differential radiologic diagnosis of bone tumors. *CA* 24:194–211, 1974.

89. KRASNOW AZ, ISITMAN AT, COLLIER BD, ET AL.: Flow study and SPECT imaging for the diagnosis of giant cell tumor of bone. *Clin Nucl Med* 13:89–92, 1988.

90. WILLIAMS HT: Multicentric giant cell tumor of bone. *Clin Nucl Med* 14:631–634, 1989.

91. GOORIN AM, ABELSON HT, FREI E III: Osteosarcoma: Fifteen years later. *N Engl J Med* 313:1637–1643, 1985.

92. McNEIL BJ: Value of bone scanning in neoplastic disease. *Semin Nucl Med* 14:277–286, 1984.

93. HOROWITZ ME, TSOKOS MG, DeLANEY TF: Ewing's sarcoma. *CA* 42:300–320, 1992.

94. HUDSON TM, CHEW FS, MANASTER BJ: Radionuclide bone scanning of medullary chondrosarcoma. *AJR* 139:1071–1076, 1982.

95. O'MARA RE: Bone scanning in osseous metastatic disease. *JAMA* 229:1915–1917, 1974.

96. ALAZRAKI N: Musculoskeletal imaging, in Taylor A Jr, Datz FL (eds): *Clinical Practice of Nuclear Medicine,* New York, Churchill Livingstone, 1991.

97. FORDHAM EW, ALI A: Skeletal imaging in malignant disease, in Gottschalk A, Hoffer PB, Potchen EJ (eds): *Diagnostic Nuclear Medicine,* Harris JH Jr (ed.): *Golden's Diagnostic Radiology Series,* Baltimore, Williams & Wilkins, 1988.

98. ROBINSON RG, BLAKE GM, PRESTON DF, ET AL.: Strontium-89: Treatment results and kinetics in patients with painful metastatic prostate and breast cancer in bone. *RadioGraphics* 9:271–281, 1989.

99. METTLER FA JR, MONSEIN L, DAVIS M, ET AL.: Three phase radionuclide bone scanning in the evaluation of local radiation injury: A case report. *Clin Nucl Med* 12:805–808, 1987.

100. JACOX RF, JOHNSON MK, KOUNTZ R: Transport of radioactive sodium across synovial membrane of normal human subjects. *Proc Soc Exp Biol* 80:655–657, 1952.

101. HARRIS R, MILLARD JB, BANERJEE SK: Radiosodium clearance from the knee joint in rheumatoid arthritis. *Ann Rheum Dis* 17:189–195, 1958.

102. AHLSTROM S, GEDDA PO, HEDBERG H: Disappearance of radioactive serum albumin from joints in rheumatoid arthritis. *Acta Rheumatol Scand* 2:129–136, 1956.

103. RODNAN GP, MacLACHLAN MJ: The absorption of serum albumin and gamma globulin from the knee joint of man and rabbit. *Arthritis Rheum* 3:152–157, 1960.

104. ST. ONGE RA, DICK WC, BELL G, ET AL.: Radioactive xenon(^{133}Xe) disappearance rates from synovial cavity of the human knee joint in normal and arthritic subjects. *Ann Rheum Dis* 27:163–166, 1968.

105. PORTER BB, NUKI G, BUCHANAN WW, ET AL.: Synovial perfusion of clinically normal knee joints in patients with rheumatoid arthritis. *Ann Rheum Dis* 29:649–652, 1970.

106. WEISS TE, MAXFIELD WS, MURISON PJ, ET AL.: Iodinated human serum albumin(^{131}I) localization of rheumatoid arthritis joints by scintiscanning. *Arthritis Rheum* 8:976–987, 1965.

107. TANNENBAUM H, ROSENTHALL L, GREENSPOON M, ET AL.: Qualitative joint imaging using gallium-67 citrate in a rabbit model of zymosan induced arthritis. *J Rheumatol* 11:687–691, 1984.

108. AL-JANOBI MA, JONES AKP, SOLANKI K, ET AL.: Tc-99m–labelled leucocyte imaging in active rheumatoid arthritis. *Nucl Med Commun* 9:987–991, 1988.

109. UNO K, MATSUI N, NOHIRA K, ET AL.: Indium-111 leucocyte imaging in patients with rheumatoid arthritis. *J Nucl Med* 27:339–344, 1986.

110. SULLIVAN MM, POWELL N, FRENCH AP, ET AL.: Inflammatory joint disease: A comparison of liposome scanning, bone scanning and radiography. *Ann Rheum Dis* 47:485–491, 1988.

111. LIBERATORE M, CLEMENTE M, LURILLI AP, ET AL.: Scintigraphic evaluation of disease activity in rheumatoid arthritis: A comparison of technetium-99m human IgG, leucocytes and albumin nanocolloids. *Eur J Nucl Med* 19:853–857, 1992.

112. SCHMERLING RH, PARKER JA, JOHNS WD, ET AL.: Measurement of joint inflammation in rheumatoid arthritis with indium-111 chloride. *Ann Rheum Dis* 49:88–92, 1990.

113. BREEVELD FC, VAN KROONENBURGH MJ, CAMPS JA, ET AL.: Imaging of inflammatory arthritis with technetium-99m labeled IgG. *J Nucl Med* 30:2017–2021, 1989.

114. LIND P, LANGSTEGER W, KOLTRINGER P, ET AL.: Immunoscintigraphy of inflammatory processes with a ^{99m}Tc-labeled monoclonal antigranulocyte antibody. *J Nucl Med* 31:417–423, 1990.

115. BECKER W, EMMERICH F, HORNELL G: Imaging rheumatoid arthritis specifically with Tc-99m CD4-specific (T-helper lymphocytes) antibodies. *Eur J Nucl Med* 17:156–159, 1990.

116. HOLOPAIENEN T, RECKONEN A: Uptake of radioactive strontium(SR-85) in joints damaged by rheumatoid arthritis by external counting of radiation. *Acta Rheumatol Scand* 12:102–106, 1966.

117. JEREMY R, CATO J, SCOTT W: Investigation of bone and joint disease using F-18. *Med J Aust* 1:492–496, 1969.

118. DESAULNIER M, ROSENTHALL L, FUKS A, ET AL.: Radiotechnetium polyphosphate joint imaging. *J Nucl Med* 15:417–423, 1974.

119. HAYS MT, GREEN FA: The pertechnetate joint scan: Timing. *Ann Rheum Dis* 31:272–277, 1972.

120. COHEN MB, LORBER A: Avoiding false positive joint scans by the use of labeled albumins. *Arthritis Rheum* 14:32–35, 1971.

121. MARTINEZ-VILLASENOR D, KATONA G: Scintigraphy by means of radioisotopes of short half-life for diagnosing disease of the joints, in *Medical Radioisotope Scintigraphy*, vol 2, Vienna, International Atomic Energy Agency, pp 295–305, 1968.

122. MAXFIELD WS, WEISS TE: Synovial membrane scanning in arthritic disease. *Semin Nucl Med* 2:50–61, 1972.

123. BLAKE DR, GALLAGHER PJ, POTTER AR, ET AL.: The effect of synovial iron on the progression of rheumatic disease. *Arthritis Rheum* 27:495–501, 1984.

124. KINNE RW, BECKER W, SIMON G, ET AL.: Joint uptake and body distribution of a technetium 99m–labeled anti–rat-CD4 monoclonal antibody in rat adjuvant arthritis. *J Nucl Med* 34:92–98, 1993.

125. ROSENSPIRE, KC, BLAU M, KENNEDY AC: Assessment and interpretation of radiopharmaceutical joint imaging in an animal model of arthritis. *Arthritis Rheum* 24:711–715, 1981.

126. DE BOIS MHW, ARNDT JW, VAN DER VELDE EA, ET AL.: ^{99m}Tc human immunoglobin scintigraphy: A reliable method to detect joint activity in rheumatoid arthritis. *J Rheumatol* 19:1371–1376, 1992.

127. MOTTONEN T, HANNONEN P, TOIVANEN J, ET AL.: Value of joint scintigraphy in the prediction of erosiveness in early rheumatoid arthritis. *Ann Rheum Dis* 47:183–189, 1988.

128. PITT P, BERRY H, CLARKE M, ET AL.: Metabolic activity of erosions in rheumatoid arthritis. *Ann Rheum Dis* 45:235–238, 1986.

129. VERNON-ROBERTS B: Advances in the pathology and pathogenesis of osteoarthritis. *Ann RCPSC* 19:45–48, 1986.

130. PAQUIN J, ROSENTHALL L, ESDAILE J, ET AL.: Elevated uptake of Tc-99m methylene diphosphate in the axial skeleton in ankylosing spondylitis and Reiter's: Implications for quantitative sacroiliac scintigraphy. *Arthritis Rheum* 26:217–220, 1983.

131. HUTTON CW, HIGGS ER, JACKSON PC: ^{99m}Tc-HMDP bone scanning in generalized nodal arthritis. The four-hour bone scan image predicts radiographic change. *Ann Rheum Dis* 45:622–626, 1986.

1G TECHNICAL ASPECTS: INTERVENTIONAL PROCEDURES

J.F. Naouri
L. Bellaiche
B. Hamze
J.M. Bondeville
J.M. Tubiana
J.D. Laredo

Development of radiologic guidance methods during recent decades has improved our capability for percutaneous diagnosis and treatment of some bone and joint disorders. Some of these techniques, such as aspiration of tendinous calcific deposits and management of frozen shoulders, are applicable exclusively or principally to the shoulder. Some other techniques, such as biopsy of musculoskeletal or synovial lesions and drainage of abscesses, are not specific to the shoulder but are sometimes indicated for some disorders of the shoulder. Percutaneous treatments that can be achieved without any radiologic guidance are not discussed in this chapter.

ASPIRATION OF ROTATOR CUFF TENDINOUS CALCIUM DEPOSITS

Apatite deposition disease (APD) is a common condition which is often asymptomatic, but especially in the rotator cuff of the shoulder it can be responsible for incapacitating pain. Needle aspiration of tendinous calcific deposits (NACD) was first performed in acutely painful shoulders to evacuate calcifications located in the subacromial bursa.[1] In 1978, Comfort and Arafiles first used this technique to treat intratendinous calcium deposits.[2]

Indications

This technique is indicated in selected cases of painful shoulder marked by chronic and debilitating pain that resists medical treatment and is at least partially related to the presence of calcific deposits in the rotator cuff tendons. In such instances, NACD often avoids surgery.

Selection Criteria

CLINICAL EVALUATION

The inefficacy of prior medical treatment such as nonsteroid anti-inflammatory drugs (NSAIDs), physiotherapy, and steroid injections must be established. Needle aspiration must be performed if the clinical and radiologic findings suggest that the pain is at least partially related to the presence of the calcific material in the rotator cuff. The most important clinical selection criterion for NACD is exacerbation of pain at night. Pain also typically is increased by all shoulder motions and may be associated with a decrease in joint motion involving all shoulder movements. Conversely, absence of pain at night, exacerbation of pain by a specific kind of motion, and limitation of a specific motion suggest that pain is related to a lesion of the tendon and not to the calcific deposit.

RADIOLOGIC EVALUATION

Calcific deposits frequently are multiple. To be appropriate for NACD, a calcification must be larger than 5 mm in diameter. Faint calcifications with blurred contours are usually liquid and easily aspirated. Conversely, very dense calcifications with clearly defined margins are usually very solid and, in most cases, cannot be aspirated. Striated calcifications usually are located within tendon fibers, correspond to degenerative tendinitis, and cannot be aspirated.

Association of tendinous calcific deposits with rotator cuff tear is rather uncommon; however, sonography, arthrography, or magnetic resonance imaging (MRI) evaluation must be performed to rule out such a tear conclusively.

Technique

The procedure itself has three goals: evacuation of the maximum amount of calcium; fragmentation of the residual deposits to facilitate resorption during the weeks following the procedure; reduction of the inflammatory process secondary to the presence of residual calcific deposits by in situ injection of steroids.

NACD is performed using conventional x-ray equipment with fluoroscopy. The approach of the needle to the shoulder is at the anterior and superior aspect of the shoulder, at the level of the subacromial space with the patient in a supine position. The x-ray beam is centered vertically to the shoulder. Appropriate rotation of the arm is selected according to the location of the calcification within the rotator cuff. Internal rotation is needed for infraspinatus tendon calcifications, whereas external rotation allows good visualization of supraspinatus tendon calcifications. Apatite deposits located in the subscapularis tendon area are aspirated through an anterior approach with slight external rotation of the arm.

Once the puncture point has been determined, the skin is prepared. The superficial plane is then anesthetized with 1% lidocaine. A 19-gauge needle with stylet is inserted parallel to the x-ray beam. At any step of the procedure, the x-ray beam can be successively tilted craniad and caudad to confirm that the needle tip is actually within the calcification (Figs. 1G-1, 1G-2). A syringe containing lidocaine or saline solution is used for calcium aspiration. Intermittent suctions with the syringe piston facilitate calcium aspiration. In large and lobulated calcific deposits, parallel insertion of two needles may be useful to achieve needle irrigation (Fig. 1G-4).

Aspirated calcium appears in the syringe as a white, cloudy return. The maneuver is repeated until maximal aspiration of calcium is achieved. Even in the best cases only the greater part of the calcification can be aspirated (Figs. 1G-3, 1G-5, Table 1G-1). Once maximal aspiration has been achieved, 2 to 3 ml of methyl-prednisolone acetate is injected locally. In the great majority of cases, the procedure is tolerated well. In the days following, approximately one-third of the patients experience an acutely painful crisis. Patients must be informed of this possibility. Analgesic drugs, NSAIDs, and the application of an ice pack to the shoulder must be prescribed. This painful crisis is often accompanied by almost complete resorption of the remaining calcification, as demonstrated by follow-up radiographic examinations.

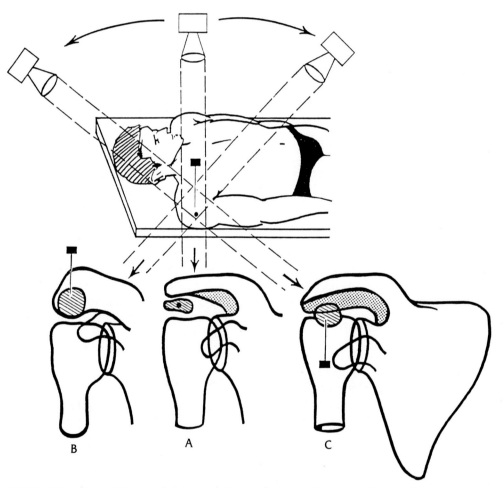

Figure 1G-1 Fluoroscopic procedure to check that needle tip is within the calcific deposits: when the x-ray beam is directed along the needle axis, the needle appears as a dot in the center of the calcification, **A.** The x-ray beam is then successively tilted cephalad, **B,** and caudad, **C,** as far as possible. Correctly placed, the needle tip will remain within the calcification during all three fluoroscopic views. (Normandin C, et al.: Aspiration of tendinous calcific deposits, in Bard M, Laredo JD (eds): *Interventional Radiology in Bone and Joint,* Vienna, Springer-Verlag, 1988, pp 258–270, with permission.)

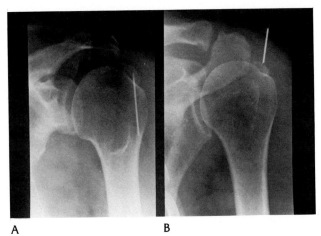

A   **B**

Figure 1G-2 Aspiration of infraspinatous calcific deposits. Example of fluoroscopic control of needle position. The x-ray beam is tilted caudad, **A,** and cephalad, **B.** The needle tip is within the calcification on both views.

Results

Four criteria were used to evaluate results of the needle aspiration technique in a previous study by one of the authors: sleep recovery, percentage of subjective improvement, recovery of normal range of motion, pain relief, and ultimate resorption of calcific deposits.[3] The

first sign of clinical improvement is the disappearance of pain at night. Daytime pain later resolves. In the best cases the ability to carry out normal activities is regained. In this study good and excellent results were obtained in 61 to 70 percent of 69 cases.[3] Eight patients of this series (11 percent) showed a poor result and finally underwent operation. The percentage of good and excellent results in other previous reports has varied from 49 to 100 percent.[1,2,4–6]

MANAGEMENT OF THE FROZEN SHOULDER SYNDROME

Background

The terms *adhesive capsulitis* and *frozen shoulder* refer to the clinical symptoms of pain and decreased joint motion associated with fibrosis and contraction of the joint capsule. Frozen shoulder is an idiopathic condition. The pathologic abnormality occurs in the fibrous layer of the capsule, which is thickened by dense and compact bundles of connective tissue containing new fibrocytes along with inflammatory cells.[7–9] This fibrous tissue develops along the joint capsule and obliterates joint recesses. In the description of typical cases of the frozen shoulder syndrome, three clinical phases are distin-

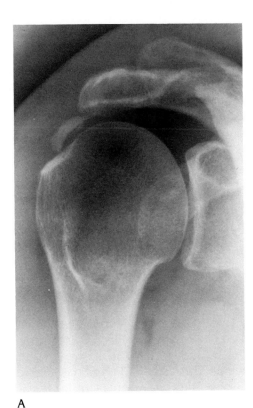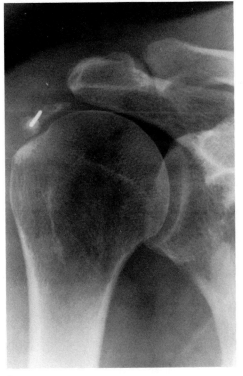

A   **B**

Figure 1G-3 Infraspinatous calcific deposits before, **A,** and after, **B,** needle aspiration. The arm is in neutral position.

Figure 1G-4 Aspiration of lobulated calcification using two needles.

guished: a painful phase, a second phase of progressive stiffness, and a third phase of gradual return to motion. The symptoms may last several years. There is a female predominance. The patients are usually between 40 and 60 years of age, and usually the nondominant shoulder is involved. All joint motions are limited, especially external rotation. Intense pain is noted at extremes of motion, especially external rotation. Sleep is often disturbed. Partial resolution may occur spontaneously after a delay of a year or more.

Arthroscopically, four different stages have been described: an early fibrinous synovial reaction, a phase of adhesive synovitis, loss of the axillary fold, and a chronic phase of restrictive adhesions.[10,11] Plain radiographic examination of the shoulder usually is negative or sometimes shows mild osteopenia of the humeral head. Arthrography typically shows a decrease in the amount of fluid that can be accepted by the joint, which is typically less than 5 ml. In addition, the axillary recess and the subcoracoid bursa are absent. Injection of an anesthetic

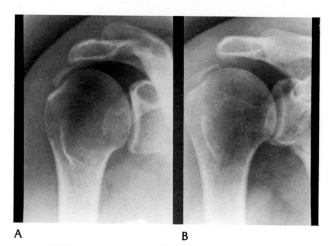

A   B

Figure 1G-5 Supraspinatous calcific deposit before, **A,** and after, **B,** needle aspiration. The arm is in an external position.

Table 1G-1 Results of Aspiration of Tendinous Calcific Deposits of the Shoulder

INVESTIGATOR	CASES (NO.)	CLINICAL CONDITION	FOLLOW-UP*	GOOD OR EXCELLENT RESULT (%)
Patterson[1] (1937)	63	Acute painful shoulders (76%)	NR	90
Comfort and Arafiles[2] (1978)	9	NR*	9 yr	100
Gross and Siegrist[5] (1981)	60	NR*	NR	70
Cabanel[6] (1983)	58	Chronic painful shoulders (93%)	10 mo	58
Normandin et al.[3] (1987)	69	Chronic painful shoulders (90%)	11–45 mo	61

*NR = Not reported.

into the joint relieves pain but without significantly improving range of motion.

Several types of treatment—medication (such as NSAIDS), local or oral steroids, physiotherapy, surgical joint release, manipulation under anesthesia, and arthroscopic treatment—have been proposed for this condition. Local anesthetic and steroid injections are among the treatments most frequently used. Many different techniques have been proposed, but repeated injections appear to be mandatory to obtain significant improvement.[12,13] Physical therapy, especially exercise, is recommended to gradually increase shoulder mobility. Early motion should be passive, of the pendular type, graduating to more active motion.

Before 1982 manipulation was the treatment of choice for adhesive capsulitis. Both closed and open manipulation under anesthesia have been advocated.[21] Loyd and Loyd reported a 94 percent rate of significant pain relief and restoration of function in a series of 31 patients treated with manipulation after intraarticular injection of local anesthetic.[14] This treatment is controversial, and some surgeons are reluctant to use it because of the delicacy of the structures involved. Shoulder manipulation under anesthesia should be considered in refractory cases.

Technique of Hydraulic Distension with Steroids and Motion Exercise Program

Hydraulic distension in adhesive capsulitis was described after arthrographic investigations showed the presence of adhesions and the reduction of the amount of fluid accepted by the joint. Various investigators used saline or air to distend the capsule.[15–18] More recently, several authors reported that hydraulic distension of the glenohumeral joint using intraarticular injection of an anesthetic and steroids can be a very successful alternative to the other types of treatments for frozen shoulder syndrome mentioned previously.[8,16,19] Good results were obtained by these authors for this condition; however, according to others,[20] there is no significant difference in the results obtained by distensive (with Xylocaine solution) and nondistensive arthrography combined with the intraarticular injection of steroids.[20] Hydraulic distension has been performed in our institution during the last 2 years. This procedure is based on the technique discussed by Fareed and coworkers.[16] Three milliliters of 1% lidocaine followed by 1 ml of betamethasone sodium and 2 ml of 1% lidocaine are injected into the joint (Fig. 1G-6A). This is done after checking the position of the needle using 3 ml of contrast material. Distension of the capsule is then performed by injecting one to four 10-ml syringefuls of refrigerated sterile saline solution through a 22-gauge needle (Fig. 1G-6B). The maximum volume accepted by the joint depends on the distensibility of the joint capsule. Afterward the patient does active and passive motion exercises under the supervision of a physician or a physical therapist. Patients continue practicing regular physical therapy exercises for a total of 4 weeks after treatment. These consist of pendular exercises, resisted flexion, extension, internal and external rotation, and abduction exercises performed four times daily.

Results of Hydraulic Distension with Steroids and Motion Exercise Program

In the series of Fareed[16] all 20 patients noted immediate resolution of previous pain and resumption of normal sleep. At the 4-week follow-up, all patients had gained normal function. For all of them, shoulder function remained normal at follow-up examinations 6 months to 10 years later. Our preliminary results confirm that local infiltration of anesthetic and steroids coupled with hydraulic distension of the glenohumeral joint can be a highly successful alternative for the management of this

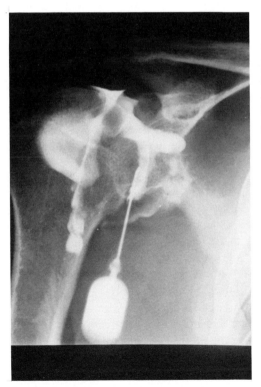 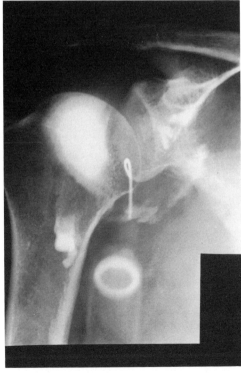

A   B

Figure 1G-6 Frozen shoulder before, **A,** and after, **B,** distension with saline and lidocaine solution.

condition. This has proved to be a safe, direct, effective, and cost-efficient method of treatment for frozen shoulder syndrome. Within about 6 months after the procedure, a return to normal painless shoulder motion is gradually obtained. A good result was achieved in 28 of our 30 patients treated with hydraulic distension.

PERCUTANEOUS BIOPSY OF MUSCULOSKELETAL LESIONS

Technologic advances in radiology, as well as new pathologic and bacteriologic capabilities, have dramatically improved treatment of skeletal disorders. In many clinical situations, percutaneous biopsy (PB) of musculoskeletal or synovial lesions under radiographic guidance can help in establishing a definitive diagnosis without the disadvantages of surgery.[21–23] To achieve optimal results, the radiologist must be a member of a team that includes the referring physician, a pathologist, and a microbiologist. Biopsies should be planned and performed in a way that would not adversely affect subsequent definitive surgical procedures. Surgical advice concerning the biopsy approach should be sought each time surgical treatment is to be considered. In this article, needle aspiration biopsy will be distinguished from trephine biopsy. Needle aspiration biopsy consists of aspiration of fluid for cytologic and bacteriologic studies. Trephine biopsy (also called core, or needle biopsy) is a process by which a core of tissue is obtained percutaneously for histologic studies.

Indications

BONE TUMOR

According to recent reports, PB has a high rate of accuracy, superior to 90 percent, in tumors with a uniform cytologic pattern such as bone metastases, multiple myeloma, lymphomas, Ewing's tumor, and solitary plasmacytoma.[21,22,24] PB is less accurate in bone tumors with a complex pathologic architecture and cellular pleomorphism such as giant cell tumors and most of the bone sarcomas. In these cases, open biopsy performed by the orthopedic surgeon is preferable for the first stage of tumor treatment. When a primary bone tumor is suspected, indications for PB and the choice of an adequate approach must be made in cooperation with the orthopedic surgeon because of the risk of tumor cell spread along the biopsy path. In such cases, the biopsy tract must be excised en bloc with the tumor at the time of radical surgery. When multiple bone lesions are present, other skeletal sites, such as the spine or the iliac bone, may occasionally be preferred to the shoulder.

BONE TUBERCULOSIS AND PYOGENIC INFECTIONS

The accuracy of PB is very high for skeletal tuberculosis since both the pathologic and bacteriologic examinations may provide a definitive diagnosis. In addition, results of bacteriologic cultures are not impaired by the previous administration of nonspecific blind antibiotic treatments.

In pyogenic infections, the causative microorganism is isolated in some 55 to 80 percent of cases. In half of the cases with negative bacteriologic findings, the pathologic examination may show some features suggestive (even though nonspecific) of a pyogenic infection.

Choice of the Modality for Radiologic Guidance

This is a critical point for PB. Four modalities of biopsy under radiologic control are presently available: fluoroscopic guidance, computed tomography (CT) guidance, combined fluoroscopic and CT guidance, and sonographic guidance.

Fluoroscopic guidance remains widely used since it has several advantages. It allows permanent control of the biopsy needle position, and it is cost-effective: a standard fluoroscopic table combined with an additional mobile tube used for cross-table radiographs is sufficient to perform most musculoskeletal PB. Biplane fluoroscopy is more comfortable for PB of some difficult anatomic sites but is not absolutely necessary. In our experience, biopsy under fluoroscopic guidance remains the method of choice for most cases when the lesion can be clearly visualized on the fluoroscopic screen.

CT is the method of choice for biopsy guidance in three instances: small bone lesions not clearly seen at fluoroscopy, bone lesions close to vital anatomic structures, and soft tissue lesions (Fig. 1G-7).

Combined CT and fluoroscopic guidance was recently introduced.[24] A mobile fluoroscopic C arm is placed immediately between the CT gantry and the table. By displacing the CT table and the patient, alternative use of CT and fluoroscopic control is possible. This method combines the advantages of both methods and will probably become very popular in the near future.

Sonographic guidance may be used for biopsy of soft tissue lesions and percutaneous drainage of abscesses in musculoskeletal infections.

Biopsy Needles

A large variety of needles is available for both trephine and needle aspiration biopsy of bone and soft tissue components. We will mention only the biopsy needles used most frequently. What specific needle is used depends upon the nature, consistency (osteoblastic, osteolytic, or mixed), and site of the lesion.

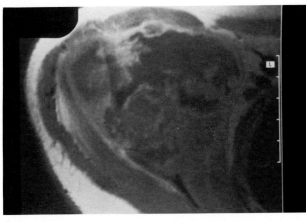

A

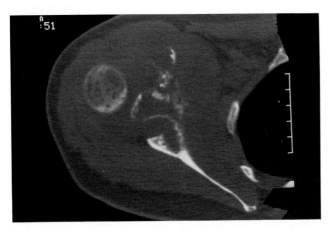

B

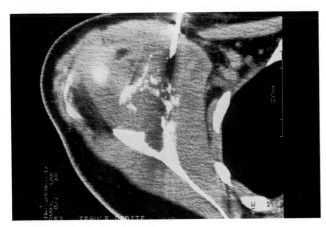

C

Figure 1G-7 **A, B.** Large necrotic bone tumor of the shoulder with soft tissue extension. **C.** The Tru-Cut needle is inserted using an anterior approach. The approach was selected according to the surgeon's recommendation.

BONE TREPHINE NEEDLES

Ackerman,[25] Craig,[26] Harlow-Wood,[27] Laredo-Bard,[28] Mac Larnon,[29] and Turkel[30] needles all have an external cannula that is advanced to the bone and a separate serrated trephine needle that is introduced through the external cannula for bone sampling. With all these needles, multiple sampling is possible while holding the external cannula against the bone; however, these needles differ from one another in their caliber and technique of placement.

The Ackerman needle[25] is a 12-gauge needle (external diameter) with a serrated trocar that provides specimens 1.6 mm in diameter.

The Craig needle is a large-caliber needle (10-gauge) approximately 3.5 mm in diameter which provides specimens 3.5 mm in caliber.[26] The 16-gauge blunt guide is inserted first through a skin stab and advanced to the biopsy site. The external cannula is slid over the guide and held firmly against the bone. The guide is removed, and the serrated trocar is inserted through the external cannula until the biopsy site is reached. With a twisting motion and a variable amount of pressure, the serrated trocar is driven into the bone to take a specimen. The external cannula can subsequently be moved to a different location to take additional specimens.

The Laredo-Bard trephine needle is used quite differently from the Ackerman, Mazabraud, or the Craig needle. The Laredo-Bard is placed via a procedure similar to vascular catheterization.[28] The Mac Larnon needle is used in a procedure similar to the Laredo-Bard procedure.[29] The Jamshidi trephine needle is designed for bone marrow biopsy but can be effective in obtaining a core biopsy of superficial and flat bones or relatively lytic lesions.[21,22] Its external cannula, which is also used as a cutting trocar, has a conical beveled tip which helps retain the specimen. The cannula is inserted with its stylet. Once the bone has been reached, the stylet is removed and the external cannula is advanced into the bone with a rotating movement. The entire needle is then removed with the specimen. Adult (8- or 11-gauge) and pediatric needles (13-gauge) of different diameters are available. They allow removal of specimens of 3.2 and 1.5 mm bore, respectively.

USE OF A HAND DRILL

A pneumatic drill may be very useful for trephination of a sclerotic lesion, especially one with a thick sclerotic cortex. Pneumatic drills are more suitable for this purpose than electric drills, owing to their lower rotation speed. Hollow pneumatic drills can be placed over a guidewire or a Kirschner wire. A trephine or a Tru-Cut needle (Travenol Labs) can easily be passed through the hole.[29]

INSTRUMENTS FOR BIOPSY OF SOFT TISSUE AND OSTEOLYTIC BONE LESIONS

The Tru-Cut needle includes an inner cannula with a 20-mm notch and a 14-gauge outer cutting cannula with a T-shaped handle. Tru-Cut needles are available in three different lengths (75, 114, and 152 mm). The needle is inserted through a skin stab and advanced until the specimen notch is within the tissue to be biopsied. Without moving the inner cannula, the outer cannula is retracted to expose the specimen notch by pulling outward on the T-shaped handle. The T-shaped handle is then quickly advanced to cut the tissue which has been drawn into the specimen notch. For multiple samplings, the inner cannula may be withdrawn with the specimen while the external cannula is left in place. Alternatively, a 15.2-cm-long Tru-Cut introduced through a 9-cm Jamshidi needle may be used.

Preoperative Assessment

Preoperative assessment is critical for this procedure. In each case the patient's file must be carefully reviewed. The patient's hemostasis must be checked a few days before the procedure. In all cases, radiographs in two projections and CT of the lesion are necessary to choose which part of the lesion to biopsy as well as the side and the angle of approach. The approach is drawn on the selected CT slice, and measurements are done according to the CT view scale. Lytic lesions must be preferred to sclerotic areas for bone biopsy. Contrast-enhanced CT may be useful when a highly vascular lesion is suspected. Frank hypervascularization may call for needle aspiration rather than trephine biopsy or for vascular embolization performed within 24 hours prior to the biopsy. Otherwise, hemostatic material (Thrombase, Spongel) must be ready to use at the time of biopsy.

The utilization of radionuclide studies to locate suitable biopsy sites must be stressed. Bone scintigraphy may identify additional lesions that are more easy to biopsy than the abnormality detected initially. Preoperative MRI may be helpful to select the optimal abnormal area to biopsy, especially in soft tissue lesions; however, CT is more appropriate than MRI for differentiating lytic bone lesions from sclerotic ones.

Anesthesia and Hospitalization

In a large majority of cases musculoskeletal biopsy is performed under local anesthesia; children and restless patients are placed under general anesthesia or given heavy sedation. Usually, the biopsy can be done on an outpatient basis. The patient should not eat on the morning of the examination. An intravenous catheter is placed and a saline solution is administered to keep the line open. Both a sedative (hydroxyzine 10 mg for an adult, 1 hour before the procedure) and pain medication are given before the examination. The procedure must be carefully explained to enlist the patient's cooperation. Biopsy of some lesions, such as osteomyelitis, frequently is very painful and should be performed under neuroleptanalgesia.

Technique of Approach

For the humerus, the approach is usually perpendicular to the bone, to avoid sliding on the round cortex (Fig. 1G-8). Normal cortex is very difficult to drill. In such cases, a pneumatic drill can be helpful. Penetration of the medullary cavity of the bone is frequently very painful, especially in the presence of osteomyelitis, and it may require neuroleptanalgesia. The biopsy approach at the level of the humeral neck should avoid the circumflex nerve. When the lesion involves the scapula, a tangential approach parallel to the long axis of the bone allows the maximal amount of bone to be sampled and avoids damage to the underlying structures in case the needle slides off the bone.

PERCUTANEOUS BIOPSY OF THE SYNOVIAL MEMBRANE OF THE GLENOHUMERAL JOINT

Arthritis is a manifestation of a wide spectrum of systemic and local diseases. In selected cases examination of the synovium may provide precise diagnostic clues or useful information about the nature of the articular process. Biopsy of the synovium can be performed through open arthrography, PB, or as part of an arthroscopic procedure during which the biopsy area can be visualized. Introduced first by Forestier[31] in 1932, PB of the synovium (PBS) permits removal of specimens from several regions of the joint lining and produces minimal trauma. PBS can be achieved in all large appendicular joints, including the glenohumeral joint; the knee does not require radiologic guidance equipment.

Indications

Suspicion of septic arthritis, either pyogenic or tuberculous, is by far the most important indication for PBS.[32,33] In such conditions PBS is indicated when a specific diagnosis cannot be obtained with usual clinical and biologic examinations and when findings of joint fluid analysis are inconclusive. Suspicion of synovial tumor, especially pigmented villonodular synovitis, is an uncommon situation in the shoulder but a good indication for PBS. PBS appears very useful in differentiating amyloidosis from arthritis in patients receiving long-term hemodialysis for chronic renal failure. It is also occasionally indicated to identify the destructive arthropathy called *Milwaukee shoulder*. Some other conditions, such

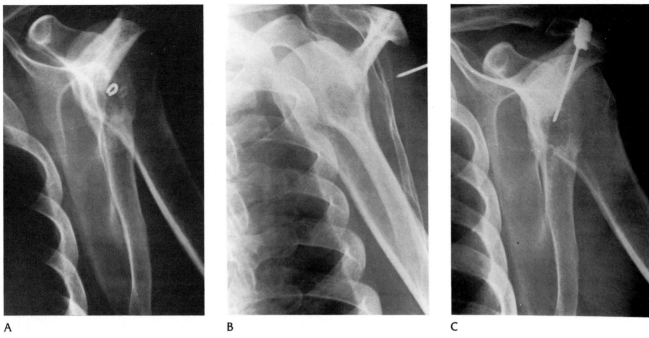

A   B   C

Figure 1G-8 Biopsy under fluoroscopic guidance of a lytic lesion of the humeral head. **A.** Roentgeno-graphic control with a metallic reference mark. **B, C.** The approach is perpendicular to the bone.

as gout, sarcoidosis, primary amyloidosis, and less often metastatic cancer, occasionally may also be diagnosed with PBS. The nonspecificity of synovial alterations in rheumatic disease has already been emphasized.[34] Even the most typical pathologic features of rheumatoid synovitis are not completely specific and may be encountered in other rheumatic diseases.[35]

Technique

GENERAL CONSIDERATIONS

PBS of the glenohumeral joint can be performed on an outpatient basis. It is accomplished under fluoroscopic guidance and local anesthesia. Preoperative evaluation must include plain films, CT, and when necessary MRI. CT combined with arthrography is very useful in localizing synovial proliferation before biopsy. PBS is performed under local anesthesia using conventional single-plane fluoroscopic guidance. The biopsy instrument consists of a 14-gauge (7.5 cm) Tru-Cut needle. The procedure always begins with a conventional arthrogram, which facilitates introduction of the biopsy instruments into the joint.

TECHNIQUE

The patient is positioned supine under the fluoroscope with the hand in external rotation anchored with a sandbag. The joint is sampled through a superoanterior approach.[32,33] The approach is through the rotator cuff interval, between the supraspinatus tendon and the long head of the biceps posteriorly and the subscapularis anteriorly. The external rotation of the shoulder protects the long head of the biceps tendon. Because of the superficial location of the shoulder, the Tru-Cut needle can be inserted directly into the joint. The needle is inserted at a point equidistant from the acromioclavicular joint and the coracoid process and 1.5 cm lateral to the vertical line passing through the glenohumeral joint space. The needle is advanced downward, 20° to 30° posteriad, and slightly mediad (Fig. 1G-9). The needle must reach the bone and then slide over the anterior and the medial aspect of the humeral head (Fig. 1G-10).

Results

Few data are available on results of PBS of the shoulder joint.[35] The glenohumeral joint space is tight and access to the synovium is more restricted than in other large appendicular joints.[36] Failure to obtain true synovial tissue is most often encountered in degenerative joint disease or other conditions commonly associated with fibrous atrophy of the synovium. The significant hypertrophy of the synovial membrane commonly found in rheumatic diseases and septic arthritis explains the higher success rate of PBS in these conditions.

Complications

Complications of PBS are rare. Some patients experience mild pain and some tenderness in the days following the

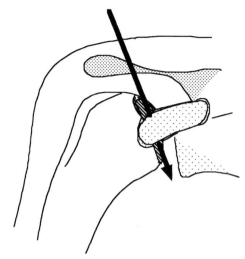

Figure 1G-9 Approach for PBS of the glenohumeral joint.

procedure. Joint effusion and hemarthrosis are rare. Strict preventive precautions make the development of secondary septic arthritis unlikely; however, the risk of this infection is higher for patients with immune deficiency, especially those who are undergoing hemodialysis for chronic renal failure.

PERCUTANEOUS DRAINAGE OF ABSCESSES IN MUSCULOSKELETAL INFECTIONS

Percutaneous drainage of abscesses (PDA) combines the principles of surgical drainage with those of vascular catheterization and percutaneous biopsy. PDA has proved to be as successful as surgical drainage in many cases and has much lower morbidity and mortality rates.[37–39]

PDA is indicated for soft tissue abscesses that are re-

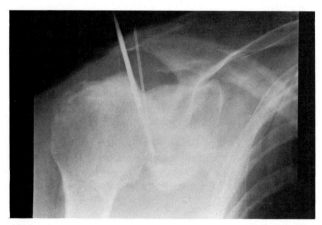

Figure 1G-10 Example of PBS of the glenohumeral joint in a Milwaukee shoulder.

fractory to medical treatment, when fistulization of the abscess into an adjacent organ may be dangerous, or when there is compression of a vital structure. PDA may also be indicated for soft tissue abscesses associated with musculoskeletal infections.

The basic steps of percutaneous abscess drainage are: percutaneous approach, pus aspiration, and drainage catheter placement.

Two single-use sets of drainage catheters are especially convenient for PDA in musculoskeletal lesions: the Ring-Mac Lean Sump (COOK Inc.)[24] and the van Sonnenberg Sump (MEDITECH)[38,39] Approach to the lesion may be performed under fluoroscopic, CT, or ultrasound guidance. When possible, drainage should be performed. A small-caliber needle (22-gauge) is first advanced and inserted into the abscess. Pus is aspirated and contrast medium opacification of the abscess is performed to help determine the need for drainage and to select the appropriate shape of the drainage catheter. A soft angiographic 4.8 French guidewire is introduced through the needle. The catheter is then advanced over the guidewire and assumes its coiled shape. When the catheter is in the abscess, pus is evacuated as completely as possible. The cavity is then irrigated with a smaller volume of saline than the total volume of aspirated pus. This minimizes the risk of bacteremia secondary to increased pressure in the abscess. A stiff exchange wire (Amplatz wire) with a flexible atraumatic distal extremity is especially well-fitted for PDA. Coaxial dilators of increasing size are used to enlarge the needle track. This facilitates placement of the drainage catheter, especially in abscesses associated with musculoskeletal infections, which usually have a thick wall. The drainage catheter itself and an internal hollow stiffening cannula are then introduced and pushed over the Amplatz guidewire. Advance of the drainage catheter is followed on the fluoroscopic screen. While the drainage catheter is advanced, the stiffening cannula is progressively withdrawn to allow the drainage catheter to wind in the abscess cavity. To check for correct placement of the drainage catheter, the abscess cavity may be opacified (Fig. 1G-11) through the double-lumen circuit. Sump-type drainage catheters are recommended for initial treatment of most abscesses. Their double-lumen configuration has two main advantages over single-lumen drainage catheters. First, the cavity can be actively drained with permanent suction and less risk of catheter clogging, and second, sump drainage catheters are less gravity-dependent than single-lumen drainage catheters.

The abscess cavity is washed out three times daily in the following days and then twice daily. Permanent suction is placed between washes. Duration of the drainage depends on the size of the collection, on the causative microorganism, and on the appearance of the abscess cavity on follow-up CT or MRI. It is usually short (several

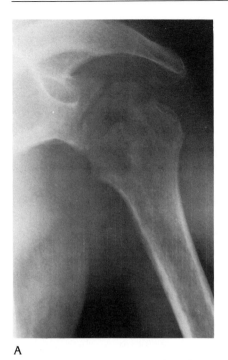
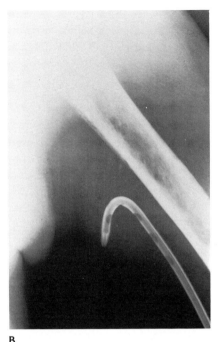
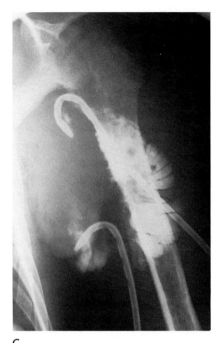

A   B   C

Figure 1G-11 **A.** Large tuberculous abscesses of the shoulder joint. **B, C.** Drainage catheter placement with opacification of two abscess cavities.

days) for pyogenic infections and longer (3 weeks) in cases of tuberculosis. Follow-up CT is performed at 4, 7, and 14 days, to follow the shrinkage of the collection. Drainage and washes are continued as long as a significant abscess cavity is seen on CT. PDA seems to be a safe and efficient procedure in our limited experience.

PERCUTANEOUS REMOVAL OF OSTEOID OSTEOMAS UNDER COMPUTED TOMOGRAPHIC GUIDANCE

Osteoid osteomas are small, benign osteogenic tumors which are responsible for debilitating long-term pain. They account for 11 percent of bone neoplasms in the series of the Mayo Clinic.[40] Osteoid osteomas are usually readily identified by means of their clinical and radiographic features. If they are left untreated or incompletely removed, the symptoms may persist for years. There are scattered reports of spontaneous regression of lesions presenting with the clinical and radiologic features of osteoid osteomas; however, biopsy proof of such lesions is lacking. The usual treatment consists of complete surgical excision of the nidus. Results are obtained rapidly, but surgical treatment is not completely free of risk and discomfort. It may require an extended skin incision or extensive bone resection, especially when the tumor is relatively inaccessible. The nidus may also be

difficult to localize at surgery because of the presence of an extensive peripheral reactive sclerosis. Perioperative radionuclide bone scan and tetracycline fluorescence techniques have been devised to help the surgeon localize the nidus, but these techniques are time consuming and cumbersome. Recurrence of symptoms is common in case of incomplete nidus removal. Several authors recently proposed percutaneous treatment of osteoid osteomas under CT guidance.[41–46]

Technique

In all cases, the nidus must be precisely localized with plain radiographs, bone scintigraphy, and CT, using 1- or 2-mm thick slices. Patients are treated under general anesthesia or regional block whenever possible (block of the brachial plexus with a supraclavicular approach).[47] There are different techniques of percutaneous removal of osteoid osteomas under CT guidance.[41–49] These techniques may be divided into two main categories, discussed next.

NIDUS REMOVAL WITH RADIOFREQUENCY ELECTRODES

Radio-frequency electrodes placed in the nidus through a trephine needle have been used by Rosenthal and coauthors.[49] The radio-frequency electrode contains an internal thermistor for simultaneous temperature measurement. The radio-frequency generator is used to heat the tip of the electrode to 90°C for 4 minutes.

NIDUS REMOVAL THROUGH BONE TREPHINATION

Mechanical removal of osteoid osteomas through bone trephination has been proposed by several authors.[41–44] Different trephine needles were used. Doyle and King used a 4-mm bore Craig needle (Codman and Shurtleff).[44] Voto and Mosheiff used a Corb needle (Zimmer).[41,46] French authors use larger needles with a 1-cm large introducing needle which is inserted on the cortical bone, bone drills to approach the nidus, and a trephine needle of 7-mm internal diameter to remove the nidus.[43,45,47] This procedure is performed in the CT suite. It is very useful to combine CT guidance with conventional fluoroscopic guidance by placing a mobile fluoroscopic C arm between the CT gantry and CT table. By displacing the CT table, alternative CT and fluoroscopic controls can be obtained. Fluoroscopic guidance is especially useful during the approach, whereas CT is necessary to check for complete nidus removal. The large introducing needle is placed against the bone, and a metallic wire is inserted into the bone at the margin of the nidus using a pneumatic hand drill. Perfect placement of this metallic wire is especially critical for successful completion of the procedure since the bone drills and trephine needle will then be inserted in the same track using a coaxial Seldinger technique.[45] When the nidus is located near a joint which could be damaged, Railhac and Assoun use a smaller trocar of 3- or 4-mm diameter.[45,47]

Results

Rosenthal used the technique of nidus removal with radio-frequency electrodes in four patients, and completely relieved the symptoms of three.[49] Percutaneous nidus removal through bone trephination was successfully performed in 23 of 24 patients in the series of Assoun's group.[47] We have a short experience of four cases with this technique, all successful. In our limited experience and in the recent report of Assoun's group this procedure is relatively safe, except for one case of the Assoun series in which subsequent surgical stabilization was necessary to prevent secondary fracture. No complications of these percutaneous treatments have been encountered to date; furthermore, this technique has several advantages over an open surgical procedure: hospitalization is shorter, bone resection is more limited, and the percutaneous treatment is more cost-effective.

References

1. PATTERSON RL, DARRACH W: Treatment of acute bursitis by needle irrigation. *J Bone Joint Surg* 19A:933, 1937.
2. COMFORT TH, ARAFILES RP: Barbotage of the shoulder with image-intensified fluoroscopic control of needle placement for calcific tendinitis. *Clin Orthop* 135:171, 1978.
3. NORMANDIN C, SEBAN E, LAREDO JD: Aspirations-triturations de calcifications tendineuses douloureuses d'épaules après echec des traitements médicaux: Apropos de 69 cas. *Rheumatology* 5:76, 1987.
4. NORMANDIN C, SEBAN E, LAREDO JD: Aspiration of tendinous calcific deposits, in Bard M, Laredo JD (eds): *Interventional Radiology in Bone and Joint,* Vienna, Springer-Verlag, 1988, pp 258–270.
5. GROSS D, SIEGRIST H: Lavage des calcifications chez la periarthrite de l'épaule (Abstract). *Rev Rheum* (suppl):853, 1981.
6. CABANEL G: La ponction aspiration lavage ou trituration: Une modalité thérapeutique des tendinites calcifiantes rebelles de l'épaule. *Memoire CES de Rhumatologie,* Paris, 1983.
7. MALONEY MD, SAUSER DD, HANSON EC: Adhesive capsulitis of the wrist: Arthrographic diagnosis. *Radiology* 167:187, 1988.
8. NEVIASER JS: Adhesive capsulitis of the shoulder: Pathologic findings in periarthritis of the shoulder. *Br J Bone Joint Surg* 27:211, 1945.
9. GOLDMAN AB, DINES DM, WARREN RE: Capsular deformities: Adhesive capsulitis, in *Shoulder Arthrography: Technique, Diagnosis, and Clinical Correlation,* Boston, Little, Brown, 1982, pp 139–149.
10. EKELUND AL RYDELL N: Combination treatment for adhesive capsulitis of the shoulder. *Clin Orthop* 282:105, 1992.
11. NEVIASER TJ: Adhesive capsulitis. *Orthop Clin North Am* 18:439, 1987.
12. RICHARDSON AT: The painful shoulder. *Proc R Soc Med* 68:731, 1975.

13. STEINBROCKER O, ARGYROS TG: Frozen shoulder: Treatment by local injection of depot corticosteroids. *Arch Phys Med Rehabil* 55:209, 1974.

14. LOYD JA LOYD HM: Adhesive capsulitis of the shoulder: Arthrographic diagnosis and treatment. *South Med J* 6:879, 1983.

15. JACOBS LGH, BARTON MAJ, WALLACE WA: Intra-articular distension and steroids in the management of capsulitis of the shoulder. *Br Med J* 302:1498, 1991.

16. FAREED DO, GALLIVAN WR: Office management of frozen shoulder syndrome. *Clin Orthop* 242:177, 1989.

17. ANDREN L, LUNDBERG BJ: Treatment of rigid shoulder by joint distension during arthrography. *Acta Orthop Scand* 36:45, 1965.

18. WALLACE WA, ECHEVERRI A: Intra-articular distension with local anesthetic, steroid and air in the treatment of capsulitis of the shoulder, in *Professional Postgraduate Services,* Tokyo 25:204–208, 1987.

19. SMITH DL, CAMPBELL SM: Painful shoulder syndromes: Diagnosis and management. *J Gen Intern Med* 7:328, 1992.

20. CORBEIL V, DUSSAULT RG, LEDUC BE: Capsulite retractile de l'epaule: Etude comparative de l'arthrographie avec corticotherapie intraarticulaire avec ou sans distension capsulaire. *Can Assoc Radiol J* 43:127, 1992.

21. LAREDO JD, BARD M, CYWINER-GOLENZER C: Percutaneous biopsy of musculo-skeletal lesions, in Bard M, Laredo JD (eds): *Interventional Radiology in Bone and Joint,* Vienna, Springer-Verlag, 1988, pp 3–50.

22. RESNICK D: Needle biopsy of bone, in Resnick D, Niwayama G (eds): *Diagnosis of Bone and Joint Disorders,* Philadelphia, Saunders, 1981, pp 692–701.

23. MURPHY WA, DESTOUET JM, GILULA LA: Percutaneous skeletal biopsy: A procedure for radiologists. Results, review and recommendations. *Radiology* 139:545, 1981.

24. GANGI A, KASTLER BA, BOUJAN F, ET AL: Interventional radiology guided with combination of CT and fluoroscopy: Advantages and indications (Abstract). *Radiology* 185 (Suppl):360, 1992.

25. ACKERMAN W: Vertebral trephine biopsy. *Ann Surg* 143:373, 1956.

26. CRAIG FS: Vertebral body biopsy. *J Bone Joint Surg* 65A:93, 1983.

27. FYFE IS, HENRY AP, MULHOLLAND RC: Closed vertebral biopsy. *J Bone Joint Surg* 65B:140, 1983.

28. LAREDO JD, BARD M: Thoracic spine: Percutaneous trephine biopsy. *Radiology* 160:485, 1986.

29. MAC LARNON JC: Biopsy of the spine using a needle with a rigid guide wire. *Clin Radiol* 33:189, 1982.

30. TURKEL H, BETHELL FH: Biopsy of bone marrow performed by a new and simple instrument. *J Lab Clin Med* 28:1246, 1943.

31. FORESTIER J: Instrumentation pour medical. *CR Soc Biol (Paris)* 110:186, 1932.

32. LAREDO JD, BARD M: Percutaneous biopsy of the synovial membrane, in Bard M, Laredo JD (eds): *Interventional Radiology in Bone and Joint,* Vienna, Springer-Verlag, 1988, pp 51–64.

33. BEAULE V, LAREDO JD, CYWINER-GOLENZER C, ET AL.: Percutaneous biopsy of the synovial membrane. *Radiology* 177:581, 1990.

34. SHERMAN MS: Non-specificity of synovial reactions. *Bull Hosp Joint Dis* 12:110, 1951.

35. GOLDENBERG DL, COHEN AS: Synovial membrane histopathology in the differential diagnosis of rheumatoid arthritis, gout, pseudogout, systemic lupus erythematosus, infectious arthritis and degenerative joint disease. *Medicine* 57:239, 1978.

36. MOON MS, KIM I, LEE HS, ET AL.: Synovial biopsy by Franklin-Silverman needle. *Clin Orthop* 150:224, 1980.

37. McLEAN GK, MACKIE JA, FREIMAN DB: Enterocutaneous fistulae: Interventional radiologic management. *AJR* 138:615, 1982.

38. VAN SONNENBERG E, MUELLER PR, FERRUCCI JT JR: Percutaneous drainage of 250 abdominal abscesses and fluid collections. Part I: Results, failures and complications. *Radiology* 151:337, 1984.

39. MUELLER PR, VAN SONNENBERG E, FERRUCCI JT JR: Percutaneous drainage of 250 abdominal abscesses and fluid collections. Part II: Current procedural concepts. *Radiology* 151:343, 1984.

40. DAHLIN DC: Osteoid osteoma, in Thomas C (ed): *Bone Tumors,* 2d ed, Springfield, Thomas, 1967, pp 62–69.

41. VOTO SJ, COOK AJ, WEINER DS: Treatment of osteoid osteoma by computed tomography guided excision in pediatric patients. *J Pediatr Orthop* 10:510, 1990.

42. ASSOUN J, RAILHAC JJ, BONNEVIALE P: Osteoid osteoma: Percutaneous resection with CT guidance. *Radiology* 188:541, 1993.

43. MAZOYER JF, KOHLER R, BOSSARD D: Osteoid osteoma: CT-guided percutaneous treatment. *Radiology* 181:269, 1991.

44. DOYLE T, KING K: Percutaneous removal of osteoid osteomas using CT control. *Clin Radiol* 40:514, 1989.

45. RAILHAC JJ, ASSOUN J, POEY C: Ablation percutanée des osteomes osteoïdes sous contrôle tomodensitometrique. *Rev Im Med* 4:463, 1992.

46. MOSHEIFF R, LIEBERGALB M, ZIV I: Osteoid osteoma of the scapula. *Clin Orthop* 262:129, 1991.

47. ASSOUN J, RAILHAC JJ, BONNEVIALLE P: Osteoid osteoma: Percutaneous resection with CT guidance. *Radiology* 188:541, 1993.

48. KOHLER R, MAZOYER JF, BESSE JL: The treatment of osteoid osteoma by percutaneous drill resection under CT scanning control. *Fr J Orthop Surg* 4:251, 1990.

49. ROSENTHAL DJ, ALEXANDER A, ROSENBERG AE: Ablation of osteoid osteomas with a percutaneous placed electrode: A new procedure. *Radiology* 183:29, 1992.

2 | NORMAL VARIANTS AND ARTIFACTS

Bttavin Jankharia
Theodore E. Keats
David J. Sartoris

VARIANTS

Knowledge of radiographic anatomy is the basis of accurate diagnosis. Familiarity with normal anatomic variation is an essential part of the radiologist's background of roentgen anatomy. This is particularly true since Mother Nature has been perverse in not structuring all of us alike—and, in fact, not even necessarily bilaterally symmetric.

A background knowledge of normal anatomic variation as it is manifested radiographically marks experienced radiologists from novices and helps them avoid many errors of commission that otherwise would lead to unnecessary diagnostic investigation and treatment.

In this chapter, a variety of anatomic variations, problems of image projection and other technical pitfalls, pertaining to conventional radiology, computed tomography (CT), magnetic resonance imaging (MRI), and CT or MRI arthrography, that might be mistaken for disease are illustrated. Many images have been taken from Dr. Keats' book *An Atlas of Normal Roentgen Variants That May Simulate Disease,* fifth edition.[1] The variants are classified according to imaging modality and specific patterns.

PLAIN RADIOGRAPHY

Ossification Centers

Ossification centers can trap unwary readers and simulate fractures.

CORACOID PROCESS

The coracoid process starts ossifying from a center in its middle in the first year of life and fuses to the rest of the scapula by age 13 to 15 years.[2–4] Another subcoracoid center appears at puberty and fuses by the 25th year (Figs. 2-1, 2-2). Sometimes, a third center may appear at the tip (Fig. 2-3), again at puberty, fusing by age 25 years.[2]

ACROMION PROCESS

The base of the acromion is formed by a normal extension from the spine of the scapula. The rest of the acromion is formed from two centers which occur at puberty (see Fig. 2-1B) and unite with the extension from the spine by age 25.[2,3] One of these secondary ossification centers may persist into adult life as a separate bone called the *os acromiale*,[5–7] and it is often mistaken for a fracture of the acromion process when seen in the axillary projection (Fig. 2-4). It is usually, but not invariably, bilateral, and its presence has been seen to be associated with an increased incidence of the impingement syndrome[6,7] usually due to instability, with consequent degeneration and repeated trauma of the rotator cuff.

GLENOID

At puberty, a horseshoe-shaped center occurs in the rim of the lower part of the glenoid cavity. A variable area of the upper third of the glenoid cavity is ossified from the subcoracoid center which occurs at the same time (Figs. 2-5, 2-6).[2] The superior center may persist unfused into adult life (Figs. 2-7, 2-8, p. 121). During growth, the glenoid margin may often seem irregular (Fig. 2-9, p. 121).

INFERIOR ANGLE OF SCAPULA

Centers occur at the inferior angle of the scapula by age 14 to 20 years and fuse to the scapula by 22 to 25 years of age (Fig. 2-10, p. 122).[2,3]

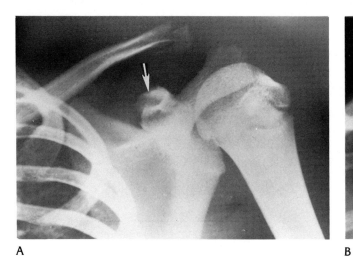

A

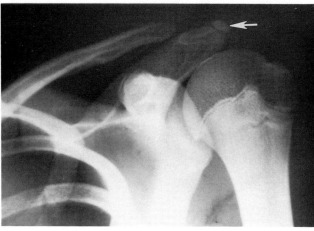

B

Figure 2-1 Normal appearance of the coracoid processes during growth. **A.** A 13-year-old boy before appearance of the subcoracoid center (*arrow*). **B.** A 15-year-old boy. Note secondary ossification centers for coracoid and acromion processes (*arrow*). (*Atlas of Normal Roentgen Variants That May Simulate Disease, Chicago, Mosby-Year Book, 1992, with permission.*)

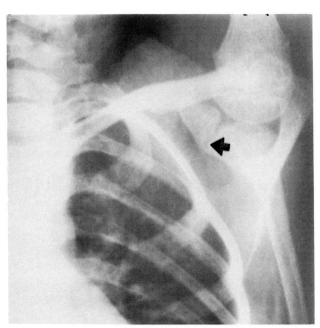

Figure 2-2 Appearance of the ossification center of the coracoid process in adolescence, before fusion occurs (*arrow*). It may be mistaken for a fracture. (*Atlas of Normal Roentgen Variants That May Simulate Disease, Chicago, Mosby-Year Book, 1992, with permission.*)

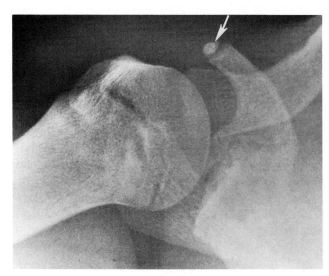

Figure 2-3 The secondary apophysis of the tip of the coracoid (*arrow*). (*Atlas of Normal Roentgen Variants That May Simulate Disease, Chicago, Mosby-Year Book, 1992, with permission.*)

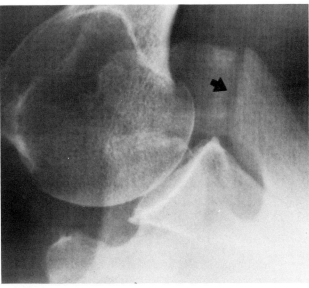

A

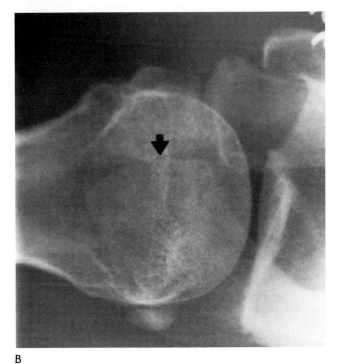

B

Figure 2-4 **A, B.** Two examples of the os acromiale (*arrows*). *(Atlas of Normal Roentgen Variants That May Simulate Disease, Chicago, Mosby-Year Book, 1992, with permission.)*

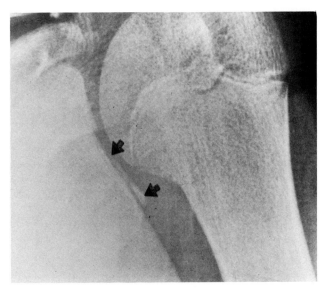

Figure 2-5 The ring apophysis of the glenoid fossa (*arrows*). *(Atlas of Normal Roentgen Variants That May Simulate Disease, Chicago, Mosby-Year Book, 1992, with permission.)*

HUMERAL HEAD

The humeral head starts ossifying by age 6 months; the centers for the greater and lesser tuberosities appear at 2 to 3 and 4 to 5 years, respectively. They fuse to each other by age 6 and to the humeral shaft by age 18 to 20 (Fig. 2-11, p. 123).[2,3]

MEDIAL END OF CLAVICLE

The ossification center of the medial end of the clavicle appears at age 18 to 20 years and fuses by age 25.[2,3] This may appear irregular (Fig. 2-12, p. 123).

Normal Defects, Thin Bones, Holes, Channels

NORMAL AREAS OF RADIOLUCENCY OR TRABECULAR PATTERN SIMULATING DISEASE

The scapular wing (Fig. 2-13, p. 124) and the greater tuberosity (Fig. 2-14, p. 124) may appear radiolucent and simulate osteolytic or cystic lesions. The scapular wing radiolucency is due to an area of relatively thin bone. The greater tuberosity lucency (humeral pseudocyst) represents an area of rarefaction in the lateral aspect of the humerus adjacent to the greater tuberosity, the inferior margin of which represents the fusion line of the lateral portion of the epiphysis of the greater tuberosity. The position of this lucency with respect to the fusion line helps differentiate it from a true lesion.[8] The trabecular pattern at the neck of the scapula may simulate a fracture in some instances (Fig. 2-15, p. 124).

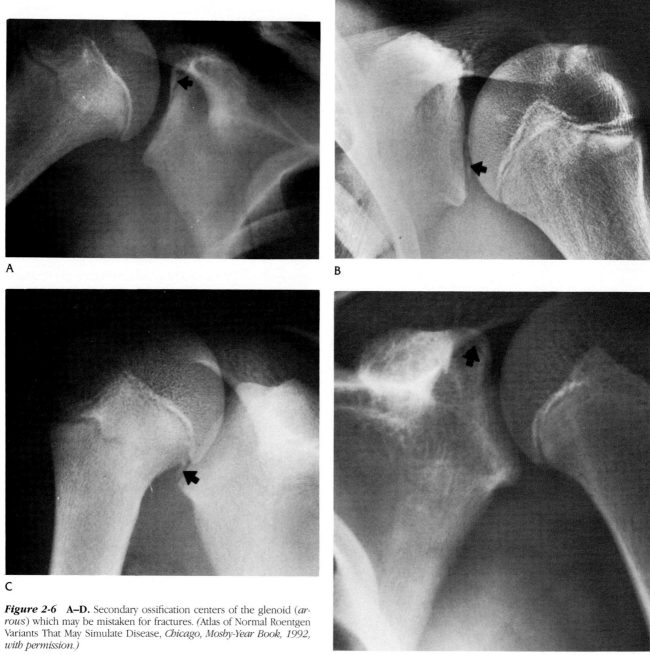

Figure 2-6 **A–D.** Secondary ossification centers of the glenoid (*arrows*) which may be mistaken for fractures. (*Atlas of Normal Roentgen Variants That May Simulate Disease, Chicago, Mosby-Year Book, 1992, with permission.*)

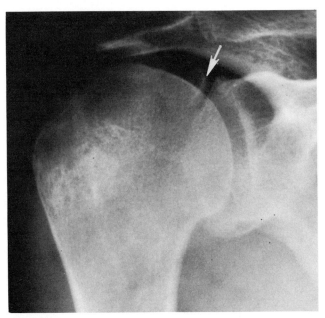

Figure 2-7 Failure of fusion of the apophysis at the superior margin of the glenoid in an adult (*arrow*). (*Atlas of Normal Roentgen Variants That May Simulate Disease, Chicago, Mosby-Year Book, 1992, with permission.*)

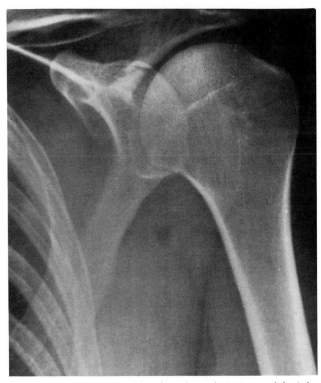

Figure 2-8 Persistence of the glenoid apophysis in an adult. (*Atlas of Normal Roentgen Variants That May Simulate Disease, Chicago, Mosby-Year Book, 1992, with permission.*)

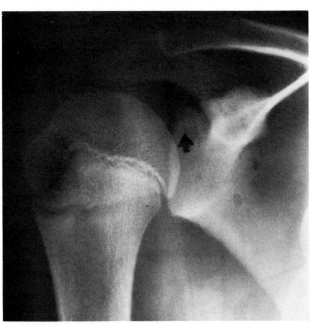

Figure 2-9 Normal irregularity of the growing glenoid processes in a 12-year-old boy (*arrow*). (*Atlas of Normal Roentgen Variants That May Simulate Disease, Chicago, Mosby-Year Book, 1992, with permission.*)

VASCULAR OR NEURAL CHANNELS SIMULATING LESIONS

Vascular channels appear as lucencies and may easily simulate fractures, especially in the body of the scapula (Fig. 2-16, p. 125) and clavicle. The latter variant is usually seen when the nutrient channel of the clavicle lies inferiorly or superiorly instead of in its normal posterior site (Fig. 2-17, p. 125). The canal of the middle supraclavicular nerve in the clavicle (Fig. 2-18, p. 125) may occasionally simulate an abnormality.

DEFECTS, NOTCHES, AND FORAMENS

Scapular foramens are well known and may be due to ossification of the superior transverse ligament or to disturbances in ossification in the body of the scapula (Fig. 2-19, p. 126). These defects may range in size from 3 to 35 mm and have to be differentiated from myeloma or metastatic lesions.[9,10]

Humeral notches are known to occur in children, usually between the ages of 10 and 16 years, situated 1 to 2 cm distal to the epiphyseal line in the medial cortex (Fig. 2-20, p. 126).[11] Though usually sharp, they may occasionally be indistinct and may be mistaken for aggressive lesions. Though the true nature of the lesion is not known, its location near the insertion of the capsule and bilateral symmetry suggest that it is an anatomic finding related to the fibroskeletal attachment.[11]

Prominent Insertions

Many areas of muscle, ligament, or tendon origins or insertions may appear irregular, thick, or deepened, sim-

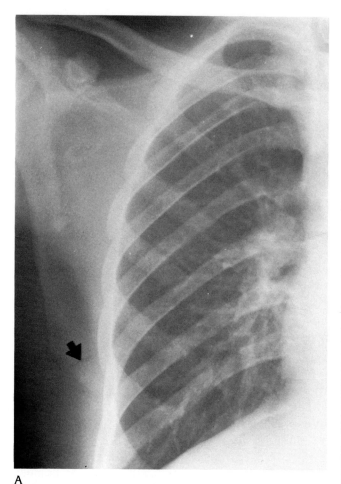

A

Figure 2-10 **A, B.** Two examples of secondary ossification centers of the inferior angle of the scapula in 16-year-old boys (*arrows*). *(Atlas of Normal Roentgen Variants That May Simulate Disease,* Chicago, *Mosby-Year Book, 1992, with permission.)*

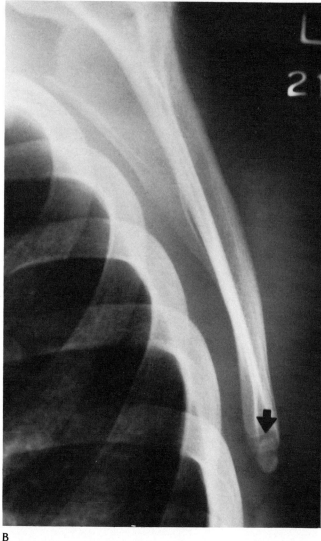

B

ulating disease. The rhomboid fossa occurs at the site of attachment of the rhomboid ligament, between the first rib and the clavicle. It is not necessarily bilaterally symmetric and may simulate bone destruction (Fig. 2-21, p. 127). It may also simulate a cavitary lesion of the lung. The attachment of the coracoclavicular ligament produces an irregular area on the inferior aspect of the clavicle (Fig. 2-22, p. 127). The prominent insertions of the deltoid muscle on the lateral aspect of the humerus may simulate periostitis or cortical thickening (Fig. 2-23, p. 128). Normal excrescences occur at the lower margin of the neck of the scapula and may occasionally be mistaken for periostitis (Fig. 2-24, p. 128).

Variants of Projection and Overlap

Overlapping of various normal structures on radiography or variations in radiographic positioning may produce apparent abnormalities. Positioning the arms in children in external rotation during shoulder radiography may

produce an appearance of acromioclavicular separation (Fig. 2-25, p. 129). Similarly, the conventional positioning of the arms during chest radiography in children may produce an appearance simulating shoulder dislocation (Fig. 2-26, p. 129). Even in adults, this appearance may occasionally be simulated (Fig. 2-27, p. 130).

With the arm of a neonate externally rotated, the shadow of the bicipital groove may simulate periostitis (Fig. 2-28, p. 130). In adults, projection of the cortex of the humeral neck can also simulate periostitis (Fig. 2-29, p. 131). Deep bicipital grooves may also be mistaken for abnormalities in children (Fig. 2-30, p. 131).

Variable, Atypical, and Pseudoarticulations

Sometimes articulations between the scapula and ribs may occur (Fig. 2-31, p. 132). Coracoclavicular joints are also known to occur as true synovial articulations (Fig. 2-32, p. 132) most commonly in Malay and Chinese

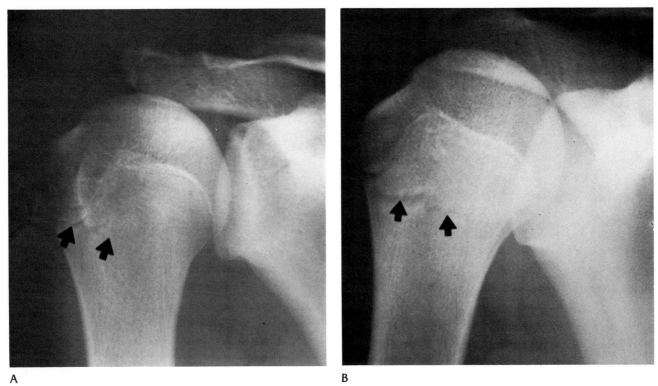

A   B

Figure 2-11   The normal epiphyseal lines of the proximal humerus in a 17-year-old boy (*arrows*). **A.** External rotation, **B,** internal rotation. The epiphyseal line in **B** at times is mistaken for a fracture. *(Atlas of Normal Roentgen Variants That May Simulate Disease, Chicago, Mosby-Year Book, 1992, with permission.)*

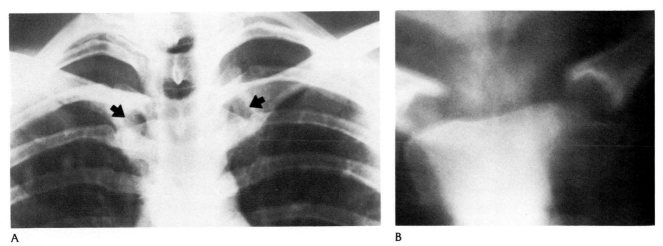

A   B

Figure 2-12   Normal irregular appearance of the medial ends of the clavicles in an 18-year-old man (*arrows*). This appearance, before completion of development, may be misinterpreted as evidence of disease. **A.** Plain film, **B,** laminagram. *(Atlas of Normal Roentgen Variants That May Simulate Disease, Chicago, Mosby-Year Book, 1992, with permission.)*

peoples[12] and usually are not significant. Marked calcification of the coracoclavicular ligament may occur (Fig. 2-33, p. 133)[13] which sometimes simulates a joint (pseudojoint).

The acromioclavicular joints show wide variation in configuration. Normally (Fig. 2-34A, p. 133), the inferior aspect of the clavicle is at the same level as the inferior aspect of the acromion. In a small percentage, the distal end of the clavicle may lie above or below the acromion (Fig. 2-34, p. 133).[14] Some individuals have wide acromioclavicular joints (Figs. 2-35, 2-36, p. 133). Comparison with the opposite side usually resolves the problem.

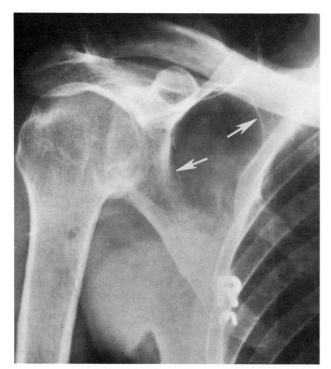

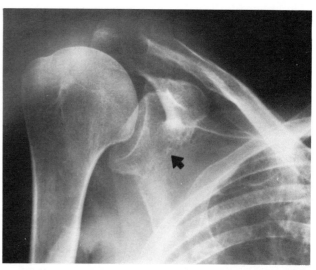

Figure 2-15 Simulated fracture of the scapula produced by trabecular pattern (*arrow*). (Atlas of Normal Roentgen Variants That May Simulate Disease, *Chicago, Mosby-Year Book, 1992, with permission.*)

Figure 2-13 Normal radiolucency of the wing of the scapula, which may resemble a cystic lesion (*arrows*). (Atlas of Normal Roentgen Variants That May Simulate Disease, *Chicago, Mosby-Year Book, 1992, with permission.*)

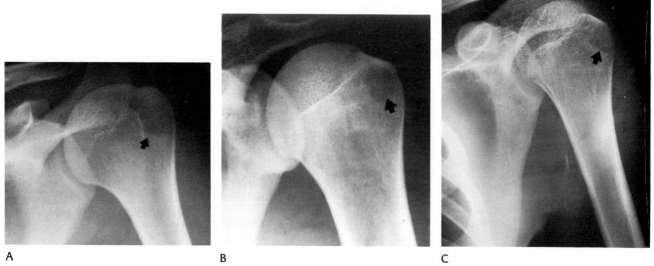

A

B

C

Figure 2-14 **A–C.** Examples of simulated destruction of the greater tuberosity (*arrows*). (Atlas of Normal Roentgen Variants That May Simulate Disease, *Chicago, Mosby-Year Book, 1992, with permission.*)

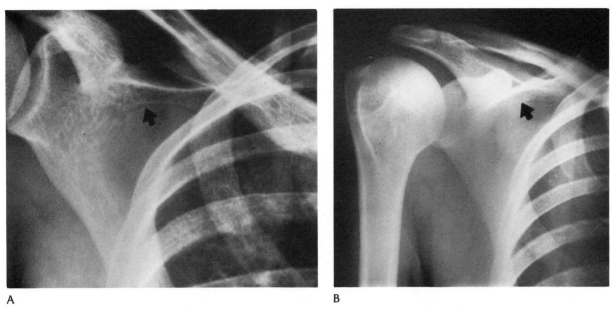

A   B

Figure 2-16 **A, B.** Two examples of vascular channels that may be mistaken for fractures (*arrows*). *(*Atlas of Normal Roentgen Variants That May Simulate Disease, *Chicago, Mosby-Year Book, 1992, with permission.)*

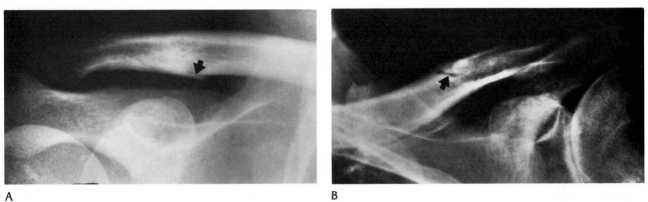

A   B

Figure 2-17   The nutrient canal of the clavicle, if seen on the inferior, **A,** or superior **B,** borders, may be mistaken for incomplete fractures (*arrows*). *(*Atlas of Normal Roentgen Variants That May Simulate Disease, *Chicago, Mosby-Year Book, 1992, with permission.)*

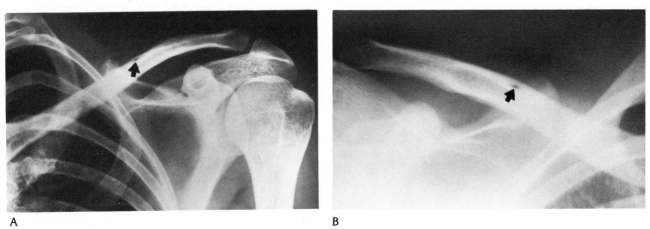

A   B

Figure 2-18 **A, B.** Two examples of the canal of the middle supraclavicular nerve (*arrows*). *(*Atlas of Normal Roentgen Variants That May Simulate Disease, *Chicago, Mosby-Year Book, 1992, with permission.)*

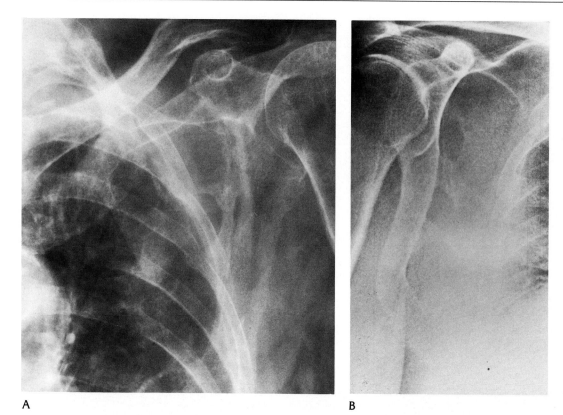

A   B

Figure 2-19 **A, B.** Developmental defects of the scapula that may be mistaken for a pathologic process. *(*Atlas of Normal Roentgen Variants That May Simulate Disease, *Chicago, Mosby-Year Book, 1992, with permission.)*

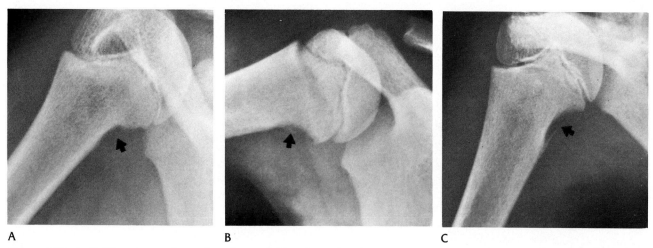

A   B   C

Figure 2-20 **A–C.** Bilateral upper humeral notches in children (*arrows*). *(*Atlas of Normal Roentgen Variants That May Simulate Disease, *Chicago, Mosby-Year Book, 1992, with permission.)*

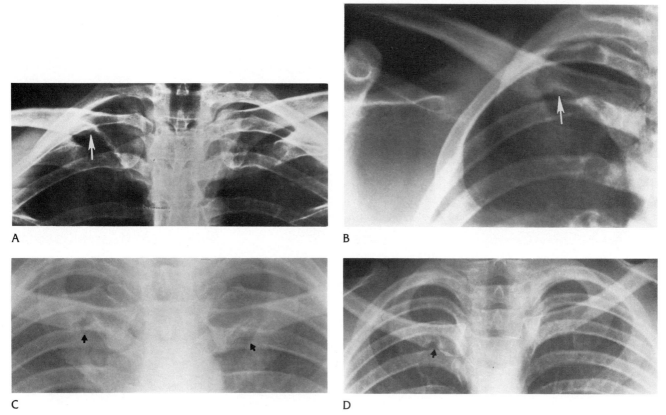

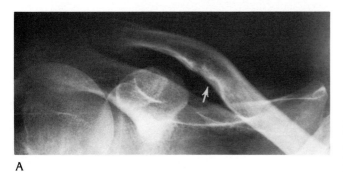

Figure 2-21 **A–D.** Examples of rhomboid fossas (*arrows*). *(*Atlas of Normal Roentgen Variants That May Simulate Disease, *Chicago, Mosby-Year Book, 1992, with permission.)*

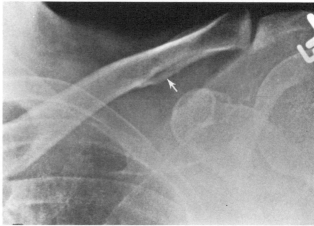

Figure 2-22 **A, B.** Grooves for the insertion of the coracoclavicular ligament (*arrows*). *(*Atlas of Normal Roentgen Variants That May Simulate Disease, *Chicago, Mosby-Year Book, 1992, with permission.)*

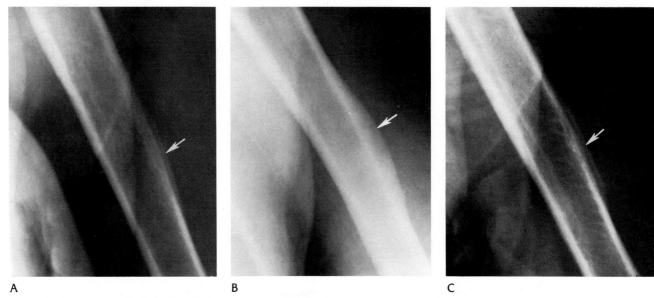

A

B

C

Figure 2-23 **A–C.** Prominent deltoid muscle insertions that may simulate periostitis (*arrows*). (Atlas of Normal Roentgen Variants That May Simulate Disease, *Chicago, Mosby-Year Book, 1992, with permission.*)

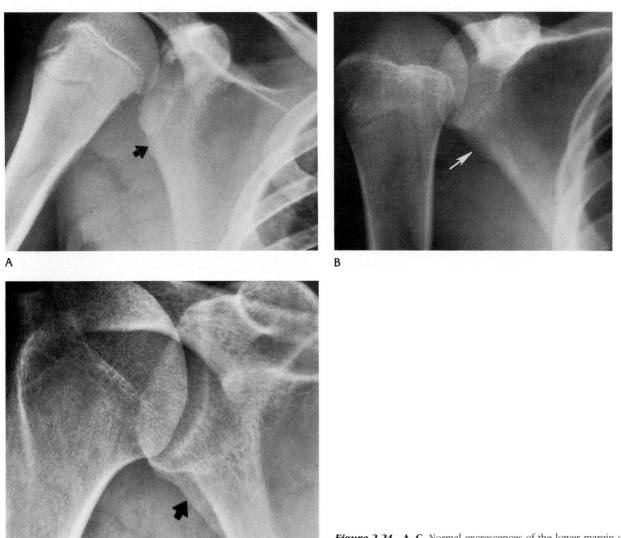

A

B

C

Figure 2-24 **A–C.** Normal excrescences of the lower margin of the neck of the scapula that may be mistaken for periostitis (*arrows*). (Atlas of Normal Roentgen Variants That May Simulate Disease, *Chicago, Mosby-Year Book, 1992, with permission.*)

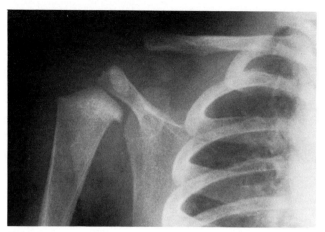

A

Figure 2-25 Positioning of the arms of children may produce an appearance simulating acromioclavicular separation. **A.** External rotation, **B,** internal rotation. (Atlas of Normal Roentgen Variants That May Simulate Disease, *Chicago, Mosby-Year Book, 1992, with permission.)*

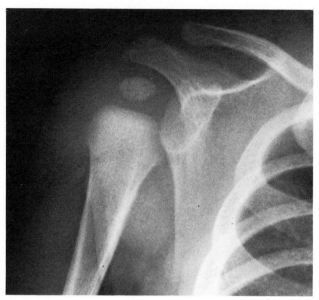

B

Figure 2-26 Conventional positioning of the arms for chest radiography may produce an appearance simulating dislocations of the shoulders in children. (Atlas of Normal Roentgen Variants That May Simulate Disease, *Chicago, Mosby-Year Book, 1992, with permission.)*

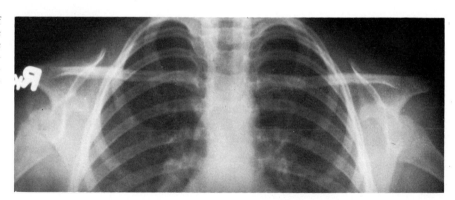

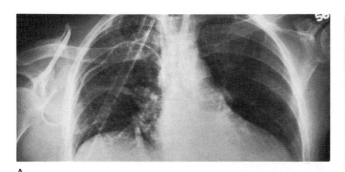

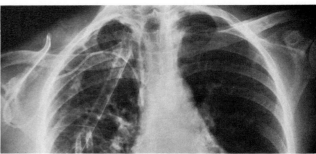

A

B

Figure 2-27 **A.** Simulated dislocation of the right shoulder secondary to positioning in an elderly person. **B.** Repeat examination shows improved relationships. *(Atlas of Normal Roentgen Variants That May Simulate Disease, Chicago, Mosby-Year Book, 1992, with permission.)*

Figure 2-28 **A, B.** Two examples of simulated periostitis produced by the shadow of the bicipital groove in neonates, seen with the arm externally rotated or elevated (*arrows*). *(Atlas of Normal Roentgen Variants That May Simulate Disease, Chicago, Mosby-Year Book, 1992, with permission.)*

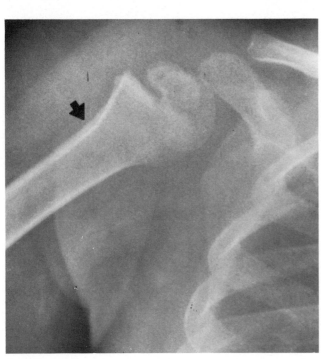

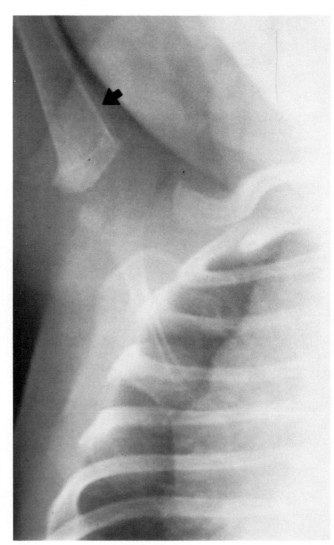

A

B

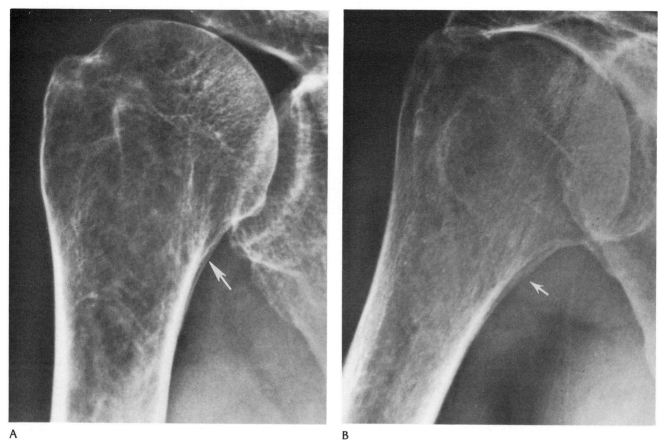

A   B

Figure 2-29 **A, B.** Two examples of how projection of the cortex of the humeral neck can simulate periostitis (*arrows*). *(Atlas of Normal Roentgen Variants That May Simulate Disease, Chicago, Mosby-Year Book, 1992, with permission.)*

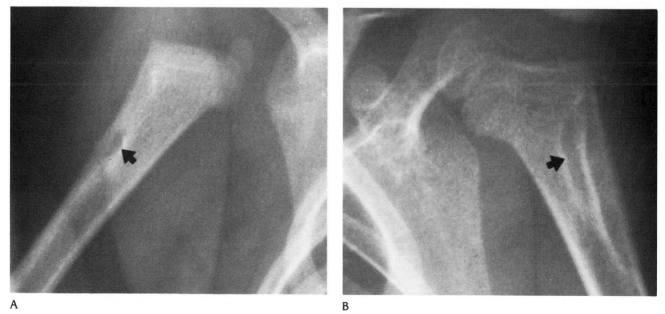

A   B

Figure 2-30 Deep bicipital grooves may be mistaken for an abnormality (*arrows*). Subjects are, **A,** 7 months old and, **B,** 2 years old. *(Atlas of Normal Roentgen Variants That May Simulate Disease, Chicago, Mosby-Year Book, 1992, with permission.)*

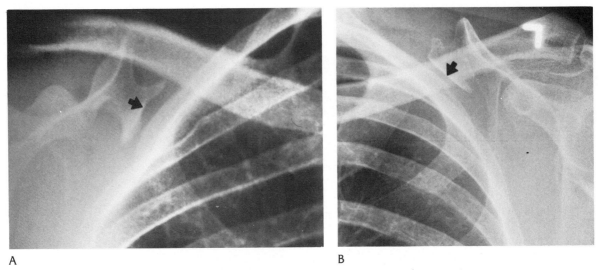

A

B

Figure 2-31 **A, B.** Two examples of articulations between the scapula and adjacent ribs (*arrows*). *(Atlas of Normal Roentgen Variants That May Simulate Disease, Chicago, Mosby-Year Book, 1992, with permission.)*

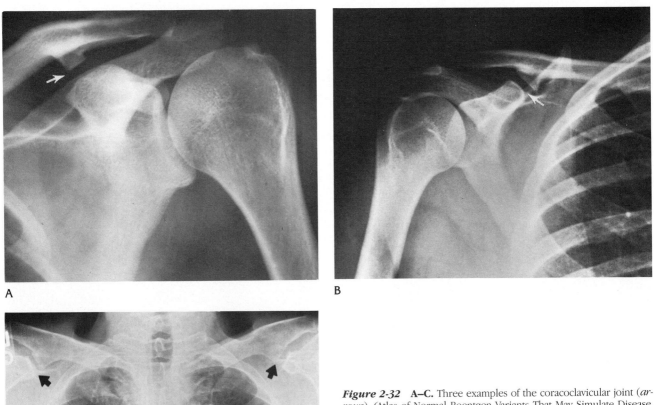

A

B

C

Figure 2-32 **A–C.** Three examples of the coracoclavicular joint (*arrows*). *(Atlas of Normal Roentgen Variants That May Simulate Disease, Chicago, Mosby-Year Book, 1992, with permission.)*

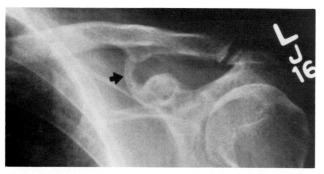

Figure 2-33 Calcifications in the coracoclavicular ligament (*arrow*). (Atlas of Normal Roentgen Variants That May Simulate Disease, *Chicago, Mosby-Year Book, 1992, with permission.*)

Miscellaneous

VACUUM PHENOMENON

Gas within the glenohumeral joint space is seen commonly in the chest radiographs of infants whose arms are elevated and distracted during positioning (Fig. 2-37A) and sometimes in adults (Fig. 2-37B).

BIFID MEDIAL END OF CLAVICLE

The medial end of the clavicle can assume unusual, bifid appearances that may be unilateral (Fig. 2-38).

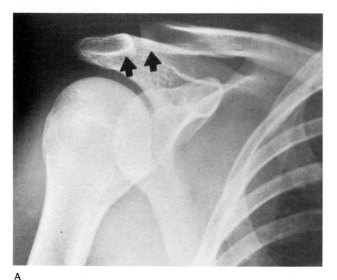

A

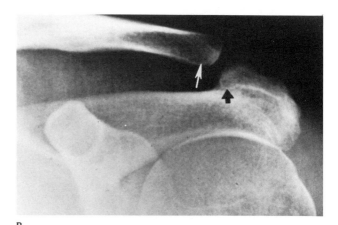

B

Figure 2-34 Variations in the configuration of the acromioclavicular joint. **A,** In most normal persons the inferior aspect of the clavicle is at the same level as the inferior aspect of the acromion (*arrows*). **B, C.** In a small percentage of normal persons, the distal end of the clavicle lies above or below the acromion and might be interpreted as an acromioclavicular separation (*arrows*). The variation emphasizes the value of examining both sides. (Atlas of Normal Roentgen Variants That May Simulate Disease, *Chicago, Mosby-Year Book, 1992, with permission.*)

C

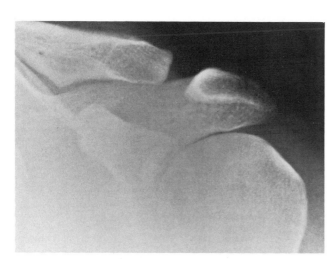

Figure 2-35 Unusually wide acromioclavicular joint in a normal individual. (Atlas of Normal Roentgen Variants That May Simulate Disease, *Chicago, Mosby-Year Book, 1992, with permission.*)

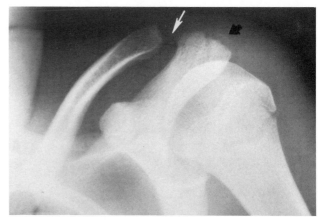

Figure 2-36 Normally wide acromioclavicular joint and apparent malalignment in a 14-year-old girl. Note also the secondary ossification center for the tip of the acromion process (*arrows*). (Atlas of Normal Roentgen Variants That May Simulate Disease, *Chicago, Mosby-Year Book, 1992, with permission.*)

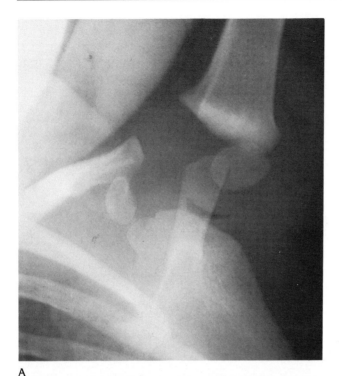

A

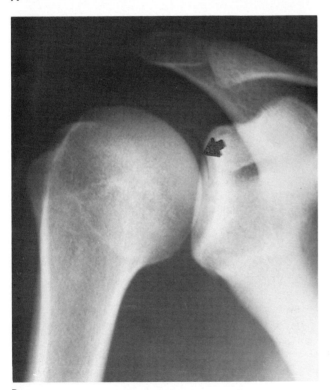

B

Figure 2-37 **A, B.** Examples of the normal "vacuum" phenomenon in the shoulder joint (*arrow*). (*Atlas of Normal Roentgen Variants That May Simulate Disease, Chicago, Mosby-Year Book, 1992, with permission.*)

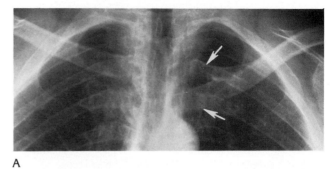

A

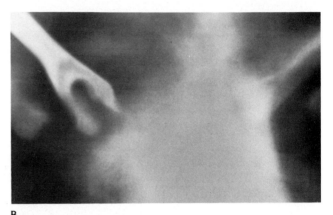

B

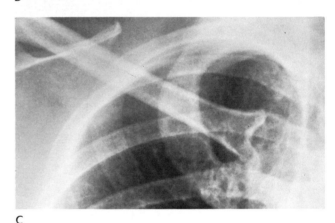

C

Figure 2-38 **A–C.** Three examples of unilateral bifid medial ends of the clavicle (*arrows*). (*Atlas of Normal Roentgen Variants That May Simulate Disease, Chicago, Mosby-Year Book, 1992, with permission.*)

COMPUTED TOMOGRAPHY

Humeral Pseudocyst

The humeral pseudocyst described above may, as in plain radiographs,[8] simulate an osteolytic lesion involving the greater tuberosity (Fig. 2-39).

Zebra Stripe Artifacts

Scanning with thin sections and improper algorithms, especially in a thick limb, can see produced streak artifacts due to beam hardening over the shoulder, obscuring detail (see Fig. 2-39).

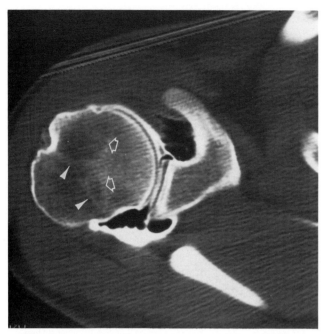

Figure 2-39 CT arthrogram of the shoulder. The humeral pseudocyst is well seen (*open arrows*) simulating a lesion involving the greater tuberosity. Note the closed physeal line (*arrowheads*) and the zebra-stripe artifacts due to beam hardening. (*Atlas of Normal Roentgen Variants That May Simulate Disease, Chicago, Mosby-Year Book, 1992, with permission.*)

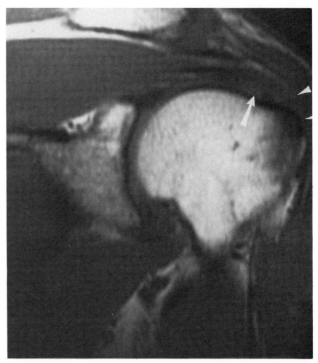

Figure 2-40 T1-weighted oblique coronal MRI. The supraspinatus tendon shows increased signal distally (*arrow*). Note the focal obliteration of the subdeltoid fat plane adjacent to the greater tuberosity (*arrowheads*). (*Atlas of Normal Roentgen Variants That May Simulate Disease, Chicago, Mosby-Year Book, 1992, with permission.*)

Closed Physeal Line

The fused physeal line on axial sections appears as an irregular, sclerotic area and should not be mistaken for a lesion. It can be recognized readily by its characteristic location, separating the epiphysis from the metaphysis (see Figs. 2-39, 2-50).

MRI

Supraspinatus Tendon

FOCAL INCREASED SIGNAL AT THE CRITICAL ZONE

An area of increased signal may be seen in the supraspinatus tendon,[15-19] 1 cm proximal to the insertion, in the region of the critical zone (Fig. 2-40). Multiple causes have been described in the literature.[16,17,20] With the arm internally rotated during imaging, the distal tendon rotates anteriorly and is not imaged in continuity, as it is not completely parallel to the imaging plane, leading to an increased signal.[16] However, increased signal is seen even in external rotation and neutral position, suggesting that positioning is not the likely cause.[15] Relative hypovascularity in the critical zone may be responsible for the increased signal.[17] Imaging tendons at angles of 55° relative to the constant magnetic induction field may produce increased signal in them, the *Magic-angle effect*.[20] This may be the most plausible cause for the

increased signal, as it is in the area of the critical zone that the tendon changes its course and angles anteriorly. The high signal intensity may represent muscle between two tendon slips or muscle interposed between the infraspinatus tendon and the supraspinatus tendon in internal rotation.[16] Thus, increased signal in the supraspinatus tendon, unless accompanied by increased signal in the infraspinatus tendon, should be considered normal. The *anterior interval pitfall*[19] ascribes the increased signal to a normally occurring area called the anterior rotator interval, the space where the superior border of the subscapularis muscle and tendon, the adjacent supraspinatus muscle and tendon, and the biceps tendon are seen together.

VARIED APPEARANCES OF THE TENDON

Multiple normal appearances have been described,[18] and Liou and coworkers divided these into five types, four basic ones and Type 5, representing any of the previous four with focal increased signal. Types 1 and 3 represent long and short central tendons, respectively; Type 2, parallel tendon slips with interdigitating muscle slips; and Type 4, muscle fibers only.[18]

Subacromial Pseudospur[15]

Sometimes a small structure of low signal intensity is seen projecting inferolaterad from the undersurface of

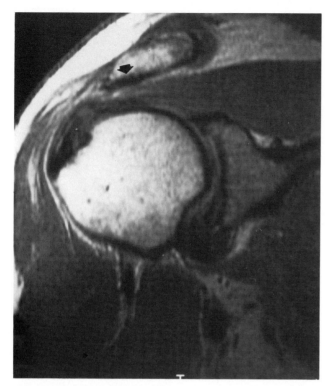

Figure 2-41   T1-weighted oblique coronal MRI. The inferior tendon slip of the deltoid muscle simulates an acromial spur (*arrow*). (Atlas of Normal Roentgen Variants That May Simulate Disease, *Chicago, Mosby-Year Book, 1992, with permission.*)

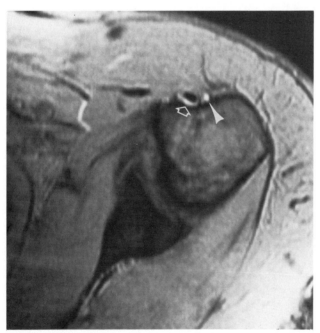

Figure 2-42   Gradient-recalled axial MRI. Hyperintense fluid (*arrow*) is seen around the hypointense biceps tendon within the biceps sheath. Note the hyperintense, laterally placed anterior circumflex humeral vessels within the bicipital groove (*arrowhead*). (Atlas of Normal Roentgen Variants That May Simulate Disease, *Chicago, Mosby-Year Book, 1992, with permission.*)

the acromion simulating a spur (Fig. 2-41). The attachment of the normal inferior tendon slip of the deltoid muscle to the acromion, especially when only a small section is seen, may sometimes be responsible for this appearance.

True spurs usually (1) have fatty marrow with high signal intensity[15] and (2) point inferomediad, as they usually represent an enthesopathy of the acromial attachment of the coracoacromial ligament.[21]

Fluid in the Biceps Tendon Sheath[15]

Fluid in the biceps tendon sheath is normal (Fig. 2-42), but usually does not completely surround the tendon. Fluid surrounding the tendon should be considered abnormal if it occurs without glenohumeral joint effusion. In the presence of joint effusion, however, fluid usually descends into the tendon sheath and distends it because the two spaces are in direct communication.

On gradient axial images the anterolateral branch of the anterior circumflex humeral vessels on the lateral aspect of the biceps tendon sheath may show increased signal, owing to slow flow, and may simulate fluid (see Fig. 2-42).[15]

Focal Obliteration of the Subacromial-Subdeltoid Fat Plane[15]

Focal obliteration of the subacromial-subdeltoid fat plane has been considered a significant ancillary sign of rotator cuff tears[22]; however, it may be seen in normal subjects, especially adjacent to the greater tuberosity. The cause is not known (see Fig. 2-40).[15,17]

Glenoid Labrum

PSEUDOTEARS

Undercutting by the hyaline cartilage on gradient axial images may suggest a tear (Figs. 2-43, 2-48). The high signal intensity of the hyaline cartilage may appear to extend into the anterior aspect of the labrum, but it can be differentiated from a true tear by the absence of irregularity of the labrum and the fact that the high-intensity signal does not completely traverse the labrum.[15] Liou and coworkers[18] have even observed full-thickness undercutting of the labrum by the hyaline cartilage.

The middle glenohumeral ligament as it courses laterad from its attachment to the glenoid rim toward the lesser tuberosity runs parallel to the anterior surface of the anterior labrum and may simulate a tear (Figs. 2-44, 2-51). Again, absence of irregularity, the otherwise normal configuration of the labrum, and tracing the course

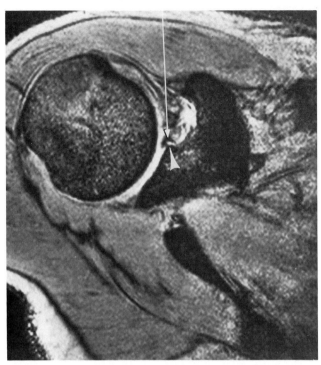

Figure 2-43 Gradient-recalled axial MRI. The hypointense anterior labrum (*arrow*) is undercut by the hyperintense hyaline cartilage (*arrowhead*). *(Atlas of Normal Roentgen Variants That May Simulate Disease, Chicago, Mosby-Year Book, 1992, with permission.)*

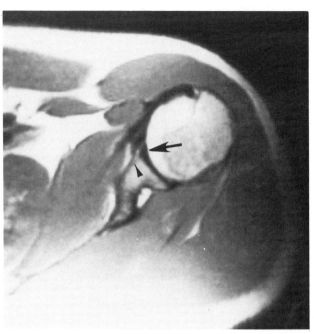

Figure 2-45 T1-weighted axial MRI. The anterior labrum is pointed and triangular (*arrow*). Note the Type II capsule (*arrowhead*). *(Atlas of Normal Roentgen Variants That May Simulate Disease, Chicago, Mosby-Year Book, 1992, with permission.)*

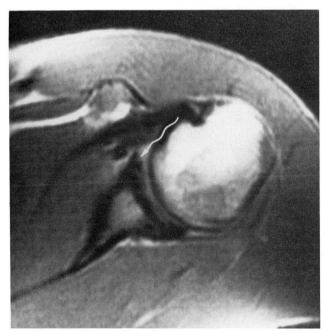

Figure 2-44 T1-weighted axial MRI. The anterior labrum (*arrow*) shows a notched appearance due to the origin of the middle glenohumeral ligament. This may easily simulate a tear. *(Atlas of Normal Roentgen Variants That May Simulate Disease, Chicago, Mosby-Year Book, 1992, with permission.)*

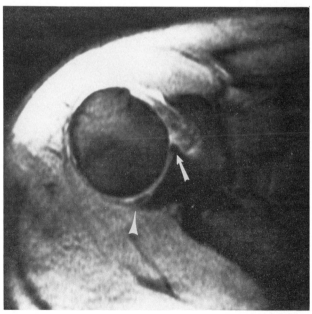

Figure 2-46 Gradient-recalled axial MRI. The anterior labrum is stubby and rounded (*arrow*). Note the posterior Type 1 capsule (*arrowhead*). *(Atlas of Normal Roentgen Variants That May Simulate Disease, Chicago, Mosby-Year Book, 1992, with permission.)*

of the middle glenohumeral ligament help to distinguish this feature from a true tear.[15]

LABRAL SHAPES

The labrum may have different shapes: triangular (Figs. 2-45, 2-49), rounded and stubby (Fig. 2-46), flat, notched, and cleaved (Fig. 2-44) have been described in normal volunteers.[23] Absent labrum, especially superiorly, is not uncommon. There are certain caveats, however. The cleaved and notched pattern, though commonly seen anteriorly, is rare posteriorly and if seen in this location should raise suspicion of a tear.[23] Absent labrum is most commonly seen posterosuperiorly but rarely inferiorly or in the midportion posteriorly. The notched and cleaved appearances may be due to the variable origin of the inferior or middle glenohumeral ligament.[18]

Capsule[23]

Three types of anterior capsular attachments are known. In Type 1, the capsule attaches on the labral tip or its outer surface (Fig. 2-47). In Type 2, it inserts immediately medial to the labrum on the glenoid rim (Figs. 2-45, 2-48). In Type 3, the capsule inserts 1 cm or more medial to the cartilaginous labral tip on the cortical surface of the glenoid neck (Figs. 2-49 through 2-51). Posteriorly,

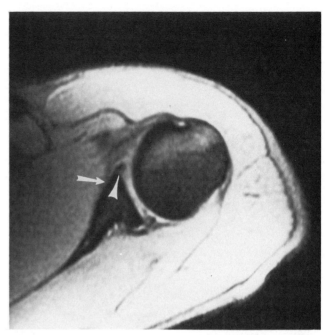

Figure 2-48 Gradient-recalled axial MRI showing a Type II capsule anteriorly (*arrow*). Note the partial undercutting of the anterior labrum by the hyaline cartilage (*arrowhead*). (Atlas of Normal Roentgen Variants That May Simulate Disease, *Chicago, Mosby-Year Book, 1992, with permission.*)

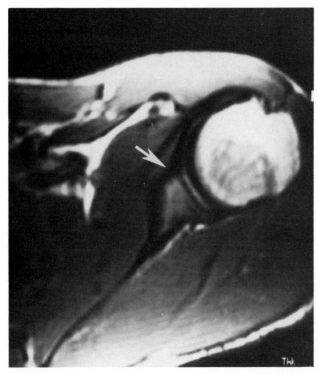

Figure 2-47 T1-weighted axial MRI showing a Type I capsule anteriorly (*arrow*). (Atlas of Normal Roentgen Variants That May Simulate Disease, *Chicago, Mosby-Year Book, 1992, with permission.*)

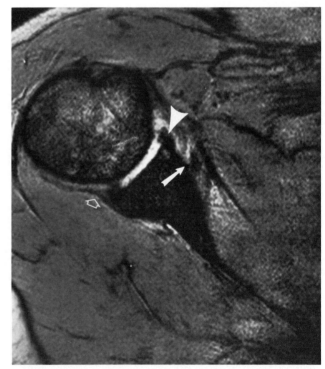

Figure 2-49 Gradient-recalled axial MRI. A Type III capsule is seen anteriorly (*closed arrow*). Note the triangular, pointed anterior labrum (*arrowhead*) and the Type I posterior capsule (*open arrow*). (Atlas of Normal Roentgen Variants That May Simulate Disease, *Chicago, Mosby-Year Book, 1992, with permission.*)

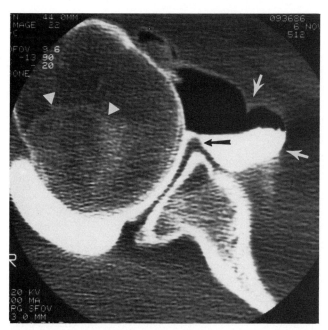

Figure 2-50   CT arthrogram. The axial image shows a deficient middle glenohumeral ligament with a distended subscapularis bursa (*white arrows*). The ligament was not visualized in any section. Note the closed physeal line (*arrowheads*) and the triangular anterior labrum (*black arrow*). (Atlas of Normal Roentgen Variants That May Simulate Disease, *Chicago, Mosby-Year Book, 1992, with permission.*)

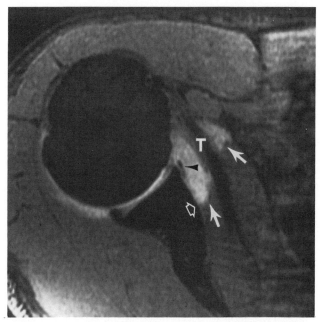

Figure 2-51   MR arthrogram with intraarticular saline. The gradient-recalled axial MRI shows a distended subscapularis bursa (*closed arrows*) with the subscapularis tendon (T) seen coursing through it. Note the origin of the middle glenohumeral ligament (*arrowhead*) and the Type III capsule anteriorly (*open arrow*). (Atlas of Normal Roentgen Variants That May Simulate Disease, *Chicago, Mosby-Year Book, 1992, with permission.*)

only Type 1 attachments (see Figs. 2-46, 2-49) are seen; any other configuration is abnormal.

CT/MRI ARTHROGRAPHY

Many of the variants seen on MRI are also seen on CT arthrography, especially those related to the labrum and capsule.

Labrum

The labrum may be rounded (see Fig. 2-50), triangular, notched, cleaved, small, or absent, leading to various appearances.[24]

Capsule

The capsule anteriorly has three types of insertions medially, as described in the section on MRI.

Glenohumeral Ligaments

Any of the three ligaments may be absent or hypoplastic, the most variable being the medial glenohumeral ligament. Absence of the middle glenohumeral ligament (see Fig. 2-50) manifests as[25] (1) failure to depict the middle glenohumeral ligament at or near its origin in a well-distended joint, (2) enlargement of the subscapularis recess, or (3) a more cephaled origin of the inferior glenohumeral ligament.

Subscapularis Bursa

In the superior aspect of the bursa, folds of capsular tissue may appear as isodense strands, and these should not be mistaken for pathologic structures.[26] Occasionally, the bursa may be markedly distended, especially in patients with instability. It may then extend anterior to the subscapularis tendon by arching superiorly over it (see Fig. 2-51).

References

1. KEATS TE: *Atlas of Normal Roentgen Variants That May Simulate Disease*, 5th ed, St. Louis: Mosby–Year Book, 1992.

2. WILLIAMS PL, WARWICK R: *Gray's Anatomy*, 36th ed, Philadelphia, Saunders, 1980, pp 353–364.

3. SUTTON D: *Textbook of Radiology and Imaging*, 4th ed, Edinburgh, Churchill Livingstone, 1987, pp 1850–1852.

4. OGDEN JA, PHILIPS SB: Radiology of postnatal skeletal development VII. The scapula. *Skel Radiol* 9:157–169, 1983.

5. FERY A, SOMMELET J: Os acromiale: Diagnosis, pathology and clinical significance. *Fr J Orthop* 2:190–104, 1988.

6. EDELSON JG, TAITZ C: Anatomy of the coraco-acromial arch—relation to degeneration of the acromion. *J Bone Joint Surg* 74B:589–594, 1992.

7. MUDGE MK, WOOD VE, FRYKMAN GK: Rotator cuff tears associated with os acromiale. *J Bone Joint Surg* 66A:427–431, 1984.

8. RESNICK D, CONE RO III: The nature of humeral pseudocysts. *Radiology* 150:27–28, 1984.

9. CIGTAY OS, MASCATELLO VJ: Scapular defects: A normal variation. *AJR* 132:239–240, 1979.

10. PATE D, KURSUNOGLU S, RESNICK D, RESNIK CS: Scapular foramina. *Skel Radiol* 14:270–275, 1985.

11. OZONOFF MB, ZITER FMH JR: The upper humeral notch. *Radiology* 113:699–701, 1974.

12. COCKSHOTT WP: The coracoclavicular joint. *Radiology* 131:313–316, 1979.

13. CHEN YM, BOHRER SP: Coracoclavicular and coracoacromial ligament calcification and ossification. *Skel Radiol* 19:263–266, 1990.

14. KEATS TE, THOMAS LP: The acromio-clavicular joint: Normal variation and the diagnosis of dislocation. *Skel Radiol* 17:159–162, 1988.

15. KAPLAN PA, BRYANS KC, DAVICK JP, OTTE M, STINSON WW, DUSSAULT RG: MR imaging of the normal shoulder: Variants and pitfalls. *Radiology* 184:519–524, 1992.

16. DAVIS ST, TERESI LM, BRADLEY WG, RESSLER JA, ETO RT: Effect of arm rotation on MR imaging of the rotator cuff. *Radiology* 181:265–268, 1991.

17. MIROWITZ SA: Normal rotator cuff: MR imaging with conventional and fat-suppression techniques. *Radiology* 180:735–740, 1991.

18. LIOU JTS, WILSON AJ, TOTTY WG, BROWN JJ: The normal shoulder: Common variations that simulate pathologic conditions at MR imaging. *Radiology* 186:435–441, 1993.

19. ZLATKIN MB: Anatomy of the shoulder, in Zlatkin MB (ed): *MRI of the Shoulder*, New York, Raven, 1991, pp 31–32.

20. ERICKSON SJ, COX IH, HYDE JS, CARRERA GF, STRANDT JA, ESTKOWKSI LD: Effect of tendon orientation on MR imaging signal intensity: A manifestation of the "magic angle" phenomenon. *Radiology* 181:389–392, 1991.

21. EDELSON JG, TAITZ C: Anatomy of the coraco-acromial arch—relation to degeneration of the acromion. *J Bone Joint Dis* 74B:589–594, 1992.

22. RAFII M, HOSSEIN F, SHERMAN O, ET AL.: Rotator cuff lesions: Signal patterns at MR imaging. *Radiology* 177:817–823, 1990.

23. NEUMANN CH, PETERSEN SA, JAHNKE AH: MR imaging of the labral-capsular complex: Normal variations. *AJR* 157:1021–1051, 1991.

24. McNIESH LM, CALLAGHAN JJ: CT arthrography of the shoulder: Variations of the glenoid labrum. *AJR* 149:963–966, 1987.

25. COUMAS JM, HOWARD BA, GUILFORD WB: Instability: CT and MR imaging of the shoulder, in *RSNA Categorical Course in Musculoskeletal Radiology,* 1993, pp 113–125.

26. ZLATKIN MB, BJORKENGREN AG, GYLYS-MORIN V, RESNICK D, SARTORIS DJ: Cross-sectional imaging of the capsular mechanism of the gleno-humeral joint. *AJR* 150:151–158, 1988.

3 CONGENITAL AND DEVELOPMENTAL DISORDERS OF THE SHOULDER: IMAGING PRINCIPLES

Joan K. Zawin
Andrew K. Poznanski

In this chapter normal growth and development and congenital anomalies of the shoulder girdle are reviewed. Embryonic development, anatomic variations, and isolated congenital structural abnormalities of the clavicle, scapula, and proximal humerus are discussed in the first section. In the second section, abnormalities about the shoulder girdle seen in congenital malformation syndromes are reviewed. The syndromes are arranged alphabetically in accordance with existing international nomenclature.[1] A brief clinical description of each syndrome is provided, with an overview of additional characteristic radiographic findings.

CLAVICLE

Growth and Development

The clavicle is an S-shaped, tubular bone that articulates medially with the manubrium to form the sternoclavicular joint and laterally with the scapula to form the acromioclavicular joint. The clavicle is formed via intramembranous bone formation and, later, by development of cartilaginous growth areas at both medial and lateral ends that contribute to longitudinal growth.[2,3] The clavicle is the first bone to ossify in the fetus: the medial and lateral primary ossification centers appear during the 5th to the 6th fetal week. These two ossification centers fuse to form the body of the clavicle by the 7th fetal week. An epiphyseal center of ossification occasionally appears at the acromial end of the clavicle during adolescence and quickly unites with the shaft.[2] Another epiphysis that more regularly appears at the sternal end of the clavicle (Fig. 3-1) is the last epiphysis in the body to ossify, usually between age 11 and 20 years. It is also the last epiphysis to fuse, usually by 25 to 26 years of age.[4] Occasionally, it remains unfused.[5]

Prenatal sonographic determination of clavicular length has been used to assess gestational age.[6] The length of the clavicle in millimeters correlates in a linear fashion with the gestational age in weeks. Clavicular bone marrow undergoes normal conversion from hematopoietic to fatty marrow. With magnetic resonance imaging (MRI) this conversion has been observed to occur after age 15 years.[7]

Normal Variants

An irregular concavity is sometimes noted along the inferior surface of the medial clavicle. A normal variant called the *rhomboid fossa* (Fig. 3-2) represents the insertion site of the costoclavicular (or rhomboid) ligament, which connects the clavicle to the first rib.[5,8] This is seen in fewer than 1 percent of the population and should not be confused with a destructive bony process.[9]

The contour of the sternal end of the clavicle can be quite variable. During the first decade of life it is more rounded or mushroom shaped, becoming more cup shaped during the second decade.[3] Occasionally, the sternal end of the clavicle can have a forked configuration.[5]

Another normal variant is the *conoid tubercle* (conoideum), a small bony protuberance extending from the posteroinferior aspect of the distal third of the clavicle.[10] The conoid tubercle is the attachment site of the coracoid portion of the coracoclavicular ligaments. The trapezoid portion of this ligament attaches to the *trapezoid line*, a bony ridge located lateral to the conoid tubercle.

A small foramen can be seen along the superior border of the midclavicle in some 2 to 6 percent of the population (Fig. 3-3).[5] This foramen transmits a nutrient artery[10] and the medial branch of the supraclavicular nerve.[5,11] Occasionally, this foramen is mistaken for a fracture, which it can simulate secondary to projection or rotation on a frontal radiograph of the chest. If displacement or rotation of the clavicle occurs, neck pain can result owing to traction on the supraclavicular nerve.[11]

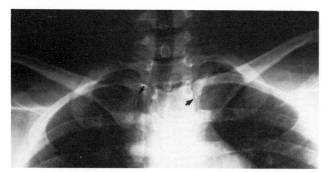

Figure 3-1 Medial clavicular epiphyses (*arrows*) in a 19-year-old girl.

Anomalies

CONGENITAL PSEUDOARTHROSIS OF THE CLAVICLE

Congenital pseudoarthrosis of the clavicle is a rare condition that usually presents as a painless mass in the midclavicular region (Fig. 3-4). In almost all cases the right side is involved, though bilateral cases and one left-sided case have been reported.[12,13] Approximately half of these lesions are detected in the first 2 weeks of life. The abnormality is usually sporadic but occasionally it is familial and autosomal recessive.[14] At least 100 cases have been reported in the literature.[15]

The exact cause of congenital pseudoarthrosis of the clavicle is not known. One theory suggests that pulsations from the relatively high-riding right subclavian artery, which passes just posterior to the midclavicle, prevents fusion of the mesenchyme situated between the two primary clavicular ossification centers during the 7th week of gestation.[16] This theory is supported by the finding of one case of a left clavicular pseudoarthrosis in a child with dextrocardia.

Radiographically, there is a defect in the midclavicle

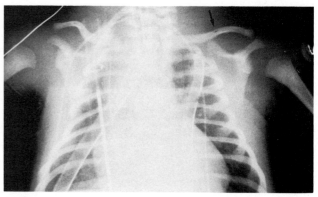

Figure 3-3 Clavicular nutrient foramen. Arrow points to small nutrient foramen in the midportion of the left clavicle. This should not be confused with a fracture.

with the medial segment displaced anterosuperiorly and the lateral segment displaced posterioinferiorly. This displacement accounts for the "mass" and has been referred to as the *lanceolate deformity*.[17] The bony ends on either side of the defect are sclerotic and capped by hyaline cartilage,[18] and they form a diarthrodial joint.[17] Often, the lateral aspect of the medial segment is tapered, while the medial end of the lateral segment is bulbous. Unlike posttraumatic pseudoarthroses, there is no periosteal reaction or callus formation in congenital pseudoarthrosis of the clavicle. Thus, the anomaly is usually easy to distinguish from postnatal fractures. Some difficulty may arise in excluding the diagnosis of cleidocranial dysplasia when evaluating the shoulder girdle alone. A skeletal survey will reveal other bony abnormalities involving the skull, mandible, pelvis, spine, and hands in cleidocranial dysplasia.

HOOKED CLAVICLE

Occasionally, an exaggerated upward convexity of the lateral clavicle is seen that has been termed the *lateral*

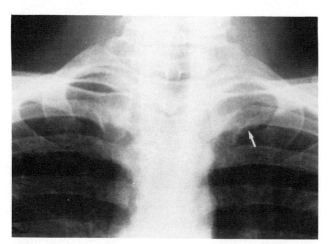

Figure 3-2 Rhomboid fossae. Irregular concavity along the undersurface of the medial clavicles (*arrow*) is consistent with rhomboid fossae.

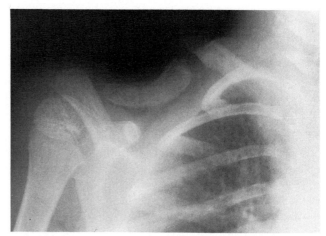

Figure 3-4 Right congenital pseudoarthrosis of the clavicle. The absence of periosteal reaction and callus formation distinguishes this entity from an acute fracture.

Table 3-1   Syndromes Associated with Lateral Hooking of the Clavicle

Campomelic dysplasia
Chondrodysplasia punctata
De Lange syndrome
Diastrophic dysplasia
First and second branchial arch syndrome
Holt-Oram syndrome
Meckel syndrome
Osteogenesis imperfecta
Pierre-Robin syndrome
Scapuloiliac dysostosis
Thrombocytopenia–absent radius syndrome
Trisomy 18

(Modified from Taybi H. Lachman RS: Radiology of Syndromes, Metabolic Disorders, and Skeletal Dysplasias, 3d ed, Chicago, Year Book, 1990.)

clavicular hook.[19] The cause of this contour abnormality is unknown. In some instances it is acquired, either as a result of fracture as in cases of severe osteogenesis imperfecta; sometimes it is postulated to result from an ipsilateral neuromuscular abnormality such as a previous brachial plexus injury.[20] There are also many syndromes that are associated with the lateral clavicular hook deformity (Table 3-1)[20,21], most often, the thrombocytopenia–absent radius (TAR) syndrome, in which it is virtually always present. When the lateral clavicular hook is noted in association with malformation syndromes it is

Table 3-2   Syndromes Associated with Clavicular Aplasia or Hypoplasia

CHILD syndrome
Cleidocranial dysplasia
First and second branchial arch syndrome
Fucosidosis
Goltz syndrome
Holt-Oram syndrome
Mandibuloacral dysplasia
Mannosidosis
Melnick-Needles syndrome
Parietal "foraminae"-clavicular hypoplasia
Progeria
Pycnodysostosis
Say-Poznanski syndrome
Scapuloiliac dysostosis
Trisomy 18
Yunis-Varón syndrome

(Modified from Taybi H. Lachman RS: Radiology of Syndromes, Metabolic Disorders, and Skeletal Dysplasias, 3d ed, Chicago, Year Book, 1990.)

often accompanied by additional deficiencies of the ipsilateral upper extremity.

APLASIA AND HYPOPLASIA

Complete absence of the clavicle can be seen in many conditions (Table 3-2),[21,22] but it is usually linked to cleidocranial dysplasia, a bone dysplasia affecting intramembranous bone formation that accounts for most cases of congenital clavicular absence or hypoplasia.

Duplication of the Clavicle

Duplication of the clavicle is an extremely rare abnormality that has been described only twice in the literature.[23,24] This anatomic variation, which has also been termed *os subclaviculare*, appears to be of no clinical significance. It consists of a small bony segment located just inferior to the distal clavicle. The lateral aspect of the os subclaviculare appears rounded and articulates with the coracoid process; the medial end has no visible bony attachments. This anomaly most likely results from displacement or duplication of the lateral clavicular ossification center during the 6th week of gestation.

OTHER CONGENITAL CLAVICULAR ABNORMALITIES

Aside from complete absence or hypoplasia of the clavicle, many syndromes are associated with abnormally long or straight clavicles (Table 3-3).[25] In addition, the clavicles can be abnormally broadened in persons with many bone dysplasias and inherited metabolic abnormalities (Table 3-4).[21,25] Perhaps the most commonly encountered of these abnormalities are the mucopolysaccharidoses, particularly Hurler syndrome, in which the clavicles are quite short and broad. Abnormally thick-

Table 3-3   Syndromes Associated with Straight/Long Clavicles

Acrodysostosis
Atelosteogenesis
Boomerang dysplasia
Homozygous achondroplasia
Larsen syndrome
Lethal chondrodysplasia, Greenberg-Rimoin type
Lethal metaphyseal dysplasia
Otopalatodigital syndrome, type 2
Pycnodysostosis
Scapuloiliac dysostosis
Schneckenbecken dysplasia
Thanatophoric dysplasia
Winchester syndrome

(Modified from OSSUM (25))

Table 3-4 Conditions Associated with Broad or Thickened Clavicles

Craniodiaphyseal dysplasia
Craniometaphyseal dysplasia
Diaphyseal dysplasia
Distal osteosclerosis
Dysplastic cortical hyperostosis
Endosteal hyperostosis (Van Buchem)
Endosteal hyperostosis (Worth)
Fucosidosis
Geleophysic dysplasia
Holt-Oram syndrome
Infantile cortical hyperostosis
Mannosidosis
Megaepiphyseal dysplasia
Melnick-Needles syndrome
Menke syndrome
Metaphyseal dysplasia
Mucolipidoses
Mucopolysaccharidoses
Oculodentodigital dysplasia
Osteogenesis imperfecta, Type II
Osteopetrosis
Pachydermoperiostosis
Pyle syndrome
Say-Poznanski syndrome
Winchester syndrome

(Modified from Taybi H, Lachman RS: Radiology of Syndromes, Metabolic Disorders, and Skeletal Dysplasias, 3d ed, Chicago, Year Book, 1990.) (Modified from OSSUM (25))

ened clavicles can also be relatively hyperostotic, as in diaphyseal dysplasia, or quite osteoporotic, as in osteogenesis imperfecta Type II.

SCAPULA

Growth and Development

The scapula is formed by endochondral ossification. The first scapular ossification center to appear is that of the glenoid fossa, usually by the 7th to 8th fetal week.[5] Shortly thereafter, normal scapular descent to the T2 to T8 level begins, usually during the 9th to 12th weeks of gestation.[11] At birth, a large portion of the scapula, including the body, is ossified; however, most of the coracoid process, acromion, glenoid, medial border, and inferior angle remain cartilaginous. Scapular development continues postnatally with the subsequent development of numerous centers of ossification.[26,27]

During the first year of life, an ossification center appears in the region of the coracoid process and ultimately fuses with the scapula by age 15 to 20 years.[5] The glenoid fossa ossification appears quite shallow in infants and between age 8 and 13 years appears rather irregular in contour, having a ring apophysis. This apophysis serves to deepen the apparent glenoid fossa and ultimately fuses with the remainder of the glenoid by 18 years of age.[5] Between age 15 and 18 years, ossification centers appear at the lateral end of the acromion and the superior and inferior angles of the scapula (Fig. 3-5). In all, at least seven secondary centers of ossification take part in the formation of the adult scapula. Normally, they have completely united with the scapula by age 25 years.[27]

Normal Variants

During both prenatal and postnatal periods, the scapula is greater in its craniocaudal dimension than in its transverse dimension.[26] The medial or vertebral scapular margin is usually straight or convex. Occasionally, this medial margin may be concave and has been referred to as the *scaphoid scapula*.[27] The superomedial border of the scapula can have a variable contour. Normally, the inferomedial border of the scapula is smooth and rounded. Occasionally, however, two small bony processes separated by a semielliptical notch are noted along the inferomedial aspect of the scapula. This abnormality has been termed the *swallowtail malformation* of the scapula[5]; it is believed to result from the absence of an ossification nucleus in this region.[27]

In addition to having normal variations in shape and contour, the scapula often has normal, albeit somewhat atypical, radiolucent zones. Occasionally, incomplete ossification can be noted in the supraspinatus or infraspinatus fossa. Nutrient foramina can also be quite prominent, and may suggest the presence of a lytic process, particularly in the region of the junction of the scapular neck and body and at the base of the coracoid process.[5] A larger radiolucent defect may occur along the superior scapular border. This is of no clinical significance and often resembles a clasp or handle.[5] Occasionally, the transverse scapular ligament, which runs superior to the suprascapular nerve as it traverses the scapular notch, ossifies. This creates what has been called the *incisura scapulae* between the coracoid process and the superior margin of the scapula. This effectively converts the scapular notch into a foramen and can lead to entrapment of the suprascapular nerve.

Many other developmental variants of the scapula involve the formation of accessory centers of ossification or the persistence of the normal centers of ossification, which fail to unite with the scapula. Though these variants are rarely symptomatic, familiarity with their radiographic appearance is useful, as they must be differentiated from fractures.

Normally, the acromion has three centers of ossification, which fuse with each other between 15 and 18 years of age and ultimately unite with the scapula by age 25 years. If these fusions are not completed by 25 years of age, the resulting bony segment is called the *os acromiale*. The os acromiale, which is best visualized on axillary views of the shoulder, occurs in up to 15 percent of the population, and some series report a 62 percent prevalence of bilaterality.[28] The radiolucent interval between the os acromiale and the remainder of the scapula is usually composed of fibrous tissue, but in some cases a distinct joint cavity with a synovial lining may exist.[27] The os acromiale is usually easily distinguished from an acute fracture, since its borders are smooth and the radiolucent interval between it and the remainder of the scapula is uniform, unlike the sharp, irregular appearance of a fracture. Usually, the os acromiale is an isolated anomaly and an incidental finding on radiography; however, recent reports link this variant with rotator cuff tear,[29] degenerative changes, and subsequent impingement syndrome.[30,31] It is postulated that the irregular undersurface of the acromion applies direct pressure to the rotator cuff when the deltoid muscle contracts, leading ultimately to rotator cuff tear.

Developmental variants involving the coracoid process also occur and include failure of union of the coracoid ossification center with the remainder of the scapula by age 20 years. An additional center of ossification, the os infracoracoideum, is occasionally observed and is separated from the base of the coracoid process by an irregular cleft. A small apical coracoid ossification center has also been observed.[5] A rare developmental anomaly involves the presence of an os coracosternale vestigiale.[32] This very rare anomaly, reported only once in the literature, consists of a tapering bony structure arising from the base of the coracoid process and extending outward and medially toward the cervical spine without fusion. The os coracosternale vestigiale is associated with an ipsilateral Sprengel's deformity, and is thought to be an embryonic remnant of a mesenchymal bar which connects the coracoid and sternum.

Occasionally, a small oval, smoothly marginated, well-corticated bony structure is seen at the scapular tip (see Fig. 3-5). This represents a normal ossification center or an accessory center for ossification at the scapular tip and has been called the *os infrascapulare* or the *infrascapular bone*.[5,27] This infrascapular bone is usually present bilaterally and so should not be mistaken for a fracture fragment. One must be aware of this normal anatomic variant, as the infrascapular bone can be mistaken for a pulmonary parenchymal nodule on a routine chest film. Should this finding be observed, a tangential view of the scapula can confirm the extrathoracic location of the infrascapular bone.

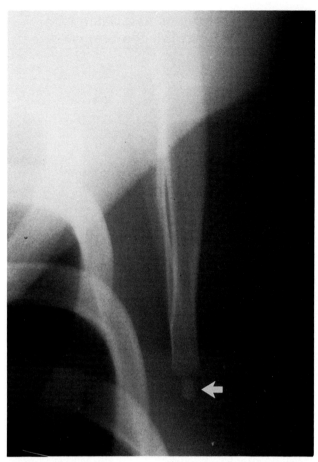

Figure 3-5 Os infrascapulare. Tangential view demonstrates the ossification center at the inferior tip of the scapula, the os infrascapulare (*arrow*).

Anomalies

SPRENGEL DEFORMITY

Sprengel deformity, or congenital undescended scapula, is the most common congenital anomaly of the shoulder. It can occur alone or as part of a syndrome (Table 3-5).[25] Sprengel deformity occasionally is inherited as an autosomal-dominant trait but usually occurs sporadically, with a 3:1 male predominance.[11] The left shoulder is more commonly affected than the right, and the deformity may be bilateral.[33] The cause of Sprengel deformity is unclear, but several theories exist[34]; increased intrauterine pressure, defective musculature about the scapula, and possibly abnormal articulations between the vertebral column and the scapula.

Congenital undescended scapula is thought to result from failure of the scapula to descend to the T2-T7 level during the 9th to 12th weeks of gestation. The scapula not only is elevated on the chest wall but is also adducted, with medial rotation of the inferior angle. The scapula in Sprengel deformity is hypoplastic with a diminished

Table 3-5   Conditions Associated with Sprengel Deformity/Winged Scapula

3M syndrome
Basal cell nevus syndrome
Holt-Oram syndrome
Klippel-Feil syndrome
Say-Poznanski syndrome
Sacroiliac dysostosis
Spondylomegaepiphyseal metaphyseal dysplasia
Trichorhinophalangeal dysplasia

(Modified from OSSUM (25))

vertical-horizontal ratio.[35] The glenoid fossa faces downward with resultant limitation of glenohumeral and scapulothoracic mobility, particularly abduction.

Associated deformities of the cervicothoracic spine, thorax, and shoulder girdle are found in at least two thirds of patients with Sprengel deformity.[11] Associated spinal abnormalities include the Klippel-Feil syndrome, scoliosis, cervical spina bifida, and diastematomyelia. Rib abnormalities have been reported in as many as 38 percent of patients—synostoses, absent or duplicated ribs, and cervical ribs (Fig. 3-6).[11] The clavicle can be straight, laterally hooked, or hypoplastic, with absence of the acromioclavicular articulation.[33] An anomalous osseous bridge between the midclavicle and the spine of the undescended scapula has also been reported in the literature.[36] The musculature of the shoulder girdle is usually defective, marked by hypoplasia or absence of the trapezius, levator scapulae, and/or rhomboid muscle groups. The latissimus dorsi, pectoralis major, sternocleidomastoid, and serratus anterior muscles may also be involved.[11,33]

In as many as 50 percent of patients an abnormal

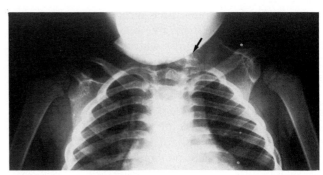

Figure 3-7 Left-sided Sprengel deformity with omovertebral bone (*arrow*).

connection exists between the superomedial angle of the scapula and the lower cervical spine. This has been termed an *omovertebral bone,* and it extends superiorly and medially from the scapula to attach to the lamina, spinous process, or transverse process of the cervical spine, usually at the C6 level (Fig. 3-7).[11] This connection can be composed of fibrous elements, but in 20 to 30 percent of patients, it is actually a chondroosseous bar. A diarthrodial joint has also been described.[37] The omovertebral bone is best imaged in the anteroposterior projection or with computed tomography (CT), espe-

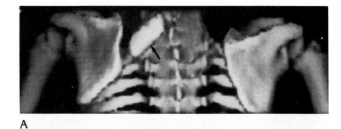

A

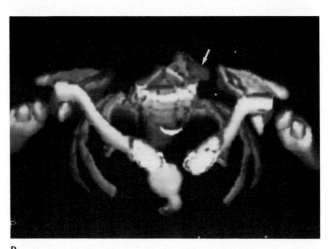

B

Figure 3-8 Sprengel deformity. **A.** Posterior projection of a three-dimensional CT reconstruction demonstrates left-sided Sprengel deformity with an omovertebral bone (*arrow*). **B.** Axial projection of the three-dimensional CT reconstruction in the same patient demonstrates left scapular rotation and an omovertebral bone (*arrow*).

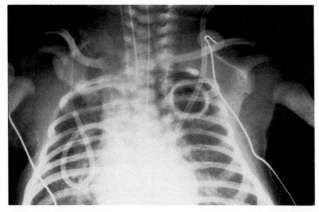

Figure 3-6 Right-sided Sprengel deformity. There are associated lateral hooking of the right clavicle, right rib anomalies, and right apical lung herniation.

cially using three-dimensional reconstructions (Fig. 3-8). When an omovertebral bone is present, motion about the shoulder is more limited.

OBSTETRIC BRACHIAL PLEXUS INJURY (ERB PALSY)

Although technically Erb palsy is an acquired condition resulting from injury to the brachial plexus during the birth process, its discussion at this time is appropriate, as it must be distinguished from Sprengel deformity. Erb palsy results from injury to the C5-C6 nerve roots, causing paralysis of the muscles of external rotation about the shoulder. Less often, injury to the C7-C8 nerve roots results in Klumpke palsy, which causes paralysis of the small muscles of the hand and wrist drop. Occasionally, both of these deficits occur together, and if there is associated injury to the cervical sympathetic chain, Horner syndrome also results.[33,38] The palsy is usually unilateral, but occasionally bilateral (Fig. 3-9). Overall, the reported incidence of birth palsy varies from 0.4 to 2.5 per 1000 births.[39]

In both Erb palsy and Sprengel deformity, the scapula is hypoplastic and elevated. In contrast to Sprengel deformity, where the inferomedial border of the scapula is deviated toward the spine, in Erb palsy the inferomedial angle of the scapula is deviated away from the spine.[40] Films obtained during the newborn period in a child who has an obstetric brachial plexus injury often show the metaphysis of the humerus to be displaced from the glenoid fossa. There is delayed ossification of the epiphysis of the humeral head (Fig. 3-10), and ultimately the humeral head is often hypoplastic.[41] Patients with Erb palsy often have posterior subluxation of the hypoplastic humeral head, which most likely is due to surrounding muscle imbalances. The glenoid fossa is usually quite shallow as well. The degree of humeral head subluxation is best evaluated with CT[42] or with MRI. Other musculoskeletal abnormalities observed in Erb palsy include

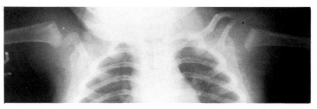

Figure 3-10 Left-sided Erb palsy. There is delayed ossification of the left humeral head, a shallow left glenoid fossa, and lateral hooking of the left clavicle.

hypoplasia or lateral hooking of the clavicle with elongation of the acromion and coracoid processes of the scapula. The elongated, downward-hooking coracoid process can in fact interfere with return of the humeral head to its normal position.[33] Retrotorsion of the proximal humerus is also seen in Erb palsy.[33]

CORACOCLAVICULAR AND ACROMIOCLAVICULAR ABNORMALITIES

Usually, mesenchymal tissue between the clavicle and the coracoid process of the scapula form the conoid and trapezoid portions of the coracoclavicular ligament. Occasionally, however, a bony, cartilaginous, or fibrous bar may form in this region, the so-called *coracoclavicular bar* or *ligament*. This connection may be partial or complete, and occasionally a diarthrodial joint may actually be present at this site.[12] This coracoclavicular articulation can be found in up to 1.2 percent of the general population[43] and also commonly occurs in the Holt-Oram syndrome. Usually, the coracoclavicular bar is an asymptomatic incidental finding on chest radiographs; however, if complete, it can interfere with scapular rotation. Coracoclavicular articulations have also been linked to compression of the nearby subclavian artery and brachial plexus[11,44] and to premature osteoarthritic changes of the acromioclavicular and sternoclavicular joints.[12]

Cases of congenital dislocation or subluxation of the acromioclavicular joints have been described.[12,45] This is an extremely rare condition characterized by hypermobility of the lateral end of the clavicle, often with associated abnormal ossification of the lateral clavicle or the acromion. Clinically, the acromioclavicular joint is prominent. The bilateral nature of this condition helps to distinguish it from posttraumatic acromioclavicular joint instability.

DUPLICATION OF THE SCAPULA

Unilateral duplication of the acromion and coracoid processes was reported by McClure and Raney[46] in a middle-aged man who had some limitation in shoulder abduction. Radiographically, there was an upper acromion that articulated normally with the clavicle at the acromioclavicular joint and a more inferior acromion that had a

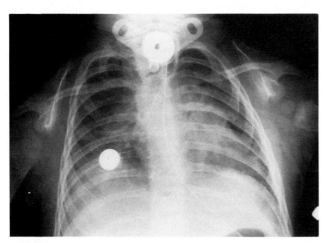

Figure 3-9 Bilateral Erb palsy.

normal relation with the humerus at the glenohumeral joint. Associated anomalies included anterolateral rib fusions, hemivertebrae, scoliosis, and unilateral renal agenesis. The embryonic basis for this anomaly is unknown.

Two cases of complete scapular duplication were reported by Martini and Neusel.[47] In both cases, there was asymptomatic complete duplication of the right scapula with depression of the shoulder joint. In both patients, the superomedial scapula articulated with the single clavicle whereas the inferolateral scapula articulated with the humeral head. There were no other duplications of the involved upper extremity, and the contralateral scapula was normal. Associated anomalies included ipsilateral syndactyly, scoliosis, neural arch defects, and lower extremity abnormalities. It is postulated that this rare scapular duplication was the result of formation of two centers of ossification for the scapular body that failed to fuse.

CONGENITAL ABSENCE OF THE SCAPULA

Congenital absence of the entire scapula is a rare anomaly and is associated with absence of the entire ipsilateral upper extremity (amelia).[11,12] It can be unilateral or bilateral.

ABNORMALITIES OF THE GLENOID FOSSA

The normal glenoid is formed in three sections. The central portion is part of the scapular body and ossifies during the 8th week of gestation. At 10 years of age, an apophysis forming the upper rim of the glenoid fossa and the base of the coracoid process appears. Approximately 3 to 4 years later, another center of ossification appears, forming the inferior glenoid rim.[11,48] If the ossification center which forms the inferior glenoid rim fails to develop, a dentate or hypoplastic glenoid results.

Glenoid hypoplasia is an uncommon condition: some 40 to 50 cases are described in the literature.[49] This condition usually occurs bilaterally and is inherited as an autosomal-dominant trait. Radiographically, the glenoid articular surface ossification is irregular and there is hypoplasia of the scapular neck.[41,48] The humeral head is flattened and there is a varus deformity of the humeral neck. The clavicle may be bowed, and there may be enlargement of the acromion. Recently, MRI has been used to clarify the status of the cartilaginous anlagen in these cases.[49]

Glenoid hypoplasia may be asymptomatic or may lead to recurrent shoulder dislocation and early osteoarthritic changes. Associated skeletal abnormalities include cervical ribs, thoracic hemivertebrae, and spina bifida.[49] True congenital glenoid hypoplasia must be differentiated from other conditions which can result in a shallow glenoid fossa (Table 3-6).[21] These conditions include epiphyseal dysplasias, neuromuscular conditions such as

Table 3-6 Syndromes Associated with Shallow Glenoid Fossa

Fucosidosis
Glenoid hypoplasia
Grant syndrome
Mucopolysaccharidoses
Multiple epiphyseal dysplasia
Neuromuscular abnormalities
Ophthalmomandibulomelic dysplasia
TAR syndrome
Vitamin deficiencies (C and D)

(Modified from Taybi H, Lachman RS: Radiology of Syndromes, Metabolic Disorders, and Skeletal Dysplasias, 3d ed, Chicago, Year Book, 1990.)

Erb palsy, and metabolic abnormalities such as vitamin C or vitamin D deficiency.[11,49]

THE HUMERUS

Growth and Development

The humerus is formed by endochondral ossification. The center of ossification in the humeral head almost never is present before 36 weeks gestation.[50] Usually, the medial ossific center in the humeral head appears between the 4th and the 8th month of life.[5] The lateral center of ossification in the humeral head generally appears between the 1st and 2d year of life whereas that of the lesser tuberosity appears by the 5th year.[11] The centers for ossification of the greater and lesser tuberosities fuse with each other between 5 and 8 years of age, and ultimately fuse with the humeral head by 14 years.[5] The epiphysis of the humeral head normally fuses with the humeral shaft by age 20 years.[5] Humeral bone marrow undergoes a well-described sequence of transformation from hematopoietic marrow to fatty marrow.[7] This normal marrow conversion is seen initially in the proximal epiphysis, followed by the diaphysis, then the distal metaphysis, and finally in the proximal metaphysis. Hematopoietic marrow can persist in the proximal humeral metaphysis in adulthood and should not be confused with a pathologic process on MR images.

Normal Variants

Anatomic variations in the depth and angulation of the bicipital groove have been described.[51] If this intertubercular groove is too shallow the patient is at risk for medial dislocation of the biceps tendon. The bicipital groove is best imaged on axial views, particularly with CT.

In 1928, Meyer described the presence of a "supratubercular bony ridge," which arises just proximal to the medial wall of the bicipital groove. Meyer found this bony protuberance in 17.5 percent of the humeri he examined[52]; in a later series by Hitchcock[51] it was noted in 59 percent of cases. The protuberance has been linked to inflammation of the biceps tendon as well as impingement upon this tendon. The supratubercular ridge of Meyer is also best appreciated on axial imaging but occasionally can be seen on an anteroposterior view with the arm held in external rotation.

Anomalies

ABSENCE OF THE HUMERUS
Complete absence of the humerus, an exceedingly rare condition, can be associated with amelia or with phocomelia. It can be unilateral or bilateral (Fig. 3-11) and is associated with glenoid underdevelopment.

ABSENCE OF THE HUMERAL HEAD
Congenital partial or complete absence of the humeral head is a rare anomaly that can be unilateral or bilateral (Fig. 3-12). The exact cause is uncertain; however, it is postulated that a defect occurs during early embryonic life that results in absence of the tissue from which the humeral capital epiphysis should form.[53] The ipsilateral glenoid cavity is usually quite hypoplastic or even convex in configuration. The extracapsular structures about the shoulder are, however, normal. Congenital absence of the humeral head can occur as an isolated condition or in association with other abnormalities, including ipsilateral Madelung deformity.[53]

HUMERUS VARUS
Normally, the angle between the humeral head and humeral shaft measures approximately 135°, but in humer-

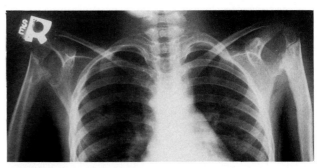

Figure 3-12   Bilateral absence of the medial ossification centers of the humeral heads.

us varus it approaches 90°.[5] Varus deformity of the proximal humerus can be seen in a variety of conditions and is perhaps most common with rickets.[12,33] Two cases of humerus varus were described by Lucas and coworkers[54] and were felt to result from physeal trauma sustained during the birth process. In both cases, the humeral shaft was in varus position relative to the humeral head and the humeral neck narrowed just distal to the physis. Other conditions that have been associated with humerus varus include neurofibromatosis[33] and glenoid hypoplasia[12,49] as well as hemiplegia, osteomalacia, and hypothyroidism.[5]

CONGENITAL GLENOHUMERAL DISLOCATIONS
True congenital glenohumeral dislocations are rare and most likely result from defective development of the cartilaginous anlagen about the glenohumeral joint.[5] True congenital dislocation of the shoulder is usually bilateral.[5,55] In these cases, both the scapula and the humeral head are hypoplastic and the glenoid fossa is underdeveloped. The coracoid process can be enlarged as well.

It is felt that more common glenohumeral dislocations are the result of paralytic injury during the birth process (Erb palsy). Several syndromes can be associated with glenohumeral dislocation, including Holt-Oram syndrome and arthrogryposis multiplex congenita.[11] Excessive anteversion or retroversion of the humeral head can also be associated with shoulder dislocation.[33]

MISCELLANEOUS ABNORMALITIES
Mineralization of the proximal humeral metaphysis closely reflects the well-being of a child. Normally, mineralization of the proximal humeral metaphysis should be uniform. When growth and maturation of physeal cartilage are delayed for any reason, bony trabeculae are not formed and a lucent band is visible in the proximal humeral metaphysis (Fig. 3-13). This can be seen in the neonate as the result of intrauterine stress such as

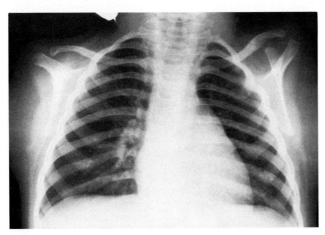

Figure 3-11   Bilateral amelia with very shallow glenoid fossae.

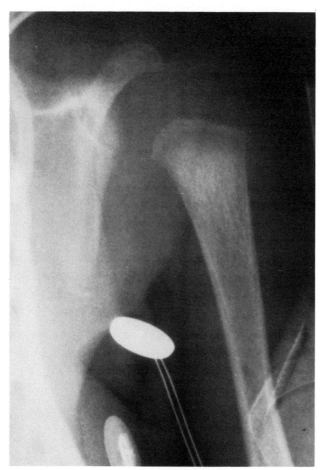

Figure 3-13 Lucent proximal humeral metaphyseal line in a premature neonate with hyaline membrane disease.

(TORCH) infections or as the result of postnatal stress such as hyaline membrane disease.

When growth resumes, the cartilage at the physis is converted to bone and subsequently advances down the diaphysis as a unit, resulting in the formation of sclerotic lines referred to as *transverse lines of Park* or *growth recovery lines of Harris*.[56] If a fetus is transiently stressed in utero, as with meconium peritonitis, these growth lines can be seen in the proximal humeral metaphysis of the newborn.[57]

Growth of the proximal humeral physis is also reflective of a large number of underlying bony dysplasias and metabolic abnormalities (Table 3-7).[56] For example, "fraying" of the proximal humeral metaphysis with associated widening of the proximal humeral physis can be seen in a number of disorders, such as rickets, metaphyseal chondrodysplasias (Fig. 3-14), and hypophosphatasia. Whereas rickets and the metaphyseal chondrodystrophies may be quite difficult to distinguish radiographically, patients with hypophosphatasia often have well-defined, punched-out lucencies in the proxi-

mal humeral metaphysis, which aid in the diagnosis (Fig. 3-15).

CONGENITAL DISORDERS ASSOCIATED WITH SHOULDER ABNORMALITIES

Atelosteogenesis

Atelosteogenesis, also known as *spondylohumerofemoral hypoplasia*, is a rare lethal chondrodysplasia. Characterized histologically by abnormal epiphyseal and physeal cartilage, its cause is unknown and most cases are sporadic.[58,59] Affected children have marked rhizomelic dwarfism with midfacial hypoplasia, micrognathia, narrow chest, incurving limbs, clubfeet, and knee or elbow dislocations. Many are stillborn, and the remainder succumb in the neonatal period, often to respiratory complications.[59]

RADIOGRAPHIC ABNORMALITIES IN THE SHOULDER

Characteristically, the humeri are hypoplastic, and in some instances absent. Usually, the humeri are club

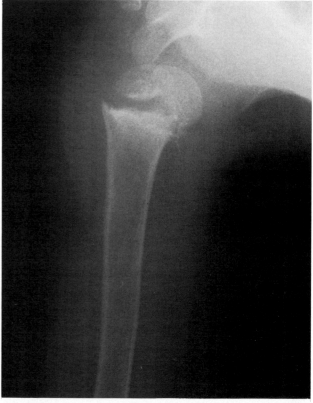

Figure 3-14 Metaphyseal chondrodysplasia, Schmid type. There is widening of the proximal humeral physis and irregular fraying of the proximal humeral metaphysis resembling that seen in rickets.

Table 3-7 Conditions Associated with Widened Physes

Aminoacidurias (phenylketonuria, homocystinuria)
Growth hormone therapy
Hypophosphatasia
Menkes kinky hair syndrome*
Metaphyseal chondrodysplasia
Rickets
Rubella
Scurvy*
Syphilis*

Secondary to fractures through the growth plate.
(Modified from Poznanski AK: Diagnostic clues in the growing ends of bone. J Can Assoc Radiol 29:7, 1978.)

shaped and distally attenuated with a hooklike appearance.[58] Premature ossification of the proximal humeral epiphysis has also been reported.[21] The scapulae are generally well-formed with mild glenoid hypoplasia.[59]

OTHER RADIOGRAPHIC FINDINGS

In addition to marked humeral hypoplasia, the femurs are short and bowed, rather broad proximally, and ta-

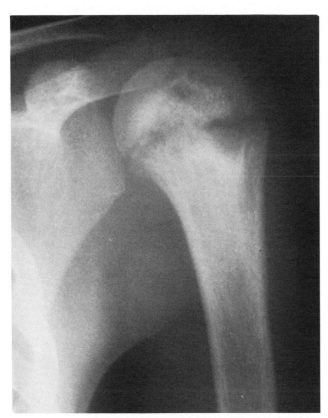

Figure 3-15 Hypophosphatasia. There is irregular narrowing of the proximal humeral physis with metaphyseal lucencies and fraying.

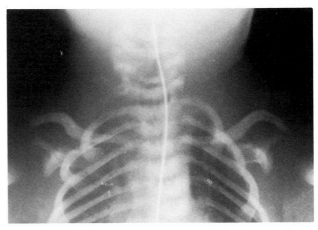

Figure 3-16 Campomelic dysplasia. The scapulae are markedly hypoplastic, particularly the infraspinous portions. There is also lateral hooking of the clavicles.

pered distally. The upper thoracic vertebrae are often hypoplastic and scoliosis is associated. Coronal clefts of the lower thoracic and lumbar vertebrae are also seen. There is usually a lack of ossification of the majority of the proximal and middle phalanges of the hands and feet, and fibular absence or hypoplasia has also been reported.[21,58,59]

Campomelic Dysplasia

Campomelic dysplasia is a rare autosomal-recessive mesomelic, short-limbed dwarfism, its incidence approximately 0.5 per 100,000 live births.[21] At birth, affected infants are very hypotonic, with macrocephaly, micrognathia, cleft palate, hypertelorism, and malformed ears.[60] The most characteristic physical finding involves symmetric shortening and bowing of the lower extremities, particularly the tibia, and the presence of cutaneous pretibial dimples.[60,61] These children are at relatively high risk for congenital heart disease (21 percent) and renal abnormalities, especially hydronephrosis (38 percent).[61] Most die in early infancy, owing to respiratory complications related to a high incidence of laryngotracheal abnormalities such as tracheomalacia[60] and incomplete tracheal rings.[61]

RADIOGRAPHIC FINDINGS IN THE SHOULDER

Classically, the scapula is absent or very hypoplastic, particularly the infraspinous portion (Fig. 3-16).[60,61] The clavicle is normal but appears disproportionately long. Occasionally, lateral hooking of the clavicle is seen.[21,62] Though there may be some mild shortening of the upper extremities, they are rarely bowed, and the humeri are usually normal.[60] Often there are 11 pairs of ribs, which are quite thin. In addition, there can be a marked delay or total absence of ossification of the sternal segments.[60,61]

OTHER RADIOGRAPHIC FINDINGS

The tibia and fibula are the most hypoplastic long bones in campomelic dysplasia.[60] One of the characteristic radiographic findings is symmetric broadening, shortening, and anterior bowing of the tibiae. Talipes equinovarus deformity is usually associated. The femora are often bowed but generally are not broadened,[60] and there is deviation of the lower ends of the ischia laterally. The incidence of hip, knee, and elbow dislocations is increased, and there is delayed ossification of the pubis, talus, and epiphyses about the knee.[60,61] Other radiographic findings include nonmineralization of thoracic pedicles, narrow vertical iliac bones, and hypoplastic cervical vertebrae.[60]

The CHILD Syndrome

The CHILD syndrome (congenital *h*emidysplasia with *i*chthyosiform erythroderma and *l*imb *d*efects) is a very rare syndrome characterized by unilateral erythema and scaling with ipsilateral visceral (e.g., renal and cardiac), central nervous system, and limb abnormalities.[63,64] The dermatologic abnormalities are usually present at birth or shortly thereafter and are characterized by unilateral distribution with strict demarcation by the midline. Occasionally, minor abnormalities of the contralateral skin, viscera, or bones are seen.[63] The face is usually spared. CHILD syndrome, thought to be inherited via an X-linked dominant gene, affects mostly females. The severity of the dermatosis is thought to reflect the severity of the associated visceral and skeletal abnormalities.[63]

RADIOGRAPHIC ABNORMALITIES IN THE SHOULDER

Patients with CHILD syndrome can have hypoplasia of the ipsilateral clavicle, scapula, and ribs. In some cases, punctate calcifications are seen in epiphyseal cartilage. As in chondrodysplasia calcificans punctata, these nonspecific cartilaginous calcifications usually disappear during the first few years of life.[64]

OTHER RADIOGRAPHIC FINDINGS

Newborns with CHILD syndrome can have variable limb defects ranging from hypoplasia of some of the digits to complete absence of an extremity.[21,63] Long bone hypoplasia can result in limb contractures.

Chondrodysplasia Punctata

Chondrodysplasia punctata refers to a heterogeneous group of rare familial conditions whose radiographic hallmark is stippled calcification in the epiphyseal regions. The most common type, affecting two thirds to

three quarters of the patients, is the nonrhizomelic, autosomal-dominant *inherited* Conradi-Hünermann (C-H) type, which itself has variable clinical and radiographic findings.[65] Patients with the C-H subtype have limb shortening, and have ichthyotic skin lesions, cataracts, craniofacial dysmorphism, and scoliosis.[21,66] The next most common type of chondrodysplasia punctata is the rhizomelic, autosomal-recessive type; these patients often die in infancy from respiratory failure.[65] The rhizomelic type is a peroxisomal disorder.[67]

RADIOGRAPHIC ABNORMALITIES IN THE SHOULDER

In the C-H type of chondrodysplasia punctata, there may be mild shortening of the humerus. The more characteristic radiographic findings about the shoulder girdle involve punctate calcific stippling in the cartilaginous anlagen of the sternum, rib ends, coracoid process, and glenoid fossa (Fig. 3-17).[21,65,66] In the rhizomelic forms, there is more severe symmetric shortening of the humeri with associated splaying of the metaphyses and the characteristic stippling in the epiphyseal regions (Fig. 3-18).[65]

OTHER RADIOGRAPHIC FINDINGS

Patients with the C-H type often have scoliosis with vertebral and paravertebral calcific stippling and vertebral body deformities. There are also frequent calcifications in the laryngeal and tracheal cartilage. In contrast, patients with the rhizomelic form tend to have milder vertebral and paravertebral calcific stippling and often have no laryngeal or tracheal cartilaginous calcifications.[65,66] They usually have coronal clefts in the vertebrae. While the radiologic findings in chondrodysplasia punctata are quite characteristic, it may be difficult to confirm the diagnosis radiographically after infancy, as the characteristic epiphyseal stippling disappears within the first 1 to 3 years of life.[66]

Cleidocranial Dysplasia

Cleidocranial dysplasia (CCD) is an autosomal-dominant skeletal dysplasia which involves membranous and endochondral bones. Typically, patients are short, with brachycephaly, frontal and parietal bossing, hypertelorism, and dental abnormalities.[68–71] One of the most characteristic clinical findings is excessive anterior mobility of the shoulders toward the midline owing to absence or hypoplasia of the clavicles.

RADIOGRAPHIC ABNORMALITIES IN THE SHOULDER

In 10 percent of cases the clavicles are entirely absent (Fig. 3-19).[21] The most common clavicular defect is absence of the lateral end of the clavicle; the least common one is absence of the medial third. With absence of the

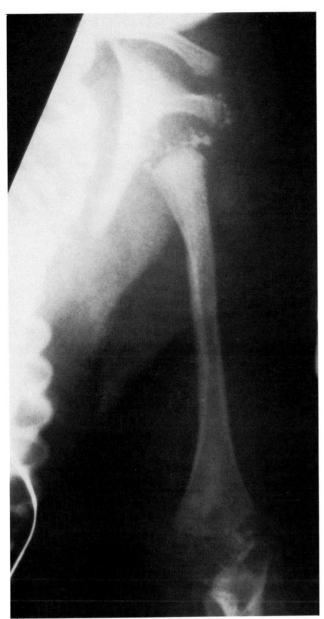

Figure 3-17 Chondrodysplasia punctata, Conradi-Hünermann type. Stippled calcifications are present in the cartilaginous portions of the coracoid, acromion, humeral head, and distal humeral epiphysis.

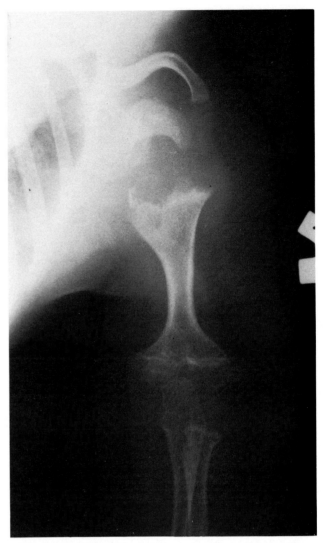

Figure 3-18 Chondrodysplasia punctata, rhizomelic type. Young child with characteristic metaphyseal splaying and marked humeral shortening. The stippled epiphyseal calcifications are no longer seen.

OTHER RADIOGRAPHIC FINDINGS

CCD is characterized by poor mineralization of the membranous bony calvarium with delayed sutural closure and multiple wormian bones. The paranasal sinuses and mas-

middle clavicular ossification center, two unfused segments are present. This situation resembles pseudoarthrosis of the clavicle with the larger medial fragment positioned anterior and superior to the smaller lateral fragment.[11,69] Clavicular abnormalities are found in virtually all patients with CCD; they are usually bilateral, but not always symmetric (Fig. 3-20). The scapula is small and winged, and normal sternal ossification often is absent.[21] These patients are said to have a cone-shaped thorax, which principally reflects abnormal development of the thoracic vertebral bodies.[69]

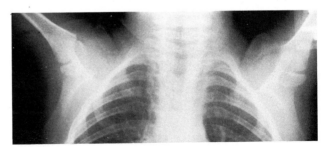

Figure 3-19 Cleidocranial dysplasia. There is complete absence of both clavicles.

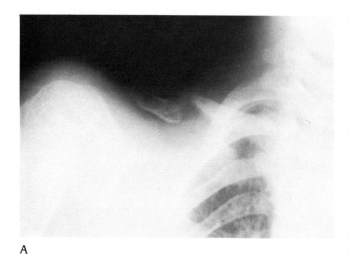

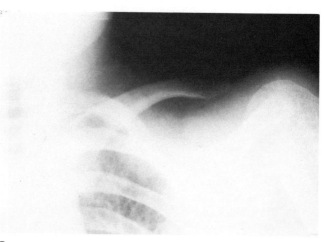

A   B

Figure 3-20 Cleidocranial dysplasia with bilateral but asymmetric clavicular defects. **A.** On the right, there is absence of the middle clavicular ossification center resembling congenital pseudoarthrosis of the clavicle. **B.** On the left, in the same patient, there is absence of the lateral clavicular end.

toid air cell complexes are poorly developed and there is delayed fusion of the mandibular symphysis. Delayed rupture of permanent teeth and supernumerary teeth is characteristic.[69] There is also poor ossification of the pubic symphysis and undertubulation of the long bone metaphyses. Findings in the hand include clinodactyly, long second metacarpal, pseudoepiphyses, and cone shaped epiphyses.[68]

Diaphyseal Dysplasia (Engelmann-Camurati Disease)

Diaphyseal dysplasia is a rare autosomal-dominant inherited bone dysplasia characterized by sclerosis and fusiform thickening of the diaphyseal cortex of the long tubular bones. Diaphyseal dysplasia is usually diagnosed in early childhood, when the presenting symptoms are waddling gait, muscle weakness, extremity pain, and failure to gain weight.[72,73]

RADIOGRAPHIC ABNORMALITIES IN THE SHOULDER

Radiographs of the shoulders may show sclerosis and thickening of the humeral diaphyseal cortex with loss of the medullary space. While diaphyseal dysplasia predominantly involves bones formed by endochondral ossification, occasionally bones that are membranous in origin are involved. In advanced cases, there may be partial involvement of the scapula and thickening of the clavicle, especially the medial two thirds (Fig. 3-21).[21,72,74] In rare cases the ribs may be involved.

OTHER RADIOGRAPHIC FINDINGS

Radiographically, there is thickening of the periosteal— and particularly endosteal—surfaces of the long bone

diaphyses, usually in a bilaterally symmetric fashion.[74] The metaphyses and epiphyses are usually spared, though there may be Erlenmeyer flask deformities and, in some cases, eventual flattening and broadening of the epiphyses.[75]

The lower extremities are more frequently involved than the upper ones, the tibia being the bone most commonly affected in patients with diaphyseal dysplasia.[72] Other commonly affected bones include the femur, fibula, ulna, radius, and the base of the skull. In rare cases, the mandible, posterior elements of the spine, metacarpals, and metatarsals may be involved. The bony changes in diaphyseal dysplasia may be progressive and are irreversible. Bone scintigraphy has been used to assess disease activity.[76] Areas which show increased activity on bone scan but no radiographic abnormalities are felt to represent early areas of active disease, whereas areas that appear radiographically abnormal but display normal uptake on the bone scan are felt to represent more mature and quiescent involvement.[76]

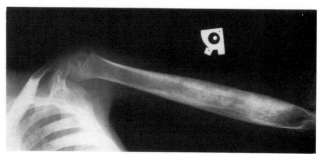

Figure 3-21 Diaphyseal dysplasia. There is marked cortical thickening involving the humeral diaphysis and medial two thirds of the clavicle.

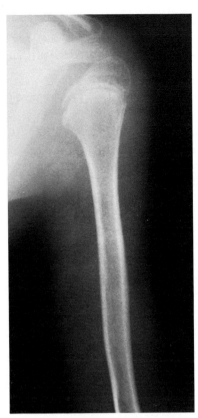

Figure 3-22   Diastrophic dysplasia. There is flattening of the humeral head and associated underdevelopment of the glenoid fossa in an older child.

Diastrophic Dysplasia

Diastrophic dysplasia is a form of dwarfism inherited via autosomal-recessive transmission. It is recognizable during the neonatal period and can even be diagnosed with prenatal sonography.[77,78] Clinically, patients have normal intelligence but are very short, with marked scoliosis, talipes equinovarus, joint contractures, and dislocations.[77,79] Approximately 84 percent of patients exhibit a deformity in calcification of the pinnae of the ear resulting in a "cauliflower ear deformity."[77] The thumb tends to be hypermobile and proximally located, resembling a hitchhiker's thumb.[68,77,79] A small percentage of patients succumb in the neonatal period, most often owing to cervical cord compression.

RADIOGRAPHIC ABNORMALITIES IN THE SHOULDER

Abnormalities about the shoulder in diastrophic dysplasia primarily involve the humerus, which is quite short. There is delayed development of the proximal humeral epiphyseal ossification center, and eventually the humeral head becomes broad, flat, and irregularly ossified (Fig. 3-22).[80] There is widening of the proximal humeral metaphysis and undertubulation of the proximal diaphysis. The glenoid fossa is often wide and shallow, relecting the abnormal contour of the humeral head.[21,80] Flexion contractures and shoulder dislocations can lead to early degenerative changes.

OTHER RADIOGRAPHIC FINDINGS

There is a generalized delay in epiphyseal development in diastrophic dysplasia, with later appearance of flat, irregular epiphyses and broadening of the neighboring metaphyses.[72,74] The long bones of the extremities, as well as the tubular bones of the hands and feet, tend to be broad and short. The first metacarpals and metatarsals are very hypoplastic or ovoid and associated with hitchhiker's thumbs.[68] The carpal and tarsal bones are quite irregular in contour, and there is bilateral talipes equinovarus deformity. The cervical vertebral bodies, including the odontoid process, are hypoplastic with cervical kyphosis.[21,77,79] In approximately 15 percent of cases this causes quadriplegia and death. There is often thoracic scoliosis as well as exaggerated lumbar lordosis.

Fibrodysplasia Ossificans Progressiva

Fibrodysplasia ossificans progressiva (FOP) is a rare mesodermal disorder characterized by progressive ossification of connective tissues and surrounding striated muscles with digital anomalies.[68] This disorder, previously called *myositis ossificans progressiva*, usually occurs sporadically. Virtually all affected children have abnormally small great toes and hallux valgus deformity.[81,82] Short thumbs may also be noted. The correct diagnosis usually is not entertained until the child presents with localized soft tissue swelling accompanied by heat, pain, and low-grade fever. Most children are diagnosed by age 4 years. There is no known cure for the disease, and many patients succumb early to restrictive pulmonary disease or pneumonia.[82] Because trauma tends to increase the ossification, biopsy of the nodules is not recommended.

RADIOGRAPHIC ABNORMALITIES IN THE SHOULDER

The initial finding is soft tissue swelling, which usually evolves into a soft, painless mass in the neck, shoulders, or paravertebral areas.[81,82] This either resolves or ossifies over the course of several months.[83] Eventually, bony bridges are formed throughout the soft tissues. In some cases, bands of ectopic bone extend from the paravertebral region and appear to form false joints or synarthroses; similar bands may arise in the extremities (Fig. 3-23). This most frequently occurs around the shoulder girdle, often a region of severely restricted motion by 10 years of age, with resultant pulmonary complications.[82]

OTHER RADIOGRAPHIC FINDINGS

The most important radiographic finding in FOP is a short great toe with absence or hypoplasia of the prox-

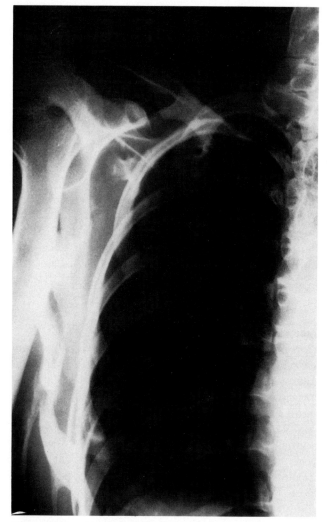

Figure 3-23 Fibrodysplasia ossificans progressiva. There are extensive soft tissue calcifications and bony bridges.

imal phalanx and hallux valgus deformity.[21,81] The thumb is often short because of a short first metacarpal,[68] and with progression of the disease there can be ankylosis of the cervical spine or long bone exostoses.

Goldenhar Syndrome (Oculoauriculovertebral Dysplasia, First and Second Branchial Arch Syndrome)

Goldenhar syndrome, also known as *first and second branchial arch syndrome*, is an uncommon, sporadically occurring syndrome characterized by vertebral abnormalities coupled with a triad of ocular dermoids, ear appendages, and fistulas.[21,84] This syndrome occurs in approximately one in 3500 to 5000 live births and is also characterized by asymmetric development of the craniofacial structures.[84,85] While the exact cause of the syn-

drome is unknown, it is postulated that there is an interruption of the blood supply to the structures of the first and second branchial arches early in embryonic life.[85]

RADIOGRAPHIC ABNORMALITIES IN THE SHOULDER

Radiographic abnormalities about the shoulder are known to occur in Goldenhar syndrome: Sprengel deformity, lateral hooking or absence of the clavicle, and multiple rib anomalies.[84]

OTHER RADIOGRAPHIC FINDINGS

Skeletal abnormalities are present in 40 to 60 percent of patients with Goldenhar syndrome; most commonly they involve the spine.[84,85] These spinal abnormalities include hemivertebrae, blocked vertebrae, occipitalization of the atlas, and scoliosis. This syndrome is also characterized by hypoplasia of the mandible, the ipsilateral maxilla, and the temporal bone. Multiple intracranial abnormalities have been documented, including lipomas, dermoids, and encephaloceles.[21] Absence of the radius has been reported, as has absence of the thumb.[68]

Goltz Syndrome

Goltz syndrome, also known as focal dermal hypoplasia, is a rare disease characterized predominantly by dermatologic abnormalities, including macules, telangiectasias, and lipomatous nodules.[86,87] In addition to having skin abnormalities, patients are often mentally retarded and have dystrophic nails, brittle hair, and ocular and dental abnormalities.

RADIOGRAPHIC ABNORMALITIES IN THE SHOULDER

Skeletal abnormalities, found in most patients with Goltz syndrome, can include absence of a portion of or an entire upper extremity.[86] Hypoplastic or bifid ribs have been described, and there may be aplasia or hypoplasia of the middle portion of the clavicle.[21]

OTHER RADIOGRAPHIC FINDINGS

The skeletal abnormalities in Goltz syndrome are variable and usually asymmetric. In 60 to 70 percent of patients, abnormalities of the hands and feet are noted: syndactyly, polydactyly, absence or hypoplasia of digits, and even lobster claw deformity.[68,86] Additional skeletal abnormalities include vertebral segmentation anomalies, scoliosis, osteopathia striata,[88] and lytic bone lesions resembling giant cell tumors.[89]

Holt-Oram Syndrome

Holt-Oram syndrome, also known as the *cardiomelic syndrome*, is an inherited autosomal-dominant condition with variable expressivity. The syndrome consists of congenital heart disease (atrial-septal or ventricular-septal defect and/or conduction abnormalities) and upper extremity or shoulder girdle malformation.[90,91] There is no association between the severity of the cardiac abnormalities and the extent of upper extremity malformations.[91,92] Typically, the most marked skeletal changes involve the hands; these range from subtle abnormalities of the thumb to phocomelia. Upper extremity involvement is usually bilateral but asymmetric. Clinically, patients have narrow, sloping shoulders and decreased range of motion.[91] The lower extremities and face are normal in this condition.

RADIOGRAPHIC ABNORMALITIES IN THE SHOULDER

The most common abnormality of the shoulder is rotation of the scapula, which is usually hypoplastic and elevated, with a shallow glenoid fossa. In infants, the short clavicles have prominent lateral hooks; in adults, the broadened clavicular ends and coracoclavicular articulations become the more prominent features.[93] Accessory ossicles, such as os acromiale and os coracoidale, are occasionally seen. The humerus can be hypoplastic or absent in patients with phocomelia. Deformity of the humeral head and prominence of the deltoid ridge have also been described.[94] The sternum may be unusually straight or short and bowed. Both pectus excavatum and pectus carinatum have been seen in these patients.[93]

OTHER RADIOGRAPHIC FINDINGS

Thumb abnormalities are present in almost all patients—triphalangeal ("fingerlike") thumb, or hypoplasia, or even absence of the thumb. Distinctive carpal abnormalities include scaphoid malformations, extra carpal bones (os centrale), and carpal fusion. The radial head may be deformed, but absence of the radius is rare in this syndrome.[68,93,94]

Hyperphosphatasia

Hyperphosphatasia, also known as *juvenile Paget disease*, is a rare, autosomal-recessive metabolic bone disorder in which abnormal membranous bone formation is characterized by the presence of immature woven bone instead of mature lamellar bone.[95,96] Patients usually present by 18 months of age with a large head, short stature, bowed extremities, and muscle weakness. Biochemically, the serum alkaline- and acid-phosphatase and urinary hydroxyproline values are elevated.[96] Diffuse skeletal involvement in hyperphosphatasia is characterized by coarsening of the bony trabecular pattern with diffuse thickening of the bones, which are "undertubulated." The cortex of the bone is markedly thin whereas the medullary cavities are dilated, often having cystlike changes within.[97]

RADIOGRAPHIC ABNORMALITIES IN THE SHOULDER

Radiologic evaluation of the shoulder demonstrates the typical broadening and undertubulation of the proximal humerus with associated coarsened bony trabeculae and bowing (Fig. 3-24). Similar changes are noted to involve the clavicle, scapula, and ribs as well.

OTHER RADIOGRAPHIC FINDINGS

Other characteristic radiologic findings include macrocranium with widening of the diploic space, patchy "cotton wool" calvarial densities, and marked thinning or absence of the outer table of the skull.[95] There is platyspondyly with biconcave vertebral bodies. The hips and pelvis often resemble those seen in osteomalacia with coxa vara and protrusio acetabuli.[97] The tubular bones of the hands and feet also have an increased diameter with coarsened trabecular markings.

Hypophosphatasia

Hypophosphatasia has a wide spectrum of severity—a lethal infantile form, a mild childhood form, and adult disease. Most cases are inherited by autosomal-recessive transmission, but some childhood and most adult cases are thought to have autosomal-dominant inheritance.[21,98] Clinically, affected young children exhibit short stature and failure to thrive, bowed extremities, and premature loss of teeth. Many of the clinical and radiologic findings resemble those seen with rickets. Biochemically, serum and tissue alkaline phosphatase levels are diminished, while there is an elevation of urinary phosphoethanolamine.[99] The primary radiographic feature of hypophosphatasia involves abnormal mineralization of membranous and endochondral bones, the degree of skeletal abnormality being inversely related to the level of alka-

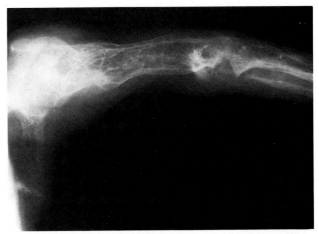

Figure 3-24 Hyperphosphatasia. There is diffuse demineralization, coarsening of the bony trabeculae, and undertubulation of the humerus. (Courtesy of Dr. Ernesto Menoc.)

line phosphatase activity[98] and to the age at which the skeletal abnormalities are noted.[100]

RADIOGRAPHIC ABNORMALITIES IN THE SHOULDER

The radiographic findings about the shoulder vary with the severity of the hypophosphatasia, but in each case there are features that resemble those found in rickets or osteomalacia. In the severe infantile form there is marked undermineralization of the entire skeleton, with short, thin, and poorly ossified ribs. The humeri are characteristically quite short and poorly ossified, with deep proximal metaphyseal cupping and fraying.[98,99,101] The scapulae also demonstrate abnormal ossification,[101] whereas the clavicle usually is the least affected bone in the body. Children with the perinatal form of hypophosphatasia usually succumb to respiratory complications as a result of underdevelopment of the thorax.[101]

In the less severe forms of hypophosphatasia the appearance of the proximal humerus also resembles that seen in rickets (i.e., diffuse osteoporosis with metaphyseal fraying and irregularity). There is widening of the physis that is not uniform across the growth plate, a feature that helps distinguish this entity from rickets. Small cystic changes are seen within the proximal humeral metaphysis (see Fig. 3-15). The anterior aspects of the ribs are noted to be cupped, resembling a "rachitic rosary." Irregular calcification at the anterior rib ends also helps to differentiate this syndrome from rickets.[99] Scalloping of the scapula is occasionally seen.[100]

OTHER RADIOGRAPHIC FINDINGS

All forms of hypophosphatasia demonstrate an increased incidence of fracture and subsequent bowing of the long bones. In addition, initial apparent widening of the cranial sutures is followed by premature craniosynostosis.[99,100]

Mandibuloacral Dysplasia

Mandibuloacral dysplasia is a very rare autosomal-recessive syndrome: approximately 20 cases are described in the literature.[102,103] This syndrome is characterized by short stature, joint stiffness, underdeveloped facial structures, and multiple abnormalities of the integument. Clinically, patients resemble those with progeria.

RADIOGRAPHIC FINDINGS IN THE SHOULDER

Mandibuloacral dysplasia is associated with progressive osteolysis resulting in postnatal hypoplasia or absence of the clavicles (Fig. 3-25).[68,102,103] Rib hypoplasia may also be seen.[21]

OTHER RADIOGRAPHIC FINDINGS

Characteristically, there is progressive acroosteolysis. Mandibular hypoplasia, multiple wormian bones, as well

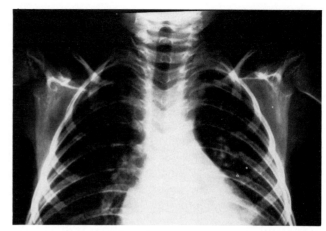

Figure 3-25   Mandibuloacral dysplasia. There is bilateral clavicular hypoplasia.

as delayed closure of the cranial sutures and fontanelles are also seen.[68,102]

Mannosidosis

Mannosidosis is a rare inherited autosomal-recessive lysosomal storage disease which usually presents during the first 3 years of life.[104,105] Two forms of mannosidosis are thought to exist, and they are differentiated by their severity.[104] Clinically, patients resemble those with mucopolysaccharidoses, having coarse facial features, mental retardation, short stature, hepatosplenomegaly, and occasionally, corneal clouding.[106] The diagnosis is made by correlating radiographic findings with clinical and biochemical data.

RADIOGRAPHIC FINDINGS IN THE SHOULDER

Typically, there is diffuse osteoporosis with coarsening of the bony trabeculae. The clavicles may be somewhat hypoplastic and broadened, particularly medially. There is also widening of the ribs, though they do not have the classic oar shape seen in the mucopolysaccharidoses.[105] Slight irregularity of the proximal humeral metaphysis with "undertubulation" of the proximal humeral diaphysis is also seen (Fig. 3-26).

OTHER RADIOGRAPHIC FINDINGS

Characteristically, there is thickening of the skull vault, particularly in the occipital and frontal regions. The vertebral bodies may be flattened with anterior beaking seen at the thoracolumbar junction.[104,105] Undertubulation of the diaphyses of the long bones as well as of the short tubular bones of the hand also occurs.

Metaphyseal Chondrodysplasia, Jansen Type

Metaphyseal chondrodysplasia, Jansen type is a rare autosomal-dominant inherited malformation syndrome

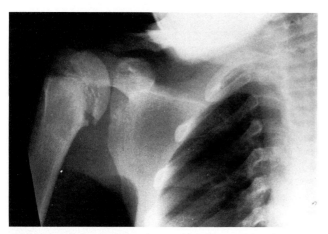

Figure 3-26 Mannosidosis. There is broadening of the ribs, irregularity of the proximal humeral metaphysis, and humerus varus.

characterized by persistence of physeal cartilage with abnormal endochondral bone formation.[107] Clinically, these patients are very short and have bowed extremities, especially the legs. This results in a peculiar apelike stance and waddling gait.[108,109] Characteristically, there is hypertelorism, exophthalmos, micrognathia, and swelling of multiple joints, including the knees and wrists. Hypercalcemia is noted in most patients.[107,109]

RADIOGRAPHIC ABNORMALITIES IN THE SHOULDER

The manifestations of this syndrome vary from infancy to adulthood. In infants, there is diffuse skeletal demineralization with coarsening of the bony trabeculae and cortical erosions (Fig. 3-27A).[108] The metaphyses, including those of the proximal humeri, become frayed and cupped, and their appearance may mimic rickets (Fig. 3-27B). As the patient matures the demineralization is no longer evident. The abnormal cartilage that was present at the metaphyseal ends is converted to bone. There is a resultant bulbous configuration as well as persistent irregular areas of lucency intermixed with large spotty calcifications or ossifications (Fig. 3-27C).[108]

In infancy, the ribs are "stringy" and irregular, with poor mineralization and cupping anteriorly, resembling the rachitic rosary. In older children, the medial ends of the clavicle are also poorly mineralized while the lateral aspect is broadened.[109] Pectus excavatum has also been noted in these patients.[25]

OTHER RADIOGRAPHIC FINDINGS

In older children, there may be sclerosis of the skull base, with underdevelopment of the paranasal sinuses and a reticular pattern involving the calvarium. Once the patient reaches adulthood, the dwarfism and extremity bowing persist, though with time the irregular pattern of calcification or ossification formerly present in the metaphyseal regions disappears.

Metatropic Dysplasia

Metatropic dysplasia is a rare inherited spondyloepimetaphyseal dysplasia that is thought to result from disordered endochondral ossification.[110] Currently, four types of this disorder are recognized that are differentiated by the mode of inheritance and severity of disease.[111] Most cases of metatropic dysplasia are inherited via an autosomal-recessive mode of transmission and are diagnosed at birth or shortly thereafter. In infancy, these patients have relatively long and narrow trunks with very short limbs. Later in life, this relationship reverses and disproportionate truncal shortening is due in part to progressive kyphoscoliosis.[112] Some affected persons have a 1- to 3-cm-long appendage or skin tag arising from the proximal gluteal fold—a "coccygeal tail."[110,112]

RADIOGRAPHIC ABNORMALITIES IN THE SHOULDER

Classically, there is marked shortening of all the long bones, including the humerus, with flaring of the metaphyses giving them a dumbbell or trumpet configuration (Fig. 3-28). Epiphyseal development, including that of the humeral head, is delayed with the eventual formation of small, flat humeral heads. The scapulae are short and squared, with hypoplasia of the glenoid fossae.[21] The clavicles can be elongated[21] and may be thickened.[113] In infancy, the thorax is long with a decreased anteroposterior diameter and short, deformed, widened ribs.[111,112] As these patients grow, they develop pectus carinatum deformity.[112]

OTHER RADIOGRAPHIC FINDINGS

Characteristically, there is platyspondyly, odontoid hypoplasia, and progressive kyphoscoliosis. A halberd-shaped pelvis with short, squared iliac wings, narrow sacrosciatic notches, and flattened acetabular roofs is noted.[111] The femurs are quite short with enlarged trochanters. The carpal and tarsal bones are deformed, whereas the tubular bones of the hands and feet are quite short.[112]

Mucolipidoses

The mucolipidoses are rare inherited lysosomal storage diseases. The best known is mucolipidosis II, also known as I-cell disease. This autosomal-recessive inherited condition is often fatal in the neonatal period and may be clinically indistinguishable from GM_1 gangliosidosis.[68] Patients with I-cell disease may resemble patients with Hurler syndrome; however, the clinical and radiologic manifestations of I-cell disease are present earlier in life.

RADIOGRAPHIC ABNORMALITIES IN THE SHOULDER

The bony changes in I-cell disease evolve with increasing age. During the first 2 months of life the bony changes

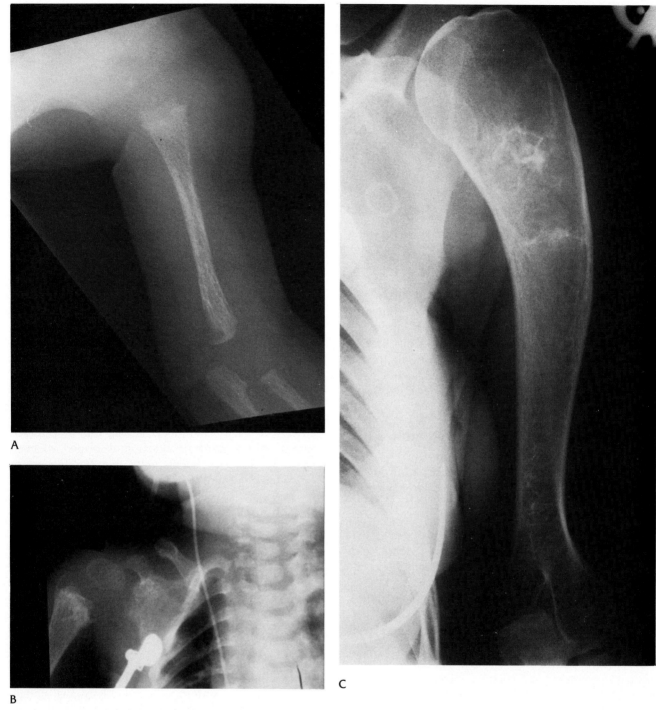

Figure 3-27 Metaphyseal chondrodysplasia, Jansen type. Radiographic findings change with increasing age. **A.** Characteristic cortical erosions and coarsened trabeculae are seen in infancy. **B.** The same child, now 2 years old, exhibits proximal humeral metaphyseal cupping and fraying. The clavicle is short and broad. **C.** The mother of the child in photos **A** and **B** has spotty calcifications in the bulbous proximal humeral shaft.

resemble those seen in congenital syphilis, rickets, and neonatal hyperparathyroidism (Fig. 3-29A).[114–116] In neonates there is diffuse osteopenia with coarse bony trabeculae and subperiosteal resorption. This is particularly

noticeable in the proximal humeral metaphysis, which is cupped and frayed and displays a peculiar notching.[114–116] The ribs are thin and poorly mineralized, often with anterior cupping. The scapulae are also poorly formed

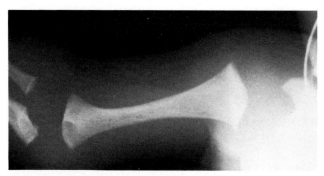

Figure 3-28 Metatropic dysplasia. The classic trumpet configuration of the humeral metaphyses is seen.

with shallow glenoid fossae. Pathologic fractures can involve the shoulder girdle, particularly the clavicle, during the birth process.

By 4 to 6 months of age, the bony abnormalities of I-cell disease resemble those seen in Hurler syndrome.[114,115] An oar-shaped deformity with characteristic broadening of the ribs also develops. The clavicles become quite broad and deformed. The scapulae, in particular the glenoid fossae, are quite hypoplastic. The humerus is short with metaphyseal widening and undertubulation of the diaphyses. Humerus varus is noted, with a peculiar narrowing at the humeral neck resembling the hatchet deformity seen in the mucopolysaccharidoses (Fig. 3-29B).[21,114,117]

OTHER RADIOGRAPHIC FINDINGS

During the early, neonatal stage of I-cell disease, stippled calcifications are seen in the epiphyseal regions, particularly the calcaneus.[114] The vertebral bodies are ovoid

with narrowing of the interpediculate distance and intervertebral disc calcifications.[21]

During the later stage of I-cell disease the bony changes closely resemble those seen in the mucopolysaccharidoses. These include the characteristic inferior beaking of the vertebral bodies at the thoracolumbar junction as well as tapering at the bases of the second through the fifth metacarpals, findings closely resembling those seen in Hurler syndrome.

Mucopolysaccharidoses

The mucopolysaccharidoses (MPS) are a group of inherited disorders involving abnormal mucopolysaccharide storage and urinary excretion owing to deficiency of lysosomal enzymes.[68] Eight distinct forms are now recognized that are differentiated by their varied clinical, radiologic, and biochemical features. The most common of these conditions is Hurler syndrome (MPS-I), an autosomal-recessive inherited condition. Typically, these patients are short, with coarse facial features, corneal clouding, and severe mental retardation. They have a protuberant abdomen, owing partially to hepatosplenomegaly, as well as flexion contractures, including claw hand deformity.[118,119] In contradistinction, patients with Morquio syndrome (MPS-IV) have normal mentation and better life expectancy, with hyperextensible joints and only mildly coarsened facial features.[21,68,118]

RADIOGRAPHIC ABNORMALITIES IN THE SHOULDER

While no radiologic abnormalities may be noted at birth, alterations about the shoulder girdle are quite common in Hurler syndrome as the child becomes older. The

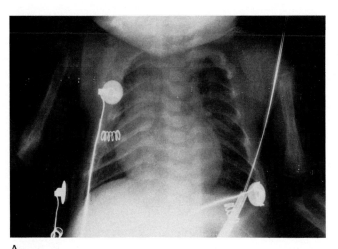

A

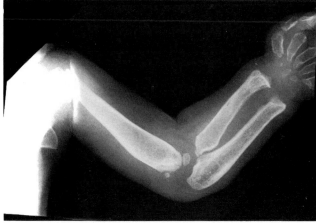

B

Figure 3-29 Mucolipidosis II (I-cell disease). Radiographic features change with increasing age. **A.** Neonate with typical osteopenia, coarsened trabeculae, proximal humeral metaphyseal fraying, and hypoplastic scapulae. (Courtesy of Dr. Ronald Glass.) **B.** Older child with typical humerus varus resembling a "hatchet," and undertubulation of the humeral diaphysis. Tapering of the bases of the second through fifth metacarpals is also demonstrated.

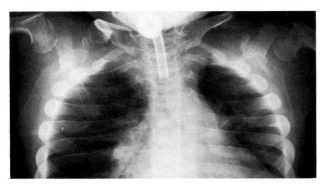

Figure 3-30 Mucopolysaccharidosis I (Hurler syndrome). Typical findings, including hypoplastic broad clavicles, oar-shaped ribs, hypoplastic glenoid fossae, and humerus varus, are illustrated.

scapulae are elevated, hypoplastic, and thickened, with poor delineation of the scapular angles and underdevelopment of the glenoid fossae. The clavicles are also short and broad, with thickening being most pronounced medially.[118,119] There is often lateral hooking of the clavicle as well.[21,119] Characteristically, the ribs are broadened with medial tapering, giving an oarlike configuration. Patients also have varus deformity of the humeral neck, which in MPS-IV is accompanied by constriction at the humeral neck resulting in a hatchetlike appearance (Fig. 3-30).[120]

Occasionally, the clavicles appear normal in Morquio disease.[121] While pectus excavatum and pectus carinatum deformities can be seen in Hurler syndrome,[118] abnormalities of the sternum are particularly prominent in Morquio disease, in which there is thickening of the sternum with premature fusion of sternal ossification centers and pectus carinatum deformity.[21,120,121]

OTHER RADIOGRAPHIC FINDINGS

In Hurler syndrome a large skull with a J-shaped sella turcica is commonly seen. In infants there is anteroinferior beaking of the vertebral bodies, thoracolumbar scoliosis and kyphosis, flared iliac wings with tapering of the inferior iliac bone, coxa valga, and shortened tubular bones of the hands with proximal tapering of the second through the fifth metacarpals.[68,118,119] Some radiographic findings peculiar to Morquio syndrome include universal platyspondyly, hypoplasia or absence of the odontoid process, central anterior vertebral body beaking, and gradual disappearance of the ossified femoral capital epiphyses.[21,119–121]

Multiple Cartilaginous Exostoses

Multiple cartilaginous exostoses, also known as *diaphyseal aclasis,* is an autosomal-dominant inherited bone dysplasia characterized by the presence of multiple cartilage-capped exostoses arising in bones formed by endochondral ossification. The earliest lesions may be present at birth, and approximately 80 percent of patients are

diagnosed by 10 years of age.[122] These patients present with palpable or visible deformities, most often in the knees and shoulder girdle. The patients with multiple hereditary exostoses may also have pain due to local pressure and mechanical alterations produced by the exostoses.[21,122,123]

RADIOGRAPHIC ABNORMALITIES IN THE SHOULDER

Typically, the exostoses in this syndrome are most numerous at the ends of actively growing bones, particularly the long tubular bones. A characteristic club-shaped broadening of the proximal humeral metaphysis is seen with multiple small, sessile exostoses.[122] Sometimes only the metaphyseal broadening may be seen. Numerous exostoses may also be noted along the vertebral border of the scapula as well as the ribs.[122–124] The exostoses involving the proximal humerus and scapula can also be large, pedunculated, cauliflower-like masses that cause considerable deformity (Fig. 3-31). Exostoses involving the clavicle and acromion can also be associated with a subacromial impingement syndrome.[125] Rarely, exostoses involving the sternum have been documented.[122]

OTHER RADIOGRAPHIC ABNORMALITIES

Exostoses in this syndrome can be quite numerous in the lower extremities, including the iliac crests. These patients may develop coxa valga, femora vara, tibia valga, as well as tibiotalar slant.[123] Deformities about the wrists can also be quite severe, simulating Madelung deformity. Previously, malignant degeneration of these exostoses to chondrosarcoma was thought to occur in approximately 5 to 25 percent of cases.[125] Currently, the prevalence is believed to be closer to 1 percent.[126]

Multiple Enchondromatosis

Multiple enchondromatosis, also known as *Ollier disease,* is an uncommon, nonhereditary condition characterized by the presence of benign cartilaginous masses or columnar streaks of unossified cartilage in the metaphyses of primarily tubular bones, with occasional extension into the diaphyses.[127] The cause of this disorder is unknown. The abnormally situated cartilage may present as a single lytic lesion or as multiple lucent linear streaks in the metaphyseal regions, which are often broadened. The adjacent epiphysis may be irregular as well. The enchondromas are usually bilateral, but often asymmetric, in distribution.[127]

Patients with multiple enchondromatosis typically present with leg length discrepancy, pathologic fractures, or angular deformity of the tubular bones.[127–129] Occasionally, the diagnosis can be made at birth.[127,128] Maffucci syndrome is a related condition consisting of multiple enchondromas with cutaneous, and occasionally visceral, cavernous hemangiomas.[130] The skeletal lesions are often

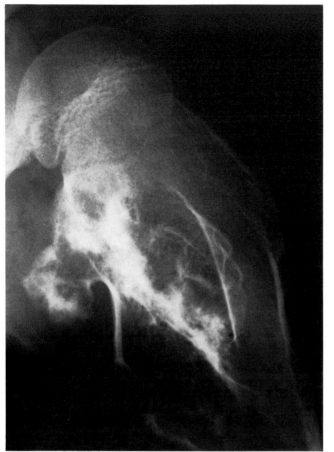

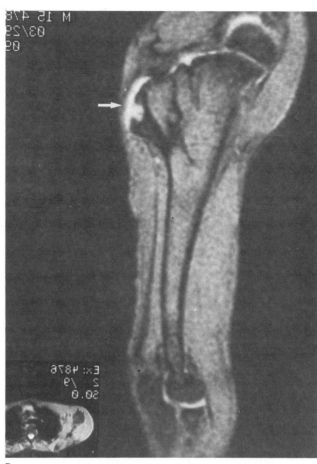

A   B

Figure 3-31 Multiple cartilaginous exostoses. **A.** A plain radiograph demonstrates proximal humeral metaphyseal broadening with a large pedunculated exostosis medially. **B.** Corresponding coronal MPGR (TR 600, TE 15, flip ∡20°) MRI of the same patient illustrates the medullary and cortical continuity between the humeral metaphysis and the exostosis. The high–signal intensity cartilaginous cap of the exostosis (*arrow*) is well seen.

asymmetric but rarely unilateral in distribution, usually with a parallel distribution of the cutaneous hemangiomas. The prevalence of sarcomatous degeneration of the enchondromas is as great as 25 to 30 percent for patients with multiple enchondromatosis[21,131] and at least 50 percent for those with Maffucci syndrome.[130,131] An increased incidence of certain nonosseous malignancies also has been documented in Maffucci syndrome.[130,131]

RADIOGRAPHIC ABNORMALITIES IN THE SHOULDER

In both multiple enchondromatosis and Maffucci syndrome, typical broadening and irregular lucencies can be seen in the proximal humeral metaphyses. The abnormal cartilage can appear as a single lytic lesion or as multiple linear streaks in the metaphysis, occasionally extending into the diaphysis (Fig. 3-32A, B). The humeral head may be irregular. Occasionally, enchondromas are seen in the scapula (Fig. 3-32C) and within the ribs. In Maffucci syndrome, multiple soft tissue calcifications and soft tissue masses are seen about the involved bony

structures; these calcifications represent phleboliths in the cutaneous venous malformations.

The abnormal cartilaginous masses generally do not continue to proliferate after puberty.[127] Adults with these syndromes may have persistent metaphyseal broadening and lucencies, or the affected areas can develop an entirely normal appearance or irregular calcifications.

OTHER RADIOGRAPHIC FINDINGS

Aside from the long tubular bones, the short tubular bones of the hands and feet and the pelvic bones are commonly involved in the syndrome. Rarely, enchondromas can be noted in the spine, base of skull, and the carpal or tarsal regions.[21,127,130]

Multiple Epiphyseal Dysplasia

Multiple epiphyseal dysplasia (MED), also known as *dysplasia epiphysealis multiplex,* is an inherited autosomal-dominant condition characterized by the delayed appearance of small, fragmented, irregular epiphyseal ossification centers. Patients with MED usually present in

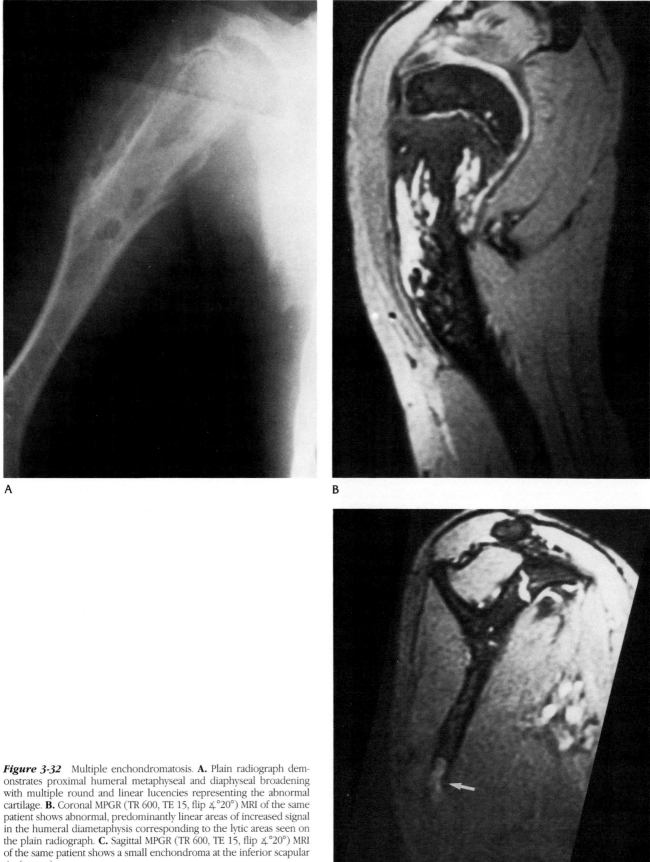

Figure 3-32 Multiple enchondromatosis. **A.** Plain radiograph demonstrates proximal humeral metaphyseal and diaphyseal broadening with multiple round and linear lucencies representing the abnormal cartilage. **B.** Coronal MPGR (TR 600, TE 15, flip ∡°20°) MRI of the same patient shows abnormal, predominantly linear areas of increased signal in the humeral diametaphysis corresponding to the lytic areas seen on the plain radiograph. **C.** Sagittal MPGR (TR 600, TE 15, flip ∡°20°) MRI of the same patient shows a small enchondroma at the inferior scapular tip (*arrow*).

late childhood or adolescence with short stature and symmetric joint pain, most commonly involving the hips, knees, and ankles.[21,132,133]

RADIOGRAPHIC ABNORMALITIES IN THE SHOULDER

Findings about the shoulder include delayed appearance of the humeral head ossification center. Ultimately, there is flattening and deformity of the humeral head with an associated hypoplastic, shallow glenoid fossa.[133] After physeal closure, the humeral head articular surface remains deformed, a condition that ultimately leads to early onset of degenerative arthritis.

OTHER RADIOGRAPHIC FINDINGS

Most epiphyses are affected in MED, but the most severe changes involve the hip. The epiphyseal ossification centers of the long tubular bones as well as the short tubular bones of the hands and feet are delayed in appearance and are ultimately irregular in configuration. There may be slight flattening of the vertebral bodies with irregular end plates, resembling Scheuermann disease.[132] Coronal clefting of the patella may also be seen.[68] In young infants, MED has a radiographic appearance similar to that of hypothyroidism. Thyroid function studies are often needed to distinguish between these two entities.

Noonan Syndrome

Noonan syndrome is a congenital malformation syndrome consisting of short stature with hypertelorism, webbed neck, cubitus valgus, mental retardation, and an increased incidence of congenital heart disease.[134-136] Many of the clinical features of Noonan syndrome resemble those seen in Turner syndrome, including the presence of a broad, shieldlike chest with widely spaced nipples. Unlike Turner syndrome, however, both males and females are affected by Noonan syndrome and the patients have a normal karyotype.[135,137]

RADIOGRAPHIC ABNORMALITIES IN THE SHOULDER

While scapula alta can be seen in this syndrome, the most common radiographic abnormality of the chest and shoulder girdle involves the sternum.[134,136,137] Typically, the sternum is short with an increased posterior concavity. There is a sharp angulation at or above the angle of Louis, with resultant pectus carinatum deformity.[136] Occasionally, there is a concurrent pectus excavatum deformity more inferiorly.[134] There is often premature fusion of the sternal ossification centers, and the manubrium is longer relative to the sternal body.[136]

OTHER RADIOGRAPHIC FINDINGS

None of the skeletal abnormalities encountered in Noonan syndrome are pathognomonic. Skeletal matura-

tion may be retarded.[137] Other radiographic findings include kyphosis, scoliosis, Klippel-Feil syndrome, cubitus valgus, flattened distal femoral and tibial epiphyses, and clinodactyly of the fifth finger.[68,134,137] Lymphangiectasia of the lungs may occur.

Osteodysplasty

Osteodysplasty, also known as *Melnick-Needles syndrome*, is a rare dysplasia initially suspected in infancy or childhood based on characteristic craniofacial dysmorphic features and radiographic skeletal abnormalities. Osteodysplasty is usually a dominant X-linked trait; several cases of a lethal, recessively inherited type are also reported in the literature.[138] With both types, males are more seriously affected than females. Clinically, patients with osteodysplasty are short with hypertelorism, full cheeks, micrognathia, malaligned teeth, and bowed extremities.[25,138,139]

RADIOGRAPHIC ABNORMALITIES IN THE SHOULDER

The most characteristic radiographic abnormalities in osteodysplasty involve the presence of thin, irregular, distorted ribs, having a "ribbonlike" appearance.[138-140] The clavicles are also wavy and tend to be small, often with lateral hooking.[21,138,141] Similarly, the scapula is often hypoplastic and elevated, and it may have irregular cortical undulations along the lateral margin.[139,140] The sternum may be abnormal, with fewer ossification centers delayed appearance thereof.[138,139] Changes involve the scapula, which is small and often elevated. The humerus is short with proximal metaphyseal flaring, diaphyseal constriction, and irregular cortical defects.

OTHER RADIOGRAPHIC FINDINGS

Characteristically, there is metaphyseal flaring, diaphyseal narrowing, and irregular cortical thickening in the long bones. There may be associated S-shaped bowing of the long bone diaphyses, particularly the tibia and radius. Other radiographic features include mandibular hypoplasia, sclerotic skull base, tall vertebral bodies, kyphosis, and scoliosis.[25,138,139]

Osteogenesis Imperfecta

The term *osteogenesis imperfecta* (OI) actually encompasses a heterogeneous group of disorders characterized by defects of collagen, mostly Type I collagen.[142] Many different classifications for OI have been devised, and they are principally based on a variety of clinical and radiographic criteria, as well as the mode of inheritance.[21,143,144] It may be difficult to distinguish between the various types purely on radiographic criteria, since the bony changes are dynamic in nature. The classical description usually involves short stature, fragile bones, blue sclerae, and deafness.[143,145] In the most severe forms, fractures can occur in utero.

RADIOGRAPHIC ABNORMALITIES IN THE SHOULDER

The primary radiographic feature of OI is diffuse osteopenia with marked cortical thinning and multiple fractures, which in infantile forms can involve the ribs, clavicles, and humeri (Fig. 3-33). There is often resultant deformity of the ribs, with severe posterior angulation posteriorly and callus formation.[146] The humerus may be fractured multiple times, with resultant bowing and an accordion-like appearance that can be seen in severely affected neonates. Hyperplastic callus formation is often seen in OI, and it is more common in the lower extremities than in the upper ones.[143]

OTHER RADIOGRAPHIC FINDINGS

Other characteristic features of OI include poor ossification of the cranium, basilar invagination, multiple wormian bones, platyspondyly, kyphoscoliosis, and dentinogenesis imperfecta.[143–145] There is often protrusio acetabuli, coxa vara, anterolateral femoral bowing, and anterior tibial bowing. The long bones may be short and broad, with a bamboolike appearance owing to multiple fractures, or alternatively may be quite thin and gracile. No fractures are specific for OI, so this diagnosis must be entertained whenever a child has a history of fractures in the absence of significant trauma.[147]

Massive Osteolysis

Massive osteolysis, also known as Gorham syndrome, is a rare disease of unknown cause that is characterized by the spontaneous dissolution of bone. It appears to be related to a hemangiomatous or lymphangiomatous process; a nonmalignant proliferation of thin-walled vessels

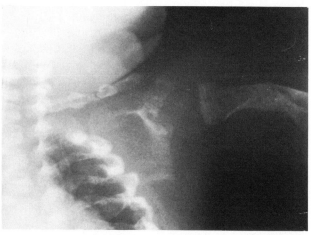

Figure 3-33 Osteogenesis imperfecta, Type II. There is typical diffuse osteopenia and severe deformity of the clavicle, scapula, humerus, and ribs due to multiple fractures.

is seen on histologic examination.[148–150] Massive osteolysis usually occurs in children and young adults of both sexes. Patients typically present with dull localized pain and weakness, without a history of significant trauma.

Massive osteolysis can occur anywhere in the skeleton but remains localized to one area, involving neighboring bones but without skipped areas or multicentricity. The most common sites for massive osteolysis are the shoulders and hips.[150,151]

RADIOGRAPHIC ABNORMALITIES IN THE SHOULDER

Massive osteolysis commonly involves the scapula and clavicle. The earliest radiologic sign of massive osteolysis is localized osteoporosis, followed by the appearance of lytic intramedullary lesions which subsequently coalesce.[150,151] When this disease involves the end of a bone such as the clavicle, there is concentric erosion that can be likened to a piece of "sucked candy."[149,151] In this syndrome the osteolysis can cross articulations.

OTHER RADIOGRAPHIC FINDINGS

Ultimately, the angiomatous or lymphangiomatous process can spread to the surrounding soft tissue structures, a phenomenon associated with a poorer prognosis. Currently, there is no known successful treatment for massive osteolysis, but radiation therapy, steroids, and chemotherapy are employed.[150] Spontaneous remissions can occur. Massive osteolysis can, however, result in death if there is extensive involvement of the thoracic cage.

The term *idiopathic osteolysis* has also been used to encompass a rare group of disorders characterized by spontaneous disappearance of bone in a multicentric distribution. Various classifications have been applied to this group of disorders.[149] While they share the same basic radiologic features of massive osteolysis, they can be inherited autosomally and may be associated with systemic abnormalities such as nephropathy.

Osteopetrosis

Osteopetrosis, also known as *Albers-Schonberg disease* or *marble bone disease,* is a rare inherited bone dysplasia characterized by diffuse osteosclerosis involving endochondral and membranous bones. Currently, several types are thought to exist, some autosomal dominant and some autosomal recessive.[21,152,153] The pathophysiology common to all types involves a failure of osteoclasts to resorb bone and calcified cartilage.[153] Patients with the infantile autosomal-recessive form of osteopetrosis present clinically with failure to thrive, hepatosplenomegaly, and anemia, and they die early, most often as a result of overwhelming infection or uncontrolled bleeding. These children can develop vitamin D–resistant rickets and often have encroachment on the neural foraminae at the skull base with resultant cranial nerve abnormalities such as blindness and deafness.[152] Patients with the milder autosomal-dominant or "tarda" form may be asymptomatic and simply have the characteristic radiographic findings of universal osteosclerosis.

RADIOGRAPHIC ABNORMALITIES IN THE SHOULDER

The earliest radiologic change in osteopetrosis involves increased bony density in the diaphyses of growing bones.[152] Later, there is more universal increased bone density. As the marrow space is encroached upon, undertubulation of the bone results. This is manifested in the shoulder as broadening of the proximal humeral metaphysis as well as the clavicle and ribs. Owing to the abnormal composition of the bones, there is an increased incidence of fractures in osteopetrosis. Pectus deformities have also been described in this syndrome.[152]

OTHER RADIOGRAPHIC FINDINGS

In addition to universal increased bone density, a bone-within-bone appearance can also be seen. There is nonpneumatization of the paranasal sinuses and mastoid air cells. In some cases of osteopetrosis associated with acroosteolysis and widened cranial sutures have also been described.[154] Presently, bone marrow transplantation is the treatment of choice. Normalization of bony corticomedullary differentiation has been noted radiographically in children following successful transplantation.[155]

Poland Syndrome

Poland syndrome is a nonhereditary condition characterized by congenital absence of the pectoralis major muscle and ipsilateral upper extremity abnormalities, particularly syndactyly.[156,157] This syndrome occurs in one in 30,000 to 50,000 live births, is more common in males, and most frequently involves the right side.[156,158,159] The pectoralis major muscle may be completely absent, but the most common abnormality is absence of the sternoclavicular head of that muscle. Deficiencies of the surrounding muscles such as the deltoid, latissimus dorsi, pectoralis minor, serratus anterior, and infraspinatus have been described.[156,159] The cause of Poland syndrome is not known, but it may be related to hypoplasia of the ipsilateral subclavian artery[158] or to a fetal injury incurred around the 7th gestational week, when the limb bud is close to the chest wall structures.[157]

Clinically, there is flattening of the involved side of the chest with ipsilateral absence of the anterior axillary fold and hypoplasia of the ipsilateral nipple or breast. This condition is associated with an increased incidence of renal anomalies and cryptorchidism and has been linked to Mobius syndrome.[156,160]

RADIOGRAPHIC ABNORMALITIES IN THE SHOULDER

Patients have hyperlucency of the involved hemithorax on chest radiographs. The ipsilateral scapula is often hypoplastic and elevated, with winging of the medial border, all signs consistent with Sprengel deformity.[156,160,161] There may be hypoplasia of the clavicle or the ipsilateral bony rib cage with apical lung herniation. Pectus excavatum and pectus carinatum deformities have also been described.[156,158] There may be hypoplasia of the ipsilateral humerus.

OTHER RADIOGRAPHIC FINDINGS

The hand is classically involved. Syndactyly may be partial or complete. The phalanges, metacarpals, and carpal bones may be hypoplastic or absent; the middle phalanges are most consistently and severely involved. There may be hypoplasia of the forearm.[68,156–161]

Progeria

Progeria, also known as Hutchinson-Gilford syndrome, is a rare disease of unknown cause characterized by premature aging. Affected persons die by the second or third decade of life, usually as the result of coronary or cerebral vascular disease.[162,163] Patients with progeria typically look normal at birth, and develop the typical physical manifestations during the first few years of life. They are quite small in stature with large heads, alopecia, prominent eyes and scalp veins, pointed nose, small chin, and a wizened elderly appearance. Other characteristic clinical findings include diminished subcutaneous fat, atrophic skin changes resembling scleroderma, and a stooped posture due to impaired hip and knee extension.[162–165]

RADIOGRAPHIC ABNORMALITIES IN THE SHOULDER

Typically, the ribs are thin and ribbonlike and the clavicles are also short and thin. Progressive osteolysis tends to involve the lateral clavicular ends as well as the posterior portions of the upper ribs, and it can even result in complete disappearance of these bony structures with time.[162,163,166] The pathophysiology of this bone resorption is unknown. Autopsy studies have shown replacement of the clavicle by fibrous tissue[165,166] but no evidence of angiomatous malformation or abnormal osteoclastic activity has been found. Valgus deformity of the humeral head and neck has also been described.[167] Ozonoff and Clemett[166] also described a peculiar area of proximal humeral diaphyseal narrowing and sclerosis where, eventually, pathologic fractures occurred.

OTHER RADIOGRAPHIC FINDINGS

Characteristically, there is diffuse osteopenia with an increased incidence of fractures and depressed bone healing. Other findings include widened cranial sutures with persistent opening of the fontanells, mandibular hypoplasia, avascular necrosis of the capital femoral epiphyses, coxa valga, hip dislocations, and acroosteolysis.[162–167] Owing to the presence of hypoplastic clavicles and skull dysplasia, progeria can resemble cleidocranial dysplasia in a very young child.

Pycnodysostosis

Pycnodysostosis, the *maladie de Toulouse-Lautrec*, is a rare inherited autosomal-recessive bone dysplasia characterized by a generalized increase in bone density.[168–170] This is felt to reflect inadequate osteoclastic activity.[171] Clinically, patients are quite short, with frontal bossing, small facies, dental abnormalities, short fingers, and an increased incidence of bone fractures. Occasionally, mental retardation has been reported in this syndrome.[168]

RADIOGRAPHIC ABNORMALITIES IN THE SHOULDER

The bones of the shoulder girdle have a diffuse sclerotic density with an increased incidence of fracture, often with poor callus formation. Clavicular dysplasia is a characteristic feature; hypoplasia or absence of the lateral ends is the most common manifestation. Occasionally, complete absence of the clavicle can be noted.[168]

OTHER RADIOGRAPHIC FINDINGS

Characteristically, there is evidence of acroosteolysis. Other findings include widened cranial sutures with a persistent open anterior fontanel, wormian bones, obtuse mandibular angle, hypoplasia of the facial bones with nonpneumatization of the paranasal sinuses, and persistence of the deciduous teeth.[21,168–171]

Scapuloiliac Dysostosis

Scapuloiliac dysostosis is a rare bone dysplasia; only four cases are reported in the literature.[172,173] This syndrome may be inherited via an autosomal-dominant mode of transmission. Clinically these patients have low-set malformed ears, micrognathia, and multiple ocular abnormalities, which include microphthalmos, coloboma of the retina and eyelids, corneal opacification, and ectopic pupils.[21,172,173]

RADIOGRAPHIC ABNORMALITIES IN THE SHOULDER

Characteristically, there is bilateral symmetry, with scapular hypoplasia involving predominantly the infraspinous portion of the scapula.[172] A case with coracoclavicular synostosis has also been reported.[173] The clavicles are also malformed, having a long, thin, "stretched" appearance, with narrowing of the medial ends.[172,173]

OTHER RADIOGRAPHIC FINDINGS

There is bilateral symmetric hypoplasia of the iliac bones, which may be associated with unstable hips in infancy.[172] Other findings include narrowing of the femoral and tibial diaphyses, radioulnar synostosis, and clinodactyly.

Thrombocytopenia–Absent Radius Syndrome

Thrombocytopenia–absent radius (TAR) syndrome is a rare autosomal-recessive inherited syndrome characterized by congenital or neonatal thrombocytopenia with bilateral radial aplasia.[174,175] Patients present at birth with obvious upper extremity deformities and with hemorrhagic tendencies. The most striking hematologic abnormality is thrombocytopenia, but there can also be anemia, leukemoid reactions, and hepatosplenomegaly.[176] Cardiac abnormalities are found in approximately 30 percent of cases.[174]

RADIOGRAPHIC ABNORMALITIES IN THE SHOULDER

Complete absence of the humerus is seen bilaterally in approximately 5 to 10 percent of cases[174] with phocomelia. Alternatively, the humeri can be quite hypoplastic (Fig. 3-34). There may be absence or marked hypoplasia of the scapula, particularly the glenoid fossa or acromion.[21,174] Similarly, the clavicles may be absent or hypoplastic; lateral hooking of the clavicles is also seen.[21]

OTHER RADIOGRAPHIC FINDINGS

In addition to bilateral absence of the radii, the ulna is also abnormal in TAR syndrome, being hypoplastic and malformed in all cases and absent in approximately 10 to 20 percent of cases.[174] Patients with TAR syndrome

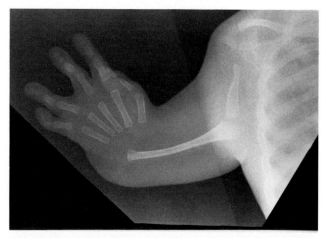

Figure 3-34 TAR syndrome. The humerus is markedly hypoplastic with absence of the humeral head and hypoplasia of the scapula, especially the glenoid fossa. There is lateral hooking of the clavicle. The radius is absent in this child with five digits (including a thumb). This is characteristic of TAR syndrome.

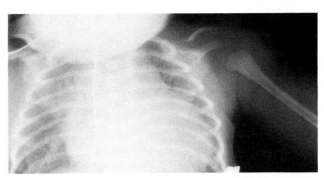

Figure 3-35 Trisomy 18. The medial aspect of the clavicle is missing, whereas the remaining lateral portion is thin and hooked.

have a thumb, unlike those with other syndromes manifesting radial aplasia. Lower limb abnormalities can be seen in as many as 50 percent of patients and include hip dislocations, coxa valga, tibial and femoral torsion, and clubfoot deformities.[174,176]

Trisomy 18

Trisomy 18 occurs sporadically, is more common in females, and is associated with increased maternal age.[177,178] Clinically, affected babies are small and exhibit failure to thrive, generalized hypertonicity, and mental retardation. There is a high incidence of cardiovascular malformations, renal anomalies, hernias, and peculiar dermatoglyphics.[21,68,177] Most children die within the first year of life.

RADIOGRAPHIC ABNORMALITIES IN THE SHOULDER

Clinically, trisomy 18 patients have a broad, shieldlike chest with widely spaced nipples. The ribs are very thin, while the sternum is short and undersegmented.[21,177,178] The clavicles are thin with lateral hooking.[21,177] There may also be hypoplasia or absence of the medial third of the clavicles (Fig. 3-35).[93] A case of trisomy 18 with a tripartite clavicle has also been reported.[178]

OTHER RADIOGRAPHIC FINDINGS

Skeletal maturation is delayed, especially about the knees. Other abnormalities found in this syndrome include mandibular hypoplasia; narrow, anteriorly rotated iliac bones; rockerbottom feet with associated vertical talus; and short, dorsiflexed great toes.[177,178] The hand is often held in a clenched position with the second digit overlapping the third. The digits often deviate medially, and clinodactyly is common.[68]

Yunis-Varón Syndrome

Yunis-Varón syndrome is a rare autosomal-recessive inherited skeletal dysplasia which has features of cleidocranial dysplasia, with severe micrognathia and absence of the thumbs.[179–180] Clinically, there is marked mental retardation, facial hypoplasia, sparse hair, and malformed ears. Patients usually die in the neonatal period.[181]

RADIOGRAPHIC ABNORMALITIES IN THE SHOULDER GIRDLE

The clavicles are variably described as being thin, hypoplastic, or absent. Involvement is usually bilateral, but need not be symmetric.[179] In addition, absence of the sternal ossification centers is often noted.[179]

OTHER RADIOGRAPHIC FINDINGS

Digital abnormalities are an integral part of the Yunis-Varón syndrome, particularly those involving the first digit of the hands and feet. There may be bilateral absence of the thumbs and of the distal phalanges of the remaining digits. Absence of the first metatarsal bone is also seen with hypoplasia or agenesis of the phalanges of the great toe.[179–181] Other findings include hypoplastic facial bones and iliac bones.[179]

References

1. THE INTERNATIONAL WORKING GROUP ON CONSTITUTIONAL DISEASES OF BONE (Communicated by Spranger J): International classification of osteochondrodysplasias. *Eur J Pediatr* 151:407–415, 1992.
2. GARDNER E: The embryology of the clavicle. *Clin Orthop* 58:9, 1968.
3. OGDEN JA, CONLOGUE GJ, BRONSON ML: Radiology of postnatal skeletal development. III. The clavicle. *Skel Radiol* 4:196, 1979.
4. JIT L, KULKARNI M: Times of appearance and fusion of epiphysis at the medial end of the clavicle. *Indian J Med Res* 64:773, 1976.

5. SCHMIDT H, FREYSCHMIDT J: *Köhler and Zimmer's Borderlands of Normal and Early Pathologic Findings in Skeletal Radiography,* 4th ed, New York, Thieme, 1993.

6. YARKONI S, SCHMIDT W, JEANTY P, REECE EA, HOBBINS JC: Clavicular measurement: A new biometric parameter for fetal evaluation. *J Ultrasound Med* 4:467, 1985.

7. ZAWIN JK, JARAMILLO D: Conversion of bone marrow in the humerus, sternum, and clavicle: Changes with age on MR images. *Radiology* 188:159, 1993.

8. KEATS TE: *Atlas of Normal Roentgen Variants That May Simulate Disease,* 5th ed, St. Louis, Mosby, 1992.

9. SHAUFFER IA, COLLINS WV: Deep clavicle rhomboid fossa. *JAMA* 195:778, 1966.

10. KUMAR R, MADEWELL JE, SWISCHUK LE, LINDELL MM, DAVID R: The clavicle: Normal and abnormal. *Radio-Graphics* 9:677, 1989.

11. WOOD VE, MARCHINSKI L: Congenital anomalies of the shoulder, in Rockwood CA Jr, Matsen FA III (eds): *The Shoulder,* Philadelphia, Saunders, 1990, pp 98–148.

12. SAMILSON RL: Congenital and developmental anomalies of the shoulder girdle. *Orthop Clin North Am* 11:219, 1980.

13. GIBSON DA, CARROLL N: Congenital pseudoarthrosis of the clavicle. *J Bone Joint Surg* 52B:629, 1970.

14. AHMADI B, STEEL HH: Congenital pseudoarthrosis of the clavicle. *Clin Orthop* 126:130, 1977.

15. SCHNALL SB, KING JD, MARRERO G: Congenital pseudoarthrosis of the clavicle: A review of the literature and surgical results of six cases. *J Pediatr Orthop* 8:316, 1988.

16. LLOYD-ROBERTS GC, APLEY AG, OWEN R: Reflections upon the aetiology of congenital pseudoarthrosis of the clavicle. *J Bone Joint Surg* 57B:24, 1975.

17. OWEN R: Congenital pseudoarthrosis of the clavicle. *J Bone Joint Surg* 52B:644, 1970.

18. ALLDRED AJ: Congenital pseudoarthrosis of the clavicle. *J Bone Joint Surg* 45B:312, 1963.

19. IGUAL M, GIEDION A: The lateral clavicle hook: Its objective measurement and its diagnostic value in Holt-Oram syndrome, diastrophic dwarfism, thrombocytopenia–absent radius syndrome and trisomy 18. *Ann Radiol* 22:136, 1979.

20. OESTREICH AE: The lateral clavicle hook—an acquired as well as a congenital anomaly. *Pediatr Radiol* 11:147, 1981.

21. TAYBI H, LACHMAN RS: *Radiology of Syndromes, Metabolic Disorders, and Skeletal Dysplasias,* 3d ed, Chicago, Year Book, 1990.

22. HALL BD: Syndromes and situations associated with congenital clavicular hypoplasia or agenesis. *Progr Clin Biol Res* 104:279, 1982.

23. GOLTHAMER CR: Duplication of the clavicle ("os subclaviculare"). *Radiology* 68:576, 1957.

24. TWIGG HL, ROSENBAUM RC: Duplication of the clavicle. *Skel Radiol* 6:281, 1981.

25. OSSUM, Parkville, Victoria: Murdoch Institute, 1991.

26. OGDEN JA, PHILLIPS SB: Radiology of postnatal skeletal development. VII. The scapula. *Skel Radiol* 9:157, 1983.

27. McCLURE JG, RANEY RB: Anomalies of the scapula. *Clin Orthop* 110:22, 1975.

28. LIBERSON F: Os acromiale—a contested anomaly. *J Bone Joint Surg* 19:683, 1937.

29. MUDGE MK, BERNARDINO S, WOOD VE, FRYKMAN GK: Rotator cuff tears associated with os acromiale. *J Bone Joint Surg* 66A:427, 1984.

30. NORRIS TR, FISCHER J, BIGLIANI LU, NEER CS II: The unfused acromial epiphysis and its relationship to impingement syndrome. *Orthop Trans* 7:505, 1983.

31. EDELSON JG, ZUCKERMAN J, HERSHKOVITZ I: Os acromiale: Anatomy and surgical implications. *J Bone Joint Surg* 74B:551, 1993.

32. FINDER JG: Congenital anomaly of the coracoid: Os coracosternale vestigiale. *J Bone Joint Surg* 18:148, 1936.

33. TACHDJIAN MO: *Pediatric Orthopedics,* 2d ed, Philadelphia, Saunders, 1990.

34. HOROWITZ AE: Congenital elevation of the scapula—Sprengel's deformity. *Am J Orthop Surg* 6:260, 1908.

35. CARSON WG, LOVELL WW, WHITESIDES TE JR: Congenital elevation of the scapula: Surgical correction by the Woodward procedure. *J Bone Joint Surg* 63A:1199, 1981.

36. ORRELL KG, BELL DF: Structural abnormality of the clavicle associated with Sprengel deformity. *Clin Orthop* 258:157, 1990.

37. JEANNOPOULOS CL: Congenital elevation of the scapula. *J Bone Joint Surg* 34A:883, 1952.

38. GREENWALD AG, SCHUTE PC, SHIVELEY JL: Brachial plexus birth palsy: A 10-year report on the incidence and prognosis. *J Pediatr Orthop* 4:689, 1984.

39. SJÖBERG I, ERICHS K, BJERRE I: Cause and effect of obstetric (neonatal) brachial plexus palsy. *Acta Paediatr Scand* 77:357, 1988.

40. KATTAN KR, SPITZ HB: Roentgen findings in obstetrical injuries to the brachial plexus. *Radiology* 91:462, 1968.

41. RESNICK D: Additional congenital or heritable anomalies and syndromes, in Resnick D, Niwayama G (eds): *Diagnosis of Bone and Joint Disorders,* 2d ed, Philadelphia, Saunders, 1988, pp 3540–3600.

42. HERNANDEZ RJ, DIAS L: CT evaluation of the shoulder in children with Erb's palsy. *Pediatr Radiol* 18:333, 1988.

43. NUTTER PD: Coracoclavicular articulations. *J Bone Joint Surg* 23:177, 1941.

44. HALL FJS: Coracoclavicular joint: A rare condition treated successfully by operation. *Br Med J* 1:766, 1950.

45. CHUNG SMK, NISSENBAUM MM: Congenital and developmental defects of the shoulder. *Orthop Clin North Am* 6:381, 1975.

46. McCLURE JG, RANEY RB: Double acromion and coracoid processes—a case report of an anomaly of the scapula. *J Bone Joint Surg* 56A:830, 1974.

47. MARTINI AK, NEUSEL E: Duplication of the scapula. *Int Orthop* 11:361, 1987.

48. OWEN R: Bilateral glenoid hypoplasia. *J Bone Joint Surg* 35B:262, 1953.

49. LINTNER DM, SEBASTIANELLI WJ, HANKS GA, KALENAK A: Glenoid dysplasia—a case report and review of the literature. *Clin Orthop* 283:145, 1992.

50. KUHNS LR, FINNSTROM O: New standards of ossification of the newborn. *Radiology* 119:655, 1976.

51. HITCHCOCK HH, BECHTOL CO: Painful shoulder: Observations on the role of the tendon of the long head of the biceps brachii in its causation. *J Bone Joint Surg* 30A:263, 1948.

52. MEYER AW: Spontaneous dislocation and destruction of

tendon of long head of biceps brachii. Fifty-nine instances. *Arch Surg* 17:493, 1928.

53. ANDREASEN AT: Congenital absence of the humeral head. Report of two cases. *J Bone Joint Surg* 30B:333, 1948.

54. LUCAS LS, GILL JH: Humerus varus following birth injury to the proximal humeral epiphysis. *J Bone Joint Surg* 29:367, 1947.

55. COZEN L: Congenital dislocation of the shoulder and other anomalies. Report of a case and review of the literature. *Arch Surg* 35:956, 1937.

56. POZNANSKI AK: Diagnostic clues in the growing ends of bone. *J Can Assoc Radiol* 29:7, 1978.

57. WOLFSON JJ, ENGEL RR: Anticipating meconium peritonitis from metaphyseal bands. *Radiology* 92:1055, 1969.

58. SILLENCE DO, LACHMAN RS, JENKINS T, RICCARDI VM, RIMOIN DL: Spondylohumerofemoral hypoplasia (giant cell chondrodysplasia): A neonatally lethal short-limb skeletal dysplasia. *Am J Med Genet* 13:7, 1982.

59. MAROTEAUX P, SPRANGER J, STANESCU V, LE MAREC B, PFEIFFER RA, BEIGHTON P, MATTEI JF: Atelosteogenesis. *Am J Med Genet* 13:15, 1982.

60. STORER J, GROSSMAN H: The campomelic syndrome. Congenital bowing of limbs and other skeletal and extraskeletal anomalies. *Radiology* 111:673, 1974.

61. HALL BD, SPRANGER JW: Campomelic dysplasia. Further elucidation of a distinct entity. *Am J Dis Child* 134:285, 1980.

62. PAZZAGLIA UE, BELUFFI G: Radiology and histopathology of the bent limbs in campomelic dysplasia: Implications in the aetiology of the disease and review of theories. *Pediatr Radiol* 17:50, 1987.

63. HAPPLE R, KOCH H, LENZ W: The CHILD syndrome: Congenital hemidysplasia with ichthyosiform erythroderma and limb defects. *Eur J Pediatr* 134:27, 1980.

64. HEBERT AA, ESTERLY NB, HOLBROOK KA, HALL JC: The CHILD syndrome: Histologic and ultrastructural studies. *Arch Dermatol* 123:503, 1987.

65. HESELSON NG, CREMIN BJ, BREIGHTON P: Lethal chondrodysplasia punctata. *Clin Radiol* 29:679, 1978.

66. ANDERSEN PE JR, JUSTESEN P: Chondrodysplasia punctata: Report of two cases. *Skel Radiol* 16:223, 1987.

67. NAIDU S, MOSER HW: Peroxisomal disorders. *Neurol Clin* 8:507, 1990.

68. POZNANSKI AK: *The Hand in Radiologic Diagnosis, with Gamuts and Pattern Profiles,* 2d ed, Philadelphia, Saunders, 1984.

69. JARVIS JL, KEATS TE: Cleidocranial dysostosis: A review of 40 new cases. *AJR* 121:5, 1974.

70. POZNANSKI AK, HOLT JF: Cleidocranial dysplasia. *Semin Roentgenol* 8:150, 1973.

71. CHITAYAT D, HODGKINSON KA, AZOUZ EM: Intrafamilial variability in cleidocranial dysplasia: A three generation family. *Am J Med Genet* 42:298, 1992.

72. HUNDLEY JD, WILSON FC: Progressive diaphyseal dysplasia. Review of the literature and report of seven cases in one family. *J Bone Joint Surg* 55A:461, 1973.

73. AGGARWAL P, WALI JP, SHARMA SK: Progressive diaphyseal dysplasia: Case report and literature review. *Orthopedics* 13:901, 1990.

74. KAFTORI JK, KLEINHAUS U, NAVEH Y: Progressive dia-

75. CLAWSON DK, LOOP JW: Progressive diaphyseal dysplasia (Engelmann's disease). *J Bone Joint Surg* 46A:143, 1964.

76. KUMAR B, MURPHY WA, WHYTE MP: Progressive diaphyseal dysplasia (Engelmann's disease): Scintigraphic-radiographic-clinical correlations. *Radiology* 140:87, 1981.

77. WALKER BA, SCOTT CI, HALL JG, MURDOCH JL, McKUSICK VA: Diastrophic dwarfism. *Medicine* 51:41, 1972.

78. GEMBRUCH U, NIESEN M, KEHRBERG H, HENSMANN M: Diastrophic dysplasia: A specific prenatal diagnosis by ultrasound. *Prenatal Diagn* 8:539, 1988.

79. TABER P, FREEDMAN S, LACKEY DA: Diastrophic dwarfism, in Kaufmann HJ (ed): *Progress in Pediatric Radiology,* vol. 4, *Intrinsic Diseases of Bones,* Basel, Karger, 1973, pp 152–166.

80. TAYBI H: Diastrophic dwarfism. *Radiology* 80:1, 1963.

81. ROGERS JG, GEHO WB: Fibrodysplasia ossificans progressiva. A survey of forty-two cases. *J Bone Joint Surg* 61A:909, 1979.

82. THICKMAN D, BONAKDAR-POUR A, CLANCY M, VAN ORDEN J, STEEL H: Fibrodysplasia ossificans progressiva. *AJR* 139:935, 1982.

83. REINIG JW, HILL SC, FANG M, MARINI J, ZASLOFF MA: Fibrodysplasia ossificans progressiva: CT appearance. *Radiology* 159:153, 1986.

84. AVON SW, SHIVELY JL: Orthopedic manifestations of Goldenhar syndrome. *J Pediatr Orthop* 8:683, 1988.

85. DARLING DB, FEINGOLD M, BERKMAN M: The roentgenological aspects of Goldenhar's syndrome (oculoauriculovertebral dysplasia). *Radiology* 91:254, 1968.

86. TEMPLE IK, MacDOWALL P, BARAITSER M, ATHERTON DJ: Syndrome of the month: Focal dermal hypoplasia (Goltz syndrome). *J Med Genet* 27:180, 1990.

87. GINSBURG LD, SEDANO HO, GORLIN RJ: Focal dermal hypoplasia syndrome. *AJR* 110:561, 1970.

88. KNOCKAERT D, DEQUECKER J: Osteopathia striata and focal dermal hypoplasia. *Skel Radiol* 4:223, 1979.

89. SELZER G, DAVID R, REVACH M, CVIBAH TJ, FRIED A: Goltz syndrome with multiple giant-cell tumor-like lesions in bones. A case report. *Ann Intern Med* 80:714, 1974.

90. KAUFMAN RL, RIMOIN DL, McALISTER WH, HARTMANN AF: Variable expression of the Holt-Oram syndrome. *Am J Dis Child* 127:21, 1974.

91. HURST JA, HALL CM, BARAITSER M: The Holt-Oram syndrome. *J Med Genet* 28:406, 1991.

92. SMITH AT, SACK GH JR, TAYLOR GJ: Holt-Oram syndrome. *J Pediatr* 95:538, 1979.

93. POZNANSKI AK, STERN AM, GALL JC JR: Skeletal anomalies in genetically determined congenital heart disease. *Radiol Clin North Am* 9:435, 1971.

94. POZNANSKI AK, GALL JC JR, STERN AM: Skeletal manifestations of the Holt-Oram syndrome. *Radiology* 94:45, 1970.

95. CAFFEY J: Familial hyperphosphatasemia with ateliosis and hypermetabolism of growing membranous bone: Review of the clinical, radiographic, and chemical features. *Bull Hosp Joint Dis* 33:81, 1972.

96. WHALEN JP, HORWITH M, KROOK L, MacINTYRE I, MENA E, VITERI F, TORUN B, NUNEZ EA: Calcitonin treatment in hereditary bone dysplasia with hyperphosphatasemia:

physeal dysplasia (Camurati-Engelmann): Radiographic follow-up and CT findings. *Radiology* 164:777, 1987.

A radiographic and histologic study of bone. *AJR* 129:29, 1977.

97. IANCU TC, ALMAGOR G, FRIEDMAN E, HARDOFF R, FRONT D: Chronic familial hyperphosphatasemia. *Radiology* 129:669, 1978.

98. FALLON MD, TEITELBAUM SL, WEINSTEIN RS, GOLD-FISCHER S, BROWN DM, WHYTE MP: Hypophosphatasia: Clinicopathologic comparison of the infantile, childhood, and adult forms. *Medicine* 63:12, 1984.

99. KOZLOWSKI K, SUTCLIFFE J, BARYLAK A, HARRINGTON G, KEMPERDICK H, NOLTE K, RHEINWEIN H, THOMAS PS, UNIECKA W: Hypophosphatasia. *Pediatr Radiol* 5:103, 1976.

100. CURRARINO G, NEUHAUSER EBD, REYERSBACH GC, SOBEL EH: Hypophosphatasia. *AJR* 78:392, 1957.

101. SHOHAT M, RIMOIN DL, GRUBER HE, LACHMAN RS: Perinatal lethal hypophosphatasia; clinical, radiologic and morphologic findings. *Pediatr Radiol* 21:421, 1991.

102. SCHRANDER-STUMPEL C, SPAEPEN A, FRYNS JP, DUMON J: A severe case of mandibuloacral dysplasia in a girl. *Am J Med Genet* 43:877, 1992.

103. PALLOTTA R, MORGESE G: Mandibuloacral dysplasia: A rare progeroid syndrome. Two brothers confirm autosomal recessive inheritance. *Clin Genet* 26:133, 1984.

104. MITCHELL ML, ERICKSON RP, SCHMID D, HIEBER V, POZNANSKI AK, HICKS SP: Mannosidosis: Two brothers with different degrees of disease severity. *Clin Genet* 20:191, 1981.

105. SPRANGER J, GEHLER J, CANTZ M: The radiographic features of mannosidosis. *Radiology* 119:401, 1976.

106. VIDGOFF J, LOVRIEN EW, BEALS RK, BUIST NRM: Mannosidosis in three brothers—a review of the literature. *Medicine* 56:335, 1977.

107. GRAM PB, FLEMING JL, FRAME B, FINE G: Metaphyseal chondrodysplasia of Jansen. *J Bone Joint Surg* 41A:951, 1959.

108. CHARROW J, POZNANSKI AK: The Jansen type of metaphyseal chondrodysplasia: Confirmation of dominant inheritance and review of radiographic manifestations in the newborn and adult. *Am J Med Genet* 18:321, 1984.

109. SILVERTHORN KG, HOUSTON CS, DUNCAN BP: Murk Jansen's metaphyseal chondrodysplasia with long-term follow-up. *Pediatr Radiol* 17:119, 1987.

110. BODEN SD, KAPLAN FS, FALLON MD, RUDDY R, BELIK J, ANDAY E, ZACKAI E, ELLIS J: Metatropic dwarfism. Uncoupling of endochondral and perichondral growth. *J Bone Joint Surg* 69A:174, 1987.

111. KOZLOWSKI K, CAMPBELL J, ANDERSON B, ERKEN EHW, JEQUIER S, NELSON M, SLIMAN N, SPRAQUE P, TAMAELA LA: Metatropic dysplasia and its variants (analysis of 14 cases). *Australas Radiol* 32:325, 1988.

112. MAROTEAUX P: Spondyloepiphyseal dysplasias and metatropic dwarfism. *Birth Defects* 5:35, 1969.

113. KOZLOWSKI K, MORRIS L, REINWEIN H, SPRAGUE P, TAMAELA LA: Metatropic dwarfism and its variants (report of six cases). *Australas Radiol* 20:367, 1976.

114. LEMAITRE L, REMY J, FARRIAUX JP, DHONDT JL, WALBAUM R: Radiological signs of mucolipidosis II or I-cell disease. A study of nine cases. *Pediatr Radiol* 7:97, 1978.

115. PAZZAGLIA UE, BELUFFI G, CASTELLO A, COCI A, ZATTI G: Bone changes of mucolipidosis II at different ages. Postmortem study of three cases. *Clin Orthop* 276:283, 1992.

116. PAZZAGLIA UE, BELUFFI G, BIANCHI E, CASTELLO A, COCI A, MARCHI A: Study of the bone pathology in early mucolipidosis II (I-cell disease). *Eur J Pediatr* 148:553, 1989.

117. TABER P, GYEPES MT, PHILIPPART M, LING S: Roentgenographic manifestations of Leroy's I-cell disease. *AJR* 118:213, 1973.

118. BUYSE ML: *Birth Defects Encyclopedia,* Dover, Blackwell, 1990.

119. EGGLI KD, DORST JP: The mucopolysaccharidosis and related conditions. *Semin Roentgenol* 21:275, 1986.

120. GROSSMAN H: The mucopolysaccharidoses and mucolipidoses, in Kaufmann HJ (ed): *Progress in Pediatric Radiology,* vol 4, *Intrinsic Diseases of Bones,* Basel, Karger, 1973, pp 495–544.

121. LANGER LO JR, CAREY LS: The roentgenographic features of the KS mucopolysaccharidosis of Morquio (Morquio-Brailsford's disease). *AJR* 97:1, 1966.

122. SOLOMON L: Hereditary multiple exostoses. *J Bone Joint Surg* 45:292, 1963.

123. SHAPIRO F, SIMON S, GLIMCHER MJ: Hereditary multiple exostoses. Anthropometric roentgenographic, and clinical aspects. *J Bone Joint Surg* 61A:815, 1979.

124. GIEDION A, KESZTLER R, MUGGIASCA F: The widened spectrum of multiple cartilaginous exostosis (MCE). *Pediatr Radiol* 3: 93, 1975.

125. CRAIG EV: Subacromial impingement syndrome in hereditary multiple exostoses. *Clin Orthop* 209:182, 1986.

126. VOUTSINAS S, WYNNE-DAVIES R: The infrequency of malignant disease in disphyseal aclasis and neurofibromatosis. *J Med Genet* 20:345, 1983.

127. MAINZER F, MINAGI H, STEINBACH HL: The variable manifestations of multiple enchondromatosis. *Radiology* 99:377, 1971.

128. RAUPP P, KEMPERDICK H: Neonatal radiological aspect of enchondromatosis (Ollier's disease). *Pediatr Radiol* 20: 377, 1990.

129. SHAPIRO F: Ollier's disease. An assessment of angular deformity, shortening, and pathological fracture in twenty-one patients. *J Bone Joint Surg* 64A:95, 1982.

130. LEWIS RJ, KETCHAM AS: Maffucci's syndrome: Functional and neoplastic significance. *J Bone Joint Surg* 55A:1465, 1973.

131. SCHWARTZ HS, ZIMMERMAN NB, SIMON MA, WROBLE RR, MILLAR EA, BONFIGLIO M: The malignant potential of enchondromatosis. *J Bone Joint Surg* 69A:269, 1987.

132. SPRANGER J: The epiphyseal dysplasias. *Clin Orthop* 114:46, 1976.

133. MURPHY MC, SHINE IB, STEVENS DB: Multiple epiphyseal dysplasia. Report of a pedigree. *J Bone Joint Surg* 55A:814, 1973.

134. ALLANSON JE: Noonan syndrome. *J Med Genet* 24:9, 1987.

135. MENDEZ HMM, OPITZ JM: Noonan syndrome: A review. *J Med Genet* 21:493, 1985.

136. HOEFFEL JC, PERNOT C, JUNCKER P: Radiologic patterns of the sternum in Noonan's syndrome with congenital heart disease. *Am J Dis Child* 135:1044, 1981.

137. RIGGS W JR: Roentgen findings in Noonan's syndrome. *Radiology* 96:393, 1970.

138. DONNENFELD AE, CONARD KA, ROBERTS NS, BORNS PF, ZACKAI EH: Melnick-Needles syndrome in males: A lethal multiple congenital anomalies syndrome. *Am J Med Genet* 27:159, 1987.

139. MELNICK JC, NEEDLES CF: An undiagnosed bone dysplasia. A two family study of four generations and three generations. *AJR* 97:39, 1966.

140. MEMIS A, USTUN EE, SENER RN: Case report 717: Osteodysplasty (Melnick-Needles syndrome). *Skel Radiol* 21:132, 1992.

141. THEANDER G, EKBERG O: Congenital malformations associated with maternal osteodysplasty. A new malformation complex. *Acta Radiol Diagn* 22:369, 1981.

142. WENSTRUP RJ, LEVER LW, PHILLIPS CL, QUARLES LD: Mutations in the COL 1A2 gene of type I collagen that result in nonlethal forms of osteogenesis imperfecta. *Am J Med Genet* 45:228, 1993.

143. SHOENFELD Y, FRIED A, EHRENFELD NE: Osteogenesis imperfecta. Review of the literature with presentation of twenty-nine cases. *Am J Dis Child* 129:679, 1975.

144. ANDERSEN PE JR, HAUGE M: Osteogenesis imperfecta: A genetic, radiological, and epidemiological study. *Clin Genet* 36:250, 1989.

145. KING JD, BOBECHKO WP: Osteogenesis imperfecta. An orthopedic description and surgical review. *J Bone Joint Surg* 53B:72, 1971.

146. VERSFELD GA, BEIGHTON PH, KATZ K, SOLOMON A: Costovertebral anomalies in osteogenesis imperfecta. *J Bone Joint Surg* 67B:602, 1985.

147. PATERSON CR, BURNS J, McALLION SJ: Osteogenesis imperfecta: The distinction from child abuse and the recognition of a variant form. *Am J Med Genet* 45:187, 1993.

148. GORHAM LW, STOUT AP: Massive osteolysis (acute spontaneous absorption of bone, phantom bone, disappearing bone). Its relation to hemangiomatosis. *J Bone Joint Surg* 37A:985, 1955.

149. HARDEGGER F, SIMPSON LA, SEGMUELLER G: The syndrome of idiopathic osteolysis. Classification, review, and case report. *J Bone Joint Surg* 67B:89, 1985.

150. JOSEPH J, BARTAL E: Disappearing bone disease: A case report and review of the literature. *J Pediatr Orthop* 7:584, 1987.

151. ABRAHAMS J, GANICK D, GILBERT E, WOLFSON J: Massive osteolysis in an infant. *AJR* 135:1084, 1980.

152. JOHNSTON CC JR, LAVY N, LORD T, VELLIOS F, MERRITT AD, DEISS WP JR: Osteopetrosis. A clinical, genetic, metabolic, and morphologic study of the dominantly inherited, benign form. *Medicine* 47:149, 1968.

153. EL KHAZEN N, FAVERLY D, VAMOS E, VAN REGEMORTER N, FLAMENT-DURAND J, CARTON B, CREMER-PERLMUTTER N: Lethal osteopetrosis with multiple fractures in utero. *Am J Med Genet* 23:811, 1986.

154. ANDREN L, DYMLING JF, HOGEMAN KE, WENDEBERG B: Osteopetrosis acro-osteolytica. A syndrome of osteopetrosis, acro-osteolysis and open sutures of the skull. *Acta Chir Scand* 124:496, 1962.

155. KAPLAN FS, AUGUST CS, FALLON MD, DALINKA M, AXEL L, HADDAD JG: Successful treatment of infantile malignant osteopetrosis by bone-marrow transplantation. *J Bone Joint Surg* 70A:617, 1988.

156. IRELAND DCR, TAKAYAMA N, FLATT AE: Poland's syndrome. A review of forty-three cases. *J Bone Joint Surg* 58A:52, 1976.

157. GOLDBERG MJ, MAZZAEI RJ: Poland syndrome: A concept of pathogenesis based on limb bud embryology. *Birth Defects* 13:103, 1977.

158. BOUVET JP, LEVEQUE D, BERNETIERES F, GROS JJ: Vascular origin of Poland syndrome? A comparative radiographic study of the vascularization of the arms of eight patients. *Eur J Pediatr* 128:17, 1978.

159. HEGDE HR, SHOKEIR MHK: Posterior shoulder girdle abnormalities with absence of pectoralis major muscle. *Am J Med Genet* 13:285, 1982.

160. WILSON MR, LOUIS DS, STEVENSON TR: Poland's syndrome: Variable expression and associated anomalies. *J Hand Surg* 13A:880, 1988.

161. HADLEY MDM: Carpal coalition and Sprengel's shoulder in Poland's syndrome. *J Hand Surg* 10B:253, 1985.

162. MONU JUV, BENKA-COKER LBO, FATUNDE Y: Hutchinson-Gilford progeria syndrome in siblings. *Skel Radiol* 19:585, 1990.

163. MOEN C: Orthopedic aspects of progeria. *J Bone Joint Surg* 64A:542, 1982.

164. SCHWARZ E: Roentgen findings in progeria. *Radiology* 79:411, 1962.

165. GABR M, HASHEM N, HASHEM M: Progeria, a pathologic study. *J Pediatr* 57:70, 1960.

166. OZONOFF MB, CLEMETT AR: Progressive osteolysis in progeria. *AJR* 100:75, 1967.

167. REICHEL W, BAILEY JA III, ZIGEL S, GARCIA-BUNUEL R, KNOX G: Radiological findings in progeria. *J Am Genet Soc* 19:657, 1971.

168. ELMORE SM: Pycnodysostosis: A review. *J Bone Joint Surg* 49A:153, 1967.

169. SEDANO HD, GORLIN RJ, ANDERSON VE: Pycnodysostosis. Clinical and genetic considerations. *Am J Dis Child* 116:70, 1968.

170. MEREDITH SC, SIMON MA, LAROS GS, JACKSON MA: Pycnodysostosis. *J Bone Joint Surg* 60A:1122, 1978.

171. SOTO RJ, MAUTALEN CA, HOJMAN D, CODEVILLA A, PIQUE J, PANGARO JA: Pycnodysostosis: Metabolic and histologic studies. *Birth Defects* 5:109, 1969.

172. THOMAS PS, REID MM, McCURDY AM: Pelvis-shoulder dysplasia. *Pediatr Radiol* 5:219, 1977.

173. BLANE CE, HOLT JF, VINE AK: Scapuloiliac dysostosis. *Br J Radiol* 57:526, 1984.

174. HALL JG: Thrombocytopenia and absent radius (TAR) syndrome. *J Med Genet* 24:79, 1987.

175. GIUFFRE L, CAMMARATA M, CORSELLO G, VITALITI SM: Two new cases of thrombocytopenia absent radius (TAR) syndrome: Clinical, genetic, and nosologic features. *Klin Padiatr* 200:10, 1988.

176. HAYS RM, BARTOSHESKY LE, FEINGOLD M: New features of thrombocytopenia and absent radius syndrome. *Birth Defects* 18:115, 1982.

177. ASTLEY R: Trisomy 17/18. *Br J Radiol* 39:86, 1966.

178. OZONOFF MB, STEINBACH HL, MAMUNES P: The trisomy 18 syndrome. *AJR* 91:618, 1964.

179. YUNIS E, VARON H: Cleidocranial dysotosis, severe micrognathism, bilateral absence of thumbs and first metatarsal bone, and distal aphalangia. A new genetic syndrome. *Am J Dis Child* 134:649, 1980.

180. HUGHES HE, PARTINGTON MW: Brief clinical report: The syndrome of Yunis and Varon—report of a further case. *Am J Med Genet* 14:539, 1983.

181. HENNEKAM RCM, VERMEULEN-MEINERS C: Further delineation of the Yunis-Varon syndrome. *J Med Genet* 26:55, 1989.

IMAGING OF SHOULDER INFECTIONS

Cheryl A. Petersilge

The shoulder girdle is an infrequent site of musculoskeletal infection. Though the humerus may rank as the third most common site of osteomyelitis, it is involved in only 10 to 14 percent of cases.[1,2] The prevalence of clavicular and scapular involvement by osteomyelitis is less than 5 percent.[1,2] Glenohumeral septic arthritis accounts for only 6 to 12 percent of all cases of septic arthritis[2,3,4]; septic arthritis of the sternoclavicular joint is rare.

The young and elderly are at increased risk, as are drug abusers, diabetics, patients with vascular disease, and patients with human immunodeficiency virus (HIV) infection and other forms of immunocompromise, patients with chronic debilitating illnesses, and patients with preexisting arthritis. A growing elderly population, an increasing incidence of trauma, and the use of intraarticular and periarticular steroids have all been proposed as factors associated with a rising incidence of glenohumeral septic arthritis.[5,6]

Patients with rheumatoid arthritis are at increased risk for the development of spontaneous septic arthritis, and the shoulder and sternoclavicular joints are frequent sites of infection.[7–9] The sternoclavicular joint is a common site of infection for intravenous drug abusers, who have a high prevalence of gram-negative infections, especially with *Pseudomonas aeruginosa*.[10] Clavicular osteomyelitis has been described in patients with long-standing tracheitis[11] and in those with a history of subclavian vein catheterization.[12–14]

PATHOPHYSIOLOGY[15,16]

Osteomyelitis

Knowledge of the pathophysiology of bone and soft tissue infections is essential to understanding the age dependence of major sites of osteomyelitis and the radiographic manifestations of the infectious process and its healing. The osseous and articular structures may become infected via a number of different mechanisms—hematogenous seeding during silent or symptomatic bacteremia, spread from adjacent soft tissue infection, direct implantation secondary to puncture or penetrating injury, and postoperative infection.

Acute hematogenous osteomyelitis is most common in children and accounts for 80 to 90 percent of childhood osteomyelitis. *Staphylococcus aureus* is the most common pathogen of neonatal and childhood acute hematogenous osteomyelitis. Group B streptococci are also common organisms in neonatal osteomyelitis and they have a predilection for the proximal humerus.[17] Patients with sickle cell disease have a high incidence of *Salmonella* osteomyelitis.[18,19] A second peak of hematogenous osteomyelitis is seen in the elderly, typically involving the vertebrae. Hematogenous osteomyelitis in the elderly population is often associated with a distant focus of infection, usually in the genitourinary tract. Gram-negative organisms predominate in these infections. In adults, direct extension from wounds or foreign bodies and postoperative infections are the most common mechanisms of osteomyelitis and septic arthritis.[6,20]

The vascular anatomy at the epiphyseal-metaphyseal junction greatly influences the location of hematogenous osteomyelitis. In children older than 1 year or after the development of the physis, the distal branches of the nutrient artery become sharply angulated as they approach the physis. The vessels curve away from the growth plate and flow into metaphyseal venous sinusoids. At the junction with sinusoids blood flow slows, creating an ideal environment for the seeding of bacteria. Thus, osteomyelitis is most commonly seen in the metaphysis between age 1 year and the age of skeletal maturity. In the proximal humerus metaphyseal osteomyelitis may result in septic arthritis since the portion of the metaphysis where the axillary recess of the glenohumeral joint capsule inserts lies within the joint.

Until the first birthday, there is no physis to obstruct the course of the arterioles, and direct communications exist between the metaphyseal and epiphyseal vasculature. As the vessels enter the epiphysis they flow into

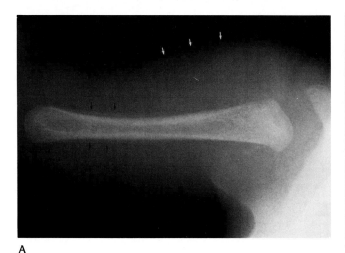
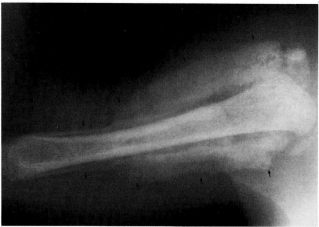

A   B

Figure 4-1 Anteroposterior (AP) views of the humerus obtained 7 days apart in a 6-week-old boy with staphylococcal osteomyelitis. Initial examination, **A,** demonstrates diffuse soft tissue swelling of the arm with subcutaneous edema and loss of the normal sharp margin between the muscle tissue and subcutaneous fat (*white arrows*). Faint periosteal new bone formation is present along the distal diaphysis (*black arrows*). No areas of osteoporosis or osteolysis are evident. **B.** Exuberant periosteal new bone formation (*black arrows*) is visible along the entire diaphysis of the humerus. Again, no changes of osseous destruction are demonstrated.

large venous lakes. Subsequent slowing of blood flow occurs, similar to that previously described in the metaphysis. Thus, bacterial seeding occurs in the epiphysis in this age group. The intraarticular location of the infected epiphysis may result in associated septic arthritis. In adults, a similar situation occurs following resorption of the cartilaginous growth plate.

In osteomyelitis due to direct extension, direct implantation, or prior surgery no predominant focus of infection can be identified; rather, osteomyelitis is seen at whatever site is affected by the soft tissue trauma. Postoperative infection that occurs early is usually the result of contamination during surgery. After joint replacement, late infections are typically the result of seeding to the hardware during bacteremia.

The site of bone involvement varies with a patient's age and so does the course and healing of osteomyelitis. Once seeding of the bone has occurred, a series of events begins that is reflected in the clinical and radiographic course of osteomyelitis.[21] First, hyperemia occurs with subsequent vascular dilatation and increased capillary permeability. Increased vascular permeability leads to accumulation of exudate within the medullary space. This early state is accompanied by surrounding soft tissue swelling. Eventually, increased medullary pressure by the exudate results in diminution of blood flow and vascular thrombosis, and is accompanied by migration of inflammatory cells into the medullary space. The exudate and inflammatory cells are responsible for the eventual bone destruction. If osteomyelitis is recognized and treated at or before this stage, little osseous destruction occurs.

As the inflammatory response proceeds, medullary

pressure continues to increase and the infectious process spreads. In neonates and children exudate escapes from the medullary space via haversian and Volkmann's canals. The looser attachment of the periosteum in infants and children results in stripping of the periosteum from the cortex and trapping of the exudate beneath the periosteum. Owing to this easy separation between periosteum and cortex, the frequency of subperiosteal abscess is greater in the pediatric population. This lifted periosteum produces new bone in the form of lamellar or solid periostitis. During the acute phase, periosteal new bone formation may be quite extensive in the infant (Fig. 4-1), yet the incredible healing properties of this age group lead to such extensive remodeling that there is little long-term evidence of infection. With more chronic infection, this periosteal reaction may encompass the entire bone; this periosteal reaction is known as *involucrum.* A tract, known as a cloacae, may develop through the involucrum, allowing infected material and sequestra access to the soft tissues. The stripping of the periosteum that accompanies the escape of exudate from the medullary space further compromises blood supply to a cortex already compromised by vascular thrombosis. Osseous necrosis ensues, with the formation of sequestra, which are devitalized fragments of cortical or cancellous bone. They are engulfed by the inflammatory exudate, and antibiotics may not reach these devascularized pieces of bone. Failure to remove sequestra predisposes to recurrent bouts of active osteomyelitis. In adults the infection is more likely to spread throughout the length of the medullary canal before escaping that space. Subperiosteal abscess, involucrum, and sequestrum are not frequently observed in the adult population, owing to the tight adherence between periosteum and cortex; rather, infection is more likely to spread along the medullary canal and may involve the entire shaft. The close union between periosteum and cortex ensures that a good blood supply is maintained to the infected bone in adults. Pathologic fracture, however, is more common in adults.

Subacute osteomyelitis is a sequela of infection with "low virulence" organisms or inadequate treatment. This form of osteomyelitis is typically seen as a localized abscess with a well-defined border. Chronic osteomyelitis develops following inadequate or inappropriate treatment of osteomyelitis. No time frame adequately separates acute from subacute or from chronic osteomyelitis. Clinical presentation, in association with radiographic findings, usually helps to characterize these different subtypes of osteomyelitis.

Septic Arthritis

Gonococcal arthritis is the most common cause of septic arthritis and usually is seen in sexually active young adults.[20] Nongonococcal septic arthritis is a disease of infants and adults; the incidence during childhood is low.[20] The more frequent infection of infants and adults is explained by the vascular anatomy previously described. In these patient populations, blood vessels have easy access to the epiphysis and subchondral bone. Gram-positive cocci are the most frequent pathogens of septic arthritis in children and adults. *Haemophilus influenzae* is commonly cultured from septic joints in patients aged 6 months to 2 years.[3,4] Gram-negative organisms are seen in infants younger than 6 months and in the elderly. Prior use of antibiotics or immunosuppressive medications and chronic debilitating illnesses predispose older individuals to gram-negative septic arthritis, which has a high rate of associated morbidity.[3,22]

Following hematogenous seeding of the joint, bacteria first invade the synovial membrane, and at this stage examination of the joint fluid may reveal no bacteria. A synovial inflammatory process ensues, with hyperemia and the development of pannus. With progression of the inflammatory process, the surrounding soft tissues become edematous. As the inflammatory pannus grows it destroys cartilage at the margins of the articular surface as well as along the central portions of the articular surface. As these destructive changes occur there is increased production of joint fluid, migration of inflammatory cells into the fluid, and subsequently, development of frank pus. Cartilaginous erosions lead eventually to destruction of the subchondral bone. In the extreme case, fibrous or osseous ankylosis may occur. A direct correlation has been shown between patient outcome and the time to diagnosis.[23] Because of the rapidity with which destructive changes occur, septic arthritis is treated as an emergent situation requiring immediate diagnosis and treatment.

Soft Tissue Infection

Cellulitis—infection confined to the subcutaneous soft tissues—can occur anywhere in the body. Patients present with erythema, warmth, and swelling of the involved extremity. Soft tissue abscess may develop with more aggressive infections. Infection of the muscles, known as pyomyositis, is extremely rare owing to the unexplained ability of muscle tissue to resist infection.

CLINICAL PRESENTATION

Pain, erythema, warmth, decreased range of motion, and joint effusion in association with fever alert the clinician to the possibility of septic arthritis. In the shoulder, recognition of this entity is often delayed because of the absence of systemic symptoms and often a paucity of local signs and symptoms other than pain. Failure to consider the diagnosis of pyoarthritis is the main cause of failure to diagnose.[5] The clinical presentation of septic arthritis mimics many other entities, including rotator cuff tear, rheumatoid flares, pseudogout, and calcific tendinitis.

Osteomyelitis may present with vague symptoms of pain without systemic manifestations,[1] although acute hematogenous osteomyelitis usually presents as an acute febrile illness with focal symptoms of pain, swelling, and erythema overlying the site of infection. In young children, refusal to use a limb may be the earliest indicator of infection.[24] In the neonate, systemic signs of infection are often lacking despite multifocal osteomyelitis.[2,25] Laboratory indicators of infection include an elevated white cell count with a left shift and an erythrocyte sedimentation rate. Symptoms may be altered in patients with an abnormal immune system or a history of antibiotic treatment.

In today's society, persons infected with HIV represent a large population at increased risk for musculoskeletal infection. The infections seen in these patients involve the soft tissues and bones. Pathogens are frequently opportunistic ones such as *Cryptococcus neoformans* and *Neisseria asteroides*,[26] although common pathogens such as *Staphylococcus aureus* or *Salmonella* species are also commonly found. In HIV-infected patients, cat scratch disease causes an unusual systemic infection associated with angiomatous cutaneous lesions and osteolytic lesions.[26–29] These lytic lesions may be associated with periostitis and a soft tissue mass.[26,27] The presence of these bone lesions helps to distinguish this disease, with its vascular cutaneous lesions, from Kaposi's sarcoma.[27]

Pyomyositis is a soft tissue infection caused by *S. aureus* which was rare in the United States until the acquired immunodeficiency syndrome (AIDS) epidemic.

This muscle infection is easily treated but may be fatal if not recognized early in its course.[30] Often multifocal, it presents with deceptively mild clinical symptoms and a "woody" stiffness of the involved muscles.[26,30]

The AIDS population also suffers from a high incidence of reactivation tuberculosis.[34] Musculoskeletal manifestations include infectious arthritis, osteomyelitis, and pyomyositis.[26]

Recognition of infection early in its course is essential to the establishment of appropriate antibiotic treatment and early surgical intervention. Failure to treat early infection can lead to disabling destructive changes, especially in the pediatric population, where damage to the growth plate and extensive bone destruction can result in devastating growth abnormalities. Joint infection may severely damage articular cartilage, leading to degenerative changes which progress long beyond the resolution of the infectious process. Improperly treated osteomyelitis, including failure to fully debride all necrotic tissue, may lead to the development of lifelong problems with recurrent bouts of reactivation. Chronic osteomyelitis and long-standing sinus tracts are associated with increased risk of malignancy, particularly squamous cell carcinoma.[32–35]

IMAGING EVALUATION

In cases of uncomplicated septic arthritis the clinical diagnosis is easily established and imaging evaluation is not a major part of the clinical evaluation. Aspiration of the joint for culture is usually performed at the bedside. Rarely, the radiologist may be requested to perform fluoroscopically guided aspiration if no fluid can otherwise be aspirated. Imaging evaluation may be requested in cases of suspected osteomyelitis.

The radiologist is more frequently involved in the evaluation of suspected osteomyelitis and soft tissue abscesses. In these patients, symptoms may be nonfocal and nonspecific, especially in children. Imaging evaluation is performed not only to confirm the presence of disease and to construct the differential diagnosis but also to localize disease as part of preoperative planning. Imaging is required when the extent of osteomyelitis is critical to surgical planning, when the extent of soft tissue involvement is unknown, to differentiate soft tissue infection from bone infection, and to determine disease activity in patients with chronic osteomyelitis.

Plain Films and Tomography

Plain film examination should be the first imaging study for suspected infection of the shoulder. Plain film examination is limited, however, owing to the absence of changes associated with septic arthritis, cellulitis, and soft tissue abscess and the delayed occurrence of plain film changes in patients with osteomyelitis. Typical radio-graphic findings of osteomyelitis do not occur until 7 to 14 days after the onset of infection. Radiographic evidence of osseous destruction is not present until some 35 to 40 percent of the bone has been destroyed.[36]

The first radiographic changes of osteomyelitis are deep soft tissue swelling adjacent to the infected bone.[21] This swelling is manifested as bulging or displacement of the muscle from the adjacent bone (Fig. 4-2). Films obtained with soft tissue technique or with the opposite side for comparison may enhance recognition of this finding.[21,37] Next, the surrounding muscles—and subsequently the subcutaneous tissues—become edematous, and the intermuscular (fascial) and muscular-subcutaneous fascial planes are obliterated. Thin linear periostitis is frequently seen in children and precedes changes of bone destruction (see Fig. 4-1). Periostitis may occur in association with cellulitis and soft tissue abscesses, even in the absence of osteomyelitis, and care should be taken in interpretation of radiographs in these patients.[38] Regional osteoporosis is a result of the hyperemia. Focal osteoporosis may be the earliest indicator of bone destruction. As the inflammatory exudate escapes from the medullary space via haversian and Volkmann's canals, bone destruction occurs along the canals, resulting in visible lucencies producing the appearance of cortical fissuring.[39] Although cortical fissuring is not specific for osteomyelitis, in the appropriate clinical setting it is an early radiographic indicator of osteomyelitis. Eventually, osseous destruction may manifest as a permeative or moth-eaten pattern or as a well-defined area of lysis (Figs. 4-2, 4-3).[37] These changes may progress for a time following the institution of appropriate antibiotic therapy.[1,15]

Brodie's abscess, or subacute osteomyelitis, is a focal, well-defined metaphyseal lytic lesion with sclerotic margins which usually occurs in the tibia in young males and is associated with local tenderness and intermittent episodes of pain.[40,41] Sinus tracts extending to the physis may be visible.[40,41] The shoulder is rarely involved. The cause of this local inflammatory process is unknown. When cultures grow a pathogen, Staphylococcus aureus is usually the offending agent.[40] The lesion is typically eccentrically located and may be intracortical. Associated findings include sinus tracts, which may be intraosseous and extend to the physis, sequestra, and periosteal new bone formation.

Chronic osteomyelitis is associated with extensive bony sclerosis, which occurs in response to a chronic inflammatory stimulus. Radiographic changes include extensive sclerosis, focal areas of lucency, and mature periosteal new bone formation. Cloacae may be present. Radiographic indicators of activity in chronic osteomyelitis, including a change from previous examinations, ill-defined osteolysis, thin linear periostitis, and sequestration,[15] are quite insensitive.[42,43]

Radiographic changes in septic arthritis are also quite

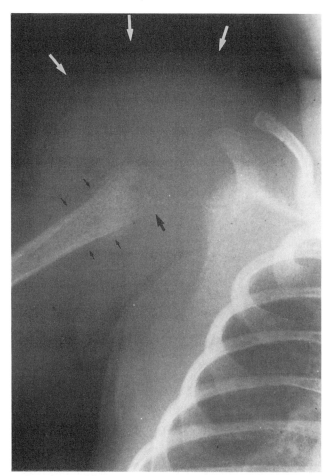

Figure 4-2 AP view of the right shoulder in a 2-week-old infant demonstrates extensive soft tissue swelling around the shoulder (*white arrows*). The epiphysis is not yet formed. The metaphysis demonstrates extensive osteoporosis with ill-defined osteolysis along the medial aspect (*large black arrow*). Immature periosteal new bone formation is present along the diaphysis (*small black arrows*).

insensitive.[15] Films are usually normal early in the disease course. As with osteomyelitis, surrounding soft tissue swelling may be one of the first indicators of infection. Joint space widening is an early finding resulting from the joint effusion, especially in children.[24] Inferior subluxation of the humeral head may occur.[23,44–46] Rarely, large effusions lead to dislocation of the humeral head.[47] Superior migration of the humeral head indicates associated rotator cuff tear.[46] Air within the joint (pneumoarthropathy) is indicative of gram-negative septic arthritis[48] or infection with facultative organisms capable of growth in aerobic and anaerobic environments.[49] The associated hyperemia may cause osteoporosis even in the absence of osteomyelitis. This is especially true of neonates with septic arthritis, where loss of mineralization in the epiphysis and metaphysis may create a misleading ominous appearance of extensive destruction.[50] Joint space loss indicates that cartilage destruction has already occurred. Marginal and central erosions are also late findings resulting from inflammatory pannus erosion through cartilage and subchondral bone. These erosions are irregular, lack sclerosis or a well-defined margin, and on the humeral head typically occur at the site of rotator cuff insertion (Figure 4-4). Tuberculous arthritis results in a characteristic constellation of findings known as Phemister's triad.[51] The triad includes juxtaarticular osteoporosis, marginal erosions, and slowly progressive loss of joint space. These changes help to differentiate tuberculous infection from bacterial infection, which is usually associated with early joint space loss and less significant osteoporosis.[51] Bony ankylosis is an unfortunate sequela of infection.

Superficial cellulitis creates only changes of soft tissue swelling, including obliteration of the normal fat planes.

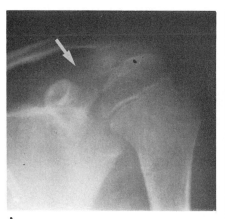

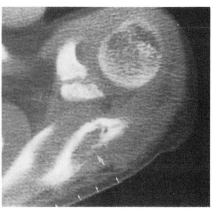

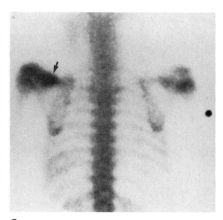

A   B   C

Figure 4-3 AP radiograph, **A,** axial CT, **B,** and delayed uptake images from a bone scan in the posterior projection, **C,** in a 9-year-old boy with cryptococcal osteomyelitis of the acromion. **A.** The AP radiograph of the left shoulder demonstrates osseous destruction at the base of the acromion (*arrow*). **C.** Bone scan demonstrates a focal area of increased uptake in the left scapular spine and no other lesions (*arrow*). CT examination, **B,** demonstrates changes typical of osteomyelitis, including ill-defined destruction of the acromion with loss of the overlying cortex (*large arrow*). Adjacent soft tissue edema is present with reticulated intermediate signal in the subcutaneous fat (*small arrows*).

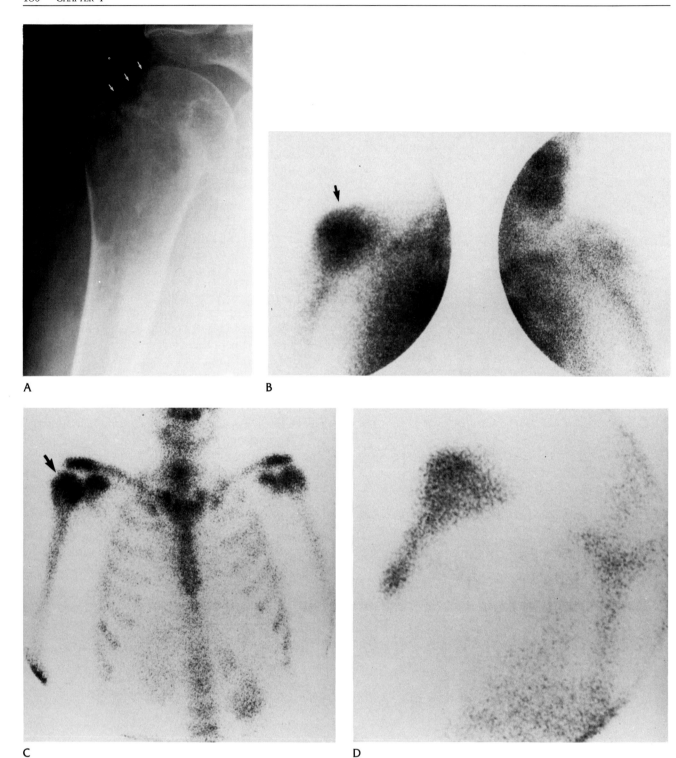

A   B   C   D

Figure 4-4   AP radiograph of the right shoulder, **A,** blood pool, and 4-hour uptake images from a bone scan, **B, C,** and 72-hour gallium scan, **D,** of the right shoulder in a patient with septic arthritis. AP radiograph demonstrates typical erosion of the humeral head associated with glenohumeral septic arthritis. This erosion occurs on the greater tuberosity at the rotator cuff insertion (*arrows*). **B.** Blood pool image demonstrates increased uptake in the right shoulder when compared to the left (*arrow*). This asymmetric uptake is also evident on the delayed image, with relatively increased uptake affecting both sides of the glenohumeral joint on the right as compared with the left (*arrow in* **C**). Gallium scan demonstrates increased uptake in the right shoulder and proximal humerus in a geographic distribution similar to the uptake on bone scan. The poor resolution prohibits distinction between the glenoid, humeral head, and acromion.

Soft tissue gas is a very specific sign of infection. Unless they contain air, soft tissue abscesses have no particular radiographic signs which help to identify them.

Currently, conventional tomography is rarely used in the evaluation of osteomyelitis or septic arthritis. No significant study of its use in these diseases has been reported in the literature. Information that might previously have been obtained from this study is now demonstrated by computed tomography (CT).

Aspiration, Arthrography, and Sinography

Fluoroscopically guided joint aspiration may be requested when the shoulder is not easily aspirated at the bedside. The technique is the same as that used for diagnostic arthrography discussed in an earlier chapter. Meticulous attention should be paid to aseptic technique, to avoid contamination. Since some concern has been raised about the bacteriostatic properties of lidocaine,[52] it is wise to limit anesthesia to the subcutaneous and periarticular soft tissues and to use a separate needle for the aspiration. At minimum, a 20-gauge needle should be used; an 18-gauge needle may be preferable, since infected fluid may be quite viscous and difficult to aspirate through a small needle. If despite local attempts to reposition the needle the initial aspirate is dry, nonbacteriostatic normal saline solution should be injected and reaspirated. Sometimes 10 ml is sufficient, but if large extraarticular collections have formed, larger amounts of saline solution may have to be injected to reaspirate an amount sufficient for culture. Optimally, at least 1 ml of fluid should be aspirated. It is recommended that the operator take care to avoid increased pressure during injection of the infected shoulder and that the patient be cautioned against exercise, to avoid bacteremia.[46]

If the initial aspirate yields any fluid, it should be sent for cell count and differential glucose determination plus gram stain, culture, and sensitivity studies. Reaspirated saline should be sent for Gram stain, culture, and sensitivity. Fungal, mycobacterial, and anaerobic cultures should also be considered in the discussion with the referring physician.

Once the aspiration is completed, contrast material should be injected to document the intraarticular position of the needle. Since some concern has been raised over the bacteriostatic properties of contrast, this step should not be performed until material for culture has been obtained. In cases of septic arthritis of the shoulder arthrography may document synovial irregularity, rotator cuff tears, and irregular extraarticular cavities.[23,46]

Sinography is performed by inserting a catheter into the exit of the sinus tract and injecting contrast material. This may be done under fluoroscopic control or, for increased sensitivity, CT guidance. Sinography is per-

formed to document the extent of a sinus tract and to determine communication with abscess cavities, bursal sacs, and joint spaces. Frequently the procedure is compromised by the inability to seal the catheter–soft tissue interface at the sinus opening, thus limiting injection pressures and retrograde filling of the tract. In the author's experience, direct injection of the joint has been the more definitive means to confirm or exclude communication with a sinus tract. Other modalities, such as magnetic resonance imaging (MRI), have also proven extremely useful in the evaluation of sinus tracts.

Computed Tomography

CT has played only a limited role in the evaluation of suspected musculoskeletal infection, usually as an adjunct to radiography and scintigraphy. CT provides a more thorough depiction of the extent of soft tissue and osseous abnormalities.[53,54] Unlike scintigraphy, CT aids in the differentiation of soft tissue infection from osseous infection[53,55] and is able to differentiate abscess from cellulitis. Most of the reported experience in the literature has been anecdotal, and only two series have reported on more than nine patients.[55,56] These studies comprised 25 and 40 patients, respectively. In addition to its role as an imaging tool, CT may be used to guide percutaneous biopsy of infected tissue (Fig. 4-5).[54] The usefulness of CT is limited because of beam-hardening artifacts which obscure subtle changes in the surrounding soft tissues. CT, however, is the study of choice for evaluation of the sternoclavicular joint.[12,57]

Cellulitis is seen as poor definition of the fascial planes and may be an isolated finding or one associated with soft tissue abscesses or osteomyelitis. Cellulitis without osteomyelitis does not appear to alter intramedullary density.[55] Abscesses appear as well-defined low-attenuation fluid collections within the soft tissues. In some situations the abscesses may be isodense relative to surrounding musculature and not easily identified before administration of contrast medium.[58] Following intravenous administration of iodinated contrast, the abscess rim is enhanced.[36] In cases of soft tissue abscess, CT helps delineate secondary osseous involvement, even when it is confined to cortical bone. Identification of osseous involvement is an important determinant of appropriate therapy.[55]

Increased intramedullary density is a nonspecific but early finding in osteomyelitis and is identifiable before radiographic changes of osteomyelitis appear.[36,53,55,59,60] Cortical and medullary destruction, cortical fissuring, intracortical gas, and fluid-fluid or fat-pus levels are all CT findings of osteomyelitis.[36,61,62] Surrounding soft tissue edema is easily identified as alteration of the surrounding fat (see Fig. 4-3).[53] Detection of intramedullary gas is essentially pathognomonic for osteomyelitis and indi-

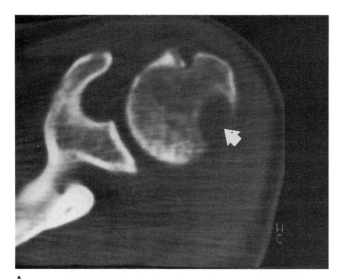

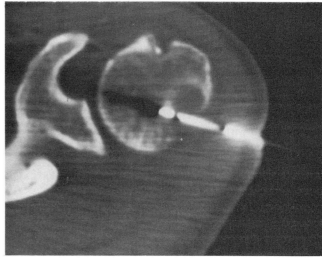

A   B

Figure 4-5 Axial images of a CT scan in a patient with septic arthritis. A previous bone scan, not shown, demonstrated increased uptake in the region of the left humeral head and the T8 vertebral body. CT was performed for diagnosis and biopsy. **A.** Axial image demonstrates a well-defined erosion along the posterior superior aspect of the humeral head (*large arrow*). The glenohumeral joint space was preserved and no other osseous or soft tissue abnormalities were seen. **B.** A percutaneous cutting needle biopsy of the area of destruction was easily performed. At the same time, 5 ml of purulent material was obtained from a CT-guided aspirate of the glenohumeral joint (not shown).

cates anaerobic infection.[63] Identification of normal intramedullary density helps to exclude osteomyelitis.[55]

Typical changes of chronic osteomyelitis are evident, including cortical thickening, medullary sclerosis, and mature periosteal new bone formation. CT is helpful in identifying activity superimposed on these long-term changes. CT is the most sensitive imaging examination for the identification of sequestra.[53,54,56,64,65] These isolated fragments of bone are a very specific indicator of activity,[42,56] and precise localization of the sequestrum is useful in preoperative planning. Other indicators of activity include intraosseous cavity formation, intraosseous gas, frank destruction, cortical channels, involucrum, cloaca, adjacent soft tissue edema, and abscesses.[54,56,60,62] CT aids in the detection of associated soft tissue abscesses, which may not have been recognized preoperatively in patients with positive scintigraphic studies.[54] Sinus tracts are also a specific sign of activity. Sinus tracts must be identified preoperatively so that they may be excised. As with sequestra these tracts may harbor bacteria and provide a source for reactivation of infection.[56] Such tracts are seen as linear soft tissue abnormalities tracking from an area of cortical disruption to the subcutaneous tissue.[56,60] They enhance after intravenous administration of contrast material.

CT is rarely employed in cases of septic arthritis. In these cases, CT offers the greatest overall evaluation of the articular surfaces[53] and is useful in identifying early changes when osteomyelitis is superimposed. Surrounding soft tissue abscesses are also visible.

Scintigraphy

Scintigraphic imaging is ordered to confirm or rule out bone infection in patients with normal or nonspecific radiographs and to exclude it in patients with soft tissue infections.[66] Three-phase bone scanning is the initial procedure of choice in any nuclear medicine department for the evaluation of the patient with suspected osteomyelitis. The addition of gallium imaging or indium 111–labeled white blood cell scans increases specificity in equivocal cases or when strong clinical suspicion prompts the physician to question a negative bone scan.[67,68] Gallium or indium-111 labeled white cell scans also help to rule out active disease in cases of chronic complicated osteomyelitis following surgery, infection, or fracture.[67] All scintigraphic examinations are limited by poor spatial resolution, which contributes to the difficulty of separating soft tissue uptake from osseous uptake and which limits the usefulness of these examinations for preoperative planning (see Fig. 4-4). The time required to obtain a diagnosis also limits the usefulness of scintigraphy. Although bone scans can be completed on the same day, if a 24-hour image is required diagnosis is delayed. Subsequent use of gallium or leukocyte imaging may contribute to further delay.

Technetium 99m-MDP bone scans are extremely sensitive for the detection of osteomyelitis before radiographic changes are evident[66,69]; findings may be positive within the first 24 hours following onset of symptoms.[66,70] Reported sensitivity and specificity for osteomyelitis range from 89 to 99 percent and 91 to 100 percent, respectively.[66,67,71–73] Such a sensitive test allows for immediate institution of antibiotic therapy. Bone scans, however, have a high rate of false positive results reflecting any change which results in increased blood flow or an increase in bone turnover. The use of the three-phase bone scan—angiogram, blood pool, and delayed uptake images—increases the specificity from 75 percent for delayed images alone to 94 percent.[73] A positive examination is based on increased blood flow, increased uptake on the blood pool image, and increased uptake in the underlying bone on the delayed images.[73,74] Lack of increased blood flow and increased uptake on the blood pool image help to distinguish noninfectious causes of increased skeletal uptake from osteomyelitis.[73] Lack of focal osseous uptake in the setting of increased blood flow differentiates cellulitis from osteomyelitis.[72] A negative three-phase bone scan essentially excludes the diagnosis of osteomyelitis,[43,75] except in the neonatal population, where a high incidence of false negative bone scans occur, regardless of the interval between onset of symptoms and imaging.[76] Septic arthritis is differentiated by diffuse radionuclide uptake on both sides of the joint rather than focal uptake (see Fig. 4-4).[67,74]

Many noninfectious disease processes may result in a positive three-phase bone scan, most notably overlying soft tissue infection, prior fracture, surgery (including joint replacement), and previous infection. To differentiate osseous uptake secondary to the hyperemia associated with soft tissue infection from osteomyelitis, a 24-hour image has been proposed.[77] Uptake in reparative bone continues beyond 4 hours and shows more intense uptake on the 24-hour scan, whereas in normal lamellar bone increased skeletal uptake secondary to the hyperemia peaks at 4 hours. The 24-hour scan has not been widely accepted, and in most instances subsequent gallium imaging or labeled leukocyte scans will help to exclude osteomyelitis.

Rarely, the bone scan may demonstrate normal or diminished uptake in an area that subsequently is proven to be involved by osteomyelitis.[67,70,78–84] These photopenic areas are thought to be the result of compromised blood supply, from either increased intramedullary pressure or stripping of the periosteum by subperiosteal abscess. In any patient with a normal or equivocal bone scan and a strong clinical suspicion of infection, an additional examination should be considered. Additional studies are also frequently required when bones are "complicated" by previous surgery, trauma, or infection.

Gallium scanning was the first scintigraphic study to be used in conjunction with bone scanning to increase specificity for infection; however, gallium is also a weak bone-seeking agent and is deposited in sites of increased bone turnover, a phenomenon that severely compromises its specificity.[85,86] Gallium scans may be interpreted

in isolation or in conjunction with the bone scan. Close correlation between the geographic distribution and the relative intensity of uptake on the bone scan and gallium scan helps establish the likelihood of infection in bones complicated by prior fracture, surgery, or infection.[85,87] This combination is very insensitive but extremely specific. Only when the gallium uptake is in a similar geographic distribution and more intense than the uptake on bone scan is the bone scan–gallium scan combination diagnostic of osteomyelitis in these patients.[87] Used alone, gallium imaging has a sensitivity of 22 to 100 percent and specificity of zero to 100 percent for the diagnosis of osteomyelitis.[43,67,85,88–91] A negative gallium scan essentially excludes the diagnosis of osteomyelitis.[85] In combination with bone scanning, sensitivity or specificity may increase, depending on what criteria are used; however, since indium scanning performs consistently better it is now preferred over gallium scanning.[85,89]

White blood cell scans, labeled with either indium 111 or, more recently, technetium 99m, alone or in conjunction with the three-phase bone scan, have reported sensitivity of 83 to 100 percent and specificity of 86 to 96 percent for the diagnosis and exclusion, respectively, of osteomyelitis and soft tissue abscesses.[85,89,92–95] The limitations of this examination lie in differentiating between soft tissue versus osseous uptake[68,93,94,96] and in the evaluation of chronic complicated osteomyelitis, where sensitivity falls to 45 to 88 percent and specificity to 58 to 75 percent.[43,85,97]

As with bone scanning, interpretation is based on the relative intensity of uptake between (1) the area of interest and adjacent bone and (2) the opposite extremity.[68,93] Focal areas of increased uptake confined to bone are diagnostic of osteomyelitis. The absence of uptake essentially rules out osteomyelitis[68,75,97] (negative predictive value 89 percent).[68] Rarely, diminished uptake may be demonstrated in sites of infection, but it is a nonspecific finding.[75,97,98] Interpretation of labeled leukocyte scans in conjunction with bone scans increases specificity.[97] In these cases, leukocyte uptake which is incongruent with or of greater intensity than the bone scan is indicative of infection.[43,97] Timing bone scan images to be immediately followed by scanning of leukocytes affords the opportunity to directly overlay the images, which aids in differentiating soft tissue uptake from osseous uptake.[75,85,94] Obtaining images in multiple projections also helps to overcome this problem.[73,85]

Initial reports indicated that the sensitivity of leukocyte scanning diminished with the "chronicity" of the infection.[43,75,85,86,97,99,100] This decreased sensitivity was attributed to the mild inflammatory response associated with chronic infections. Subsequent reports have refuted this.[92,93] In patients with suspected osteomyelitis following fracture, when indium leukocyte scans demonstrate intense uptake or uptake of greater intensity or larger in area than the bone scan, the diagnosis of osteomyelitis is easily confirmed.[94,101,102] However, a significant number of patients with osteomyelitis following fracture may have only mild to moderate uptake,[101] which may also be seen in uncomplicated fractures.[94,102]

Current recommendations for the use of scintigraphy in the evaluation of osteomyelitis are summarized by Schauwecker.[103] If the radiographic examination is normal, three-phase bone scan should be the initial examination. The addition of any subsequent examination is unlikely. In the neonatal patient, a three-phase bone scan should be performed first; however, if the examination is negative, a gallium scan should be performed. Acute and chronic complicated osteomyelitis should be evaluated by three-phase bone scan followed by indium-111 leukocyte imaging, as necessary.

Magnetic Resonance Imaging

Magnetic resonance imaging (MRI), because of its multiplanar capability and its excellent spatial resolution, is rapidly becoming the preferred advanced imaging modality for the evaluation of musculoskeletal infection, in many instances replacing scintigraphy as the procedure of choice following radiographic evaluation. MRI has proven to be of equal or greater sensitivity and specificity than scintigraphy for the identification of osteomyelitis.[104–107] The benefits of MRI include a dramatic increase in resolution and increased sensitivity for the detection of soft tissue processes[105,106] and the ability to differentiate cellulitis from abscess.[105–108] MRI demonstrates greater sensitivity than CT in the detection of both osteomyelitis and soft tissue abscesses[36] and has replaced CT as the imaging method of choice for the evaluation of the extent of soft tissue infection. The sensitivity of MRI for the detection of osteomyelitis and abscess ranges from 92 to 98 percent.[36,104,107,109] The specificity of MRI ranges from 75 to 96 percent for the exclusion of osteomyelitis[36,104,107,109] and 93 percent for the exclusion of abscess.[36]

MRI is more limited than scintigraphy only in that it cannot be used as a whole body screening examination. To be properly performed, MRI examinations must be directed to an area of interest. Cost constraints are a consideration, though the cost of an MRI examination is roughly equivalent to the cost of a three-phase bone scan combined with either gallium imaging or labeled leukocyte scans, a combination frequently used to rule out infection. Other general limitations of MRI are discussed in more detail in an earlier chapter. MRI is not useful for evaluating patients with total shoulder replacements; for such patients, indium 111-labeled leukocyte imaging is more specific.[96]

MRI directly visualizes the changes of infection, including decreased marrow fat and increased water, from hyperemia, edema, exudate, or ischemia.[104,107,110] These

are nonspecific and have been described in a variety of other entities. Previous surgery, recent fracture, healed osteomyelitis, sickle cell disease, gout, neoplasm, radiation necrosis, and sarcoidosis all mimic changes of osteomyelitis.[109] Clinical correlation is essential to appropriate interpretation of these MRI changes.

MRI examination typically is performed with the smallest field of view which covers adequately the area of concern. The use of surface coils improves resolution and the signal-to-noise ratio. Views should be obtained in at least two orthogonal planes. Evaluation of the opposite extremity on at least one image is recommended. T1- and T2-weighted spin-echo sequences are necessary for appropriate recognition of changes of infection. (STIR) images aid in the detection of disease but do not readily distinguish between soft tissue edema and abscess, and they may be overly sensitive to marrow abnormalities.[109] Intravenous gadolinium-DTPA administration results in enhancement of inflammatory tissue, increasing its conspicuousness.[111] Recently, fat-suppression examinations following intravenous gadolinium administration have proven equally sensitive and more specific than nonenhanced examinations for the identification of infection.[112] The use of gradient echo imaging for evaluation of musculoskeletal infection has not been studied extensively. We perform any examination to rule out osteomyelitis or soft tissue abscess with a multiecho spin-echo axial sequence and a T1-weighted spin-echo sequence along the long axis of the extremity, typically the coronal plane. If these two sequences demonstrate no abnormality, STIR images may be performed. If an abnormality is identified, T1-weighted fat-saturated axial and coronal sequences are performed following intravenous administration of gadolinium-DTPA.

Criteria for MRI diagnosis of acute osteomyelitis include a diffuse or focal increase in the marrow signal on T2-weighted images in association with normal or decreased marrow signal on the T1-weighted images.[36,104,106–110,113,114] The margins of the lesion are usually ill-defined.[90,110] Bright marrow signal is present on STIR images.[107,109] Diffuse enhancement of the abnormal marrow follows intravenous administration of gadolinium-DTPA.[112,115] Necrotic material is not enhanced.[115] These different patterns of enhancement help to distinguish inflammatory tissue from abscess formation.[115] The normal low signal intensity of cortical bone is usually preserved in cases of acute hematogenous osteomyelitis, though with advanced disease abnormal cortical signal may be evident and frank cortical disruption may be seen. Cortical disruption and abnormal intracortical signal typically are seen in cases of osteomyelitis secondary to contiguous spread from soft tissue disease.[109] Acute osteomyelitis almost always is associated with soft tissue edema.[107,109] In some cases, subperiosteal elevation by pus may be seen.[109,115]

MRI has proven useful in the evaluation of bones that

previously were involved by trauma or surgery but currently exhibit signs of infection, and in the evaluation of chronic osteomyelitis. In such cases scintigraphy is extremely nonspecific, reflecting the increased bone turnover associated with healing bone. As with uncomplicated acute osteomyelitis, areas of low signal intensity on T1-weighted images and increased intensity on T2-weighted images are indicative of active osteomyelitis.[110,114–116] In 93 percent of their cases of posttraumatic chronic active osteomyelitis, Erdman and coworkers found a low–signal intensity rim, presumably fibrous tissue, surrounding the areas of infection, which demonstrated decreased T1- and increased T2-weighted signal.[109] The specificity of these findings has not yet been determined, and similar findings may be present in such cases even in the absence of active disease.[109] In patients with a recent history of fracture or surgery, the noninfectious inflammatory changes mimic those of osteomyelitis.[96,108,109] However, as fractures heal, they appear as low to intermediate areas on T1-weighted images and exhibit slightly increased signal on T2-weighted images without discrete bright foci.[106] Previous pin sites are seen as linear bands of low signal on T1- and T2-weighted studies.[110] Posttraumatic, postsurgical, and postinfectious areas of fibrosis demonstrate low T1 signal without increase on the T2-weighted images.[110,114,115] In areas of healed osteomyelitis, high T1-weighted signal indicative of fat and the lack of bright T2-weighted signal eliminates the diagnosis of active or recurrent infection.[107,110]

Changes other than abnormal marrow signal are useful for identifying ongoing infection in the setting of suspected chronic osteomyelitis. Sequestra and sinus tracts are quite specific. Soft tissue edema is less striking than in acute osteomyelitis.[109] Soft tissue changes are extremely important in the evaluation of patients with chronic osteomyelitis. Sinus tracts are readily identified as areas of linear bright signal tracking from abnormal marrow through a cortical defect to the skin.[109,114,116] These areas are also enhanced following intravenous administration of gadolinium-DTPA.[112,115] In a patient who recently underwent surgery, identification of soft tissue fluid collections is indicative of infection.[96] Sequestra, though more easily visualized by CT, are identifiable on MRI as areas of decreased signal on T1- and T2-weighted images in the areas of abnormal marrow.[110,115,116] If the fragment originates from cancellous bone marrow, normal marrow signal characteristics will be identified surrounded by inflammatory exudate.[110] These areas do not enhance with gadolinium-DTPA.

Subacute osteomyelitis with Brodie's abscess is seen as a well-demarcated area of intermediate T1 signal and bright T2 signal, with a thick sclerotic rim which manifests as low T1- and T2-weighted signal and enhances with gadolinium-DTPA.[110,115] A more complex structure may be seen with a multilayered appearance.[117]

Ill-defined bright signal in soft tissue on the T2-weighted and STIR images is a nonspecific change indicative of edema or inflammatory change[106,108,110] (Fig. 4-6). Extensive soft tissue edema may be the result of osteomyelitis or may indicate infection limited to the soft tissue. In edematous muscle the normal intermediate signal is replaced by bright signal on the T2-weighted images. Subcutaneous edema is identified as reticulated intermediate T1 signal coursing through the normally bright signal of fat, which brightens on the T2-weighted images. Soft tissue plane distortion and mass effect help to distinguish infection from nonspecific soft tissue edema.[109,114] Cellulitis alone does not alter marrow signal,[90,107,110] but it may cause periostitis, even in the absence of osteomyelitis.[38] Diffuse enhancement of the inflammatory tissue occurs after injection of gadolinium-DTPA.[111,112] When there is secondary involvement of the cortex by an adjacent soft tissue abscess intermediate signal will be present in the otherwise low–signal intensity cortical bone.[116] Demonstration of normal marrow signal excludes osteomyelitis.

Abscesses appear as well-demarcated collections of homogeneous or heterogeneous low signal intensity on T1-weighted images and increased signal on T2-weighted images[36,58,106–108,115] (see Fig. 4-6). A low–signal intensity rim surrounding abscesses has been described by some[58,106] but has not been seen by others.[107] Pathologically, this rim represents a fibrous capsule.[106] Gas may be seen within abscesses as an area of signal void. Following intravenous administration of gadolinium-DTPA, the periphery of the abscess is enhanced,[111,112,115] and after a time diffuse enhancement of the entire abscess is observed.[111] Histologically, the area of peripheral enhancement corresponds to the inflammatory zone; the areas of delayed enhancement are the necrotic center. Rim enhancement does not occur in all abscesses.[115] In some instances immediate diffuse enhancement may be observed, which may be the result of gadolinium-DTPA diffusion into avascular tissue or into highly vascular inflammatory tissue without abscess formation.[112,115]

The soft tissue abscesses of pyomyositis are readily identified on MRI.[26,30,118] An unusual appearance of these lesions has been observed on MRI examination. The lesions are associated with a hyperintense rim on the T1-weighted images; the reason is not known.[26,30] To date, this increased signal on T1-weighted images has been described only in AIDS patients with bacterial myositis, and the significance of the association is not known.[30] Diffuse increased T1-weighted signal with persistent increased signal on T2-weighted images has also been observed in these lesions.[30] Pyomyositis is confined to muscle tissue, with little or no signal abnormality in the adjacent subcutaneous tissues. This lack of subcutaneous abnormality helps to differentiate pyomyositis from Kaposi's sarcoma, lymphoma, lymphedema, and carbunculosis.[30]

Joint effusion may be the only finding in septic arthri-

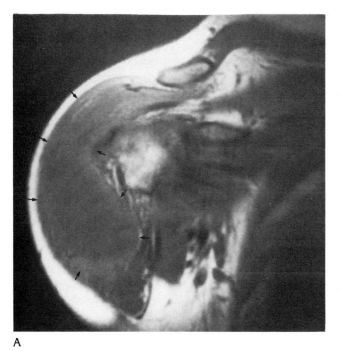

A

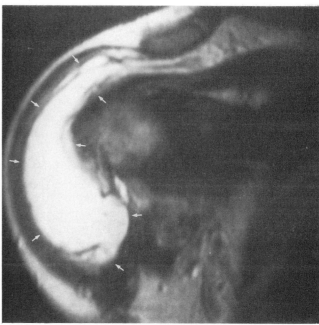

B

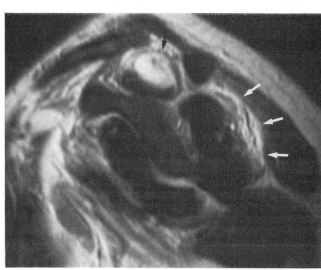

C

Figure 4-6 T1-weighted oblique coronal, **A,** and fast T2-weighted spin-echo oblique coronal, **B,** and sagittal images, **C,** of the right shoulder in the patient with staphylococcal septic bursitis demonstrate a large collection of fluid in the subacromial-subdeltoid bursa (*arrows in* **A, B**). **C.** Sagittal T2-weighted images at the level of the coracoid process clearly demonstrate extensive subcutaneous edema between the deltoid muscle and infraspinatus teres minor muscles (*white arrows*) as well as in the anterior soft tissue surrounding the subscapularis muscle. This soft tissue edema adjacent to the fluid-filled bursa suggests infection. Fluid in the subacromial bursa is seen compressing the supraspinatus muscle (*black arrow*). Normal marrow signal in the humeral head and the absence of joint effusion help to exclude associated osteomyelitis and septic arthritis.

tis, and infected fluid has no distinguishing characteristics. More advanced disease may result in joint space narrowing secondary to loss of articular cartilage.[110] With severe cartilage destruction, abutment of subchondral bone against subchondral bone creates lower than normal intensity and gives better definition to the joint space.[110] In septic arthritis and infectious tenosynovitis, the joint and tendon fluid demonstrate no characteristics specific for infection. The fluid appears hypointense gray on T1-weighted images and bright on T2-weighted images. Beltran and coworkers suggest that if increased T2-weighted signal is identified in the surrounding soft tissue or if other signs of bone or soft tissue infection are present, the joint or tendon fluid may be presumed to be infectious[106] (see Fig. 4-6). Hypointense T1 signal and

bright signal on STIR images may be seen on both sides of a joint in a patient with septic arthritis, even in the absence of osteomyelitis.[109] In the few cases in which they were available, T2-weighted images correctly identified normal marrow[109]; however, Unger and colleagues found no marrow abnormalities in patients with septic arthritis.[107] Increased T2 marrow signal has also been reported in association with noninfectious tenosynovitis.[106]

Ultrasonography

Limited experience with ultrasonographic diagnosis of osteomyelitis is reported in the literature.[119–122] The main criteria for ultrasound confirmation of osteomyelitis is the identification of a fluid collection adjacent to the cortical surface without intervening soft tissue.[119,120] Subperiosteal abscesses in the absence of osteomyelitis yield a false positive sonogram. Ultrasound is able to distinguish between cellulitis and abscess, a problematic area in scintigraphy.[119] The soft tissue abscesses are distinguished from the fluid collections associated with osteomyelitis by the presence of soft tissue intervening between these collections and the adjacent cortical bone.

The exact role of ultrasound in the diagnosis of osteomyelitis remains questionable, since in the majority of the reported cases plain film findings were already present at the time of sonography.[119,121] Ultrasound may be helpful for guiding needle aspiration and in some cases for the detection of cortical disruption or localization of sequestra.[47,120,127] Ultrasound is of little use in the diagnosis of osteomyelitis associated with septic arthritis.[119] Although ultrasound appears quite sensitive in the diagnosis of osteomyelitis, its specificity is unknown.[122]

SHOULDER REPLACEMENT

Shoulder replacement is an infrequent operation performed to relieve pain and improve function for patients with rheumatoid arthritis, primary or posttraumatic osteoarthritis, other degenerative disease, or a neoplasm of the proximal humerus. Infection is a rare complication.[123,124] Following total shoulder replacement, pain relief is usually dramatic. Any complaints of continued or worsening pain should alert the physician to the possibility of infection.[6] Distinguishing infection from other causes of pain in these patients is important in prerevision surgical planning, since infection is usually treated with arthrodesis rather than revision.[125] Local erythema, swelling, warmth, fever, and sinus tracts are strong but insensitive clinical indicators of infection.[126]

Radiographic assessment of infection in any joint replacement is insensitive. Lucent lines surrounding the bone-prosthesis and cement-bone interfaces may be a normal finding in asymptomatic patients and are frequently seen along the glenoid–cement interface.[123,127,128] These lines are typically less than 2 mm thick.[127,129] Lucency thicker than 2 mm indicates loosening,[124,129] but aseptic loosening is not readily distinguished from loosening secondary to infection. It has been suggested that the lack of a sclerotic line adjacent to the lucency indicates septic loosening.[124] If areas of frank cortical destruction are identified, infection is highly likely. Focal medullary lucencies may be seen with infection as well as in areas of foreign body reaction at the hip, although such lucencies have not been described in the shoulder.

Scintigraphy has been widely studied as a method of confirming loosening and distinguishing between infectious and noninfectious causes; however, the results of these studies have been less than convincing, regardless of what modality is used—bone scan, bone scan in combination with gallium scan, or bone scan followed by labeled leukocyte study.[130,131] Of these tests, labeled leukocytes perform best,[89,95,97,126,132] with reported sensitivities and specificities of 85 to 100 percent and 85 percent, respectively.[89,97,133] Specificity is improved when the leukocyte scans are interpreted in conjunction with the bone scan.[97,133] Few of these studies have investigated efficacy in the evaluation of shoulder replacements. At the author's institution little reliability is given to these examinations, and they are rarely ordered.

Clinical suspicion and the results of aspiration arthrography are the mainstay of the diagnosis of septic loosening. In a patient being evaluated for shoulder replacement revision, clinical suspicion determines whether or not aspiration arthrography is required. Arthrography may be performed in the absence of signs of infection to document loosening. In the recent past, every prerevision joint was aspirated. The change in approach has been supported by several recent studies on the utility of hip joint aspiration before revision.[134–136] A large percentage of the results are false positive when all prerevision joints are aspirated.[137]

Fibrin deposition on the hardware has been proposed as one of the factors inciting infection in prosthetic joints. The fibrin layer provides a surface to which bacteria may adhere. In patients with early infection, we have experimented with intraarticular urokinase as a treatment modality. Injection of urokinase dissolves the fibrin, destroying the surface to which bacteria adhere. If such therapy is instituted before loosening occurs, surgery may be avoided.

References

1. WALDVOGEL FA, MEDOFF G, SWARTZ MN: Osteomyelitis: A review of clinical features, therapeutic considerations and unusual aspects (first of three parts). *N Engl J Med* 282:198–206, 1970.

2. MOK PM, REILLY BJ, ASH JM: Osteomyelitis in the neonate. *Radiology* 145:677–682, 1982.

3. GOLDENBERG DL, COHEN AS: Acute infectious arthritis: A review of patients with nongonoccocal joint infections (with emphasis on therapy and prognosis). *Am J Med* 60:369–377, 1976.

4. NELSON JD, KOONTZ WC: Septic arthritis in infants and children. A review of 117 cases. *Pediatrics* 38:966–971, 1986.

5. KELLY PJ, COVENTRY MB, MARTIN WJ: Bacterial arthritis of the shoulder. *Mayo Clin Proc* 40:695–699, 1965.

6. GRISTINA AG, KAMMIRE G, VOYLEK A, WEBB LX: Sepsis of the shoulder: Molecular mechanisms and pathogenesis, in Rockwood CA Jr, Matsen FA III (eds): *The Shoulder,* Philadelphia, Saunders, 1990, pp 920–939.

7. GRISTINA AG, ROVERE GD, SHOJI H: Spontaneous septic arthritis complicating rheumatoid arthritis. *J Bone Joint Surg* 56A:1180–1184, 1974.

8. KARTEN I: Septic arthritis complicating rheumatoid arthritis. *Ann Intern Med* 70:1147–1158, 1960.

9. KELLGREN JH, BALL J, FAIRBROTHER RW, BARNES KL: Suppurative arthritis complicating rheumatoid arthritis. *Br Med J* 1:1193–1200, 1958.

10. KIDO D, BRYAN D, HALPERN M: Hematogenous osteomyelitis in drug addicts. *AJR* 118:356–363, 1973.

11. KRESPI YP, MONSELL EM, SISSON GA: Osteomyelitis of the clavicle. *Ann Otol Rhinol Laryngol* 92:525–527, 1983.

12. LINDSEY RW, LEACH JA: Sternoclavicular osteomyelitis and pyoarthrosis as a complication of subclavian vein catheterization: A case report and review of the literature. *Orthopedics* 7:1017–1021, 1984.

13. MANNY J, HARUZI I, YOSIPOVITCH Z: Osteomyelitis of the clavicle following subclavian vein catheterization. *Arch Surg* 106:342–343, 1973.

14. HUNTER D, MORAN JF, VENEZIO FR: Osteomyelitis of the clavicle after Swan-Ganz catheterization. *Arch Intern Med* 143:153–156, 1983.

15. RESNICK D, NIWAYAMA G: Osteomyelitis, septic arthritis, and soft tissue infection: The mechanisms and situation, in Resnick D, Niwayama G. (eds): *Diagnosis of Bone and Joint Disorders,* 2d ed, Philadelphia, Saunders, 1988, pp 2524–2618.

16. TRUETA J: The three types of acute haematogenous osteomyelitis: A clinical and vascular study. *J Bone Joint Surg* 41B:671–680, 1959.

17. EDWARDS MS, BAKER CJ, WAGNER ML, TABER LH, BAR-
RETT FF: An etiologic shift in infantile osteomyelitis: The emergence of the group B streptococcus. *J Pediatr* 93:578–583, 1978.

18. WALDVOGEL FA, MEDOFF G, SWARTZ MN: Osteomyelitis: A review of clinical features, therapeutic considerations and unusual aspects (third of three parts). *N Engl J Med* 282:316–322, 1970.

19. BARRETT-CONNOR E: Bacterial infection and sickle cell anemia: An analysis of 250 infections in 166 patients and a review of the literature. *Medicine* 50:97–112, 1971.

20. O'MEARA PM, BARTAL E: Septic arthritis: Process, etiology, treatment outcome: A literature review. *Orthopedics* 11:623–628, 1988.

21. CAPITANIO MA, KIRKPATRICK JA: Early roentgen observations in acute osteomyelitis. *AJR* 108:488–496, 1970.

22. GOLDENBERG DL, BRANDT KD, CATHCART ES, COHEN AS: Acute arthritis caused by gram-negative bacilli: A clinical characterization. *Medicine* 53:197–208, 1974.

23. MASTER R, WEISMAN MH, ARMBUSTER TG, SLIVKA J, RESNICK D, GOERGEN TG: Septic arthritis of the glenohumeral joint, unique clinical and radiographic features and a favorable outcome. *Arthritis Rheum* 20:1500–1506, 1977.

24. SCHMIDT D, MUBARAK S, GELBERMAN R: Septic shoulders in children. *J Pediatr Orthop* 1:67–72, 1981.

25. BRILL PW, WINCHESTER P, KRAUSS AN, SYMCHYCH P: Osteomyelitis in a neonatal intensive care unit. *Radiology* 131:83–87, 1979.

26. STEINBACH LS, TEHRANZADEH J, FLECKENSTEIN JL, VANARTHOS WJ, PAIS MJ: Human immunodeficiency virus infection: Musculoskeletal manifestations. *Radiology* 186:833–838, 1993.

27. BARON AL, STEINBACH LS, LEBOIT PE, MILLS CM, GEE JH, BERGER TG: Osteolytic lesions and bacillary angiomatosis in HIV infection: Radiologic differentiation from AIDS-related Kaposi sarcoma. *Radiology* 177:77–81, 1990.

28. HERTS BR, RAFII M, SPIEGEL G: Soft-tissue and osseous lesions caused by bacillary angiomatosis: Unusual manifestations of cat-scratch fever in patients with AIDS. *AJR* 157:1249–1251, 1991.

29. KOEHLER JE, LEBOIT PE, EGBERT BM, BERGER TG: Cutaneous vascular lesions and disseminated cat-scratch disease in patients with the acquired immunodeficiency syndrome (AIDS) and AIDS-related complex. *Ann Intern Med* 109:449–455, 1988.

30. FLECKENSTEIN JL, BURNS DK, MURPHY FK, JAYSON HT, BONTE JF: Differential diagnosis of bacterial myositis in AIDS: Evaluation with MR imaging. *Radiology* 179:653–658, 1991.

31. BUCKNER CB, LEITHISER RE, WALKER CW, ALLISON JW:

The changing epidemiology of tuberculosis and other mycobacterial infections in the United States: Implications for the radiologist. *AJR* 156:255–264, 1991.

32. LIFESO RM, BULL CA: Squamous cell carcinoma of the extremities. *Cancer* 55:2862–2867, 1985.

33. UNNI KK, DAHLIN DC: Premalignant tumors and conditions of bone. *Am J Surg Pathol* 3:47–60, 1979.

34. FITZGERALD RH JR, BREWER NS, DAHLIN DC: Squamous-cell carcinoma complicating chronic osteomyelitis. *J Bone Joint Surg* 58A:1146–1148, 1976.

35. BENEDICT EB: Carcinoma in osteomyelitis. *Surg Gynecol Obstet* 53:1–11, 1931.

36. CHANDNANI VP, BELTRAN J, MORRIS CS, KHALIL SN, MUELLER CF, BURK JM, BENNETT WF, SHAFFER PB, VASILA MS, REESE J, RIDGEWAY JA: Acute experimental osteomyelitis and abscesses: Detection with MR imaging versus CT. *Radiology* 174:233–236, 1990.

37. DAVID R, BARRON BJ, MADEWELL JE: Osteomyelitis, acute and chronic. *Radiol Clin North Am* 25:1171–1201, 1987.

38. SUYDAM MJ, MIKITY VG: Cellulitis with underlying inflammatory periostitis of the mandible. *AJR* 106:133–135, 1969.

39. ROSEN RA, MOREHOUSE HT, KARP HJ, YU GSM: Intracortical fissuring in osteomyelitis. *Radiology* 141:17–20, 1981.

40. MILLER WB, MURPHY WA, GILULA LA: Brodie abscess: Reappraisal. *Radiology* 132:15–23, 1979.

41. KING DM, MAYO KM: Subacute haematogenous osteomyelitis. *J Bone Joint Surg* 51B:458–463, 1969.

42. TUMEH SS, ALIABADI P, WEISSMAN BN, McNEIL BJ: Disease activity in osteomyelitis: Role of radiography. *Radiology* 165:781–784, 1987.

43. AL-SHEIKH W, SFAKIANAKIS GN, MNAYMNEH W, HOURANI M, HEAL A, DUNCAN RC, BARNETT A, ASHKAR FS, SERAFINA AN: Subacute and chronic bone infections: Diagnosis using In-111, Ga-67 and Tc-99m MDP bone scintigraphy, and radiography. *Radiology* 155:501–506, 1985.

44. GORDON EJ, HUTCHFUL GA: Pyarthrosis simulating ruptured rotator cuff syndrome. *South Med J* 75:759–762, 1982.

45. RESNIK CS: Septic arthritis: A rare cause of drooping shoulder. *Skel Radiol* 21:307–309, 1992.

46. ARMBUSTER TG, SLIVKA J, RESNICK D, GOERGEN TG, WEISMAN M, MASTER R: Extraarticular manifestations of septic arthritis of the glenohumeral joint. *AJR* 129:667–672, 1977.

47. GOMPELS BM, DARLINGTON LG: Septic arthritis in rheumatoid disease causing bilateral shoulder dislocation: Diagnosis and treatment assisted by grey scale ultrasonography. *Ann Rheum Dis* 40:609–611, 1981.

48. MEREDITH HC, RITTENBERG GM: Pneumoarthropathy: An unusual radiographic sign of gram-negative septic arthritis. *Radiology* 129:642, 1978.

49. ANDERSON RB, DORWART BB: Pneumarthrosis in a shoulder infected with *Serratia Liquefasciens:* Case report and literature review. *Arthritis Rheum* 26:1166–1168, 1983.

50. LLOYD-ROBERTS GC: Suppurative arthritis of infancy. *J Bone Joint Surg* 42B:706–720, 1960.

51. RESNICK D, NIWAYAMA G: Osteomyelitis, septic arthritis, and soft tissue infection. The organisms, in Resnick D,

Niwayama G (eds): *Diagnosis of Bone and Joint Disorders,* 2d ed, Philadelphia, Saunders, 1988, pp 2647–2755.

52. SCHMIDT RM, ROSENKRANZ NS: Antimicrobial activity of local anesthetics: Lidocaine and procaine. *J Infect Dis* 121:597, 1970.

53. AZOUZ EM: Computed tomography in bone and joint infections. *J Can Assoc Radiol* 32:102–106, 1981.

54. SELTZER SE: Value of computed tomography in planning medical and surgical treatment of chronic osteomyelitis. *J Comput Assist Tomogr* 8:482–487, 1984.

55. KUHN JP, BERGER PE: Computed tomographic diagnosis of osteomyelitis. *Radiology* 130:503–506, 1979.

56. WING VW, JEFFREY RB JR, FEDERLE MP, HELMS CA, TRAFTON P: Chronic osteomyelitis examined by CT. *Radiology* 154:171–174, 1985.

57. ALEXANDER PW, SHIN MS: CT manifestation of sternoclavicular pyoarthrosis in patients with intravenous drug abuse. *J Comput Assist Tomogr* 14:104–106, 1990.

58. WALL SD, FISHER MR, AMPARO EG, HRICAK H, HIGGINS CB: Magnetic resonance imaging in the evaluation of abscesses. *AJR* 144:1217–1221, 1985.

59. HALD JK JR, SUDMANN E: Acute hematogenous osteomyelitis: Early diagnosis with computed tomography. *Acta Radiol [Diagn]* 23:55–58, 1982.

60. HERMANN G, ROSE JS: Computed tomography in bone and soft tissue pathology of the extremities. *J Comput Assist Tomogr* 3:58–66, 1979.

61. RAFII M, FIROOZNIA H, GOLIMBU C, McCAULEY DI: Hematogenous osteomyelitis with fat-fluid level shown by CT. *Radiology* 153:493–494, 1984.

62. TOTTY WG: Radiographic evaluation of osteomyelitis using magnetic resonance imaging. *Orthop Rev* 18:587–592, 1989.

63. RAM PC, MARTINEZ S, KOROBKIN M, BREIMAN RS, GALLIS HR, HARRELSON JM: CT detection of intraosseous gas: A new sign of osteomyelitis. *AJR* 137:721–723, 1991.

64. HELMS CA, JEFFREY RB, WING VW: Computed tomography and plain film appearance of a bony sequestration: Significance and differential diagnosis. *Skel Radiol* 16:117–120, 1987.

65. HERNANDEZ RJ: Visualization of small sequestra by computerized tomography: Report of 6 cases. *Pediatr Radiol* 15:238–241, 1985.

66. GILDAY DL, PAUL DJ, PATERSON J: Diagnosis of osteomyelitis in children by combined blood pool and bone imaging. *Radiology* 117:331–335, 1975.

67. LISBONA R, ROSENTHALL L: Observations on the sequential use of ^{99m}Tc-phosphate complex and ^{67}Ga imaging in osteomyelitis, cellulitis, and septic arthritis. *Radiology* 123:123–129, 1977.

68. MAURER AH, MILLMOND SH, KNIGHT LC, MESGARZADEH M, SIEGEL JA, SHUMAN CR, ADLER LP, GREENE GS, MALMUD LS: Infection in diabetic osteoarthropathy: Use of indium-labeled leukocytes for diagnosis. *Radiology* 161:221–225, 1986.

69. DUSZYNSKI DO, KUHN JP, AFSHANI E, RIDDLESBERGER MM JR: Early radionuclide diagnosis of acute osteomyelitis. *Radiology* 117:337–340, 1975.

70. HANDMAKER H, LEONARDS R: The bone scan in inflammatory osseous disease. *Semin Nucl Med* 6:95–105, 1976.

71. HOWIE DW, SAVAGE JP, WILSON TG, PATERSON D: The technetium phosphate bone scan in the diagnosis of osteomyelitis in childhood. *J Bone Joint Surg* 65A:431–437, 1983.

72. MAJD M, FRANKEL RS: Radionuclide imaging in skeletal inflammatory and ischemic disease in children. *AJR* 126:832–841, 1976.

73. MAURER AH, CHEN DCP, CAMARGO EE, WONG DF, WAGNER HN JR, ALDERSON PO: Utility of three-phase skeletal scintigraphy in suspected osteomyelitis: Concise communication. *J Nucl Med* 22:941–949, 1981.

74. PARK HM, ROTHSCHILD PA, KERNEK CB: Scintigraphic evaluation of extremity pain in children: Its efficacy and pitfalls. *AJR* 145:1079–1084, 1985.

75. JACOBSON AF, HARLEY JD, LIPSKY BA, PECORARO RE: Diagnosis of osteomyelitis in the presence of soft-tissue infection and radiologic evidence of osseous abnormalities: Value of leukocyte scintigraphy. *AJR* 157:807–812, 1991.

76. ASH JM, GILDAY DL: The futility of bone scanning in neonatal osteomyelitis: Concise communication. *J Nucl Med* 21:417–420, 1980.

77. ISRAEL O, GIPS S, JERUSHALMI J, FRENKEL A, FRONT D: Osteomyelitis and soft-tissue infection: Differential diagnosis with 24 hour/4 hour ratio of Tc-99m MDP uptake. *Radiology* 163:725–726, 1987.

78. TEATES CD, WILLIAMSON BRJ: "Hot and cold" bone lesion in acute osteomyelitis. *AJR* 29:517–518, 1977.

79. BARRON BJ, DHEKNE RD: Cold osteomyelitis radionuclide bone scan findings. *Clin Nucl Med* 7:392–393, 1984.

80. GARNETT ES, COCKSHOTT WP, JACOBS J: Classical acute osteomyelitis with a negative bone scan. *Br J Radiol* 50:757–760, 1977.

81. SULLIVAN DC, ROSENFIELD NS, OGDEN J, GOTTSCHALK A: Problems in the scintigraphic detection of osteomyelitis in children. *Radiology* 135:731–736, 1980.

82. RUSSIN LD, STAAB EV: Unusual bone-scan findings in acute osteomyelitis: Case report. *J Nucl Med* 17:617–619, 1976.

83. ALLWRIGHT SJ, MILLER JH, GILSANZ V: Subperiosteal abscess in children: Scintigraphic appearance. *Radiology* 179:725–729, 1991.

84. BERKOWITZ ID, WENZEL W: "Normal" technetium bone scans in patients with acute osteomyelitis. *Am J Dis Child* 134:828–830, 1980.

85. SCHAUWECKER DS, PARK HM, MOCK BH, BURT RW, KERNICK CB, RUOFF AC III, SINN HJ, WELLMAN HN: Evaluation of complicating osteomyelitis with TC-99m MDP, In-111 granulocytes, and Ga-67 citrate. *J Nucl Med* 25:849–853, 1984.

86. McAFEE JG, SAMIN A: In-111 labeled leukocytes: A review of problems in image interpretation. *Radiology* 155:221–229, 1985.

87. TUMEH SS, ALIABADI P, WEISSMAN BN, McNEIL BJ: Chronic osteomyelitis: Bone and gallium scan patterns associated with active disease. *Radiology* 158:685–688, 1986.

88. ESTERHAI J, ALAVI A, MANDELL GA, BROWN J: Sequential technetium 99m gallium-67 scintigraphic evaluation of subclinical osteomyelitis complicating fracture non-union. *J Orthop Res* 3:219–225, 1985.

89. MERKEL KD, BROWN ML, DEWANJEE MK, FITZGERALD RH JR: Comparison of indium-labeled-leukocyte imaging with sequential technetium-gallium scanning in the diagnosis of low-grade musculoskeletal sepsis. *J Bone Joint Surg* 67A:465–476, 1985.

90. MODIC MT, PFLANZE W, FEIGLIN DHI, BELHOBEK G: Magnetic resonance imaging of musculoskeletal infections. *Radiol Clin North Am* 24:247–258, 1986.

91. SEABOLD JE, NEPOLA JV, CONRAD GR, MARSH JL, MONTGOMERY WJ, BRICKER JA, KIRCHNER PT: Detection of osteomyelitis at fracture nonunion sites: Comparison of two scintigraphic methods. *AJR* 152:1021–1027, 1989.

92. DATZ FL, THORNE DA: Effect of chronicity of infection on the sensitivity of the In-111–labeled leukocyte scan. *AJR* 147:809–812, 1986.

93. McCARTHY K, VELCHIK MG, ALAVI A, MANDELL GA, ESTERHAI JL, GOLL S: Indium-111–labeled white blood cells in the detection of osteomyelitis complicated by a preexisting condition. *J Nucl Med* 29:1015–1021, 1988.

94. SCHAUWECKER DS: Osteomyelitis: Diagnosis with In-111–labeled leukocytes. *Radiology* 171:141–146, 1989.

95. COPPING C, DALGLIESH SM, DUDLEY NJ, GRIFFITHS PA, HARRINGTON M, POTTER R, SMITH BD: The role of ^{99}Tc^m-HMPAO white cell imaging in suspected orthopaedic infection. *Br J Radiol* 65:309–312, 1992.

96. BERQUIST TH, BROWN ML, FITZGERALD RH JR, MAY GR: Magnetic resonance imaging: Application in musculoskeletal infection. *Magn Reson Imaging* 3:219–230, 1985.

97. WUKICH DK, ABREU SH, CALLAGHAN JJ, VAN NOSTRAND D, SAVORY CG, EGGLI DF, GARCIA JE, BERREY BH: Diagnosis of infection by preoperative scintigraphy with indium-labeled white blood cells. *J Bone Joint Surg* 69A:1353–1360, 1987.

98. DATZ FL, THORNE DA: Cause and significance of cold bone defects on indium-111–labeled leukocyte imaging. *J Nucl Med* 28:820–823, 1987.

99. McDOUGALL IR, BAUMERT JE, LANTIERI RL: Evaluation of ^{111}In leukocyte whole body scanning. *AJR* 133:849–854, 1979.

100. SFAKIANAKIS GN, AL-SHEIKH W, HEAL A, RODMAN G, ZEPPA R, SERAFINI A: Comparisons of scintigraphy with In-111 leukocytes and Ga-67 in the diagnosis of occult sepsis. *J Nucl Med* 23:618–626, 1982.

101. KIM EE, PJURA GA, LOWRY PA, GOBUTY AH, TRAINA JF: Osteomyelitis complicating fracture: Pitfalls of ^{111}In leukocyte scintigraphy. *AJR* 148:927–930, 1987.

102. VAN NOSTRAND D, ABREU SH, CALLAGHAN JJ, ATKINS FB, STOOPS HC, SAVORY CG: In-111–labeled white blood cell uptake in noninfected closed fracture in humans: Prospective study. *Radiology* 167:495–498, 1988.

103. SCHAUWECKER DS: The scintigraphic diagnosis of osteomyelitis. *AJR* 158:9–18, 1992.

104. MODIC MT, FEIGLIN DH, PIRAINO DW, BOUMPHREY F, WEINSTEIN MA, DUCHESNEAU PM, REHM S: Vertebral osteomyelitis: Assessment using MR. *Radiology* 157:157–166, 1985.

105. BELTRAN J, McGHEE RB, SHAFFER PB, OLSEN JO, BEN-

NETT WF, FOSTER TR, McCALLA MS, ISKRA LA, BLAGG RL, BILLER DS: Experimental infections of the musculoskeletal system: Evaluation with MR imaging and Tc-99m MDP and Ga-67 scintigraphy. *Radiology* 167:167–172, 1988.

106. BELTRAN J, NOTO AM, McGHEE RB, FREEDY RM, McCALLA MS: Infections of the musculoskeletal system: High-field-strength MR imaging. *Radiology* 164:449–454, 1987.

107. UNGER E, MOLDOFSKY P, GATENBY R, HARTZ W, BRODER G: Diagnosis of osteomyelitis by MR imaging. *AJR* 150:605–610, 1988.

108. YUH WTC, CORSON JD, BARANIEWSKI HM, REZAI K, SHAMMA AR, KATHOL MH, YUTAKA S, EL-KHOURY GY, HAWES DR, PLATZ CE, COOPER RR, CORRY RJ: Osteomyelitis of the foot in diabetic patients: Evaluation with plain film, ^{99m}Tc-MDP bone scintigraphy, and MR imaging. *AJR* 152:795–800, 1989.

109. ERDMAN WA, TAMBURRO F, JAYSON HT, WEATHERALL PT, FERRY KB, PESHOCK RM: Osteomyelitis: Characteristics and pitfalls of diagnosis with MR imaging. *Radiology* 180:533–539, 1991.

110. TANG JSH, GOLD RH, BASSETT LW, SEEGER LL: Musculoskeletal infection of the extremities: Evaluation with MR imaging. *Radiology* 166:205–209, 1988.

111. PAAJANEN H, GRODD W, REVEL D, ENGELSTAD B, BRASCH RC: Gadolinium-DTPA enhanced MR imaging of intramuscular abscesses. *Magn Reson Imaging* 5:109–115, 1987.

112. MORRISON WB, SCHWEITZER ME, BOCK GW, MITCHELL DG, HUME EL, PATHRIA MN, RESNICK D: Diagnosis of osteomyelitis: Utility of fat-suppressed contrast-enhanced MR imaging. *Radiology* 189:251–257, 1993.

113. FLETCHER BD, SCOLES PV, NELSON AD: Osteomyelitis in children: Detection by magnetic resonance. *Radiology* 150:57–60, 1984.

114. MASON MD, ZLATKIN MB, ESTERHAI JL, DALINKA MK, VELCHIK MG, KRESSEL HY: Chronic complicated osteomyelitis of the lower extremity: Evaluation with MR imaging. *Radiology* 173:355–359, 1989.

115. DANGMAN BC, HOFFER FA, RAND FF, O'ROURKE EJ: Osteomyelitis in children: Gadolinium-enhanced MR imaging. *Radiology* 182:743–747, 1992.

116. QUINN SF, MURRAY W, CLARK RA, COCHRAN C: MR imaging of chronic osteomyelitis. *J Comput Assist Tomogr* 12:113–117, 1988.

117. MARTI-BONMATI L, APARISI F, POYATOS C, VILAR J: Brodie abscess: MR imaging appearance in 10 patients. *J Magn Reson Imaging* 3:543–546, 1993.

118. YUH WTC, SCHREIBER AE, MONTGOMERY WJ, EHARA S: Magnetic resonance imaging of pyomyositis. *Skel Radiol* 17:190–193, 1988.

119. ABIRI MM, KIRPEKAR M, ABLOW RC: Osteomyelitis: Detection with US. *Radiology* 172:509–511, 1989.

120. ABIRI MM, DeANGELIS GA, KIRPEKAR M, ABOU A-NA, ABLOW RC: Ultrasonic detection of osteomyelitis: Pathologic correlation in an animal model. *Invest Radiol* 27:111–113, 1992.

121. WILLIAMSON SL, SEIBERT JJ, GLASIER CM, LEITHISER RE, ARONSON J: Ultrasound in advanced pediatric osteomyelitis: A report of 5 cases. *Pediatr Radiol* 21:288–290, 1991.

122. PARK CM, CHUNG KB, SUH WHS: Osteomyelitis: Detection with US. *Radiology* 178:890, 1991.

123. NEER CS, WATSON KC, STANTON FJ: Recent experience in total shoulder replacement. *J Bone Joint Surg* 64A:319–337, 1982.

124. ALIABADI P, WEISSMAN BN, THORNHILL T, NIKPOOR N, SOSMAN JL: Evaluation of a nonconstrained total shoulder prosthesis. *AJR* 151:1169–1172, 1988.

125. NEER CS, KIRBY RM: Revision of humeral head and total shoulder arthroplasties. *Clin Orthop* 107:189–195, 1982.

126. MAGNUSON JE, BROWN ML, HAUSER MF, BERQUIST TH, FITZGERALD RH JR, KLEE GG: In-111-labeled leukocyte scintigraphy in suspected orthopedic prosthesis infection: Comparison with other imaging modalities. *Radiology* 168:235–239, 1988.

127. COFIELD RH: Total shoulder arthroplasty with the Neer prosthesis. *J Bone Joint Surg* 66A:899–906, 1984.

128. POST M, HASKELL SS, JABLON M: Total shoulder replacement with a constrained prosthesis. *J Bone Joint Surg* 62A:327–335, 1980.

129. GRISTINA AG, ROMANO RL, KAMMIRE GC, WEBB LX: Total shoulder replacement. *Orthop Clin North Am* 18:445–453, 1987.

130. ROSENTHALL L, LISBONA R, HERNANDEZ M, HADJIPAVLOU A: 99mTc-PP and 67Ga imaging following insertion of orthopedic devices. *Radiology* 133:717–721, 1979.

131. WILLIAMSON BRJ, McLAUGHLIN RE, WANG GJ, MILLER CW, TEATES CD, BRAY ST: Radionuclide bone imaging as a means of differentiating loosening and infection in patients with a painful total hip prosthesis. *Radiology* 133:723–725, 1979.

132. MULAMBA L, FERRANT A, LENERS N, DeNAYER P, ROMBOUTS JJ, VINCENT A: Indium-111 leucocyte scanning in the evaluation of painful hip arthroplasty. *Acta Orthop Scand* 54:695–697, 1983.

133. JOHNSON JA, CHRISTIE MJ, SANDLER MP, PARKS PF JR, HOMRA L, KAYE JJ: Detection of occult infection following total joint arthroplasty using sequential technetium-99m HDP bone scintigraphy and indium-111 WBC imaging. *J Nucl Med* 29:1347–1353, 1988.

134. TIGGES S, STILES RG, MELI RJ, ROBERSON JR: Hip aspiration: A cost-effective and accurate method of evaluating the potentially infected hip prosthesis. *Radiology* 189:485–488, 1993.

135. BARRACK RL, HARRIS WH: The value of aspiration of the hip joint before revision total hip arthroplasty. *J Bone Joint Surg* 75A:66–76, 1993.

136. GOULD ES, POTTER HG, BOBER SE: Role of routine percutaneous hip aspirations prior to prosthesis revision. *Skel Radiol* 19:427–430, 1990.

137. PHILLIPS WC, KATTAPURAM SV: Efficacy of preoperative hip aspiration performed in the radiology department. *Clin Orthop* 179:141–146, 1983.

5 IMAGING OF BONE TUMORS IN THE SHOULDER

Roger Kerr
Bruce Wollman
David J. Sartoris

Radiologic imaging plays a major role in the diagnosis of bone tumors. While both computed tomography (CT) and magnetic resonance imaging (MRI) can be very useful in determining the precise extent of neoplasia, plain films (along with histologic analysis) are crucial for making a correct diagnosis. Furthermore, posttreatment imaging of tumors has emerged as a very accurate means of assessing response to therapy.

Unlike the proximal humerus, the clavicle and scapula are uncommon sites of primary bone neoplasms. Review of the small existing body of literature on primary tumors of the clavicle and scapula is useful to determine the relative frequency and distribution of lesions arising at these sites.

Smith and coworkers reviewed 58 patients diagnosed with clavicle lesions over a 50-year period at the Memorial Sloan-Kettering Cancer Center.[1] Thirty of the tumors were malignant, 5 were benign, and the remaining 23 were tumorlike lesions. The overall distribution of tumors resembled that observed on long bones; that is, distal sites were more common. Also, the researchers noted that 24 small lesions (<3cm) were found on the acromion but only 8 in the sternal end. It was noted that this information is not helpful in the diagnosis because metastases are commonly found at the ends of bones (Fig. 5-1). They stressed that though the diagnosis may be suggested radiographically, frequently a biopsy is needed to confirm the histologic nature of the lesion.

Samilson and coworkers conducted a review of the totality of cases of scapular tumors reported in English from 1925 to 1968.[2] Of the 271 patients, 79 had benign tumors, 168 were primary malignant neoplasms, and 24 were metastatic malignant tumors, most commonly (75 percent) from cancer of the breast. Osteochondroma (49 percent) and giant cell tumor (18 percent) were the most common benign lesions. The most frequently observed malignant tumors were osteogenic sarcoma (33 percent), Ewing's sarcoma (22 percent), and chondrosarcoma (20 percent). The same group then reviewed the 31 cases of tumor of the scapula diagnosed at the University of Cal-

ifornia Medical Center in San Francisco between 1943 and 1968. Of these 31 cases, 12 were benign (8 osteochondromas), 6 were malignant, and 13 were metastatic.

Smith's group also reviewed patients with tumors of the clavicle or scapula from three sources: The Memorial Sloan-Kettering Cancer Center, Dahlin's monograph from the Mayo Clinic, and the *Radiological Atlas* from the Netherlands Committee on Bone Tumors.[3] The following data are from the combination of the results from these three sources. Of all 66 clavicular tumors, 12 percent were benign, 62 percent were malignant, and 26 percent were tumorlike lesions. Of the 204 scapular tumors, 70 percent were malignant, 23 percent benign, and 7 percent tumorlike. Osteochondroma was the most common benign tumor, and the most frequently seen tumorlike lesions were aneurysmal bone cysts or eosinophilic granulomas. Of the malignant scapular tumors, chondrosarcoma was the most common, followed by Ewing's and osteogenic sarcomas. These three diseases were equally prevalent in malignant clavicular tumors, although myeloma was especially common in Dahlin's monograph.

Aoki and associates studied 13 cases of giant cell tumor in the scapula.[4] This study was unusual for the fact that eight of the patients were younger than 20 years (mean overall age was 20 years) whereas the majority of people with giant cell tumor (usually found in the femur, tibia, and radius) are between 20 and 40 years (mean 30). Ten of the tumors were laterally situated and involved the shoulder articulations. This was reasonable, owing to the fact that embryologically the glenoid, acromion, and coracoid process all correspond to the distal end of a long bone, the most common site of giant cell tumors. In addition, histologic and radiologic appearances were similar to those observed in tumors of long bones.

Gerscovich and colleagues submitted the radiologic studies of 17 patients with proven benign tumors of the clavicle for further review to three radiologists who had no prior knowledge of the cases.[5] The physicians concurred that nine were indeed benign, but the eight others had aggressive-looking features that allowed for possible

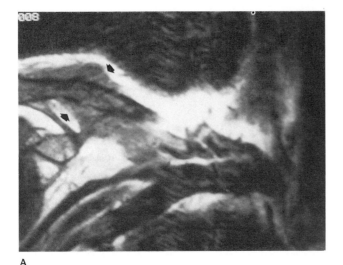

A

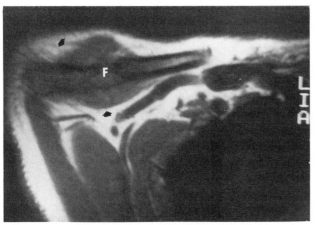

B

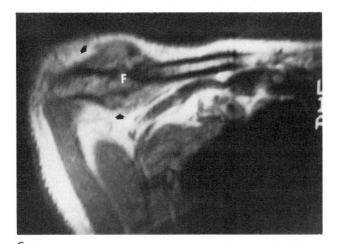

C

Figure 5-1 Metastatic breast cancer involving the clavicle. **A.** T1-weighted coronal MRI reveals soft tissue extension of the process (*arrows*). **B, C.** Transaxial proton-density and T2-weighted images document a pathologic fracture (F) within the lesion (*arrows*). Signal intensity is higher with T2 weighting.

malignancy in the differential diagnosis. Interestingly, these concerns were also raised in these same eight individuals at the original interpretation. The authors felt that the clavicle's unique embryologic development, shape, and variable cortical thickness were responsible for benign tumors mimicking malignant ones.

Franklin and coworkers reviewed 16 children (mean age 7.4 years) with nontraumatic lesions of the clavicle diagnosed between 1963 and 1983 at the Children's Orthopedic Hospital and Medical Center in Seattle.[6] Six of the lesions were due to infection (acute or chronic osteomyelitis) and four were developmental anomalies. The remaining six lesions were neoplasms, but only one was malignant. This was unusual, owing to the fact that the majority of clavicular tumors were malignant in the other studies. Also, the authors noted that pain may be an important symptom in diagnosis. While all of the children with infection had pain, only half of those with neoplasms and none with developmental anomalies complained of pain in the clavicle region.

CARTILAGE-FORMING TUMORS

Osteochondroma

An osteochondroma (or osteocartilaginous exostosis) is a bony projection covered by a cap of hyaline cartilage. The hallmark of osteochondroma is continuity of the cortical and trabecular bone of the lesion with that of the host bone. The pathogenesis has not been established, but it is thought that an osteochondroma develops when a portion of the physeal cartilage separates from the physis and proliferates in an abnormal direction.[7,8] It may occur in any bone that develops by endochondral ossification and usually stops growing when skeletal maturity is reached. Osteochondroma is the most common benign tumor of bone, representing approximately 50 percent of benign bone tumors and 10 to 15 percent of all bone tumors.[9] Patients are usually diagnosed before age 20 years[9,10] and usually present with a painless, palpable mass. Pain may develop because of impingement on adjacent muscle, tendon, or bone, fracture of the lesion, formation and subsequent inflammation of an overlying bursa, or malignant degeneration. An osteochondroma arising from the deep surface of the scapula may produce an audible snapping sound with shoulder girdle movement and give rise to crepitus or discomfort and winging of the scapula.[11] In the knee, popliteal vein thrombosis and popliteal artery pseudoaneurysm may occur, owing to a mechanical effect of an osteochondroma.[12,13] The most common sites of osteochondroma are the distal femur, proximal tibia, and proximal humerus. Some 14 to 25 percent of osteochondromas involve the proximal humerus.[9,14,15] Fewer than 1 percent of cases involve the clavicle. As many as 5 percent of osteochondromas involve the scapula, and, in fact, osteochondroma is the most common benign tumor of the scapula.[2,3]

In long bones, osteochondroma typically has a metaphyseal location. It may occur as a broad-based sessile lesion or as a pedunculated lesion. The stalk of a pedunculated lesion points away from the nearest joint. The cartilage cap ossifies with skeletal maturation and is usually only 2 or 3 mm thick in an adult.[14] Osteochondromas with a cartilage cap thicker than 2 to 3 cm are believed to be at increased risk for malignant transformation to chondrosarcoma.[16,17]

Hereditary multiple osteochondromatosis is an autosomal-dominant disorder that is usually detected in the first decade of life. The most frequently affected areas are the long bones, pelvis, scapulae, and ribs. In children, lesions of the scapulae and tibiae are typically the most conspicuous and are usually discovered first.[18] Both sessile and pedunculated forms coexist, among multiple bones or within a single bone. Retardation of diaphyseal bone growth is common, creating short stature and other deformities. Malignant degeneration is estimated to occur in not more than 1 percent of solitary osteochondromas and in 1 to 30 percent of patients with hereditary multiple osteochondromatosis.[9,10,19,20] Malignant degeneration must be considered whenever an adult patient with osteochondroma presents with pain or an enlarging mass.

The radiographic appearance of a pedunculated osteochondroma is typical: the stalk, composed of mature cortical and trabecular bone, is continuous with the host bone (Fig. 5-2). The calcified or ossified cap is often smooth and regular but may be lobulated and cauliflower-like. Sessile lesions also arise in continuity with the host bone, but because they often have a broad base of attachment this feature may be less conspicuous than in pedunculated forms. Pedunculated lesions grow away from the nearest joint. In addition to shortening of the bone, failure of normal tubulation may occur at the site of an osteochondroma, especially in patients with multiple osteochondromas, producing an abnormally wide bone.

Further imaging of an osteochondroma may be performed if a patient is symptomatic, if the diagnosis is uncertain, and if surgery is being considered. With MRI, continuity of the cortical and trabecular bone of an osteochondroma with that of host bone is readily identified (see Fig. 5-2). This may be useful in diagnosing sessile lesions, in which this relationship may not be clear on radiographs, and in distinguishing sessile lesions from other surface lesions of bone. The cartilage cap is well visualized on MRI as a region of intermediate signal intensity on T1-weighted images and of high signal intensity on T2-weighted images (see Fig. 5-2D, E). With MRI, the thickness of the cartilage cap may be determined to within 2 mm, and caps as small as 3 mm may reliably be demonstrated.[21] MRI also reveals the low–signal intensity perichondrium overlying the cartilage cap. When malignant transformation is suspected, MRI or CT may be used to search for destruction of cortical or trabecular bone or the development of a soft tissue mass. In a patient with an osteochondroma, a bone scan may be useful to search for additional lesions.

Enchondroma

Enchondroma is a benign tumor composed of mature hyaline cartilage that arises in the medullary space of bone. It is thought to arise from heterotopic cartilage cell nests derived from the epiphyseal cartilage plate.[22] An enchondroma is usually asymptomatic and is discovered incidentally on a radiograph or detected because of a pathologic fracture. The average age at presentation is 35 years, though the lesion may be found at almost any age.[9,10] Patients may complain of pain or swelling. The incidence of pathologic fracture increases with the tumor's size and is greater with more eccentric lesions.[9,10] The onset of pain or an enlarging mass, in the absence of trauma, is worrisome and may signify malignant transformation.

Enchondroma is the most common bone tumor of the hand, and this site accounts for 28 to 35 percent of enchondromas.[9,10,14] The proximal humerus is the next most common site of involvement, accounting for 5 to 12 percent of lesions.[9,14,23] Enchondroma originates in the metaphysis of a long bone but may be found within the diaphysis. The risk of malignant transformation of a solitary enchondroma is low, the greatest risk being associated with lesions of the shoulder or pelvic girdle.[24]

Ollier's disease is a nonheritable disorder characterized by multiple enchondromas, most often involving the bones of the hands and feet. The lesions are usually more expansile and deforming than are solitary enchondromas. Ollier's disease is often bilateral but is characterized by disproportionate involvement of one side of the body. The risk of malignant transformation is estimated at 30 percent.[9,10]

Radiographically, enchondroma typically appears as a round, oval, or lobulated lytic lesion with well-defined, often thinly sclerotic, margins. Punctate, flocculent, or ringlike calcifications often are present. Long-standing lesions may be completely mineralized without evidence of a lytic component.[25] Endosteal scalloping is common, but cortical expansion is infrequent except in thin bones such as the fibula or a rib. In a tubular bone, enchondroma is usually centrally located and involves the metaphysis, metadiaphysis, or diaphysis. Radiographic signs suggestive of malignant transformation include loss of definition of the lesion margin, cortical destruction, path-

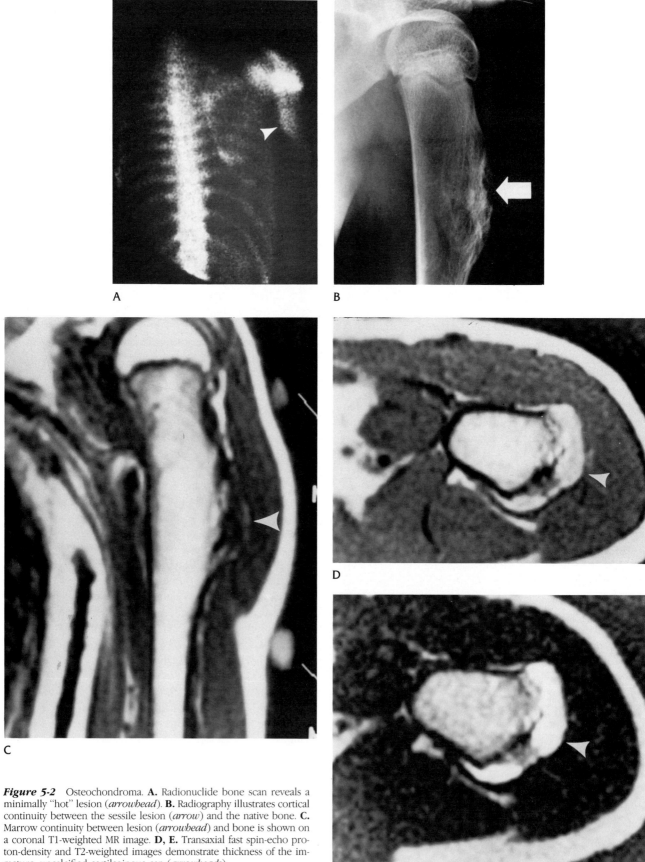

Figure 5-2 Osteochondroma. **A.** Radionuclide bone scan reveals a minimally "hot" lesion (*arrowhead*). **B.** Radiography illustrates cortical continuity between the sessile lesion (*arrow*) and the native bone. **C.** Marrow continuity between lesion (*arrowhead*) and bone is shown on a coronal T1-weighted MR image. **D, E.** Transaxial fast spin-echo proton-density and T2-weighted images demonstrate thickness of the immature, uncalcified cartilaginous cap (*arrowheads*).

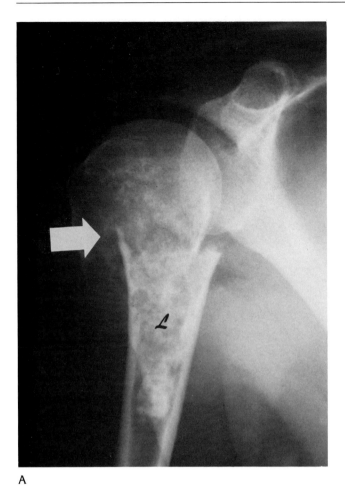

A

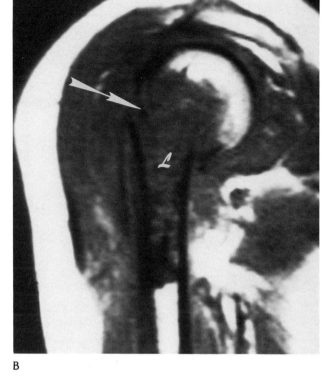

B

Figure 5-3 Pathologic fracture through large humeral enchondroma. **A.** The heavily calcified lesion (L) has fractured through its superior aspect (*arrow*) following trauma. **B.** T1-weighted sagittal MR image demonstrates low signal intensity within the lesion (L) as well as displacement at the fracture site (*arrow*).

ologic fracture (except for lesions of the phalanges) (Fig. 5-3), and development of a soft tissue mass. CT may be useful to demonstrate subtle matrix mineralization and to assess the adjacent cortical bone. On MRI, enchondromas and other lesions composed of hyaline cartilage matrix with low cellularity produce a characteristic pattern of signal abnormality (Figs. 5-4, 5-5).[26] On T1-weighted images, the lesion reveals a homogeneous pattern of low to intermediate signal intensity. T2-weighted images reveal lobules of homogeneous, diffuse high signal intensity with thin intervening septa of low signal intensity. Mineralized portions of an enchondroma appear as areas of low signal intensity, although very small foci may not be visible with MRI. It may be difficult to distinguish a small, well-differentiated chondrosarcoma from enchondroma unless there is cortical destruction or a soft tissue component.

Periosteal Chondroma

Periosteal chondroma is a benign, slow-growing cartilage tumor that arises under the periosteum.[27–29] It has a predilection for the proximal humerus (involved in 27 percent of reported cases) and the bones of the hand (involved in 17 percent of reported cases).[30] The lesion is usually 2 to 3 cm but may measure up to 7 cm.[27] Most

patients present in the second or third decade of life with pain and swelling. Symptoms are often long standing (average in one study, 21 months).[27] Histologically, periosteal chondroma consists of benign hyaline cartilage underlying the periosteum. At its external boundary the tumor is enclosed by a fibrous capsule.[30]

On radiographs, periosteal chondroma is associated with scalloping or remodeling of the cortex with a well-defined inner margin. Cortical buttressing and an overhanging edge of reactive periosteal bone may be seen at the superior and inferior margins of the lesion. This reactive bone may completely encircle the lesion. A variable degree of calcification or ossification of the cartilage matrix may be present. In one study, a soft tissue mass was visible on radiographs in one-third of cases.[28] On MRI, periosteal chondroma has imaging features similar to an enchondroma, with high signal intensity on T2-weighted images and variable foci of low signal intensity, depending on the extent of matrix calcification.[31]

It is important to distinguish periosteal chondroma from periosteal chondrosarcoma, as a well-differentiated chondrosarcoma and periosteal chondroma may have similar histologic features.[28] Periosteal chondroma is treated by simple curettage, whereas periosteal chondrosarcoma requires wide surgical resection. On radio-

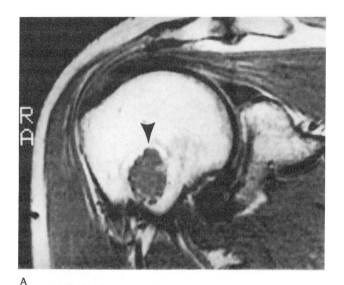

A

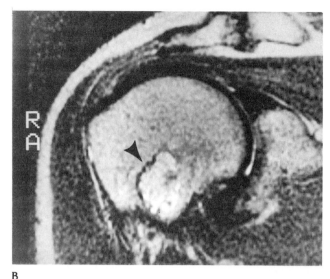

B

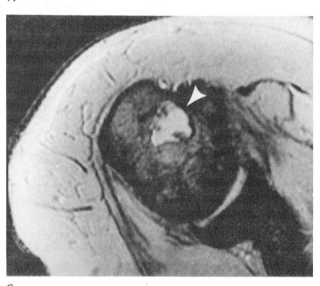

C

Figure 5-4 Enchondroma. **A, B.** Coronal proton-density and T2-weighted MR images reveal low and high signal intensity, respectively, within the well-defined metaphyseal lesion (*arrowheads*). **C.** Transaxial gradient-echo image also demonstrates high signal intensity in the tumor (*arrowhead*). *Courtesy of Randall Patten, MD, Kirkland, WA.*

graphs, a periosteal chondrosarcoma is usually larger and more exophytic than periosteal chondroma and often has less mass effect upon the adjacent cortex.[27,28] Periosteal chondrosarcoma is usually seen in a slightly older age group, during the fourth decade of life.[32] Periosteal osteosarcoma usually presents with a large soft tissue mass, bony spiculation, and cortical thickening, rather than scalloping. Small periosteal osteosarcomas and chondrosarcomas may, however, be difficult to distinguish from periosteal chondroma.

Chondroblastoma

Chondroblastoma is a rare benign tumor of cartilage cell origin. The tumor is composed of chondroblasts and chondroid matrix and originates from the epiphyseal side of the cartilage plate.[10,33–35] Most patients present

between age 5 and 25 years (average 16 to 18 years). An average age of 28 years has been reported when chondroblastoma arises in flat or short tubular bones.[33] Because chondroblastoma is an epiphyseal lesion, it often produces synovitis and presents with symptoms referable to a joint.[35] A joint effusion has been noted in one-third of patients.[36] Some 70 to 80 percent of chondroblastomas arise in long bones, and as many as 20 to 25 percent arise within the humeral head.[10,33,35] Involvement of the scapula or clavicle is rare.

On histologic examination, chondroblastoma is composed of chondroblasts, scattered multinucleated giant cells, and chondroid matrix. Typically, cellular elements predominate and chondroid matrix constitutes less than 30 percent of the lesion.[23] A characteristic pattern of chicken wire calcification is variably present.[9] Development of a secondary aneurysmal bone cyst and a locally aggressive pattern of growth may also be observed. Aggressive chondroblastoma may metastasize to lung, yet the primary lesion and metastatic tumors reveal the typical benign histologic appearance of chondroblastoma.[37]

On radiographs, chondroblastoma is centered in the epiphysis or an apophysis and often extends into the metaphysis. Rarely, there is isolated involvement of only the metaphysis. Chondroblastomas usually measure 1–6 cm in size, though larger lesions have been encountered. Chondroblastoma typically appears as a well-defined, geographic, lytic lesion with a thin sclerotic margin. Cortical expansion or endosteal scalloping may also be observed. Chondroblastoma rarely demonstrates an aggressive pattern of growth with penetration of subchondral bone and the overlying articular cartilage or violation of the cortex. This is especially true for lesions that arise in

the bony pelvis.[38] Varying degrees of matrix mineralization have been reported in 25 to 60 percent of lesions.[39,40] A distinctive pattern of thick, solid or layered periosteal reaction has been observed involving the metadiaphyseal shaft distal to the lesion in 53 percent of chondroblastomas involving the long bones.[41] Periostitis was observed in 73 percent of lesions involving the proximal humerus.[41] It is believed to reflect an inflammatory reaction, the mechanism that probably also underlies the development of joint effusion with chondroblastoma. This periosteal reaction is a useful radiographic sign for distinguishing chondroblastoma from other epiphysis-centered lesions. Clear cell chondrosarcoma (discussed below) is a rare malignant tumor of the epiphysis that may appear similar to chondroblastoma but usually presents at a later age.

On MRI, chondroblastoma usually reveals intermediate

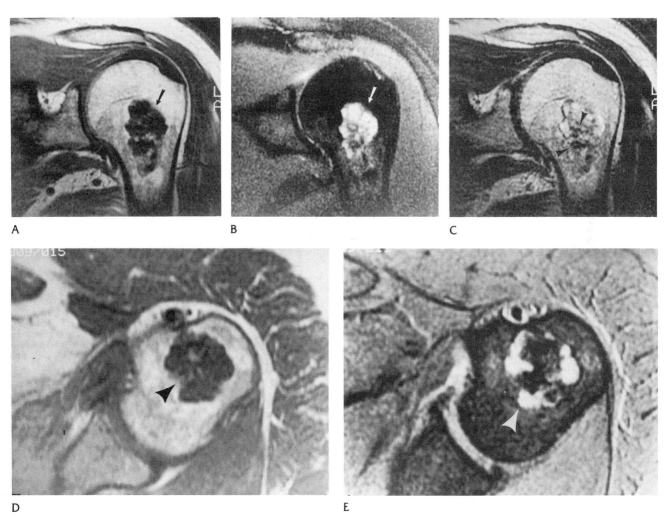

Figure 5-5 Enchondroma. **A.** Coronal T1-weighted MR image demonstrates a well-defined lesion (*arrow*) of low signal intensity. **B.** Fast spin-echo inversion recovery image in the same plane exhibits high signal intensity within the lesion (*arrow*). **C.** Corresponding fast spin-echo T2-weighted image documents chondroid matrix of low signal intensity (*arrowheads*). **D.** Transaxial T1-weighted image exhibits findings similar to those in **A** (*arrowhead*). **E.** Corresponding gradient-echo image reveals high–signal intensity lesion with internal low–signal intensity matrix (*arrowhead*).

signal intensity on both T1-weighted and T2-weighted images.[42] Low, high, or inhomogeneous signal intensity has been reported on T2-weighted images.[43] The usual lack of high signal intensity on T2-weighted images reflects the predominant cellular nature of chondroblastoma and lack of hyaline cartilage.[26] Chondroblastoma may undergo cystic change or develop a secondary aneurysmal bone cyst, resulting in focal regions of high signal intensity on T2-weighted images and fluid-fluid levels.[44] MRI may overestimate the extent of chondroblastoma due to perilesional edema within the intramedullary space and the adjacent soft tissues.[43] CT may suggest the diagnosis by detecting intralesional calcification not apparent on radiographs.

Chondromyxoid Fibroma

Chondromyxoid fibroma is a rare benign tumor of cartilage origin that also contains varying amounts of myxoid and fibrous tissue elements. It is most common in the second decade of life, and 60 to 75 percent of lesions present by age 30.[9,23,45] Symptoms usually evolve slowly; pain develops first, followed by swelling. It is not unusual for symptoms to be present for 2 years or more.[9,45] Chondromyxoid fibroma has a predilection for the bones of the lower extremity, especially around the knee. In multiple series, 67 to 90 percent of chondromyxoid fibromas occurred in the lower extremity, the proximal tibia being the site most frequently affected.[9,14,44] Involvement of the shoulder region is uncommon; no more than 3 percent of cases involve the proximal humerus and no more than 2 percent the scapula.[15]

On radiographs chondromyxoid fibroma typically presents as an eccentric metaphyseal or metadiaphyseal lytic lesion with a sclerotic margin and lobulated contour.[46] Extension into the epiphysis may also be observed. Chondromyxoid fibroma often appears trabeculated owing to reactive bony ridges at the periphery of the lesion. The lesion is often expansile, rarely destroys cortical bone, and extends into soft tissue. Matrix mineralization is rare. On MRI, chondromyxoid fibroma produces low to intermediate signal intensity on T1-weighted images and high signal intensity on T2-weighted images. A heterogeneous pattern of signal abnormality may be produced by cystic or hemorrhagic regions within the tumor.[10]

Chondrosarcoma

Chondrosarcoma is the third most common primary malignant bone tumor, following multiple myeloma and osteosarcoma. It accounts for 17 to 22 percent of such tumors.[9,14,17] Most chondrosarcomas arise de novo in bone (primary chondrosarcoma), but a significant percentage develops from a preexisting benign cartilage tumor (secondary chondrosarcoma). Secondary chon-

drosarcoma usually occurs in patients with hereditary multiple exostoses or Ollier's disease. Chondrosarcoma is classified as *central* when it arises from the medullary space and *peripheral* when it arises on the surface of the affected bone. The rare *extraskeletal* chondrosarcoma originates in soft tissue.

Patients with central, de novo chondrosarcoma present at an average age of 50 years, whereas secondary central lesions typically develop between age 30 and 40.[10] Pain, tenderness, and local swelling are frequent. Because these tumors often grow slowly, symptoms may be present for at least 1 or 2 years.[9] Pain and tenderness are valuable diagnostic signs of malignancy as benign cartilage tumors are asymptomatic. Central chondrosarcoma most often arises in the proximal femur, pelvic bones, proximal humerus, and ribs.[23] The prevalence is 12 percent in the proximal humerus, and 6 percent in the scapula; the clavicle rarely is involved.[9,23]

The histologic diagnosis of chondrosarcoma is not always straightforward, as it may be difficult to distinguish a low-grade chondrosarcoma from an enchondroma.[10,17,25] In such cases, the radiographic findings may be useful for predicting the benign or malignant nature of a lesion.[47] In general, the higher the histologic grade of a chondrosarcoma, the poorer the prognosis.[10]

The radiologic appearance of chondrosarcoma varies, depending on its histologic grade.[47] Typically it appears as a multilobulated, lytic lesion with variable calcification (Figs. 5-6 through 5-8). The margins vary from well defined and sclerotic to ill defined. The cortical bone may be intact, may reveal endosteal scalloping or bony expansion, or may be violated in association with a soft tissue mass. Low-grade lesions demonstrate an eccentric, lobular growth pattern with sclerotic or well-defined margins and extensive regions of dense calcification forming rings or spicules (Fig. 5-9).[47] High-grade lesions reveal a concentric patten of growth with ill-defined,

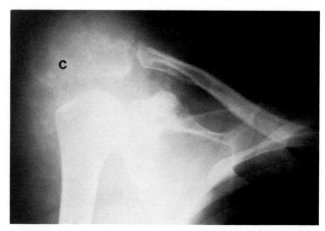

Figure 5-6 Chondrosarcoma. A large mass with typical diffuse chondroid calcification (C) arises from and destroys the acromion process.

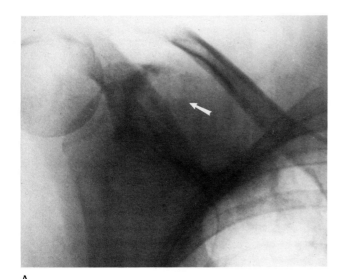

A

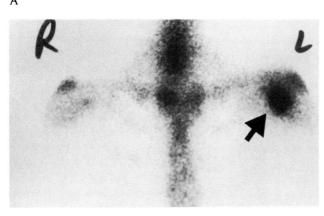

B

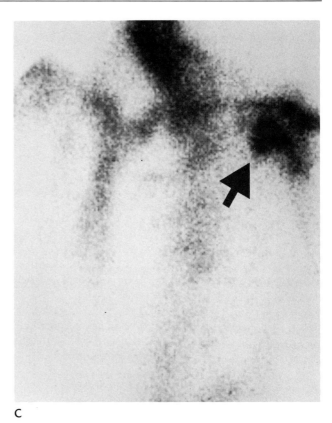

C

Figure 5-7   Chondrosarcoma. **A.** Destruction of the coracoid process is associated with typical chondroid calcification (*arrow*). **B, C.** The lesion exhibits prominent increased activity (*arrows*) on a radionuclide bone scan (frontal and oblique views).

moth-eaten or permeative margins, large noncalcified areas, and faint, amorphous calcification.[47] On CT, low-density areas, representing necrosis, are an additional sign of a high-grade lesion.[47] On MRI, well-differentiated, low-grade chondrosarcoma is characterized by a lobular pattern of low signal intensity on T1-weighted images and high signal intensity on T2-weighted images owing to the hyaline cartilage matrix.[26] On gadolinium-enhanced T1-weighted images, low-grade chondrosarcoma reveals enhancing, curvilinear septae, reflecting fibrovascular tissue between cartilage lobules.[48] Intralesional calcifications appear as foci of low signal intensity. In high-grade chondrosarcoma hyaline cartilage is replaced by myxoid matrix, and a heterogeneous pattern of intermediate or high signal intensity is observed on T2-weighted images. Highly cellular areas in high-grade chondrosarcoma reveal homogeneous or heterogeneous enhancement on gadolinium-enhanced T1-weighted images.[48]

Most peripheral or surface chondrosarcomas arise from a sessile osteochondroma.[10] These secondary chondrosarcomas become clinically apparent because of pain or the presence of an enlarging mass. Peripheral chondrosarcoma is distinguished from an osteochondroma by the presence of bone destruction and a soft tissue mass that usually contains scattered regions of calcification.[49,50] A low-grade peripheral chondrosarcoma may be difficult to distinguish from osteochondroma[51]; however, it is hypothesized that a septal pattern of gadolinium enhancement on MR images may be specific for low-grade chondrosarcoma and may be used to distinguish it from enchondroma or osteochondroma.[48] The demonstration of a cartilage cap thickness greater than 3 cm is suggestive of malignancy and may be accurately revealed with MRI.[21]

Periosteal chondrosarcoma, a rare tumor, is the malignant counterpart of periosteal chondroma.[52,53] This lesion has a strong predilection for the distal femoral diaphysis or metaphysis and the proximal humerus.[9] It may occur in the second to the seventh decade of life. The histologic findings are those of a low-grade chondrosarcoma, and the prognosis is relatively favorable in comparison with that for central chondrosarcoma.[32,52,53] A periosteal chondrosarcoma is usually greater than 5 cm

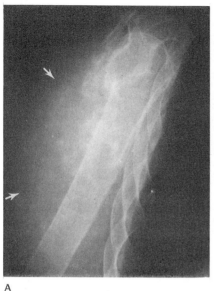

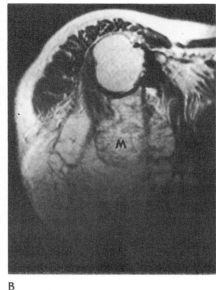

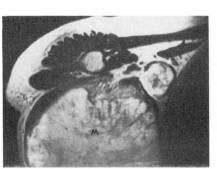

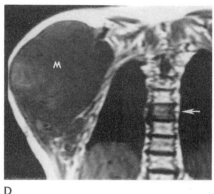

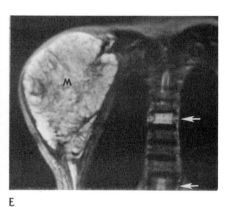

Figure 5-8 Chondrosarcoma. **A.** Radiography reveals a massive lesion arising from the scapula with internal calcifications (*arrows*). **B, C.** Transaxial fast spin-echo T2-weighted MR images reveal predominantly high signal intensity within the mass (M). **D.** Coronal T1-weighted image demonstrates the mass (M) and a metastasis to T6 (*arrow*). **E.** Corresponding fast spin-echo T2-weighted image reveals high signal intensity within the mass (M) and its vertebral metastases (*arrows*).

in diameter, whereas periosteal chondroma is usually less than 3 cm.[9] Radiographically, periosteal chondrosarcoma appears as a soft tissue mass with granular or "popcorn" calcification (Fig. 5-10). The underlying cortex is usually thickened and sclerotic and may reveal mild saucerization. Invasion of the medullary cavity does not occur. Periosteal osteosarcoma may have a similar radiographic appearance but usually affects the middiaphysis and is associated with spicules of reactive bone perpendicular to the underlying cortex.[52]

Dedifferentiated chondrosarcoma is a highly malignant variant of chondrosarcoma.[54,55] It is a lesion that consists of a chondrosarcoma and an additional high-grade malignant tumor (osteosarcoma, fibrosarcoma, or malignant fibrous histiocytoma). The secondary sarcoma is thought to arise from undifferentiated mesenchymal cells within a chondrosarcoma.[56] Approximately 90 percent of these lesions occur within a central chondrosarcoma.[54,55] This pattern of sarcomatous transformation occurs in 10 to 11 percent of chondrosarcomas. The scapula and proximal humerus are not uncommon sites for this lesion. Radiographically, the lesion appears as a chondrosarcoma with

an aggressive, lytic component, representing the second sarcoma. Cortical destruction and a large, uncalcified soft tissue mass are common features.[57] The 5-year survival rate is only 10 percent.[55]

Clear cell chondrosarcoma is an uncommon, low-grade malignant tumor that occurs in an epiphyseal location, usually the proximal femur or proximal humerus.[58,59] There is a mild tendency to involve multiple bones.[59] It usually occurs in the third to fifth decade of life; mean age is 39 years.[10] It is a slow-growing tumor, and symptoms of pain and limited range of motion are often present for 1 or 2 years prior to presentation. Histologically, the tumor is characterized by the presence of clear cells, although areas of conventional chondrosarcoma may be seen in as many as 50 percent of cases.[60] Radiographs reveal a lytic, often expansile lesion of the epiphysis with margins that are usually well-defined or sclerotic. Larger lesions extend into the metaphysis and may have ill-defined margins. Cortical violation and soft tissue extension are rare and periosteal reaction does not occur. A variable degree of matrix calcification is observed in one-third of cases.[10] The epiphyseal location, distinct borders, and occasional calcification may produce an appearance identical to that of chondroblastoma. In such instances, the lack of periosteal reaction and older age of the patient are features that may be used to distinguish clear cell chondrosarcoma from chondroblastoma. When treated by wide excision, clear cell chondrosarcoma has a much better prognosis than conventional chondrosarcoma. On MRI, clear cell chondrosarcoma has a nonspecific appearance with low to intermediate signal intensity on T1-weighted images and predominant high signal intensity on T2-weighted images.[26,42,61]

BONE-FORMING TUMORS

Osteoid Osteoma

Osteoid osteoma is a benign lesion of bone with a self-limited growth potential. It is usually seen in patients aged 10 to 25 years and is rare after age 30.[62] Osteoid osteoma is composed of a nidus of partially calcified

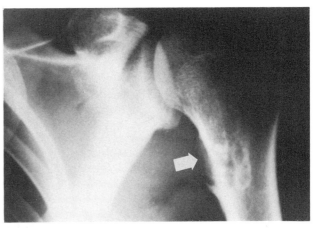

Figure 5-10 Juxtacortical chondrosarcoma. A cortically based lesion with chondroid calcification and a poorly defined margin (*arrow*) is present in the humeral metadiaphysis.

osteoid trabeculae and a highly vascular connective tissue stroma. There is variable calcification of the nidus, the most pronounced calcification occurring within the center and less or none in the periphery.[17] The lesion (which consists of the nidus) may measure 1.5 to 2 cm in diameter; larger lesions are classified as osteoblastoma.[63] Most osteoid osteomas occur in or near cortical bone and are surrounded by extensive reactive sclerosis. Intramedullary or intraarticular, subcortical lesions do not provoke reactive bone formation.[63,64] Intraarticular lesions produce joint-related symptoms with inflammatory synovitis and joint effusion.[65,66] Weakness, flexion deformity, or muscle atrophy may occur with these lesions. Premature development of osteoarthritis of the hip has been reported in association with an intraarticular lesion.[66] Patients with intraarticular osteoid osteoma are often treated for arthritis for months or years as radiographs reveal periarticular osteopenia but typically not the nidus.[63,65]

Osteoid osteoma is classically associated with pain, worse at night, that is relieved by aspirin. Pain is thought to be related to production of prostaglandins by the tumor. This may cause increased vascular pressure and stimulate afferent nerves within the nidus, producing pain.[62,63] Osteoid osteoma most commonly involves the femur (especially the femoral neck), the tibia, the vertebral column, or the bones of the hand or foot. Spinal lesions are often associated with scoliosis, local tenderness, and paraspinal muscle atrophy.[67] The proximal humerus is involved in 2 to 5 percent of cases, the scapula in 1 to 2 percent, and the clavicle in 1 to 3 percent.[9,14,23,68,69] In the long bones most osteoid osteomas are diaphyseal, but extension into the metaphysis may be observed.

On radiographs, a classic osteoid osteoma appears as a round or ovoid intracortical radiolucency surrounded by a broad zone of sclerosis (Fig. 5-11). Solid or lamellar

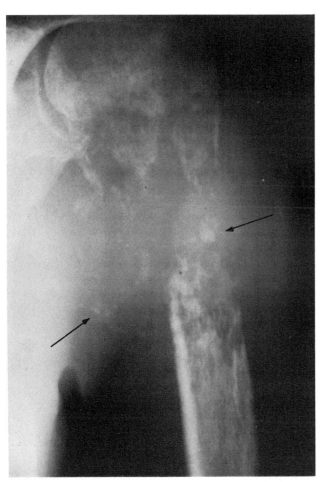

Figure 5-9 Chondrosarcoma. Permeative destruction of the humeral metadiaphysis indicates a high-grade lesion. *Arrows* indicate chondroid calcification.

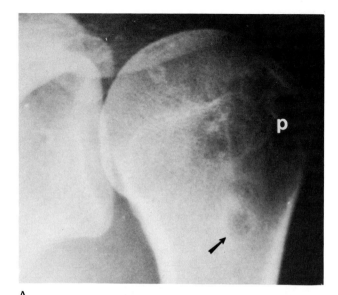

Figure 5-11 Osteoid osteoma. External, **A,** and internal, **B,** rotation views reveal a small cortically based lytic nidus with a sclerotic margin (*arrows*). A prominent humeral pseudocyst (P) is also evident.

periosteal reaction is present in approximately 60 percent of patients.[64] The nidus is usually partially mineralized, but it may be completely radiolucent or, rarely, fully calcified. Intraarticular lesions and those involving the spine or pelvis are often radiographically occult. If osteoid osteoma is suspected clinically but is not evident on radiographs, CT (using 1.5-mm thick slices) is the best imaging examination to detect the nidus.[70,71] A three-phase bone scan is useful for lesions that are poorly localized, as the highly vascular nidus avidly takes up the radionuclide. A pattern of focal increased uptake within a larger region of increased uptake (the double-density sign) has been described in osteoid osteoma and may be used to distinguish it from osteomyelitis.[72] Osteoid osteoma is the only primary bone tumor that is diag-

nosed more accurately by CT than by MRI, as detection of the nidus is most accurately accomplished with CT.[43] On MRI, the nidus of osteoid osteoma demonstrates low to intermediate signal intensity on T1-weighted images and low, intermediate, or high signal intensity on T2-weighted images.[73–77] There is variable enhancement of the hypervascular nidus following intravenous injection of gadolinium.[76] MRI may also reveal extensive intraosseous and soft tissue edema or inflammation adjacent to an osteoid osteoma.[73,74,77] Joint effusion and synovial thickening are often seen on MRI with intra-articular lesions.

Osteoid osteoma is usually treated by complete en bloc resection; it is essential that the entire nidus be removed. Surgical localization of the nidus may be accomplished with intraoperative bone scintigraphy, CT, guidance, or tetracycline fluorescence.[63,70,78,79] Percutaneous excision or ablation of osteoid osteoma has recently been described and represents a promising alternative to open surgery.[80–82]

Osteoblastoma

Osteoblastoma is histologically similar to osteoid osteoma but is distinguished by its larger size (1.5 to 2.0 cm) and progressive pattern of growth.[83,84] It occurs most often during the second and third decades of life; 90 percent of affected patients are younger than 30 years of age.[83] Most patients complain of pain, often of 1 to 2 years' duration. Osteoblastoma most often involves the vertebral column, femur, tibia, talus, skull, and facial bones. The proximal humerus is involved in 8 to 10 percent of cases, the scapula in 1 percent, and the clavicle in less than 1 percent.[14,23] Histologically, osteoblastoma consists of osteoid trabeculae with irregular bone formation, large numbers of osteoblasts, a fibrovascular stroma, and multinucleated giant cells.[9] Histologic differentiation from osteoid osteoma may be difficult or impossible; however, in osteoblastoma the bone trabeculae are broader, longer, and less densely packed.[84] A subset of osteoblastomas resemble low-grade osteosarcoma histologically and radiographically. These lesions have been termed *aggressive osteoblastoma* and *malignant osteoblastoma* but are best considered to represent low-grade osteosarcoma.[84,85] Such lesions are locally aggressive and have the ability to metastasize. Histologic features that favor the diagnosis of osteosarcoma include anaplasia, permeative growth and margins, and "trapping" of host lamellar bone by tumor bone.[23]

On radiographs, osteoblastoma involving a long bone appears as a round or oval lytic lesion with a variable amount of intralesional and perilesional sclerosis. Cortical expansion is common, and solid, lamellar, or spiculated periosteal reaction may be observed. An aggressive pattern of growth, with cortical destruction and a soft tissue mass, may also occur. Most lesions arise within the cortex or eccentrically within the medullary space. Intracortical lesions are surrounded by abundant reactive sclerosis. Approximately three-fourths of lesions are diaphyseal and the remainder metaphyseal.[83] CT may be useful to demonstrate matrix ossification and a surrounding bony shell. On MRI, osteoblastoma reveals low to intermediate signal intensity on T1-weighted images and high signal intensity or a mixed pattern of intermediate and high signal intensity on T2-weighted images.[70,84] Edema or inflammation of the adjacent marrow and soft tissues may also be present and may obscure the tumor boundaries on MRI.[84,86] Atrophy of adjacent muscle may be identified on CT or MRI.[84]

Osteosarcoma

Osteosarcoma is one of the most common primary malignant bone tumors, second in prevalence only to multiple myeloma.[87] Histologically, a malignant proliferating spindle-cell stroma produces osteoid or immature bone. This neoplasm is classified by a variety of characteristics, including location in bone, histologic composition, level of differentiation, status of underlying tissue, and number of foci involved.[88]

The most common type of this lesion is the conventional medullary osteosarcoma. This neoplasm presents more frequently in males (60 percent) and in younger people (85 percent under age 30).[89] Patients usually present with increasing pain and swelling; the symptoms usually persist for a few months before diagnosis.[87] The disease is most commonly found in the legs but also can be present in the proximal humerus (10 percent), clavicle (1 percent), or scapula (1 percent).[89] Most of these tumors originate in the metaphysis.[88]

The radiologic appearance of conventional osteosarcoma often depends on the degree of bone production by the lesion. It is usually a mixture of osteolysis and osteosclerosis with fluffy, cloudlike densities (Fig. 5-12).[89] Periosteal reactions are common, often in the form of radiating spiculation (sunburst) or Codman's triangle.[87] Other typical features are periostitis, cortical destruction, and a soft tissue mass.[88]

The intramedullary extent and soft tissue component of osteosarcoma are most accurately determined with MRI (Fig. 5-13).[64] Furthermore, MRI may be used to assist biopsy planning by identifying the various tumor components (e.g., cellular areas, compact bone, cartilage, necrosis, and hemorrhage). Tc-99m MDP radionuclide bone imaging shows the primary neoplasm (and any metastases) avidly taking up bone-seeking compounds. Accurate depiction of tumor extent is difficult, owing to the fact that this accumulation often occurs beyond the boundaries of the tumor.[88]

The mortality rate for patients with osteosarcoma was quite high before the use of effective chemotherapies; now the estimated 5-year survival rate can be as high as 80 percent.[90]

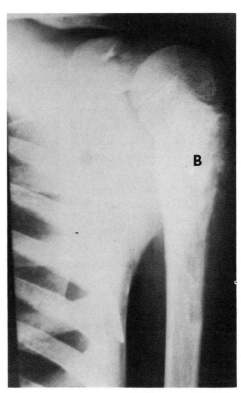

Figure 5-12 Osteosarcoma. Tumor bone formation (B) is evident within the medullary space of the humeral metadiaphysis, with lateral extension into the soft tissues.

Telangiectatic osteosarcoma represents 11 percent of all osteosarcomas and is characterized by the presence of multiple, large blood-filled cystic cavities.[87] This disease usually affects the femur (54 percent) but it is also found in the humerus (14 percent) and scapula (2 percent).[88] It is metaphyseal in origin and purely osteolytic.[90] The tumor itself is expansile, multilocular, and not sclerotic.[89] Other radiologic features are soft tissue mass and pathologic fracture. The diagnosis of this disease is often difficult, owing to the fact that both radiographic and histologic characteristics are similar to those of other lesions, such as giant cell tumor and aneurysmal bone cyst.[88]

Small cell osteosarcoma is more rare, comprising only 1 percent of all such tumors.[89] Patients with this lesion are usually between the second and fourth decades of life and present with pain and swelling in the femur or the humerus.[88] The lesion extends from the metaphysis to the diaphysis with a permeative osteolytic pattern.[87] In about half of cases, the tumor is present in conjunction with a soft tissue mass or periostitis.[88]

Periosteal (juxtacortical) osteosarcoma (Fig. 5-14) originates at the margin of the cortex and periosteum[90] and most frequently involves the diaphysis of long tubular bones such as the femur (44 percent) or the humerus (7 percent).[88] Two percent of all osteosarcomas are periosteal, and the mean patient age is around 22 years.[89] Unlike a parosteal osteosarcoma, a distal periosteal lesion

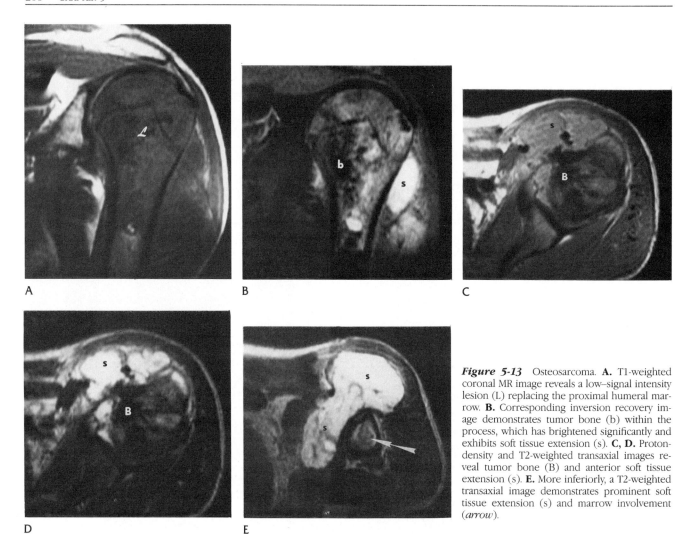

Figure 5-13 Osteosarcoma. **A.** T1-weighted coronal MR image reveals a low–signal intensity lesion (L) replacing the proximal humeral marrow. **B.** Corresponding inversion recovery image demonstrates tumor bone (b) within the process, which has brightened significantly and exhibits soft tissue extension (s). **C, D.** Proton-density and T2-weighted transaxial images reveal tumor bone (B) and anterior soft tissue extension (s). **E.** More inferiorly, a T2-weighted transaxial image demonstrates prominent soft tissue extension (s) and marrow involvement (*arrow*).

is located in the medial, lateral, or anterior surface of the bone. The neoplasm is confined to the cortex (which is thickened) and often is seen in conjunction with radiating osseous spicules.[88] Also common is an accompanying uncalcified soft tissue mass.[87] After adequate local resection, the prognosis is better than in conventional osteosarcoma.[88]

Parosteal osteosarcoma primarily (80 percent) affects people between 20 and 50 years old, women (58 percent) slightly more often than men.[89] This tumor usually originates in the metaphyseal area of long bones such as the femur (64 percent), the proximal humerus (15 percent), and very rarely the scapula (<1 percent).[88] The main symptom is a slow-growing mass that hinders movement about a joint; other signs are pain and swelling.

Parosteal lesions appear as a large mass, often with homogeneous ivory density due to bone production by the tumor.[87] The lesion is attached to the bone surface and tends to encircle it. Often, a thin radiolucent line, representing the fibrous periosteum,[90] separates the

mass from the bone, but this may be destroyed at later stages. Intramedullary involvement is most accurately demonstrated with MRI and tends to occur with high grade lesions.[9] CT may distinguish intralesional radiolucent regions that may represent high-grade dedifferentiated tumor.[88]

Ossification of the tumor starts at the base, unlike the similar-looking myositis ossificans which initiates ossification at the periphery.[88] It is also important to differentiate this disease from cortical desmoid[90] and sessile osteochondroma.[88] After amputation, the 5-year survival rate is 60 to 80 percent.[90]

Multicentric (multifocal) osteosarcoma may occur by one of several different mechanisms. Simultaneous generation of tumors (osteosarcomatosis) is usually seen in children.[88] These neoplasms are similar in size and appearance and are present in the absence of a dominant tumor. In general, these bilateral, symmetrical osteosclerotic foci present in the metaphyseal regions of long bones but are also found in the clavicles.[87] Prognosis is very poor for patients with osteosarcomatosis.[89]

Multifocal tumors may also be metachronous, arising 5 to 44 months after the primary lesion.[89] They vary in size, are distributed asymmetrically, and are not always osteosclerotic. Long-term survival is not incompatible with this disease.[88]

Sarcomatous transformation is a complication in about 1 percent of cases of Paget's disease.[9] Approximately half of these sarcomas are osteosarcomas; the next most frequently observed is fibrosarcoma (25 percent). The age of such patients ranges from 46 to 91 years (mean 55),

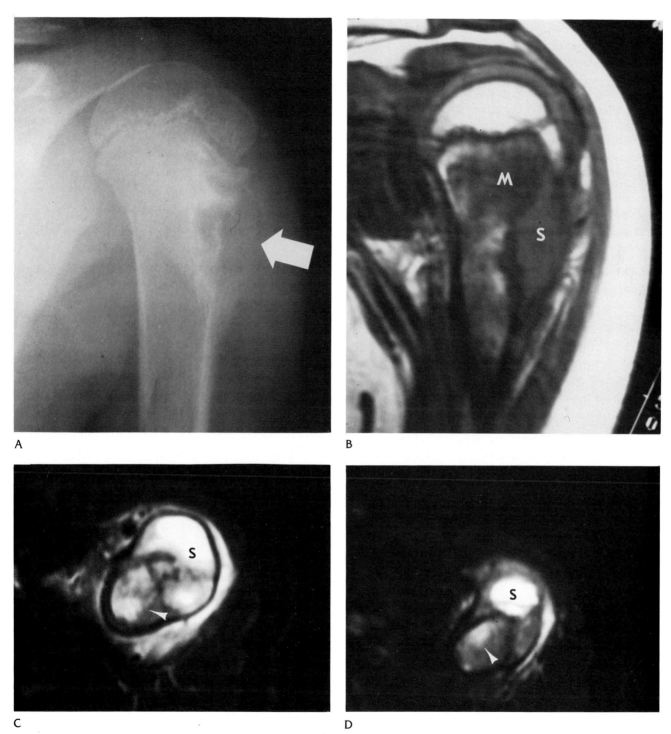

Figure 5-14   Periosteal osteosarcoma. **A.** Frontal radiograph demonstrates a cortically based lytic process (*arrow*) with associated periosteal reaction. **B.** Coronal T1-weighted MR image documents marrow (M) and soft tissue (S) involvement. **C, D.** Fast spin-echo T2-weighted transaxial images with fat suppression reveal high signal intensity within the marrow (*arrowheads*) as well as the prominent soft tissue mass (S).

and men are affected about twice as often as women.[87] Osteosarcoma from Paget's disease is observed in the humerus (18 percent), clavicle (2 percent), and scapula (<1 percent).[89]

These osteosarcomas are predominantly osteolytic; other common radiographic features are bone spiculation, cortical destruction, soft tissue mass, and fracture without signs of healing (Fig. 5-15).[88] In general, the prognosis for these patients is quite poor. Death usually occurs within 6 to 9 months, and 5-year survival rates are less than 10 percent.[89]

Osteosarcoma is also seen following radiation exposure, both internally (as documented in radium watch dial painters) and externally (cancer therapy).[90] This tumor is often seen in tubular bones (50 percent) but also presents in the clavicle, ribs, and spine (13 percent).[89] A formal set of criteria for diagnosis of such osteosarcomas follows[88]:

1. The disease for which radiation therapy was administered must be shown to be nonmalignant via microscopic or radiographic evidence.
2. The osteosarcoma must be present in the irradiated field.
3. The latent period must be at least 4 years.
4. There must be histologic evidence of osteosarcoma.

Doses as low as 800 cGy have been reported to induce sarcoma, but the usual dose needed is 3000 cGy.[88] After

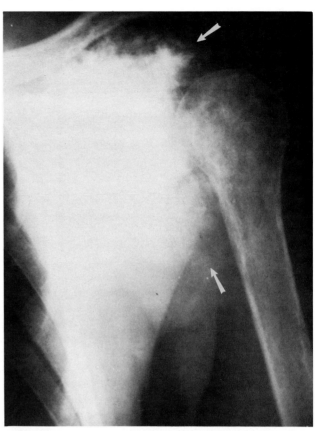

Figure 5-16   Radiation-induced osteosarcoma. A large sclerotic mass of immature tumor bone (*arrows*) arises from the scapula.

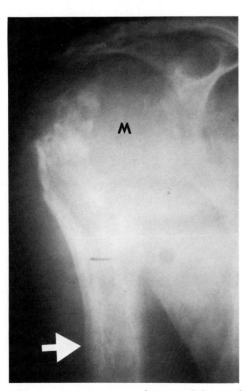

Figure 5-15   Paget sarcoma. An osteolytic mass (M) arises from the humeral head. Typical pagetic alterations are evident in the diaphysis (*arrow*).

the latent period, swelling, pain, and a soft tissue mass suddenly appear. Development of sarcoma is often preceded by osteosclerotic changes (Fig. 5-16).

High grade surface osteosarcoma is a rare lesion that is indistinguishable histologically from conventional osteosarcoma. On radiographs it appears similar to periosteal osteosarcoma.

FIBROUS BONE TUMORS

Benign Fibrous Lesions

There are four principal benign fibrous lesions of bone: metaphyseal fibrous defect, benign fibrous histiocytoma, desmoplastic fibroma, and fibrous dysplasia.[91,92] The term *metaphyseal fibrous defect* (or *fibroxanthoma*) refers to two lesions: fibrous cortical defect and nonossifying fibroma. Fibrous cortical defect is a small intracortical lesion, whereas nonossifying fibroma is an eccentric, variable-sized intramedullary lesion. Nonossifying fibroma is thought to represent medullary extension of a fibrous cortical defect.[92] Both lesions are found principally in children and usually involve the lower extremities, especially the distal femur. These lesions rarely involve the shoulder region. It has been estimated that fibrous cortical defect occurs in 30 to 40 percent of children older than 2 years.[93] Nonossifying fibroma is somewhat less common. Both lesions are identical histologically, consisting of fibroblasts arranged in a storiform pattern, multinucleated giant cells, and lipid-laden xanthoma cells. These lesions are thought to represent a developmental anomaly rather than a true neoplasm.[93] Affected patients are usually asymptomatic, and the lesions are discovered incidentally, although pathologic fracture may occur through a large nonossifying fibroma, and there may be a propensity toward avulsion fracture at the site of a fibrous cortical defect.[94,95]

On radiographs, fibrous cortical defect appears as a well-demarcated, intracortical radiolucency in the metaphysis or metadiaphysis (Fig. 5-17). It is usually less than 2 cm in its greatest dimension, with sclerotic margins. Nonossifying fibroma presents as a lobulated, multilocular, well-demarcated lesion with a sclerotic margin. This lesion also may reveal endosteal cortical scalloping and cortical expansion or thickening. Fibroxanthomas typically heal spontaneously. The diagnosis of fibrous cortical defect or nonossifying fibroma is usually readily made by conventional radiography; CT, MRI, or bone scan is rarely necessary. In one report of 10 fibroxanthomas studied with MRI, 8 lesions revealed diffuse, very low signal intensity on both T1-weighted and T2-weighted images.[96] This pattern of signal abnormality is related to the fibrous content of these lesions and/or to hemosiderin deposition.[91,96]

Benign fibrous histiocytoma is histologically identical to fibroxanthoma and differs only in that it occurs in older patients, usually between age 20 and 50 years.[9,91,97] This lesion is infrequent and most often involves the femur, tibia, and ilium. Radiographs typically reveal a well-defined, lytic lesion with bony ridges and a sclerotic margin. Cortical thinning or expansion is common; however, a more aggressive pattern with cortical breakthrough and soft tissue extension may occur.[97]

Desmoplastic fibroma is a rare, benign, locally aggressive tumor of bone that is histologically identical to the soft tissue desmoid tumor.[98] It usually occurs during the first four decades of life, and as many as 46 percent of cases present during the second decade.[99,100] The lesion most often involves the mandible, femur, tibia, bony pelvis, or humerus. The humerus is involved in 11 to 12 percent of patients, the scapula in 3 to 4 percent, and the clavicle in 1 to 2 percent.[99,100] Patients usually present with pain and swelling. In long bones, desmoplastic fibroma usually arises in the metaphysis. Histologically, desmoplastic fibroma consists of fibroblasts separated by irregularly arranged bundles of collagen with an infiltrating border into the marrow.[100] It may be difficult, histologically, to distinguish desmoplastic fibroma from a Grade I spindle cell sarcoma.[99] Because of its infiltrating pattern of growth, treatment by curettage results in a high rate of recurrence.[100]

On radiographs, desmoplastic fibroma usually appears as a geographic lytic lesion, causing bony expansion with a well-defined, nonsclerotic intraosseous margin. Bony ridges on the surface typically produce a multilocular, trabeculated appearance ranging from fine to coarse. Cortical breakthrough with soft tissue extension and pathologic fracture are additional features that are not uncommon.[99,101] Periosteal reaction is very rare.[99] Owing to its fibrous composition, desmoplastic fibroma would be expected to reveal low to intermediate signal intensity on T1-weighted and T2-weighted MR images.

Fibrous dysplasia is a developmental abnormality in which normal marrow is replaced by fibrous tissue and multiple small, abnormally arranged bone trabeculae.[9,23,102] The monostotic form accounts for 75 to 85 percent of patients with fibrous dysplasia and is usually diagnosed between age 5 and 20 years.[23,91] Monostotic lesions most often involve the femur, tibia, craniofacial bones, or ribs.[103,104] Some 5 to 7 percent of monostotic lesions involve the humerus; involvement of the scapula or clavicle is rare.[102,105] Monostotic lesions are often asymptomatic. Long bone lesions usually are discovered because of pain related to pathologic fracture.

Polyostotic fibrous dysplasia may be associated with café-au-lait spots and endocrine dysfunction, most notably McCune-Albright syndrome. Two-thirds of patients with polyostotic fibrous dysplasia become symptomatic before age 10 years.[103] Approximately 70 percent of such patients present with leg pain, limp, or pathologic fracture.[103] Patients with polyostotic disease present at a younger average age those with monostotic disease owing to the more extensive skeletal involvement. Polyostotic fibrous dysplasia is often widespread and most often

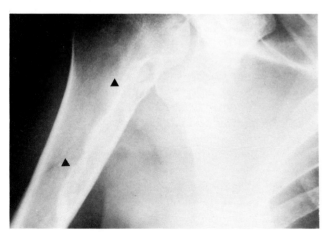

Figure 5-17 Fibrous cortical defect. An unusually long cortically based lytic lesion with a sclerotic margin (*arrowheads*) involves the humeral metadiaphysis.

involves the bones of the lower extremity and pelvis. The humerus is involved in 50 percent of patients, the scapula in 33 percent, and the clavicle in 10 percent.[103] Lesions of the scapula usually appear as a multilocular lytic process with well-defined margins and are most often found in the region of the glenoid, coracoid, or acromion processes.[15] Skeletal deformity is common in polyostotic fibrous dysplasia secondary to pathologic fracture or chronic stress loading of weakened bone. The most common deformities are leg length discrepancy, shepherd's crook deformity of the proximal femur, tibial bowing, and curved ribs.[91] Malignant transformation occurs in fewer than 1 percent of all patients with fibrous dysplasia.[9,15]

Pathologically, fibrous dysplasia is composed of a mature fibrous stroma and small, variously shaped islands of woven bone. The bone has no structural organization and does not strengthen the preexisting bone. Small, well-differentiated cartilage nodules may be seen, usually in patients with polyostotic disease.[103] Fluid-filled regions may develop owing to necrosis.

The radiographic appearance of fibrous dysplasia varies considerably. The lesion may by purely lytic or demonstrate a hazy, increased radiodensity likened to ground glass, depending on the extent of bone formation. In long bones, fibrous dysplasia often appears as a diaphyseal or metadiaphyseal eccentric lytic lesion with cortical thinning and expansion (Fig. 5-18). Rarely, fibrous dysplasia may extend through the cortex into the soft tissue.[106] The intraosseous margin is usually well-defined and may be densely sclerotic. There may be cortical thickening. Bony ridging on the surface may produce a trabeculated appearance, and punctate or flocculent calcification may develop within cartilage nodules. Compared to monostotic lesions, polyostotic lesions more commonly reveal a wide zone of transition with adjacent normal bone, have a ground glass appearance, or produce bowing of the long bones of the lower extremity.[9]

On bone scan, fibrous dysplasia often reveals extremely intense increased uptake.[91,107] CT is most useful in defining the extent of craniofacial disease.[106] On MRI, fibrous dysplasia usually exhibits low signal intensity on T1-weighted images and high signal intensity on T2-weighted images.[107] There may be mild inhomogeneity or low–signal intensity linear septations on T2-weighted images. A pattern of diffuse low or intermediate signal intensity may also be observed on T2-weighted images.[107]

Malignant Fibrous Lesions

Malignant fibrous histiocytoma of bone is an uncommon malignant tumor composed primarily of fibroblasts and histiocytes. Malignant fibrous histiocytoma may occur as a primary lesion or in a bone with a preexisting abnormality. It has been reported in association with bone infarct, Paget's disease, previous radiation therapy, chronic osteomyelitis, and joint prostheses.[108–110] It may occur at any age and has a relatively broad age distribution pattern, from the second to the eighth decade of life.[9] A bimodal age distribution has been described: primary lesions most often occur during the second and third decades of life and secondary lesions during the sixth and seventh decades.[111] Malignant fibrous histiocytoma most often involves the femur, tibia, and bony pelvis. In one series of 130 cases, the proximal humerus was involved in 9 percent, the scapula in 5 percent, and the clavicle in 2 percent of affected patients.[111] Multifocal osseous involvement has been reported.[112,113] Patients usually complain of pain and swelling. Pathologic fracture occurs in approximately one-fourth of patients.[111] The histologic appearance of malignant fibrous histiocytoma is variable and is characterized by fibroblasts arranged in a storiform pattern, histiocytes, giant cells, and an absence of osteoid production by tumor cells.[108] The latter feature is used to distinguish malignant fibrous histiocytoma from osteosarcoma.

On radiographs, malignant fibrous histiocytoma usually produces an aggressive moth-eaten or permeative pattern of bone destruction with ill-defined margins (Fig. 5-19). The lesion is usually centered in the metaphysis of a long bone with extension into the diaphysis or, less commonly, the epiphysis. Soft tissue extension is common.[114] On MRI, malignant fibrous histiocytoma reveals a nonspecific pattern of low signal intensity on T1-weighted images and high signal intensity on T2-weighted images.[91,115] Intratumoral necrosis or hemorrhage will lead to an inhomogeneous pattern of varied signal intensities.

Fibrosarcoma of bone is a rare malignant tumor, comprising only 3.2 percent of malignant primary bone tu-

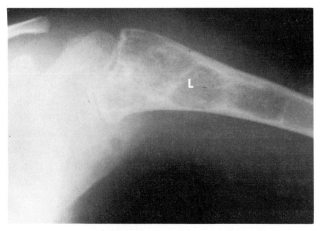

Figure 5-18 Fibrous dysplasia. A well-defined lytic lesion with septations (L) involves the humeral metadiaphysis.

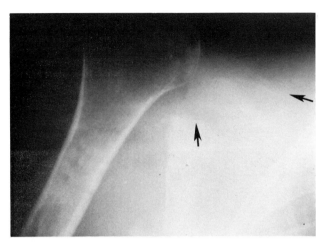

Figure 5-19 Malignant fibrous histiocytoma. A purely lytic process has completely destroyed the glenoid, acromion, and coracoid (*arrows*).

mors.[14] It is a malignant fibroblastic tumor that produces varying amounts of collagen and does not produce cartilage or osteoid matrix.[9,14] The tumor has a broad age distribution from age 4 to 83 years (average 38 years).[9] Patients usually present with pain that, on average, has been present for 2 years.[9] Approximately 25 to 30 percent of fibrosarcomas occur as secondary lesions in bones involved by preexisting benign conditions or in previously irradiated bone.[116] Most fibrosarcomas are intramedullary in location, but as many as 30 percent may arise in the periosteum.[117] Intramedullary lesions usually arise in the metaphysis and most often affect the distal femur, bony pelvis, proximal tibia, and proximal humerus. The proximal humerus is affected in 7 to 10 percent of patients; the scapula and clavicle are rarely involved.[9,14,23] Histologically, fibrosarcoma is characterized by proliferation of fibroblasts arranged in a distinctive herringbone growth pattern with varied amounts of intercellular collagen and myxoid material.[117] Well-differentiated lesions may be difficult to distinguish from desmoplastic fibroma. In the past, many malignant fibrous histiocytomas were mistakenly diagnosed as fibrosarcoma.[9] The histologic grade tends to correlate with the radiographic appearance and with the prognosis. On radiographs, fibrosarcoma usually reveals a moth-eaten or permeative pattern of bone destruction or, less commonly, a geographic pattern (Fig. 5-20).[118] There is usually cortical thinning and destruction with soft tissue extension and some periosteal reaction. Lesions are often large, measuring more than 7 cm in diameter. On bone scan there is increased uptake of radionuclide, sometimes in an extended pattern, and a central photopenic ("cold spot") region has been reported.[119] The MRI features of fibrosarcoma have not been well established.

GIANT CELL TUMOR

Giant cell tumor of bone is a benign neoplasm composed of poorly differentiated mononuclear cells and multinucleated giant cells.[120–122] It is a locally aggressive lesion with a strong tendency toward local recurrence and may metastasize as a histologically benign lesion.[121,123–125] Approximately 75 percent of affected persons are between age 15 and 40 years, and the incidence is greatest during the third decade of life.[120,121] Most patients present with pain and tenderness. Pathologic fracture is common with lesions of the lower extremity but is uncommon in giant cell tumor of the upper extremity.[126] The most commonly affected sites are the distal femur, the proximal tibia, and the distal radius. The proximal humerus accounts for 5 to 6 percent of giant cell tumors; the clavicle and scapula are rare sites of involvement.[14,15,23,126] Nevertheless, giant cell tumor is the second most common primary neoplasm of the scapula and tends to involve the coracoid, acromion, glenoid processes, and body.[4,15] Giant cell tumor arises in the metaphysis and characteristically extends into the adjacent epiphysis to the subarticular plate. In skeletally immature persons, its prevalence is 1.7 percent.[127]

Giant cell tumor may have a heterogeneous composition, with hemorrhage, necrosis, cyst formation, edema, lipid, and calcium.[120,126] Histologic grading of giant cell tumor has been unrewarding, owing to poor correlation with the growth rate and aggressiveness of the tumor.[120] Tumor recurrence after surgical removal is principally related to the adequacy of the surgical margin rather than the histologic or radiographic features of the lesion. This is reflected in one series where the recurrence rate for patients treated with curettage was 34 percent but only 7 percent for those treated with wide resection.[122] Enneking has developed a staging system for giant cell tumors that has proved helpful in planning the appropriate surgical approach.[128] Stages I, II, and III, respectively, correspond to latent, active, and aggressive clinical

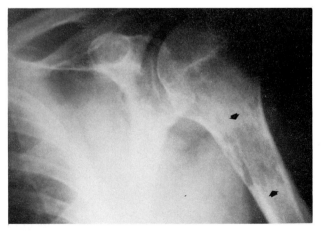

Figure 5-20 Fibrosarcoma. A purely lytic permeative process (*arrows*) involves the humeral metadiaphysis.

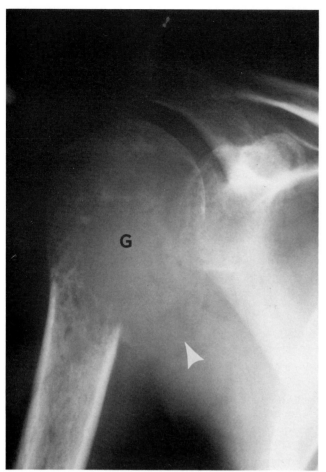

A

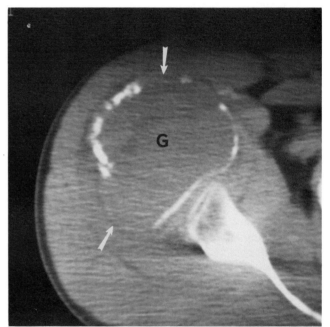

Figure 5-21 Giant cell tumor. **A.** The tumor (G) manifests a geographic, aggressive (*arrowhead*) pattern by radiography. **B.** CT image reveals marrow replacement by the tumor (G) and optimally depicts cortical destruction (*arrows*). **C.** Coronal T1-weighted MR image demonstrates extent of marrow (G) and soft tissue (s) involvement. **D.** Transaxial T2-weighted image reveals predominantly high signal intensity within the lesion (G).

B

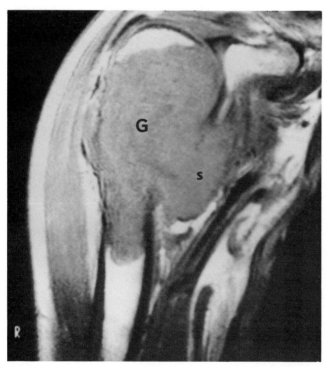

C

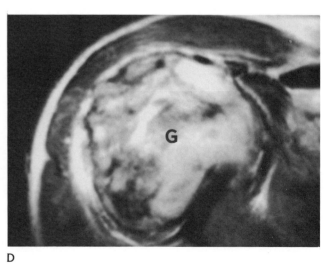

D

and radiologic presentations. Curettage is performed on Stage I and less aggressive Stage II tumors; resection en bloc is carried out for stage III lesions. Using this approach, the recurrence rate has been diminished.[129] The previously reported rates of recurrence of 40 to 60 percent resulted from indiscriminate use of curettage for all lesions, including Stage III lesions.[129] Approximately 2 to 3 percent of giant cell tumors are associated with histologically benign pulmonary metastases.[124] This most often occurs with recurrent local disease and with radiographically aggressive lesions.[124,130] Pulmonary metastases are optimally treated by wedge resection or lobectomy and may be associated with long-term survival. Overall mortality in this setting is 23 to 25 percent.[124,130] Secondary malignant giant cell tumor of bone usually represents a fibrosarcoma or osteosarcoma arising in a previously irradiated giant cell tumor.[130] Primary malignant giant cell tumor is a very rare lesion.

On radiographs, giant cell tumor typically presents as a geographic, lytic lesion eccentrically located in the metaphysis (Fig. 5-21A). The tumor characteristically extends into the epiphysis to within 1 cm or less of the subchondral cortex (Fig. 5-22). Erosion or penetration of this subarticular cortical bone has been reported in 27 to 80 percent of lesions.[122,131,132] The margin is usually well-defined and nonsclerotic, but it may be mildly sclerotic. Small intralesional foci of dystrophic mineralization may be present. There may be cortical thinning or expansion, but periostitis is rare. Giant cell tumor may appear trabeculated on radiographs but, rather than representing bony septae, this appearance reflects bony ridges on the surface.[126] Aggressive lesions demonstrate cortical breakthrough and a soft tissue mass. This soft

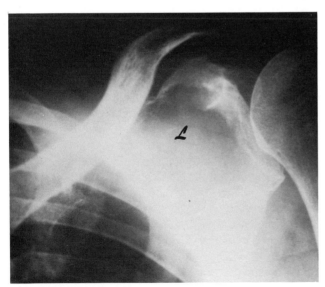

Figure 5-22 Giant cell tumor. A large expansile lytic process (L) involves the glenoid region, an epiphyseal-equivalent area.

tissue component is usually delineated by a thin cortical rim that may be visible only on CT (Fig. 5-21B). On MRI, giant cell tumor reveals variable patterns of signal intensity, depending on its contents (Fig. 5-21C, D). A nonspecific pattern of low to intermediate signal intensity on T1-weighted images and intermediate to high signal intensity on T2-weighted images is common.[133,134] Prominent regions of very low signal intensity on T1-weighted and T2-weighted images have been reported due to hemosiderin deposition.[4] Fluid-fluid levels may also be present.[126]

ROUND CELL TUMORS OF BONE

Ewing's Sarcoma

Ewing's sarcoma is a malignant bone tumor composed of densely packed small cells. The cell of origin has not been established, but recent work suggests a neural origin, linking Ewing's sarcoma to the rare primitive neuroectodermal tumor of bone.[135] Ewing's sarcoma accounts for approximately 10 percent of malignant bone tumors.[9] It is rare after age 30, and 95 percent of affected patients are between 4 and 25 years of age.[136] Ewing's sarcoma has a predilection for Caucasians, whereas Blacks and Asians are uncommonly affected.[137] Patients usually complain of pain and swelling. Fever, weight loss, anemia, leukocytosis, and an elevated sedimentation rate may occur and lead to a clinical impression of osteomyelitis. More than 60 percent of Ewing's sarcomas involve the bony pelvis or lower extremity.[137,138] The proximal humerus is involved in 7 percent of cases, the scapula in 4 to 5 percent, and the clavicle in 2 percent.[14,23] In long bones, 45 to 59 percent of Ewing's sarcomas are metadiaphyseal and roughly one-third are diaphyseal.[23,137] Metaphyseal lesions are not uncommon, but an epiphyseal origin is rare.

Pathologically, Ewing's sarcoma is an intramedullary lesion that classically spreads through the haversian canals into the adjacent soft tissue with relatively little bone destruction. Ewing's sarcomas usually are large (5 to 10 cm) at initial presentation, and the extraosseous component is typically larger than the intraosseous tumor. In its early stages, Ewing's sarcoma is a solid tumor; however, with cortical violation there are areas of hemorrhage and cyst formation producing a semiliquid consistency.[138] On radiographs, Ewing's sarcoma typically presents as a poorly marginated, permeative lytic lesion with a lamellar periosteal reaction and a soft tissue component (Fig. 5-23). Focal or diffuse sclerosis is common owing to reactive bone formation in regions of bone necrosis.[139] Uncommon radiographic findings, occurring in 10 to 30 percent of cases, include spiculated or "hair-on-end" periosteal reaction, cortical thickening, cortical

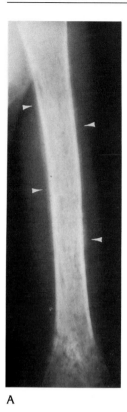

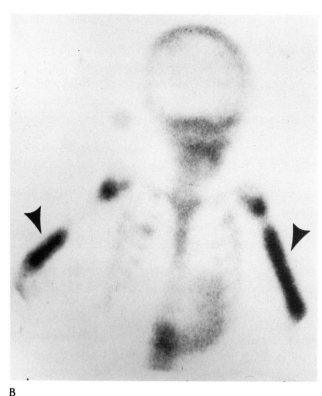

A   B

Figure 5-23 Ewing's sarcoma. **A.** Permeative osteolysis and periosteal reaction (*arrowheads*) involve the humeral diaphysis. **B.** Radionuclide bone scan documents increased activity within the lesion as well as a metastasis in the opposite humerus (*arrowheads*).

destruction, pure osteolysis, pathologic fracture, bony expansion, and a cystic component.[137] Rarely present (< 10 percent) are soft tissue calcification, cortical saucerization, a honeycomb pattern, or a well-defined margin.[137] When Ewing's sarcoma involves flat bones, a prominent soft tissue component is characteristic.[138] Ewing's sarcoma demonstrates nonspecific features on MRI: low to intermediate signal intensity on T1-weighted images, high signal intensity on T2-weighted images, and signal heterogeneity if hemorrhage or necrosis is present.[138,139]

Several features of Ewing's sarcoma have been shown to have prognostic significance. In terms of tumor location, pelvic lesions have the least favorable prognosis, and lesions of the femur or humerus are associated with a poorer chance of survival than those located elsewhere.[140–142] Decreased survival is also observed with increasing intraosseous dimension of the tumor.[142] Other adverse prognostic signs include lesion diameter greater than 8 cm, older age, increased leukocyte count, and increased sedimentation rate.[141] A poor histologic response to chemotherapy also correlates with decreased survival.[141] The current treatment of Ewing's sarcoma utilizes neoadjuvant chemotherapy with multiple drugs, surgical excision of the primary tumor, and/or radiation therapy, followed by adjuvant chemotherapy. Surgical excision of the primary lesion rather than radiation therapy is now recommended whenever feasible and provides improved local control, and possibly a better chance for survival.[141]

Multiple Myeloma

Multiple myeloma is a malignant tumor of plasma cells that typically presents with multifocal skeletal involvement but may appear as a solitary lesion (solitary myeloma, plasmacytoma; Fig. 5-24). It is the most common neoplasm of bone in adults and accounts for almost half of all malignant bone tumors.[9,14] Affected patients are usually between age 50 and 70 years and are rarely younger than 40. Patients present with bone pain, weakness, fatigue, and normochromic, normocytic anemia. This disease may be associated with a variety of systemic complications, including renal insufficiency, congestive heart failure, amyloidosis, increased susceptibility to infection, and gouty arthritis. Any bone may be involved, but the vertebrae, ribs, bony pelvis, and skull are affected most often. The proximal humerus, scapula, and clavicle are each involved in 2 to 4 percent of cases.[14] Histologically, multiple myeloma is composed of plasmacytic cells of varying maturity.[9] It has been proposed that an osteoclasis-stimulating factor, produced by the plasma cells of myeloma, is responsible for the osteolytic lesions that develop.[143]

In as many as one-fourth of patients with multiple myeloma no abnormality is detected on radiographs.[144]

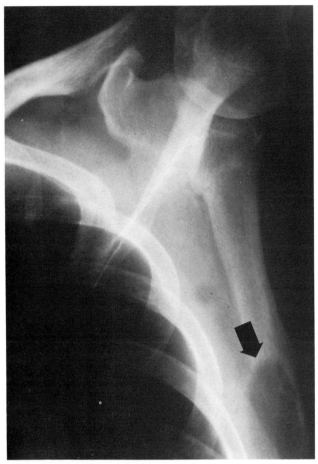

Figure 5-24 Plasmacytoma. A well-defined lytic lesion without marginal sclerosis (*arrow*) involves the inferior aspect of the scapula.

Diffuse osteopenia without focal lytic lesions is common, usually involving the spine and pelvis. Multiple, variable-sized, punched-out lytic lesions with endosteal cortical scalloping is also a common radiographic pattern. Lesions may be expansile. Multiple sclerotic lesions occur in fewer than 3 percent of patients and are often associated with polyneuropathy in the form of polyneuropathy, organomegaly, endocrinopathy, myeloma, and skin disease (POEMS) syndrome.[145,146]

Bone scintigraphy is notoriously insensitive to the lesions of multiple myeloma.[147] Scintigraphy is, however, more sensitive than radiography for detecting lesions of the ribs, shoulder girdle, and cervical spine.[147,148] Bone scintigraphy may also be useful in determining response to chemotherapy, as diminished radionuclide uptake is associated with remission.[147] CT may be useful for demonstrating bone destruction not evident on radiographs.[149] The accuracy of MRI in diagnosing multiple myeloma has not been established. In one study, focal regions of abnormal signal intensity were detected on T1-weighted images in 25 percent and on T2-weighted images in 53 percent of patients with multiple myeloma

of the lumbar spine and on either T1-weighted or T2-weighted images in 50 percent of patients with multiple myeloma and lumbar vertebral compression fractures.[150] Many patients with multiple myeloma of the vertebral column reveal intermediate signal intensity or inhomogeneous signal intensity on both T1-weighted and T2-weighted images, precluding confident diagnosis of multiple myeloma.[150,151] Comparable MRI studies of multiple myeloma involving the appendicular skeleton have not been performed.

Lymphoma of Bone

In both Hodgkin's disease and non-Hodgkin's lymphoma, skeletal involvement is uncommon at initial presentation but may be seen later as a manifestation of disease progression. Skeletal, or more precisely, bone marrow, involvement eventually occurs in 10 to 25 percent of patients with Hodgkin's disease and in 25 to 45 percent of patients with non-Hodgkin's lymphoma.[144,152] Bone involvement may occur by hematogenous spread or by direct extension from a contiguous involved lymph node. Primary lymphoma of bone is a non-Hodgkin's lymphoma (usually diffuse histiocytic type) that arises initially in bone. To diagnose primary lymphoma of bone, some investigators require that regional or distant metastases not be present for at least 6 months after the onset of symptoms, whereas others state that regional lymph node involvement does not exclude the diagnosis.[9] Primary lymphoma of bone constitutes 10 percent of cases of non-Hodgkin's lymphoma and 5 percent of primary malignant bone tumors.[9] All forms of lymphoma tend to involve the bony pelvis, spine, and femur; less commonly involved are the humerus and tibia.[9,144] Lesions of the humerus usually involve the proximal or middle portion.[153,154] The clavicle and scapula are uncommon sites of involvement.

In addition to cytologic parameters, clinical staging of patients with lymphoma of bone is important in determining prognosis and therapy.[155] Patients with primary lymphoma of bone who have no evidence of disease elsewhere for at least 6 months after diagnosis have a 55 percent 5-year survival rate.[156] This compares favorably to those with lymphoma of bone with nodal or other soft tissue involvement, for whom the 5-year survival rate is 22 percent.[156] Local soft tissue extension of primary lymphoma of bone involving a long bone makes the prognosis worse.[157]

On radiographs, primary lymphoma of bone typically reveals moth-eaten or permeative osteolysis with a variable degree of cortical bone destruction and indistinct margins. Bone sclerosis, usually mild or moderate in degree, occurs in as many as 45 percent of cases.[154] Periosteal reaction (usually lamellar), cortical thickening, and pathologic fracture are additional features that are

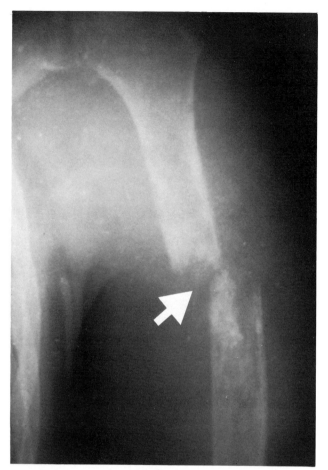

Figure 5-25 Non-Hodgkin's lymphoma. Pathologic fracture (*arrow*) has occurred through an area of permeative osteolysis in the humeral diaphysis.

not uncommon. Soft tissue extension is common. Radiographic signs that reflect imminent or actual soft tissue extension are associated with a worse prognosis:[158] pathologic fracture (Fig. 5-25), lamellar or interrupted periosteal reaction, cortical destruction with a soft tissue mass, or soft tissue swelling.[158]

In a series of seven patients with primary lymphoma of bone, MRI revealed homogeneous low signal intensity on TI-weighted images and inhomogeneous low signal intensity on T2-weighted images.[159] This was attributed to a high fibrous content of these lesions, demonstrated on histologic examination. One lesion revealed moderate hyperintensity on T2-weighted images, and all lesions contained small high–signal intensity foci on T2-weighted images. All lesions revealed moderate or marked enhancement following gadolinium-DTPA administration and were located at the end of a long bone. Direct tumor extension into the adjacent joint was observed in five cases. These results are of interest when viewed in contrast to other malignant small cell neoplasms of bone marrow such as Ewing's sarcoma and primitive neuroectodermal tumor, which demonstrate homogeneous or

predominantly high signal intensity on T2-weighted images.[159]

TUMORLIKE LESIONS OF BONE

Simple Bone Cyst

A simple (or unicameral) bone cyst is a nonneoplastic, fluid-filled lesion of bone. It is usually discovered during the first or second decade of life. As many as two-thirds of patients with simple cysts present with pathologic fracture.[9] In one study, 81 percent of simple bone cysts occurring in children and adolescents involved the proximal humerus or proximal femur, whereas 52 percent of such lesions in adults involved the ilium or calcaneus.[160] The proximal humerus is involved in 38 to 54 percent of cases.[9,15,144] The scapula and clavicle are rarely involved.[161]

The pathogenesis of simple bone cyst is unproven but is thought to relate to venous obstruction and the development of increased intraosseous pressure.[144] A sim-

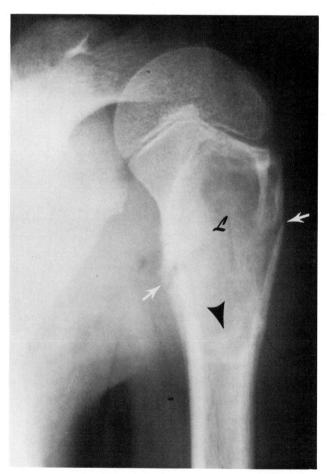

Figure 5-26 Simple bone cyst. A lytic and slightly expansile lesion (L) in the humeral metaphysis exhibits a pathologic fracture (*arrows*) and the "fallen fragment" sign (*arrowhead*) of a fluid-filled process.

ple bone cyst consists of serous or blood-tinged fluid and is diagnosed histologically by demonstration of a fibrous wall.[9] A cementum-like calcified material may be identified within the cyst.[162]

In long bones, simple bone cyst has a characteristic radiographic appearance consisting of a centrally located metaphyseal or diaphyseal lytic lesion with cortical thinning and mild expansion in all directions. A simple bone cyst in a long bone is always longer in the longitudinal dimension of the parent bone than it is wide. Rarely, a simple bone cyst may extend across an open growth plate to involve an epiphysis or apophysis.[163] A thin sclerotic margin is typical, although the diaphyseal margin is often indistinct. Bony ridges on the surface of the lesion may give the impression of a multilocular lesion.[164] A simple bone cyst does not produce cortical violation or a soft tissue mass.[9] Pathologic fracture of a simple bone cyst may result in displacement of a fragment of cortical bone into the cyst. This bone fragment drops to the bottom of the cyst cavity, producing the *fallen fragment sign* (Fig. 5-26).[165] This sign may be used to determine the true distal extent of a simple bone cyst.[166] In one series, the fallen fragment sign was present in 20 percent of cases.[166] Fallen fragments may be single or multiple. A *trap door fragment* is produced when a cortical fragment is displaced inwardly but remains partially attached or hinged to the periosteum.

On MRI, a simple bone cyst appears as a well-demarcated lesion of low to intermediate signal intensity on TI-weighted images and high signal intensity on T2-weighted images. With pathologic fracture, a fluid-fluid level occurs secondary to settling of blood products, and a low–signal intensity fallen fragment may be evident.[167]

Aneurysmal Bone Cyst

Aneurysmal bone cyst is a nonneoplastic lesion of bone that consists of multiple thin-walled, blood-filled spaces. It is believed to result from a local hemodynamic disturbance, such as arteriovenous fistula or a venous obstruction, and may be a posttraumatic lesion.[144] Aneurysmal bone cyst may be found in association with several primary bone tumors, including chondroblastoma, osteoblastoma, and giant cell tumor. Approximately 80 percent of affected patients are younger than age 20 years, and almost all patients are less than 30 years of age.[9,11] Patients usually present with pain and swelling. The sites most commonly affected are the femur, tibia, and vertebrae.[168] The proximal humerus (3 to 4 percent), the scapula (2 to 3 percent), and the clavicle (2 to 3 percent) are less frequent sites of involvement.[9,14,15] In the long bones the typical radiographic appearance of aneurysmal bone cyst is an eccentric, lytic, expansile lesion, centered in the metaphysis (Fig. 5-27A). Aneurysmal bone cyst may also develop centrally within the metaphysis, eccentri-

cally in the metadiaphysis, or subperiosteally. When aneurysmal bone cyst arises adjacent to an open epiphyseal plate, extension across the plate into the epiphysis has been reported to occur in 23 percent of cases.[169,170] The intraosseous margin is well-defined and may be sclerotic. The expanded extracortical portion of an aneurysmal bone cyst is usually contained by a complete or incomplete periosteal shell of bone. More aggressive lesions reveal an ill-defined endosteal margin and no delimiting periosteal shell.[9,23] Periosteal reaction may be evident in a long bone at the periphery of an aneurysmal bone cyst. Calcified chondroid material has been reported in association with aneurysmal bone cyst.[171]

CT may be useful to demonstrate a thin, calcified rim surrounding the soft tissue component of an aneurysmal bone cyst. On MRI, aneurysmal bone cyst appears as an expansile lesion with small diverticulae or lobulations (Fig. 5-27B). A thin, well-defined low–signal intensity rim is identified on all pulse sequences and consists of fibrous or calcified tissue.[172–174] Within an aneurysmal bone cyst are multiple, variable-sized cysts. These cysts reveal a wide range of signal intensities and may contain fluid-fluid levels.[175,176] The conspicuousness of fluid-fluid levels is variable, as it may be more evident on T1-weighted or T2-weighted images, depending on the fluid content (Fig. 5-27C)[173,177]. The fluid-fluid levels are generated by the layering of products of blood degradation.

Eosinophilic Granuloma

Eosinophilic granuloma of bone is one of three variants of Langerhans' cell histiocytosis (LCH) of bone (formerly known as histiocytosis X). This group of diseases is characterized by abnormal proliferation of histiocytes and granuloma formation and is believed to represent a disorder of immune regulation.[178,179] Hand-Schüller-Christian disease is the chronic, recurring form of LCH that usually affects children between age 1 and 5 years, involves bone and extraskeletal sites, and is fatal in approximately 15 percent of patients.[179] Letterer-Siwe disease, the fulminant form of Langerhans' cell histiocytosis, usually develops during the first 2 years of life and typically has a rapidly progressive, fatal course. Eosinophilic granuloma is the localized form of LCH and accounts for 70 percent of cases. Affected patients are usually between age 5 and 15 years, and the average age at onset is between 10 and 14 years.[179] Local pain is the most common symptom; however, swelling, tenderness, fever, and an elevated sedimentation rate are also common. Combined with the radiographic findings, these clinical features are suggestive of osteomyelitis or Ewing's sarcoma.

The histologic features of eosinophilic granuloma vary, depending on the phase or age of the lesions.[23] Varying amounts of histiocytes, eosinophils, lymphocytes, polymorphonuclear cells, giant cells, and hemorrhage are

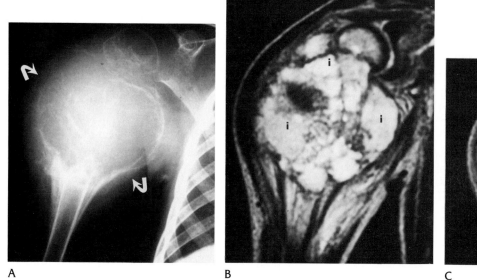

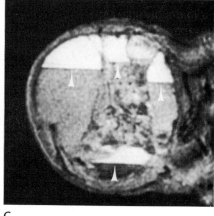

A   B   C

Figure 5-27   Aneurysmal bone cyst. **A.** A markedly expansile lesion (*arrows*) is present on the radiograph. **B.** Sagittal fast spin-echo T2-weighted MR image reveals multiple lobules of high signal intensity (i). **C.** Fluid levels (*arrowheads*) indicating hemorrhage are evident on a transaxial gradient-echo image.

observed. Older lesions contain abundant scar tissue.[23] The treatment of the eosinophilic granuloma is controversial, as lesions may heal spontaneously.[180] Excision, curettage, and intralesional corticosteroid injection each have produced good results.[179,181]

Some 10 to 20 percent of patients with eosinophilic granuloma have multiple bone lesions.[179,181,182] Any bone can be involved, but most often the skull, spine, pelvis, ribs, mandible, femur, tibia, and humerus are affected.[179,182] The scapula and clavicle are affected in 2 to 6 percent of cases.[23,179,181] The bones of the hands and feet are rarely affected. In the long bones most lesions arise in the diaphysis, although metaphyseal origin is not uncommon. Metadiaphyseal lesions are less common; epiphyseal lesions are rare.[179]

The radiographic appearance of eosinophilic granuloma varies with the phase of disease and the bone involved.[23] In the early phase long bone lesions reveal a central, intramedullary lytic lesion with an ill-defined margin. Cortical thinning, endosteal scalloping, linear or lamellar periosteal reaction, and a hole-within-a-hole appearance may also be observed (Fig. 5-28). A soft tissue mass and pathologic fracture are not uncommon. As the lesion matures, the borders become more sharply defined, and sometimes densely sclerotic. Remodeling of periosteal reaction may produce an expanded appearance.[23] Clavicle lesions vary from permeative to expansile and often exhibit abundant periosteal reaction.[179,181] Scapular lesions appear as lytic ovoid lesions with margins ranging from well-defined and sclerotic to indistinct.[179,181]

Eosinophilic granuloma of bone may not be detected on bone scan in as many as 35 percent of cases and may appear as "cold" regions of diminished uptake of radionuclide.[179,183] On MRI eosinophilic granuloma appears as a diffuse, ill-defined region of decreased signal intensity on T1-weighted images and increased signal intensity on T2-weighted images. Reactive changes consistent with edema or inflammation are common in the adjacent marrow and soft tissues in early or midphase lesions.[43,184] A low–signal intensity rim may be seen around the lesion in the middle or late phase. Marked contrast enhancement is observed in early-phase lesions following intravenous administration of gadolinium-DTPA.[185] A pattern of intermediate to high signal intensity on T1-weighted images and high signal intensity on T2-weighted images has also been reported in early-phase lesions of eosinophilic granuloma.[185]

VASCULAR TUMORS

Bones have a vascular supply—arteries, capillaries, sinusoids, veins—and thus can develop vascular tumors. In general, vascular tumors are uncommon, and they are especially rare in the shoulder.

Hemangiomas

The most common vascular neoplasms, hemangiomas, represent about 1 percent of all biopsied primary bone tumors. Most patients with the disease are between 20 and 60 years old, and females present more often than

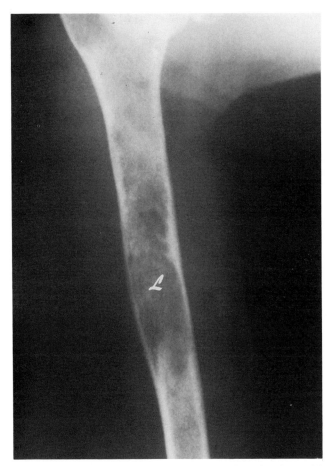

Figure 5-28 Eosinophilic granuloma. A well-defined lytic lesion (L) without a sclerotic margin exhibits endosteal scalloping but no periosteal reaction.

males. Hemangiomas are most commonly diagnosed in the skull and spine; 2 percent of such tumors present in the proximal humerus and fewer than 2 percent are found in the scapula or clavicle.[89]

These benign lesions are divided into capillary and cavernous types and may involve a wide variety of tissues, such as muscle, tendon, connective tissue, fatty tissue, and synovium, as well as bone.[88] Hemangiomas are mainly asymptomatic and appear as a nonhomogeneous mass of water density.[88] A typical radiologic feature in flat bones is the "sunburst"[87] of bone spicules radiating toward the periphery from a central focus. Also seen are coarse trabecular responses of a honeycombed or striated nature.[186] Intravascular phlebolith calcifications are also seen in focal hemangiomas (ones that involve contiguous bones, soft tissues, and joint structures).[89]

Angiosarcoma (Hemangiosarcoma, Hemangioendothelioma)

This malignant tumor consists of anastomosing vascular channels lined by an irregular endothelium layer.[88] Angiosarcomas represent 0.2 to 8 percent of biopsied pri-

mary bone tumors; the mean age of a patient with this disease is about 35 to 40 years, and males present more often. The disease manifests predominantly in the limbs: 13 percent of angiosarcomas are found in the proximal humerus but in only about 5 percent of cases is the scapula or clavicle involved.[89]

Common symptoms of angiosarcoma are local pain and swelling. Pathologic fracture occurs less frequently. Such a tumor has roundish, lytic and highly destructive radiographic features (Fig. 5-29).[89] The lesions vary in size, but a very elongated tumor (one whose greatest diameter is at least 1.5 times the least diameter) may be indicative of angiosarcoma.[186] Other common features are mild or moderate osseous expansion and cortical thinning or destruction.[88]

Angiosarcoma has both solitary and multifocal variants, the latter involving either contiguous or noncontiguous bones.[89] While surgical excision of well-differentiated lesions has a favorable prognosis, even aggressive treatment of high-grade tumors is associated with poor long-term survival rates.[88]

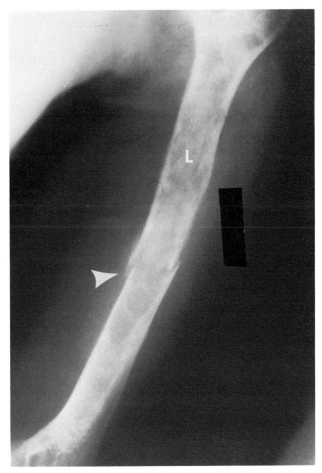

Figure 5-29 Hemangioendothelioma. Pathologic fracture (*arrowhead*) has occurred through an extensive lytic lesion (L) in the humeral diaphysis.

Hemangiopericytoma

This slow-growing, often malignant vascular tumor is derived from the pericytes of Zimmerman that surround small vessels.[88] It is very rare, accounting for only 5 percent of primary vascular tumors, and predominantly presents in the femur and sacroiliac region. Only 8.8 percent of these cases are seen in the humerus and 2.2 percent in the clavicle. The mean age of patients with hemangiopericytoma is 46 years, and males present more frequently than females.[89] Typical radiologic features include nonspecific soft tissue masses, often with lytic destruction and stippled calcification resembling synovial sarcoma.[186]

Angioblastoma (Adamantinoma)

This extremely rare malignant or locally aggressive tumor is a dense fibrous stroma formed by rows of epithelium-like cells.[88] While the pathogenesis is not completely known, lesions have an endothelial nature. The mean age of patients with angioblastoma is 28 years, and the disease is most commonly found in the long bones (especially the tibia) and occasionally in the scapula and clavicle.[89] The neoplasm has the radiographic appearance of a multilocular, expansile, osteolytic lesion.[87] Multiple lesions begin as punched-out holes that ultimately merge into larger tumors.[89] Angioblastoma can metastasize, and inadequate treatment results in tumor recurrence, which increasingly resembles sarcoma.

LIPOMA

Lipomas are common benign neoplasms of soft tissue but are very rarely found in bone. They are categorized by the location of the tumor in the bone: intraosseous, parosteal, or intracortical.

Intraosseous lipoma represents 0.1 percent of bone tumors and affects men and women of all ages with relatively equal frequency. This tumor presents most frequently (60 percent) in the long bones, with the proximal humerus being involved in about 8 percent of cases.[89] Patients present with localized pain and swelling approximately 70 percent of the time.[88]

Common radiologic findings are metaphyseal to epiphyseal location, bone expansion, sclerotic border, predominant central lysis, and cortical thinning without destruction (Fig. 5-30). Central calcifications and lobulated bone expansion are less frequently observed, and periosteal reaction and cortical destruction are absent.[89]

Parosteal lipoma represents 0.3 percent of biopsy-analyzed primary bone tumors and presents most frequently in the long tubular bones.[89] This disease shows no predilection for either sex or age group. The key radiographic finding in this lipoma is a radiolucent mass of

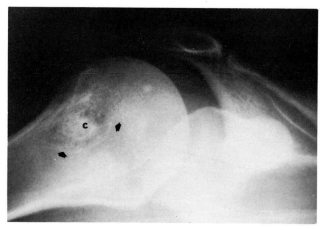

Figure 5-30 Intraosseous lipoma. A well-defined radiolucent lesion with a thin sclerotic margin (*arrows*) and central calcification (c) is present in the greater tuberosity.

fat density in conjunction with cortical hyperostosis, cortical erosion, or bowing of the bone away from the tumor.

POSTTREATMENT IMAGING

Preoperative chemotherapy is a common mode of treatment for cancer of the shoulder for a variety of reasons, such as facilitating limb-sparing surgery and increasing long-term survival. Because of the high morbidity of chemotherapy and the fact that surgery is postponed to administer it, it is important to be able to determine the response to the preoperative therapy during the course of the treatment. There are several means of accomplishing this by imaging methods.

Serial Thallium 201 Scintigraphy

Twenty-seven patients with extremity lesions (24 of them osteosarcoma) were classified into three categories based on tumor uptake of thallium-201.[187] This radionuclide uptake was imaged by thallium scintigraphy and provided an estimate of tumor viability. The three categories were (I) no response, (II) reduction but not obliteration of the lesion, and (III) lesion barely or not at all discernible. The histologic grading came from pathologic inspection of the surgical specimen; a good result had greater than 95 percent necrosis.

The breakdown of patients into categories was I, 10; II, 9; and III, 8. After histologic inspection, while 90 percent of those in category I had a bad response, 67 percent and 100 percent of category II and III lesions, respectively, had a good response. Category I thus correlated statistically to a bad response, and categories II and III to a good response, which in this study meant 100 percent relapse-free survival at 4 years. Furthermore, the predictive value of serial thallium-201 scintigraphy was evident in as early as 2 weeks after the initiation of chemotherapy.

Spin-Echo Magnetic Resonance Imaging

Spin-echo MRI was used to evaluate the effects of preoperative chemotherapy in 57 patients with osteosarcoma.[188] The investigators observed a variety of tumor characteristics: margin, volume, homogeneity, edema, joint effusion, and fracture. Histopathologic response was designated exactly as in the previous procedure (good represents less than 5 percent viable tumor). It was discovered that an increase in tumor volume after the preoperative treatment was predictive of a poor response (88 to 92 percent predictive value) but the converse was not true. Similarly, an increase or a stable level of edema was also predictive of a poor response (85 to 89 percent predictive value), and again the converse was not valid. Not surprisingly, the combination of increased tumor volume and increased or stable edema level was very predictive of a poor response (93 to 95 percent predictive value). Changes in the other tumor characteristics occurred independently of pathologic response in many of the patients, and they could not serve as prognostic indicators.

Contrast–Enhanced Subtraction Magnetic Resonance Imaging

Gadolinium-enhanced subtraction MRI has been shown to be useful in determining response of 10 osteosarcoma patients to preoperative chemotherapy.[189] This type of MR imaging is useful because neither nonenhanced T2-weighted MR nor gadopentate dimeglumine-enhanced T1-weighted MR could distinguish viable tumor from postchemotherapy inflammation.

The 10 patients were imaged after the course of chemotherapy. Four had no enhancing mass more than 3 mm wide. After histopathologic examination, all of these four had less than 3 percent viable tumor. The other six had enhancing masses greater than 3 mm wide, and five of them had large osteosarcomas with viable tumor ranging from 18 to 48 percent.

Dynamic, Contrast-Enhanced Magnetic Resonance Imaging

The response to chemotherapy in 20 pediatric patients (mean age 15 years) was determined by measuring tumor signal intensity with FLASH (*fast low-angle shot*) gradient-echo images obtained at 15-second intervals before and 3 or more minutes after intravenous injection of gadopentate dimeglumine.[190] These images were taken before, during, and after the course of chemotherapy and then compared to the histologic findings. Eleven patients had tumors with more than 90 percent necrosis and were designated as good responders.

For the procedure, the signal intensity was plotted against time and the slopes were measured as percentage of increase per minute. Before the chemotherapy, the difference in slopes between ultimate responders and nonresponders was not significant. That is, these slopes did not correlate with histologic outcome. During chemotherapy, however, the slopes correlated to the ultimate histologic response ($P = .02$). Post chemotherapy, the slopes were highly correlated to histologic outcome ($P = .007$). At this stage, all responders had less than a 40 percent increase per minute slope, and all but one nonresponder had a greater slope. Initial size of the tumor and size changes were also measured in this study, but at no point did these variables significantly relate to outcome.

References

1. SMITH J, YUPPA F, WATSON RC: Primary tumors and tumor-like lesions of the clavicle. *Skel Radiol* 17:235–246, 1988.
2. SAMILSON RL, MORRIS JM, THOMPSON RW: Tumors of the scapula. A review of the literature and an analysis of 31 cases. *Clin Orthop* 58:105–115, 1968.
3. SMITH J, MCLACHLAN DL, HUVOS AG, ET AL.: Primary tumors of the clavicle and scapula. *AJR* 124:113–123, 1975.
4. AOKI J, MOSER RP JR, VINH TN: Giant cell tumor of the scapula. A review of 13 cases. *Skel Radiol* 18:427–434, 1989.
5. GERSCOVICH EO, GREENSPAN A, SZABO RM: Benign

clavicular lesions that may mimic malignancy. *Skel Radiol* 20:173–180, 1991.

6. FRANKLIN JL, PARKER JC, KING HA: Nontraumatic clavicle lesions in children. *J Pediatr Orthop* 7:575–578, 1987.

7. D'AMBROSIA R, FERGUSON AB JR: The formation of osteochondroma by epiphyseal cartilage transplantation. *Clin Orthop* 61:103–115, 1968.

8. MILGRAM JW: The origins of osteochondromas and enchondromas. A histopathologic study. *Clin Orthop* 174:264–294, 1983.

9. HUVOS AG: *Bone Tumors. Diagnosis, Treatment, and Prognosis,* 2d ed, Philadelphia, Saunders, 1991.

10. GIUDICI MA, MOSER RP JR, KRANSDORF MJ: Cartilaginous bone tumors. *Radiol Clin North Am* 31:237–259, 1993.

11. PARSONS TA: The snapping scapula and subscapular exostoses. *J Bone Joint Surg* 55B:345–349, 1973.

12. LIZAMA VA, ZERBINI MA, GAGLIARDI R, ET AL.: Popliteal vein thrombosis and popliteal artery pseudoaneurysm complicating osteochondroma of the femur. *AJR* 148:783–784, 1987.

13. VALLANCE R, HAMBLEN DL, KELLY IG: Vascular complications of osteochondromas. *Clin Radiol* 36:639–642, 1985.

14. DAHLIN DC, UNNI KK: *Bone Tumors: General Aspects and Data on 8,542 Cases,* 4th ed, Springfield, IL, Charles C Thomas, 1986.

15. WILNER D: *Radiology of Bone Tumors and Allied Disorders,* Philadelphia, Saunders, 1982.

16. HUDSON TM, SPRINGFIELD DS, SPANIER SS, ET AL.: Benign exostoses and exostotic chondrosarcomas: Evaluation of cartilage thickness by CT. *Radiology* 152:595, 1984.

17. SPJUT HJ, DORFMAN HD, FECHNER RE, ET AL.: *Tumors of Bone and Cartilage,* Washington, D.C., Armed Forces Institute of Pathology, 1971.

18. SOLOMON L: Hereditary multiple exostosis. *J Bone Joint Surg* 45B:292–304, 1963.

19. GARRISON RC, UNNI KK, MCLEOD RA, ET AL.: Chondrosarcoma arising in osteochondroma. *Cancer* 49:1890–1897, 1982.

20. PETERSON HA: Multiple hereditary osteochondromata. *Clin Orthop* 239:222–230, 1989.

21. LEE JK, YAO L, WIRTH CR: MR imaging of solitary osteochondromas: Report of eight cases. *AJR* 149:557–560, 1987.

22. JAFFE HL, LICHTENSTEIN L: Solitary benign enchondroma of bone. *Arch Surg* 46:480–493, 1943.

23. MIRRA JM: *Bone Tumors: Diagnosis and Treatment,* 2nd ed, Philadelphia, Lippincott, 1990.

24. LEVY WM, AEGERTER EE, KIRKPATRICK JA JR.: The nature of cartilaginous tumors. *Radiol Clin North Am* 2:327–336, 1964.

25. RAGSDALE BE, SWEET DE, VINH TN: Radiology as gross pathology in evaluating chondroid lesions. *Hum Pathol* 20:930–951, 1989.

26. COHEN EK, KRESSEL HY, FRANK TS, ET AL.: Hyaline cartilage origin bone and soft-tissue neoplasms: MR appearance and histologic correlation. *Radiology* 167:477–481, 1988.

27. BORIANI S, BACCHINI P, BERTONI F, ET AL.: Periosteal chondroma. A review of twenty cases. *J Bone Joint Surg* 65A:205–212, 1983.

28. DESANTOS LA, SPJUT HJ: Periosteal chondroma—a radiographic spectrum. *Skel Radiol* 6:15–20, 1981.

29. ROCKWELL MA, SAITER ET, ENNEKING WF: Periosteal chondroma. *J Bone Joint Surg* 54A:102–108, 1972.

30. LEWIS MN, KENAN S, YABUT SM, ET AL.: Periosteal chondroma. A report of ten cases and review of the literature. *Clin Orthop* 256:185–191, 1990.

31. VARMA DGK, KUMAR R, CARRASCO CH, ET AL.: MR imaging of periosteal chondroma. *J Comput Assist Tomogr* 15:1008–1010, 1991.

32. KENAN S, ABDELWAHAB IF, KLEIN MJ,' ET AL.: Lesions of juxtacortical origin (surface lesions of bone). *Skel Radiol* 22:337–357, 1993.

33. BLOEM JL, MULDER JD: Chondroblastoma: A clinical and radiological study of 104 cases. *Skel Radiol* 14:1–9, 1985.

34. DAHLIN DC, IVINS JC: Benign chondroblastoma. A study of 125 cases. *Cancer* 30:401–413, 1972.

35. SPRINGFIELD DS, CAPANNA R, GHERLINZONI R, ET AL.: Chondroblastoma. A review of 70 cases. *J Bone Joint Surg* 67A:748–755, 1985.

36. SCHAJOWICZ F, GALLARDO H: Epiphysial chondroblastoma of bone. A clinicopathologic study of 69 cases. *J Bone Joint Surg* 52B:205–226, 1970.

37. KYRIAKOS M, LAND VJ, PENNING HL, ET AL.: Metastatic chondroblastoma. Report of a fatal case with a review of the literature on atypical, aggressive, and malignant chondroblastoma. *Cancer* 55:1770–1789, 1985.

38. MATSUNO T, HASEGAWA I, MASUDA T: Chondroblastoma arising in the triradiate cartilage. Report of two cases with review of the literature. *Skel Radiol* 16:216–222, 1987.

39. KURT AM, UNNI KK, SIM FH, ET AL.: Chondroblastoma of bone. *Hum Pathol* 20:965–976, 1989.

40. MCLEOD RA, BEABOUT JW: The roentgenographic features of chondroblastoma. *AJR* 118:464–478, 1973.

41. BROWER AC, MOSER RP, KRANSDORF MJ: The frequency and diagnostic significance of periostitis in chondroblastoma. *AJR* 154:309–314, 1990.

42. FOBBEN ES, DALINKA MK, SCHEIBLER ML, ET AL.: The magnetic resonance imaging appearance at 1.5 Tesla of cartilaginous tumors involving the epiphysis. *Skel Radiol* 16:647–651, 1987.

43. HAYES CW, CONWAY WF, SUNDARAM M: Misleading aggressive MR imaging appearance of some benign musculoskeletal lesions. *RadioGraphics* 12:1119–1134, 1992.

44. KAHMANN R, GOLD RH, ECKARDT JJ, ET AL.: Case report 337. *Skel Radiol* 14:301–304, 1985.

45. GHERLINZONI F, ROCK M, PICCI P: Chondromyxoid fibroma—the experience at the Instituto Ortopedico Rizzoli. *J Bone Joint Surg* 65A:198–203, 1983.

46. WILSON AJ, KYRIAKOS M, ACKERMAN LV: Chondromyxoid fibroma—appearance in 38 cases and a review of the literature. *Radiology* 179:513–518, 1991.

47. ROSENTHAL DI, SCHILLER AL, MANKIN HJ: Chondrosarcoma—correlation of radiological and histologic grade. *Radiology* 150:21–26, 1984.

48. GEIRNAERDT MJA, BLOEM JL, EULDERINK F, ET AL.: Cartilaginous tumors—correlation of gadolinium-enhanced

MR imaging and histopathologic findings. *Radiology* 186:813–817, 1993.

49. KENNEY PJ, GILULA LA, MURPHY WA: The use of computed tomography to distinguish osteochondroma and chondrosarcoma. *Radiology* 139:129–137, 1981.

50. NORMAN A, SISSONS HA: Radiographic hallmarks of peripheral chondrosarcoma. *Radiology* 151:589–596, 1984.

51. HUDSON TM, SPRINGFIELD DS, SPANIER SS, ET AL.: Benign exostoses and exostotic chondrosarcomas—evaluation of cartilage thickness by CT. *Radiology* 152:595–599, 1984.

52. BERTONI F, BORIANI S, LAUS M, ET AL.: Periosteal chondrosarcoma and periosteal osteosarcoma—two distinct entities. *J Bone Joint Surg* 64B:370–376, 1982.

53. SCHAJOWICZ F: Juxtacortical chondrosarcoma. *J Bone Joint Surg* 59B:473–480, 1977.

54. CAPANNA R, BETTONI G, BETTELI G, ET AL.: Dedifferentiated chondrosarcoma. *J Bone Joint Surg* 70A:60–69, 1988.

55. FRASSICA FJ, UNNI KK, BEABOUT JW, ET AL.: Dedifferentiated chondrosarcoma. A report of the clinicopathological features and treatment of 78 cases. *J Bone Joint Surg* 68A:1197–1205, 1986.

56. TETU B, ORDONEZ NG, AYALA AG, ET AL.: Chondrosarcoma with additional mesenchymal component (dedifferentiated chondrosarcoma). II. An immunohistochemical and electron microscopic study. *Cancer* 58:287–298, 1986.

57. DE LANGE EE, POPE TL JR, FECHNER RE: Dedifferentiated chondrosarcoma: Radiographic features. *Radiology* 160:489–492, 1986.

58. PRESENT D, BACCHINI P, PIGNATTI G, ET AL.: Clear cell chondrosarcoma of bone. A report of 8 cases. *Skel Radiol* 20:187–191, 1991.

59. UNNI KK, DAHLIN DC, BEABOUT JW, ET AL.: Chondrosarcoma: Clear cell variant. *J Bone Joint Surg* 58A:676–683, 1976.

60. KUMAR R, DAVID R, CIERNEY G III: Clear cell chondrosarcoma. *Radiology* 154:45–48, 1985.

61. VARMA DGK, AYALA AG, CARRASCO CH: Chondrosarcoma—MR imaging with pathologic correlation. *RadioGraphics* 12:687–704, 1992.

62. HEALEY JH, GHELMAN B: Osteoid osteoma and osteoblastoma. Current concepts and recent advances. *Clin Orthop* 204:76–85, 1986.

63. KLEIN MH, SKANKMAN S: Osteoid osteoma: Radiologic and pathologic correlation. *Skel Radiol* 21:23–31, 1992.

64. BLOEM JL, KROON HM: Osseous lesions. *Radiol Clin North Am* 31:261–278, 1993.

65. KATTAPURAM SV, KUSHNER DC, PHILLIPS WC, ET AL.: Osteoid osteoma: An unusual case of articular pain. *Radiology* 147:383–387, 1983.

66. NORMAN A, ABDELWAHAB IF, BUYON J, ET AL.: Osteoid osteoma of the hip stimulating an early onset of osteoarthritis. *Radiology* 158:417–420, 1986.

67. KRANSDORF MJ, STULL MA, GILKEY FW, ET AL.: Osteoid osteoma. *RadioGraphics* 11:671–696, 1991.

68. KLEIN MJ, LUSSKIN R, BECKER MH, ET AL.: Osteoid osteoma of the clavicle. *Clin Orthop* 143:162, 1979.

69. MOSHEIFF R, LIEBERGALL M, ZIV I, ET AL.: Osteoid osteoma of the scapula. A case report and review of the literature. *Clin Orthop* 262:129–131, 1991.

70. GREENSPAN A: Benign bone-forming lesions: Osteoma, osteoid osteoma, and osteoblastoma. *Skel Radiol* 22:485–500, 1993.

71. HERRLIN K, EKELUND L, LOVDAHL R, ET AL.: Computed tomography in suspected osteoid osteomas of tubular bones. *Skel Radiol* 9:92, 1982.

72. HELMS CA, HATTNER RS, VOLGER JB III: Osteoid osteoma: Radionuclide diagnosis. *Radiology* 151:779–784, 1984.

73. BIEBUYCK, JC, KATZ LD, MCCAULEY T: Soft tissue edema in osteoid osteoma. *Skel Radiol* 22:37–41, 1993.

74. GLASS RBJ, POZNANSKI AK, FISHER MR, ET AL.: Case report. MR imaging of osteoid osteoma. *J Comput Assist Tomogr* 10:1065–1067, 1986.

75. GOLDMAN AB, SCHNEIDER R, PAVLOV H: Osteoid osteoma of the femoral neck: Report of four cases evaluated with isotopic bone scanning, CT and MR imaging. *Radiology* 186:227, 1993.

76. WOODS ER, MATTEL W, MANDELL SH, ET AL.: Reactive soft tissue mass associated with osteoid osteoma: Correlation of MR imaging features with pathologic findings. *Radiology* 186:221, 1993.

77. YEAGER DA, SCHIEBLER ML, WERTHEIM S, ET AL.: Case report. MR imaging of osteoid osteoma of the talus. *J Comput Assist Tomogr* 11:916–917, 1987.

78. AYALA AG, MURRAY JA, ERLING MA, ET AL.: Osteoid osteoma: Intraoperative tetracycline-fluorescence demonstration of the nidus. *J Bone Joint Surg* 68A:747, 1986.

79. STEINBERG GG, COUMAS JM, BREEN T: Preoperative localization of osteoid osteoma: A new technique that uses CT. *AJR* 155:883–885, 1990.

80. DOYLE T, KING K: Percutaneous removal of osteoid osteoma using CT control. *Clin Radiol* 40:514–517, 1989.

81. MAZOYER J-F, KOHLER R, BOSSARD D: Osteoid osteoma: CT-guided percutaneous treatment. *Radiology* 181:269–271, 1991.

82. ROSENTHAL DI, ALEXANDER A, ROSENBERG AE, ET AL.: Ablation of osteoid osteoma with a percutaneously placed electrode: A new procedure. *Radiology* 183:29–33, 1992.

83. MCLEOD RA, DAHLIN DC, BEABOUT JW: The spectrum of osteoblastoma. *AJR* 126:321–335, 1976.

84. KROON HM, SCHURMANS J: Osteoblastoma: Clinical and radiologic findings in 98 new cases. *Radiology* 175:783–790, 1990.

85. BERTONI F, UNNI KK, MCLEOD RA, ET AL.: Osteosarcoma resembling osteoblastoma. *Cancer* 55:416–426, 1985.

86. CRIM JR, MIRRA JM, ECKARDT JJ, ET AL.: Widespread inflammatory response to osteoblastoma—the flare phenomenon. *Radiology* 177:835–836, 1990.

87. GREENFIELD GB: *Radiology of Bone Diseases,* 5th ed, Philadelphia, JB Lippincott, 1990.

88. RESNICK D: *Bone and Joint Imaging,* Philadelphia, Saunders, 1989.

89. MIRRA JM: *Bone Tumors: Clinical, Radiologic, and Pathologic Correlations,* Philadelphia, Lea & Febiger, 1989.

90. GRIFFITHS HJ: *Basic Bone Radiology,* 2nd ed, Norwalk, CT, Appleton & Lange, 1987.

91. HUDSON TM, STILES RG, MONSON DK: Fibrous lesions of bone. *Radiol Clin North Am* 31:279–297, 1993.

92. KUMAR R, MADEWELL JE, LINDELL MM, ET AL.: Fibrous lesions of bone. *RadioGraphics* 10:237–256, 1990.

93. CAFFEY J: On fibrous defects in cortical walls of growing tubular bones: Their radiologic appearance, structure, prevalence, natural course and diagnostic significance. *Adv Pediatr* 7:13–51, 1955.

94. DRENNAN DB, MAYLAHN DJ, FAHEY JJ: Fracture through large nonossifying fibromas. *Clin Orthop* 103:82–88, 1974.

95. KUMAR R, SWISCHUK LE, MADEWELL JE: Benign cortical defect: Site for an avulsion fracture. *Skel Radiol* 15:553–555, 1986.

96. KRANSDORF MJ, UTZ JA, GILKEY FW, ET AL.: MR appearance of fibroxanthoma. *J Comput Assist Tomogr* 12:612–615, 1988.

97. BETTONI F, CALDERONI P, BACCHINI P, ET AL.: Benign fibrous histiocytoma of bone. *J Bone Joint Surg* 68A:1225–1230, 1986.

98. RABHAN WN, ROSAI J: Desmoplastic fibroma. Report of ten cases and review of the literature. *J Bone Joint Surg* 50A:487–502, 1968.

99. CRIM JR, GOLD RH, MIRRA JM, ET AL.: Desmoplastic fibroma of bone: Radiographic analysis. *Radiology* 172:827–832, 1989.

100. GEBHARDT MC, CAMPBELL CJ, SCHILLER AL, ET AL.: Desmoplastic fibroma of bone. A report of eight cases and review of the literature. *J Bone Joint Surg* 67A:732–747, 1985.

101. YOUNG JWR, AISNER SC, LEVINE AM, ET AL.: Computed tomography of desmoid tumors of bone: Desmoplastic fibroma of bone. *Skel Radiol* 17:333–337, 1988.

102. KRANSDORF MJ, MOSER RP JR, GILKEY FW: Fibrous dysplasia. *RadioGraphics* 10:519–537, 1990.

103. HARRIS WH, DUDLEY HR JR, BARRY RJ: The natural history of fibrous dysplasia. An orthopaedic, pathological, and roentgenographic study. *J Bone Joint Surg* 44A:207–233, 1962.

104. HENRY A: Monostotic fibrous dysplasia. *J Bone Joint Surg* 51B:300–306, 1969.

105. SCHAJOWICZ F: *Tumors and Tumor-Like Lesions of Bone and Joints,* New York, Springer-Verlag, 1981.

106. DAFFNER RH, KIRKS DR, GEHWEILER JA JR, ET AL.: Computed tomography of fibrous dysplasia. *AJR* 139:943–948, 1982.

107. UTZ JA, KRANSDORF MJ, JELINEK JS, ET AL.: MR appearance of fibrous dysplasia. *J Comput Assist Tomogr* 13:845–851, 1989.

108. CAPANNA R, BERTONI F, BACCHINI P, ET AL.: Malignant fibrous histiocytoma of bone. The experience at the Rizzoli Institute: Report of 90 cases. *Cancer* 54:177–187, 1984.

109. HAAG M, ADLER CP: Malignant fibrous histiocytoma in association with hip replacement. *J Bone Joint Surg* 71B:701, 1989.

110. ROS PR, VIAMONTE M JR, RYWLIN AM: Malignant fibrous histiocytoma: Mesenchymal tumor of ubiquitous origin. *AJR* 142:753–759, 1984.

111. HUVOS AG, HEILWEIL M, BRETSKY SS: The pathology of malignant fibrous histiocytoma of bone. A study of 130 patients. *Am J Surg Pathol* 9:853–871, 1985.

112. CASTILLO M, TEHRANZADEH J, BECERRA J, ET AL.: Case report 408. *Skel Radiol* 16:74–77, 1987.

113. SPJUT HJ, FECHNER RE, ACKERMAN LV: *Tumors of Bone and Cartilage (Supplement),* Washington, DC, Armed Forces Institute of Pathology, 1981.

114. SPANIER SS: Malignant fibrous histiocytoma of bone. *Orthop Clin North Am* 8:947–961, 1977.

115. SUNDARAM M, MCLEOD RA: MR imaging of tumor and tumor-like lesions of bone and soft tissue. *AJR* 155:817–824, 1990.

116. DAHLIN DC, IVINS JC: Fibrosarcoma of bone. A study of 114 cases. *Cancer* 23:35–41, 1969.

117. HUVOS AG, HIGINBOTHAM NL: Primary fibrosarcoma of bone. A clinicopathologic study of 130 patients. *Cancer* 35:837–847, 1975.

118. TACONIS WK, MULDER JD: Fibrosarcoma and malignant fibrous histiocytoma of long bones: Radiographic features and grading. *Skel Radiol* 11:237–245, 1984.

119. LYSKO JE, GUILFORD WB, SEIGAL GP: Case report 362. *Skel Radiol* 15:268–272, 1986.

120. CAMPANACCI M, BALDINI N, BORIANI S, ET AL.: Giant-cell tumor of bone. *J Bone Joint Surg* 69A:106–114, 1987.

121. DAHLIN DC: Giant cell tumor of bone: Highlights of 407 cases. *AJR* 144:955–960, 1985.

122. MCDONALD DJ, SIRE FH, MCLEOD RA, ET AL.: Giant-cell tumor of bone. *J Bone Joint Surg* 68A:235–241, 1986.

123. BERTONI F, PRESENT D, ENNEKING WF: Giant-cell tumor of bone with pulmonary metastases. *J Bone Joint Surg* 67A:890–900, 1985.

124. TUBBS WS, BROWN LR, BEABOUT JW, ET AL.: Benign giant-cell tumor of bone with pulmonary metastases: Clinical findings and radiologic appearance of metastases in 13 cases. *AJR* 158:331–334, 1992.

125. VANEL D, CONTESSO G, REBIBO G, ET AL.: Benign giant-cell tumors of bone with pulmonary metastases and favourable prognosis. Report on two cases and review of the literature. *Skel Radiol* 10:221–226, 1983.

126. MOSER RP JR, KRANSDORF MJ, GILKEY FW, ET AL.: Giant cell tumor of the upper extremity. *RadioGraphics* 10:83–102, 1990.

127. KRANSDORF MJ, SWEET DE, BUETOW PC, ET AL.: Giant cell tumor in skeletally immature patients. *Radiology* 184:233–237, 1992.

128. ENNEKING WF: *Musculoskeletal Tumor Surgery,* New York, Churchill Livingstone, 1983.

129. ECKARDT JJ, GROGAN TJ: Giant cell tumor of bone. *Clin Orthop* 204:45–58, 1986.

130. ROCK MG, PRITCHARD DJ, UNNI KK: Metastases from histologically benign giant-cell tumor of bone. *J Bone Joint Surg* 66A:269–274, 1984.

131. HUDSON TM, SCHEIBLER M, SPRINGFIELD DS, ET AL.: Radiology of giant-cell tumors of bone: Computed tomography, arthro-tomography and scintigraphy. *Skel Radiol* 11:85–95, 1984.

132. LEVINE E, DESMET AA, NEFF JR: Role of radiologic imaging in management planning of giant cell tumor of bone. *Skel Radiol* 12:79–89, 1984.

133. HERMAN SD, MESGARZADEH M, BONAKDARPOUR A, ET AL.: The role of magnetic resonance imaging in giant cell tumor of bone. *Skel Radiol* 16:635–643, 1987.

134. MANASTER BJ, DOYLE AJ: Giant cell tumors of bone. *Radiol Clin North Am* 31:299–323, 1993.

135. CAVAZANNA AO, MISER JS, JEFFERSON J, ET AL.: Experimental evidence for a neural origin of Ewing's sarcoma of bone. *Am J Pathol* 127:507–518, 1987.

136. NESBIT ME: Ewing's sarcoma. *CA* 26:174–180, 1976.

137. REINUS WR, GILULA LA: Radiology of Ewing's sarcoma: Intergroup Ewing's Sarcoma Study (IESS). *RadioGraphics* 4:929–944, 1984.

138. EGGII KD, QUIOGUE T, MOSER RP JR: Ewing's sarcoma. *Radiol Clin North Am* 31:325–337, 1993.

139. SHIRLEY SK, GILULA LA, SIEGEL GP, ET AL.: Roentgenographic-pathologic correlation of diffuse sclerosis in Ewing's sarcoma of bone. *Skel Radiol* 12:69–78, 1984.

140. BACCI G, TONI A, MADDELANA A, ET AL.: Long-term results in 144 localized Ewing's sarcoma patients treated with combined therapy. *Cancer* 63:1477, 1989.

141. O'CONNOR MI, PRITCHARD DJ: Ewing's sarcoma. Prognostic factors, disease control, and the reemerging role of surgical treatment. *Clin Orthop* 262:78–87, 1991.

142. REINUS WR, GEHAN EA, GILULA LA, ET AL.: Plain radiographic predictors of survival in treated Ewing's sarcoma. *Skel Radiol* 21:287–291, 1992.

143. MUNDY GR, RAISZ LG, COOPER RA, ET AL.: Evidence for the secretion of an osteoclast-stimulating factor in myeloma. *N Engl J Med* 291:1041, 1974.

144. RESNICK D, NIWAYAMA G: *Diagnosis of Bone and Joint Disorders,* 2d ed, Philadelphia, Saunders, 1988.

145. AGGARWAL S, GOULATIA RK, SOOD A, ET AL.: POEMS syndrome: A rare variety of plasma cell dyscrasia. *AJR* 155:339–341, 1990.

146. RESNICK D, GREENWAY GD, BARDWICK PA, ET AL.: Plasma-cell dyscrasia with polyneuropathy, organomegaly, endocrinopathy, M-protein and skin changes: The POEMS syndrome. *Radiology* 140:17–22, 1981.

147. BATAILLE R, CHEVALIER J, ROSSI M, ET AL.: Bone scintigraphy in plasma-cell myeloma. A perspective study of 70 patients. *Radiology* 145:801–804, 1982.

148. LEONARD RCF, OWEN JP, PROCTOR SJ, ET AL.: Multiple myeloma: Radiology or bone scanning? *Clin Radiol* 32:291–295, 1981.

149. SCHREIMAN JS, MCLEOD RA, KYLE RA, ET AL.: Multiple myeloma: Evaluation by CT. *Radiology* 154:483–486, 1985.

150. LIBSHITZ HI, MALTHOUSE SR, CUNNINGHAM D: Multiple myeloma: Appearance at MR imaging. *Radiology* 182:833–837, 1992.

151. FRUEHWALD FXJ, TSCHOLAKOFF D, SCHWAIGHOFER B, ET AL.: Magnetic resonance imaging of the lower vertebral column in patients with multiple myeloma. *Invest Radiol* 23:193–199, 1988.

152. LINDEN A, ZANKOVICH R, THEISSEN P, ET AL.: Malignant lymphoma: Bone marrow imaging versus biopsy. *Radiology* 173:335, 1988.

153. IVINS JC, DAHLIN DC: Reticulum-cell sarcoma of bone. *J Bone Joint Surg* 35A:835–842, 1953.

154. WILSON TW, PUGH DG: Primary reticulum-cell sarcoma of bone, with emphasis on roentgen aspects. *Radiology* 65:343–351, 1955.

155. REIMER RR, CHABNER BA, YOUNG RC, ET AL.: Lymphoma presenting in bone. Results of histopathology, staging, and therapy. *Ann Intern Med* 87:50–55, 1977.

156. OSTROWSKI ML, UNNI KK, BANKS PM, ET AL.: Malignant lymphoma of bone. *Cancer* 58:2646–2655, 1986.

157. SHOJI H, MILLER TR: Primary reticulum cell sarcoma of bone. Significance of clinical features upon the prognosis. *Cancer* 28:1234–1244, 1971.

158. PHILLIPS WC, KATTAPURAN SV, DOSERETZ DE, ET AL.: Primary lymphoma of bone: Relationship of radiographic appearance and prognosis. *Radiology* 144:285–290, 1982.

159. STIGLBAUER R, AUGUSTIN I, KRAMER J, ET AL.: MRI in the diagnosis of primary lymphoma of bone: Correlation with histopathology. *J Comput Assist Tomogr* 16:248–253, 1992.

160. NORMAN A, SCHIFFMAN M: Simple bone cysts: Factors of age dependency. *Radiology* 124:779–782, 1977.

161. PRIETTO C, OROFINO CF, WAUGH TR: Unicameral bone cyst in the scapula. *Clin Orthop* 125:183, 1977.

162. STELLING CB, MARTIN W, FECHNER RE, ET AL.: Case report 150. Diagnosis: Solitary bone cyst with cementum-like bone production. *Skel Radiol* 6:213–215, 1981.

163. CAPANNA R, VAN HORN J, RUGGIERI P, ET AL.: Epiphyseal involvement in unicameral bone cysts. *Skel Radiol* 15:428–432, 1986.

164. RUGGIERI P, BIAGINI R, PICCI P: Case report 437. Diagnosis: Solitary bone cyst of the scapula. *Skel Radiol* 16:493–497, 1987.

165. REYNOLDS J: The "fallen fragment sign" in the diagnosis of unicameral bone cysts. *Radiology* 92:949, 1969.

166. STRUHL S, EDELSON C, PRITZKER H, ET AL.: Solitary (unicameral) bone cyst. The fallen fragment sign revisited. *Skel Radiol* 18:261–265, 1989.

167. CONWAY WF, HAYES CW: Miscellaneous lesions of bone. *Radiol Clin North Am* 31:339–358, 1993.

168. DAHLIN DC, MCLEOD RA: Aneurysmal bone cyst and other non-neoplastic conditions. *Skel Radiol* 8:243–250, 1982.

169. CAPANNA R, SPRINGFIELD DS, BIAGINI R, ET AL.: Juxta-epiphyseal aneurysmal bone cyst. *Skel Radiol* 13:21–25, 1985.

170. DYER R, STELLING CB, FECHNER RE: Epiphyseal extension of an aneurysmal bone cyst. *AJR* 137:172–173, 1981.

171. GOLD RH, MIRRA JM: Case report 234. Diagnosis: Aneurysmal bone cyst of left scapula with intramural calcified chondroid. *Skel Radiol* 10:57–60, 1983.

172. BELTRAN J, SIMON DC, LEVY M, ET AL.: Aneurysmal bone cysts: MR imaging at 1.5 T. *Radiology* 158:689–690, 1986.

173. MUNK PL, HELMS CA, HOLT RG, ET AL.: MR imaging of aneurysmal bone cysts. *AJR* 153:99–101, 1989.

174. ZIMMER WD, BERQUIST TH, SIM FH, ET AL.: Magnetic resonance imaging of aneurysmal bone cyst. *Mayo Clin Proc* 59:633–636, 1984.

175. HUDSON TM: Fluid levels in aneurysmal bone cysts: A CT feature. *AJR* 141:1001–1004, 1984.

176. HUDSON TM, HAMLIN DJ, FITZSIMMONS JR: Magnetic resonance imaging of fluid levels in an aneurysmal bone cyst and in anticoagulated human blood. *Skel Radiol* 13:267–270, 1985.

177. CORY DA, FRITSCH SA, COHEN MD, ET AL.: Aneurysmal

bone cysts: Imaging findings and embolotherapy. *AJR* 153:369–373, 1989.

178. OSBAND ME: Histiocytosis X: Langerhans' cell histiocytosis. *Hematol Oncol Clin North Am* 1:737–751, 1987.

179. STULL MA, KRANSDORF MJ, DEVANEY KO: Langerhans' cell histiocytosis of bone. *RadioGraphics* 12:801–823, 1992.

180. SARTORIS DJ, PARKER BR: Histiocytosis X: Rate and pattern of resolution oil osseous lesions. *Radiology* 152:679–684, 1984.

181. NAUERT C, ZORNOZA J, AYALA A, ET AL.: Eosinophilic granuloma of bone: Diagnosis and management. *Skel Radiol* 10:227–235, 1983.

182. DAVID R, ORIA RA, KUMAR R, ET AL.: Radiologic features of eosinophilic granuloma of bone. *AJR* 153:1021–1026, 1989.

183. CRONE-MUNZEBROCK W, BRASSOW F: A comparison of radiographic and bone scan findings in histiocytosis X. *Skel Radiol* 9:170–173, 1983.

184. BELTRAN J, APARISI F, BONMATI LM, ET AL.: Eosinophilic granuloma: MRI manifestations. *Skel Radiol* 22:157–161, 1993.

185. DESCHEPPER AMA, RAMON F, VAN MARCK E: MR imaging of eosinophilic granuloma: Report of 11 cases. *Skel Radiol* 22:163–166, 1993.

186. RESNICK D, PETTERSSON H: *Skeletal Radiology,* Florida, Merit Communications, 1992.

187. ROSEN G, LOREN GJ, BRIEN EW, ET AL.: Serial thallium 201 scintigraphy in osteosarcoma. *Clin Orthop* 293:302–306, 1993.

188. HOLSCHER HC, BLOEM JL, VANEL D, ET AL.: Osteosarcoma: Chemotherapy-induced changes at MR imaging. *Radiology* 182:839–844, 1992.

189. DE BAERE T, VANEL D, SHAPEERO LG: Osteosarcoma after chemotherapy: Evaluation with contrast material–enhanced subtraction MR imaging. *Radiology* 185:587–592, 1992.

190. FLETCHER BD, HANNA SL, FAIRCLOUGH DL, ET AL.: Pediatric musculoskeletal tumors: Use of dynamic, contrast-enhanced MR imaging to monitor response to chemotherapy. *Radiology* 184:243–248, 1992.

6 IMAGING OF SOFT TISSUE NEOPLASMS IN THE SHOULDER

Philip M. Hughes
Charles S. Resnik

The upper extremity is not uncommonly affected by soft tissue neoplasms, most of which arise about the shoulder girdle.[1] The importance of detection, characterization, and staging of these lesions has been emphasized with the introduction of new treatment techniques. Staging is influenced by anatomic location, anatomic extent, and histologic grade. Imaging contributes to this process by determining whether a neoplasm is confined to its compartment of origin and by establishing its relationship to critical neurovascular structures and adjacent bone. This information aids appropriate decision making about limb salvage procedures, chemotherapy, radiation therapy, or combinations thereof.

Magnetic resonance imaging (MRI) is now widely regarded as the premier imaging modality for the investigation of soft tissue lesions.[2–4] Advantages of MRI over computed tomography (CT) include superior soft tissue contrast and characterization, multiplanar imaging, no beam-hardening artifact, and avoidance of iodinated intravenous contrast agents. Conventional radiographs retain a role as an adjunct to MRI in the identification of diagnostic features such as soft tissue calcification and ossification, which might otherwise be overlooked. This discussion of soft tissue neoplasms of the shoulder will place emphasis on lesions with specific appearances and on the features and limitations of imaging characteristics used to differentiate benign lesions from malignant ones.

TECHNIQUE

Patient Positioning and Coil Selection

Patient positioning in the investigation of soft tissue shoulder neoplasms is determined by the site of the lesion. In general, imaging is performed with the patient in the supine position, but prone positioning is preferable for investigating posteriorly located neoplasms, to avoid tumor compression and distortion and local imaging artifacts secondary to the proximity of the coil.

Movement artifact is minimized by positioning the arm by the side with the wrist in pronation. Respiratory artifact is diminished by a variety of compensatory techniques which depend on the imaging system used. A dedicated shoulder coil, either single- or double-loop configuration, should be used to maximize the signal-to-noise ratio. Tumors that extend beyond the field of these coils should be imaged using the body coil.

Imaging Plane and Sequence Selection

Numerous pulse sequences can be used to evaluate soft tissue neoplasms including spin-echo (SE) sequences (short TR/TE and long TR/TE), gradient echo (GE) sequences, short tau inversion recovery (STIR) sequences, and chemical shift imaging. Newer sequences as yet incompletely evaluated include fast spin-echo (FSE) imaging, which offers the ability to generate heavily T2-weighted SE images in relatively short acquisition time. SE images are usually adequate for identification and staging of most soft tissue neoplasms. Diseased tissue generally has longer T1 and T2 relaxation times than muscle and so appears hypointense or isointense on T1-weighted images and hyperintense on T2-weighted images. Tumor conspicuousness is usually maximal on T2-weighted images, but T1-weighting provides better anatomic detail and contrast between fat and muscle.

We use a double-echo T2-weighted SE sequence (TR/TE, 2200/20-70 msec) in the axial plane, with 5 to 7 mm slice thickness and a 1-mm interslice gap. A T1-weighted sequence is then performed in either a coronal (lateral lesion) or sagittal (anterior or posterior lesion) plane using similar section thickness. We now commonly perform a T2-weighted FSE (TR/TE, 4000/105) sequence in this second plane, but T2 GE (T2*) sequences may be substituted. Fat suppression is necessary when using the T2-weighted FSE sequence. When contrast enhancement is desired, intravenous injection of 0.1 mmol/kg of gadolinium-DTPA (Gd-DTPA) is usually used.

DIFFERENTIATING BENIGN AND MALIGNANT NEOPLASMS

MRI and CT both accurately localize soft tissue neoplasms, but differentiating between benign and malignant lesions has proven difficult.[5–8] Clinical data, particularly age and duration of symptoms, have been demonstrated to improve the diagnostic accuracy of MRI with respect to benign lesions.[3,9] Classically, benign lesions tend to be well-marginated and have homogeneous signal intensity whereas malignant lesions have irregular margins, are inhomogeneous, and more often encase neurovascular structures.[7] The use of these features yields a negative predictive value for malignancy on the order of 94 percent. Despite this, surgery is routinely undertaken for lesions that look benign since exceptions undermine the reliability and practicality of these features to exclude malignant neoplasms. Benign tumors that are often misclassified as malignant by virtue of these imaging features include aggressive fibromatosis, which is often locally infiltrative, cavernous hemangiomas, and large necrotic benign neoplasms (neurofibromas and leiomyomas), which exhibit heterogeneous signal intensity. The malignant neoplasm most commonly misdiagnosed as benign is synovial sarcoma. This is often well-marginated, and its MRI appearance often simulates a cyst or a hematoma, since intralesional hemorrhage is common (Table 6-1). In addition, many nonneoplastic processes may simulate either benign or malignant neoplasms (Table 6-2).

NEOPLASMS WITH SPECIFIC APPEARANCES

Benign Lesions

SIMPLE LIPOMA

Lipomas are common mesenchymal neoplasms that consist of a localized collection of adipose tissue. Multiple lesions, referred to as *lipomatosis* (Dirkum's disease),

Table 6-1 Commonly Misdiagnosed Neoplasms

Misdiagnosed as malignant
  Aggressive fibromatosis
  Cavernous hemangioma
  Neurofibroma
  Leiomyoma
Misdiagnosed as benign
  Synovial sarcoma

Table 6-2 Nonneoplastic Lesions That Simulate Neoplasms

Hematoma
Abscess
Cyst (ganglion, sebaceous)
Myositis ossificans

are encountered in 7 percent of cases.[10] The upper arm, shoulder, trunk, and thigh are most commonly affected. Lipomas may arise within muscle, between muscles, or in the subcutaneous soft tissues. Malignant degeneration is rare.

A lipoma is usually distinguishable from neighboring soft tissues on plain films as a well-defined area of translucency, either in subcutaneous tissues or deep to a fascial plane or muscular aponeurosis. A variable fibrous component can contribute to septation, causing a reduction in the expected degree of translucency. This can create uncertainty about the benign nature of the lesion.

The efficacy of CT and MRI in the diagnosis of benign lipomatous neoplasms is well established.[9,11,12] The CT characteristics include a well-defined margin, homogeneous low attenuation (range -60 to -100 Hounsfield units [HU]),[9] and absence of tumor contrast enhancement (Fig. 6-1). CT is often sufficient for diagnosis and is less costly than MRI; however, if enhanced CT imaging is also to be employed, the cost saving is less significant and may be offset by MRI's superior soft tissue contrast, multiplanar delineation, and absence of ionizing radiation.

Lipomas evaluated with MRI demonstrate equivalent signal characteristics to those of the subcutaneous fat: high signal intensity on T1-weighted sequences and lower intensity on intermediate- and T2-weighted sequences (Figs. 6-2, 6-3). Lesions are usually well marginated and may exhibit fibrous septation. It is not uncommon for part of the periphery to appear irregular. Areas of in-

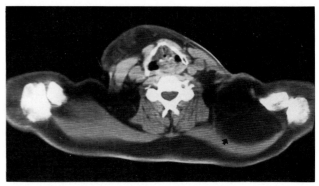

Figure 6-1 Intramuscular lipoma. Axial CT image at the level of the acromioclavicular joint demonstrates a septated lipoma (*arrow*) in the supraclavicular fossa.

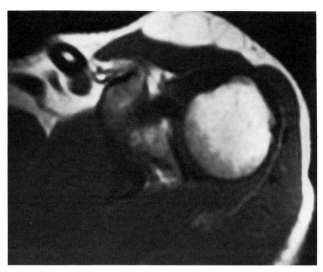

Figure 6-2 Subcutaneous lipoma. Axial T1-weighted SE image demonstrates a lobulated lipoma in the subcutaneous soft tissues anterior to the shoulder that is isointense to the surrounding fat.

creased signal intensity on T2-weighted sequences within or adjacent to the lesion suggest malignancy, and excision is usually advised in these circumstances. Intravenous Gd-DTPA enhancement generally does not improve evaluation or characterization beyond that achieved with standard T1- and T2-weighted sequences.

A subacute hematoma can simulate a lipoma on T1-weighted sequences, and occasionally on T2-weighted sequences. Chemical shift artifacts seen at the interface between the lipoma and adjacent soft tissue on T1-weighted sequences[13] or techniques aimed at fat suppression can help distinguish these entities.

INFILTRATING INTRAMUSCULAR LIPOMA

A variant of the encapsulated lipoma is the infiltrating intramuscular lipoma, which has a predilection for the large muscle groups of the shoulder, upper arm, hip,

and thigh (Fig. 6-4).[14–16] These lesions are characteristically large and infiltrating and can undergo necrosis, which may make them difficult to differentiate from liposarcomas. The absence of enhancement following intravenous Gd-DTPA is a useful additional indicator of a benign lesion in these circumstances. Fine-needle aspiration cytologic examination has been proposed,[17] but owing to the inhomogeneity of liposarcomas this is not a practical alternative to excisional biopsy when the diagnosis of an infiltrating lipoma is questionable. Recurrence following resection is frequent; whenever possible, complete muscle resection is considered the treatment of choice.[14,15]

LIPOBLASTOMA AND LIPOBLASTOMATOSIS

These benign lipomatous tumors are considered to originate from fetal white fat[18] and are found almost exclusively in children younger than 1 year. A male predominance has been reported, and sites of primitive adipose tissue such as the chest, neck, axilla, and extremities are most commonly affected.[19] Maturation of fat cells has been observed on follow-up.

The radiographic appearance of these conditions depends on the maturity of the lipocytes.[11] A lesion with predominantly mature lipocytes has mainly fatty CT attenuation characteristics, whereas lesions composed of less mature lipoblasts and myxoid components demonstrate higher attenuation. Lipoblastomas are well-circumscribed and lobular and often contain fibrous septa. The less well-circumscribed lipoblastoma, often termed *lipoblastomatosis,* is more locally infiltrative and frequently recurs following surgery. Based purely on the CT appearances there are similarities in appearance between these benign lesions and well-differentiated liposarcomas. Liposarcomas are, however, particularly rare in infants. To date there are no reports documenting the use of MRI in the evaluation of lipoblastomas.

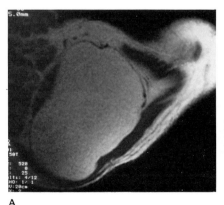

A

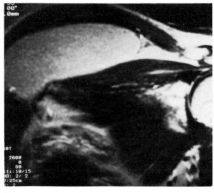

B

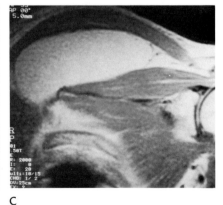

C

Figure 6-3 Intermuscular lipoma. Axial T1-weighted, **A,** coronal oblique T2-weighted, **B,** and coronal oblique proton-weighted, **C,** SE images show a large intermuscular lipoma arising between the deltoid and supraspinatus muscles. (Courtesy of Dr. J.P.R. Jenkins.)

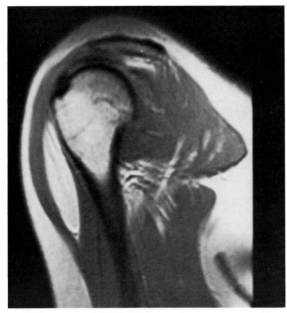

A

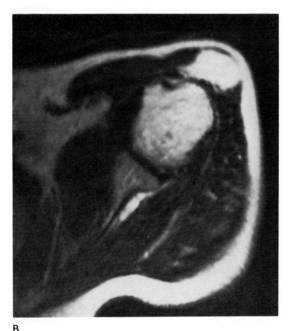

B

Figure 6-4 Infiltrating intramuscular lipoma. Coronal T1-weighted, **A,** and axial T2-weighted, **B,** SE images demonstrate a homogeneous nonencapsulated fatty tumor within the lateral aspect of the deltoid. (Courtesy of Dr. J. Hawnaur.)

HEMANGIOMA

Skeletal muscle hemangiomas account for 70 percent of all benign soft tissue neoplasms. They occur primarily in children and young adults. Patients can present with a palpable mass, muscle atrophy, limb overgrowth, or cutaneous hypersensitivity overlying the involved muscle. Hemangiomas are often deep seated and variable in both size and consistency, so clinical misdiagnosis is not uncommon.[20]

There are three categories of extremity vascular malformations: hemangiomas, arteriovenous malformations (AVMs), and purely venous malformations.[21] Hemangiomas are further subdivided according to the size of the aberrant vessels. Lesions with mostly small vessels (diameter smaller than 20 red blood cells) are termed *capillary hemangiomas;* those with larger vessels are commonly referred to as *cavernous* or *large-vessel hemangiomas.*[22] Mixed-type hemangiomas composed of equal portions of small and large vessels are also recognized.[23]

Cavernous hemangiomas are the most frequently encountered vascular malformation of the extremities.[24] In addition to large vessels they include a variable amount of nonvascular tissue, particularly adipose tissue. A cavernous hemangioma may occasionally be indistinguishable from a lipoma.[23]

Radiographs reveal phleboliths in as many as 45 percent of hemangiomas[22] and may show evidence of osseous infiltration or localized limb overgrowth; however, cross-sectional imaging is now central to the diagnosis and evaluation of the extent of vascular malformations. In this respect, the superiority of MRI over CT and angiography is well-established.[25,26] Angiography is still used occasionally to identify feeding and draining vessels preoperatively, but it often underestimates the size of the vascular malformation and the extent of osseous involvement.[22,25,26] The introduction of MR angiography has further challenged the already diminishing role of conventional angiography.

The MR appearance of hemangiomas reflects their morphology. On T1-weighted images, cavernous hemangiomas demonstrate isointense or mildly hyperintense signal relative to muscle but remain hypointense relative to subcutaneous fat.[22,24,27] Localized areas of high signal may be identified within these lesions, representing fibrofatty septa between vessels.[27] On T2-weighted images the signal intensity is increased relative to muscle and fat as a result of the increased free water in stagnant blood in the large vessels and sinusoids. Numerous feeding and draining vessels are usually obvious as serpentine areas of high signal on T2-weighted sequences; however, differentiation of veins, arteries, and lymphatics usually is not possible. Linear areas of low signal may also be seen which correspond to the high-signal septa on T1-weighted sequences. Other diagnostic features include the identification of phleboliths, which appear round and hypointense on all sequences (Fig. 6-5).

Accentuated T2-weighted SE sequences (TE 150 msec) have been shown to be more sensitive than conventional sequences (TE 80 msec) in diagnosing hemangiomas and evaluating their extent.[24] Our initial experience using

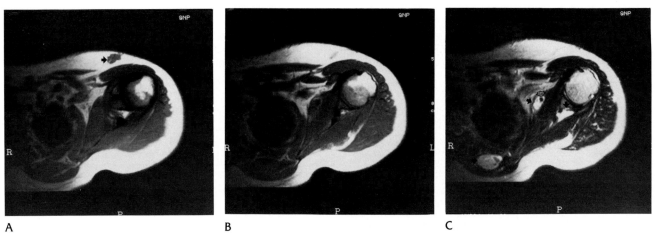

Figure 6-5 Multiple hemangiomas in a 30-year-old woman. Axial T1-weighted, **A, B,** and T2-weighted, **C,** SE images demonstrate multiple deep and superficial hemangiomas (*arrows*). Phleboliths are also identified on the T2-weighted image (*open arrow*). (Courtesy of Dr. J. Hawnaur.)

FSE imaging (TE > 100 msecs) for hemangiomas at other extremity sites supports this observation.

The ill-defined areas of fat frequently identified within hemangiomas may make them difficult to distinguish from a poorly differentiated liposarcoma. The basis for correct preoperative diagnosis of hemangioma rests on the identification of phleboliths on plain films and aberrant vessels on MRI.

DIFFUSE NEONATAL HEMANGIOMATOSIS

Hemangiomas occur in 10 percent of newborns, most often as solitary cutaneous lesions. Multiple hemangiomas limited to the skin are less common and are referred to as *benign neonatal hemangiomatosis.* These lesions usually regress spontaneously by age 2 years.[28] Diffuse neonatal hemangiomatosis refers to a condition characterized by the presence of multiple soft tissue and visceral hemangiomas. This condition, often termed the *blue rubber bleb nevus syndrome* (BRBNS) by virtue of the appearance of the cutaneous lesions, manifests progressively during childhood and affects particularly the trunk and upper extremities. Complaints referable to the skin lesions are concerned mainly with their cosmetic effect, but they can be painful and tender. The most commonly affected organs include the liver (60 to 100 percent), gastrointestinal tract (50 percent), lungs (50 percent), and central nervous system (30 to 50 percent).[29] Histologically, the extremity hemangiomas in this condition are of the cavernous type characterized by dilated, irregular vascular spaces.

MRI has proven useful for evaluating the extent of soft tissue and visceral involvement in BRBNS. Hemangiomas demonstrate MRI signal characteristics similar to those previously described for cavernous hemangiomas (Fig. 6-6).[30,31] The soft tissue contrast of MRI is superior to that of CT, and MRI should be regarded as the primary imaging modality for determining the extent of BRBNS.

PERIPHERAL NERVE NEOPLASMS

Peripheral nerve neoplasms are common, originating from the Schwann cells of the nerve sheath. There are four principal types of nerve sheath neoplasm: schwannoma (neurilemmoma), neurofibroma, plexiform neurofibroma, and malignant schwannoma.[32] These are most common in areas of neural abundance such as nerve roots and the brachial and pelvic neural plexuses. The presence of a plexiform neurofibroma or more than two neurofibromas is considered pathognomonic of von Recklinghausen's neurofibromatosis.[33]

Schwannomas are often encapsulated (more than 70 percent), and the nerve of origin is seen displaced toward the periphery of the lesion in 90 percent of cases.[16,34] In contrast, the nerve of origin of a neurofibroma is visible either in the center of the tumor or, more often, is not visible. Encapsulation is also less common in neurofibromas. The differentiation of schwannoma from neurofibroma is of surgical relevance since the former is easily shelled out while the latter often requires nerve resection with the tumor and subsequent nerve grafting. Plexiform neurofibromas are fusiform, lobulated lesions that extend along neural bundles and can compress and destroy tissue as they expand. Associated findings include adjacent bony dysplasia and overgrowth.

MRI and CT usually demonstrate well-defined tumor margins. Inhomogeneity or irregularity is less common. These features do not reliably distinguish between benign and malignant neural lesions. The signal intensity of peripheral neurofibromas and schwannomas is invariably isointense to muscle on T1-weighted sequences and

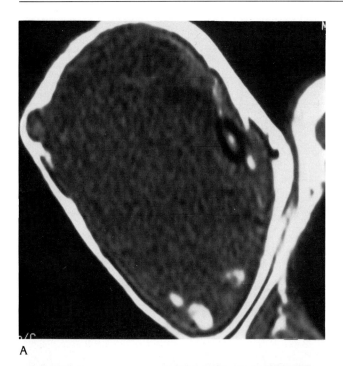

A

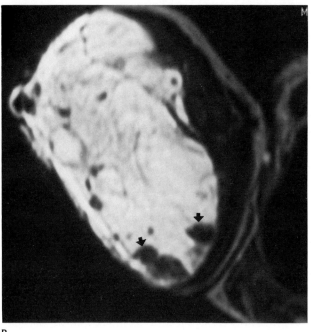

B

Figure 6-6 BRBNS in a 2-year-old girl who presented with progressive deformity of the right shoulder and arm. T1-weighted, **A,** and T2-weighted, **B,** SE images demonstrate a large septated angiomatous mass infiltrating the deltoid, biceps, and triceps muscle groups. Areas of high signal on T1-weighted images and low signal on T2-weighted images (*arrows*) are consistent with focal calcifications.

hyperintense on T2-weighted sequences.[34] The T2 relaxation times are often more characteristic of fluids, reflecting the high water content of the myxoid matrix of the neurofibroma; true cystic change is uncommon. Areas of low signal intensity, representing fibrosis, are

frequently recognized in neurofibromas (83 percent) and schwannomas (40 percent) and cannot be used for differential purposes.[34,35] Plexiform neurofibromas are more commonly homogeneous on T2-weighted sequences (Fig. 6-7). Enhancement with iodinated contrast medium in CT studies and gadolinium in MRI studies is highly variable but is most commonly homogeneous, occasionally heterogeneous, and rarely peripheral.

Malignant Liposarcoma

Liposarcoma, the most common of the soft tissue sarcomas,[36] usually occurs in adults over age 40 years. The lower limb is more commonly affected than the shoulder or arm. Lesions are slow growing and usually painless, often attaining large proportions by the time of presentation. Liposarcomas are classified into four groups by the Armed Forces Institute of Pathology (AFIP): myxoid, well-differentiated (lipoma-like), round cell, and pleomorphic.

On plain radiographs, liposarcomas appear inhomogeneous and may exhibit areas of fatlike lucency. The MRI and CT appearances frequently allow diagnosis of these lesions and can often presumptively differentiate well-differentiated liposarcoma from myxoid liposarcoma.[9,36] The most common type of liposarcoma is myxoid (prevalence 40 to 50 percent), comprising a myxoid matrix, areas of necrosis, and less than 10 percent fat, which may be either amorphous or linear.[36] In contrast, the lipoma-like liposarcoma contains predominantly adult-type fat with scattered lipoblasts.[16,36] The heterogeneous fatty characteristics and ill-defined margins demonstrated by most liposarcomas on CT and MRI allow differentiation from other soft tissue sarcomas and simple lipomas.

Myxoid liposarcomas demonstrate CT attenuation which can vary from +30 to −30 HU in contrast to the −60 to −100 HU demonstrated by lipomas and well-differentiated liposarcomas. If CT is utilized to distinguish neoplasms with a predominant myxoid component from the surrounding soft tissue, intravenous contrast enhancement is required.

Despite the accuracy of CT, MRI is now widely preferred as the method of choice for characterizing and staging liposarcomas. T1-weighted sequences are most sensitive and specific for diagnosis of liposarcoma.[36] The fatty component of the myxoid type appears as areas of linear, lacy, or amorphous high signal intensity on T1-weighted images which become "dark" on T2-weighted images, paralleling the signal intensity of the subcutaneous fat (Fig. 6-8).[36,37] The bulk of the myxoid matrix appears isointense or hyperintense relative to muscle on T1- and T2-weighted sequences, respectively. Areas of low signal on T1- and T2-weighted sequences, representing hemosiderin deposition secondary to hemor-

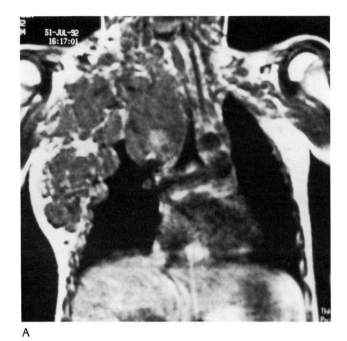

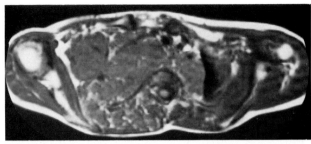

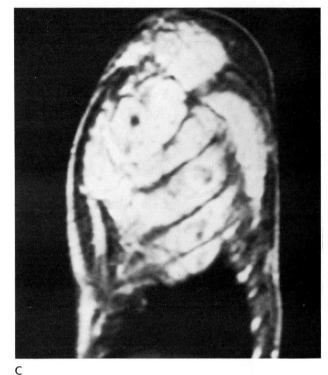

Figure 6-7 Plexiform neurofibroma in a 45-year-old man. Coronal T1-weighted, **A,** and axial proton-weighted, **B,** SE images demonstrate a lobulated tumor isointense with muscle involving the chest wall and supraclavicular fossa. **C.** Sagittal T2-weighted SE image demonstrates intense high signal within the mass.

rhage, have also been documented.[36] Despite the aggressive nature of this neoplasm, the margins are often well defined. In the absence of high-signal foci on T1-weighted images, myxoid liposarcoma is indistinguishable from other soft tissue sarcomas.

Well-differentiated liposarcomas exhibit a signal intensity similar to that of fat on T1-weighted images. They are distinguished from benign lipomas by their heterogeneity and irregularity of outline. Areas of intermediate or high signal may be seen, but they are not a prominent feature. Gadolinium-DTPA–enhanced images offer no obvious advantage over nonenhanced T2-weighted images.

The principal differential considerations raised by areas of high signal within a soft tissue lesion on T1-weighted images include hemorrhage and cavernous hemangioma. Hemorrhage demonstrates variable appearances but may "mirror" the signal intensity of fat. Fat suppression and STIR sequences can be used to nullify the high signal from fat and help differentiate from hemorrhage. Serpentine areas of high signal on T2-weighted images, representing dilated vessels, usually allow accurate diagnosis of cavernous hemangioma.

NEOPLASMS WITH NONSPECIFIC APPEARANCES

Benign Lesions

AGGRESSIVE FIBROMATOSIS

Although numerous designations (desmoid, fibromatosis, extraabdominal desmoid) have been utilized, *aggressive fibromatosis* (AF) is the term recommended by the AFIP to describe this locally invasive fibroproliferative tumor that often recurs following surgical excision but does not metastasize. The lesion is characterized by interlacing bundles of spindle cells alternating with varying

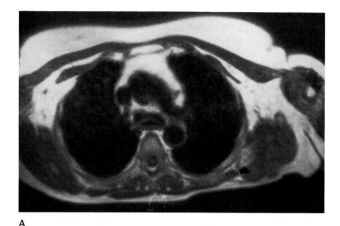

A

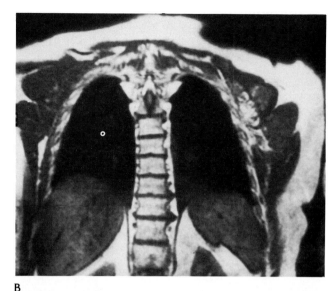

B

Figure 6-8 Myxoid liposarcoma in a 58-year-old woman involving the subscapularis muscle and scapula. **A.** Axial T1-weighted SE image demonstrates a soft tissue mass predominantly isointense to surrounding muscle with amorphous areas of high signal (*arrow*) corresponding to fat within the tumor. Coronal proton density-weighted, **B,** and T2-weighted, **C,** SE images demonstrate high signal generated by the myxoid tumor component.

C

amounts of collagen. It is less frequent in the extremities than in the thorax, abdomen, and retroperitoneum.

The MRI appearance of AF was initially suggested to be distinctive, with low signal on all sequences indicating the high collagen content. It is now recognized that most cases of AF demonstrate areas of high signal on T2-weighted sequences, depending on tumor cellularity (Fig. 6-9).[38] This may make AF indistinguishable from other benign or malignant processes. It may also be difficult to distinguish recurrent tumor from postoperative fibrous granulation. Therefore, a baseline postoperative scan is essential.

MYXOMA

A myxoma is a benign mesenchymal lesion whose cause is considered to be an altered fibroblast which produces an excess of mucopolysaccharide. Most myxomas are intramuscular, involving the thigh, shoulder, or upper arm. They are most common in the fifth through the seventh decades of life.

Myxomas typically appear well defined from surrounding muscle with MRI. They exhibit uniformly low and high signal intensities, respectively, on T1- and T2-weighted images. Contrast-enhanced images demonstrate inhomogeneous enhancement.[39]

Malignant Lesions

MALIGNANT FIBROUS HISTIOCYTOMA

Malignant fibrous histiocytoma (MFH) is the commonest type of adult soft tissue sarcoma and involves the extremities, including the shoulder, in 70 percent of cases.[40] The incidence of MFH is increased in persons who previously were treated with radiotherapy.[41,42]

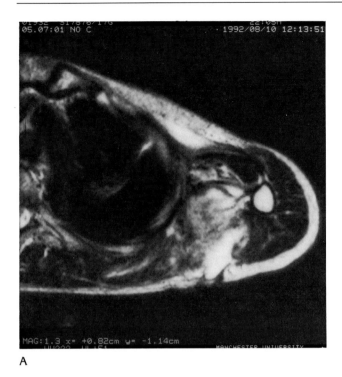

A

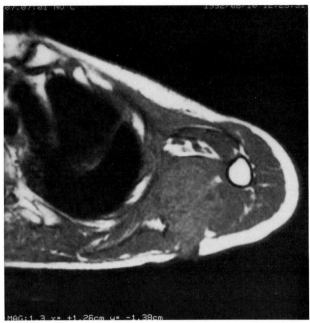

B

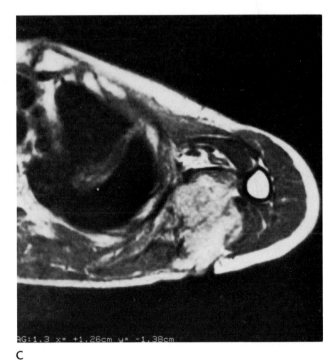

C

Figure 6-9 Recurrent aggressive fibromatosis of the right shoulder in a 22-year-old man. **A.** Axial T2-weighted image demonstrates a high signal mass infiltrating deep and superficial muscle groups. Axial unenhanced T1-weighted image, **B,** and Gd-DTPA–enhanced T1-weighted image, **C,** demonstrate uniform enhancement of the mass. (Courtesy of Dr. J. Hawnaur.)

The radiographic appearance is very variable, as MFH may be either solid or cystic with a nodular component. Histologic subtypes include pleomorphic, storiform, inflammatory, and myxoid.[43] The CT and MRI appearances reflect these different subtypes but do not accurately allow them to be distinguished from one another or from other malignant neoplasms. MFH usually appears isointense to muscle on T1-weighted sequences and hyperintense on T2-weighted images. The margin is often well defined (Fig. 6-10). Additional features include punctate calcifications, which are far less common than in synovial sarcoma and are better demonstrated by plain radiography and CT than by MRI. Bone involvement, also better demonstrated by plain radiographs and CT, is found in association with 25 percent of MFH. Of these, 75 percent represent localized infiltration by an MFH arising in the soft tissues, and the remainder are considered to have arisen primarily from bone.[44]

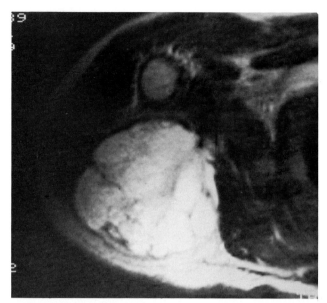

Figure 6-10 Malignant fibrous histiocytoma in a 51-year-old man arising within the posterior aspect of the deltoid. Axial T2-weighted SE image demonstrates a well-defined high-signal mass with internal septation.

SYNOVIAL SARCOMA

Synovial sarcomas account for approximately 10 percent of all soft tissue sarcomas and usually occur before age 40 years.[45] They arise from undifferentiated mesenchymal cells in relation to tendons and their sheaths, but despite their name they do not usually arise within joints or bursae. Growth is usually slow, with the mass developing over several years before pain or its size prompts the patient to seek medical attention. Histologically, synovial sarcomas are divided into monophasic and biphasic types, the latter being more aggressive and prone to metastasize.

Amorphous or punctate calcification is visible radiographically in 30 percent of synovial sarcomas[45] but is commonly overlooked with MRI.[46] The MRI appearance most indicative of a synovial sarcoma is an inhomogenous septate mass with infiltrative margins located close to a joint, a tendon, or a bursa, especially if calcifications are seen by CT or plain radiography. Synovial sarcomas have occasionally been mistaken for benign lesions when they appeared small, well marginated, and cystic.[3] Fluid-fluid levels within synovial sarcomas have also been reported. This reflects the propensity of these lesions to undergo necrotic liquefaction and hemorrhage with subsequent sedimentation of blood products, yielding "fluids" of different signal intensities.[47] The appearance may be similar to that of a soft tissue hemangioma.[47] MRI demonstrates no difference in signal characteristics between the biphasic and monophasic types. Additional features include lymph node involvement in 12 to 23 percent of patients, bone involvement in 10 to 20 percent, and lung metastases in 74 to 81 percent.[45,48]

OTHER MALIGNANT NEOPLASMS

Less common neoplasms that may present as a shoulder mass include rhabdomyosarcoma, lymphoma, fibrosarcoma, Kaposi's sarcoma, and metastases. Imaging characteristics are variable and nonspecific, but the presence of infiltration of surrounding soft tissue structures strongly suggests malignancy.

GADOLINIUM ENHANCEMENT

The precise role of intravenous paramagnetic agents such as Gd-DTPA in the evaluation of musculoskeletal neoplasms is currently under investigation. Since the musculoskeletal system has no barrier to extracellular distribution of Gd-DTPA, this compound is distributed relative to regional blood flow after intravenous injection. Increased vascularity due to either neoplasia or inflammation will cause localized accumulation of the contrast agent within a few minutes of injection. Clearance is also less rapid than in surrounding normal tissues. This provides sufficient contrast enhancement to be detected on T1-weighted images. Limited contrast between fat and enhancing neoplastic tissue on conventional T1-weighted images can be circumvented by the use of fat suppression techniques, including chemical shift selective saturation, STIR sequences, and phase cycling (Dixon technique). Although the contrast-to-noise ratio between neoplastic tissue and muscle is increased on T1-weighted images following gadolinium enhancement, it has been shown to remain 44 percent lower than that achieved on comparable T2-weighted images.[49]

Important parameters to be determined include differentiation of neoplastic tissue from surrounding edema, differentiation of viable from nonviable tissue, and differentiation of benign neoplasms from malignant ones. The high-signal halo that often surrounds malignant neoplasms on T2-weighted images can represent either neoplastic infiltration or reactive edema. With gadolinium, T1-weighted images demonstrate strong enhancement of viable neoplastic tissue relative to edema.[50] Viable neoplastic tissue also demonstrates more rapid enhancement than edema on dynamic enhanced studies.[51] Distinguishing between viable and nonviable tissue can be impossible using T2-weighted sequences, since both demonstrate high signal. With gadolinium, however, T1-weighted images clearly define the enhancing viable neoplastic tissue (see Fig. 6-9). Unfortunately, differentiation of benign from malignant lesions using enhancement characteristics has not proven clinically useful, since both can demonstrate variable patterns and rates of enhancement.[51]

POSTTREATMENT EVALUATION

The presence of residual or recurrent tumor following chemotherapy, radiotherapy, or surgery is often difficult to determine. In the early postoperative period (the first 3 months), inflammatory change and resolving hematoma are often indistinguishable from tumor. MRI has improved posttreatment evaluation, particularly after these early changes have subsided.

Residual or recurrent tumor exhibits higher signal intensity on T2-weighted images than scar tissue, which appears isointense or hypointense to muscle on T1- and T2-weighted sequences. One study has demonstrated with 96 percent sensitivity that low signal on T2-weighted sequences, indicates absence of active neoplasm in patients treated with surgery, radiotherapy, and/or chemotherapy.[50] High–signal intensity lesions demonstrated 70 percent sensitivity for active neoplasm. This increased to 100 percent if patients treated with radiotherapy were excluded, since radiation-induced reactive lesions simulate neoplasm on T1- and T2-weighted sequences. Conventional T1- and T2-weighted sequences are usually adequate for follow-up, but standardization of the imaging parameters on sequential examinations is essential to allow valid comparison of serial images.

T2-weighted SE images and intravenous Gd-DTPA–enhanced T1-weighted images correlate closely in the identification of neoplastic tissue. A potential role for Gd-DTPA, however, is suggested by its ability through dynamic studies to identify good responders to treatment by quantifying the reduction of signal increase relative to previous examinations.[50] Poor responders to chemotherapy reveal no reduction or only a minor one. Further research in this area is under way to determine its clinical application.

SPECTROSCOPY

Spectroscopy has not yet achieved widespread clinical use, but recent studies of a variety of neoplasms have shown increased levels of phosphomonoesters, phosphodiesters, and inorganic phosphates and a decrease in phosphocreatine.[52] The increased phosphomonoester peak indicates increased glycolysis and has been demonstrated to regress during chemotherapy and return in patients with recurrent disease.[53] Results indicate a role for spectroscopy in following the response of neoplasms to therapy.

CONCLUSION

Although imaging characteristics may offer specificity and accuracy of diagnosis in close to 90 percent of some benign and malignant lesions, this is insufficient to avoid biopsy in all but the most characteristic of benign lesions, since delay in diagnosis and institution of appropriate treatment can detrimentally affect prognosis. Nevertheless, MRI is an invaluable asset in the staging of soft tissue neoplasms and in posttreatment evaluation.

References

1. ROSENBERG SA, SUIT F, BAKER L: Sarcomas of soft tissue, in De Vita VT, Hellman S, Rosenberg SA (eds): *Cancer. Principles and Practice of Oncology*, 2d ed, Philadelphia, Lippincott, 1985, pp 1243–1293.
2. SUNDARAM M, MCGUIRE MH, HERBOLD DR: Magnetic resonance imaging of soft tissue masses: An evaluation of fifty-three histology-proven tumors. *Magn Reson Imaging* 6:237–248, 1982.
3. BERQUIST TH, EHMAN RL, KING BF, HODGMAN CG, ILSTRUP DM: Value of MR imaging in differentiating benign from malignant soft-tissue masses: Study of 95 lesions. *AJR* 155:109–113, 1990.
4. FIROOZNIA H, GOLIMBU CN, RAFII M, RAUSCHNING W, WEINREB J: *MR and CT of the Musculoskeletal System*, St Louis, Mosby–Year Book, 1992.
5. BELTRAN J, SIMON DC, KATZ W, WEIS LD: Increased MR signal intensity in skeletal muscle adjacent to malignant tumors: Pathologic correlation and clinical relevance. *Radiology* 162:251–255, 1987.
6. BLAND K, MCCOY DM, KINARD RE, COPELAND EM III:

Applications of magnetic resonance imaging and computed tomography as an adjunct to surgical management of soft tissue sarcomas. *Ann Surg* 205:473–481, 1987.

7. BERQUIST TH: Magnetic resonance imaging of musculoskeletal neoplasms. *Clin Orthop* 244:101–118, 1989.

8. MOSKOVIC E, SERPELL JW, PARSONS C, FISHER C, THOMAS JR: Benign mimics of soft tissue sarcomas. *Clin Radiol* 40:248–252, 1992.

9. DOOMS GC, HRICAK H, SOLLITTO RA, HIGGINS CB: Lipomatous tumors and tumors with fatty component: MR imaging potential and comparison of MR and CT results. *Radiology* 157:479–483, 1985.

10. MINK JH, DEUTSCH AL: *MRI of the Musculoskeletal System: A Teaching File*, New York, Raven, 1990, pp 451–453.

11. WALIGORE MP, STEPHENS DH, SOULE EH: Lipomatous tumors of the abdominal cavity: CT appearances and pathological correlation. *AJR* 137:539–545, 1981.

12. HALLDORSDOTTIR A, EKELUND L, RYDHOLM A: CT diagnosis of lipomatous tumors of soft tissues. *Arch Orthop Trauma Surg* 100:211–216, 1982.

13. ROSEN BR, CARTER EA, PYKETT IL: Proton chemical shift imaging, an evaluation of its clinical potential using an in vivo fatty liver model. *Radiology* 185:469–472, 1985.

14. KINGBLOM LG, ANGERVALL L, STENER B: Intermuscular and intramuscular lipomas and hibernomas: A clinical, roentgenologic, histologic, and prognostic study of 46 cases. *Cancer* 33:754–762, 1974.

15. BJERREGAARD P, HAGEN K, DAUGAARD S, KOFOED H: Intramuscular lipoma of the lower limb: Long-term follow-up after local resection. *J Bone Joint Surg* 71B:812–815, 1989.

16. ENZINGER FM, WEISS SW: *Soft Tissue Tumors*, 2d ed, St Louis, Mosby, 1983.

17. RYDHOLM A, AKERMAN H, IDVALL I, PERSSON BM: Aspiration cytology of soft tissue tumors: A prospective study of its influence on choice of surgical procedure. *Int Orthop* 6:209–214, 1982.

18. ALBA GM, GARCIA RL, VULETIN JC: Benign lipoblastomatosis. Ultrastructure and histogenesis. *Cancer* 45:511–515, 1980.

19. CHUNG EB, ENZINGER FM: Benign lipoblastomatosis: An analysis of 35 cases. *Cancer* 32:482–492, 1973.

20. CRUES JV: *MRI of the Musculoskeletal System*, New York, Raven, 1991, pp 212–213.

21. RESNICK D, NIWAYAMA G: *Diagnosis of Bone and Joint Disorders*, 2d ed, Philadelphia, Saunders, 1987.

22. BUETOW PC, KRANSDORF MJ, MOSER RP, JELINEK JS, BERREY BH: Radiologic appearance of intramuscular hemangioma with emphasis on MR imaging. *AJR* 154:563–567, 1990.

23. ALLEN PB, ENZINGER FM: Hemangioma of skeletal muscle: Analysis of 89 cases. *Cancer* 29:8–22, 1972.

24. NELSON MC, STULL MA, TEITELBAUM P, PATT RH, LACK EE, BOGUMILL GP, FREEDMAN MT: Magnetic resonance imaging of peripheral soft tissue hemangiomas. *Skel Radiol* 19:477–482, 1990.

25. BURROW PE, MULLIKEN JB, FELLOWS KE, STAND RD: Childhood hemangiomas and vascular malformations: Angiographic differentiation. *AJR* 141:483–488, 1983.

26. RAUCH RF, SILVERMAN PM, KOROBKIN M, DUNNICK NR,

MOORE AV, WESTMAN D, MARTINEZ S: CT of benign angiomatous lesions of the extremities. *J Comput Assist Tomogr* 8:1143–1146, 1984.

27. LEVINE E, WETZEL L, NEFF J: MR imaging and CT of extrahepatic cavernous hemangiomas. *AJR* 147:1299–1304, 1986.

28. MESSARITARKIS J, ANAGNOSTAKIS D: Benign neonatal hemangiomatosis. *Am J Dis Child* 140:447–448, 1986.

29. HOLDEN KR, ALEXANDER F: Diffuse neonatal hemangiomatosis. *Pediatrics* 46:411–421, 1970.

30. BREE R, SCHWAB R, GLAZR G, FINK-BENNETT D: The varied appearance of hepatic cavernous hemangiomas with sonography, computed tomography, magnetic resonance imaging and scintigraphy. *RadioGraphics* 7:1153–1175, 1987.

31. MONTGOMERY SP, GUILLOT AP, BARTH RA: MRI of disseminated neonatal hemangiomatosis: Case report. *Pediatr Radiol* 20:204–205, 1990.

32. HARKIN JC: Pathology of nerve sheath tumors. *Ann NY Acad Sci* 486:147–154, 1986.

33. NATIONAL INSTITUTES OF HEALTH CONSENSUS DEVELOPMENT CONFERENCE: Neurofibromatosis. *Arch Neurol* 45:575–578, 1987.

34. CEROFOLINI E, LANDI A, DESANTIS G, MAIORANA A, CANOSSI G, ROMAGNOLI R: MR of benign peripheral nerve sheath tumors. *J Comput Assist Tomogr* 15:593–597, 1991.

35. BURK DL, BRUNBERG JA, KANAL E, LATCHAW RE, WOLF GL: Spinal and paraspinal neurofibromatosis. Surface coil MR imaging at 1.5 T. *Radiology* 162:797–801, 1987.

36. SUNDARAM M, BARAN G, MERENDA G, MCDONALD D: Myxoid liposarcoma: Magnetic resonance appearances with clinical and histological correlation. *Skel Radiol* 19:359–362, 1990.

37. LONDON J, KIM EE, WALLACE S, SHIRKHODA A, COAN J, EVAN J: MR imaging of liposarcoma: Correlation of MR features and histology. *J Comput Assist Tomogr* 143:832–835, 1989.

38. FELD R, BURK DL, MCCUE P, MITCHELL DG, LACKMAN R, RIFKIN MD: MRI of aggressive fibromatosis: Frequent appearance of high signal intensity on T2-weighted images. *Magn Reson Imaging* 8:583–588, 1990.

39. PETERSON KK, RENFREW DL, FEDDERSON RM, BUCKWALTER JA, EL-KHOURY GY: Magnetic resonance imaging of myxoid containing tumors. *Skel Radiol* 20:245–250, 1991.

40. WEISS SW, ENZINGER FM: Malignant fibrous histiocytoma. Analysis of 200 cases. *Cancer* 41:2250–2266, 1978.

41. KEPES JJ, KEPES M, SLOWIK F: Fibrous xanthomas and xanthosarcomas of the meninges and the brain. *Acta Neuropathol* 23:187–199, 1973.

42. AMENDOLA BE, AMENDOLA MA, MCCLATCHEY KD: Radiation induced malignant fibrous histiocytoma: A report of five cases including two occurring post-whole brain irradiation. *Cancer Invest* 3:507–513, 1985.

43. KATENKAMP D: Das maligne fibrose Histiozytom des Weichgewebes. *Dtsch Gesundheitswies* 38:1633–1640, 1983.

44. FELDMAN F, NEWMAN D: Intra- and extraosseous malignant fibrous histiocytoma (malignant fibrous xanthoma). *Radiology* 104:497–508, 1972.

45. CADMAN NL, SOULE EH, KELLY PJ: Synovial sarcoma: An analysis of 134 tumors. *Cancer* 18:613–627, 1965.

46. MORTON MJ, BERQUIST TH, MCLEOD RA, UNNI KK, SIM

FH: MR imaging of synovial sarcoma. *AJR* 156:337–340, 1990.

47. TSAI JC, DALINKA MK, FALLON MD, ZLATKIN MB, KRESSEL HY: Fluid-fluid level: A non-specific finding in tumors of bone and soft tissue. *Radiology* 175:779–782, 1990.

48. HAJDU SI, SHIU MH, FORTNER JG: Tendosynovial sarcoma: A clinicopathological study of 136 cases. *Cancer* 39:1201–1217, 1977.

49. ERLEMAN R, REISER MF, PETERS PE: Musculoskeletal neoplasms: Static and dynamic Gd-DTPA–enhanced MR imaging. *Radiology* 170:767–773, 1989.

50. VANEL D, LACOMBE MJ, COUANET D, KALIFA C, SPIELMAN M, GENIN J: Musculoskeletal tumors: Follow-up with MR imaging after treatment with surgery and radiation therapy. *Radiology* 164:243–245, 1987.

51. BLOEM JL, MAXIMILIAN FR, VANEL D: Magnetic resonance contrast agents in the evaluation of the musculoskeletal system. *Magn Reson Q* 6:136–163, 1990.

52. ZLATKIN MB, LENKINSKI RE, SHINKWIN M, SCHMIDT RG, DALY JM, HOLLAND GA, FRANK T, KRESSEL HY: Combined MR imaging and spectroscopy of bone and soft tissue tumors. *J Comput Assist Tomogr* 14:1–10, 1990.

53. ROSS B, HELSPER JT, COX IJ, YOUNG IR, KEMPF R, MAKEPEACE A, PENNOCK J: Osteosarcoma and other neoplasms of bone. Magnetic spectroscopy to monitor therapy. *Arch Surg* 122:1464–1469, 1987.

7 IMAGING OF BONE MARROW DISORDERS IN THE SHOULDER

Joseph S. Yu
Bor-Yau Yang
David J. Sartoris

The bone marrow is one of the largest organs in the body. By weight, it is exceeded only by bone, muscle, and fat, and approaches nearly 3000 gm in the adult male and 2600 gm in the adult female.[1] It is one of the primary organs of hematopoiesis and functions as a reservoir of stem cells, providing a stable environment for the orderly proliferation and differentiation of precursor cells and for their release into the vascular system as fully differentiated cells. In the human adult, all of the erythrocytes, granulocytes, and platelets circulating in the peripheral blood are produced in the bone marrow. Historically, patients required an invasive procedure for evaluation of marrow abnormalities because imaging methods lacked either the ability to directly visualize the marrow space or the necessary resolution to assess its contents. With the advent of magnetic resonance imaging (MRI), sufficient information about marrow content and its relative cellular composition can now be obtained noninvasively.

In this chapter, the normal development and physiology of the bone marrow are discussed with the characteristic age-related imaging findings, emphasizing MRI. In the latter portion of the chapter we discuss pathologic processes that involve the bone marrow and their associated imaging findings.

NORMAL BONE MARROW

Physiology and Microanatomy

In utero, hematopoietic tissue initially is contained in the yolk sac, functioning as the main source of hematopoiesis until the 6th gestational week.[2] From approximately the 4th week of gestation, the liver and spleen begin to assume this role and continue this function to about the 21st week. Subsequently, as liver hematopoiesis declines, the bone marrow overtakes the liver as the major and definitive organ of blood cell synthesis.[3] Marrow hematopoiesis is related to the onset of bone ossification. Blood vessels and nerves penetrate the ossifying mem-

brane simultaneously with mesenchymal cells, and as the bone cavities enlarge, the venous sinusoids and nutrient vessels sprout along the marrow cylinder. Between the vessels and the newly formed bone trabeculae a network of fine reticulin fibers containing reticulum cells is deposited.[3] At the end of the second trimester, the concentration of hematopoietic cells in the bone marrow reaches its peak, henceforth rendering the bone marrow the primary source of blood cells throughout life.[4]

The nutrient arteries are the major blood supply of the bone marrow. Having entered the bone via the nutrient foramen, an artery penetrates the center of the marrow and divides into an ascending and a descending branch,[5] which run parallel to the long axis of the bone. The sinusoidal system is composed of vascular spaces which are supplied by perforating vessels in the osteal canals,[6] from which the capillary network sends the small transosteal branches. The sinusoids form an extensive and abundantly anastomosing network of thin-walled vascular channels.[5] The sinusoids then drain into the central venous sinus of the medullary canal, which exits through the nutrient foramen.[1]

The bone marrow is innervated by the periosteal nerve, which branches to form a network over the surface of the bone. The medullary branch of the nerve enters through the nutrient foramen and arborizes in a pattern similar to that of the nutrient artery.[5] The nerve supply is composed of sympathetic and afferent nerve fibers, which may influence the release of marrow cells.[1,7]

The three major marrow constituents consist of the osseous matrix, hematopoietic marrow, and fatty marrow. The osseous component of the marrow, cancellous bone,[1] is composed of primary and secondary trabeculae. This trabecular framework provides the architectural support to the medullary space and contains a rich supply of minerals, including calcium and phosphorus.

Hematopoietic, or red, marrow is actively involved in the production of red cells, white cells, and platelets from pluripotent progenitor cells. Other functions of the hematopoietic marrow are destruction of erythrocytes with subsequent storage of iron and production of undifferentiated lymphocytes.[8] Yellow marrow is composed mainly of fat cells and is considered hematopoietically inactive.

The adipose cells in yellow marrow account for roughly 50 percent of the total bone marrow weight.[9] Because half of red marrow is also composed of adipose cells, approximately 75 percent of the adult bone marrow consists of fat cells.[1,10] Morphologically, the marrow fat cell is identical to those of extramedullary sites except for being smaller.[5] The origin of the marrow fat cell is believed to be the adventitial cell of the sinusoidal wall.[11] Although the physiologic role of fat cells has not been clearly defined, their primary function appears to be that of passive space fillers,[5] though there is some evidence that they may participate actively in hematopoiesis by providing nutritional support, and perhaps growth factors.[12] The volume and number of adipose tissue is influenced by the hematopoietic demand for peripheral blood cells. When the bone marrow is not producing hematopoietic cells, there is a relative increase in the volume and number of adipose cells, but in times of increased cell production the adipose cells atrophy.[2]

The chemical composition of the two types of marrow differ: red marrow is composed of 40 percent water, 40 percent fat, and 20 percent protein, whereas yellow marrow is composed of 15 percent water, 80 percent fat, and 5 percent protein.[9] Structurally, red and yellow marrow also differ in their vascular supply. The vast sinusoidal system in the hematopoietic marrow is replaced in the fatty marrow with capillaries, venules, and thin-walled veins, reflecting a relative decrease in overall vascularity.[1]

The reticulin fibers form the structural scaffold that supports the sinusoids and the hematopoietic elements. The reticular cells are intimately associated with these fibers. Two types of reticular cells have been identified, the phagocytic cell and the undifferentiated nonphagocytic cell,[13] and though these cells are present in regions of hematopoietic activity, their role remains unclear.[1]

Marrow Conversion

The proportion of osseous tissue to total bone volume is relatively constant from childhood to about the 6th decade of life, when the effects of osteoporosis become more evident.[14–16] In the bone marrow, however, there is a steady and progressive conversion of the cellular constituents to fat, so that the proportion of fatty marrow increases incrementally with age.

In utero, the fetal marrow is completely dedicated to hematopoiesis. In theory, this may be related to the higher body temperature of the fetus in utero.[17] With birth, marrow conversion begins and becomes evident first in the terminal phalanges of the hands and feet.[18]

In the skeleton, the process of conversion occurs in a predictable and orderly sequence: peripheral bones undergo this change before the axial skeleton does and generally conversion is earlier at the more distal bones.[2,19–21] In the long bones, conversion initially occurs in the diaphysis and with maturation progresses to the metaphysis.[19–21] At birth, the cartilaginous epiphyses contain no marrow, but they will when they become ossified.[19] The epiphyseal and apophyseal marrow usually undergoes conversion very early and is composed of fatty marrow throughout a person's life. Occasionally, hematopoietic marrow is seen in a normal infant. By age 1 year, conversion is complete in the phalanges of the hands and feet, and by age 7 years, fat is macroscopically evident in the distal epiphyses of the peripheral long bones such as the tibia, fibula, radius, and ulna.[22] At puberty, the epiphyses of all of the distal long bones contain significantly more fat than do the femora or humeri.[19]

By the 3rd decade of life, a typical adult pattern is achieved and hematopoietic marrow is distributed in the vertebrae, sternum, ribs, pelvis, skull, and proximal metadiaphysis of the femora and humeri.[22,23] Conversion is usually symmetric; however, this process can also occur heterogeneously so that it is not uncommon to have focal islands of hematopoietic marrow in the fatty marrow. In addition, residual foci of red marrow may persist in some people—as a physiologic response to menstruation, cigarette smoking, or obesity, and in marathon runners.[24] As aging continues, a dynamic balance is achieved between red and yellow marrow, with slower and more gradual conversion toward fatty marrow. As one becomes older, the effect of trabecular bone loss in association with osteoporosis increases the demand for additional volume of fatty marrow to replace the lost bone mass.[14] In some elderly persons, the bone marrow may appear entirely fatty, although microscopic rests of hematopoietic marrow may be present.[25,26] Accounting for the relative increase in bone loss seen in elderly females, marrow conversion appears to occur equally in both men and women.[27]

Reconversion of inactive yellow marrow to active red marrows occurs rapidly when, owing to an increased requirement of peripheral red blood cells, the hematopoietic system is stressed, or when it is replaced.[25,28–30] Pathologic disorders associated with increased demand for hematopoiesis include those due to ineffective synthesis, increased erythrocyte destruction, or failure of oxygenation of normal blood. Reconversion occurs in a sequence the reverse of initial marrow conversion. Therefore, the changes occur initially in the axial skeleton and proceed peripherally, and they occur in the metaphyses before involving the diaphyses of a long bone.[2,19] The early physiologic alteration that heralds reconversion in the bone marrow takes place subendos-

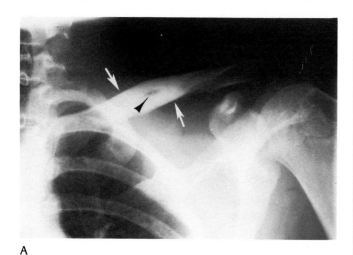

A

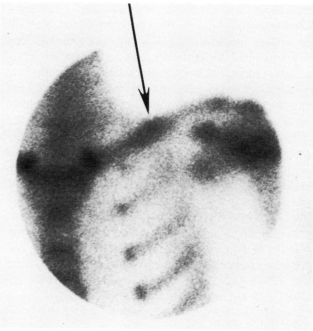

B

Figure 7-1 Plasma cell osteomyelitis of the clavicle in 16-year-old boy. **A.** Radiography shows osteosclerosis (*white arrows*) with a central osteolytic focus (*black arrowhead*) in the middle third of the clavicle; bony expansion is noted. **B.** Bone scan shows increased uptake at the site of involvement (*arrow*).

teally with hyperemia, capillary proliferation, and sinusoid formation.[1,30]

The factors that initiate reconversion are not entirely known. Several stimuli have been implicated, among them changes in temperature, low oxygen tension, and elevated erythropoietin level.[17,22,31,32] The degree of reconversion is determined by the severity and duration of the inciting stimulus; however, when the stimulus is severe, areas that normally contain fatty marrow throughout life, such as the epiphysis, may undergo cellular conversion.[33]

IMAGING

Conventional Radiography

For initial assessment of the bone marrow conventional radiographs routinely are obtained. The plain radiograph is an adequate method for evaluating the integrity of the osseous structures and a screening tool for detection of processes that may originate in the bone marrow but extend to the endosteum, cause a periosteal reaction, or cause the bone to fracture. Marrow abnormalities that remain contained in the medullary cavity and cause minimal trabecular changes often go undetected because considerable bone loss is necessary before it becomes radiographically evident.[1] Prior investigations indicate that at least 50 percent of trabecular bone must be absent or destroyed before the loss is discernible by conventional radiography.[34,35] Another limitation to the plain radiograph is that it is difficult to elicit from it physiologic

information because the cellular composition of the marrow cannot be ascertained. As a screening method, it is useful for assessing the bony architecture.

Scintigraphy

Scintigraphy of the bone and bone marrow can be achieved with several different techniques. Nevertheless, scintigraphy allows for the assessment of physiologic function of the marrow that is not possible with the plain radiograph. Skeletal or bone scintigraphy utilizes technetium-labeled bone-seeking pharmaceuticals, which commonly are analogues of calcium, hydroxyl groups, or phosphates. The most commonly utilized radiopharmaceuticals for skeletal imaging are technetium-labeled phosphate analogues.[36] Increased activity in the bone may be related to increased vascularity or alterations in the bone metabolism in response to osteoclastic, osteoblastic, or neoplastic cellular activity (Fig. 7-1). It also is determined in part by the baseline quantity of mineralization. Bone scans, therefore, reflect processes that are occurring in the bone marrow; that is, the marrow is indirectly evaluated by the overall assessment of the entire skeleton. A major limiting factor is that certain neoplasms may not be detected by bone scintigraphy, even if there is significant involvement of the bone marrow. Such neoplastic processes include highly anaplastic tumors, reticulum cell sarcomas, renal cell carcinoma, thyroid carcinoma, histiocytosis, neuroblastoma, and multiple myeloma.[36]

Bone marrow scans, in contradistinction to bone scans, evaluate activity in the marrow space and therefore directly assess changes due to processes that alter marrow distribution, replace or displace marrow, or affect its physiologic function. Two techniques are available. One technique assesses hematopoiesis and the other evaluates the function of the reticuloendothelial system.

Radionuclide-labeled iron and analogues that bind transferrin target the erythroid precursors, allowing functional imaging of the cells that are involved in the hematopoietic process. In the evaluation of the reticuloendothelial system, technetium-labeled sulfur colloid particles introduced into the bloodstream are phagocytosed by reticulum cells that line the bone marrow sinusoids; this phenomenon affords imaging of the reticuloendothelial element of the marrow.

In general, the erythroid and reticuloendothelial components of the bone marrow have similar imaging patterns by scintigraphy in circumstances that are normal and pathologic, but there are conditions in which imaging with sulfur colloid and radiolabeled iron yield disparate distributions. This is most notable in processes that result in ineffective hematopoiesis thus resulting in expansion of the granulocytic marrow elements.[37] Examples of such processes include red blood cell aplasia, hematologic malignancies, aplastic anemia, and advanced myeloid metaplasia with myelofibrosis.[37]

The distinct advantage of scintigraphy over conventional radiography is the capability to assess the physiologic function of the marrow (i.e., hemodynamics, cellular function, and active marrow distribution). The acute sensitivity to marrow disorders and reactive osseous changes indicates that this imaging method has an important role in the screening evaluation of marrow dysfunction. The major limitations obviously include limited spatial resolution (so that small structures in close proximity cannot be differentiated), systemic exposure to radiation, and lack of specificity.[1]

Computed Tomography

Computed tomography (CT) has a restricted role in the assessment of bone marrow disorders. Certain advantages over conventional radiography and scintigraphy are evident. The capability of visualizing exquisite anatomic detail is an obvious advantage of CT, and the cross-sectional acquisition of images eliminates confusion that is often created by the superimposition of structures. Spatial resolution is unparalleled, and contrast between bone, fat, and soft tissues is excellent. Contrast resolution between soft tissues has been a limiting factor for CT, and although Hounsfield values can be advantageous in distinguishing between fat and other soft tissues, differences in CT attenuation between normal and abnormal marrow may be difficult to detect.[37a]

The image obtained with CT is determined by the degree of x-ray beam attenuation by the various tissues of bone. Because the distribution of hematopoietic marrow and fatty marrow is location dependent, different regions in a bone may have different appearances.[1] The contribution of trabecular bone to the attenuation value should be considered when comparing different areas in the bone as well, since the significance of its contribution is more evident toward the metaphyseal and epiphyseal areas.

The large volume of adipose cells in the adult marrow results in a negative Hounsfield value, with typical values of −100 HU.[38] A positive Hounsfield value in the diaphysis of a long bone should be suspected to represent tumor infiltration, marrow replacement, or marrow reconversion (Fig. 7-2).[39] When measuring the attenuation values of bone marrow, asymmetry with regard to the contralateral side is often diagnostic of disease, and, generally, a discrepancy of 20 HU is considered abnormal.[1] In the metaphyseal and epiphyseal regions, attenuation values are generally positive, sometimes approaching 100 HU, reflecting an increase in the proportion of hematopoietic marrow and trabecular density.

Although spatial resolution and contrast between bone, fat, and soft tissues are excellent with CT, it has not become a preferred method for evaluating the bone marrow because contrast differences between normal and abnormal marrow in the medullary cavity have been insufficient for optimal assessment of marrow disorders. Beam hardening also limits the utility of CT, as the area of interest may be obscured by artifacts (Fig. 7-3).[38]

Magnetic Resonance Imaging

MRI has emerged as the preferred imaging method for evaluation of bone marrow processes. It is superior to other techniques because of its ability to clearly separate fat from other tissues (see Figs. 7-4, 7-5) and allows direct visualization of the bone marrow.[2]

Each marrow constituent (osseous matrix, hematopoietic marrow, fatty marrow) contributes signal intensities to the formation of the MR image. Virtually no signal is exhibited by trabecular and cortical bone, owing to a lack of mobile protons.[1,40,41] In addition, local field gradients are produced owing to heterogeneous magnetic susceptibility at fat-water interfaces which alter the signal character at these areas.[42]

The MRI appearance of bone marrow depends on what pulse sequence is selected. Fatty marrow appears bright in signal intensity on T1-weighted spin-echo images, reflecting the short T1 relaxation time of fat owing to hydrophobic side groups that make up the bulk of fat protons.[43] Because hematopoietic marrow contains a larger volume of water (40 percent) and smaller volume of fat (40 percent) than the fatty marrow (15 percent water, 80 percent fat), the signal intensity reflects the longer T1 and T2 relaxation time of water. The role of

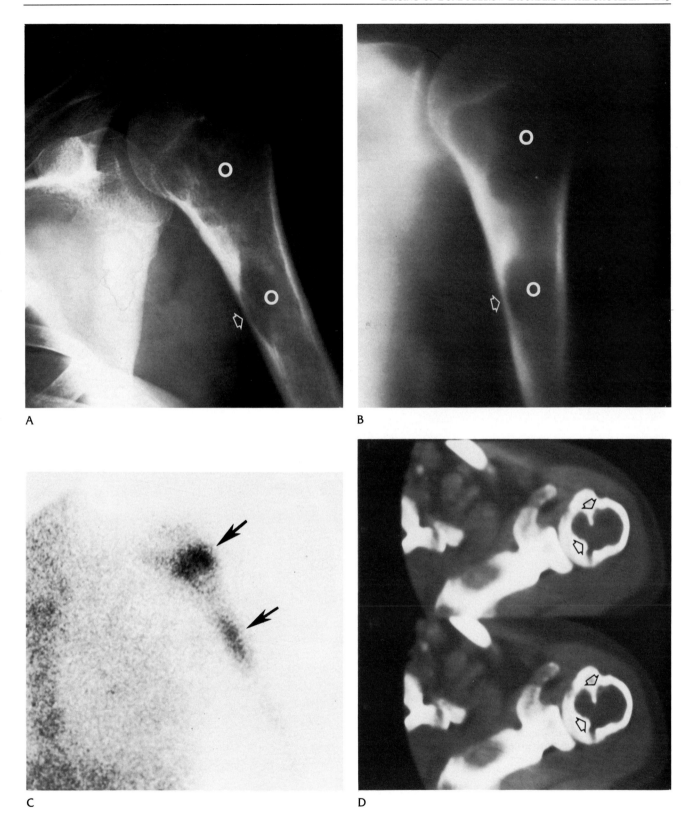

Figure 7-2 Staphylococcal osteomyelitis of the proximal humerus in a 26-year-old woman. Radiography, **A,** and conventional tomography, **B,** show an osteolytic process (O) involving the proximal humerus, with scalloping of the endosteal surface (*arrow*). **C.** Bone scan shows increased uptake at involved sites (*arrows*). **D.** CT of the proximal humerus shows endosteal scalloping and increased attenuation of the marrow from replacement by infection (*arrows*).

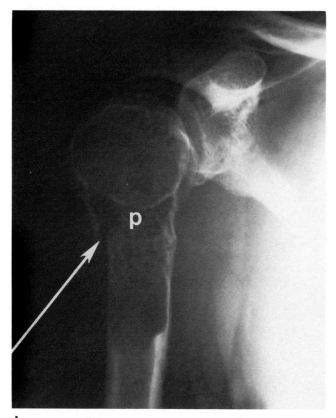

A

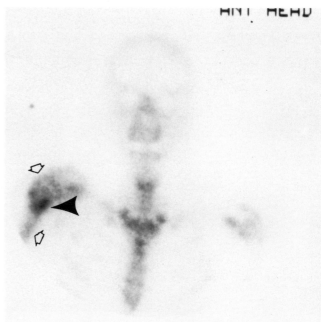

B

Figure 7-3 Plasmacytoma of the shoulder girdle in a 40-year-old man. **A.** Radiography shows an expansile osteolytic lesion (p) in the proximal humerus with pathologic fracture (*arrow*). **B.** Bone scan shows increased uptake in the lesion (*white arrows*), particularly at the site of pathologic fracture (*arrowhead*). **C.** CT shows the humeral lesion (p) to better advantage, along with a scapular lesion (*arrow*) which was radiographically and scintigraphically occult.

C

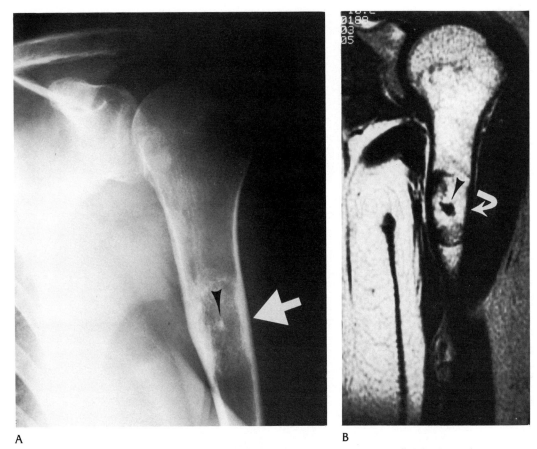

A   B

Figure 7-4 Intraosseous lipoma in a 48-year-old woman. **A.** Radiography shows a well-defined mixed sclerotic and lytic lesion (*white arrow*) in the proximal humerus. Central calcification (*black arrowhead*) is also noted. **B.** Coronal MR (TR 500 msec/TE 25 msec) image shows high-intensity lesion (*white arrow*) in the proximal humerus, with dark peripheral margin and central calcification (*black arrowhead*).

marrow protein in MRI is unclear since it can exist in either a bound state, with longer T1 relaxation time, or in solution, with relatively shortened T1 relaxation time.[41,44]

Low–signal intensity marrow on T1-weighted images is a normal finding in children and in the axial hematopoietic marrow of young adults.[1,2,21,27,44,45] Both the T1 and T2 relaxation times of marrow decrease with normal aging, but the decrease in the T1 relaxation time is proportionately greater.[14,27,46] The largest decrease in T1 relaxation time takes place during the second decade of life. Some investigators have suggested using T1-T2 ratios to characterize marrow disorders to correct for this normal effect of aging, but most centers do not routinely obtain quantitative values for T1 and T2.[47] Other studies suggest that quantitative MRI does not enhance diagnostic accuracy over that of visual inspection alone.

Diffuse low–signal intensity marrow in the diaphysis is normal in the first decade of life.[1,2,44,48,49] Diffuse low signal intensity in the metaphysis is normal until the end

of the second decade.[1,2,44] If diffuse low–signal intensity marrow is visualized in persons beyond these ages it should be investigated. Marrow signal less than that of muscle is always abnormal. Low–signal intensity marrow on T1-weighted spin-echo images in mature adults is an abnormal but nonspecific finding associated with numerous diseases that alter the medullary space.[24,42,50–57] Many of these abnormal entities show brighter signal on T2-weighted sequences (Fig. 7-6), but some remain of low signal intensity on long TR and long TE spin-echo sequences. Entities such as osteopetrosis, sclerotic metastases, hemosiderosis, marrow fibrosis, and leukemia may show low signal intensity on all imaging sequences.

It is doubtful that conventional spin-echo imaging alone is adequate for the complete assessment of marrow disorders. Spin-echo techniques are valuable for identifying focal lesions and advanced disease, but subtle changes in free water concentration are seen to far better advantage on alternate sequences. Spin-echo underestimates the proportion of hematopoietic marrow because

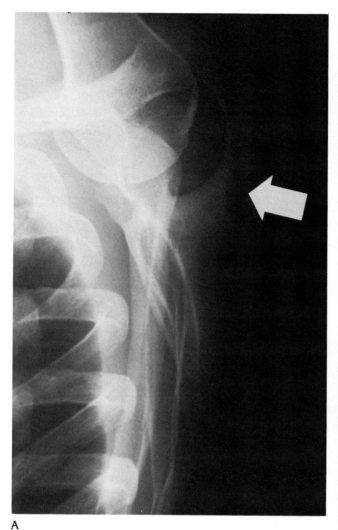

A

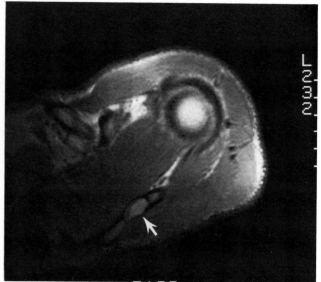

B

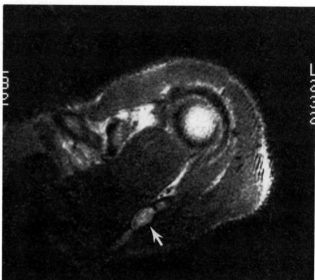

C

Figure 7-5   Intraosseous lipoma in a 50-year-old man. **A.** Radiography shows a well-marginated osteolytic lesion (*arrow*) in the base of the acromion. **B.** Axial proton-density (TR 2000 msec/TE 30 msec) and, **C,** T2-weighted (TR 2000 msec/TE 80 msec) MR images show that the lesion (*arrow*) has signal intensity compatible with fat.

the short T1 of fat overwhelms the longer T1 of red marrow. The bone may appear completely fatty on MR images whereas on histologic examination, islands of red marrow may be observed.

Short tau inversion recovery (STIR) is widely used for marrow assessment because of its acute sensitivity.[58] The STIR sequence suppresses the fat signal; thus, abnormal bone marrow disorders that have a longer T1 relaxation time than that of fat give off a significantly more intense signal against the black (suppressed) fatty marrow.[1] Selective fat-saturation sequences provide the same effect as long as the TR and TE are established for T2-weighted imaging. Lesion conspicuousness on T1-weighted fat-saturated images is very poor unless gadolinium is admin-

istered intravenously and enhancement of tissue involved by the disease process occurs (Fig. 7-7).[59–61] Gadolinium cannot be used effectively with STIR sequences because there is suppression of all short-T1 substances, not only fat. T2-weighted gradient-echo sequences also suppress fatty marrow and offer another alternative for marrow imaging. The magnetic inhomogeneity effects produced by trabecular bone are significant with gradient-echo techniques and may make it difficult to detect lesions.[42] Using gradient recalled echo sequences, increasing TE produces a decrease in marrow signal relative to that of subcutaneous fat, particularly in the epiphysis.[2] These subtle changes may not be visible if there is poor field homogeneity.

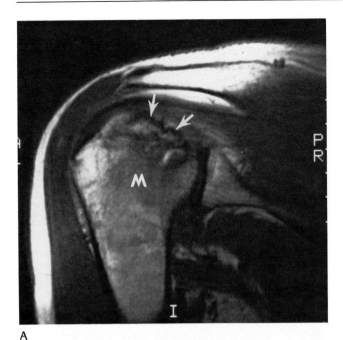

A

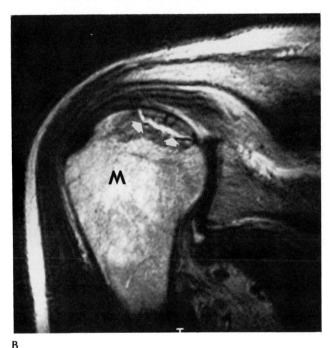

B

Figure 7-6 Osteochondritis dissecans involving the humerus of a 20-year-old man. **A.** Oblique coronal MR (TR 600 msec/TE 20 msec) image shows osteochondral fracture (*arrows*) on the superomedial aspect of the humeral head with patchy low-intensity areas in the metaphysis (M). **B.** Oblique coronal T2-weighted (TR 2616 msec/TE 96 msec) image show a high-intensity line (*arrows*) beneath the osteochondral fragment, consistent with loosening in situ. Patchy high-intensity areas in the proximal humeral metaphysis (M) represent bone marrow edema.

Chemical shift imaging has potential as another method for evaluating bone marrow, but currently only limited data are available. These methods rely on the different precession rates or resonance frequencies of aliphatic and water portions in biologic tissues.[1] The difference has been reported to be approximately 3.5 ppm, or 75 to 150 Hz, at an external field ranging from 0.5 to 1 T.[62] Chemical shift imaging produces images that emphasize the water or fat component of marrow by separating the returning MR signals and temporally dephasing fat and water protons, thereby suppressing either fat or water signal.[63–65]

BONE MARROW DISORDERS

Failure of Conversion and Reconversion

Numerous disorders are associated with an increased need for hematopoietic marrow, owing to ineffective hematopoiesis, erythrocyte destruction, or failure of oxygenation of normal blood. *Failure of conversion* occurs when the disorder develops in childhood. *Reconversion* occurs when the adult marrow is stressed. Reconversion occurs in the reverse order of normal conversion, progressing from central to distal bones. Examples of these disorders include thalassemia (Fig. 7-8), chronic hemolytic anemias such as spherocytosis, congenital heart disease, and diffuse marrow replacement processes. Sickle cell disease also results in abnormal conversion, but the appearance of marrow also is altered by the development of infarcts, resulting quite often in considerable marrow inhomogeneity in this disease (Fig. 7-9). Similarly, myelofibrosis produces abnormally dark bone marrow, owing to processes other than reconversion. The marrow signal intensity in these disorders is similar to that of normal childhood marrow. Osseous expansions, extramedullary hematopoiesis, and epiphyseal reconversion are late features of these disorders.

Myeloid Depletion

Accelerated replacement of hematopoietic tissue by fatty tissue can be seen following radiation therapy (Fig. 7-10) and chemotherapy. After radiation, a sharp line of demarcation between the bright fatty marrow and the less intense hematopoietic marrow is noted at the margin of the radiation field on T1-weighted images. This change becomes evident within weeks of the radiation therapy and probably persists indefinitely. The conversion to fatty marrow progresses rapidly for the initial 6 weeks of therapy, and then more slowly. The changes are more apparent in younger patients, owing to their higher pro-

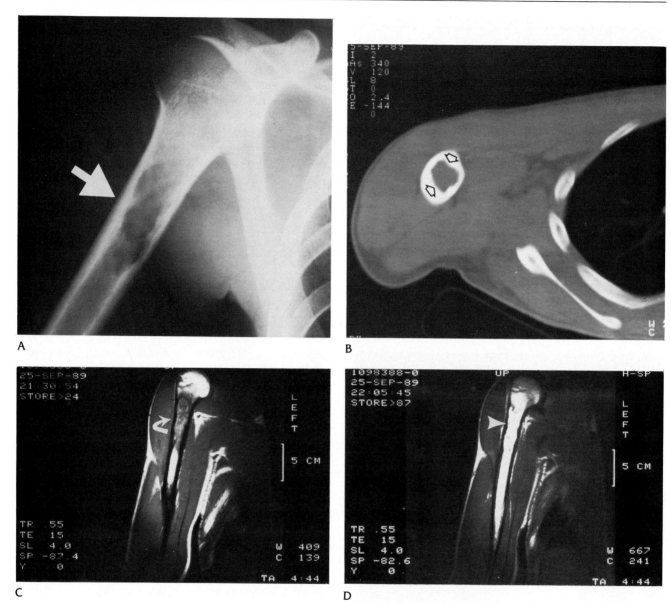

Figure **7-7**   Eosinophilic granuloma of the humerus in a 20-year-old man. **A.** Radiography shows a well-defined osteolytic lesion (*arrow*) in the proximal humerus with endosteal scalloping. **B.** CT shows replacement of the marrow fat and endosteal scalloping (*arrows*) to better advantage. Coronal T1-weighted (TR 550 msec/TE 15 msec) before, **C,** and after, **D,** gadolinium-DTPA enhancement, MR images show a low– to intermediate–signal intensity lesion (*arrow*) in the proximal humerus, which brightens following intravenous contrast administration (*arrowhead*).

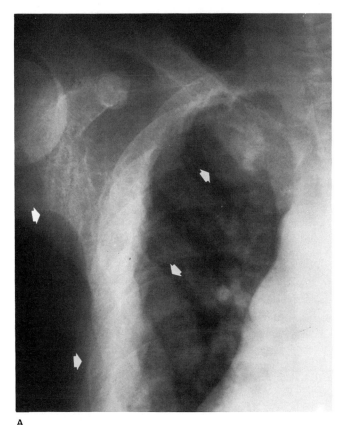

A

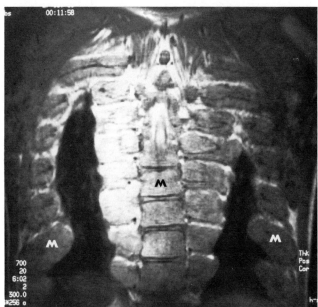

B

Figure 7-8 Thalassemia major with marrow hyperplasia in a 29-year-old man. **A.** Radiography of the shoulder and hemithorax shows widespread and marked osseous expansion (*arrows*) secondary to marrow hyperplasia; extramedullary hematopoiesis is also noted around the mediastinum and thoracic cage. **B.** Coronal MR image of the thorax (TR 700 msec/TE 20 msec) shows diffuse low signal intensity in the expanded marrow (M) secondary to the hematopoietic reconversion process. **C.** Radiograph of another patient shows similar findings; pathologic fracture (*white arrowhead*) of the proximal humerus, related to diffuse osteopenia induced by the process; and osseous expansion (*black arrow*).

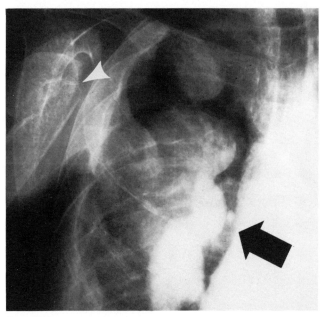

C

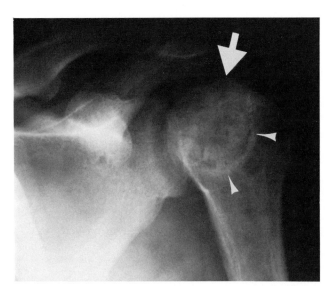

A

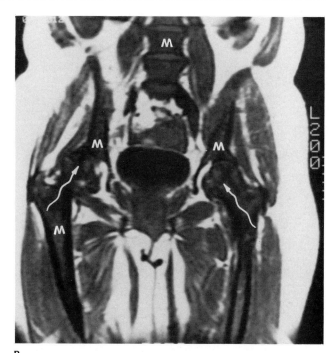

B

Figure 7-9 Avascular necrosis of the humeral head and both femoral heads secondary to sickle cell anemia in a 26-year-old woman. **A.** Radiograph of the shoulder shows mixed lytic and sclerotic areas in the humeral head (*arrowheads*); collapse of the articular surface and subchondral fracture (*arrow*) are evident. **B.** Coronal MR image of both hips (TR 600 msec/TE 20 msec) shows osteonecrosis in both femoral heads (*arrows*). Diffuse low signal intensity in the marrow (M) of the lumbar spine, pelvis, and proximal femurs represents hematopoietic marrow and hemosiderin deposition.

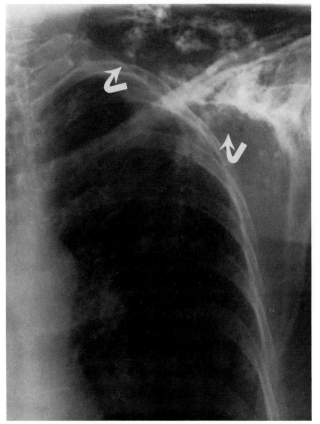

A

Figure 7-10 Sequelae of radiation following mastectomy for breast carcinoma. **A.** Radiograph of the shoulder and hemithorax shows patchy dystrophic soft tissue calcification (*arrows*) with radiation pneumonitis in the upper lung field. **B.** Another patient shows typical findings of radiation, including osteonecrosis, sclerosis (*arrowhead*), fragmentation (*arrow*), and osteolysis (O).

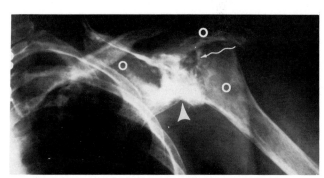

B

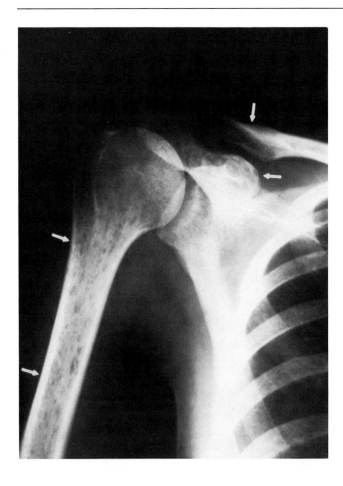

Figure 7-11 Acute leukemia of the shoulder girdle in a 27-year-old woman. Radiography shows numerous small osteolytic lesions (*arrows*) in the proximal humerus, distal clavicle, and scapula.

portion of hematopoietic marrow. Regeneration of marrow, if it occurs, usually is evident within a year of therapy. Regeneration characteristically develops at the periphery of an irradiated vertebral body, producing a band pattern. Similar findings are seen following successful bone marrow transplantation.

Aplastic anemia is a disorder of myeloid depletion associated with pancytopenia that can be idiopathic or induced by diverse factors such as drugs, toxins, viral infections, and hepatitis. There are conflicting reports describing the appearance of marrow. Patients with very fatty marrow, normal MR studies, and patchy areas of fatty marrow have all been described with this disorder.

Marrow Infiltration

Most cases of marrow infiltration are due to neoplastic disease. Leukemia (Fig. 7-11), lymphoma (Fig. 7-12), multiple myeloma (Figs. 7-13, 7-14), and metastatic disease (Fig. 7-15) all are common malignancies associated with marrow infiltration. These disorders may be diffuse, disseminated, or solitary. The diffuse forms are the most difficult to recognize, particularly on spin-echo imaging. The disseminated and focal forms are easily identified as long as the appropriate area is imaged. These disorders on T1-weighted sequences are characterized by low signal intensity. Their appearance on T2-weighted images is

highly variable. Lytic metastases are bright; sclerotic metastases may be dark, intermediate, or bright. Leukemia and lymphoma also are highly variable on T2-weighted spin-echo sequences and often do not appear bright, possibly owing to the presence of free radicals. They may be difficult to detect in children.

Nonneoplastic disorders associated with marrow infiltration include eosinophilic granuloma, Gaucher's disease, systemic mastocytosis (Fig. 7-16), Erdheim-Chester disease (Fig. 7-17), and the mucopolysaccharidoses. Eosinophilic granuloma produces a wide spectrum of changes, ranging from solitary tumorlike deposits to diffuse marrow infiltration (Fig. 7-18). Periostitis and extensive soft tissue edema also may be present (Fig. 7-19), leading to confusion with Ewing's sarcoma or osteomyelitis. In Gaucher's disease, replacement of marrow by glycocerebroside-filled reticulum cells produces low–signal intensity marrow on both T1- and T2-weighted sequences in the metaphyses and diaphyses of the skeleton. With more advanced disease, epiphyseal involvement and osteonecrosis become evident (Fig. 7-20).

Marrow Edema

"Edema" of bone marrow can result from trauma, infection, or reaction to an adjacent neoplasm, or it may be idiopathic. The exact histopathologic basis of bone mar-

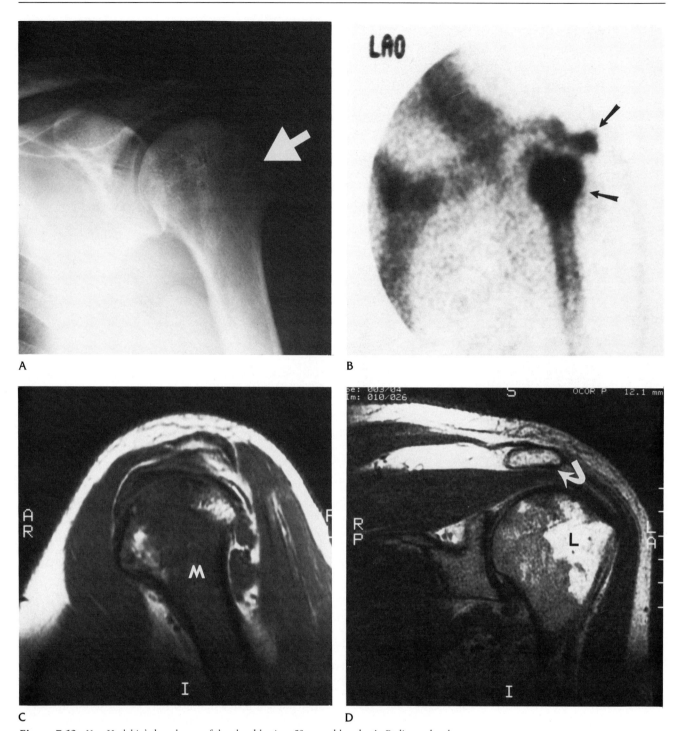

A

B

C

D

Figure 7-12 Non-Hodgkin's lymphoma of the shoulder in a 53-year-old male. **A.** Radiography shows a subtle osteolytic process in the superolateral aspect of the proximal humerus (*arrow*). **B.** Bone scan shows increased uptake in the proximal humerus and acromion (*arrows*). **C.** Oblique sagittal MR (TR 300 msec/ TE 15 msec) image shows diffuse low signal intensity of the humeral marrow (M). **D.** Oblique coronal MR (TR 2000 msec/TE 70 msec) image shows a patchy high–signal intensity lesion (L) involving both the humeral epiphysis and metaphysis; similar findings are also noted in the acromion (*arrow*).

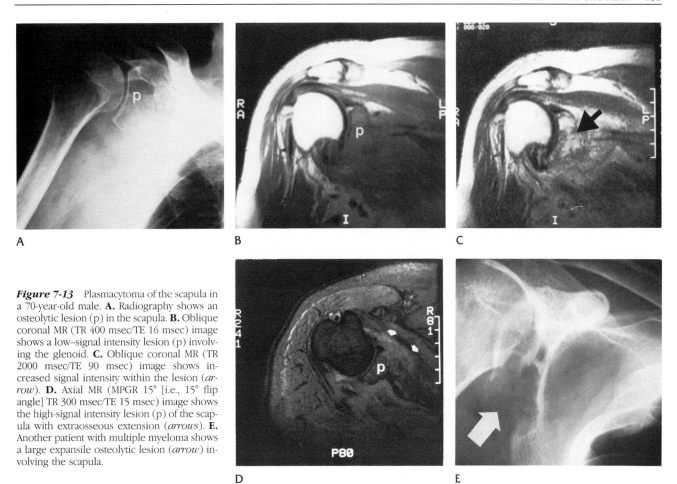

Figure 7-13 Plasmacytoma of the scapula in a 70-year-old male. **A.** Radiography shows an osteolytic lesion (p) in the scapula. **B.** Oblique coronal MR (TR 400 msec/TE 16 msec) image shows a low–signal intensity lesion (p) involving the glenoid. **C.** Oblique coronal MR (TR 2000 msec/TE 90 msec) image shows increased signal intensity within the lesion (*arrow*). **D.** Axial MR (MPGR 15° [i.e., 15° flip angle] TR 300 msec/TE 15 msec) image shows the high-signal intensity lesion (p) of the scapula with extraosseous extension (*arrows*). **E.** Another patient with multiple myeloma shows a large expansile osteolytic lesion (*arrow*) involving the scapula.

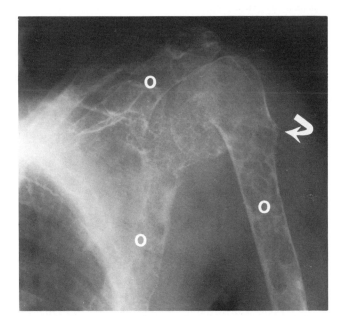

Figure 7-14 Multiple myeloma with diffuse bony involvement in a 50-year-old man. Radiography shows extensive osteolytic lesions (O) involving the shoulder girdle and hemithorax with osteoporosis; also note the pathologic fracture (*arrow*) of the proximal humerus.

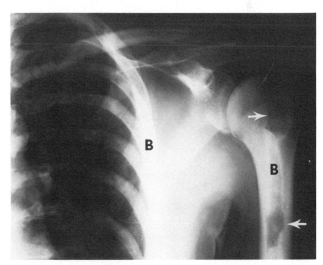

Figure 7-15 Metastatic prostate carcinoma in a 51-year-old man. Radiography shows diffuse osteoblastic disease (B) involving the shoulder girdle and hemithorax; patchy areas of osteolysis (*arrows*) are noted in the proximal humerus.

row edema is not known. All these entities produce low–signal intensity marrow on T1-weighted images and high–signal intensity marrow on T2-weighted and STIR images (see Fig. 7-4).

Traumatic edema, like that associated with a bone bruise, is a transient abnormality of medullary bone that is presumably secondary to microfractures. Edema may also be seen adjacent to occult or stress fractures. The fracture line maintains low signal intensity on T2-weighted images, whereas the edema becomes high signal intensity. STIR may be more sensitive than spin-echo for identifying these changes. Osteomyelitis produces alterations in bone marrow owing to the intense inflammatory reaction and release of free water (Fig. 7-21). MRI is extremely sensitive for detection of early infection, but its specificity is only moderate. Abnormal marrow signal can be seen adjacent to septic arthritis in the absence of osteomyelitis. A well-known example of an idiopathic disorder associated with bone marrow edema is "transient osteoporosis of the hip." Diffuse transient loss of fat signal is seen in the femoral head and neck. This condition is self-limited and has a good prognosis.

Marrow Ischemia and Osteonecrosis

MRI is the most sensitive imaging method available for detection of osteonecrosis (see Figs. 7-7, 7-18). The patterns seen with infarction depend on its location, duration, and stage. Subarticular avascular necrosis of the femoral head has been most widely studied. It produces a variety of appearances, including the ring or band

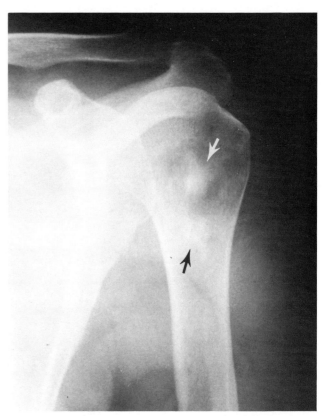

Figure 7-17 Erdheim-Chester disease involving the humerus of a 52-year-old woman. Note osteosclerotic areas (*arrows*) involving the proximal humeral metaphysis.

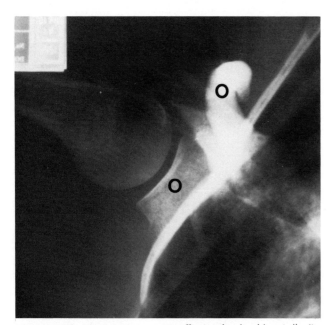

Figure 7-16 Systemic mastocytosis affecting the shoulder girdle. Radiography demonstrates diffuse osteosclerosis (O) of the osseous structures, related to marrow infiltration by mast cells.

pattern, the double-line sign, and inhomogeneous areas of low signal intensity on T1-weighted images. The location of avascular necrosis tends to be anterolateral, and the defects are often wedge-shaped as they abut the cortex. Early noncollapsed areas of avascular necrosis tend to maintain fat signal on T2-weighted sequences, whereas advanced disease with collapse typically exhibits low signal intensity on these images. The Ficat staging system for avascular necrosis is based on the plain film findings:

- Stage 1: Normal
- Stage 2: Sclerosis and lucency
- Stage 3: Subchondral fracture
- Stage 4: Collapse
- Stage 5: Osteoarthritis

Early detection of Stage 1 or 2 disease may improve the patient's outcome; however, there is considerable controversy about early management. Early therapies include core decompression, osteotomy, and vascularization procedures using allografts. Lesions that encompass more than 50 percent of the head tend to collapse, regardless of the procedure.

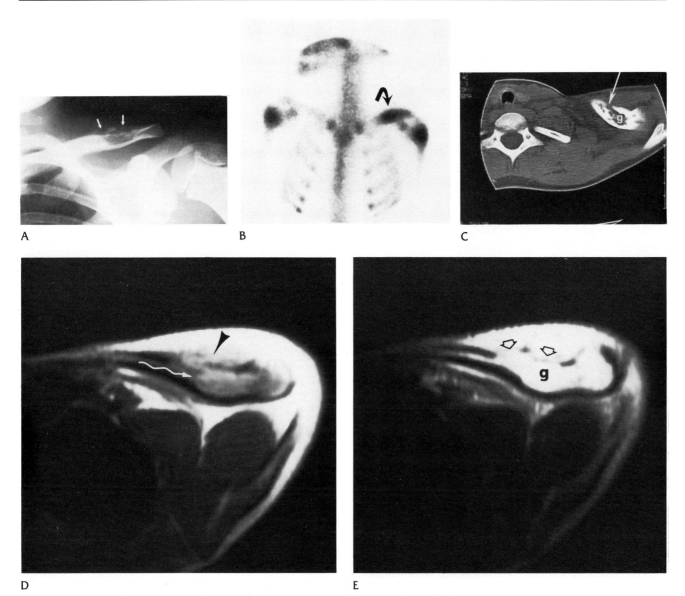

Figure 7-18 Eosinophilic granuloma of the distal clavicle in a 9-year-old boy. **A.** Radiography shows a well-marginated osteolytic lesion with cortical breakthrough (*arrows*). **B.** Bone scan shows increased uptake at the site of involvement (*arrow*). **C.** CT shows the osteolytic lesion (g) with interruption of the cortex (*arrow*). **D.** Axial-weighted (TR 650 msec/20 msec) MR image shows an intermediate–signal intensity lesion (*white arrow*) in the distal clavicle with extraosseous extension (*black arrowhead*). **E.** Axial-weighted 12 (TR 2000 msec/TE 80 msec) image shows high signal intensity within the lesion (g) as well as cortical disruption (*arrows*).

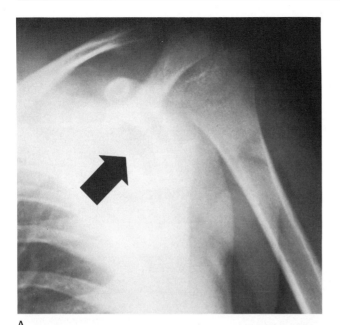

A

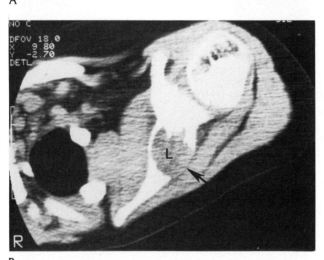

B

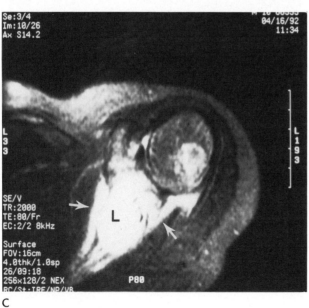

C

Figure 7-19 Eosinophilic granuloma of the scapula in a 10-year-old boy. **A.** Radiography shows a well-defined osteolytic lesion (*arrow*) in the scapula. **B.** CT shows the lesion (L) to be intrascapular, with cortical interruption (*arrow*). **C.** Axial MR (TR 2000 msec/TE 80 msec) image shows high signal intensity within the lesion (L) and surrounding soft tissues (*arrows*).

Figure 7-20 Gaucher's disease in a 36-year-old man with humeral involvement and bilateral femoral head osteonecrosis. **A.** Radiography shows septate lytic Gaucher cell deposits (G) in the proximal humerus. **B.** Coronal MR (TR 500 msec/TE 20 msec) image shows osteonecrosis of the right femoral head (*arrow*). Signal void on the left side represents joint arthroplasty (A) for previous osteonecrosis. The mottled appearance of the marrow (M) in the pelvis, spine, and right proximal femur is consistent with Gaucher cell infiltration.

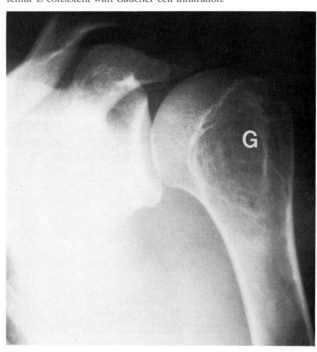

A

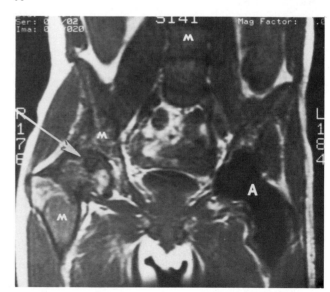

B

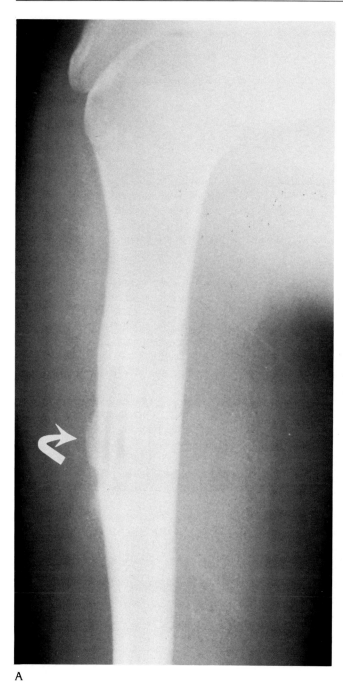

A

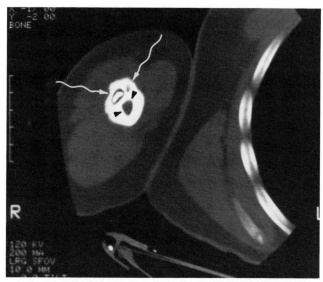

B

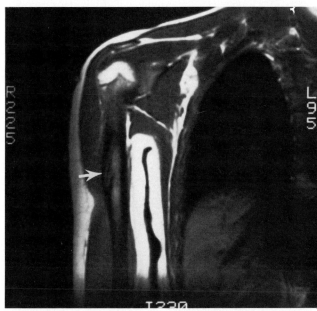

C

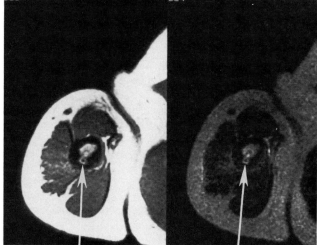

D

Figure 7-21 Cortical abscess in a 15-year-old girl. **A.** Radiography shows linear osteolytic areas with surrounding sclerosis (*arrow*) involving the lateral aspect of the proximal humeral cortex. **B.** CT shows the lesions (*arrows*) to better advantage; note the relatively preserved marrow fat morphology and attenuation (*arrowheads*). Coronal, **C,** (TR 600 msec/TE 20 msec) and axial, **D,** MR (TR 2000 msec/TE 20/80 msec) images show central calcification surrounded by a rim of increased signal intensity (*arrows*) corresponding to an abscess with sequestrum formation. Early marrow inflammation is more conspicuous than on CT.

References

1. VOGLER JB III, MURPHY WA: Bone marrow imaging. *Radiology* 168:679, 1988.

2. STEINER RM, MITCHELL DG, RAO VM, SCHWEITZER ME: Magnetic resonance imaging of diffuse bone marrow disease. *Radiol Clin North Am* 31:383, 1993.

3. KELEMEN E, CAZVO W: Prenatal hematopoiesis in human bone marrow and its developmental antecedents, in Trubowitz S, Davis S (eds): *The Human Bone Marrow: Anatomy, Physiology, and Pathophysiology*, vol 1, Boca Raton, FL, CRC Press, 1982, pp 3–41.

4. ERSLEV AJ: Medullary and extramedullary blood formation. *Clin Orthop* 52:25, 1967.

5. TRUBOWITZ S, DAVIS S: The bone marrow matrix, in Trubowitz S, Davis S (eds): *The Human Bone Marrow: Anatomy, Physiology, and Pathophysiology*, vol 1, Boca Raton, FL, CRC Press, 1982, pp 43–75.

6. DE BRUYN PPH, BREEN PC, THOMAS TB: The microcirculation of the bone marrow. *Anat Rec* 168:55, 1970.

7. KUNTZ A, RICHINS CA: Innervation of the bone marrow. *J Comp Neurol* 83:213, 1945.

8. JUNQUEIRA LC, CARNEIRO J: The life cycle of blood cells, in Junqueira LC, Carneiro J (eds): *Basic Histology*, 4th ed, Los Altos, CA, Lange, 1983, pp 275–292.

9. SNYDER WS, COOK MJ, NASSET ES, KARHAUSEN LR, HOWELLS GP, TIPTON IH: *Report on the Task Group on Reference Man*, Oxford, Pergamon, 1974, pp 72–98.

10. ROHR K: Das menschliche Knochenmark, Stuttgart, Thieme, 1960.

11. WEISS L: The histology of the bone marrow, in Gordon AS (ed): *Regulation of Hematopoiesis*, vol 1, New York, Appleton-Century-Crofts, 1970, p 79.

12. DOAN CA, CUNNINGHAM RS, SABIN FR: Experimental studies on the origin and maturation of avian and mammalian red blood cells. *Contrib Embryol Carnegie Inst Wash* 16:163, 1925.

13. BIERMANN HR: Leukopoiesis in health and disease. *Ann NY Acad Sci* 113:511, 1964.

14. DUNNILL MS, ANDERSON JA, WHITEHEAD R: Quantitative histological studies on age changes in bone. *J Pathol Bacteriol* 94:275, 1967.

15. GENANT HK, CANN CE: Quantitative computed tomography for assessing vertebral bone mineral, in Genant HK, Chafetz N, Helms CA (eds): *Computed Tomography of the Lumbar Spine*, San Francisco, University of California, 1982, pp 289–314.

16. GORDAN GS, GENANT HK: Aging of bone in the two sexes, in Marini L, Gordan GS, Sciarra F (eds): *Steroid Modulation of Neuroendocrine Function, Sterols, Steroids, and Bone Metabolism*. New York, Elsevier, 1984, pp 139–153.

17. HUGGINS C, BLOCKSOM BH JR: Changes in outlying bone marrow accompanying a local increase of temperature within physiological limits. *J Exp Med* 64:253, 1936.

18. EMERY JL, FOLLETT GF: Regression of bone-marrow haemopoiesis from the terminal digits in the foetus and infant. *Br J Haemotol* 10:485, 1964.

19. KRICUN ME: Red-yellow marrow conversion: Its effect on the location of some solitary bone lesions. *Skel Radiol* 14:10, 1985.

20. MOORE SG, DAWSON KL: Red and yellow marrow in the femur. Age related changes in appearance at MR imaging. *Radiology* 175:219, 1990.

21. RICCI C, COVA M, KANG YS, YANG A, RAHMOUNI A, SCOTT WW, ZERHOUNI EA: Normal age-related patterns of cellular and fatty bone marrow distribution in the axial skeleton: MR imaging study. *Radiology* 177:83, 1990.

22. PINEY A: The anatomy of the bone marrow. *Br Med J* II:792, 1922.

23. NEUMANN E: Das Gesetz der Verbreitung des gelben und roten Markes in den Extremitatenknochen. *Zentralblatt Med Wissenschaft* 20:321, 1882.

24. SHELLOCK FG, MORRIS E, DEUTSCH AL, MINK JH, KERR R, BODEN SD: Hematopoietic bone marrow hyperplasia: High prevalence on MR images of the knee in asymptomatic marathon runners. *AJR* 158:335, 1992.

25. HASHIMOTO M: The distribution of active marrow in the bones of normal adult. *Kyushu J Med Sci* 11:103, 1960.

26. HAJEK PC, BAKER LL, GOOBAR JE, ET AL.: Focal fat deposition in axial bone marrow: MR characteristics. *Radiology* 162:245, 1987.

27. DOOMS GC, FISHER MR, HRICAK H, RICHARDSON M, CROOKS LE, GENANT HK: Bone marrow imaging: Magnetic resonance studies related to age and sex. *Radiology* 155:429, 1985.

28. CUSTER RP, AHFELD FE: Studies on the structure and function of the bone marrow. *J Lab Clin Med* 17:951, 1932.

29. OEHLBECK LWF, ROBSHEIT-ROBBINS FS, WHIPPLE GH: Marrow hyperplasia and hemoglobin reserve in experimental anemia due to bleeding. *J Exp Med* 56:425, 1932.

30. SABIN FR: Bone marrow. *Physiol Rev* 8:191, 1928.

31. TRIBUKAIT B: Experimental studies on the regulation of erythropoiesis with special reference to the importance of oxygen. *Acta Physiol Scand* 58(Suppl 208):1, 1963.

32. JACOBSEN EM, DAVIS AK, ALPEN EL: Relative effectiveness of phenylhydrazine treatment and hemorrhage in the production of an erythropoietic factor. *Blood* 11:937, 1956.

33. RAO VM, FISHMAN M, MITCHELL DG, ET AL: Painful sickle cell crisis: Bone marrow patterns observed with MR imaging. *Radiology* 161:211, 1986.

34. ARDRAN GM: Bone destruction not demonstrable by radiography. *Br J Radiol* 24:107, 1951.

35. EDELSTYN GA, GILLESPIE PJ, GREBBELL FS: The radiological demonstration of osseous metastasis: Experimental observations. *Clin Radiol* 18:158, 1967.

36. METTLER FA, GUIBERTEAU MJ: Skeletal system, in Mettler FA, Guiberteau MJ (eds): *Essentials of Nuclear Medicine Imaging*, 3d ed, Philadelphia, Saunders, 1991, pp 209–236.

37. DATZ FL, TAYLOR A JR: The clinical use of radionuclide bone marrow imaging. *Semin Nucl Med* 15:239, 1985.

37a. RICHARDSON ML: Optimizing pulse sequences for magnetic resonance imaging of the musculoskeletal system. *Radiol Clin North Am* 24:137, 1986.

38. HELMS CA, CANN CE, BRUNELLE FO, GILULA LA, CHAFETZ N, GENANT HK: Detection of bone-marrow metastases using quantitative computed tomography. *Radiology* 140:745, 1981.

39. HERMANN G, ROSE JS, STRAUSS L: Tumor infiltration of the bone marrow: Comparative study using computed tomography. *Skel Radiol* 11:17, 1984.

40. MAJUMDAR S, THOMASSON D, SHIMAKARA A, ET AL.: Quantitation of the susceptibility difference between trabecular bone and bone marrow: Experimental studies. *Magn Reson Med* 22:111, 1990.

41. MITCHELL DG, BURK DL JR, VINITSKI S, ET AL.: The biophysical basis of tissue contrast in extracranial MR imaging. *AJR* 149:831, 1987.

42. ROSENTHAL H, THULBORN KR, ROSENTHAL DI, KIM SH, ROSEN BR: Magnetic susceptibility effects of trabecular bone on magnetic resonance imaging of bone marrow. *Invest Radiol* 25:173, 1990.

43. WEHRLI FW, MacFALL JR, SHUTTS D, BREGER R, HERFKENS RJ: Mechanisms of contrast in NMR imaging. *J Comput Assist Tomogr* 8:369, 1984.

44. MOORE SG, SEBAG GH: Primary disorders of the bone marrow, in Cohen MD, Edwards MK (eds): *Magnetic Resonance Imaging of Children,* Philadelphia, Decker, 1990, p 765.

45. DAWSON KL, MOORE SG, ROWLAND JM: Age-related marrow changes in the pelvis: MR and anatomic findings. *Radiology* 183:47, 1992.

46. RICHARDS MA, WEBB JAW, JEWELL SE, ET AL.: In-vivo measurement of spin-lattice relaxation time (T1) of bone marrow in healthy volunteers: The effects of age and sex. *Br J Radiol* 61:30, 1988.

47. SMITH SR, WILLIAMS CE, DAVIES JM, EDWARDS RH: Bone marrow disorders: characterization with quantitative MR imaging. *Radiology* 172:805, 1989.

48. COHEN MD, KLATTE EC, BACHNER R, ET AL: Magnetic resonance imaging of bone marrow disease in children. *Radiology* 151:715, 1984.

49. WEINREB JC: MR imaging of bone marrow: a map could help. *Radiology* 177:23, 1990.

50. JOHNSON LA, HOPPEL BE, GERARD EL, ET AL.: Quantitative chemical shift imaging of vertebral bone marrow in patients with Gaucher disease. *Radiology* 182:451, 1992.

51. GERARD EL, FERRY JA, AMREIN PC, ET AL.: Compositional changes in vertebral bone marrow during treatment for acute leukemia: Assessment with quantitative chemical shift imaging. *Radiology* 183:39, 1992.

52. DEUTSCH AL, MINK JH, ROSENFELD FP, WAXMAN AD: Incidental detection of hematopoietic hyperplasia on routine knee MR imaging. *AJR* 152:333, 1989.

53. LINDEN A, ZANKOVICH R, THEISSEN P, DIEHL V, SCHICHA H: Malignant lymphoma: Bone marrow imaging versus biopsy. *Radiology* 173:335, 1989.

54. LIBSHITZ HI, MALTHOUSE SR, CUNNINGHAM D, MacVICAR AD, HUSBAND JE: Multiple myeloma: Appearance at MR imaging. *Radiology* 182:833, 1992.

55. MOULOPOULOS LA, VARMA DGK, DIMOPOULOS MA, ET AL.: Multiple myeloma: Spinal MR imaging in patients with untreated newly diagnosed disease. *Radiology* 185:833, 1992.

56. MIROWITZ SA, APICELLA P, REINUS WR, HAMMERMAN AM: MR imaging of bone marrow lesions: Relative conspicuousness on T1-weighted, fat-suppressed T2-weighted, and STIR images. *AJR* 162:215, 1994.

57. DAFFNER RH, LUPETIN AR, DASH N, DEEB ZL, SEFCZEK RJ, SCHAPIRO RL: MRI in the detection of malignant infiltration of bone marrow. *AJR* 146:353, 1986.

58. BYDDER GM, YOUNG IR: MR imaging: Clinical use of the inversion recovery sequence. *J Comput Assist Tomogr* 9:695, 1985.

59. MORRISON WB, SCHWEITZER ME, BOCK GW, ET AL.: Diagnosis of osteomyelitis: Utility of fat-suppressed contrast-enhanced MR imaging. *Radiology* 189:251, 1993.

60. BELTRAN J, CHANDNANI V, McGHEE RA JR, KURSUNOGLU-BRAHME S: Gadopentate dimeglumine–enhanced MR imaging of the musculoskeletal system. *AJR* 156:457, 1991.

61. COVA M, KANG YS, TSUKAMOTO H, ET AL.: Bone marrow perfusion evaluated with gadolinium-enhanced dynamic fast MR imaging in a dog model. *Radiology* 179:535, 1991.

62. WISMER GL, ROSEN BR, BUXTON R, STARK DD, BRADY TJ: Chemical shift imaging of the bone marrow: Preliminary experience. *AJR* 145:1031, 1985.

63. ROSENTHAL DI, BARTON NW, McKUSICK KA, ET AL.: Quantitative imaging of Gaucher disease. *Radiology* 185:841, 1992.

64. ROSEN BR, FLEMING DM, KUSHNER DC, ET AL.: Hematologic bone marrow disorders: Quantitative chemical shift MR imaging. *Radiology* 169:799, 1988.

65. ISHIZAKA H, TOMIYOSHI K, MATSUMOTO M: MR quantification of bone marrow cellularity: Use of chemical-shift misregistration artifact. *AJR* 160:572, 1993.

8 OSSEOUS TRAUMA TO THE SHOULDER: IMAGING PRINCIPLES

Ronald Hendrix
Lee F. Rogers

Trauma to the shoulder results most commonly from a fall onto an outstretched hand or from a direct blow to the shoulder that causes various fractures, dislocations, and soft tissue injuries. Our task is to image the shoulder in such manner as to demonstrate most easily and clearly the injury, so that it can be treated. Conventional plain film radiography is used as a general screening or survey tool to distinguish between normal and abnormal shoulders and to demonstrate significant lesions. Shoulders that appear abnormal on routine radiographs may need further examination using nonroutine views or other imaging modalities, as do those that are radiographically normal but painful. In both situations the choice of additional studies must be tailored to the trauma and symptoms, as discussed herein. Injuries to the soft tissues are discussed elsewhere.

Shoulder injury occurs in all age groups but tends to be age dependent. Clavicle fracture is the most common skeletal birth injury (Fig. 8-1) and childhood skeletal injury. Shoulder dislocation and acromioclavicular separation are common in the 20- to 40-year age range. Fractures of the surgical neck and associated humeral head fractures are most common in elderly persons.

RADIOGRAPHIC EXAMINATION

There is no consensus about the best views to evaluate the shoulder although anteroposterior (AP) views in internal and external rotation are the standard radiographic study of the shoulder. This is true even though the common radiographic dictum that two views obtained at 90° to one another is the minimum needed to make sense of a three-dimensional object on the two-dimensional format of radiographs. It is nearly impossible to obtain two radiographs of the shoulder at 90° to each other. The AP view is easily obtained, but a transthoracic view is almost useless because of the superimposed ribs and chest. An axillary view is not too difficult to obtain, but the information derived from it has limitations as do all views. The axillary view allows evaluation for fracture or

dislocation of the humeral head and fracture of the glenoid, coracoid, and acromion. A major drawback is that abduction of the shoulder is needed to position a curved film cassette in the axilla for the radiograph. If this is a routine part of the shoulder radiographic study, a technician will be found manipulating or trying to move unstable fractures, frequently before they are known to exist. Even if no fracture or dislocation is present, a significant number of patients with shoulder trauma refuse to move their shoulder for the view. In such cases it is possible for the patient while standing to hold a flat cassette on top of the shoulder parallel to the floor. The patient leans backward over an x-ray tube on a crane placed at floor level pointing toward the ceiling. The resulting image is an axillary view.

The primary problem with imaging of the shoulder is due to the overlap of multiple structures. Each anatomic structure and each abnormality of the shoulder can best be seen on a particular view, but the impracticality of obtaining all views on every patient should be evident. Instead, the study has to be "tailor made," more so than for other areas of the body. We routinely obtain an AP view in external rotation and a Grashey view; other views are added as indicated by the clinical findings and findings on the first two radiographs.

A scapular Y view visualizes the body of the scapula in profile and the coracoid and acromion in lateral view. Fractures of these three structures may be seen with this view that are not seen or are difficult to see with AP views. The humeral head and neck also are seen well, which is especially useful for evaluating displaced proximal humeral fractures.

We began routinely obtaining a 45° posterior oblique view called the Grashey view, which sights down the glenohumeral joint line, after being embarrassed once too often by missing a posterior dislocation. This view clearly demonstrates posterior dislocations, of which at least half typically are missed on the initial radiographic examination of the shoulder.[1] It is also more useful than the routine AP views for detecting glenoid rim fractures.

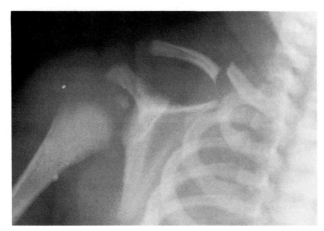

Figure 8-1   Birth fracture of the middle third of the clavicle in a 1-day-old baby.

The Grashey view is easily obtained even in the severely multiple injured patient; it requires minimal moving of the body and none of the arm. The cassette can be placed posterior to the shoulder with its lateral margin elevated enough to make a 45° angle with the table and the x-ray tube angled at 45° (medial to lateral) with the patient supine. This view also throws the humeral head laterally, so that the humeral head, surgical neck, anatomic neck, and greater tuberosity are well visualized. The coracoid process is seen in partial profile and projects over the joint. The glenoid and scapular neck are clearly seen also. An apical oblique view provides information similar to that obtained with a Grashey view. As with the Grashey view the apical oblique view is obtained with the patient turned in a 45° posterior oblique position, but the x-ray beam is oriented 45° caudad instead of parallel to the horizontal plane.

AP views of the shoulder superimpose the clavicle on the scapula and ribs, and its distal end is often overexposed. A view with 15° cephalad angulation[2] throws the distal two-thirds of the clavicle off the ribs and scapula, and as much as 40° of angulation may be necessary to throw the proximal clavicle free of the ribs and spine.

Computed tomography (CT) of the shoulder is of limited value for acute trauma diagnosis but is often helpful for evaluating complex fractures and fracture dislocations of the shoulder.[3–5] The relation of the glenoid to the humeral head fragments is demonstrated better than with conventional radiographs, and structures are not superimposed. Compression fractures, split fractures of the humeral head, and glenoid rim fractures are all demonstrated well with CT. If there is difficulty moving the patient for routine radiographs because of multiple injuries, CT can be obtained with minimal repositioning. CT also provides the most definitive study of the sternoclavicular joint for fracture or dislocation.[3]

FRACTURES

Clavicle Fractures

Clavicle fracture is the most frequent fracture of childhood: half occur in children younger than 10 years (see Fig. 8-1). Often these fractures cause bowing or angulation but not a discernible cortical break.[6] A direct fall onto the shoulder or a direct blow to the clavicle is the mechanism of more than 90 percent of clavicular fractures; a fall onto an outstretched hand rarely is the cause.[7]

The distribution of clavicular fractures is 65 to 80 percent in the middle third, 15 to 30 percent in the lateral third, and 5 percent in the medial third.[7,8] Middle-third fractures are usually transverse or oblique and often are comminuted (Fig. 8-2).[9] The sternocleidomastoid muscle pulls up the medial fragment, and the lateral fragment is depressed by the weight of the upper extremity. This allows the distal fragment to slip under the proximal fragment, causing the frequent finding of overriding. Neurologic injury and vascular compromise are possible complications, but these are rare.[9] Nondisplaced fractures of the middle third may be missed with AP radiographs if the x-ray beam is not tilted 15° cephalad (Fig. 8-3). Treatment consists of immobilization with a figure-of-eight harness, limiting abduction to no more than 30°, and limiting forward flexion to prevent motion at the fracture site and possible delayed union or nonunion.[9] Healing occasionally occurs with massive callus formation and a visible lump, which must be partially resected for cosmetic reasons.

The distal third of the clavicle is tightly bound to the coracoid by the coracoclavicular ligaments—the conoid medially and the trapezoid laterally (Fig. 8-4). Outer third fractures occur either between the conoid and trapezoid

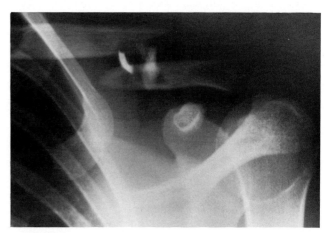

Figure 8-2   Fracture of the middle third of the clavicle in a 19-year-old man from a fall on the shoulder. Comminution, inferior displacement, and slight overriding of the distal fracture fragment are typical findings in midclavicular fractures.

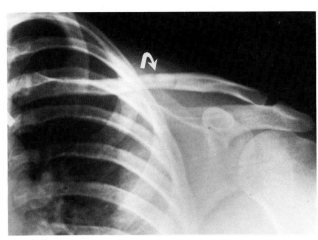

Figure 8-3 Nondisplaced fracture of the middle third of the clavicle (*arrow*) is seen with 15° of cephalad angulation of the x-ray beam in a 27-year-old women. This fracture could not be seen on the routine AP view, which is not shown.

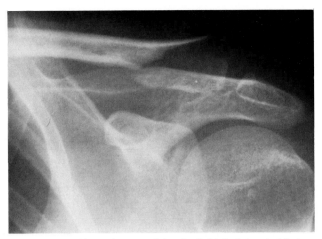

Figure 8-5 Oblique fracture of the distal third of the clavicle in a 27-year-old woman sustained from a fall on the shoulder. The separation of the fracture fragments indicates that the conoid ligament has been disrupted.

ligaments (the ligaments remaining intact or the conoid being disrupted) or with the much less frequent fracture of the coracoid process of the scapula. Radiographically these fractures can be distinguished: There is no displacement of the fracture if the ligaments are intact, but the medial bone fragment is displaced cephalad if the conoid ligament is disrupted or the coracoid process is fractured (Fig. 8-5). Stress views made with 10 to 15 lb of weight suspended from the patient's wrists should be done when a distal third fracture is encountered to determine the status of the coracoclavicular ligaments.[10] The stress views are more likely to be successful if the weights are suspended from the patient's wrists than if they are hand held, in which case muscle spasm could mask a subluxation or a dislocation. The nondisplaced distal clavicular fracture is approximately three times more frequent than the displaced type.[10]

With a displaced fracture the medial fragment is dis-

placed in a cephalad and posterior direction and the lateral fragment is pulled posteriorly by the trapezius muscle. Motion of the fracture will occur with shoulder movement, possibly interposing the trapezius muscle into the fracture site. This accounts for the high prevalence of nonunion when such fractures are treated without open reduction and internal fixation (Fig. 8-6).[10] Pin fixation has been employed in the past but it has been associated with serious consequences from pin migration. Paraplegia, pneumothorax, fatal cardiac tamponade, aortopulmonary fistula, and subclavian artery laceration are only some of the complications that have resulted from migrating pins from the shoulder.[11] A small number of distal clavicular fractures involve only the lateral mar-

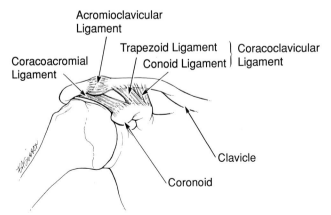

Figure 8-4 Diagram of the ligaments responsible for maintaining the position of the distal clavicle.

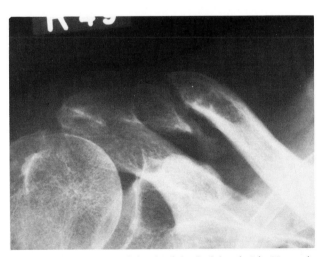

Figure 8-6 A fracture of the distal third of the clavicle 25 months earlier was treated closed and is now a nonunion in a 78-year-old woman. Disruption of the conoid ligament can be inferred from the inferior displacement of the distal fracture fragment.

gin of the clavicle and extend into the acromioclavicular joint. Degenerative arthritis may later develop in the acromioclavicular joint of these patients.[9]

Fractures of the medial third of the clavicle account for no more than 5 percent of clavicular fractures.[7,8] They usually are nondisplaced and are treated with a sling. The combination of superimposed ribs and spine and nondisplacement makes them difficult to identify. An AP view with 30° to 40° of cephalad angulation should provide adequate visualization (Fig. 8-7).

Almost all clavicular fractures heal without difficulty. Nonunion occurs most frequently in distal third fractures with disruption of the coracoclavicular ligaments or in a severely comminuted or angulated fracture (see Fig. 8-6).[8,12–15] Nonunion is nearly nonexistent in children and its prevalence is less than 1 percent in patients treated with closed reduction.[8,14] Fractures treated with open reduction and internal fixation have a 2 to 4 percent rate of nonunion, more likely owing to the severity of the fracture than to the open reduction.[13–15]

Scapular Fractures

Scapular fractures are rare because the bone is well protected. They are usually secondary to major blunt trauma from motor vehicle accidents, falls, or crush injuries.[16–18] They were conveniently grouped into three categories by Thompson and coworkers.[16] Class 1, coracoid and/or small chip fractures of the scapular body; Class 2, glenoid and/or glenoid neck fractures; Class 3, major scapular body fractures. Body and glenoid fractures constitute 80 percent of scapular fractures.[18] Some 61 to 84 percent of scapular fractures have been reported in association with a motor vehicle, though some of the injured were pedestrians.[16–18] Concomitant injuries were

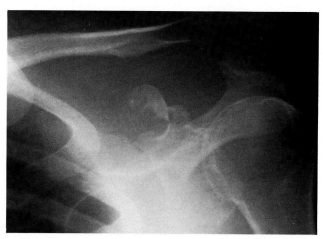

Figure 8-8 Grade 3 acromioclavicular joint separation sustained in a fall by a 46-year-old woman. A tear of the coracoclavicular ligaments is typically seen with a Grade 3 acromioclavicular separation, but a rare coracoid fracture in this case has produced the same separation.

present in 81 to 98 percent of reported cases, including rib, clavicle, spine, and extremity fractures, pulmonary contusion, vascular transection, brachial plexus injury, and central nervous system injury, among others.[16–19] These injuries were most frequent in adjacent structures on the ipsilateral side, though remote injuries on either side were not infrequent. Scapular fractures are often overlooked because of the overwhelming attention demanded by associated life-threatening injuries or are masked clinically or radiographically by injuries to adjacent structures.[19] Failure to diagnose the fracture with the initial radiographs, and in particular with the chest study, has been reported in 25 to 43 percent of cases.[16,18,19] In approximately three-fourths of these failure-to-diagnose cases the fracture was visible on initial radiographs but was not appreciated.

Avulsion fractures are seen involving the superior or lateral scapular border, the inferior angle, the acromion, or the coracoid (Fig. 8-8).[20,21] Most of these are secondary to avulsion of attached muscles.[20,21] Acromion fractures usually are caused by a direct blow, but occasionally they are associated with the rare superior dislocation of the glenohumeral joint. The fracture characteristically is vertical, occurring at the junction of the scapular spine and the acromion. Care must be exercised to differentiate nutrient foramina in the neck and body of the scapula and apophyseal lines from fractures. Fractures are usually displaced and angulated, whereas nutrient foramina and apophyses have thin, sclerotic, parallel margins with no displacement or angulation (Fig. 8-9).

Coracoid fractures have been described in association with anterior dislocation of the glenohumeral joint,[22–25] rarely in association with severe acromioclavicular dislocation (see Fig. 8-8),[22,26–30] and infrequently from direct blows.[31,32] They are usually located at the base of the coracoid process and are oriented transversely (see Fig.

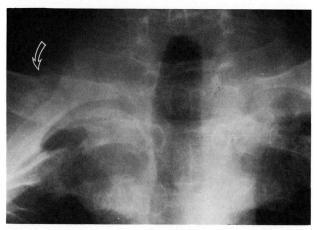

Figure 8-7 Fracture of the proximal third of the clavicle (*arrow*) is seen with difficulty even with 30° of cephalad angulation of the x-ray beam in a 70-year-old man who was blown off a ladder by 60-mph gusts of wind. CT is the best modality for evaluating fractures such as this in the most mediad portion of the clavicle, since many of them cannot be seen even with steep cephalad angulation of the x-ray beam on conventional radiographs.

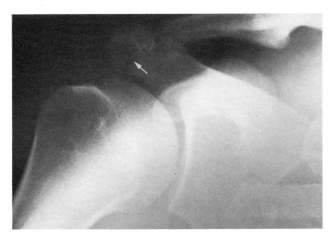

Figure 8-9 Unfused acromial apophysis (*arrow*) in a 33-year-old man can easily be mistaken for a fracture. The sclerotic opposing margins and the nondisplaced position are helpful in distinguishing this from a fracture.

8-8). Radiographically they may be demonstrated with 20° to 45° of cephalic angulation on the AP projection,[32,33] with a scapular Y view (Fig. 8-10), or with CT.[34] We have been pleased with the ease with which they can be demonstrated with a scapular Y view (see Fig. 8-10).

Class 2 fractures involve the glenoid and/or its neck (Fig. 8-11). Impaction of the humeral head into the glenoid fossa is the suspected cause of many Class 2 fractures, even though direct trauma accounts for most scapular fractures.[16] Fracture of the ipsilateral clavicle occurs twice as frequently with glenoid or glenoid neck fractures as with other scapular fractures.[16] A high incidence of residual stiffness also is seen following healing of these fractures.[18] Avulsion of the glenoid rim, also a Class 2 fracture, is seen with anterior (Fig. 8-12) or posterior (Fig. 8-13) shoulder dislocation but most often anteriorly.[35,36] When this fracture is due to anterior dislocation, it is seen as a thin curvilinear bone fragment immediately medial to the anterior inferior glenoid rim superimposed on the glenoid neck on an AP view. Usually, it is better seen with a posterior oblique (Grashey) view (see Fig. 8-12), an axillary view, or with CT.

Fractures of the scapular body, Class 3 fractures, may be vertical, horizontal, or comminuted (Fig. 8-14).[17] They are easily overlooked, for the reasons cited above. No special radiographic views are needed to identify them. They merely have to be sought. We like the Grashey view because it throws the ribs off part of the scapula and

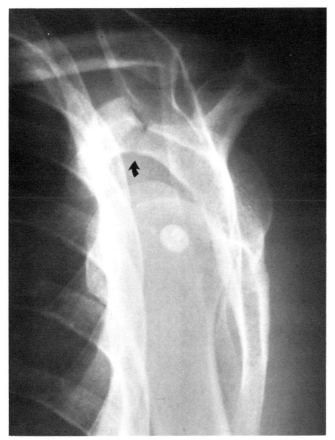

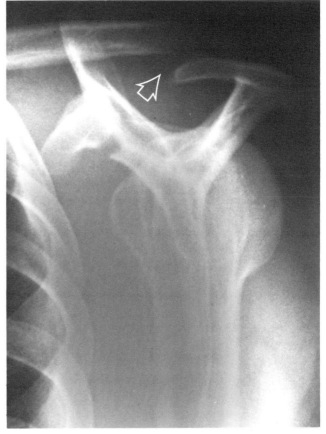

A   B

Figure 8-10 **A.** Anterior subcoracoid dislocation of the humeral head and fracture of the coracoid (*arrow*) in a 35-year-old man seen with a scapular Y view. **B.** A postreduction scapular Y view in the same patient made a few minutes later demonstrates dislocation of the acromioclavicular joint (*arrow*), which could not be appreciated on the prereduction film, **A.**

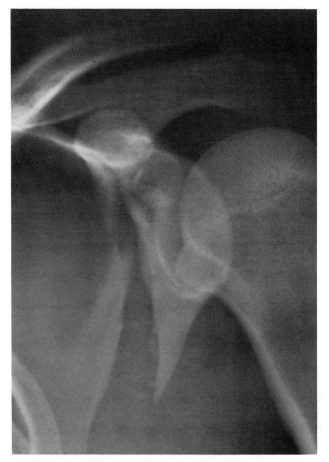

Figure 8-11 Glenoid neck fracture with modest displacement in a 22-year-old man secondary to a block to the upper chest during a football game.

Pertinent anatomic features of the proximal humerus include the greater and lesser tuberosities, the head, the anatomic neck, and the surgical neck. The supraspinatus, infraspinatus, and teres minor muscles insert in a line from anterior to posterior on the greater tuberosity and externally rotate the humeral head. The subscapularis muscle inserts on the lesser tuberosity and internally rotates the head. These four muscles and their tendons form the rotator cuff. The pectoralis major inserts on the anterior surface of the proximal humerus immediately distal to the surgical neck and adducts the humeral shaft. Medial to this insertion the latissimus dorsi and teres major muscles insert. The neurovascular bundle containing the axillary artery and vein and the ulnar, median, and radial nerves lies anterior to the glenohumeral joint on the anterior surface of the subscapularis muscle. Anterior dislocation of the humeral head and displaced fractures of the surgical neck of the humerus may injure any of these nerves or vessels.[36–38,41]

Fractures of the proximal humerus may involve the surgical or anatomic neck, the greater or lesser tuberosity, the articular surface, or various combinations of these structures. In 80 percent of these fractures there is no significant displacement of the fracture fragments.[38] Surgical neck fractures are frequently impacted and the

gives a true AP view of the bone. A scapular Y view is useful also to sight down the length of the bone, and it often best demonstrates displaced bone fragments.

The importance of scapular fractures resides not in the fracture itself but in the high incidence of associated severe, often life-threatening, injuries. Scapular fractures are sentinel injuries: they are a warning that significant ipsilateral, regional injuries of the shoulder girdle and thoracic cage likely are present and perhaps multiple remote injuries. A mortality rate of 10[17] to 16 percent[16] has been reported in association with Class 2 or 3 fractures.

Fractures of the Proximal Humerus

Fractures of the proximal humerus occur at an average age of 55 to 65 years.[37–39] Until age 45 they are evenly distributed between the sexes, but thereafter there is a steep increase in incidence, principally in women.[38–40] In older patients most proximal humerus fractures are sustained from falls onto the outstretched hand from a standing position. Fractures in younger patients tend to occur from more severe trauma.

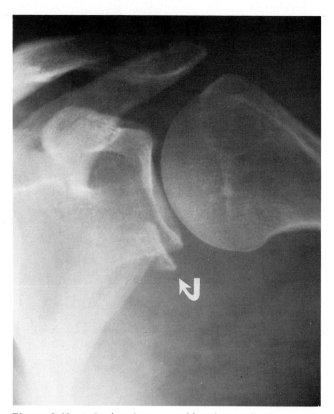

Figure 8-12 A Grashey (posterior oblique) view demonstrates an anterior inferior glenoid rim fracture (*arrow*) that a 41-year-old man sustained in a fall. The fracture was best seen with this view after reduction of an anterior dislocation.

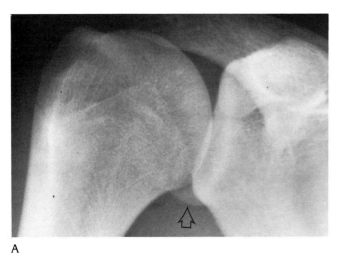

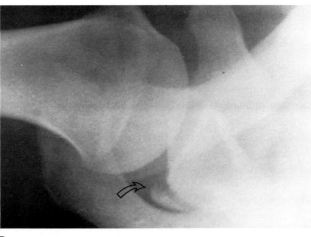

A   B

Figure 8-13 **A.** A Grashey view demonstrates a glenoid rim fracture (*arrow*) sustained by a 21-year-old professional baseball pitcher while throwing a baseball. **B.** An axillary view demonstrates that the glenoid rim fracture is a posterior (*arrow*) rim fracture rather than the more frequent anterior type.

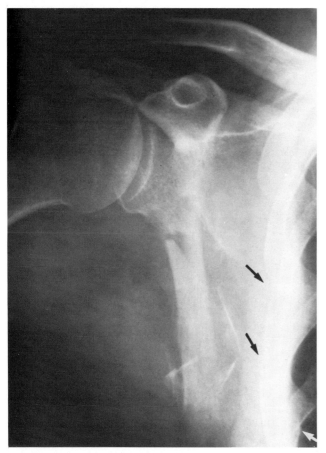

Figure 8-14 Comminuted fracture of the scapular body with fracture of multiple adjacent ribs (*arrows*) sustained in a motor vehicle accident by a 45-year-old man. This combination of fractures has been reported with approximately 50 percent of scapular fractures.[10,12] Scapular fractures are sentinel lesions usually accompanied by other significant fractures or organ injuries.

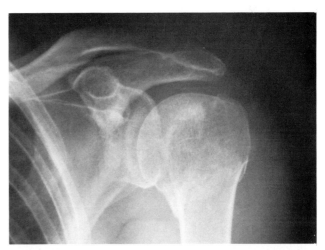

Figure 8-15 A nondisplaced fracture of the surgical neck and greater tuberosity in a 61-year-old woman who fell. This is a one-part fracture since the fracture fragments are not displaced.

adjacent tuberosities are often fractured, but these fractures are infrequently displaced (Fig. 8-15). The fragments are held in place by the rotator cuff, the partially intact periosteum, and the joint capsule. These nondisplaced fractures can be treated by closed methods. In approximately 15 percent of proximal humeral fractures one or more fragments are displaced, which often requires open reduction and internal fixation.[38] Two-part fractures account for 10 percent of proximal humeral fractures, three-part fractures for 3 percent, and four-part fractures for 4 percent.[37] The remaining 2 to 5 percent of fractures involve the humeral head. These include split fractures of the head and compression fractures of the articular surface such as a Hill-Sachs deformity or a trough line deformity sustained with dislocation.

The surgical neck is the most common site of fracture, which usually is accompanied by a nondisplaced greater tuberosity fracture. Isolated fractures of the anatomic neck are quite rare[38] and disrupt the humeral head blood supply, causing osteonecrosis, especially when they are displaced. If impaction of the anatomic neck occurs, a most unusual occurrence, there is a higher expectation of humeral head survival than without impaction. Isolated fractures of the greater tuberosity are uncommon, and those of the lesser tuberosity are rare (Fig. 8-16).[42] Greater tuberosity fractures occur most frequently in association with surgical neck fractures (Figs. 8-15, 8-17), and lesser tuberosity fractures with posterior dislocation of the shoulder.[44]

The most widely used classification of proximal humeral fractures was developed by Neer in 1970 based on a proposal by Codman in 1934 that these fractures roughly followed the anatomic lines of epiphyseal union.[38,45] The classification not only provides logical

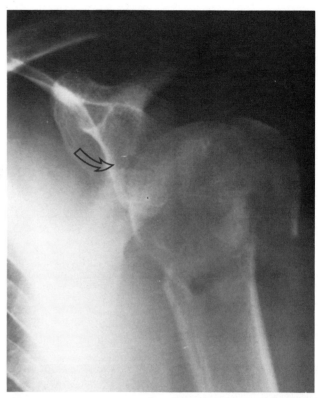

Figure 8-17 Fractures of the surgical neck and greater tuberosity of the humerus and a horizontal fracture of the glenoid (*arrow*) in a 60-year-old man. The patient was blown down by a gust of wind while walking. In spite of the comminution, this is a two-part fracture of the proximal humerus because only the greater tuberosity is displaced. A hemarthrosis causes inferior subluxation of the humeral head.

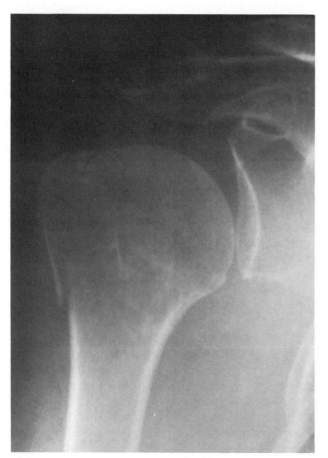

Figure 8-16 A Grashey view demonstrates an isolated nondisplaced greater tuberosity fracture in an 85-year-old woman sustained by falling down two steps. This is an unusual one-part fracture, since greater tuberosity fractures are usually associated with anterior dislocation, which was not present in this patient.

categories but also has predictive value the surgeon can use to plan treatment.[37,38] The classification is based on the presence or absence of displacement of one or more of the four major segments of the proximal humerus: the head, the greater tuberosity, the lesser tuberosity, and the shaft.[38] Fractures are classified as one-part to four-part fractures, according to how many segments are displaced. To be considered displaced a fragment must be angulated more than 45° or displaced by more than 1 cm from its normal position. A fragment may be comminuted, with several undisplaced pieces, but they should not be considered separate fragments since they are held in continuity by soft tissue. Using this classification, 80 percent of fractures of the proximal humerus are one-part fractures (see Figs. 8-15, 8-16) which are stable and not displaced and can be treated by closed means. With a two-part fracture one fragment is displaced in relation to the other three anatomic structures (see Fig. 8-17). With a three-part fracture two fragments are displaced from each other and from the two undisplaced fragments but the head remains in contact with the glenoid (see Fig. 8-18). So long as one of the tuberosities remains attached to the head, the blood supply to the humeral head can be expected to be intact. With a four-part fracture all four segments are displaced (Figs. 8-19, 8-20)[38], and osteonecrosis of the humeral head is assured. The humeral head has no soft tissue attachment and thus no restraint except the joint capsule, so its normal relation to the glenoid is easily lost. The humeral head may be angulated anteriorly, posteriorly, laterally, inferiorly, or superiorly. A torn rotator cuff occurs with a displaced fracture of either tuberosity.

Displaced fractures are displaced according to the direction of muscle pull on the loose fragment.[37] The shaft will be displaced anteriorly and medially by the pull of the pectoralis major. The lesser tuberosity is retracted by the subscapularis and the greater tuberosity by the supraspinatus, infraspinatus, and teres minor muscles. A displaced fracture of the anatomic neck separates the humeral head from its blood supply. There is no muscle attachment to the head fragment, so it can float within the joint capsule or outside of it, depending on the intactness of the capsule.

Fracture-dislocation of the proximal humerus consists

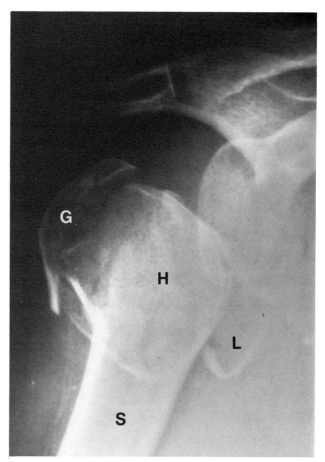

Figure 8-19 A four-part fracture of the proximal humerus in a 56-year-old woman followed a fall from a chair. The humeral head is rotated but remains in contact with the glenoid. Inferior subluxation is the result of hemarthrosis. (Key: L, lesser tuberosity; G, greater tuberosity; H, humeral head; S, humeral shaft.)

of either avulsion of the tuberosities associated with dislocation of the humeral head (Fig. 8-21) or dislocation of the articular segment accompanied by a severely comminuted fracture of the proximal humerus (see Fig. 8-20). The humeral head may be dislocated anteriorly, posteriorly, superiorly, or inferiorly with a fracture-dislocation. According to the displacement of the fracture fragments it may be classified as a two-part (see Fig. 8-21), three-part, or four-part (see Fig. 8-20) fracture-dislocation. Relation of fracture fragments to one another may be difficult to determine under these circumstances, and CT is needed to sort out their relative positions.[5] Approximately 15 percent of anterior dislocations and 15 percent of posterior dislocations are associated with avulsion of the greater and the lesser tuberosity, respectively.[44]

Impression or compression fractures of the humeral head articular surface (Fig. 8-22) and head-splitting fractures (Fig. 8-23) are special cases. Compression fractures of the articular surface are caused by anterior or poste-

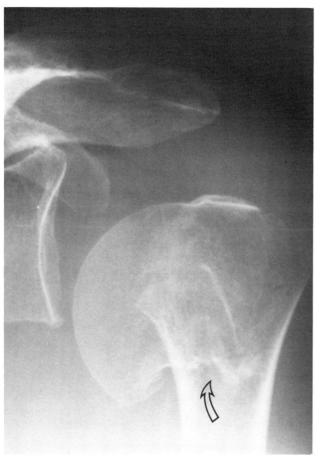

Figure 8-18 An impacted three-part fracture with more than 1 cm displacement of the fracture fragments in an 83-year-old man was sustained when he fell onto his shoulder when the bus he was riding suddenly stopped. The lesser tuberosity has been avulsed (*arrow*). The inferior subluxation of the humeral head is due to a hemarthrosis.

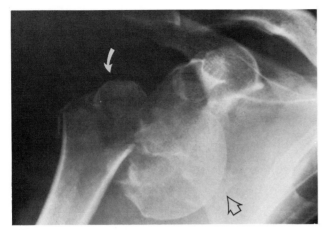

Figure 8-20 A four-part fracture-dislocation in a 66-year-old man was sustained in a fall. The fractured lesser tuberosity is seen medially (*open arrow*) and the greater tuberosity laterally (*solid arrow*).

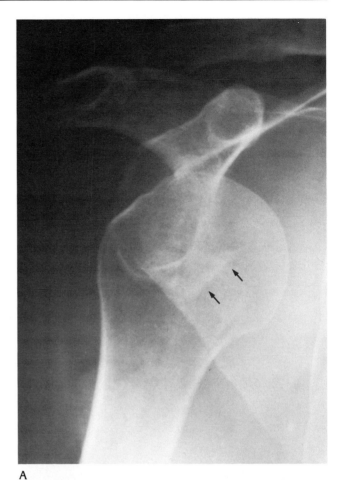

A

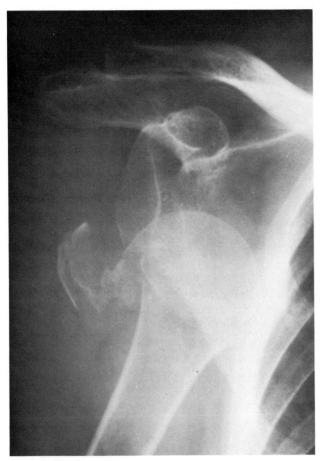

Figure 8-21 Fracture-dislocation. Anterior subcoracoid dislocation with a displaced fracture of the greater tuberosity and a fracture of the surgical neck (impossible to see on this view) in a 74-year-old woman injured in a fall.

B

Figure 8-22 **A.** Anterior subcoracoid dislocation with a bone fragment (*arrows*) superimposed on the humeral head from an anterior glenoid rim fracture in a 41-year-old man. **B.** A CT scan following reduction demonstrates a Hill-Sachs deformity (*arrow*) or impression fracture of the posterior lateral humeral head. The fractured glenoid rim is not seen on this section but was easily seen on others.

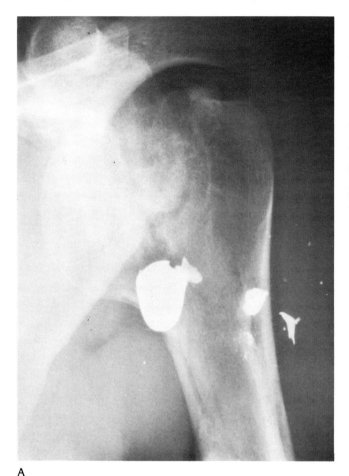

A

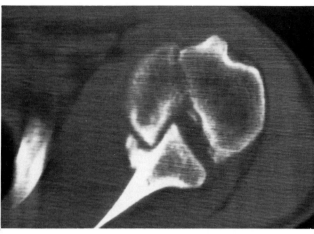

B

Figure 8-23 **A.** Fracture and anterior dislocation of the humeral head in a 19-year-old man secondary to a gunshot wound several weeks earlier. **B.** CT demonstrates a split fracture of the humeral head, the anterior dislocation of only the anterior fracture fragment of the humeral head, and a deformed anterior glenoid rim from a healed rim fracture. None of these findings was appreciated accurately on the conventional radiographic study.

rior dislocation and are graded by the percentage of the surface involved: less than 20 percent, 20 to 45 percent, and more than 45 percent. The less-than-20 percent group can be treated by closed means, the 20-to-45-percent group need surgical correction, and the greater-than-45-percent group need a head prosthesis. The head-splitting fractures fragment the articular surface into many disconnected pieces. The mechanism is a blow to the lateral aspect of the shoulder that impales the head on the glenoid. They are treated with a humeral head prosthesis.[37,38]

Complications of fractures and dislocations of the proximal humerus may occur immediately or later. Immediate complications include injury to the axillary artery or the brachial plexus, both of which course close to the coracoid, the anterior glenoid rim, the anterior humeral head, and the surgical neck of the humerus. The axillary nerve is the nerve most commonly injured. The arterial injury may consist of transection of the axillary artery, avulsion of one of its branches, or partial or complete thrombosis arising from an intimal tear.[46,47] Delayed complications include frozen shoulder, impaired motion from deformity of the articular surfaces from a healed fracture, or osteonecrosis of the humeral head. Osteonecrosis is seen almost certainly with displaced anatomic neck fractures, and often even when anatomic neck fractures are not displaced and impacted.[38]

Fractures of the Proximal Humeral Epiphysis

Injuries of the proximal humeral epiphysis account for 3 percent of all epiphyseal fractures.[48] Most such injuries demonstrate little or no displacement, are relatively uncomplicated, and can be treated by immobilization. The proximal humeral epiphysis develops from three ossification centers, which produce the humeral head, the greater tuberosity, and the lesser tuberosity.[49] They appear at approximately age 3 months, 3 years, and 5 years, respectively, and at age 7 fuse into a single center with an inverted V shape. This cone-shaped epiphysis with its cephalad convexity locks the physis and metaphysis in a highly stable configuration. Thickened periosteum posteriorly at the level of the epiphyseal plate further resists posterior displacement.

Two types of epiphyseal plate injuries are seen in the proximal humerus. Salter Type I injuries are seen most often in infants and young children and Salter Type II injuries predominate in older children and adolescents.[49] Presumably, the freedom of motion of the shoulder protects the epiphysis from Type III, IV, and V injuries. Significant growth disturbances are unusual, but when they occur they are usually seen in older adolescents or in association with marked displacement of the fracture fragments.[50] They may cause early epiphyseal plate closure with shortening of 1 to 3 cm but this is tolerated well, unlike similar shortening in the lower extremity.[51] Also, almost any deformity in patients younger than 12 years of age remodels. Acute epiphyseal separation due to throwing has also been described. Chronic stress from throwing in baseball pitchers aged 10 to 15 years has been reported, which produces widening of the epiphyseal plate and local bone demineralization.[52,53] The demineralization presumably is due to local inflammation. Comparative radiographs of the opposite shoulder are needed to make the diagnosis. The problem is self-limiting, and with rest and avoidance of throwing the associated pain subsides and the epiphyseal plate reverts to normal.[52]

DISLOCATIONS

Dislocation of the Sternoclavicular Joint

The sternoclavicular joint is the sole articulation between the upper extremity and the trunk. It infrequently sustains significant injury, indicating how well it is suited to its task. Of all dislocations of the pectoral girdle only 2 to 3 percent involve the sternoclavicular joint.[37,54] The rarity of this dislocation is fortunate since it is difficult to visualize the joint with routine radiographic projections owing to the superimposed spine and mediastinum.[55]

The sternoclavicular joint can dislocate anteriorly or posteriorly with slight superior displacement (Fig. 8-24). Anterior dislocations are variously reported as being 20 times[56] to two times[37] more common than posterior dislocations. The inferior margin of the proximal clavicle is tightly attached to the superior margin of the proximal first rib by the costoclavicular (or rhomboid) ligament.[37] This ligament acts as a fulcrum when a blow is delivered to the anterior or posterior portion of the shoulder. The clavicle may act as a lever with such trauma, causing disruption and dislocation of the proximal clavicle either anteriorly or posteriorly in the direction opposite to the direction in which the blow displaced the distal clavicle.[57,58] Posterior dislocation also can result from a direct blow to the medial part of the clavicle. Spontaneous dislocation without a history of trauma[59] or in elderly

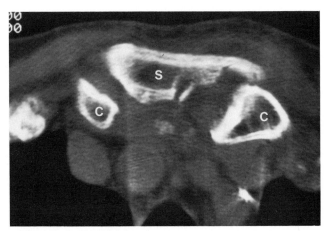

Figure 8-24   CT of the sternoclavicular joints shows posterior dislocation with typical slight superior position and, thus, larger size of the left proximal clavicle and fracture of the adjacent manubrium in this 85-year-old man. (Key: S, sternum; C, clavicle.)

women with degenerative arthritis of the sternoclavicular joint has been reported.[60]

Dislocations of the sternoclavicular joint are difficult to identify and evaluate radiographically. Even with tomographs we have found it difficult to interpret the amount of clavicular displacement. Therefore we strongly urge our clinicians to obtain a CT study of the sternoclavicular joints whenever there is a clinical possibility of a dislocation there (see Fig. 8-24).[3] Care must be exercised not to misdiagnose an unfused medial clavicle epiphysis, a thin, vertical line of ossification, as a fracture. It is not possible to angulate the x-ray beam cephalad enough to identify some fractures of the most medial part of the clavicle, and CT is necessary to evaluate this area.

Almost all complications of sternoclavicular dislocation are associated with posterior dislocation.[61,62] The lack of associated complications other than a local lump, which on occasion requires cosmetic surgery, no doubt explains why the literature mostly ignores the much more frequent anterior dislocation in favor of the posterior variety. Approximately 25 percent of posterior dislocations are associated with a complication such as laceration of the superior vena cava, thoracic outlet syndrome from venous compression, voice changes from recurrent laryngeal nerve compression, rupture or compression of the trachea, pneumothorax, esophageal rupture, or compression or occlusion of the subclavian or the carotid arteries. In spite of this intimidating list of complications, death is much more rare from any of them than from surgical treatment of the dislocated joint.[37] Therefore closed reduction and immobilization of the extremity with a sling is the therapy of choice. Open reduction and pin fixation has culminated in pin breakage in as many as 30 percent and migration of pins into the mediastinum with laceration of a great vessel, and occasionally death.[11,20,37]

Acromioclavicular Joint Injuries

SEPARATIONS AND DISLOCATIONS

Acromioclavicular joint dislocation—from a direct fall onto the shoulder or from a fall onto an outstretched hand[9,63]—accounts for 12 percent of all dislocations of the shoulder area, with 85 percent involving the glenohumeral joint and 2 to 3 percent the sternoclavicular joint.[54] They occur most commonly between ages 15 and 40 years and most often are due to an athletic injury.[10,64]

Injury to the acromioclavicular joint may include a sprain or tear of the acromioclavicular ligaments (Fig. 8-25), a tear of the coracoclavicular ligaments (Fig. 8-26), a coracoid process fracture (see Figs. 8-8, 8-10), detachment of the deltoid and trapezius muscles from the clavicle, or intraarticular fractures of the clavicle or acromion.[64] The acromioclavicular ligaments are injured first. Depending on the severity of injury the acromioclavicular joint may be widened or the distal end of the clavicle may be elevated somewhat (see Fig. 8-25). More severe injuries disrupt the coracoclavicular ligaments, allowing abnormal width of the coracoclavicular interval as well as further cephalad migration of the distal clavicle (see Fig. 8-26). This may be obvious on initial films, but if it is not, stress views with weights are needed to exclude this possible abnormality. The width of the acromioclavicular joint is normally 7 mm or less in men and 6 mm or less in women, but it decreases with age.[65] The width of the AC joints of an individual should not increase by more than 2 mm with stress views. The distance between the coracoid and the clavicle is normally 11 to 13 mm.[66] It is definitely abnormal if there is

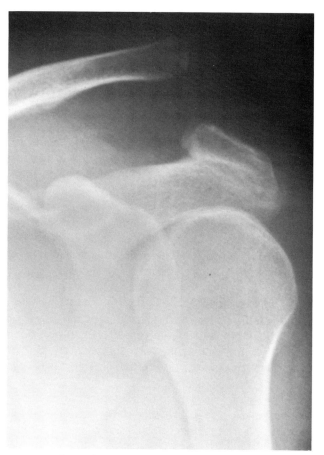

Figure 8-26 Grade 3 acromioclavicular joint separation with grossly abnormal coracoclavicular and acromioclavicular distances due to a fall onto the shoulder in a 47-year-old man.

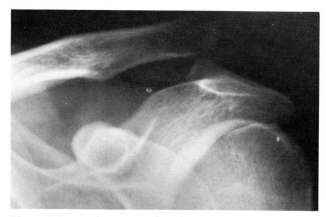

Figure 8-25 Grade 2 acromioclavicular joint disruption in a 27-year-old man occurred when he fell off a bicycle onto his shoulder. The acromioclavicular joint is dislocated but the coracoclavicular distance is normal.

a difference of 50 percent or more between the two shoulders, and it may be abnormal at half this distance.[66] Because there is a wide range of variation of alignment between the acromion and the clavicle within the population, this alignment is not diagnostically useful. Approximately 20 percent of patients demonstrate the distal clavicle projecting above, below, or superimposed on the acromion.[67] Weight-bearing views in these patients show no change in the relation between acromion and clavicle.[67]

Acromioclavicular joint separation is a common athletic injury caused by a fall onto the point of the acromion.[9] These injuries most commonly are graded 1 to 3.[9,63,68] A Grade 1 injury is a sprain with strain of the supporting ligaments. There is no widening of the joint and no displacement of the distal tip of the clavicle.[9,68] A Grade 2 injury results from dislocation of the acromioclavicular ligaments causing dislocation or subluxation of the joint but with normal coracoclavicular distance (see Fig. 8-25). In a Grade 3 injury the coracoclavicular distance also becomes abnormal, the distance being at least 50 percent greater on the affected side than on the normal side (see Fig. 8-26).[37] Rarely, a coracoid process fracture occurs, instead of coracoclavicular ligament rupture,[69] when acromioclavicular joint disruption occurs (see Figs. 8-8, 8-10). Usually this is seen in patients younger than 25 years. Since the apophysis of the coracoid does not fuse until age 21 to 25 years, many of these presumed coracoid fractures probably represent avulsion of the apophysis.[26,69] This is also a Grade 3 acromioclavicular separation. Rockwood has proposed adding three more grades of separation to the classification, Grades 4 to 6. Grade 4 represents a posterior dislocation (Fig. 8-27), Grade 5 a severe Grade 3 dislocation (see Fig. 8-26), and Grade 6 a dislocation of the distal clavicle anteriorly and beneath the coracoid.[64] Grades 4 to 6 are all rare to extremely rare lesions that are primarily surgical findings, rather than specific radiographic abnormalities, that have implications for surgery. Adding these grades seems to complicate the classification unnecessarily.

Protass and colleagues[27] advocate an axillary view or an AP view with 30° to 35° of cephalad angulation of the x-ray beam to demonstrate coracoid fractures. We have found that a scapular Y view of the shoulder is simpler and as effective a way to demonstrate these fractures (see Figs. 8-8, 8-10). The coracoid develops from five ossification centers,[22] and care must be exercised to avoid mistaking one of them for an avulsion fracture. Comparison with the normal side is useful.[27]

Although the clavicle appears to be dislocated cephalad with Grade 3 separations, it actually remains in normal position. The shoulder sags under its own weight because it has lost its normal ligamentous suspension.

POSTTRAUMATIC OSTEOLYSIS OF THE DISTAL CLAVICLE

Posttraumatic osteolysis of the distal end of the clavicle may occur from repeated injury of the acromioclavicular joint[70] or from a single injury.[71] It has been reported most frequently in weight lifters,[70] but we have also seen it in hockey players, a baseball player, and in a manual laborer who frequently shoveled large quantities of dirt above the level of his head while digging trenches. Repetitive stress of the acromioclavicular joint over a long time was the common experience of these patients. The trauma is not severe enough to cause joint dislocation. Almost all of the patients are in their third decade.[70,71] The same abnormality also is seen following a sprain of the acromioclavicular joint, though its mechanism is unknown.[71] In this situation the osteolytic process begins some 4 weeks to several months after injury, with slow onset of acromioclavicular joint pain. In the case of weight lifters, no specific injury could be recalled and radiographic findings appeared only after months or years of weight training.[70] Radiographically the earliest findings were a loss of subchondral bone detail with

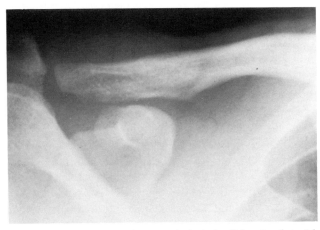

Figure 8-27 A rare posterior acromioclavicular dislocation that a 34-year-old man sustained when he ran into a wall while playing racquetball. The distal end of the clavicle is dislocated posteriorly into or through the trapezius muscle. This type of dislocation could project the clavicle at the same level as the acromion but in this patient projects it inferior to the acromion. An axillary view is usually needed to prove its posterior position.

small subchondral cystic areas with sclerotic margins (Fig. 8-28).[70] The adjacent acromion is always normal.[70] Technetium bone scan demonstrates abnormal activity in the distal clavicle, and occasionally in the acromion.[70] More pronounced findings include widening of the AC joint due to erosion of the distal 1 cm of the clavicle.[71] No synovial changes in the acromioclavicular joint have been seen in surgical specimens.[71] The osteolysis is self-limited to the distal centimeter of the clavicle, which in some cases can become tapered.[72,73] Eventually the cortical margin of the distal clavicle is partially reconstituted, but some joint widening persists.

Shoulder Dislocations

The shoulder joint is the most unstable joint in the body.[74] Dislocations of the shoulder account for more

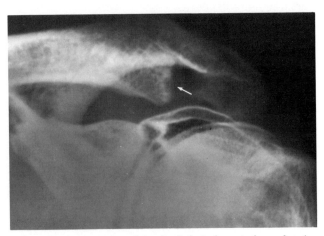

Figure 8-28 Resorption of the distal clavicular articular surface (*arrow*) in a 41-year-old longtime weight lifter. Contrast material and air in the shoulder joint are from an arthrogram.

than 50 percent of all large-joint dislocations,[75] in spite of its being uncommon in children.[37,76] The peaks are at approximately age 20 years, and again at 60 years; half occur before age 45 and half afterwards.[36,74] In decreasing order of frequency, dislocations of the glenohumeral joint are anterior, posterior, inferior (luxatio erecta), and superior dislocations.[37,77] At least 95 percent of all dislocations of the shoulder are anterior,[36,44,78] 2 to 4 percent are posterior, and the balance are inferior or superior. Dislocations of the shoulder may be recent or recurrent, traumatic or atraumatic.[36] The atraumatic type is associated with congenital deficits of the humeral head or glenoid and with lax, mobile shoulders that lack adequate muscle and soft tissue support.[36,75] In a series of 500 shoulder dislocations reported by Rowe only 22 were atraumatic.[36]

Traumatic dislocations are most often due to indirect forces. Abduction with forced external rotation of the arm causes anterior dislocation, whereas a force applied through the arm with adduction, flexion, and internal rotation, as with falls onto an outstretched hand, causes posterior dislocation.[37] Occasionally a direct force such as a blow applied directly to the anterior or posterior shoulder may cause, respectively, posterior or anterior dislocation. Seizures and electric shock are common causes of bilateral posterior dislocation, but we have seen bilateral anterior dislocation result from these as well. Inferior dislocation (luxatio erecta) is produced by hyperabduction of the arm. The neck of the humerus impinges on the acromion, using it as a fulcrum to lever the humeral head away from the glenoid, and allows it to dislocate inferiorly (Fig. 8-29). The same dislocation also can be produced by a caudally directed force acting along the length of the arm with the shoulder maximally abducted. Superior dislocation, the rarest of all shoulder dislocations, is produced by a force directed cephalad along the arm with the shoulder adducted.[77] Usually this is produced by a cephalad blow to the elbow. The humeral head is driven through the rotator cuff into the acromion.

ANTERIOR SHOULDER DISLOCATION

Anterior shoulder dislocations are classed as subcoracoid, subglenoid, subclavicular, and intrathoracic, according to where the humeral head comes to rest. The most common type, the subcoracoid, occurs when the humeral head lies inferior to the coracoid (see Fig. 8-21, 8-22).[37] The subglenoid is the next most common type, with the humeral head inferior to the glenoid rim (Fig. 8-30). The subclavicular type with the humeral head displaced medial to the coracoid and lying inferior to the clavicle is rare. The very rare intrathoracic variety is caused by a violent force dislocating the joint and then driving the humeral head through an intercostal space into the thorax.

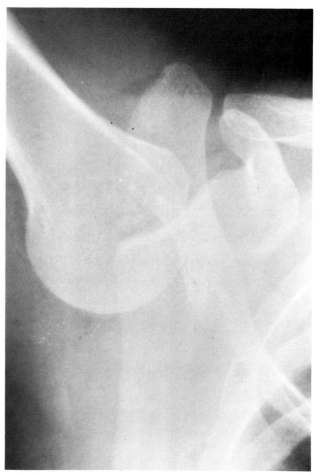

Figure 8-29 Luxatio erecta, or inferior dislocation, of the humeral head in a 31-year-old construction worker. He fell off a two-story scaffold but caught it with his hand part way down, hyperabducting his shoulder and levering the humeral head out of the glenoid. Notice that the humeral shaft and scapular spine are parallel.

As the humeral head dislocates its posterolateral surface strikes the anterior or anterior inferior glenoid rim. This may cause a compression fracture of the posterolateral humeral head, a Hill-Sachs lesion (see Fig. 8-22B), or a glenoid rim fracture (see Figs. 8-17, 8-22A) or both.[36] Fracture of the glenoid rim has been reported in 5 to 8 percent of anterior dislocations, and it may be large enough to need open reduction and internal fixation to prevent recurrent dislocation.[35,36] These fractures are difficult, if not impossible, to identify on standard AP views with internal or external rotation. They are usually best seen with axillary, Grashey, or apical oblique views. CT is an even more certain way of demonstrating either a glenoid rim fracture or a Hill-Sachs deformity (see Fig. 8-22B). The Hill-Sachs defect occurs in more than 50 percent of anterior dislocations, is usually caused by the first episode, and may enlarge with recurrent dislocations.[36,37,79] It is best seen on conventional radiographs with AP projection in internal rotation.

A fracture of the greater tuberosity has been reported

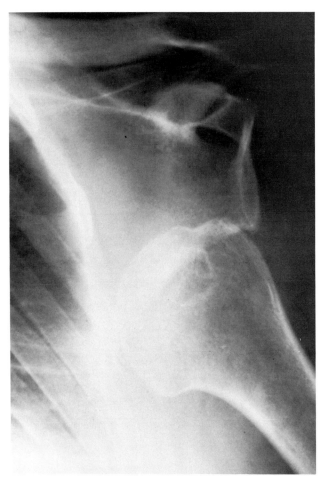

Figure 8-30 Anterior dislocation with subglenoid position of the humeral head sustained when a 71-year-old man slipped and fell on ice.

in approximately 15 percent of anterior dislocations and it may need internal fixation if it remains grossly displaced after reduction of the dislocation.[35] It is most frequent in older persons (see Fig. 8-21). Fractures of the surgical neck of the humerus (Fig. 8-31), the scapular body, the acromion, and the clavicle collectively have been reported to be associated with 2 percent of all shoulder dislocations (see Fig. 8-21).[36] Occasionally, nondisplaced fractures of the surgical neck are converted into fracture dislocations with attempted reduction of the dislocation (see Fig. 8-31).

The most common complication of anterior dislocation, recurrence, is related to the patient's age at the time of the initial dislocation.[74,79,80] The reported recurrence rate is over 90 percent for patients younger than 20 years, 75 percent for those aged 20 to 40, and 14 percent for older persons.[74,79] The more severe the trauma that caused the dislocation the less likely is recurrence.[74] When the greater tuberosity is fractured with the dislocation, the reported prevalence of recurrence is 5 to 15 percent.[74,79] Bankart[81,82] insisted that detachment of the anterior labrum and stripping of the anterior joint capsule from the glenoid rim was the cause of recurrent dislocation. Carter Rowe found defects at surgery in the anterior glenoid rim, separation of the capsule from the glenoid rim (Bankart lesion), and a Hill-Sachs lesion in almost equal numbers in 161 patients with recurrent dislocation.[74] Also, at surgery he found no abnormality in 15 percent of 161 patients. He concluded that recurrent dislocation is caused by a combination of abnormalities, not a single one.[74]

In patients older than 45 years dislocation is more frequently complicated by rotator cuff tear, greater tuberosity fracture, or nerve injury than by recurrent dislocation.[83] Nerve injury occurs in 5 to 10 percent of anterior dislocations, usually with axillary nerve or brachial plexus involvement, but most neurologic injuries are transient.[83,84] They occur when the neurovascular bundle is stretched over the subscapularis and teres major muscles as the humeral head and neck are dislocated anteriorly.[84,85] Arterial injury is usually confined to elderly patients with significant arteriosclerosis. The axillary artery or one of its branches is injured.[75]

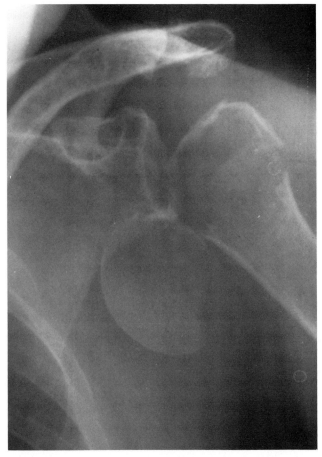

Figure 8-31 Severely displaced humeral head fracture originally was an anterior dislocation with a nondisplaced surgical neck fracture sustained by this 69-year-old woman from a fall while walking. Closed reduction was attempted, displacing the fracture and turning it into a severely displaced fracture-dislocation.

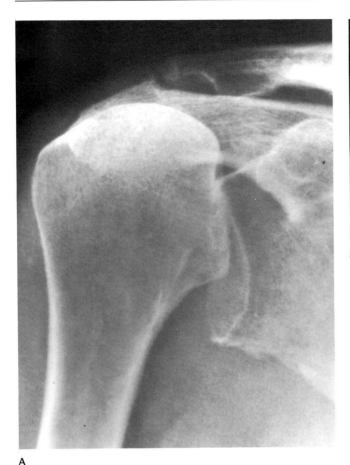

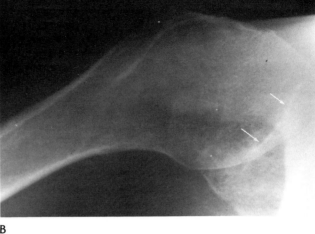

B

Figure 8-32 **A.** Superior dislocation of the humeral head in an 81-year-old woman who experienced no known trauma but had a rotator cuff tear identified a year earlier by arthroscopy that was not repaired when calcific deposits were resected. The patient plays tennis regularly but with increasing difficulty owing to pain, muscle weakness, and decreasing range of motion. Erosion of the medial articular surface of the humeral head is due to the chronic nature of the dislocation. Most superior dislocations are atraumatic. This one is due to a chronic rotator cuff tear. Erosion of the distal clavicle is from known hyperparathyroidism, which has been treated. **B.** Axillary view of the same shoulder demonstrates no anterior or posterior position of the humeral head. The glenoid rim (*arrow*) is difficult to see.

A

INFERIOR SHOULDER DISLOCATION

Luxatio erecta, inferior dislocation of the shoulder, is rare but unmistakable. The arm is abducted, elevated, and fixed with the hand and forearm resting on top of the patient's head. Clinically nothing else has this presentation, so it should present no diagnostic problem. The humeral head, levered out of the glenoid fossa by hyperabduction, slips into the subcoracoid position.[77] The entire capsule may be separated, or the head may be buttonholded through a tear in the inferior capsule.[75] Radiographically the humeral shaft is parallel to the scapular spine, the arm is abducted and fixed, and the humeral head is subcoracoid in position (see Fig. 8-29). Although the subcoracoid position of the humeral head is also seen with anterior dislocations, no confusion should exist, since the arm is adducted with the humeral shaft parallel to the chest wall in those patients. Complications include fracture of the acromion, the greater tuberosity of the humerus, or the inferior glenoid rim and rarely a neurovascular injury.[77,86]

SUPERIOR SHOULDER DISLOCATION

Superior dislocation of the shoulder is rarer still than luxatio erecta.[77] The usual cause is a strong upward force on the adducted arm, such as a cephalically directed blow to the flexed elbow. The humeral head is driven upwardly through the rotator cuff into the acromion. Radiographs demonstrate the humeral head cephalad to the glenoid fossa, close to the acromion, and often associated fracture of the clavicle, acromion, coracoid, or greater tuberosity of the humerus or separation of the acromioclavicular joint. Muscle weakness, loss or decrease of the radical pulse, and hypesthesias are often associated neurovascular complications.[75,77] Most superior dislocations are seen in older patients, who probably have preexisting rotator cuff tears or a very weak cuff that provides little resistance to a cephalad force. They may even have a chronic superior dislocation (Fig. 8-32) that is detected coincidentally when radiographs are obtained for a traumatic episode which did not in fact cause the dislocation but is blamed for it. Rotator cuff tears with superior migration of the humeral head are not infrequent, but traumatic superior dislocation is, especially in younger patients where the rotator cuff is thick and a very powerful force is needed to drive the humeral head through it to produce a superior dislocation.

POSTERIOR SHOULDER DISLOCATION

Posterior dislocations account for 2 to 4 percent of all shoulder dislocations.[36,78] Making the diagnosis is the most serious difficulty with this type of dislocation since as many as 70 percent are missed on the initial exami-

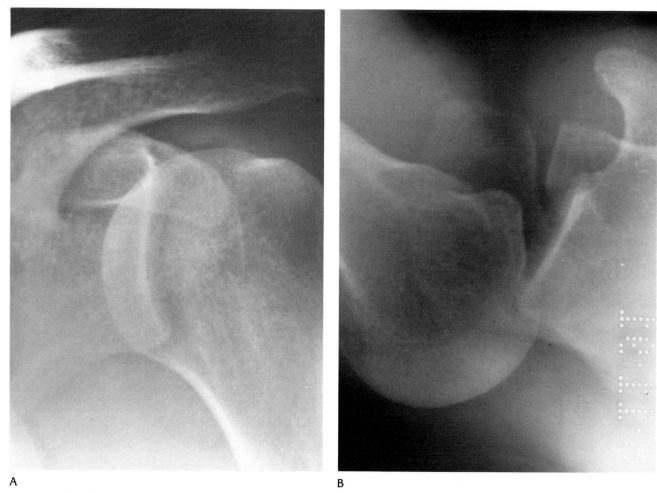

A   B

Figure 8-33 **A.** A Grashey view demonstrates overlap of the humeral head and glenoid from a posterior dislocation in a 30-year-old bicyclist struck by a taxi. **B.** An axillary view of the same patient also demonstrates the posterior dislocation and a compression fracture of the humeral head. The acromio-clavicular joint projects anterior to the glenoid. The joint space is not widened in **A** because of the deep trough line fracture of the humeral head.

nation and large numbers remain undetected even after more than a year.[1,87] The dislocation is caused by a direct blow to the anterior aspect of the shoulder or by an indirect force such as a fall onto the outstretched hand or a seizure. With either of these mechanisms the humeral head is pushed posteriorly in internal rotation, driving the anterior medial surface of the head against the posterior glenoid rim. The humeral head is softer than the glenoid rim, so a compression fracture of the head occurs at the site of impact if the force is sufficient.[44] Avulsion of the lesser tuberosity or of the posterior glenoid rim may also accompany the dislocation. Convulsive seizures and motor vehicle accidents are the most frequent causes of posterior dislocation, and bilateral dislocations are almost always due to seizures or high-voltage electric shock.[1,4,88] If following a seizure a patient has shoulder pain, a posterior dislocation must be ruled out. Conversely, a patient who presents with a posterior

shoulder dislocation and no history of trauma should prompt strong suspicion of a seizure disorder.

The findings of posterior dislocation are subtle when the routine radiographic study is confined to AP views in internal and in external rotation. They include the humeral head held in internal rotation on all views, the joint space increased because the medial humeral head is perched on the posterior glenoid rim (a *positive rim sign*), and loss of the normal half-moon overlap of the glenoid and humeral head.

We added a posterior oblique or Grashey view to our standard shoulder examination after one too many of these dislocations was missed at our institution. Since that time we are unaware of missing a posterior dislocation on the initial radiographic examination. Caution must be exercised when using the Grashey view, to be certain that the anterior and posterior glenoid rim are superimposed on one another (Fig. 8-33A). If they are not, a dislocation can be missed, as with the routine AP views, or a false positive diagnosis can be made. Diagnosis can also be made with an axillary (Fig. 8-33B) or scapular Y view. We added the Grashey view rather than either of these because it requires less movement on the patient's part. This is often important for polytrauma patients, and it also prevents the x-ray technician from manipulating an unstable fracture unawares for an axillary view before the fracture has been discovered. If a posterior dislocation is present, one sees overlap of the humeral head on the glenoid with the Grashey view rather than the clear joint space that is normally seen between the two articular surfaces (see Fig. 8-33A). The humeral head is fixed in internal rotation.

A *trough line* may be the only evidence of a posterior dislocation on the AP radiographs.[44] It is seen as a vertically oriented dense line of bone with a sharp medial margin, much less dense bone medial to the dense line, and a second more mediad dense line parallel to the lateral sclerotic line, which is the medial articular cortex of the humeral head (Fig. 8-34A).[44] The trough line is evidence of a vertical compression fracture caused by the humeral head impacting on the posterior glenoid rim. It is analogous to the Hill-Sachs defect caused by anterior dislocation. In the AP projection a posterior dislocation produces a positive rim sign, the joint appearing to be too wide, unless there is a compression fracture of the head deep enough to allow the glenoid rim to sink far enough into the impaled humeral head to cause a false negative rim sign (see Fig. 8-33).

CT establishes the diagnosis of posterior dislocation in any questionable case. It also demonstrates the size of any compression defect in the humeral head, which is useful especially when surgery is contemplated (Fig. 8-34B).[4] Avulsion fractures of the anterior or posterior glenoid rim and lesser tuberosity fractures are likewise easily demonstrated.

Scapulothoracic Dissociation

Scapulothoracic dissociation is a traumatic separation of the scapula and upper extremity from their thoracic attachments.[89,90] It is a closed forequarter amputation with intact skin caused by blunt trauma and traction to the shoulder girdle, most commonly from a motorcycle accident.[90] Most patients have multiple associated injuries: lateral displacement of the scapula, ligamentous disruption, muscular avulsion, neurovascular injury, and possibly clavicle fracture.[90,91] Partial or complete rupture of the deltoid, pectoralis minor, and trapezius muscles and avulsion of all the muscles attached to the medial border

Figure 8-34 **A.** Posterior dislocation of the right shoulder in a 44-year-old man secondary to a seizure and subsequent fall. The humeral head overlaps the glenoid rim. A dense sclerotic vertical line (*arrows*) lateral to the glenoid rim is the lateral margin of a trough line. **B.** CT of both shoulders demonstrates bilateral posterior humeral head dislocations. There is a vertical trough fracture of the right humeral head, but on the left a surgical neck fracture with displacement is seen in addition to the trough fracture. (Key: S, humeral shaft; H, humeral head.)

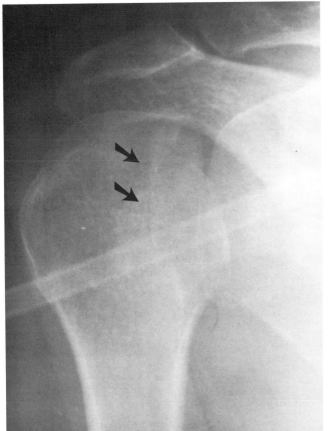

A

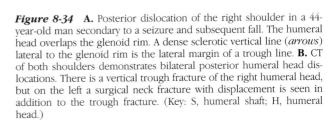

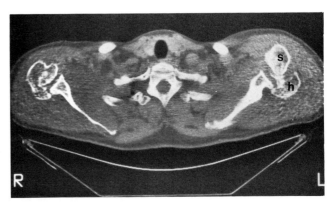

B

of the scapula are present.[89-91] Vascular disruption most often involves the subclavian artery, but axillary artery injury may occur and the subclavian vein is usually ruptured. Complete brachial plexus avulsion is most common, but incomplete reversible injury can occur.[90] A distracted clavicle fracture, sternoclavicular disruption, or a Grade 3 acromioclavicular disruption allows the upper extremity to be displaced laterally and can be seen radiographically. Scapular displacement is measured from the spinous processes of the vertebrae to the medial scapular border on a nonrotated chest radiograph with the upper extremities positioned symmetrically (Fig. 8-35). The scapula will be displaced 1 to 3 cm more on the abnormal side.[90,91] A 20 percent mortality rate has been reported, but the rate may be much greater if deaths are counted that occur before treatment can begin.[90] All patients with a complete brachial plexus avulsion are left with a flail upper extremity.

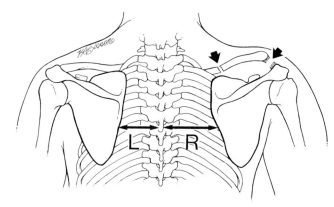

Figure 8-35 Diagram of the primary findings of traumatic scapulo-thoracic dissociation. The scapula on the affected side measures 1 to 3 cm farther from the midline than the normal side, but to prevent a false postive diagnosis care must be taken to ensure that the chest is not rotated. An associated clavicle fracture, acromioclavicular disruption, sternoclavicular dislocation, or a combination of these with distraction will also be present.

References

1. HAWKINS RJ, NEER CS II, PIANTA RM, MENDOZA FX: Locked posterior dislocation of the shoulder. *J Bone Joint Surg* 69A:9–18, 1987.
2. ZANCA P: Shoulder pain: Involvement of the acromioclavicular joint. Analysis of 100 cases. *AJR* 112:493–506, 1971.
3. DESTOUET JM, GILULA LA, MURPHY WA, SAGEL SS: Computed tomography of the sternoclavicular joint and sternum. *Radiology* 138:123–128, 1981.
4. WADLINGTON V, HENDRIX RW, ROGERS LF: CT evaluation of traumatic posterior dislocations of the shoulder. *J Trauma* 32:113–115, 1992.
5. CASTAGNO AA, SHUMAN WP, KILCOYNE RF, ET AL.: Complex fractures of the proximal humerus. Role of CT in treatment. *Radiology* 165:759–762, 1987.
6. BOWEN A: Plastic bowing of the clavicle in children. *J Bone Joint Surg* 65A:403–405, 1983.
7. STANLEY D, TROWBRIDGE EA, NORRIS SH: The mechanism of clavicular fracture. *J Bone Joint Surg* 70B:461–464, 1988.
8. ROWE CR: An atlas of anatomy and treatment of midclavicular fractures. *Clin Orthop* 58:29–42, 1968.
9. NEVIASER RJ: Injuries to the clavicle and acromioclavicular joint. *Orthop Clin North Am* 18:433–438, 1987.
10. HEPPENSTALL RB: Fractures and dislocations of the distal clavicle. *Orthop Clin North Am* 6:477–486, 1975.
11. LYONS FA, ROCKWOOD CA: Migrations of pins used in operations on the shoulder. *J Bone Joint Surg* 72A:1262–1267, 1990.
12. ESKOLA A, VAINIONPAA S, MYLLYNEN, PATIALA H, ROKKANEN P: Outcome of clavicular fracture in 89 patients. *Arch Orthop Trauma Surg* 105:337–338, 1986.
13. ZENNI EJ, KRIEG JK, ROSEN MJ: Open reduction and internal fixation of clavicular fractures. *J Bone Joint Surg* 63A:147–151, 1981.
14. NEER CS II: Nonunion of the clavicle. *JAMA* 172:1006–1011, 1960.
15. PAFFEN PJ, JANSEN EWL: Surgical treatment of clavicular fracture with Kirschner wires: A comparative study. *Arch Chir Neerland* 30:43–53, 1978.
16. THOMPSON DA, FLYNN TC, MILLER PW, FISCHER RP: The significance of scapular fractures. *J Trauma* 25:974–977, 1985.

17. IMATANI RJ: Fractures of the scapula: A review of 53 fractures. *J Trauma* 15:473–478, 1975.

18. ARMSTRONG CP, VAN DER SPUY J: The fractured scapula: Importance and management based on a series of 62 patients. *Injury* 15:324–329, 1984.

19. HARRIS RD, HARRIS JH: The prevalence and significance of missed scapular fractures in blunt chest trauma. *AJR* 151:747–750, 1988.

20. HEYSE-MOORE GH, STOKER DJ: Avulsion fractures of the scapula. *Skel Radiol* 9:27–32, 1982.

21. ISHIZUKA M, YAMAURA I, ISOBE Y, ET AL.: Avulsion fracture of the superior border of the scapula. *J Bone Joint Surg* 63A:820–822, 1981.

22. BERNARD TN, BRUNET ME, HADDAD RJ: Fractured coracoid process in acromioclavicular dislocations. *Clin Orthop* 175:227–232, 1983.

23. GARCIA-ELIAS M, SALO JM: Non-union of a fractured coracoid process after dislocation of the shoulder. *J Bone Joint Surg* 67B:722–723, 1985.

24. WONG-PACK WK, BOBEEHKO PE, BECKER EJ: Fractured coracoid with anterior shoulder dislocation. *J Can Assoc Radiol* 31:278–279, 1980.

25. BENCHETRIT E. FRIEDMAN B: Fracture of the coracoid process associated with subglenoid dislocation of the shoulder. *J Bone Joint Surg* 61A:295–296, 1979.

26. MONTGOMERY SP, LOYD DR: Avulsion fracture of the coracoid epiphysis with acromioclavicular separation. *J Bone Joint Surg* 59A:963–965, 1977.

27. PROTASS JJ, STAMPFLI RW, OSMER JC: Coracoid process fracture diagnosis in acromioclavicular separation. *Radiology* 116:61–64, 1975.

28. SMITH DM: Coracoid fracture associated with acromioclavicular dislocation. A case report. *Clin Orthop* 108:165–167, 1975.

29. CARR AJ, BROUGHTON NS: Acromioclavicular dislocation associated with fracture of the coracoid process. *J Trauma* 29:125–126, 1989.

30. LASDA NA, MURRAY DG: Fracture separation of the coracoid process associated with acromioclavicular dislocation: Conservative treatment—a case report and review of the literature. *Clin Orthop* 134:222–224, 1978.

31. FROIMSON AI: Fracture of the coracoid process of the scapula. *J Bone Joint Surg* 60A:710–711, 1978.

32. ZILBERMAN Z, REJOVITZKY R: Fracture of the coracoid process of the scapula. *Injury* 13:203–206, 1981.

33. GOLDBERG RP, VICKS B: Oblique angled view for coracoid fractures. *Skel Radiol* 9:195–197, 1983.

34. KOPECKY KK, BIES JR, ELLIS JH: CT diagnosis of fracture of the coracoid process of the scapula. *Comput Radiol* 8:325–327, 1984.

35. KUMMEL BM: Fractures of the glenoid causing chronic dislocation of the shoulder. *Clin Orthop* 69:189–191, 1970.

36. ROWE CR: Prognosis in dislocations of the shoulder. *J Bone Joint Surg* 38A:957–977, 1956.

37. NEER CS II, ROCKWOOD CA JR: Fractures and dislocations of the shoulder, in Rockwood CA, Green DP (eds): *Fractures*, Philadelphia, J.B. Lippincott, 1975, pp 585–815.

38. NEER CS II: Displaced proximal humeral fractures. *J Bone Joint Surg* 52A:1077–1089, 1970.

39. LIND T, KRONER K, JENSEN J: The epidemiology of fractures of the proximal humerus. *Arch Orthop Trauma Surg* 108:285–287, 1989.

40. HORAK J, NILSSON BE: Epidemology of fracture of the upper end of the humerus. *Clin Orthop* 112:250–253, 1975.

41. HAYES JM, VANWINKLE GN: Axillary artery injury with minimally displaced fracture of the neck of the humerus. *J Trauma* 23:431–433, 1983.

42. ROSS GJ, LOVE MD: Isolated avulsion fracture of the lesser tuberosity of the humerus: Report of two cases. *Radiology* 172:833–834, 1989.

43. SHIBUYA S, OGAWA K: Isolated avulsion fractures of the lesser tuberosity of the humerus. *Clin Orthop* 211:215–218, 1986.

44. CISTERNINO SJ, ROGERS LF, STUFFLEBAM BC, KRUGLIK GD: The trough line: A radiographic sign of posterior shoulder dislocation. *AJR* 130:951–954, 1978.

45. CODMAN EA: The shoulder: Rupture of the supraspinatus tendon and other lesions in or about the subacromial bursa, Boston, Thomas Todd, 1934, pp 262–293.

46. HAYES JM, VANWINKLE GN: Axillary artery injury with minimally displaced fracture of the neck of the humerus. *J Trauma* 23:431–433, 1983.

47. LIM EVA, DAY LJ: Thrombosis of the axillary artery complicating proximal humeral fractures. *J Bone Joint Surg* 69A:778–780, 1987.

48. NEER CS, HOROWITZ BS: Fractures of the proximal humeral epiphyseal plate. *Clin Orthop* 41:24–31, 1965.

49. SHERK HH, PROBST C: Fractures of the proximal humeral epiphysis. *Orthop Clin North Am* 6:401–413, 1975.

50. BAXTER MP, WILEY JJ: Fractures of the proximal humeral epiphysis. Their influence of humeral growth. *J Bone Joint Surg* 68B:570–573, 1986.

51. AUFRANC OE, JONES WN, BIERBAUM BE: Epiphysial fracture of the proximal humerus. *JAMA* 207:727–729, 1969.

52. ADAMS JE: Little league shoulder. Osteochondrosis of the proximal humeral epiphysis in boy baseball pitchers. *Calif Med* 105:22–25, 1966.

53. BARNETT LS: Little league shoulder syndrome: Proximal humeral epiphyseolysis in adolescent baseball pitchers. *J Bone Joint Surg* 67A:495–496, 1985.

54. CAVE ER, BURKE JF, BODY RJ: Posterior dislocations, in *Trauma Managment*. Chicago, Year Book, 1974, pp 409–437.

55. WORRELL J, FERNANDEZ GN: Retrosternal dislocation of the clavicle: An important injury easily missed. *Arch Emerg Med* 3:133–135, 1986.

56. NETTLES JL, LINSCHEID RL: Sternoclavicular dislocations. *J Trauma* 8:158–164, 1968.

57. ROGERS LF: Radiology of sports injuries. *Curr Probl Diagn Radiol* 12:1–48, 1982.

58. LEIGHTON RK, BUHR AJ, SINCLAIR AM: Posterior sternoclavicular dislocation. *Can J Surg* 29:104–106, 1986.

59. ROCKWOOD CA JR, ODOR JM: Spontaneous atraumatic anterior subluxation of the sternoclavicular joint. *J Bone Joint Surg* 71A:1280–1288, 1989.

60. BONNIN JG: Spontaneous subluxation of the sternoclavicular joint. *Br Med J* 2:274–275, 1960.

61. GANGAHAR DM, FLOGAITES T: Retrosternal dislocation of the clavicle producing thoracic outlet syndrome. *J Trauma* 18:369–372, 1978.

62. MCKENZIE JMM: Retrosternal dislocation of the clavicle. *J Bone Joint Surg* 45B:138–141, 1963.

63. SMITH MJ, STEWART MJ: Acute acromioclavicular separations: A 20-year study. *Am J Sports Med* 7:62–71, 1979.

64. ROCKWOOD CA, WILLIAMS GR, YOUNG DC: Injuries to the acromioclavicular joint, in Rockwood CA, Green DP, Bucholz RW (eds): *Fractures in Adults*, 3d ed, Philadelphia, J.B. Lippincott, 1991, pp 1181–1251.

65. PETERSSON CJ, REDLUND-JOHNELL I: Radiographic joint space in normal acromioclavicular joints. *Acta Orthop Scand* 54:431–433, 1983.

66. BEARDEN JM, HUGHSTON JC, WHATLEY GS: Acromioclavicular dislocation: Method of treatment. *J Sports Med* 1:5–17, 1973.

67. KEATS TE, POPE TL JR: The acromioclavicular joint: Normal variation and the diagnosis of dislocation. *Skel Radiol* 17:159–162, 1988.

68. ALLMAN FL JR: Fractures and ligamentous injuries of the clavicle and its articulation. *J Bone Joint Surg* 49A:774–784, 1967.

69. TAGA I, YONEDA M, ONO D: Epiphyseal separation of the coracoid process associated with acromioclavicular sprain. *Clin Orthop* 207:138–141, 1986.

70. CAHILL BR: Osteolysis of the distal part of the clavicle in male athletes. *J Bone Joint Surg* 64A:1053–1058, 1982.

71. MURPHY OB, BELLAMY R, WHEELER W, BROWER TD: Posttraumatic osteolysis of the distal clavicle. *Clin Orthop* 109:108–114, 1975.

72. LEVINE AH, PAIS MJ, SCHWARTZ EE: Posttraumatic osteolysis of the distal clavicle with emphasis on early radiologic changes. *AJR* 127:781–784, 1976.

73. MADSEN B. Osteolysis of the acromial end of the clavicle following trauma. *Br J Radiol* 36:822–828, 1963.

74. ROWE CR. Acute and recurrent anterior dislocations of the shoulder. *Orthop Clin North Am* 11:253–270, 1980.

75. ROCKWOOD CA, THOMAS SC, MATSEN FA III. Subluxations and dislocations about the glenohumeral joint, in Rockwood CA, Green DP, Bucholz RW (eds): *Fractures in Adults*, 3d ed, Philadelphia, Lippincott, 1991, pp 1021–1179.

76. ASHER MA: Dislocations of the upper extremity in children. *Orthop Clin North Am* 7:583–591, 1976.

77. DOWNEY EF, JR, CURTIS DJ, BROWER AC: Unusual dislocations of the shoulder. *AJR* 140:1207–1210, 1983.

78. KRONER K, LIND T, JENSEN J: The epidemiology of shoulder dislocations. *Arch Orthop Trauma Surg* 108:288–290, 1989.

79. HOVELIUS L: Anterior dislocation of the shoulder in teenagers and young adults. Five-year prognosis. *J Bone Joint Surg* 69A:393–399, 1987.

80. HENRY JH, GENUNG JA: Natural history of glenohumeral dislocation—revisited. *Am J Sports Med* 10:135–137, 1982.

81. BANKART ASB: Recurrent or habitual dislocation of the shoulder joint. *Br Med J* 2:1132–1133, 1923.

82. BANKART ASB: The pathology and treatment of recurrent dislocation of the shoulder joint. *Br J Surg* 26:23–29, 1938.

83. JOHNSON JR, BAYLEY JIL: Early complications of acute anterior dislocation of the shoulder in the middle-aged and elderly patient. *Injury* 13:431–434, 1982.

84. McMANUS F: Brachial plexus lesions complicating anterior fracture-dislocation of the shoulder joint. *Injury* 8:63–66, 1977.

85. McLAUGHLIN HL, MacLELLAN DI: Recurrent anterior dislocation of the shoulder: II A comparative study. *J Trauma* 7:191–201, 1967.

86. LEV-EL A, ADAR R, RUBINSTEIN Z: Axillary artery injury in erect dislocation of the shoulder. *J Trauma* 21:323–325, 1981.

87. ROWE CR, ZARINS B: Chronic unreduced dislocations of the shoulder. *J Bone Joint Surg* 64A:494–505, 1982.

88. PEARL BL: Bilateral posterior fracture dislocation of the shoulder—an uncommon complication of a convulsive seizure. *N Engl J Med* 283:135–136, 1970.

89. RUBENSTEIN JD, EBRAHEIM NA, KELLAM JF: Traumatic scapulothoracic dissociation. *Radiology* 157:297–298, 1985.

90. EBRAHEIM NA, AN HS, JACKSON WT, ET AL.: Scapulothoracic dissociation. *J Bone Joint Surg* 70A:428–432, 1988.

91. KELBEL JM, JARDON OM, HUURMAN WW: Scapulothoracic dissociation. A case report. *Clin Orthop* 209:210–214, 1986.

9 IMAGING OF SHOULDER INSTABILITY

David A. Rubin
Murray K. Dalinka
Richard J. Herzog

The anatomy of the glenohumeral joint permits a wide range of motion of the upper extremity; this same anatomy, however, makes the joint inherently unstable. The shoulder is the most frequently dislocated major joint in the body.[1] Once a dislocation occurs, the shoulder is prone to repeated dislocations and subluxations; clinical and radiologic diagnosis in these cases is relatively straightforward. Recent technical advances in arthroscopy and imaging of the shoulder have led to an enhanced interest and understanding of its anatomy and biomechanics, increasing our ability to diagnose and treat lesions of the capsulolabral structures. Furthermore, in many cases we can now define an anatomic cause for nonspecific shoulder symptoms that are due to subclinical subluxations or isolated labral injuries; this finding has been termed *functional instability*.[2]

In this chapter we first review current concepts of shoulder biomechanics and the mechanisms responsible for stability of the glenohumeral joint. Then we discuss the principles of imaging that apply to three distinct clinical circumstances: acute dislocation, recurrent instability, and nonspecific shoulder pain that may be secondary to functional instability.

MECHANISMS OF STABILITY

Normal Anatomy and Biomechanics of the Shoulder Stabilizers

The humeral head is larger than the glenoid fossa, and only one-fourth to one-third of the humeral head is in contact with the glenoid at any time.[3] This anatomic arrangement allows for extensive motion at the expense of stability. Since the glenoid is oblique to the main axis of the body, lying in a plane approximately midway between anatomic coronal and sagittal, the glenoid is positioned posteromedial to the humeral head, providing some posterior support; however, the osseous structures do not contribute to anterior stability.

Randelli and Gambrioli used computed tomography (CT) to examine the osseous relationships in stable and unstable shoulders.[4] They found no statistically significant difference in the glenohumeral index (ratio of the glenoid and humeral transverse diameters) or glenoid tilt (angle between the glenoid surface and the scapular body) between control subjects and patients with anterior instability. Three of seven patients with voluntary posterior subluxation exhibited more glenoid retrotilt than controls.[4] Findings in a larger series of patients with posterior instability confirmed this last finding.[5]

The stability of the glenohumeral joint is maintained by a complex interaction between static and dynamic mechanisms. The capsular mechanism concept recognizes the contributions of various structures to stabilizing the glenohumeral joint.[6] The anterior capsular mechanism refers to the elements that contribute to anterior stability, encompassing the capsule and glenohumeral ligaments along with the associated anterior recesses and bursae, labrum, synovium, and scapular periosteum; the anterior mechanism also includes the subscapularis muscle and tendon.[6–8] Similarly, the main posterior stabilizers depend on the integrity of the posterior capsular mechanism: the posterior capsule, recesses, synovium, periosteum, and posterior superior rotator cuff (supraspinatus, infraspinatus, and teres minor).[6] Separating the anterior and posterior capsular mechanisms anatomically are the coracohumeral ligament and the long head of the biceps tendon.

The glenoid labrum is composed of fibrocartilage in both adults and children,[9] although some authors feel that it is predominantly a fibrous structure with only a small portion, the transition zone, composed of fibrocartilage.[6,10] The labrum deepens the socket formed by the glenoid. In the normal shoulder, its attachment to the glenoid varies around the perimeter of the glenoid and is strongest inferiorly and loosest superiorly.[10,11] It is not unusual for the labrum to be partially detached in older patients.[9,12,13] Although labral tears and detachments are frequent sequelae of anterior dislocation, in the past the labrum was felt to contribute little if anything to stability.[3,7] Recent studies, however, have shown that removal of the labrum reduces the effectiveness of the concavity compression mechanism of glenohumeral stability by approximately 20 percent.[10] Concavity compression describes the stabilization of the shoulder that results from compression of the humeral head into the glenoid fossa. The compression is chiefly the result of the rotator cuff musculature. This mechanism operates in the midrange of glenohumeral motion, where the capsule and glenohumeral ligaments are lax and do not contribute to stability.[10,13a]

The joint capsule limits the excursion of the humeral head in the glenoid. As the humeral head translates in one direction, negative pressure on the contralateral side of the joint tends to invaginate the capsule inward, adding support to prevent subluxation. Howell and coworkers analyzed glenohumeral motion in the horizontal plane on axillary radiographs while varying the position of the arm.[14] They found an average of 4 mm of posterior translation in normal subjects when the arm was maximally extended in external rotation (the cocked position of throwing). The humerus did not translate within the glenoid in any other arm position. In patients with recurrent anterior instability examined in the same positions, either no posterior translation occurred or the humerus moved anteriorly within the glenoid in the cocked position. The investigators attributed the normal posterior translation seen with extension and external rotation to tension developed in the intact anterior capsular restraints and the abnormal motion found in patients with instability to disruption of the anterior capsular mechanism.[14] Howell and Kraft repeated this study in 13 patients with proven disruption of the anterior capsulolabral structures.[13a] By temporarily paralyzing the supraspinatus and infraspinatus muscles using a suprascapular nerve block, they concluded that these rotator cuff muscles were not necessary to maintain normal shoulder mechanics in the horizontal plane.[13a] In a cadaver preparation, Harryman and coworkers demonstrated anterior translation of the humeral head with flexion or cross-body movement of the humerus.[15] The amount of anterior translation increased following operative tightening of the posterior capsule and could be eliminated by sectioning of the capsule. These authors coined the term *capsular constraint mechanism* to describe the stability provided by an intact capsule.[15]

The capsule also limits the volume of the joint and, together with the tiny amount of joint fluid normally present, contributes to stability through the mechanisms of adhesion and cohesion. When the joint capsule is punctured at surgery a slight degree of inferior shoulder subluxation occurs.[1] Disruption of these mechanisms dependent on a finite joint volume may contribute to the

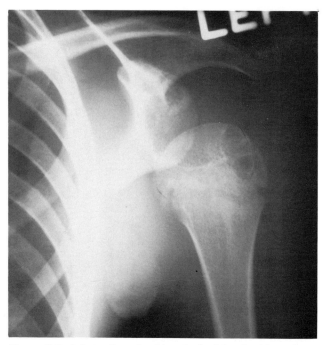

Figure 9-1 Inferior "pseudosubluxation" of the shoulder. Inferior displacement of the humeral head is due to a large hemorrhagic joint effusion. Note the cystic changes in the humerus of this child with hemophilia. (Courtesy of Lee F. Rogers.)

inferior "pseudosubluxation" seen when a large joint effusion is present (Fig. 9-1).

The glenohumeral ligaments are localized thickenings of the joint capsule (Fig. 9-2). The glenohumeral ligaments and joint capsule provide the majority of the static support for the anterior joint. These restraints are redundant at rest, contributing to stability only near the physiologic limits of motion when they become taut.[1] They are named for their attachment sites on the humerus, not for their relative positions as they traverse the glenohumeral space.[16] While the anatomy of these structures has been extensively studied and described, there is considerable variation in their presence and arrangement.

The superior glenohumeral ligament has attachments to both the apex of the labrum, where it is conjoined with the origin of the long head of the biceps, and to the scapula at the base of the coracoid.[17] The insertion is on the lesser tuberosity. It is the most constant of the glenohumeral ligaments, present in 97 percent of cadaver specimens.[6] It contributes little to anterior stability but, along with the coracohumeral ligament, may help prevent inferior dislocation.[1,17,18]

The middle glenohumeral ligament is the most variable. Some investigators suggest that it may be absent or ill defined in as many as 30 percent of cases[1,19]; other researchers found it to be present in all specimens, though ill defined in some.[6] The middle glenohumeral

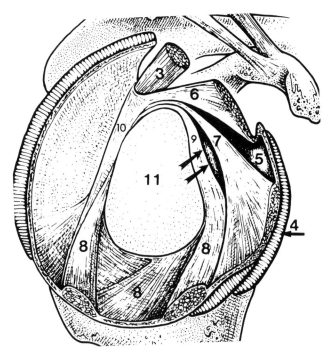

Figure 9-2 Anatomy of the glenohumeral ligaments viewed from side with humeral head removed. (Key: 3, biceps tendon, long head; 4, subscapularis muscle and tendon; 5, subscapularis recess; 6, superior glenohumeral ligament; 7, middle glenohumeral ligament; 8, anterior band, axillary pouch, and posterior band of the inferior glenohumeral ligament complex; 9, anterior labrum; 10, posterior labrum; 11, glenoid fossa.) A small anterior recess is also visible between the middle glenohumeral ligament and the anterior band of the inferior glenohumeral ligament complex (*double arrow*). (Coumas JM, Waite RJ, Goss TP, Ferrari DA, Kanzaria PK, Pappas AM: CT and MR evaluation of the labral capsular ligamentous complex of the shoulder. *AJR* 158:591, 1992. Used with permission.)

ligament inserts on the lesser tuberosity of the humerus, where it is fused with the posterior aspect of the subscapularis tendon. The attachment of the ligament to the scapula at the middle level of the joint forms the basis for the classification of capsular types. The anterior capsule may attach directly to the anterior labrum (Type I), to the glenoid adjacent to the labrum (Type II), or more medially along the scapular neck (Type III).[6] The Type III capsule is commonly a sequela of anterior dislocation, where the capsule has been stripped from the scapular neck, and it is often associated with detachment of the labrum.[20,21] Rarely, a Type III capsule may be a normal variant, and it is found in a minority of fetal and embryonic specimens.[6,22].

The anatomy of the middle glenohumeral ligament determines the size and number of anterior synovial recesses. There are openings in the anterior capsule between the glenohumeral ligaments that provide communication with the subscapularis bursa and recess(es). These recesses occur above, below, or both above and below the middle glenohumeral ligament.[23] The most common arrangement is two synovial recesses: one be-

tween the superior and middle glenohumeral ligaments and one between the middle and inferior glenohumeral ligaments (see Fig. 9-2).[6,16] When the middle glenohumeral ligament arises directly from the labrum the recesses are smaller or nonexistent and the anterior capsule is stronger. Conversely, when the ligament arises more medially on the scapular neck the recesses are larger and more numerous, providing less anterior support. Absence or severe attenuation of the middle glenohumeral ligament may be associated with a single large anterior synovial pouch.[6]

The inferior glenohumeral ligament complex represents a diffuse thickening of the inferior capsule, arising directly from the anterior-inferior, inferior, and posterior-inferior labrum.[10,17] It is composed of thick anterior and posterior bands separated by an axillary pouch.[17,19] The anterior and posterior bands differ histologically from the axillary pouch: the bands contain organized coarse collagen fibers running in the coronal plane from the glenoid to the humerus, whereas the axillary pouch consists of thinner, intermingled collagen layers.[19] The inferior glenohumeral ligament is found in all cadaver and fetal specimens.[6,17] While the anterior band has been consistently identified arthroscopically in cadaver specimens with specific positioning of the arm,[19] it is absent at gross dissection in 25 percent of cases.[17] The distal attachment of the inferior glenohumeral ligament is to the surgical neck of the humerus immediately inferior to the anatomic neck.[17,19] The ligament may form a continuous collar around the articular edge of the humeral neck, or the ligament may have a V-shaped insertion with the axillary pouch forming the apex of the V, distal to the articular edge.[19]

The posterior capsule always attaches directly to the glenoid labrum.[22] In some cases, small perforations of the posterior capsule provide communication between the glenohumeral joint and a bursa deep to the infraspinatus tendon.[23]

The passive shoulder restraints are reinforced by the active support provided by the rotator cuff muscles and tendons and the long head of the biceps muscle. The rotator cuff muscles tend to pull the humeral head into the glenoid fossa, enhancing stability resulting from the concavity compression mechanism.[10] In addition, they counteract both extrinsic and intrinsic translational forces applied to the humerus.[1] The intraarticular portion of the long head of the biceps lies superior to the humeral head. This arrangement provides a potential stabilizing mechanism to prevent superior movement of the humeral head as the biceps contracts to flex the elbow and supinate the forearm. Evidence for this role of the long head comes from cadaver studies in which superior subluxation of the humerus was seen when the short head of the biceps was tensed alone, but not with contraction of the long head alone or both heads together.[24]

Conflicting data concern the individual contributions of the static stabilizers to overall stability of the shoulder. The disagreement may result in part from the different types of studies performed to investigate instability. Some studies have looked at the anatomy, biomechanics, and movement in the intact shoulder, either in cadaver specimens or in asymptomatic volunteers.[17,19,25] Other researchers have investigated the effects of sequentially transecting supporting structures in cadaver specimens.[1,17,26] It is not clear how readily these results can be applied to patients with shoulder dislocations. Other investigators have looked at the pathologic changes in the shoulder after dislocation, either in patients with recurrent instability or in experimentally created dislocations.[3,6,20,21,26,27] In these circumstances it is difficult to separate the changes that predispose to recurrent instability from those produced at the time of initial dislocation.

In a strain gauge analysis of cadaver shoulders, Terry and coworkers concluded that tension is shared among the passive shoulder restraints depending on the position of the humerus.[25] The investigators found that maximum tension develops in the coracohumeral ligament with flexion of the arm and that this tension is distributed between the coracohumeral ligament and the glenohumeral ligaments (chiefly the inferior glenohumeral ligament) when external rotation is added to flexion. The stress is shared between the coracohumeral ligament and the lower two-thirds of the posterior capsule when internal rotation is added. The superior glenohumeral ligament functioned maximally with extension combined with external rotation. The middle glenohumeral ligament developed maximal strain with the combination of flexion and external rotation. Abduction with flexion and external rotation produced maximum tension in the inferior glenohumeral ligament. Internal rotation by itself produced tension mainly in the superior and middle portions of the posterior capsule, whereas the inferior aspect of the posterior capsule was the most stressed structure with abduction or the combination of abduction and internal rotation.[25]

By labeling the glenohumeral ligaments in cadaver specimens and radiographing the shoulders in various positions, Warner and coworkers[18] found that the middle glenohumeral ligament shortens with the humerus adducted. When the humerus is abducted to 45° the ligament is positioned anterior to the humeral head, providing a barrier against anterior translation. At up to 60° of abduction the middle glenohumeral ligament may still provide a checkrein against external rotation, but with further abduction it courses above the humeral head and no longer contributes to anterior stability. The inferior glenohumeral ligament complex tightens with abduction, and at 90° of abduction the anterior and posterior bands become parallel, demonstrating reciprocal lengthening with internal and external rotation.[18]

Turkel and coworkers investigated the stabilizing mechanisms in a cadaver preparation that included the subscapularis muscle and tendon in addition to the capsule and ligaments.[17] After examining specimens in different anatomic positions and performing sequential transections of individual components of the capsular mechanism, they concluded that the main anterior shoulder stabilizer at 0° abduction was the subscapularis with contributions from the inferior glenohumeral ligament. At 45° abduction stability was maintained by the subscapularis, middle glenohumeral ligament, and anterior band of the inferior glenohumeral ligament. The anterior band of the inferior glenohumeral ligament became the primary stabilizer when the humerus was abducted 90°, with the fibers of the axillary pouch encircling the humeral head like a Chinese fingertrap.[17] O'Brien and associates found that the anterior band of the inferior glenohumeral ligament fans out and, together with the axillary pouch, cradles the humeral head during abduction and external rotation of the arm,[19] the position that most often leads to anterior dislocation. Conversely, with abduction and internal rotation the posterior band works with the axillary pouch to form a hammock to support the posterior humeral head.[19]

Other studies involving selective transection of individual stabilizing elements as well as those involving experimentally produced dislocations have reached similar conclusions: the inferior glenohumeral ligament, especially the anterior band, together with parts of the posterior capsule, provide the primary restraint to anterior dislocation, with secondary contributions from the middle glenohumeral ligament (when present) and subscapularis.[1,26,27] The posterior capsule is the primary restraint against posterior dislocation, along with the other stabilizers, depending on the position of the humerus.[1]

Pathologic Changes Related to Instability

THE HILL-SACHS LESION

The normal humeral head is always spherical,[22] and any flattening or indentation of its surface should be considered pathologic. Defects of the superior posterolateral humeral head related to anterior instability are often referred to as Hill-Sachs lesions, though they were described long before Hill and Sachs' classic 1940 paper.[1,28] They recognized that the lesion was an impacted fracture of the humeral head that occurred at the time of initial dislocation.[28] This impaction can only occur once the anterior capsule is stretched or disrupted.[7] Analogous defects can occur in the anterior humeral head following posterior dislocation, resulting from impaction against the posterior glenoid.[20,29]

Hill-Sachs lesions have been reported in 21 to 45 percent of patients at the time of initial dislocation.[20,28,30,31] The true prevalence is probably higher, as many lesions can be demonstrated only with special radiographic projections (see Principles of Imaging Shoulder Instability). Furthermore, at arthroscopy chondral lesions in the superior posterolateral humeral head are often found following anterior shoulder dislocation.[32] Injuries confined to the cartilage of the humeral head are difficult to detect with current imaging techniques. Hill-Sachs lesions may be more common in older patients who suffer a primary acute anterior dislocation.[33] Hill-Sachs defects are much more common, and tend to be larger, with recurrent dislocations; the reported prevalence ranges from 46 to 100 percent in this setting.[6,20,21,28,30]

Although the Hill-Sachs lesion is usually the result of a traumatic shoulder dislocation,[1,7] it may also be seen in patients with shoulder instability who do not have a history of trauma.[20] Experimental evidence suggests that the Hill-Sachs lesion may be involved in recurrent instability.[26,28] In a cadaver study, Symeonides demonstrated that the defect increases instability when the subscapularis muscle has been stretched.[26] The lesion may contribute to recurrent dislocations by acting as a lever to promote displacement of the humeral head during external rotation.[34]

BANKART LESION AND RELATED ABNORMALITIES

Bankart was not the first to describe the strong association between detachment of the anterior capsulolabral complex and anterior instability,[1] but he did popularize the abnormality that now bears his name.[35,36] A Bankart deformity is a tearing or avulsion of the anterior labrum, anterior capsule, and/or fracture of the anterior glenoid rim that results from an anterior, usually traumatic, dislocation.[2,3,6,20,21,26,37] The fractures are referred to as *osseous Bankart lesions*. The definition of the classic Bankart lesion can be expanded to include other lesions that may be associated with anterior instability, such as sleeve-like medial stripping of the labroligamentous complex down the glenoid neck.[38] Analogous abnormalities secondary to posterior dislocation are sometimes called reverse Bankart lesions and include posterior capsule, labrum, and bony glenoid injuries.

Bankart believed that recurrent dislocations were not related to "ordinary traumatic dislocation" and that the capsulolabral complex injury that occurred secondary to the original dislocation was the major predisposing factor for repeated dislocation.[35,36] His surgical reattachment of the anterior labrum was designed to repair this predisposing factor.[7,21,35] Townley emphasized that the success of the Bankart repair was attributable to the reattachment of the anterior capsule, not the labrum.[7] Others have concluded that the capsulolabral detachment is the result of the first traumatic dislocation and have questioned whether it is a cause of recurrent dislocation.[26] While Bankart lesion is not invariably produced by an anterior dislocation, it is present in the majority of cases.[2,6] The reported prevalence of torn or detached labra at the time of surgery for recurrent dislocation ranges from 62 to 85 percent[20,21,26]; the incidence of capsular rupture or avulsion ranges from 16 to 100 percent.[3,20,21,26]

A fracture of the glenoid disrupts more of the socket mechanism of the shoulder than does a simple labral avulsion.[13a] Thus, patients with osseous Bankart lesions might be expected to have a higher rate of recurrent dislocation than those with soft-tissue Bankart lesions. In large series this was found to be the case: the recurrence rate for patients with an anterior glenoid rim fracture was 62 percent, as compared with 38 percent for all patients.[20] A later and larger study by the same author found that the rate of recurrent dislocation was not increased by a glenoid fracture.[21] Glenoid fractures are relatively uncommon, occurring in some 5 to 18 percent of acute dislocations.[20,26] Lesser glenoid changes, such as a rounded contour, eroded surface, or hyperostotic spur, are much more common sequelae of previous dislocations (prevalence as high as 73 percent).[20,21] These subtle changes serve as a potentially useful radiographic markers of instability.

The chances of finding an intact anterior capsulolabral complex at the time of surgery for instability vary from 10 to 28 percent.[6,21,22] In these "non-Bankart" cases the anterior capsule is often described as redundant.[22] In Moseley and Övergaard's original report, three of four patients without a Bankart lesion demonstrated a large anterior pouch that was due in part to a Type III insertion of the middle glenohumeral ligament far medial on the scapular neck; in the fourth, the middle glenohumeral ligament was ill defined.[6]

INJURIES TO THE ROTATOR CUFF

Several authors have commented on the lax subscapularis muscle and tendon universally found at the time of surgery for recurrent instability,[6,26] and they cite the high incidence of posttraumatic changes in this muscle as evidence for a major contribution of subscapularis abnormalities to instability.[26] While experimentally created dislocations lend credence to this concept,[26,27] it is not clear that the pathogenesis is the same in vivo. Other investigators report subscapularis muscle injury in only a minority of surgical cases.[3,21] Tears of the other rotator cuff tendons can be found in combination with anterior capsule derangements,[30,33,39] but in these cases the injuries may be coincident, produced by different components of the same initial force. In one series utilizing computed arthrotography, rotator cuff tears were found exclusively in patients who were older than 50 years at the time of initial dislocation.[33]

In summary, Bankart initial notion, "the essential feature [of recurrent instability] is the detachment of the capsule from the fibrocartilaginous glenoid ligament [labrum]"[35] can be broadened to include a spectrum of pathologic lesions.[2,3,37] Certainly a damaged labrum and/or anterior capsule—the classic Bankart lesion—is present in a large number of cases. Osseous abnormalities such as glenoid fractures and Hill-Sachs lesions likely contribute to instability in some patients. Excessive laxity of the subscapularis may also play a role in instability. In patients without a Bankart lesion or an equivalent one, redundancy of the joint capsule appears to be a contributing factor in instability.

CLASSIFICATION OF INSTABILITY

Etiology

Trauma, either a direct blow to the shoulder or an indirect force applied to the arm and transmitted to the glenohumeral articulation, is responsible for 86 to 96 percent of acute dislocations.[20,21] Dislocation can also result from a fall on an outstretched arm.[21,31] The force typically responsible for an anterior dislocation produces abduction, extension, and external rotation of the humerus. A combination of axial loading, adduction, and internal rotation can produce a posterior dislocation. Inferior dislocation results from forced hyperabduction.[1]

The intense muscle contraction associated with an electric shock or a convulsion can also lead to a shoulder dislocation. Because the combined force of the internal rotators exceeds that of the external rotators, forceful contraction of both sets of muscles is more likely to produce posterior dislocation.[1] Bilateral posterior dislocations are not uncommon following a seizure or electrical injury.

Some 4 to 14 percent of dislocations are not caused by a single major traumatic event but rather are the result of normal motion of the arm or seemingly insignificant trauma.[20,21] These patients often have developmental ligamentous laxity and exhibit multidirectional instability, which is commonly bilateral.[1] Finally, some dislocations are volitional; that is, the patient can voluntarily dislocate and relocate the shoulder.[40]

Direction

The majority of shoulder dislocations are anterior.[20] These injuries can be further subclassified by the final position of the humeral head. The most common type is subcoracoid, where the humeral head is located anterior and medial to the glenoid, just inferior to the coracoid process (Fig. 9-3). Subglenoid or axillary position of the humeral head results from an anterior inferior dislocation (Fig. 9-4). An anterior superior dislocation is termed *subclavicular* when the humeral head lies below the clavicle, medial to the coracoid. Rarely, the humeral head can become interposed between ribs, a condition known as *intrathoracic dislocation.*[1]

Ovesen and Søjbjerg investigated which of the supporting structures are partially or completely torn with each type of anterior dislocation.[27] After experimentally producing subcoracoid, subclavicular, and axillary anterior dislocations in 15 specimens (five of each type), they documented disruption of the anterior capsule in all cases, and complete or partial tears of the subscapularis muscle or tendon in all cases except one of the axillary dislocations. Tears of the posterior capsule and posterior rotator cuff (infraspinatus, teres minor, or both) were produced in all subclavicular and axillary dislocations, but in none of the subcoracoid dislocations.[27]

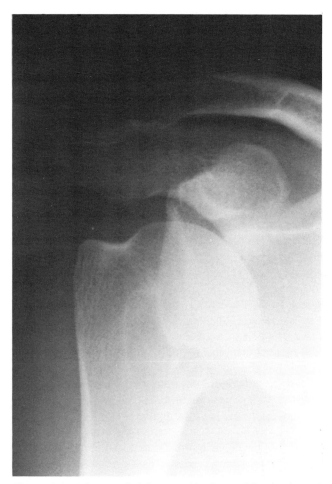

Figure 9-3 Subcoracoid dislocation. The humeral head is located inferior to the coracoid. This is the most common type of anterior dislocation.

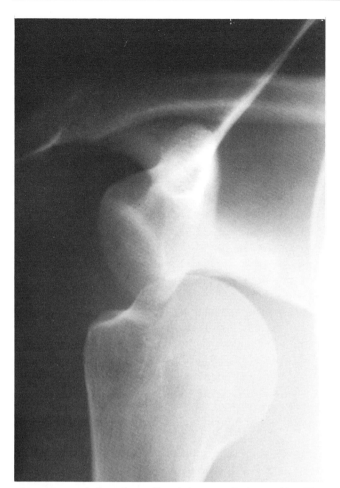

Figure 9-4 Subglenoid or axillary dislocation. The humeral head lies beneath the glenoid, farther inferior than in subcoracoid dislocations.

Posterior dislocations account for approximately 2 percent of all shoulder dislocations.[20] These injuries can be subclassified as subacromial, subglenoid, or subspinous, the last referring to the situation where the humeral head comes to rest medial to the acromion, inferior to the scapular spine.[1] The subacromial variety is the most common (Fig. 9-5). Patients with posterior instability often have bilateral instability and frequently can dislocate the shoulder voluntarily.[5]

Inferior dislocation is a rare condition in which the humeral head is forced downward into the axilla, coming to rest directly inferior to the scapula. Because of the muscular insertions on the humeral shaft, the entire upper extremity is pulled upward in abduction. The patient often presents with the arm locked in abduction with the forearm resting on the head, a presentation called *luxatio erecta* (Fig. 9-6).[41] The injury is commonly associated with fracture of the greater tuberosity, avulsion of the rotator cuff, or avulsion of the pectoralis major.[1,42]

Acute superior dislocations are exceedingly rare.[6] Normally the acromion, distal clavicle, acromioclavicular joint, coracoacromial ligament, and supraspinatus muscle and tendon provide a strong barrier that prevents superior displacement of the humeral head,[1] so this injury can be produced only by an extreme upward force. Associated fractures of the acromion, clavicle, coracoid, and humeral tuberosities would be expected with this type of dislocation.[1]

Frequency

Most acute dislocations are detected and reduced at the time of initial injury, but rarely an acute dislocation goes unrecognized and unreduced for a period of time. This condition is termed *chronic dislocation*. Various authors have defined the minimum interval that must pass between the dislocation and its detection to designate a dislocation as *chronic:* the range is from as little as 1 day[1] to as much as 3 weeks.[43] In some cases the dislocation has been present for more than a year.

As a group, patients with chronic dislocations tend to

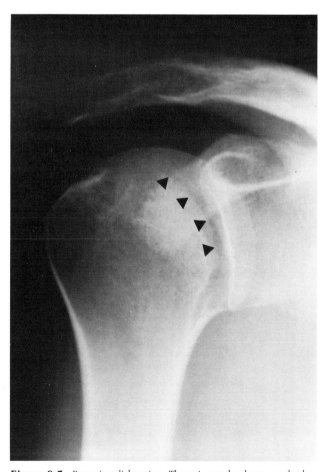

Figure 9-5 Posterior dislocation. There is overlap between the humeral head and glenoid on this AP view of the glenohumeral joint. Also observe the trough line (*arrowheads*) created by impaction of the humeral head against the posterior glenoid.

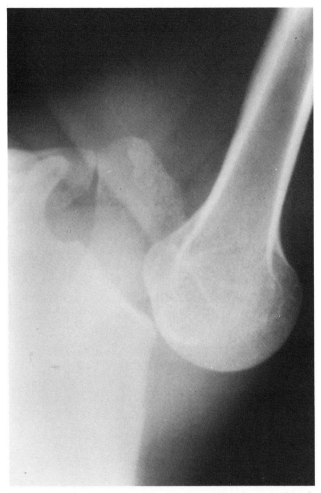

Figure 9-6 Luxatio erecta. The humeral head is dislocated inferiorly and the arm is locked in fixed abduction above the patient's head.

be older. Overall, anterior dislocations are much more common than posterior ones; however, in chronic cases, posterior dislocations make up a disproportionately large percentage of injuries, and in some series chronic posterior dislocations outnumber anterior dislocations.[43] Management of chronic dislocations depends on several factors, including the degree of functional impairment and the integrity of the humeral head and glenoid. Treatment options include rehabilitation alone for patients with acceptable shoulder function, closed or open reduction, hemiarthroplasty, and total shoulder arthroplasty.

Following an acute anterior dislocation, the overall rate of recurrence was 38 percent in a study of 500 dislocations.[20] The recurrence rate is inversely related to the age of the patient, being highest for patients younger than 20 years at the time of initial injury.[20,31] Young athletes have a particularly high rate of repeat dislocations.[31] With each subsequent dislocation less force is necessary to dislocate the shoulder, and it is not unusual for a patient to experience dislocations and subluxations more frequently as time goes on. In patients with this history,

surgery is often indicated. Most of these patients have a Bankart lesion and require a capsulolabral repair.[21]

Eighty-six percent of atraumatic dislocations recur.[20] Physical rehabilitation through muscle-strengthening exercises is the mainstay of therapy for these patients.[44,45] If conservative therapy fails, an inferior capsular shift procedure may be performed.[44] It is crucial that individuals with multidirectional instability are identified preoperatively; a unidirectional repair in these circumstances often fails owing to continued capsular redundancy, and it can lead to fixed subluxation in the opposite direction (see Fig. 9-27).[44–46]

Recurrent dislocation is particularly problematic in cases of posterior instability. In one large series, 96 percent of patients with posterior instability suffered recurrences when treated by physical rehabilitation, and 72 percent following surgical reconstruction. Interestingly, although there were more recurrences in the patients treated with rehabilitation alone, more patients in this group reported symptomatic improvement than in the group of patients who underwent surgical repair.[5]

Degree

By definition, shoulder dislocation exists when the degree of humeral head translation is such that the articular surfaces of the humeral head and glenoid are no longer in contact; lesser degrees of translation constitute subluxations. Repeated subluxations can be just as disabling as recurrent dislocations, and they may be harder to diagnose clinically as symptoms may be nonspecific.[37,45,47,48] Subclinical shoulder subluxations can cause symptoms in throwing athletes.[49,50] Although these patients may never have had a documented shoulder dislocation, Hill-Sachs and Bankart lesions are not uncommon.[37,48,49,51] Transient occult subluxations are probably also partly responsible for the symptomatic instability that patients may experience after an initial dislocation, even in the absence of repeat dislocation.[31]

Rockwood and colleagues have coined the acronyms TUBS and AMBRI to tie together the different classification schemes (etiology, direction, frequency, and degree) and the preferred methods of treatment. The terms synthesize the salient features in two distinct groups of patients. The TUBS syndrome refers to patients with *t*raumatic, *u*nidirectional instability, usually with a *B*ankart lesion, and often requiring *s*urgery. AMBRI patients have *a*traumatic, *m*ultidirectional, often *b*ilateral instability for which *r*ehabilitation is indicated, or an *i*nferior capsular shift if conservative measures fail.[1] As will be discussed, one goal of imaging patients with recurrent instability is to identify Bankart and Hill-Sachs lesions, which suggest the TUBS syndrome and that indicate the major direction of instability,[45] or to demonstrate findings of both anterior and posterior instability, which implies the AMBRI syndrome.[8]

PRINCIPLES OF IMAGING SHOULDER INSTABILITY

Conventional Radiography

Conventional or plain film radiography should always be the first imaging study obtained in patients with acute trauma or suspected instability. In addition to signs of instability, they may also reveal other possible causes for the patient's symptoms, including soft tissue calcifications, subtle fractures, arthritis, or tumors.

The primary role of imaging in acute dislocation is to confirm or establish the diagnosis. In patients with suspected acute dislocations we routinely obtain a standard "trauma series" consisting of a direct anteroposterior (AP) view of the glenohumeral joint and a lateral scapular Y view. For the direct AP view of the joint, the patient is turned into a 45° posterior oblique position. The Y view is an anterior oblique examination with the arm at the side and the scapular body perpendicular to the cassette.[52] These studies are easily obtained by turning the patient without moving the injured extremity. Interpretation of the radiographs is straightforward; on the Y view the coracoid, scapular spine, and scapular body form the limbs of the Y and intersect at the glenoid (Fig. 9-7). With anterior dislocations the humeral head lies beneath the coracoid on both the direct AP and the Y view (Fig. 9-8). In posterior dislocations the humeral head projects beneath the acromion on the Y view but overlaps with the glenoid rim on the direct AP view (see Fig. 9-5).

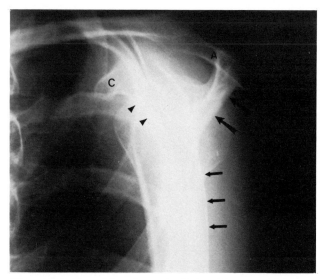

Figure 9-7 Normal lateral scapular Y view. The coracoid (*arrowheads* and C), scapular spine (*thick arrows*), and scapular body (*thin arrows*) form the limbs of the Y. The intersection of these limbs marks the position of the glenoid fossa. In this case the humeral head is directly superimposed over the glenoid. (Key: A, acromion.)

Other views may be utilized for suspected dislocations or subluxations. The anterior oblique or Garth view may replace the lateral scapular Y view.[53] An axillary view can be performed with a curved cassette placed in the axilla and the x-ray beam directed downward through the shoulder joint or with a cassette on top of the shoulder and the tube angled through the axilla (Figs. 9-8A, 9-9). The latter approach requires less movement of the shoulder. These additional views may help detect Hill-Sachs lesions or fractures of the glenoid rim. The transscapular lateral view is occasionally used, but its interpretation may be difficult, particularly in a patient who is breathing rapidly because of shoulder pain (Fig. 9-8B). Although only internal and external rotation views of the shoulder are obtained following acute trauma in some institutions, we feel that posterior dislocations can easily be overlooked with these views and therefore are not by themselves adequate as a screening examination.

The diagnosis of acute posterior dislocation deserves special comment. As with the clinical signs of this injury, the radiographic findings can be subtle, and the diagnosis requires a high degree of suspicion. Initial misdiagnosis rates of 50 percent or more have been reported.[29] An isolated avulsion of the lesser tuberosity occurs in approximately 25 percent of posterior dislocations,[29] and it can be the tip-off to an unsuspected posterior dislocation. This fracture occurs because the subscapularis muscle, which inserts on the lesser tuberosity, is stretched over the anterior glenoid as the shoulder dislocates posteriorly.

Other clues to the diagnosis of posterior dislocation include a position of fixed internal rotation of the humerus and overlap of the glenoid and humerus on a true AP view of the glenohumeral joint (see Fig. 9-5). The *rim sign* is apparent widening of the joint on a film made AP to the patient's body. Arndt and Sears determined that the width is normally no more than 6 mm; in their small series, the distance in posteriorly dislocated shoulders measured more than 10 mm.[54]

As the humeral head dislocates posteriorly it can strike the posterior rim of the glenoid, producing an impaction fracture of the anterior margin of the humeral head. The situation is analogous to a Hill-Sachs lesion seen with anterior dislocations, and the injury produced by posterior dislocations has been called a "reverse Hill-Sachs" lesion (Fig. 9-10). The impaction site, seen on the AP examination as a vertical line of cortical bone parallel to the margin of the humeral head, has been called the *trough line* (see Fig. 9-5).[29] Finally, fractures of the posterior glenoid rim can occur with posterior dislocations, analogous to the anterior glenoid fractures caused by anterior dislocations. The presence of any of these secondary signs should prompt a diligent search for other evidence of posterior dislocation; the diagnosis can be confirmed with a lateral scapular examination.

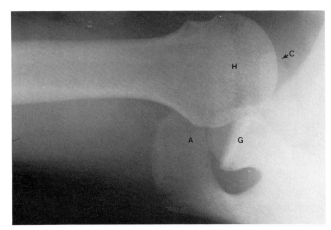

A

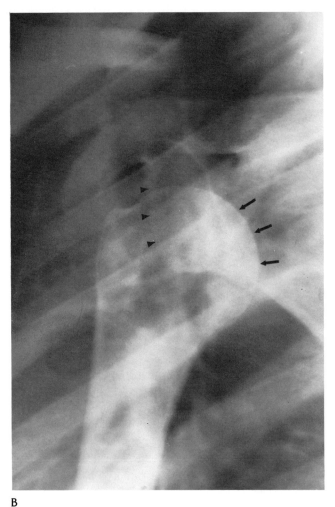

B

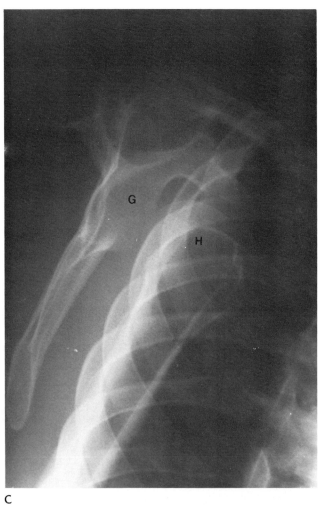

C

Figure 9-8 Three cases of anterior dislocation. **A.** An axillary radiograph demonstrates the anterior position of the humeral head (H) with respect to the glenoid (G). The coracoid (C) and acromion (A) serve as anterior and posterior markers, respectively. **B.** The lateral transthoracic examination is difficult to interpret but does show discontinuity of the articular surfaces of the glenoid (*arrowheads*) and humeral head (*arrows*). **C.** The lateral scapular study clearly shows anterior subcoracoid position of the humeral head (H). (Key: G, glenoid.)

In all cases of acute shoulder dislocation, the initial and postreduction radiographs should be carefully assessed for associated fractures, especially those that may impede reduction. Approximately 15 percent of anterior dislocations are associated with fractures of the greater tuberosity (Fig. 9-11). Interestingly, in this group only 7 percent suffer recurrent dislocation, well below the 38 percent overall recurrence rate for anterior dislocation.[20] Two facts may explain this observation. The fractures occur predominantly in older patients,[33] who have lower rates of recurrence than younger ones. Alternatively, scar tissue formed as the fracture heals may help prevent

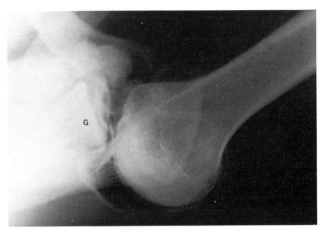

Figure 9-9   Posterior subluxation. This axillary projection was obtained as part of a double-contrast arthrogram. Note the posterior subluxation of the humeral head with respect to the glenoid (G).

future dislocations. Greater tuberosity fractures can also accompany inferior dislocations, and occasionally posterior ones.[1]

In patients with recurrent or suspected instability supplementary radiographic views may increase detection of subtle Hill-Sachs or Bankart deformities that are not demonstrated on standard examinations.[55,56] At the very least, an AP examination with the humerus in internal rotation should be obtained to bring the posterolateral humeral head into profile (Fig. 9-12).[11,57] Submaximal internal rotation should be avoided, lest a small Hill-Sachs lesion be missed.[57] Other supplementary views include the West Point, Stryker, and Didiee. The Stryker notch view may be helpful in detecting Hill-Sachs lesions (Fig. 9-13).[58,59] Subtle glenoid rim findings such as small fractures, areas of hyperostosis, or periostitis suggest a previous dislocation (Fig. 9-14). The West Point and Didiee views are modified axial projections used primarily to examine the bony glenoid.[59,60] Demonstration of these osseous lesions becomes crucial in cases of suspected recurrent instability, where they (1) provide evidence of previous dislocation in patients who do not have documented episodes of dislocation or whose clinical findings are equivocal, (2) indicate the direction of instability, and (3) usually imply trauma. Radiologic demonstration of osseous lesions can also provide evidence of unsuspected multidirectional instability when clinical findings point to only unidirectional instability.

Figure 9-10   Chronic posterior dislocation. **A.** The AP examination shows an ill-defined sclerotic trough line (*arrowheads*) in the humeral head. **B.** On the axillary projection note the large humeral head defect (*large arrows*) caused by long-term impaction against the posterior glenoid rim (*small arrows*). This study demonstrates the origin of the reverse Hill-Sachs lesion in posterior dislocations.

A

B

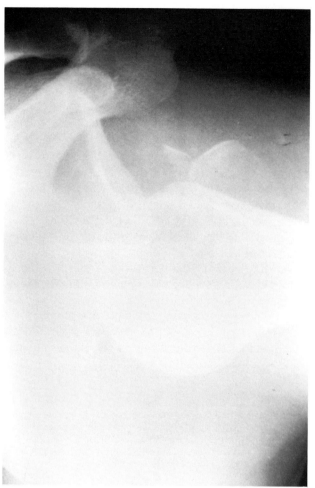

Figure 9-11 Anterior fracture-dislocation. A subglenoid dislocation is associated with a comminuted fracture of the greater tuberosity.

Computed Tomography and Computed Arthrotomography

Conventional radiographs are usually the only study needed for uncomplicated shoulder dislocations. CT, however, is often helpful with severe fracture-dislocations, as surgical planning requires an accurate depiction of all major fracture fragments. Occasionally, closed reduction is prevented by small intraarticular fragments, which are easily identified on CT (Fig. 9-15).

CT is useful in the evaluation of chronic dislocations. Virtually all patients demonstrate a Hill-Sachs or reverse Hill-Sachs deformity, and these lesions often increase in size the longer the shoulder is dislocated (see Fig. 9-10). CT can assess the size of the humeral head defect, which may determine whether open or closed reduction is attempted. Additionally, large humeral head defects may be repaired at the time of surgery, or they may require a prosthesis.[43] The glenoid should also be evaluated on CT examination, as a severely deformed glenoid may

dictate arthroplasty. In cases of chronic dislocation, magnetic resonance imaging (MRI) would probably provide the same information about the osseous structures as CT but would offer the advantage of improved detection of associated soft tissue injuries such as rotator cuff tears.

CT examination is more sensitive than conventional radiography for demonstrating Hill-Sachs lesions since it provides all possible tangential projections of the humeral head (Fig. 9-16). In one study CT demonstrated twice as many Hill-Sachs defects as conventional projections, which included an internally rotated AP examination.[61] On transaxial images of the humeral head the normal posterolateral flattening seen at the junction of the head and neck should not be interpreted as pathologic. A Hill-Sachs defect can be reliably diagnosed only in the superior portion of the humeral head. The level of the coracoid serves as a useful cross-sectional landmark for the upper portion of the humeral head when the shoulder is located normally. CT may also detect other subtle bony changes of instability that are difficult to visualize on conventional radiographs, such as periosteal new bone formation around the scapular neck (Fig. 9-17B).[62,63]

Double-contrast CT arthrography provides more information than conventional arthrography[30] or arthrotomography for the evaluation of instability.[2,12] CT arthrography provides a very detailed and accurate evaluation of both the osseous and soft tissue structures about the shoulder, including the labrum, capsule, and capsular recesses.

The normal variability in the appearance of the labrum and capsule on CT arthrography must be appreciated to avoid errors of interpretation.[64] The normal anterior labrum is usually triangular or rounded, but it can be cleaved or notched; the posterior labrum usually appears rounded (Fig. 9-18).[12,65] No correlation has been found between labrum shape and labrum tears.[61] The labrum can also vary considerably in size.[64] Air or contrast material can be visualized normally between the anterior labrum and the underlying cartilage.

Eighty percent of shoulders have synovial folds in the superior joint recess (see Fig. 9-16)[61]; these folds have no known clinical significance. The superior glenohumeral ligament is commonly visualized at CT arthrography.[64] It is best seen on the section below the origin of the long head of the biceps. The presence, size, and attachment site of the middle glenohumeral ligament is quite variable. The middle glenohumeral ligament and the anterior capsular insertion are best evaluated at the level of the midglenoid.[64,66] A superior subscapular recess may be present between the superior and middle glenohumeral ligaments.[66] The subscapularis tendon is seen outlined by air in the subscapularis bursa (Fig. 9-17). The inferior glenohumeral ligament is difficult to identify as it is inseparable from the anterior-inferior labrum.[67]

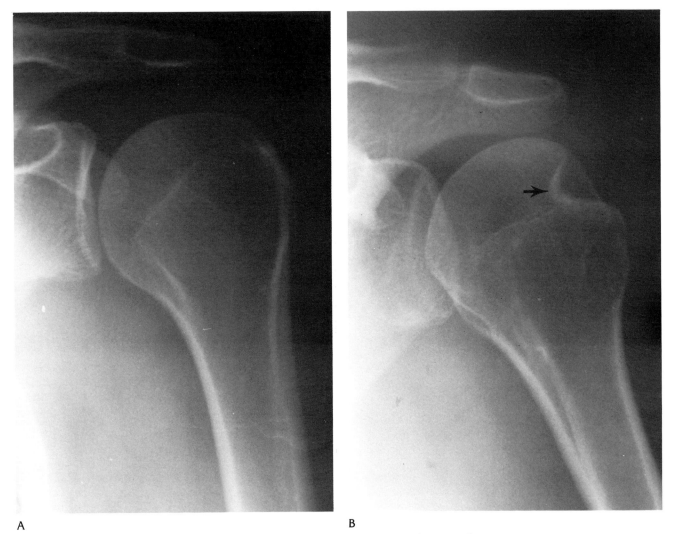

A   **B**

Figure 9-12   Hill-Sachs lesion. AP examinations with, **A,** external rotation and, **B,** internal rotation. The grooved defect in the posterolateral humeral head is optimally seen on the internal rotation view (*arrow*).

The findings of instability on CT arthrography are listed in Table 9-1. The labrum may appear deformed, fragmented, absent, attenuated, or frankly detached (see Fig. 9-17); occasionally contrast or air may be seen within the substance of a labrum tear.[61–63] Because the normal anterior labrum can at times appear hypoplastic, cleaved, or notched, care should be exercised when interpreting an isolated anterior labrum abnormality. Certainly, when accompanied by other evidence of instability (Hill-Sachs lesion, capsular abnormalities, or glenoid changes), an abnormal-looking labrum is likely to be damaged. The normal posterior labrum does not contain clefts or notches, so such changes should be regarded as abnormal.

For the detection of labral abnormalities the sensitivity of CT arthrography has been reported to be greater than 95 percent,[12,61] although the studies that reported these excellent results were biased toward patients with severe disease.[12,61] At surgery, most labra were abnormal. Furthermore, CT arthrography diagnosed labral abnormalities in 35 to 58 percent of the subjects who did not undergo surgery. Even among the few patients whose labrum was normal at surgery, 17 to 38 percent were interpreted as abnormal by CT arthrography.[12,61]

The joint distension accomplished during CT arthrography permits evaluation of the capsule. In patients with anterior instability, the anterior capsule may attach to the medial third of the scapular neck, a so-called Type III insertion.[61] While this arrangement can represent a normal variant,[6,22] it frequently is secondary to stripping of the anterior capsule down the scapular neck, which occurs at the time of dislocation.[20,21,33] Furthermore, patients with a congenital Type III capsule may be predis-

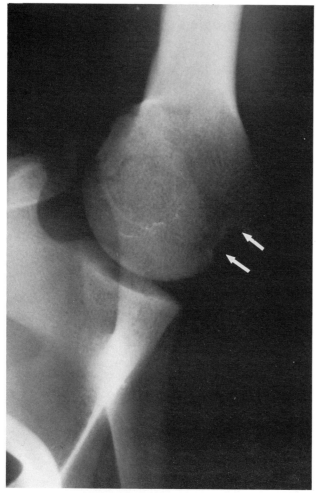

Figure 9-13 Hill-Sachs lesion. The humeral head impaction injury was not evident on the standard radiographs but is shown on the Stryker notch projection (*arrows*).

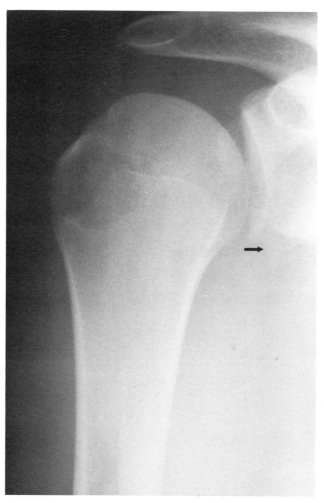

Figure 9-14 Osseous Bankart's lesion. This AP examination of the shoulder demonstrates a fracture of the anterior-inferior glenoid rim (*arrow*).

Table 9-1   CT Arthrographic Findings Associated with Instability

Labrum
   Detachment
   Absence or attenuation
   Deformation, fragmentation, irregular margins
   Contrast medium or air within substance
Capsule
   Tear (usually posterior)
   Stripping from glenoid
   Thickening or irregularity over scapula
   Ballooning or redundancy
Recesses and bursae
   Large anterior pouch (often with capsular stripping)
Bones
   Humeral head defects
   Glenoid fractures
   Scapular periosteal new bone formation
   Periosteal stripping

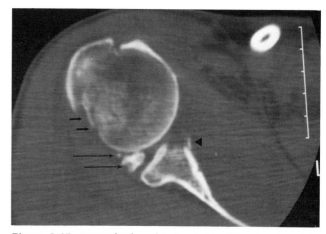

Figure 9-15 Incompletely reduced anterior dislocation due to intraarticular bone fragment. The CT examination shows a fracture of the anterior glenoid rim (*arrowhead*) with two fracture fragments (*long arrows*) displaced into the posterior compartment of the glenohumeral joint, preventing complete reduction. Note fractured greater tuberosity and Hill-Sachs defect (*short arrows*). This patient had a seizure earlier in the day that produced a transient anterior dislocation. The intraarticular position of the glenoid fracture fragments was not appreciated on the initial AP examination.

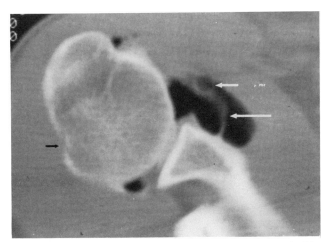

Figure 9-16 Hill-Sachs lesion. This transaxial image from a double-contrast CT arthrogram through the superior glenohumeral joint demonstrates a notched defect (*black arrow*) in the posterolateral humeral head, a sign of anterior instability. Note the synovial folds in the superior joint recess (*white arrows*); these are seen in the majority of shoulders and have no known significance.

posed to anterior instability.[8] While some authors feel that the anterior capsular insertion is a poor predictor of instability,[64] we feel that an anterior capsule that inserts far medially on the scapular neck is a marker of either prior anterior dislocation or the propensity for anterior instability. In one study all patients with medial capsular insertions who underwent surgery were also found to have labrum tears.[61] Avulsion or total absence of the labrum may be associated with a ballooned anterior capsule on CT arthrography (Fig. 9-19).[64,66]

It is unusual to visualize a frank tear of the anterior capsule on a CT arthrogram. Tears of the posterior capsule can occasionally be seen with extravasation of contrast or filling of a bursa that has formed as a result of capsular disruption.[62,63] Since the posterior capsule inserts directly into the posterior labrum, any stripping of the capsular insertion should be interpreted as pathologic. With the humerus in external rotation, normal redundancy of the posterior capsule can mimic a labrum-capsule junction tear.[67]

Occasionally, abnormalities of the posterior labrum and capsule are better demonstrated with the humerus in external rotation (Fig. 9-20A,B).[67,68] This position aids in the evaluation of the posterior structures as it displaces air posteriorly while simultaneously providing optimal contrast coating of the posterior labrum.[12,65] Conversely internal rotation, by distending the anterior joint, often demonstrates abnormalities of the anterior capsule that would not otherwise be seen.[68] Some anterior labral abnormalities can be seen only with internal rotation, probably because of the gaseous distension of the capsule (Fig. 9-20C,D).[68] However, a subset of tears or detachments of the anterior labrum may be demonstrated only when the humerus is externally rotated, placing the anterior structures under tension. Overall, Pennes and coworkers found that performing CT arthrography with

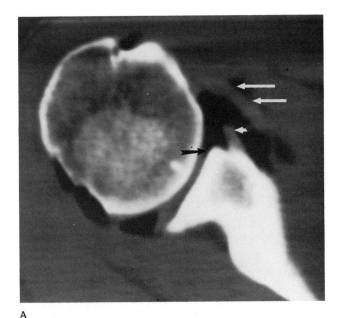

A

B

Figure 9-17 CT-arthrographic demonstration of Bankart lesion. **A.** At the midglenoid level, the anterior-inferior labrum has been avulsed (*large black arrow*). The truncated soft tissue structure attached to the anterior margin of the scapula may represent a fragment of the anterior labrum or a torn middle glenohumeral ligament (*short white arrow*). The subscapularis tendon is outlined by gas in the subscapularis recess (*long white arrows*). **B.** An osseous fragment of the glenoid rim is present on the image through the inferior joint (*small black arrow*). Observe that in this case the normal posterior labrum appears triangular at the midjoint and rounded farther inferiorly.

external rotation added information in 9 percent of cases.[68] These researchers recommend examination in both internal and external rotation for all patients.

CT arthrography can confirm the presence and direction of instability in patients with definite historical or physical evidence of instability, but in addition, the examination can suggest instability when the cause of

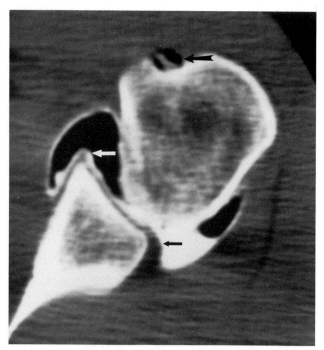

Figure 9-18 Normal double-contrast CT arthrogram. The triangular anterior labrum is well-defined, outlined by air and coated with a thin layer of contrast medium (*white arrow*). The posterior labrum appears rounded (*small black arrow*). Air in the bicipital tendon sheath outlines the tendon of the long head of the biceps (*large black arrow*).

shoulder pain is unknown. In a study of athletes with shoulder symptoms, CT arthrography provided evidence of instability in four whose instability was suspected on clinical grounds but was unconfirmed and in two patients with unsuspected instability.[62] The last two patients'

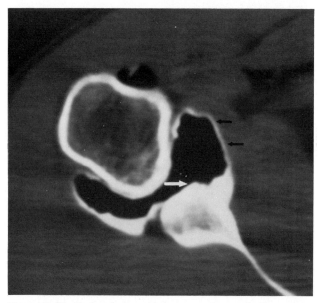

Figure 9-19 Bankart lesion with large anterior pouch. The anterior labrum is absent (*white arrow*), and the joint capsule is ballooned anteriorly (*black arrows*).

symptoms had been attributed to rotator cuff disease. Shoulder instability was eventually confirmed clinically in three of these six subjects.

Magnetic Resonance Imaging and Arthrography

MRI is rarely necessary for acute dislocation, though it may be helpful in solving specific problems. With an irreducible dislocation, MRI may demonstrate what structure is preventing relocation. For example, occasionally the tendon of the long head of the biceps becomes interposed between the humeral head and the glenoid following an anterior or posterior dislocation, preventing closed reduction. MRI can demonstrate this abnormality, which mandates open reduction.[69] Other soft tissue structures, such as an avulsed rotator cuff tendon, can be displaced into the joint, hampering reduction. With MRI examination it is possible to detect these complications as well.

In patients with instability, MRI can demonstrate many of the same findings seen on CT arthrography (Table 9-2). Unlike CT arthrography, MRI is noninvasive and does not require coordination of two examinations or transporting the patient from one room to another. The increased soft tissue contrast and multiplanar imaging capability of MRI make it superior to CT arthrography for detection of additional abnormalities such as impingement or rotator cuff disease, which may coexist with instability.[39,70] The major disadvantage of MRI is that, in the absence of joint fluid and distension, capsulolabral abnormalities that are readily detectable on CT arthrograms are easily overlooked on MRI studies.

CT arthrography and MRI examination are equivalent in the detection of Hill-Sachs lesions.[71] On transaxial images the Hill-Sachs lesion appears as a posterolateral notched defect or an area of flattening in the normally spherical superior humeral head (Fig. 9-21). Relatively large defects can also be detected on oblique coronal or oblique sagittal MRI images, which occasionally are helpful for confirmation. On T2-weighted images an area of high signal intensity may be seen in the subcortical bone subjacent to a Hill-Sachs defect, representing contusion or subchondral cyst formation.[34]

Workman and colleagues compared the MRI detection of the Hill-Sachs lesion with conventional radiography and arthroscopy.[34] When arthroscopy was used as the gold standard, the sensitivity and specificity of MRI were greater than a set of standard radiographs that included an AP examination with the humerus in internal rotation. Arthroscopy is not a true gold standard, since the entire humeral head may not be seen through a single port. When the combination of MR, arthroscopy, and plain film analysis was used as the standard (a Hill-Sachs defect was

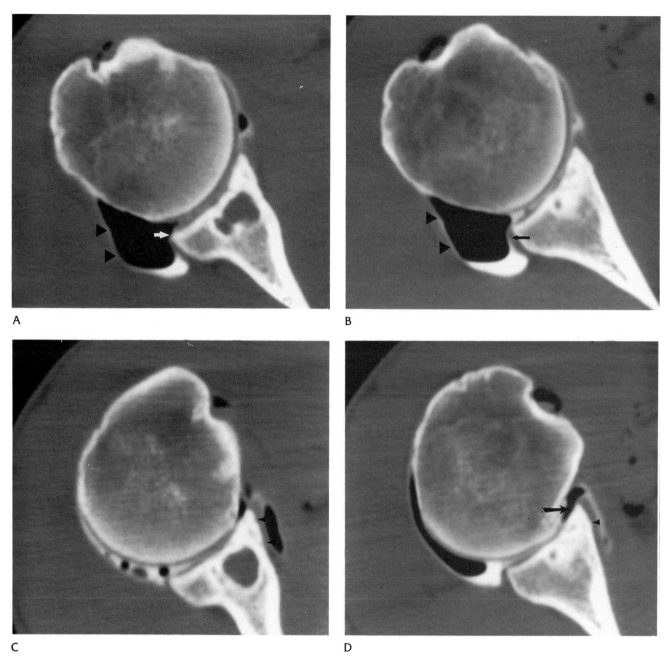

Figure 9-20 Multidirectional instability on CT arthrogram. **A,B.** Examination in external rotation shows posterior capsular redundancy (*large arrowheads*), but the attachment site to the labrum is intact (*short black arrow*). The posterior labrum is focally deficient (*short white arrow*). Posterior instability was not suspected clinically before the study was performed. **C,D.** With internal rotation air moves anteriorly and optimally demonstrates that the anterior labrum is also segmentally absent (*large black arrow*). Note the osseous changes in the anterior glenoid (*small arrowheads*). The lytic lesion within the glenoid communicates with the joint at other levels and is likely a posttraumatic cyst.

deemed present if it was detected by at least two of the three modalities), the sensitivity and specificity of MR were 97 percent and 91 percent, respectively.[34]

The shape of the anterior labrum varies from patient to patient and frequently from the right to the left shoulder of an individual. The shape can also vary within a single shoulder, appearing round superiorly and triangular on lower transaxial images.[72] The normal anterior labrum can appear crescent shaped, cleaved, notched, or flattened on MRI (Fig. 9-22).[72,74] The posterior labrum is normally smaller than the anterior labrum.[73] It usually has a triangular shape on MRI studies; however, it can

Table 9-2　MRI Findings Associated with Instability

Labrum
　Detachment
　Cleavage line of abnormal signal, cleft
　Absence or attenuation
　Deformation, truncation, blunting, fraying
Capsule
　Stripping from glenoid
　Torn middle glenohumeral ligament
Muscles
　Interruption of subscapularis tendon
　Subscapularis muscle atrophy, retraction
　Rotator cuff abnormalities
Bones
　Humeral head defects
　Glenoid fractures

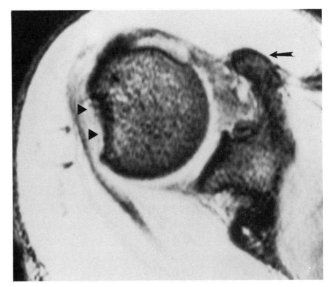

Figure 9-21 Hill-Sachs defect. Note the notched defect (*arrowheads*) in the superior posterolateral humeral head on this gradient-echo MRI image. The coracoid (*arrow*) provides a useful landmark for the superior segment of the humeral head when it is anatomically positioned in the glenoid.

appear round or flat (see Fig. 9-22).[74] In contradistinction, on CT arthrography the normal posterior labrum is often rounded, which may be secondary to gaseous distension that allows the triangular posterior labrum to flatten. Clefts and notches are not seen in the normal posterior labrum.[74]

The glenoid labrum demonstrates some signal in as many as 46 percent of normal subjects, though it is composed of fibrocartilage or a combination of fibrous tissue and fibrocartilage.[74,75] The signal is present on gradient-echo or proton-density–weighted spin-echo images, but not on T2-weighted images.[74,75] It may be globular or linear, and it can extend to both surfaces of the anterior labrum. In two studies examining asymptomatic

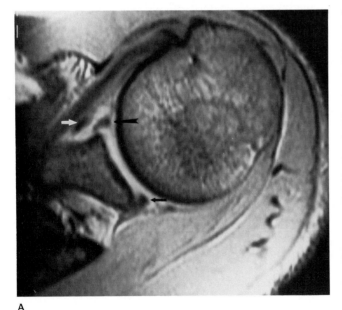

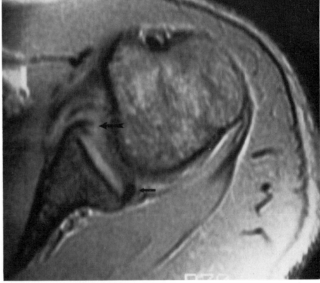

A　　　　　　　　　　　　　　　　　　　B

Figure 9-22 Variable shape of the normal labrum. Transaxial MRI images through the, **A,** middle and, **B,** inferior segment of the glenohumeral joint. **A.** The anterior labrum (*large black arrow*) is crescent-shaped and the posterior labrum (*small black arrow*) is triangular. The structure (*white arrow*) posterior to the subscapularis tendon is one of the glenohumeral ligaments, most likely the middle one. **B.** Farther inferior is an apparent cleft in the anterior labrum (*large black arrow*). This appearance may represent the normal attachment of the inferior glenohumeral ligament to the anterior inferior labrum. The posterior labrum (*small black arrow*) now appears flattened.

subjects, linear signal was seen in only one of 78 posterior labra.[74,75]

Joint fluid helps in the evaluation of the labrum, particularly if it is voluminous enough to distend the joint.[23] In patients with shoulder instability the labrum may be completely avulsed, severely truncated, or torn (Fig. 9-23).[22,75–77] When torn, the anterior labrum may be visualized as an ill-defined mass in the joint, difficult to distinguish from the glenohumeral ligaments, which may also be torn (see Fig. 9-23B).[77] When the labral abnormality is subtle (e.g., mild attenuation, fraying, or indistinctness of the labrum)[75,76,78] a diagnosis of instability should be entertained cautiously, since normal labra may exhibit similar features, especially in older patients.[70,73] The anterior labrum may occasionally be entirely absent

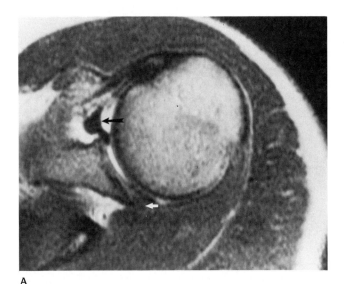

A

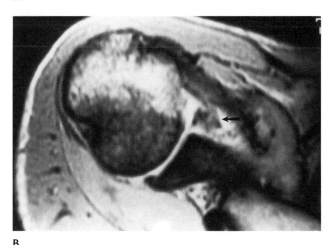

B

Figure 9-23 Two examples of Bankart lesions. **A.** The T2-weighted image shows complete avulsion of the anterior labrum (*black arrow*) surrounded by fluid. Note the abnormal high signal within the posterior labrum (*white arrow*), which still appears attached to the glenoid. An inferior capsular shift procedure was performed. **B.** In this case the avulsed anterior labrum forms an ill-defined mass (*arrow*) in the anterior joint inseparable from the anterior capsular structures.

in normal subjects.[74] When labrum abnormalities are equivocal, associated findings such as Hill-Sachs lesions and anterior capsule stripping increase the likelihood that instability is present.

In some cases of suspected instability with a normal-looking labrum, subtle abnormalities may be brought out by specific positioning of the humerus, specifically external rotation for the anterior labrum and internal rotation for the posterior labrum.[67] These maneuvers increase tension in the capsular attachments to the labrum and can enhance the detection of a torn labrum (see, for example, Fig. 9-31). Normal anatomy also often becomes better defined once the capsular attachments are stretched (Fig. 9-24). Depending on the size of the patient and the type of surface coil used, it may be more difficult to externally rotate the humerus in the small bore of the MRI scanner than in the CT gantry.

Multiple studies have addressed the performance of MRI for detecting labral abnormalities, utilizing arthroscopic surgery as the gold standard. The sensitivity ranges from 44 to 88 percent and specificity from 67 to 93 percent.[75,77–79] These studies evaluated patients with clinically unstable shoulders whose symptoms warranted surgery and who thus had a high pretest probability of having an abnormal labrum. Seeger and coworkers noted that all labral Bankart lesions were missed on MRI examination limited to T1-weighted images.[76] Other investigators have found poor interobserver and intraobserver variability in the detection of labral abnormalities by MRI.[79] Legan and colleagues demonstrated 95 percent sensitivity for tears of the anterior labrum, 40 percent for tears of the inferior labrum, and only 8 percent for posterior labrum tears.[77]

There is considerable disagreement concerning the visualization of the glenohumeral ligaments. The superior glenohumeral ligament may be difficult to identify confidently.[23,72] Some authors have stated that the inferior glenohumeral ligament is also inconsistently seen,[23] though Liou and associates claim to identify the anterior band of the inferior glenohumeral ligament at the middle level of the glenohumeral joint in 85 percent of normal shoulders, even in the absence of joint effusion.[72] The most inferior supporting structures—the axillary pouch portion of the inferior glenohumeral ligament, anterior-inferior capsule, and axillary recess—are not discernible as distinct structures on MRI.

The middle glenohumeral ligament, although the most variable, is the easiest to recognize. It appears as a linear structure parallel and deep to the subscapularis tendon (see Fig. 9-22A).[23,72] Like the other glenohumeral ligaments, it takes an oblique inferior course from the glenoid to the humeral neck, and it cannot be seen in its entirety on a single image. Although a torn middle glenohumeral ligament is a sign of anterior instability,[70] these tears are difficult to detect by MRI.

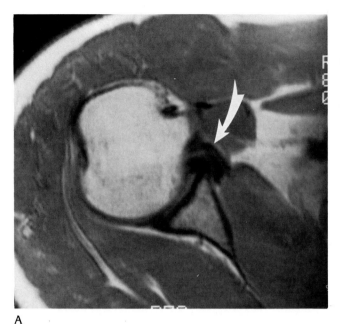
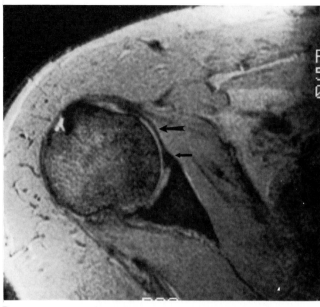

A   B

Figure 9-24 Effect of humeral position on normal capsulolabral appearance. **A.** With the humerus in internal rotation, it is difficult to distinguish individual components of the anterior capsular mechanism, which appear redundant (*curved white arrow*). **B.** External rotation stretches the subscapularis tendon and middle glenohumeral ligament (*large arrow*). The middle glenohumeral ligament attaches directly to the triangular anterior labrum (*small arrow*).

MRI of the glenoid labrum has several pitfalls. High-signal hyaline cartilage is present between the cortical bone of the glenoid rim and the base of the labrum (Fig. 9-25). This undercutting of the labrum by cartilage can normally extend to the capsular surface of the labrum and should not be mistaken for a labral tear or avulsion.[72,73,77] On gradient-echo images the signal from hyaline cartilage may be almost as bright as that of fluid, making the distinction of normal cartilage from a labral tear difficult (see Fig. 9-25). We recently abandoned gradient-echo imaging in favor of conventional dual-echo spin-echo sequences for this reason. We feel that the spin-echo images also provide better anatomic detail.

Linear high signal is occasionally seen within the substance of the anterior labrum as a normal variant. It is parallel to the sublabral cartilage near the base of the labrum[70] and can be distinguished from a labral tear by its smooth contour and its disappearance or decreased intensity on T2-weighted images. The close proximity of the glenohumeral ligaments to the anterior labrum may simulate a labral tear or detachment. This pitfall can be avoided by noting that the adjacent labrum is normal in size and shape and that the glenohumeral ligament follows its expected course (see Fig. 9-25).[73] Inferiorly, the inferior glenohumeral ligament lies very close to, and eventually fuses with, the anterior labrum; this relationship may explain the notched appearance of the labrum noted in some series (see Fig. 9-22B).[72] In cases with

questionable labral abnormalities, repeat imaging with the arm in external rotation may facilitate the evaluation of labral morphology.

Other MRI findings of instability include osseous changes in the anterior or posterior glenoid (Fig. 9-26), and abnormalities of the rotator cuff, especially the subscapularis muscle and tendon.[70,76] Complete disruption of the subscapularis may be seen with CT arthrography, but subtler changes such as myotendinous strain, partial tear, or muscle atrophy are better detected by MRI because of the superior soft tissue contrast resolution. Last, subluxation of the humeral head can be shown on MRI (Fig. 9-27).

Anterior capsular stripping or a Type III capsular insertion is common in patients with anterior instability (Fig. 9-28).[70,71] Neumann and colleagues found a Type III capsular insertion on MRI in 4 percent of normal volunteers,[74] an incidence similar to that found in fetal and cadaver studies.[6] Many investigators feel, however, that even when it is present as a developmental variant, it predisposes to anterior instability.[6,8] Occasionally, posterior capsular stripping is seen as a sign of posterior instability (Fig. 9-29).

Evaluation of the capsule and glenohumeral ligaments can be difficult in the absence of a joint effusion (Fig. 9-30). Additionally, without joint distension it may not be possible to distinguish normal changes from pathologic ones in the labrum. This limitation has motivated some

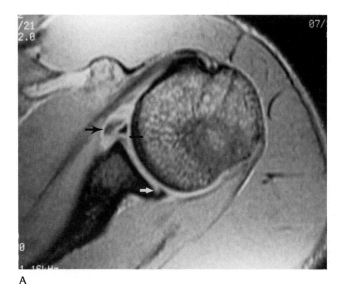

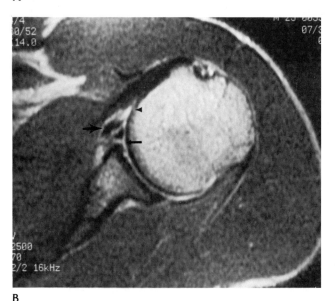

is the need for relatively time-consuming T2-weighted acquisitions. Alternatively, a dilute gadolinium solution can be injected and T1-weighted images used for diagnosis,[80,82] but since gadolinium currently is not approved for intraarticular use, this experimental technique can be performed only at centers with institutional approval.

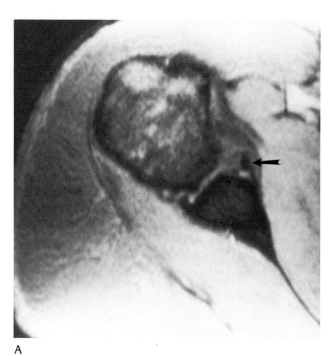

A

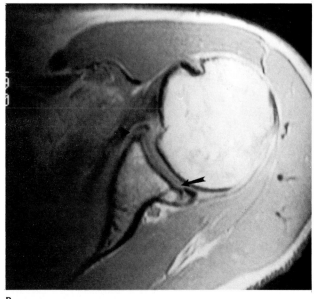

B

Figure 9-26 Osseous changes of instability. **A.** A fracture of the anterior glenoid (*arrow*), an osseous Bankart lesion. **B.** A second patient demonstrates evidence of a previous fracture of the posterior glenoid (*arrow*) secondary to a posterior dislocation. Note the severely attenuated anterior labrum (*arrowhead*) in this patient who had multidirectional instability.

Figure 9-25 Normal undercutting of the labrum. **A.** Gradient-echo image. **B.** T2-weighted spin-echo image. High-signal hyaline cartilage (*small black arrows*) is interposed between the anterior labrum and glenoid on both images. This is a normal appearance that should not be interpreted as an avulsed labrum. The signal from cartilage is indistinguishable from that of fluid on the gradient-echo image, **A,** but is slightly less than that of the small amount of joint fluid (*arrowhead*) seen on the T2-weighted image, **B.** Note the close apposition of the middle glenohumeral ligament (*large black arrows*) and anterior labrum, also a normal appearance. Undercutting of the posterior labrum by cartilage (*white arrow*) is evident on the gradient-echo image **(A).** At the time of surgery for recurrent instability, the absence of a Bankart lesion was confirmed, and an inferior capsular shift procedure was performed.

investigators to perform MRI arthrography.[80,81] This can be accomplished by injecting saline solution into the joint under fluoroscopic control before the MRI examination (Fig. 9-31).[81] The disadvantage of using saline, especially if a conventional MRI study is performed first,

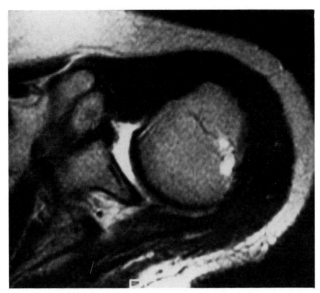

Figure 9-27 Subluxation of the humeral head. This patient with multidirectional instability underwent a procedure to tighten the anterior capsule and now has a fixed posterior subluxation.

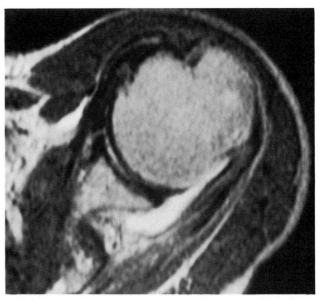

Figure 9-29 Posterior capsular stripping. The posterior capsule, which should always attach directly to the posterior labrum, is detached. This patient also had a complete rotator cuff tear.

The chief disadvantages of the technique are the conversion of a completely noninvasive test into a minimally invasive one, the logistic problems inherent in transferring a patient from the fluoroscopy suite to the MRI scanner while timing both studies to ensure optimal joint distension for the MRI study, and the increased expense of the examination.

Flannigan and coworkers prospectively detected nine of nine surgically confirmed labral tears with MRI arthrography but saw only three of them with conventional MRI.[82] Similarly, Karzel and Snyder visualized all surgically confirmed anterior labral lesions in a group of patients with unstable shoulders on MRI after intraarti-

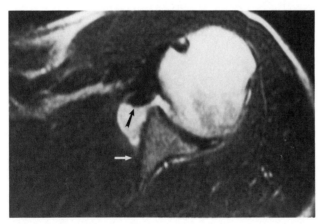

Figure 9-28 Anterior capsular stripping. The anterior capsule is distended and inserts medially on the scapular neck (*white arrow*). The anterior labrum is also avulsed (*black arrow*). A Hill-Sachs lesion was present on more superior images.

cular gadolinium administration, compared to a 50 percent detection rate without intraarticular contrast.[80] The preliminary data suggest that MRI arthrography may be a useful adjunct procedure in a select subset of patients with equivocal findings on conventional MRI study, but it still must be clarified whether this increase in sensitivity comes at the expense of an increased rate of false positive diagnoses. Alternatively, CT arthrography can be performed if findings of the conventional MRI examination are inconclusive.

IMAGING PATIENTS WITH OCCULT AND FUNCTIONAL INSTABILITY

Some patients with glenohumeral instability present with atypical clinical findings. A subset of patients have had episodes of dislocation, or more commonly subluxation, which went unrecognized either because of spontaneous reduction,[45] or because the history and physical findings were atypical.[37] This situation may best be characterized as subclinical or occult instability. In this group, the demonstration of osseous, labral, or capsular abnormalities may help clarify the symptoms and the treatment options.

Other patients have clinically stable shoulders, even when examined under anesthesia, but they have isolated labral abnormalities, most commonly lesions of the superior labrum, that account for their symptoms.[2,63] This syndrome has been called *functional instability* and is currently recognized in athletes involved in throwing and other overhead arm movements.[50,83] Management of these athletes can be particularly perplexing as their

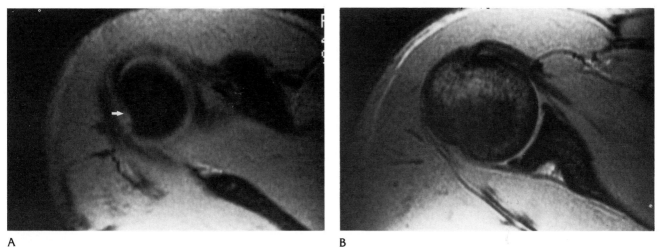

Figure 9-30 Bankart lesion with a false negative MR examination. **A.** An image through the superior humeral head demonstrates Hill-Sachs lesion (*arrow*). **B.** On a lower image the labra and capsules appear normal; however, a complete anterior capsulolabral detachment was found at arthroscopy.

symptoms may be due to isolated labral abnormalities, episodes of subclinical instability, the impingement syndrome, or a combination of causes, each of which may require different treatment.[49,50] Thus, finding objective evidence of a labral injury, instability, or impingement can alter management in these cases.

Occult Instability

Patients with unrecognized recurrent instability may present in several ways. Some develop a sharp "paralyzing" pain associated with weakness and loss of control, numbness, or heaviness of the arm on overhead positioning, a condition called the *dead arm syndrome*.[37,48,51] Others present with secondary impingement—pain due

to impingement that is secondary to recurrent anterior subluxations. Still others demonstrate an *apprehension syndrome* characterized by avoidance of activities that produce symptoms.[51] Any of these syndromes can become disabling.[37]

Rowe and Zarins examined 60 shoulders of patients with recurrent transient subluxation.[48] Although all patients demonstrated a positive apprehension test on physical examination, less than half had the subjective feeling of transient subluxation. Eighty-six percent reported an initial traumatic event, either a direct blow or a situation where the abducted humerus was forced into external rotation; the remainder had no single precipitating event but did engage in excessive throwing or overhand serving. Of the 50 patients who underwent

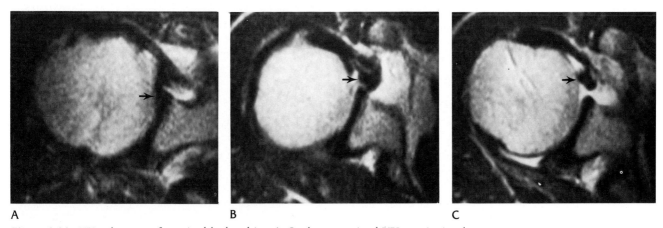

Figure 9-31 MRI arthrogram of anterior labral avulsion. **A.** On the conventional MRI examination the anterior labrum of this baseball pitcher appears irregular and ill-defined (*arrow*). Repeat MRI examination performed after intraarticular instillation of saline was done in internal, **B,** and external, **C,** rotation. The joint fluid now outlines the avulsed anterior labrum (*arrow*), which is demonstrated with the humerus in external rotation **(C).**

surgery, 64 percent had Bankart lesion, which was repaired. The other patients, several of whom demonstrated excessive laxity of the anterior capsule, underwent capsulorrhaphy. Hill-Sachs and anterior glenoid rim changes were demonstrated on conventional radiographs in 40 and 45 percent, respectively.[48] The prevalence of bone changes might have been greater had special projections been utilized. Demonstration of one of these signs on plain films, CT, or MRI examination increases the likelihood of instability when the diagnosis is in doubt.[37]

Preoperative fluoroscopy in the axillary position of the anesthetized patient has been advocated in the diagnosis of subtle instability.[47] Papilion and Shall took spot films while applying maximal anterior and posterior stress to both shoulders; the asymptomatic side served as a control. To correct for magnification, the translation of the humeral head from the neutral position compared to the glenoid centrum was expressed as a percentage. They determined that more than 14 percent anterior translation or 37 percent posterior translation was abnormal. These criteria were more successful in predicting anterior instability than the posterior type. A 10 percent difference in anterior translation between the symptomatic and asymptomatic side also predicted instability.[47]

Labral Abnormalities in the Stable Shoulder

Labral tears are usually found in association with instability. Occasionally, a labral tear may produce symptoms in an anatomically stable shoulder. Symptoms range from intermittent clicking or locking to a sensation of catching or slipping.[2] Neviaser recently reported five cases where superficial anterior inferior labral tears produced pain in patients without anterior instability,[84] and Rafii and coworkers have found symptomatic anterior labral tears in athletes with stable shoulders.[63] More commonly, however, such lesions are found in the superior labrum related to the origin of the long head of the biceps, or in the anterior superior or posterior superior segments of the labrum.[62,63,83,85]

Either CT arthrography[62,63,86] or MRI[13,87] can be used to detect abnormalities of the superior labrum and adjacent labral segments (Fig. 9-32). The normal appearance of the superior labrum should be appreciated to avoid errors in diagnosis. On MRI examination, signal may be seen normally in the superior labrum. Some superior labra demonstrate globular signal.[75] Others may have a liner band of increased signal intensity interposed between the proximal biceps tendon and the labrum.[87] Undercutting of the labrum by hyaline cartilage is normal, but in the superior labrum it should not extend to the superior margin (Fig. 9-33).[77] With aging, the superior labrum may become at least partially detached,[12,13,87]

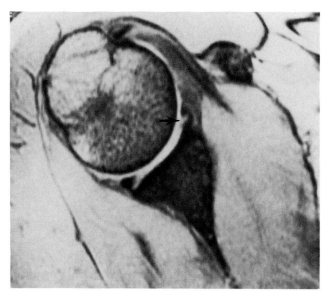

Figure 9-32 Cleft versus partial tear of anterior superior labrum. Abnormal signal (*arrow*) extends into, but does not completely traverse, the anterior superior labrum in this 34-year-old man. In addition to the cleft, fibrillation of the superior labrum was seen at arthroscopy; the changes were felt to be pathologic, and the labrum was debrided.

and even in younger patients the central portion of the superior labrum may be normally detached.[11] Partial separation of the superior labrum has been reported as a source of pain in stable shoulders,[62,63] but because this finding can be seen in asymptomatic subjects, where it is thought to represent degeneration, we are very cau-

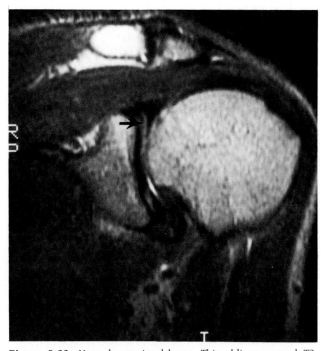

Figure 9-33 Normal superior labrum. This oblique coronal T2-weighted MR image demonstrates the normal undercutting of the superior labrum by hyaline cartilage (*arrow*).

tious about making this diagnosis in older patients. For patients with isolated labral tears, if surgical debridement or excision is contemplated, any imaging findings that suggest instability may alter the planned surgery since removal of the labrum could increase the instability.[63]

The SLAP Lesion

Snyder and colleagues recently described tears of the superior labrum that start at the biceps tendon attachment and extend into the posterior superior and anterior superior labrum.[88] They coined the acronym *SLAP lesions* (*superior labrum, anterior* and *posterior*). The common mechanism is contraction of the long head of the biceps tendon, which exerts force on the superior labrum.[62,86] The tears can be produced by a fall on the outstretched arm, by a sudden pull on the arm as when catching a heavy falling object, or by repetitive overhead motion.[86,88] Symptoms include pain exacerbated by overhead activities, catching, clicking, or popping.[86] Approximately 15 percent of these cases demonstrate anterior instability, and many have partial- or full-thickness rotator cuff tears.[88]

Snyder and colleagues have divided SLAP lesions into four types based on their findings at arthroscopy. Table 9-3 shows the arthroscopic classification and cross-sectional imaging findings in SLAP lesions. In Type I lesions the frayed superior labrum is still attached to the glenoid.[88] Type I abnormalities may be difficult to differentiate from labral degeneration commonly seen in patients over age 40 years.[86] Type II abnormalities involve stripping of the labrum and biceps tendon from the superior glenoid[88]; however, this finding can also be encountered in asymptomatic older subjects.[12,13,87] Type III lesions are bucket-handle tears of the labrum with displacement of the central fragment into the joint. Type IV lesions are characterized by a tear that extends into the proximal biceps tendon. The surgical repair of SLAP lesions depends on what type of deformity is present.[88]

Prior to the arthroscopic description of the SLAP lesions, Rafii and colleagues described separation of the superior labrum from the glenoid on CT arthrography as a source of symptoms in athletes with stable shoulders.[62,63] Several studies have examined the ability of CT arthrography[86] and MRI,[13,87] with and without intra-articular contrast,[80] to detect and classify SLAP lesions. Hunter and coworkers evaluated CT arthrograms in 17 patients with arthroscopically proven SLAP lesions. Prospectively, they reported that 16 of 17 were diagnosed as having an abnormal labrum though they did not clearly state that the labral abnormalities involved both the anterior and posterior labrum. In a retrospective analysis, the group correctly classified the subtype of SLAP lesion in 15 of 17 cases. Their criterion for a Type II lesion was a tear in the superior labrum that extended inferiorly to the level of the middle glenohumeral ligament. Type III tears characteristically showed the bucket-handle fragment as a round soft tissue structure surrounded by contrast and air. The authors likened its appearance to that of a Cheerio. The same finding associated with lack of visualization of the biceps tendon in the bicipital groove defined Type IV tears.[86]

Studies utilizing MRI and MRI arthrography have also been performed to define criteria for the diagnosis of SLAP lesions.[13,80,87] One study described the oblique coronal plane as best for visualizing the superior labrum[87]; another emphasized the axial images.[13] MRI was insensitive in the detection of Type I lesions, even with intraarticular contrast.[13] Type II tears may appear to have only partial separation of the labrum from the glenoid; whereas this appearance can be normal in older patients, its presence may suggest disease in younger ones.[13] MRI arthrography increases the sensitivity of the examination for SLAP lesions, but its utility is diminished by an increase in false positive diagnoses when fluid tracks under the lip of the superior labrum, mimicking a torn or detached labrum.[80] In a double-blind study, Karzel and

Table 9-3 Labral Findings Associated with the SLAP Lesion

TYPE	ARTHROSCOPIC APPEARANCE	IMAGING FINDINGS	
		CT ARTHROGRPAHY	MRI/MRI ARTHROGRAPHY
I	Fraying	Irregular contour	Usually normal
II	Detached with biceps tendon	Tear extending to level of middle glenohumeral ligament	Partial or complete detachment
III	Displaced bucket-handle tear	"Cheerio" sign	Tear with complete detachment
IV	Tear extending into biceps tendon	"Cheerio" sign with displaced biceps tendon	Abnormal signal extending into biceps tendon

Snyder detected none of seven SLAP lesions with conventional MRI and four of the seven with MRI arthrography; however, there were three false positive MRI arthrogram readings.[80]

The Throwing Athlete

The act of pitching places great stress on the static and dynamic shoulder stabilizers. Normally, the humeral head translates 4 mm posteriorly in the cocked position and then with throwing is propelled anteriorly into the glenoid rim, producing shearing forces on the anterior cartilage and labrum (see Fig. 9-31).[14] A complex interaction takes place among the different stabilizing mechanisms during throwing. The static stabilizers are augmented by the dynamic stabilizers: the rotator cuff musculature, the long head of the biceps muscle, and the scapular rotators (trapezius, serratus anterior, rhomboids, and levator scapulae).[50] The role of the biceps tendon is incompletely understood, but it appears that its contraction is important during the deceleration phase.[83]

Terry and coworkers performed a study utilizing strain gauge analysis of cadaver shoulders. The shoulder was put through a range of motion corresponding to cocking, acceleration, and follow-through positions. Maximum tension developed first in the coracohumeral and superior glenohumeral ligaments. It was then transferred to the posterior capsule and was finally shared between the superior glenohumeral ligament and the middle and inferior portions of the posterior capsule.[25] With repetitive throwing these static stabilizers may become attenuated. Initially, the dynamic stabilizers compensate, but when they fatigue, anterior subluxation can occur. As the elevated humeral head moves forward it can abut the coracoacromial arch and result in secondary impingement. This biomechanical imbalance may result in a rotator cuff tear.[50] The repetitive stresses placed on the superior labrum at the attachment of the long head of the biceps tendon may compound the problem by producing tears of the superior labrum or biceps tendon.[83] In addition, during the cocking phase the undersurface of the rotator cuff may impinge on the posterosuperior border of the glenoid rim.[50,85] Pitchers and other throwing athletes are thus at risk for instability, impingement, isolated labral tears, and combination lesions. Since MRI can detect changes of impingement and rotator cuff disease as well as instability, it would appear to be the ideal study for symptomatic throwing athletes. Furthermore, MRI, possibly supplemented by MRI arthrography, may identify some of the superior labral tears common to this group of athletes.

Kvitne and Jobe believe that shoulder injuries in throwing athletes occur along a continuous spectrum ranging from pure impingement to pure instability. Intermediate classifications include secondary impingement caused by chronic labral microtrauma or by generalized ligamentous laxity.[50] A precise diagnosis is extremely important, as the clinical management is directed by the specific anatomic and functional abnormality. If conservative rehabilitation fails, athletes with pure impingement will benefit from subacromial decompression whereas those with pure instability or impingement secondary to instability require a capsulolabral repair, such as a capsular shift procedure.[50]

In throwing athletes with recurrent instability the classic Bankart lesion may be absent.[89] Hill-Sachs lesions, however, are common in throwing athletes with subclinical instability. In one study the lesions were detected in 23 of 28 cases utilizing anterior oblique films of the shoulder.[49] The presence of a humeral head defect moves a patient out of the group with pure impingement and into a category of primary instability, with or without secondary impingement. Andrews and colleagues arthroscoped 73 throwing athletes with tears of the anterior superior labrum at the attachment of the biceps tendon.[83] In 23 percent the tear extended posteriorly as well; today these injuries would be classified as SLAP lesions. Ten percent also had partial tears of the biceps tendon. The vast majority of these athletes reported pain while throwing, but only 5 percent exhibited instability on clinical examination.[83] Similarly, a CT arthrographic study found no anterior inferior (classic Bankart) labral or capsular abnormalities in a group of 19 athletes with painful stable shoulders; however, the same group demonstrated tears of the superior or midanterior labrum.[63]

SUMMARY

Shoulder instability can present in a variety of ways, and the radiologic approach should be tailored to the clinical situation. For the diagnosis of acute dislocation, the roles of imaging should be to confirm the presence and direction of dislocation, to identify associated fractures or other injuries, and to evaluate the adequacy of reduction. Conventional radiographs usually suffice, although occasionally an additional study such as CT may be used. Typical indications for CT include complex fracture-dislocations, failed reductions, suspected intraarticular fragments, and chronic dislocation.

When a patient presents with known recurrent instability, imaging complements the clinical assessment. The presence of a Hill-Sachs or Bankart lesion supports the diagnosis of instability, indicates direction, and suggests a history of trauma. Studies should be carefully scrutinized for evidence of multidirectional instability, as management of these patients differs. Finally, identification of associated lesions such as rotator cuff tears or biceps tendon abnormalities will alter management. Conventional radiography, CT arthrography, and MRI may each play a role in these patients.

Finally, persons such as throwing athletes with non-specific shoulder symptoms are at risk for multiple shoulder ailments. Clinical diagnosis may be difficult since instability, impingement, labral lesions, or combinations of these abnormalities may be present. The role of imaging in this setting is still evolving, but MRI and possibly MRI arthrography certainly can contribute to the evaluation of these challenging patients.

References

1. MATSEN FA III, THOMAS SC, ROCKWOOD CA JR: Glenohumeral instability, in Rockwood CA Jr, Matsen FA III (eds): *The Shoulder*, Philadelphia, Saunders, 1990, pp 526–622.
2. PAPPAS AM, GOSS TP, KLEINMAN PK: Symptomatic shoulder instability due to lesions of the glenoid labrum. *Am J Sports Med* 11:279, 1983.
3. BOST FC, INMAN VT: The pathologic changes in recurrent dislocation of the shoulder. *J Bone Joint Surg* 24A:595, 1942.
4. RANDELLI M, GAMBRIOLI PL: Glenohumeral osteometry by computed tomography in normal and unstable shoulders. *Clin Orthop* 206:151, 1986.
5. HURLEY JA, ANDERSON TE, DEAR W, ANDRISH JT, BERGFELD JA, WEIKER GG: Posterior shoulder instability: Surgical versus conservative results with evaluation of glenoid version. *Am J Sports Med* 20:396, 1992.
6. MOSELEY HF, ÖVERGAARD B: The anterior capsular mechanism in recurrent anterior dislocation of the shoulder. *J Bone Joint Surg* 44B:913, 1962.
7. TOWNLEY CO: The capsular mechanism in recurrent dislocation of the shoulder. *J Bone Joint Surg* 32A:370, 1950.
8. TSAI JC, ZLATKIN MB: Magnetic resonance imaging of the shoulder. *Radiol Clin North Am* 28:279, 1990.
9. PRODROMOS CC, FERRY JA, SCHILLER AL, ZARINS B: Histologic studies of the glenoid labrum from fetal life to old age. *J Bone Joint Surg* 72A:1344, 1990.
10. COOPER DE, ARNOCZKY SPJ, O'BRIEN SJ, ET AL.: Anatomy, histology, and vascularity of the glenoid labrum. *J Bone Joint Surg* 74A:46, 1992.
11. RAMES RD, KARZEL RP: Injuries to the glenoid labrum, including SLAP lesions. *Orthop Clin North Am* 24:45, 1993.
12. DEUTSCH AL, RESNICK D, MINK JH, ET AL.: Computed and conventional arthrotomography of the glenohumeral joint: Normal anatomy and clinical experience. *Radiology* 153:603, 1984.
13. HODLER J, KURSUNOGLU-BRAHME S, FLANNIGAN B, SNYDER SJ, KARZEL RP, RESNICK D: Injuries of the superior portion of the glenoid labrum involving the insertion of the biceps tendon: MR imaging findings in nine cases. *AJR* 159:565, 1992.
13a. HOWELL SM, KRAFT TA: The role of the supraspinatus and infraspinatus muscles in glenohumeral kinematics of anterior shoulder instability. *Clin Orthop* 263:128, 1991.
14. HOWELL SM, GALINAT BJ, RENZI AJ, MARONE PJ: Normal and abnormal mechanisms of the glenohumeral joint in the horizontal plane. *J Bone Joint Surg* 70A:227, 1988.
15. HARRYMAN DT II, SIDLES JA, CLARK JM, McQUADE KJ, GIBB TD, MATSEN FA III: Translation of the humeral head on the glenoid with passive glenohumeral motion. *J Bone Joint Surg* 72A:1334, 1990.
16. NOTTAGE WM: Arthroscopic anatomy of the glenohumeral joint and subacromial bursa. *Orthop Clin North Am* 24:27, 1993.
17. TURKEL SJ, PANIO MW, MARSHALL JL, GIRGIS FG: Stabilizing mechanisms preventing anterior dislocation of the glenohumeral joint. *J Bone Joint Surg* 63A:1208, 1981.
18. WARNER JJP, CABORN DNM, BERGER R, FU FH, SEEL M: Dynamic capsuloligamentous anatomy of the glenohumeral joint. *J Shoulder Elbow Surg* 2:115, 1993.
19. O'BRIEN SJ, NEVES MC, ARNOCZKY SP, ET AL.: The anatomy and histology of the inferior glenohumeral ligament complex of the shoulder. *Am J Sports Med* 18:449, 1990.
20. ROWE CR: Prognosis in dislocation of the shoulder. *J Bone Joint Surg* 38A:957, 1956.
21. ROWE CR, PATEL D, SOUTHMAYD WW: The Bankart procedure: A long-term end-result study. *J Bone Joint Surg* 60A:1, 1978.
22. UHTHOFF HK, PISCOPO M: Anterior capsular redundancy of the shoulder: Congenital or traumatic? *J Bone Joint Surg* 67B:363, 1985.
23. KURSUNOGLU-BRAHME S, RESNICK D: Magnetic resonance imaging of the shoulder. *Radiol Clin North Am* 28:941, 1990.
24. KUMAR VP, SATKU K, BALASUBRAMANIAM P: The role of the long head of the biceps brachii in the stabilization of the head of the humerus. *Clin Orthop* 244;172, 1989.

25. TERRY GC, HAMMON D, FRANCE P, NORWOOD LA: The stabilizing function of the passive shoulder restraints. *Am J Sports Med* 19:26, 1991.

26. SYMEONIDES, PP: The significance of the subscapularis muscle in the pathogenesis of recurrent anterior dislocation of the shoulder. *J Bone Joint Surg* 54B:476, 1972.

27. OVESEN J, SØJBJERG JO: Lesions in different types of anterior glenohumeral joint dislocation: An experimental study. *Arch Orthop Trauma Surg* 105:216, 1986.

28. HILL HA, SACHS MD: The grooved defect of the humeral head: A frequently unrecognized complication of dislocations of the shoulder joint. *Radiology* 35:690, 1940.

29. CISTERNINO SJ, ROGERS LF, STUFFLEBAM BC, KRUGLIK GD: The trough line: A radiographic sign of posterior shoulder dislocation. *AJR* 130:951, 1978.

30. TIJMES J, LOYD HM, TULLOS HS: Arthrography in acute shoulder dislocations. *South Med J* 72:564, 1979.

31. SIMONET WT, COFIELD RH: Prognosis in anterior shoulder dislocation. *Am J Sports Med* 12:19, 1984.

32. NORLIN R: Intraarticular pathology in acute, first-time anterior shoulder dislocation: An arthroscopic study. *Arthroscopy* 9:546, 1993.

33. RIBBANS WJ, MITCHELL R, TAYLOR GJ: Computerised arthrotomography of primary anterior dislocation of the shoulder. *J Bone Joint Surg* 72B:181, 1990.

34. WORKMAN TL, BURKHARD TK, RESNICK D, ET AL.: Hill-Sachs lesion: Comparison of detection with MR imaging, radiography, and arthroscopy. *Radiology* 185:847, 1992.

35. BANKART ASB: Recurrent or habitual dislocation of the shoulder joint. *Br Med J* 2:1132, 1923.

36. BANKART ASB: The pathology and treatment of recurrent dislocation of the shoulder joint. *Br J Surg* 26:23, 1938.

37. HAWKINS R, MOKTADI NGH: Controversy in anterior shoulder instability. *Clin Orthop* 272:152, 1991.

38. NEVIASER TJ: The anterior labroligamentous periosteal sleeve avulsion lesion: A cause of anterior instability of the shoulder. *Arthroscopy* 9:17, 1993.

39. KUMMEL BM: Spectrum of lesions of the anterior capsular mechanism of the shoulder. *Am J Sports Med* 7:111, 1979.

40. BRAUNSTEIN EM, MARTELL W: Voluntary glenohumeral dislocation. *AJR* 129:911, 1977.

41. DOWNEY EF JR, CURTIS DJ, BROWER AC: Unusual dislocations of the shoulder. *AJR* 140:1207, 1983.

42. KOTHARI K, BERNSTEIN RM, GRIFFITHS H, STANDERTSKJÖLD-NORDENSTEM CG, CHOI PK: Luxatio erecta. *Skel Radiol* 11:47, 1984.

43. ROWE CR, ZARINS B: Chronic unreduced dislocations of the shoulder. *J Bone Joint Surg* 64:494, 1982.

44. NEER CS II, FOSTER CR: Inferior capsular shift for involuntary inferior and multidirectional instability of the shoulder: A preliminary report. *J Bone Joint Surg* 62A:897, 1980.

45. NEER CS II, WELSH RP: The shoulder in sports. *Orthop Clin North Am* 8:583, 1977.

46. COOPER RA, BREMS JJ: The inferior capsular shift for multidirectional instability of the shoulder. *J Bone Joint Surg* 74A:1516, 1992.

47. PAPILION JA, SHALL LM: Fluoroscopic evaluation for subtle shoulder instability. *Am J Sports Med* 20:548, 1992.

48. ROWE CR, ZARINS B: Recurrent transient subluxation of the shoulder. *J Bone Joint Surg* 63A:863, 1981.

49. GARTH WP, ALLMAN FL JR, ARMSTRONG WS: Occult anterior subluxations of the shoulder in noncontact sports. *Am J Sports Med* 15:579, 1987.

50. KVITNE RS, JOBE FW: The diagnosis and treatment of anterior instability in the throwing athlete. *Clin Orthop* 291:107, 1993.

51. McGLYNN F, CASPARI RB: Arthroscopic findings in the subluxating shoulder. *Clin Orthop* 183:173, 1984.

52. RUBIN SR, GRAY RL, GREEN WR: The scapular "Y": A diagnostic aid in shoulder trauma. *Radiology* 110:725, 1974.

53. GARTH WP JR, SLAPPEY CE, OCHS CW: Roentgenographic demonstration of instability of the shoulder: The apical oblique projection. *J Bone Joint Surg* 66A:1450, 1984.

54. ARNDT JH, SEARS AD: Posterior dislocation of the shoulder. *AJR* 94:639, 1965.

55. ENGEBRETSEN L, CRAIG EV: Radiologic features of instability. *Clin Orthop* 291:29, 1993.

56. PAVLOV H, WARREN RF, WEISS CB JR, DINES DM: The roentgenographic evaluation of anterior shoulder instability. *Clin Orthop* 194:153, 1985.

57. DANZIG LA, GREENWAY G, RESNICK D: The Hill-Sachs lesion: An experimental study. *Am J Sports Med* 8:328, 1980.

58. HALL RH, ISSAC FA, BOOTH CR: Dislocations of the shoulder with special reference to the accompanying small fractures. *J Bone Joint Surg* 41A:489, 1959.

59. ROZING PM, DeBAKKER HM, OBERMANN WR: Radiographic views in recurrent anterior shoulder dislocation. *Acta Orthop Scand* 57:328, 1986.

60. ROKOUS JR, FEAGIN JA, ABBOTT HG: Modified axillary roentgenogram: A useful adjunct in the diagnosis of recurrent instability of the shoulder. *Clin Orthop* 82:84, 1972.

61. WILSON AJ, TOTTY WG, MURPHY WA, HARDY DC: Shoulder joint: Arthrographic CT and long-term follow-up with surgical correlation. *Radiology* 173:329, 1989.

62. RAFII M, FIROONZNIA H, BONAMO JJ, MINKOFF J, GOLIMBU C: Athlete shoulder injuries: CT arthrographic findings. *Radiology* 162:559, 1987.

63. RAFII M, MINKOFF J, BONAMO J, ET AL.: Computed tomography (CT) arthrography of shoulder instabilities in athletes. *Am J Sports Med* 16:352, 1988.

64. DAVIES AM: The current role of computed tomographic arthrography of the shoulder. *Clin Radiol* 44:367, 1991.

65. McNIESH LM, CALLAGHAN JJ: CT arthrography of the shoulder: variations of the glenoid labrum. *AJR* 149:963, 1987.

66. ZLATKIN MB, BJORKENGREN AG, GYLYS-MORIN V, RESNICK D, SARTORIS DJ: Cross-sectional imaging of the capsular mechanism of the glenohumeral joint. *AJR* 150:151, 1988.

67. COUMAS JM, WAITE RJ, GOSS TP, FERRARI DA, KANZARIA PK, PAPPAS AM: CT and MR evaluation of the labral capsular ligamentous complex of the shoulder. *AJR* 158:591, 1992.

68. PENNES DR, JONSSON K, BUCKWALTER K, BRAUNSTEIN E, BLASIER R, WOJTYS E: Computer arthrotomography of the shoulder: Comparison of examinations made with internal and external rotation of the humerus. *AJR* 153:1017, 1989.

69. ALLARD JC, BANCROFT J: Irreducible posterior dislocation of the shoulder: MR and CT findings. *J Comput Assist Tomogr* 15:694, 1991.

70. HOLT GR, HELMS CA, STEINBACH L, NEUMANN C, MUNK PL, GENANT HK: Magnetic resonance imaging of the shoul-

der: Rationale and current applications. *Skel Radiol* 19:5, 1990.

71. KIEFT GJ, BLOEM JL, ROZING PM, OBERMANN WR: MR imaging of recurrent anterior dislocation of the shoulder: Comparison with CT arthrography. *AJR* 150:1083, 1988.

72. LIOU JTS, WILSON AJ, TOTTY WG, BROWN JJ: The normal shoulder: Common variations that simulate pathologic changes at MR imaging. *Radiology* 186:435, 1993.

73. KAPLAN PA, BRYANS KC, DAVICK JP, OTTE M, STINSON WW, DUSSAULT RG: MR imaging of the normal shoulder: Variants and pitfalls. *Radiology* 184:519, 1992.

74. NEUMANN CH, PETERSEN SA, JAHNKE AH: MR imaging of the labral-capsular complex: Normal variations. *AJR* 157:1015, 1991.

75. McCAULEY TR, POPE CF, JOKL P: Normal and abnormal glenoid labrum: Assessment with multiplanar gradient-echo MR imaging. *Radiology* 183:35, 1992.

76. SEEGER LL, GOLD RH, BASSETT LW: Shoulder instability: Evaluation with MR imaging. *Radiology* 168:695, 1988.

77. LEGAN JM, BURKHARD TK, GOFF WB II, ET AL.: Tears of the glenoid labrum: MR imaging of 88 arthroscopically confirmed cases. *Radiology* 179:241, 1991.

78. IANNOTTI JP, ZLATKIN MB, ESTERHAI JL, KRESSEL HY, DALINKA MK, SPINDLER KP: Magnetic resonance imaging of the shoulder: Sensitivity, specificity, and predictive value. *J Bone Joint Surg* 73A:17, 1991.

79. GARNEAU RA, RENFREW DL, MOORE TE, EL-KHOURY GY, NEPOLA JV, LEMKE JH: Glenoid labrum: Evaluation with MR imaging. *Radiology* 179:519, 1991.

80. KARZEL RP, SNYDER SJ: Magnetic resonance arthrography of the shoulder: A new technique of shoulder imaging. *Clin Sports Med* 12:123, 1993.

81. TIRMAN PFJ, STAUFFER AE, CRUES JV III, ET AL.: Saline magnetic resonance arthrography in the evaluation of glenohumeral instability. *Arthroscopy* 9:550, 1993.

82. FLANNIGAN B, KURSUNOGLU-BRAUME S, SNYDER S, KARZEL R, DEL PIZZO W, RESNICK D: MR arthrography of the shoulder: Comparison with conventional MR imaging. *AJR* 155:829, 1990.

83. ANDREWS JR, CARSON WG, McLEOD WD: Glenoid labrum tears related to the long head of the biceps. *Am J Sports Med* 13:337, 1985.

84. NEVIASER TJ: The GLAD lesion: Another cause of anterior shoulder pain. *Arthroscopy* 9:22, 1993.

85. WALCH G, BOILEAU P, NOEL E, DONNELL ST: Impingement of the deep surface of the supraspinatus tendon on the posterosuperior glenoid rim: An arthroscopic study. *J Shoulder Elbow Surg* 1:238, 1992.

86. HUNTER JC, BLATZ DJ, ESCOBEDO EM: SLAP lesions of the glenoid labrum: CT arthrographic and arthroscopic correlation. *Radiology* 184:513, 1992.

87. CARTLAND JP, CRUES JV III, STAUFFER A, NOTTAGE W, RYU RKN: MR imaging in the evaluation of SLAP injuries of the shoulder: Findings in 10 patients. *AJR* 159:787, 1992.

88. SNYDER SJ, KARZEL RP, DEL PIZZO W, FERKEL RD, FRIEDMAN MJ: SLAP lesions of the shoulder. *Arthroscopy* 6:274, 1990.

89. GLOUSMAN RE: Instability versus impingement syndrome in the throwing athlete. *Orthop Clin North Am* 24:89, 1993.

SOFT TISSUE INJURY TO THE SHOULDER: IMAGING PRINCIPLES

Curtis W. Hayes
William E. Palmer

Imaging choices for the evaluation of the shoulder for possible soft tissue injury have increased significantly over the past two decades. What was once a straightforward decision is now complicated by increasing imaging and therapeutic options. In this chapter we examine strategies for imaging soft tissue injuries around the shoulder. Although *soft tissue injury* essentially means rotator cuff disease, it would be impractical to assume that imaging of the rotator cuff is performed without concern for the other structures around the shoulder. Therefore, other common related abnormalities of the shoulder, such as labral tears, are discussed briefly where appropriate.

ANATOMIC AND FUNCTIONAL CONSIDERATIONS

Although the anatomy of the shoulder has already been covered, several features of shoulder anatomy should be considered before soft tissue injury is addressed. The glenohumeral joint is the most mobile joint in the human body. It is also one of the least inherently stable joints. The shoulder is subjected to numerous stresses which may cause acute or chronic injury related to work, sporting activities, or simple daily tasks. The combination of anatomic instability and high functional stresses make shoulder injuries one of the most common orthopedic problems.

The glenohumeral articulation is stabilized by the glenoid labrum, joint capsule, glenohumeral ligaments, and the rotator cuff. The cuff is composed of the interwoven tendons of the subscapularis, supraspinatus, infraspinatus, and teres minor muscles. The subscapularis inserts on the lesser tuberosity of the humerus anteriorly; the supraspinatus, infraspinatus, and teres minor tendons insert on the superior, middle, and inferior facets of the greater tuberosity, respectively. These tendons intermesh in the last several centimeters to form an essentially continuous supporting cuff anteriorly, superiorly, and posteriorly.

In addition to providing support, the muscles of the rotator cuff participate in these motions:[1] (1) medial rotation (subscapularis), (2) abduction (supraspinatus), and (3) lateral rotation (infraspinatus and teres minor). During elevation of the arm, the cuff muscles and the deltoid muscle behave as a force couple: the deltoid and supraspinatus elevate the arm while the subscapularis, infraspinatus, and teres minor muscles depress the humeral head in a synergistic fashion.

During elevation, the supraspinatus muscle and tendon glide through the space between the humeral head and the coracoacromial arch, the latter formed by the acromion process, coracoacromial ligament, and coracoid process. More medially, the supraspinatus muscle must also pass beneath the acromioclavicular joint. If for any reason this space is insufficient, the cuff is squeezed during motion, forming the basis of the impingement concept proposed by Neer and discussed below.

IMPINGEMENT SYNDROME

The concept that impingement syndrome is the principal cause of rotator cuff injury has been popularized by Neer.[2] According to this theory, the vast majority of rotator cuff tears result from a chronic degenerative process in which the rotator cuff, in particular the supraspinatus tendon, is repeatedly squeezed between the coracoacromial arch and the humeral head. The lack of space may be due to many conditions that narrow the outlet: anterior acromial spurs, a hooked acromion, or degenerative changes in the acromioclavicular joint. Rarely, an os acromiale[3] or a calcified coracoacromial ligament is the cause.[4]

Repetitive motion through the narrowed supraspinatus outlet produces degeneration in the cuff tendon, a process that Neer divides into three stages. Stage I occurs in young persons (usually before age 25) and is characterized by edema and hemorrhage in the cuff. Stage II is characterized by fibrosis and typically occurs between age 25 and 40. Stage III is the end result of impingement, the complete tear, and usually occurs in older persons.

Though not all authors accept that the impingement theory is the cause of rotator cuff degeneration leading to tears, there is evidence to support it. Rotator cuff tear is, by and large, a lesion of middle-aged and older persons. Only a minority of tears occur in young persons, and those are usually secondary to acute trauma. Most tears occur in the supraspinatus tendon, which is the one most likely to be mechanically compromised by the coracoacromial arch.

The site most vulnerable to impingement lies in the anterior portion of the distal supraspinatus tendon, approximately 1 to 2 cm from its insertion on the greater tuberosity. This area is hypovascular compared with other sites and is referred to as the *critical zone.* Hypovascularity may lead to ischemia under pressure, decreased capacity for repair, and eventual degeneration as a result of repetitive microtrauma. The same site in the supraspinatus tendon is commonly affected by calcified peritendinitis, a condition considered by some authors to also represent a degenerative process due to chronic hypovascularity and trauma.[5]

Thus, it appears likely that most complete rotator cuff tears are the result of a long-standing mechanical degenerative process. Therefore, current therapy is aimed not only at repairing the tear but also at removing the cause of impingement before a complete rotator cuff tear develops. In this regard, the goals of imaging should be to accurately identify tears and to identify abnormalities likely to be responsible for impingement.

Several anomalies have been identified as causative factors in impingement. The most common one is the subacromial osteophyte. This spur usually projects anteriorly and inferiorly from the acromion process, impinging on the anterior aspect of the supraspinatus tendon. The shape of the acromion has also been linked to impingement. Three variations of acromion shape have been described (Fig. 10-1).[6–8] Types 1 and 2 are not associated with increased risk of impingement. Type 3 acromion is hooked inferiorly at the anterior aspect and definitely shows an increased association with impingement.[6,7] Thickening and calcification or ossification of the coroacoacromial ligament may be an unusual cause of impingement.[4]

Degenerative changes in the acromioclavicular joint can be a cause of impingement syndrome. Inferiorly projecting spurs, in particular, may impinge on the distal supraspinatus muscle at the musculotendinous junction.

SOFT TISSUE INJURY: CHOICE OF IMAGING MODALITY

The increased choices now available for imaging the shoulder seem to have produced confusion and frustration among radiologists and clinicians. The relative roles of plain films, arthrography, arthrography plus computed tomography (arthro-CT), ultrasonography (US), and magnetic resonance imaging (MRI) have been debated keenly for the past several years. The fact is, all these modalities have merits and faults, and no single examination is appropriate for all patients.

The following considerations should inform the choice of which examination(s) to perform: (1) patient factors, (2) referring physician's needs, (3) radiologist's experience, and (4) cost. The most important patient factor is age. With older patients, the question to be answered may simply be whether or not there is a complete rotator cuff tear, and if so approximately how large it is. The presence of tendinitis or a partial tear probably will not influence therapy in older patients. On the other hand, when impingement is suspected in a young patient, the presence of a partial tear, bone changes likely to cause impingement, or other conditions such as calcific peri-

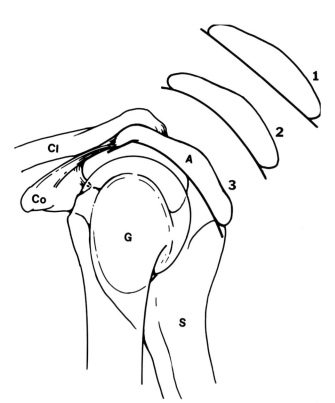

Figure 10-1 Artist's rendering of variations in acromion shape. Type 3, with an anterior hook, is associated with impingement syndrome and rotator cuff tears. (Key: 1, 2, 3, and A, acromion; Cl, clavicle; Co, coracoid; G, glenoid; S, scapula.)

tendinitis may significantly alter therapy. In young or athletic patients with impingement syndrome it may be important to evaluate for glenohumeral instability as well as rotator cuff disease.

The referring physician has expectations for diagnostic tests that are based upon treatment options for that patient. If an older patient is suspected of having a long-standing tear, the size of the defect is of critical importance for deciding whether or not (1) repair or (2) debridement should be attempted. If impingement syndrome is confirmed on the basis of clinical symptoms and a positive response to lidocaine injection, the clinician's only question may be whether there is a full tear.

The experience of a particular radiologist is an equally important factor. Shoulder US has been demonstrated to be highly reliable in the hands of a few experienced radiologists. The technique is difficult, requiring optimal equipment, highly motivated operators, and a long learning curve. The interpretation of shoulder MR images likewise has a learning curve. Shoulder arthrography and arthro-CT are less operator-dependent studies, though some technical skill is required. There appear to be fewer nuances in the interpretation of these latter tests than with MR or US, at least as far as detection of rotator cuff tear is concerned.

Finally, cost is a legitimate consideration. If an MR or arthro-CT examination informs the clinician's therapeutic decision no better than a less expensive test, it is unjustified to perform the expensive examination simply because it may be considered the gold standard.

In the remainder of this chapter specific modalities are reviewed for their merits and shortcomings in imaging rotator cuff disease and other soft tissue injuries of the shoulder.

PLAIN RADIOGRAPHY

Conventional radiography of the shoulder remains a very valuable study for the evaluation of suspected soft tissue abnormalities, especially impingement syndrome. High-quality plain films are an essential precursor to any other imaging examination of the shoulder. The inexpensive and universally available plain film examination may detect significant bone changes at the acromion, acromioclavicular joint, and humeral head that indicate the extent of underlying soft tissue abnormality and thus direct the course of treatment. In spite of the proliferation of sophisticated imaging procedures in the past few years, the value of plain radiographs of the shoulder remains high.

Standard radiographic views of the shoulder usually include anteroposterior (AP) projections with the humerus in external and internal rotation, a transscapular or Y view, and the axillary view. At some institutions a 35° posterior oblique view of the shoulder is preferred over the standard AP projection in order to view the glenohumeral joint tangentially. In assessing for impingement, two additional views have been described: the AP projection with 30° caudal angulation and the supraspinatus outlet view. Cone and colleagues found that 30° caudad angulation was approximately parallel to the angle formed by the acromion and provided optimal visualization of anterior subacromial spurs in cadaver specimens.[9] Kilcoyne stresses the importance of this view and believes that it often allows visualization of spurs that are missed on routine AP radiographs owing to superimposition of the spur over the posterior aspect of the acromion (Fig. 10-2).[10]

A supraspinatus outlet view, also described by Neer,[11] consists of a transscapular lateral view with approximately 10° to 15° caudad angulation. This view is effective in demonstrating subacromial spurs and the shape of the acromion (Fig. 10-3). Kilcoyne believes this view is difficult to obtain and prefers the AP projection with 30° caudad angulation.[10] However, since the angulation of the acromion varies from approximately 13° to 34° and is also dependent on posture, setting a fixed angulation of 30° is not optimal for all patients. Newhouse therefore recommends that for an AP view with caudad angulation the patient be positioned fluoroscopically.[12] This is accomplished by having the patient lean forward, toward the image intensifier, and requires little extra time and exposure. Since a fluoroscopy machine is required this may be impractical in some practices. Before shoulder arthrography this view can be performed routinely, adding potentially valuable information for patients suspected of having rotator cuff tears.

Many plain radiographic findings have been described in association with the impingement syndrome—subacromial bone proliferation and spurs, degenerative changes in the greater tuberosity of the humerus, decreased acromiohumeral distance, and degenerative changes at the acromioclavicular joint, among others.

The presence of a subacromial spur is an important indicator of shoulder impingement. In a study of anatomic specimens, Cone and colleagues found that these spurs arise at the site of insertion of the coracoacromial ligament at the anterior acromion and nearly always project anteriorly and inferiorly from the cortical surface of the acromion.[9] Cone and colleagues found that spurs could be identified from routine radiographs in 26 percent of male patients (mean age 52) referred for evaluation of shoulder pain. Of the patients with spurs subsequently examined by arthrography, approximately half had rotator cuff tears.[9] Hardy and colleagues studied a group of patients more selectively chosen for symptoms of impingement syndrome and found subacromial spurs in 68 percent.[13] The average age of their patients, 56

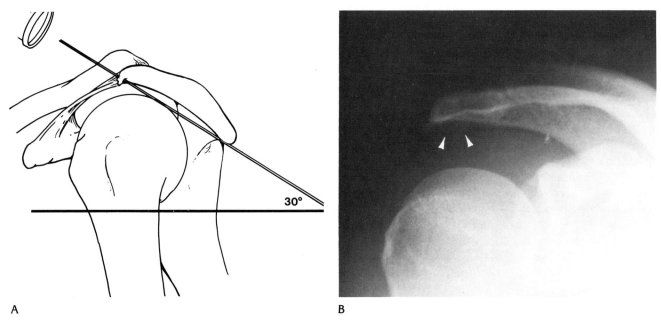

A

B

Figure 10-2 **A.** AP radiography of the shoulder with 30° caudad angulation is optimal for visualization of subacromial spurs, demonstrated in **B** (*arrowheads*).

years, emphasizes the prevalence of these changes in older patients with impingement. Both Cone and Hardy used standard AP radiographs; the incidence of spurs might have been even greater had they used the AP view with 30° caudad angulation.

Degenerative changes in the greater tuberosity of the humerus are frequently observed in association with impingement. These include bony proliferation, sclerosis, cystic changes, and flattening. Cone and coworkers reported such changes in one-third of their patients[9]; Hardy and associates found greater tuberosity changes in two-thirds of their selected group.[13] Flattening and sclerosis may be the most specific of the greater tuberosity changes. Cone and associates theorized that this appearance was due to direct bone-to-bone contact secondary to rotator cuff tear.[9]

The normal acromiohumeral distance varies with a patient's age and body size. The distance decreases with age and is approximately 8 to 9 mm in older persons[13]; a distance of less than 6 mm is considered abnormal.[13] Narrowing to this degree was reported in 21 percent of patients in the series by Hardy and colleagues.[13] As the gap narrows, the likelihood of full rotator cuff tear increases. We find that a distance less than 5 mm usually indicates a full tear. With chronic tears the deltoid muscle pulls the humeral head superiorly, obliterating the acromiohumeral space and eventually producing a concave pressure erosion on the undersurface of the acromion. While this finding is a very late one, it is important, since a large, long-standing tear is virtually ensured and additional imaging tests are of little value.

The finding of degenerative changes in the acromio-

clavicular joint deserves special consideration. Hardy and coworkers found that 66 percent of their patients showed such changes,[13] and 32 percent more specifically demonstrated inferiorly oriented acromioclavicular osteophytes. Inferiorly directed spurs are believed to be an important factor in some cases of impingement, causing pressure on the supraspinatus tendon at the musculotendinous junction (Fig. 10-4).[14] Degenerative changes of the acromioclavicular joint without inferiorly projecting spurs may have little effect on the rotator cuff. Acromioclavicular spurs may have important therapeutic consequences. Surgical therapy by anterior acromioplasty

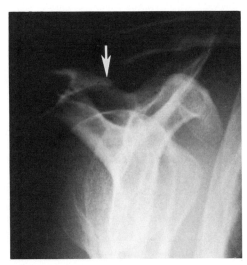

Figure 10-3 Supraspinatus outlet view demonstrates an anterior acromial spur (*arrow*).

alone may be ineffective if the primary cause of impingement is acromioclavicular spurs.

Additional plain radiographic findings reported in patients with impingement syndrome include small calcifications near the insertion of the supraspinatus tendon on the greater tuberosity[13] and obliteration of the subacromial-subdeltoid fat plane.[15] The latter finding, a nonspecific one, is seen with numerous inflammatory conditions and in some normal shoulders. The calcifications associated with impingement can be distinguished from those of calcific peritendinitis by their tiny size and their proximity to the greater tuberosity.[13]

Variation in shape of the acromion process has been described by Morrison and Bigliani.[6,7] Type 1 acromions have a flat undersurface; Type 2 are concave; and Type 3 have an anterior inferior hook. Type 3 acromions have a definite association with impingement syndrome and the development of rotator cuff tears. The supraspinatus view is the only plain radiographic view capable of accurately demonstrating the acromion's shape.

ARTHROGRAPHY

Although little attention has been paid to standard arthrography with the emergence of arthro-CT, US, and MRI, shoulder arthrography remains an accurate, safe, and cost-effective test for evaluating the rotator cuff. The accuracy of arthrography for the detection of full-thickness rotator cuff tears is well-established.[16] With proper

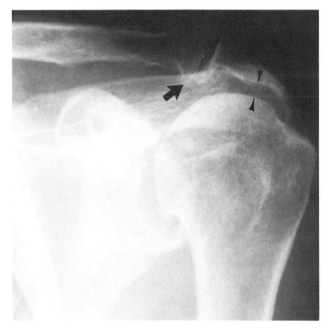

Figure 10-4 Bony degenerative changes indicative of advanced impingement syndrome seen on the AP projection. Inferiorly projecting acromioclavicular osteophytes (*arrows*), significant narrowing of the acromiohumeral distance (*arrowheads*), and sclerosis of the greater tuberosity are noted.

technique, we believe an overall accuracy rate greater than 90 percent can be expected. In a small study comparing arthrography, US, and MRI, for detecting complete tears, Burk and coworkers found conventional arthrography to be as accurate as MRI and more accurate than US.[17] Arthrography is also relatively accurate for detecting partial rotator cuff tears, though only tears on the glenohumeral side of the cuff can be detected without performing bursography. Arthrography is the least ambiguous study available for assessing the rotator cuff: contrast medium either passes out of the joint into the subacromial-subdeltoid space through a tear or it does not. There is little intra- or interobserver variation in readings as compared with MRI or US.

The technique of arthrography was reviewed in Chapter 1. To maximize accuracy a few points should be emphasized. First, the importance of exercising the shoulder following the injection cannot be overstated. We suspect that the lack of sufficient exercise is the reason for most false negative readings of arthrograms. If the postexercise views are negative in a patient though suspicion of a tear is high, we frequently repeat the exercise and filming. Finally, the addition of fluoroscopically positioned spot radiographs may be very helpful in assessing the size of a full-thickness tear or in confirming a partial tear.

The safety and patient acceptance of arthrography must be considered. Since arthrography is invasive, there is a small but measurable risk of associated morbidity. Severe complications of arthrography are rare. According to a survey reported by Newberg, no deaths occurred in more than 126,000 procedures.[18] The incidence of infection was one in 40,000 studies and of hives one in 2000.[18] Transient exacerbation of the patient's pain is common. This pain appears to be worse when ionic contrast medium is used, especially a compound containing a sodium salt.[19] Hall reported a 60 percent prevalence of moderate to severe pain with ionic contrast, as compared to 14 percent with nonionic compounds. Single-contrast studies showed a higher incidence of pain than double-contrast studies. Delayed pain is also much more likely if there is extraarticular extravasation of contrast during the procedure.[19]

Significant vasovagal reactions are uncommon with shoulder arthrography. We believe this complication can be reduced by allowing the patient to remain supine for several minutes following removal of the needle. We use this time to observe the joint under fluoroscopy while passively exercising the shoulder. If a tear is seen, further exercise is unnecessary; further spread of contrast may actually complicate the evaluation of the margins of the tear.

Findings in shoulder arthrography include detection of a full or partial tear and quantification of its size. A complete tear is demonstrated by extravasation of con-

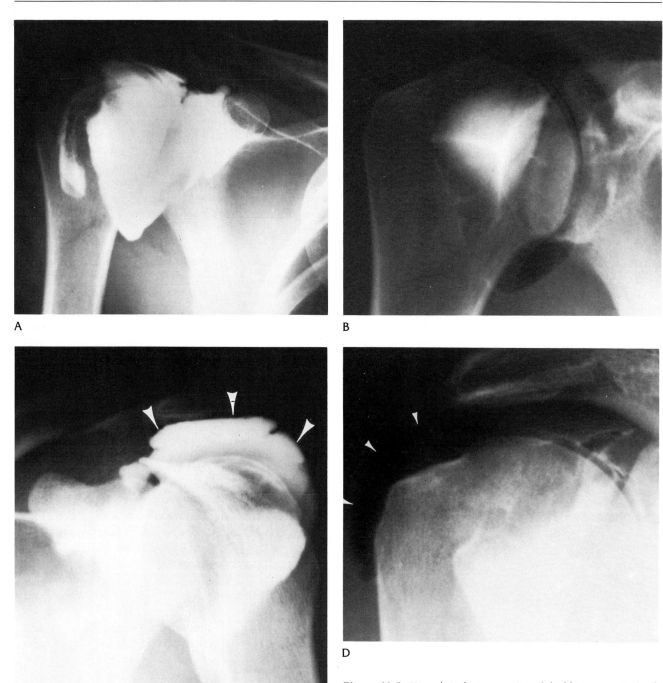

A

B

C

D

Figure 10-5 Normal single-contrast, **A,** and double-contrast, **B,** shoulder arthrograms. **C.** A tear is demonstrated by a single-contrast examination showing a large amount of contrast in the subacromial-subdeltoid space (*arrowheads*). **D.** The tear is indicated by gas in the subacromial-subdeltoid space (*arrowheads*).

trast or air through the defect into the subacromial-subdeltoid bursa (Fig. 10-5). Few errors in interpretation are possible if the patient has not previously undergone surgery. Occasionally an inexperienced arthrographer mistakes gas above in the intraarticular portion of the biceps tendon for gas in the subacromial-subdeltoid bursa and makes the false positive diagnosis of complete cuff tear. Calcifications in the cuff can also be mistaken for

contrast if the preinjection film is not compared with the postinjection image. Partial extraarticular contrast injection due to faulty needle placement usually does not compromise the study. Rarely, contrast may be inadvertently injected directly into the subacromial-subdeltoid bursa; then repeat injection at a later time is then necessary.

Detecting partial rotator cuff tears by arthrography is

slightly more difficult. If extension of contrast into but not through the cuff is suspected (on the basis of faint focal or linear increased density), it is helpful to perform fluoroscopically directed spot films in multiple positions to confirm the tear. One author sometimes obtains eight or more spot films in varying degrees of rotation, in an attempt to clearly show a linear partial tear. When caught in tangent it may be possible to estimate the depth of a partial tear. Some surgeons may elect to operate on deep partial tears and to treat superficial ones conservatively.

Shoulder arthrography is also useful for the detection of intraarticular loose bodies and in the assessment of adhesive capsulitis. Conventional arthrography is not useful for assessing tendinitis, glenohumeral instability, or partial tears on the bursal side of the cuff.

If the critical question to be answered is whether or not a full tear is present, then standard arthrography remains an excellent choice, particularly true for middle-aged or older patients who have classic signs of impingement. Confirming the presence of a full tear and estimating its size may be the only determinants of therapy in these cases.

ARTHRO-CT

Since the combination of CT and double-contrast arthrography of the shoulder was first suggested in 1981, many studies have reported the use of arthro-CT, especially for the evaluation of labral tears and abnormalities of the capsular mechanism of the shoulder.[20-30] A few reports have compared arthro-CT with MRI to determine their relative accuracy.[31,32] When evaluating for rotator cuff tears only, it is unlikely that arthro-CT has any advantage over conventional arthrography.

Arthro-CT has largely replaced conventional arthrotomography. Although arthrotomography is an effective means of evaluating the glenoid labrum following arthrography, it has several disadvantages as compared with CT. Polytomography requires specially trained technologists, dedicated equipment, and considerable space. It is time-consuming, uncomfortable for most patients, and exposes the patient to increased ionizing radiation. CT images are easier to interpret, provide better visualization of soft tissues, and offer the additional option of multiplanar reconstructions.

The technique of arthro-CT was described in Chapter 1; only a few points are reviewed here. We believe the arthrographic technique should not differ significantly from conventional arthrography, other than the addition of epinephrine (0.3 ml of 1:1000) to retard resorption of contrast medium. We use 1.5 to 2.0 ml of contrast with 10 to 12 ml of room air. The patient exercises the shoulder to a limited degree, and postexercise upright spot films are obtained before CT. Some authors who believe exercise may cause extravasation and decrease the ac-

curacy of labral evaluation perform arthro-CT without exercise.

The usefulness of arthro-CT shoulder examinations is principally in the evaluation of suspected glenohumeral instability, which was addressed in the preceding chapter. The tomographic format of CT, the addition of contrast, and the distension of the glenohumeral joint make arthro-CT one of the modalities best-suited for the evaluation of labral and capsular abnormalities, detection of loose bodies and biceps tendon abnormalities, and evaluation of cartilage. Because of the axial plane of imaging, arthro-CT is not particularly useful in the assessment of subacromial or acromioclavicular joint spurs or for assessing the shape of the acromion. Some authors have described direct sagittal and coronal CT imaging techniques for the shoulder.[23,30] While perhaps valuable in selected situations, these are impractical for most radiologic practices.

Arthro-CT findings in full rotator cuff tears are characteristic: the extension of even a tiny amount of contrast or air into the subacromial-subdeltoid bursa can be detected with much sensitivity (Fig. 10-6). The detection of partial tears can be more difficult. A partial tear should be suspected if contrast medium or air extends into the substance of the rotator cuff. Since most tears arise in the supraspinatus tendon near the greater tuberosity, volume averaging can be a problem in detecting partial tears with arthro-CT. Small deposits of hydroxyapatite in the cuff may be mistaken for contrast if the preliminary radiograph has not been evaluated. Partial tears on the bursal side of the rotator cuff cannot be detected by arthro-CT.

Arthro-CT is well-established as an accurate means of evaluating the labrum, joint capsule, and glenohumeral

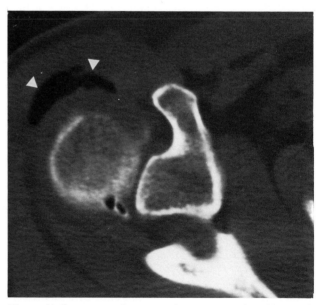

Figure 10-6 Rotator cuff tear on arthro-CT. Gas in the subacromial-subdeltoid space indicates a full-thickness tear (*arrowheads*).

ligaments (Fig. 10-7).[25,27,28,30,31] Wilson and coworkers reported a sensitivity of 100 percent and specificity of 97 percent for the detection of labral tears, using surgery as the gold standard.[28] Coumas believes that the detection of labral abnormalities by CT can be enhanced through dynamic evaluation.[33] This technique involves obtaining images with external shoulder rotation, to distract anterior labral tears, and with internal rotation, to distract posterior tears.

Arthro-CT is also useful for assessing the site of capsular insertion on the scapula. Abnormalities of articular cartilage are more readily seen on the glenoid than on the humeral head.[28] Bony abnormalities of the glenoid and humerus, both congenital and acquired, are usually seen well by arthro-CT (Fig. 10-8).

Abnormalities of the long tendon of the biceps brachii muscle are fairly common and may have a confusing clinical presentation. Medial dislocation of the tendon or frank rupture can be detected effectively by arthro-CT (Fig. 10-9) or MRI. These lesions are discussed in the following section.

Injuries to the superior margin of the glenoid labrum at the origin of the long head of the biceps brachii recently have received considerable attention in the orthopedic and radiologic literature. Tears in the superior labrum occur as a result of a fall on the outstretched hand or from stress on the biceps as in pitching or in catching a heavy object. These tears characteristically extend both anteriorly and posteriorly from the superior labrum and are termed SLAP lesions (superior labrum anterior, posterior). Four types of SLAP lesion have been described, based on arthroscopic findings.[34] Type I lesions consist of degenerative fraying at the junction of the biceps tendon and labrum. Type II lesions consist of a tear between the superior labrum at the biceps attachment and the adjacent glenoid labrum (Fig. 10-10). Type

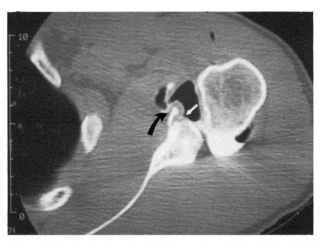

Figure 10-8 Bankart's lesion. Axial image through the inferior third of the glenohumeral joint on this arthro-CT image demonstrates a Bankart's fracture (*curved black arrow*) as well as contrast extending into a cartilage defect at the fracture site (*small white arrow*).

III is a bucket-handle tear of the central portion of the superior glenoid with the biceps insertion on the glenoid intact. In the Type IV lesion the tear extends into the proximal portion of the biceps tendon.

Preliminary reports suggest that both arthro-CT and MRI are accurate for detecting SLAP lesions.[29,33,35–38] Some authors report Type I lesions to be the most difficult to detect,[36] although Hunter and coworkers retrospectively found arthro-CT abnormalities in six patients with Type I lesions.[29] Type II lesions are diagnosed by a defect in the superior labrum that clearly extends anteriorly and posteriorly. This appearance can be confused with a recently described normal variant in which the

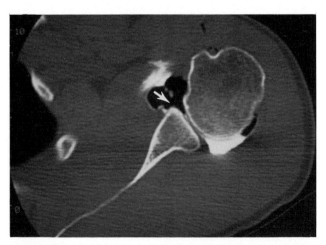

Figure 10-7 Axial image through the midportion of the glenohumeral joint on arthro-CT shows complete absence of the anterior labrum consistent with a large displaced tear (*arrow*).

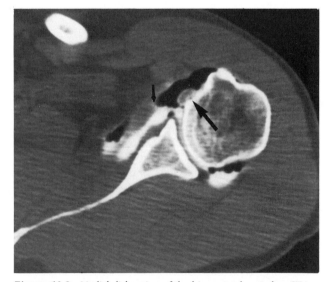

Figure 10-9 Medial dislocation of the biceps tendon. Arthro-CT image through the midportion of the glenohumeral joint demonstrates medial dislocation of the biceps tendon (*large arrow*). Note also the torn, retracted margins of the subscapularis tendon (*small arrow*).

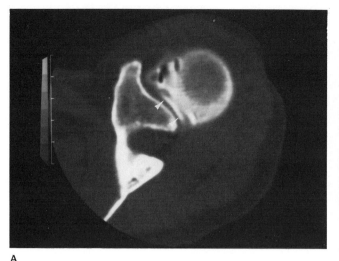
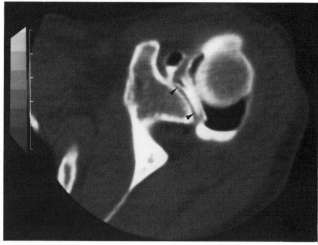

A   B

Figure 10-10 **A, B.** Type II SLAP lesion. Images through the superior aspect of the glenohumeral joint performed with the humerus in internal rotation, **A,** and external rotation, **B,** show a Type II SLAP lesion extending anteriorly and posteriorly (*arrowheads*). (Courtesy of James M. Coumas, M.D.)

anterior and posterior attachments of the biceps tendon form a hooded configuration, under which air, contrast medium, or joint fluid may accumulate and mimic a tear.[33] The lack of significant anterior-posterior extension may help differentiate this from a true tear. Better delineation of the tear by means of external rotation has been recommended by Coumas.[33]

SHOULDER ULTRASONOGRAPHY

The first reports on the use of US for the evaluation of the rotator cuff were made independently by three groups in 1985.[39–41] Since then, the technique has been the focus of considerable debate. The first reports of rotator cuff US were very encouraging; this generated a great deal of interest in the technique. Subsequent reports have shown varied results,[42–47] and interest has waned in private settings and in many academic settings. It is clear that shoulder US is one of the most technically demanding examinations. Those that have mastered the technique report excellent accuracy for full tears, comparable to that of other invasive and more expensive tests.

The demanding technical requirements for rotator cuff US have been reviewed by Middleton,[48] who emphasizes that success depends on a number of factors. First, high-resolution transducers are extremely important. Middleton recommends a 7.5-MHz linear-array transducer. A 5-MHz linear-array transducer is adequate for large patients. The patients should be scanned with the shoulder hyperextended, which exposes the maximum amount of cuff from underneath the acromion. Dynamic, real-time scanning is important, especially for the detection of subtle defects. Authors stress that assessment should be made from the image on the monitor during real-time scanning, not from hard copy. Examinations should always include both shoulders, so that a comparison can be made of overall cuff thickness and echogenicity. Comparison to plain radiographs of the shoulder avoids confusing focal calcifications with other lesions.

Several US criteria for rotator cuff tears have been described.[43,44,46] The most specific finding is nonvisualization of the cuff (Fig. 10-11). This finding represents a large tear in which the proximal end has retracted beneath the acromion. The deltoid muscle then lies directly on the humeral head. Though this is 100 percent specific, it is a late finding. When present, typically there is radiographically evident narrowing of the acromiohumeral space, and the US only serves to confirm the suspected long-standing tear.

Smaller full-thickness tears appear as a segmental loss or focal thinning of the cuff, or as a focal hypoechoic zone that extends through the entire cuff (Fig. 10-12). Focal thinning due to a tear can be distinguished from degenerative thinning by abrupt margins in the former, as compared to a more gradual change in the latter.[48]

For partial tears, Wiener and Seitz consider the following US criteria to be diagnostic: a focal hypoechoic zone within the substance of the cuff, small hypoechoic discontinuities of the internal or external surface of the cuff, or a dominant asymmetric linear echogenic focus within the cuff, with or without associated decreased thickness.[46]

Using these criteria Wiener and Seitz correctly reported the diagnosis in 206 of 225 (92 percent) patients,

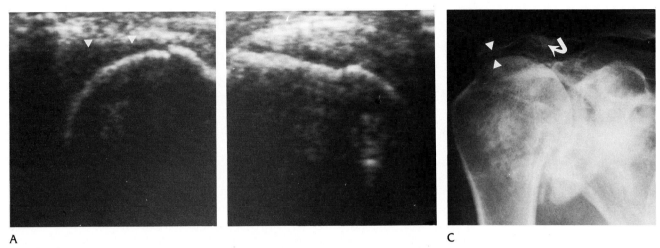

A

C

Figure 10-11   Shoulder US. A massive rotator cuff tear is demonstrated by absence of cuff, **A,** (*arrow-heads*) compared to the normal opposite shoulder, **B. C.** The arthrogram shows a decreased acromio-humeral distance (*arrowheads*), a large acromioclavicular spur (*curved arrow*), and a large tear. (Courtesy of Andrew J. Collins, M.D.)

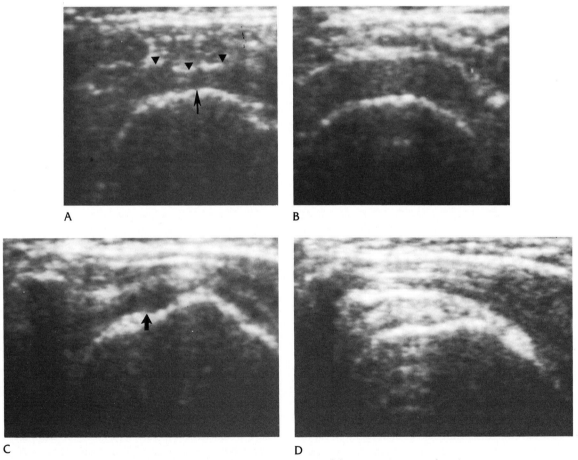

A

B

C

D

Figure 10-12   Shoulder US. Right rotator cuff tear. Transverse image of the supraspinatus tendon, **A,** demonstrates focal thinning of the cuff (*arrowheads*) associated with a focal hypoechoic area within the cuff (*arrow*). **B.** Normal left shoulder transverse image for comparison. **C.** Longitudinal image through right supraspinatus tendon confirms focal hypoechoic area, consistent with a tear (*arrow*). **D.** Longitudinal view of the normal left shoulder for comparison. (Courtesy of Andrew J. Collins, M.D.)

including 64 of 69 with partial-thickness tears.[46] Furthermore, these authors found that with US they could accurately stage full tears into small (<1 cm), large (1 to 3 cm), or massive ones (>3 cm). It is therefore apparent that in expert hands shoulder US is accurate not only for full-thickness tears but for partial tears as well.

US is limited in its usefulness to the exposed portion of the rotator cuff, subacromial-subdeltoid bursa, and the biceps tendon.[49–51] US has not been used to evaluate the labrum or glenohumeral ligaments, nor is it useful for assessing bone changes associated with impingement syndrome. A tear of the more proximal portion of the cuff may be obscured from US evaluation by the acromion process. Practically, this may be of little concern, since the vast majority of cuff tears are near the insertion on the humerus and thus easily visible by US.

What is the role of shoulder US in the management of patients with suspected soft tissue injury? If the question is whether or not a full tear is present, US should be considered as long as the operator is technically proficient. In a middle-aged or older patient with symptoms of impingement or with a positive plain-film examination, US could replace either arthrography or MR in confirming the presence of a tear and grading its size, thus influencing the surgical approach. US is not indicated in patients with glenohumeral instability and is of little use in the early evaluation of impingement syndrome, when full tears are unlikely.

MAGNETIC RESONANCE IMAGING

The use of MRI for evaluation of suspected soft tissue injuries of the shoulder has increased dramatically in the past several years. In many centers shoulder MRI has become the principal imaging modality for the evaluation of both suspected rotator cuff injury and glenohumeral instability. MRI of the shoulder has several advantages over other modalities. It is noninvasive, uses no ionizing radiation, and allows direct visualization of soft tissue and bone structures in a multiplanar tomographic format. MRI can provide a high-resolution survey of the entire shoulder joint and surrounding structures. MRI is not without drawbacks, however. MRI is an order of magnitude more costly than US, plain films, or arthrography. The quality of shoulder MR images is very dependent on technical factors. Specialized surface coils are necessary, and patient cooperation is needed, as it is necessary to remain motionless during the study.

The role that MRI ultimately will assume in the evaluation of the shoulder is evolving. As improvements accrue in spatial resolution and acquisition time, the accuracy and attraction of MRI will likely increase. A better understanding of anatomic variants, artifacts, and

the nature of rotator cuff degeneration should also increase the accuracy and clinical impact of interpretations. Ultimately MRI must compete not only with other imaging modalities but also with arthroscopy, which affords both diagnostic examination and operative treatment.

A number of technical factors are critical for successful MRI of the shoulder. The use of surface coils is mandatory. We recommend using a dedicated shoulder coil; there are many commercially available configurations that function adequately.

The choice of sequence parameters and imaging planes is important to accurate MR imaging. Most experts agree that conventional spin-echo T2-weighted images are the most reliable for detecting cuff tears. The value of fast spin-echo, multi-planar gradient echo (MPGR), and fat-suppression techniques are currently under investigation.

For the evaluation of rotator cuff tears, the paracoronal plane (parallel to the supraspinatus muscle and tendon) is most valuable. The parasagittal plane is helpful for assessing the size of a tear as well as the shape of the acromion and the supraspinatus outlet. There is less agreement about the optimal sequence for the evaluation of the glenoid labrum. Most investigators have utilized spin-echo proton weighted (PW) and T2-weighted images[52–54]; others have opted for gradient-echo (GRE) sequences.[54,55] The slice should be approximately 3 to 4 mm thick, especially for paracoronal views. A field of view (FOV) of 150 mm or less is recommended. The use of intraarticular contrast material is addressed below.

Patient positioning is important for accurate shoulder MRI. The humerus should be positioned in external rotation but the patient must be comfortable enough to remain motionless. Internal rotation can result in overlap of the supraspinatus and infraspinatus tendons in the paracoronal images, mimicking a tear.[56] The angle chosen for the paracoronal sequence should be parallel to the distal supraspinatus tendon, not to the body of the scapula. The orientation of parasagittal images should be parallel to the articular surface of the glenoid.

The MR appearance of the normal or asymptomatic rotator cuff has been a subject of controversy. Original reports stated that the rotator cuff should be visualized as low signal intensity on all sequences. Early reports judged areas of increased signal intensity on T1- and PW images to indicate tendinitis, tendinopathy, or partial tears. A number of subsequent articles have clearly shown that focal or diffuse areas of increased signal intensity are present on T1- and PW images of most asymptomatic shoulders (Fig. 10-13).[57–59] These areas do not show increasing signal intensity on T2-weighted images, and on this basis they are differentiated from tears. Therefore, most authors agree that spin-echo T2-weighted images are most valuable for diagnosing rotator cuff tears.

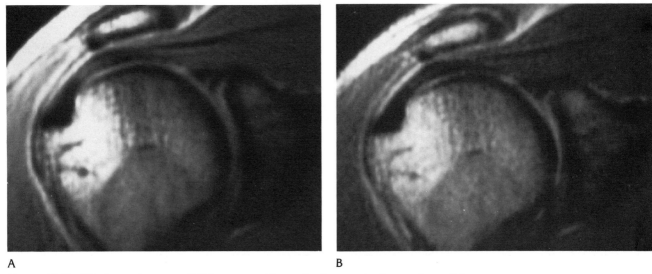

A   B

Figure 10-13 MR of normal rotator cuff. PW paracoronal image, **A,** of a normal volunteer shows slight linear increased signal in the cuff that does not increase in intensity on T2-weighted image, **B.** The signal intensity of the cuff is homogeneously low in the critical zone near the insertion on the greater tuberosity.

Several explanations have been offered for these areas of increased signal seen on T1- and PW images. In an histopathologic study of cadavers, Kjellin and coworkers[60] found that areas of increased signal corresponded to eosinophilic, fibrillar, and mucoid tendon degeneration and scarring. These findings typically occurred in the "critical zone" of the supraspinatus tendon. The investigators noted an absence of active inflammation in these areas and suggested that the term *tendinosis* or *tendinopathy* would be more appropriate than *tendinitis* for this finding. Since these changes occur in asymptomatic persons, perhaps neither term is correct. Other explanations offered for the finding of increased signal on T1- and PW images include the *magic angle effect*, internal rotation causing tendon overlap, connective tissue between tendon slips, and volume averaging of the long head of the biceps brachii tendon.[16]

Conventional MRI is accurate for the detection of full-thickness rotator cuff tears. Results have varied, but most recent studies and our own experience suggest that sensitivity and specificity of 90 percent or more can be achieved. With the addition of intraarticular contrast material, nearly 100 percent accuracy for detection of rotator cuff tear may not be unreasonable.

Several authors have proposed criteria for MR evaluation of rotator cuff tears.[61,62] In 1989, Zlatkin and associates proposed a scoring system for the evaluation of the rotator cuff, using a 7-point scale.[61] The system scored 3 points for the appearance of the supraspinatus tendon (discontinuous, signal changes, and morphology), and 1 point each for the absence of the subacromial and subdeltoid fat planes and for the presence of subacromial or subdeltoid fluid. A score of 0 to 2 was normal, 3 to 4

indicated a partial tear, and 5 or more a full tear. Applying this scale, the authors achieved 91 percent sensitivity and 100 percent specificity for complete and partial tears. It has since been reported that failure to identify the subacromial or subdeltoid fat planes may occur in normal volunteers.[59] Still, this system remains a valuable reference.

T2-weighted images are crucial for the evaluation of the rotator cuff. High intensity within the substance of the cuff is clearly abnormal. Full-thickness tears are diagnosed if the signal completely crosses the cuff (Figs. 10-14 through 10-16). If the abnormal signal extends to one surface only, the tear is partial. An accurate descrip-

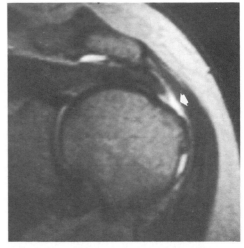

Figure 10-14 Small, full-thickness rotator cuff tear. T2-weighted paracoronal image shows high-intensity signal extending across the distal aspect of the supraspinatus tendon at the insertion on the greater tuberosity (*arrow*).

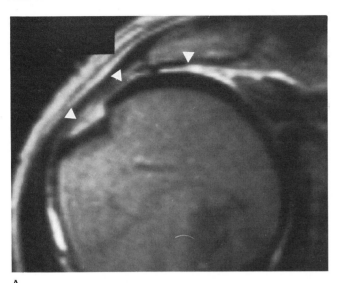

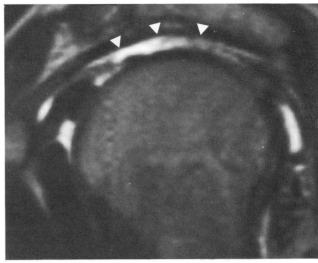

A   B

Figure 10-15 Large, chronic rotator cuff tear. T2-weighted paracoronal, **A,** and parasagittal, **B,** images show virtual absence of the rotator cuff (*arrowheads*) and marked narrowing of the acromiohumeral distance.

tion and measurement of the rotator cuff tear is also possible with MR imaging (Fig. 10-17).

In the evaluation of other aspects of the impingement syndrome, MR imaging may be useful for assessing acromion shape, subacromial spurs, degenerative changes in the acromioclavicular joint, and bursal fluid. As mentioned above, assessment of the cuff for tendinitis probably has little clinical value. It has also been noted that the normal deltoid insertion on the acromion tip may be mistaken for a pathologic subacromial spur,[57] so caution is advised. MRI also can accurately detect Hill-Sachs deformities of the humeral head.[63]

MR imaging is helpful in the evaluation of other soft tissue injuries, including labral tears (Fig. 10-18) and abnormalities of the biceps tendon. The reported accuracy of MRI is more variable in the evaluation of the glenoid labrum than for cuff tears. Legan and colleagues reported an accuracy of 92 percent for anterior labrum tears.[35] Garneau and coworkers reported rather poor results and noted "substantial intra- and interobserver

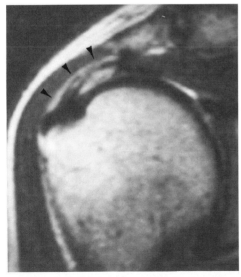

Figure 10-16 Full-thickness rotator cuff tear. T2-weighted paracoronal image demonstrates increased signal involving the critical zone of the supraspinatus tendon. Fluid is present in the subacromial-subdeltoid space (*arrowheads*). Although there appeared to be a few intact fibers, a moderate-sized full-thickness tear was confirmed surgically.

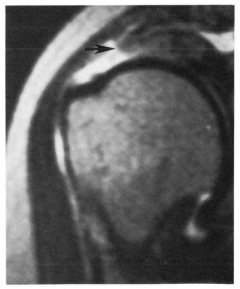

Figure 10-17 T2-weighted paracoronal image demonstrates a full-thickness rotator cuff tear with moderate retraction of the proximal tendon (*arrow*). The amount of retraction can be accurately measured by MR imaging in most cases.

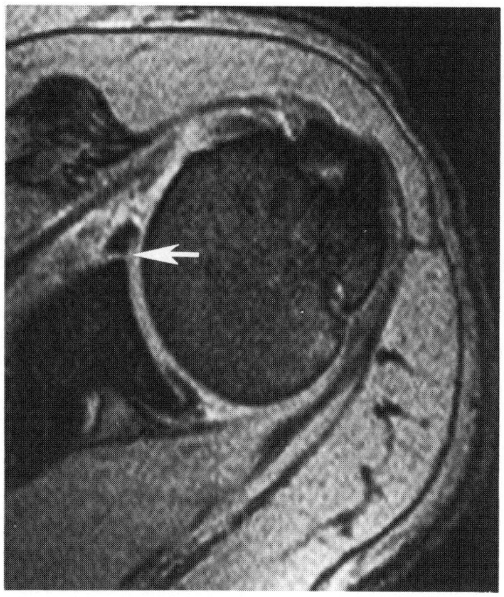

Figure 10-18 Axial GRE image through the glenohumeral joint shows a nondisplaced anterior labral tear (*arrow*).

variability."[53] The reason for this discrepancy is unclear, since both studies used similar PW and T2-weighted sequences and similar criteria for labrum tears.

The MR findings in SLAP lesions of the glenoid labrum have been described.[35–38] Several authors have reported in retrospective reviews that MR abnormalities could be identified in most SLAP lesions. According to one report, Type 1 lesions, characterized by degenerative fraying, could not be detected.[36] Legan's group reported a sensitivity rate of 75 percent and overall accuracy of 95 percent for superior labrum tears in a carefully selected population.[35] They noted that the most common MRI findings in superior labrum tears were absence of the labrum and increased signal intensity across the entire labrum. They stressed that the latter criterion must be differentiated from normal undercutting of the labrum, in which increased signal extends into the labrum from below but not all the way to the superior surface.

Abnormalities of the long tendon of the biceps brachii muscle are common. Distension of the biceps tendon sheath is commonly associated with tears of the rotator cuff.[64] Loose bodies can be found in the tendon sheath. Calcifications in the biceps tendon or at its origin may be overlooked by MRI. Rupture of the biceps tendon can be identified by MRI, though this abnormality rarely occurs in isolation and is usually clinically apparent.[64]

Medial dislocation of the biceps tendon is a relatively common injury. This injury occurs in association with partial or complete tears of the subscapularis tendon or with injuries of the superior capsule and supraspinatus tendon.[65] Plain radiography is not helpful for evaluating this injury. Arthro-CT and MRI are most helpful for confirming these injuries. Cervilla and coworkers described two types of medial dislocation.[65] The most common

type was associated with a complete tear of the subscapularis tendon, with entrapment of the biceps tendon in the anterior aspect of the joint. The second type was an incomplete dislocation in which the tendon lay between partly disrupted fibers of the subscapularis tendon. Patten further described the MRI appearance of subscapularis tears, noting increased signal on T2-weighted images in the tendon, discontinuity, and retraction.[66] In his series, most subscapularis tears were associated with biceps tendon abnormalities.

MR ARTHROGRAPHY

To capitalize on the advantages of joint distension and intraarticular contrast, some radiologists have combined MRI with arthrography to evaluate the rotator cuff, capsule, and glenoid labrum.[67–69] A dilute solution of gadopentate dimeglumine or saline is injected into the glenohumeral joint under fluoroscopic guidance. The fluid outlines the inferior surface of the cuff and fills tears (Fig. 10-19). With full-thickness tears, contrast solution enters the subacromial-subdeltoid space (Fig. 10-20). Diagnostic difficulties may arise because fat and gadopentetate dimeglumine have similar signal intensities on T1-weighted images. The use of fat-suppression techniques has been proposed to selectively decrease the signal from fat while the signal from contrast solution remains unaffected.[69]

MR arthrography requires single-contrast techniques to avoid susceptibility artifact from intraarticular gas. Gadopentetate dimeglumine is injected in a concentration of 2 mmol. Two ml Magnevist (Berlex Laboratories)

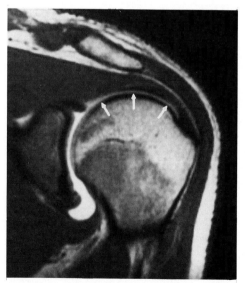

Figure 10-19 MR arthrography of a normal rotator cuff. Following intraarticular injection of gadopentate dimeglumine, T1-weighted paracoronal image shows high-signal contrast material outlining the inferior surface (*arrows*) of the distal supraspinatus tendon.

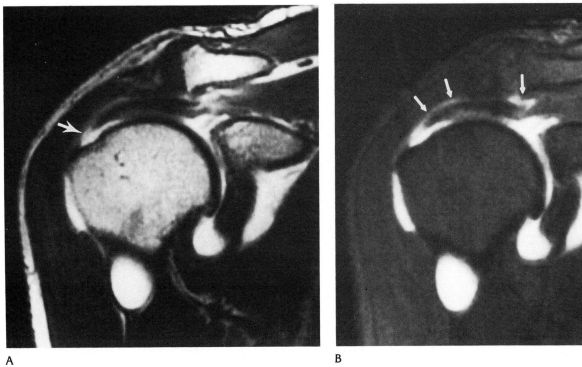

A   B

Figure 10-20 **A,B.** MR arthrography: complete rotator cuff tear. **A.** T1-weighted paracoronal image shows high-signal contrast solution (*arrow*) crossing the critical zone of the rotator cuff. The distal supraspinatus tendon is mildly retracted. **B.** T1-weighted fat-suppressed paracoronal image at the same level shows contrast solution extending into the subacromial-subdeltoid space (*arrows*).

is added to 250 ml normal saline. Ten milliliters of this solution is mixed with 5 ml 60% meglumine diatrizoate (Reno-M-60; Squibb), 5 ml lidocaine 1%, and 0.3 ml epinephrine 1:1000. A volume of 10 to 15 ml of contrast solution is injected into the glenohumeral joint under fluoroscopic guidance; then, radiographs are made before the shoulder is exercised and afterward. Since intraarticular injection of gadopentetate dimeglumine has not been approved by the Federal Drug Administration, this procedure must be sanctioned by the Institutional Review Board.

MRI of the shoulder is begun within 30 minutes of the intraarticular injection. T1-weighted sequences are performed in axial, paracoronal, and parasagittal planes. A second T1-weighted paracoronal sequence using fat-suppression (frequency-selective presaturation of fat) is also performed. T1-weighted sequences take advantage of the paramagnetic effect of gadopentetate dimeglumine on T1 relaxation and generate high signal-to-noise ratio, excellent spatial resolution, and contiguous slices in a relatively short examination time.

The optimal imaging protocol for MR arthrography depends on the nature of the contrast solution. If saline is used, T2-weighted (or GRE) images maximize the signal from the contrast solution. Fast spin-echo T2-weighted images can be obtained as rapidly as T1-weighted images, and they allow similar signal-to-noise

ratio and spatial resolution. T2-weighted images also have the advantage of showing partial tears on the bursal side of the cuff and edema due to tendinitis. Although fat-suppressed T2-weighted images help to distinguish subacromial-subdeltoid fat from fluid, they cannot be used to distinguish a fluid collection secondary to bursitis from saline that has leaked from the glenohumeral joint through a cuff tear. Thus, saline MR arthrography may not be able to distinguish partial and complete rotator cuff tears as accurately as can gadopentetate dimeglumine MR arthrography.

The criteria for detecting tears by MR arthrography are similar to standard arthrographic criteria. With complete tears, contrast fluid passes through a defect and extends into the subacromial-subdeltoid bursa. With partial tears, contrast extends into the cuff but not into the subacromial-subdeltoid bursa (Fig. 10-21). In MR arthrography, as with conventional arthrography, postinjection exercise of the joint is important. To identify small full-thickness tears, the subacromial-subdeltoid space must be carefully examined for the presence of contrast fluid.

MR arthrography aids in the evaluation of the glenoid labrum. Flannigan and colleagues reported greater accuracy for MR arthrography than for conventional MRI.[67] The conspicuousness of labral tears is increased because a detached labrum can be displaced from the glenoid rim by the glenohumeral ligaments and because nondis-

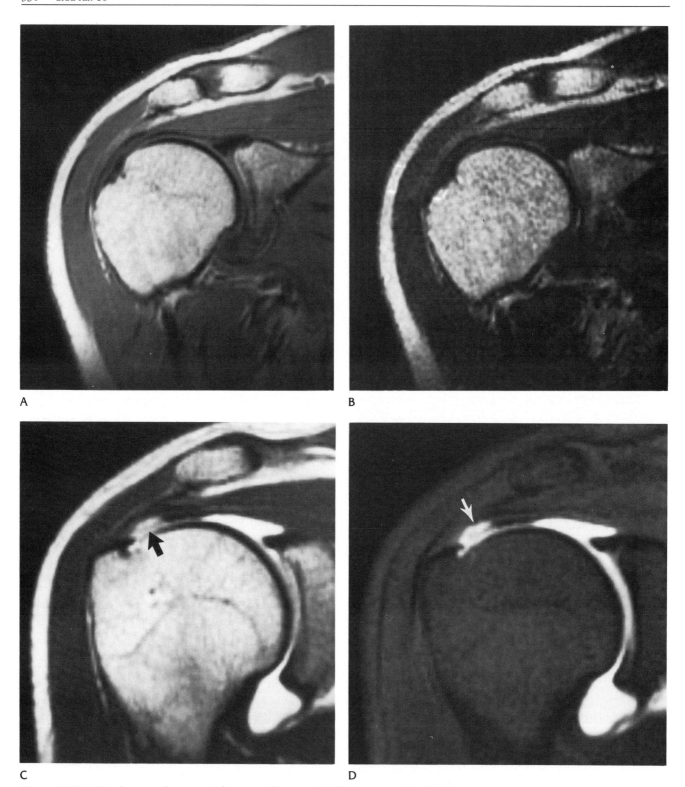

A

B

C

D

Figure 10-21 MR arthrogram shows a partial rotator cuff tear not identified on conventional MR images. **A,B.** PW and T2-weighted paracoronal conventional MR images show normal thickness of the tendon, with no abnormal signal at the critical zone. **C, D.** Following arthrography, T1-weighted and T1-weighted fat-suppressed images at the same level show disruption of the inferior fibers (*arrow*) of the cuff and contrast solution confined to the partial tear, without extension into the subacromial-subdeltoid space.

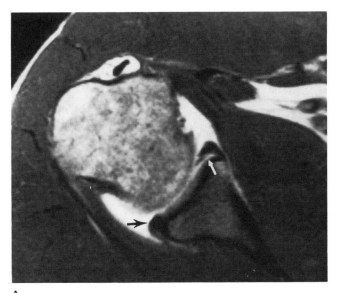

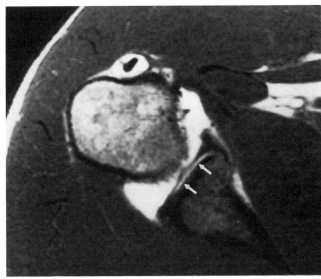

A   B

Figure 10-22 MR arthrography of Bankart's lesion. **A.** T1-weighted axial image shows a normal posterior labrum (*black arrow*) and underlying hyaline cartilage. Contrast solution (*white arrow*) extends beneath the anterior labrum, which remains partially attached to the glenoid rim. **B.** Farther caudad, the nondisplaced anteroinferior labral tear is filled by contrast solution (*arrows*).

placed tears collect contrast solution (Fig. 10-22). Pseudotears, common to conventional MRI, cause fewer diagnostic difficulties. Hyaline cartilage is lower in signal intensity than the gadopentetate dimeglumine solution and is uniform in thickness, whereas tears show irregular contours. The glenohumeral ligaments can be distinguished from labral fragments because they are separated from the labrum by the distended capsule and can be followed to their capsular insertion sites. The normal superior sublabral sulcus is localized to the bicipital

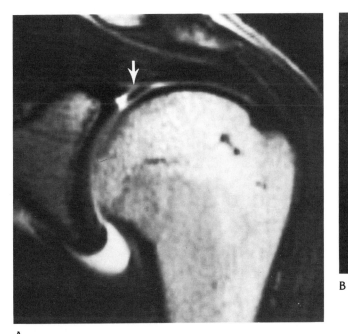

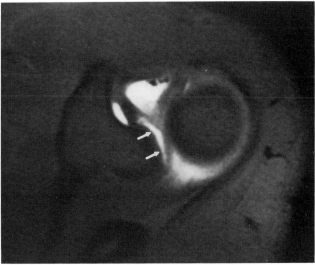

A   B

Figure 10-23 MR arthrography shows a superior labrum tear. **A.** T1-weighted paracoronal image posterior to the bicipital anchor shows contrast solution separating the detached superior labral fragment from the glenoid rim (*arrow*). **B.** T1-weighted fat-suppressed axial image at the level of the superior glenohumeral ligament and bicipital tendon shows contrast solution under the displaced superior labral fragment (*arrows*).

anchor, whereas tears of the superior labrum extend anterior and posterior to the bicipital tendon (Fig. 10-23) and often show labral displacement from the glenoid rim.

SUMMARY

As the sophistication of clinical diagnosis and treatment options for shoulder abnormalities have increased, so have the options for diagnostic imaging. When performed and interpreted optimally, all the techniques described in this chapter are useful. No single modality can be recommended for all clinical circumstances, so the choice should be "tailored" to the situation at hand.

Plain radiographs remain a cost-effective test for all cases of suspected shoulder pathology. Particular attention should be paid to subacromial spurs, acromioclavicular joint arthritis, humeral changes, and the shape of the acromion. Specific radiographic projections designed to evaluate these bony changes are helpful and should be added, routinely or as necessary. Significant narrowing of the acromiohumeral gap indicates that rotator cuff tear is likely. The plain radiograph may also demonstrate soft tissue calcifications; US and MRI examinations should not be interpreted without reference to plain radiographs.

Conventional arthrography is quite accurate for detecting full-thickness rotator cuff tears. If attention is given to technique, partial tears can also be identified with reasonable accuracy. If the clinical question is simply whether or not a full-thickness tear is present, arthrography is an excellent test because results are unambiguous.

Arthro-CT is accurate for the evaluation of labral ab-normalities. At many institutions it is the gold standard for the evaluation of capsular and labral abnormalities in patients with symptoms of glenohumeral instability. If the area of clinical concern is confined to the rotator cuff alone, arthro-CT offers no advantage over conventional arthrography.

Sonography is a difficult technique to apply successfully for rotator cuff evaluation, but it has been shown to be accurate in the hands of the few who master it. A long learning curve can be expected. For those who have adequate experience with it, US may replace arthrography or MRI when the question is whether or not a full-thickness tear is present. US is not useful for detecting bone changes or assessing the glenoid labrum.

Conventional MRI is an accurate but expensive non-invasive test for detecting full-thickness rotator cuff tears. The accuracy of MRI for partial tears and labrum abnormalities has not yet been adequately confirmed. It is uncertain whether or not the additional information or increased discrimination capability of MRI, plus its non-invasive nature, justify its cost. Future cost-benefit studies will be required to address this question.

MR arthrography combines the benefits of intraartic-ular contrast with superb soft tissue detail, at the cost of turning a noninvasive test into an invasive one. MR arthrography may prove to be the ultimate "all-in-one" test, affording precise diagnosis of full-thickness and partial rotator cuff tears as well as labrum and capsule abnormalities. Though such precise information may be indispensable in guiding therapy for some patients, such as professional or high-performance athletes, it is impractical to consider MR arthrography appropriate for investigation of all shoulder symptoms.

References

1. GRAY H: *Anatomy of the Human Body*, 29th ed, Chap 12, Philadelphia, Lea & Febiger, 1973, pp 371–526.
2. NEER CS: Impingement lesions. *Clin Orthop* 173:70–77, 1983.
3. MUDGE MK, WOOD VE, FRYKMAN GK: Rotator cuff tears associated with os acromiale. *J Bone Joint Surg* 66A:427, 1984.
4. MORIMOTO K, MORI E, NAKAGAWA Y: Calcifications of the coracoacromial ligament. A case report of shoulder impingement syndrome. *Am J Sports Med* 16:80, 1988.
5. UHTHOFF H, KIRITI S, MAYNARD J: Calcifying tendinitis: A new concept of its pathogenesis. *Clin Orthop* 18:164–168, 1976.
6. BIGLIANI LU, MORRISON DS: The morphology of the ac-

romion and its relationship to rotator cuff tears. *Orthop Trans* 10:228, 1986.

7. MORRISON DS, BIGLIANI LU: The clinical significance of variations in acromial morphology. *Orthop Trans* 11:234, 1987.

8. EPSTEIN RE, SCHWEITZER ME, FRIEMAN BG, FENLIN JM, MITCHELL DG: Hooked acromion: Prevalence of MR images of painful shoulders. *Radiology* 187:479–481, 1993.

9. CONE RO, RESNICK D, DANZIG L: Shoulder impingement syndrome: Radiographic evaluation. *Radiology* 150:29–33, 1984.

10. KILCOYNE RF, REDDY PK, LYONS F, ROCKWOOD CA: Optimal plain film imaging of the shoulder impingement syndrome. *AJR* 153:795–797, 1989.

11. NEER CS, POPPEN NK: Supraspinatus outlet. *Orthop Trans* 11:234, 1987.

12. NEWHOUSE KE, EL-KHOURY GY, NEPOLA JV, MONTGO-MERY WJ: The shoulder impingement view: A fluoroscopic technique for the detection of subacromial spurs. *AJR* 151:539–541, 1988.

13. HARDY DC, VOGLER JB, WHITE RH: The shoulder impingement syndrome: Prevalence of radiographic findings and correlation with response to therapy. *AJR* 147:557–561, 1986.

14. PETERSON CJ, GENTZ CF: The significance of distally pointing acromioclavicular osteophytes in ruptures of the supraspinatus tendon, in Bateman JE, Welsh RP (eds): *Surgery of the Shoulder*, Philadelphia, Decker, 1984, pp 129–133.

15. MITCHELL MJ, CAUSEY G, BERTHOTY DP, SARTORIS DJ, RESNICK D: Peribursal fat plane of the shoulder: Anatomic study and clinical experience. *Radiology* 168:699–704, 1988.

16. STILES RG, OTTE MT: Imaging of the shoulder. *Radiology* 188:603–613, 1993.

17. BURK DL, KARASICK D, KURTZ AB, MITCHELL DG, RIFKIN MD, MILLER CL, LEVY DW, FENLIN JM, BARTOLOZZI AR: Rotator cuff tears: Prospective comparison of MR imaging with arthrography, sonography, and surgery. *AJR* 153:87–92, 1989.

18. NEWBERG AH, MUNN CS, ROBBINS AH: Complications of arthrography. *Radiology* 155:605–606, 1985.

19. HALL FM, GOLDBERG RP, WYSHAK G, KILCOYNE RF: Shoulder arthrography: Comparison of morbidity after use of various contrast media. *Radiology* 154:339–341, 1985.

20. DANZIG L, RESNICK D, GREENWAY G: Evaluation of unstable shoulders by computed tomography. *Am J Sports Med* 10:138–141, 1982.

21. SHUMAN WP, KILCOYNE RF, MATSEN FA, ROGERS JV, MACK LA: Double-contrast computed tomography of the glenoid labrum. *AJR* 141:581–584, 1983.

22. RAFII M, FIROOZNIA H, GOLIMBU C, MINKOFF J, BONAMO J: CT arthrography of capsular structures of the shoulder. *AJR* 146:361–367, 1986.

23. BELTRAN J, GRAY LA, ROOLS JC, ZUELZER W, WEIS LD, UNVERFERTH LJ: Rotator cuff lesions of the shoulder: Evaluation by direct sagittal CT arthrography. *Radiology* 160:161–165, 1986.

24. RAFII M, FIROOZNIA H, BONAMO JJ, MINKOFF J, GOL-IMBU C: Athlete shoulder injuries: CT arthrographic findings. *Radiology* 162:559–564, 1987.

25. SINGSON RD, FELDMAN F, BIGLIANI L: CT arthrographic patterns in recurrent glenohumeral instability. *AJR* 149:749–753, 1987.

26. McNIESH LM, CALLAGHAN JJ: CT arthrography of the shoulder: Variations of the glenoid labrum. *AJR* 149:963–966, 1987.

27. PENNES DR, JONSSON K, BUCKWALTER K, BRAUNSTEIN E, BLASIER R, WOJTYS E: Computed arthrotomography of the shoulder: Comparison of examinations made with internal and external rotation of the humerus. *AJR* 153:1017–1019, 1989.

28. WILSON AJ, TOTTY WG, MURPHY WA, HARDY DC: Shoulder joint: Arthrographic CT and long-term follow-up, with surgical correlation. *Radiology* 173:329–333, 1989.

29. HUNTER JC, BLATZ DJ, ESCOBEDO EM: SLAP lesions of the glenoid labrum: CT arthrographic and arthroscopic correlation. *Radiology* 184:513–518, 1992.

30. BLUM A, BOYER B, REGENT D, SIMON JM, CLAUDON M, MOLE D: Direct coronal view of the shoulder with arthrographic CT. *Radiology* 188:677–681, 1993.

31. KIEFT GJ, BLOEM JL, ROZING PM, OBERMANN WR: MR imaging of recurrent anterior dislocation of the shoulder: Comparison with CT arthrography. *AJR* 150:1083–1087, 1988.

32. CHANDNANI VP, YEAGER TD, DEBERRARDINO T, CHIS-TENSEN K, GAGLIARDI TA, HEITZ DR, BAIRD DE, HANSEN MF: Glenoid labral tears: Prospective evaluation with MR imaging, MR arthrography, and CT arthrography. *AJR* 161:1229–1235, 1993.

33. COUMAS JM, HOWARD BA, GUILFORD WB: Instability: CT and MR imaging of the shoulder, in Weissman BN (ed): *Syllabus: A Categorical Course in Musculoskeletal Radiology. Advanced Imaging of Joints: Theory and Practice,* Oak Brook, IL, RSNA Publications, 1993, pp. 113–125.

34. SNYDER SJ, KARZEL RP, DEL PIZZO W, FERKEL RD, FRIED-MAN MJ: SLAP lesions of the shoulder. *Arthroscopy* 6:274–279, 1990.

35. LEGAN JM, BURKHARD TK, GOFF WB, BALSARA ZN, MAR-TINEZ AJ, BURKS DD, KALLMAN DA, O'BRIEN TJ, LAPOINT JM: Tears of the glenoid labrum: MR imaging of 88 arthroscopically confirmed cases. *Radiology* 179:241–246, 1991.

36. HODLER J, KURSUNOGLU-BRAHME S, FLANNIGAN B, SNYDER SJ, KARZEL RP, RESNICK D: Injuries of the superior portion of the glenoid labrum involving the insertion of the biceps tendon: MR imaging findings in nine cases. *AJR* 159:565–568, 1992.

37. CARTLAND JP, CRUES JV, STAUFFER A, NOTTAGE W, RYU RKN: MR imaging in the evaluation of SLAP injuries of the shoulder: Findings in ten patients. *AJR* 159:787–792, 1992.

38. SMITH AM, McCAULEY TR, JOKL P: SLAP lesions of the glenoid labrum diagnosed with MR imaging. *Skel Radiol* 22:507–510, 1993.

39. BRETZKE CA, CRASS JR, CRAIG EV: Ultrasonography of the ratator cuff: Normal and pathologic anatomy. *Invest Radiol* 20:311–315, 1985.

40. MIDDLETON WD, EDELSTEIN G, REINUS WR, ET AL.: Sonographic detection of rotator cuff tears. *AJR* 144:349–353, 1985.

41. MACK LA, MATSEN FA, KILCOYNE RF, DAVIES PK, SICKLER

ME: Ultrasound evaluation of the rotator cuff. *Radiology* 157:205–209, 1985.

42. CRASS JR, CRAIG EV, BRETZKE C, FEINBERG SB: Ultrasonography of the rotator cuff. *RadioGraphics* 5:941–953, 1985.

43. SOBLE MG, KAYE AD, GUAY RC: Rotator cuff tear: Clinical experience with sonographic detection. *Radiology* 173:319–321, 1989.

44. HODLER J, FRETZ CJ, TERRIE F, GERBER C: Rotator cuff tears: Correlation of sonographic and surgical findings. *Radiology* 169:791–794, 1988.

45. VICK CW, BELL SA: Rotator cuff tears: Diagnosis with sonography. *AJR* 154:121–123, 1990.

46. WIENER SN, SEITZ WH: Sonography of the shoulder in patients with tears of the rotator cuff: Accuracy and value for selecting surgical options. *AJR* 160:103–107, 1993.

47. BRANDT TD, CARDONE BW, GRANT TH, POST M, WEISS CA: Rotator cuff sonography: A reassessment. *Radiology* 173:323–327, 1989.

48. MIDDLETON WD: Status of rotator cuff sonography. *Radiology* 173:307–309, 1989.

49. FARIN PU, JAROMA H, HARJU A, SOIMAKALLIO: Shoulder impingement syndrome: Sonographic evaluation. *Radiology* 176:845–849, 1990.

50. VON HOLSBEECK M, STROUSE PJ: Sonography of the shoulder: Evaluation of the subacromial-subdeltoid space. *AJR* 160:561–564, 1993.

51. MIDDLETON WD, REINUS WR, TOTTY WG, MELSON GL, MURPHY WA: US of the biceps tendon apparatus. *Radiology* 157:211–215, 1985.

52. SEEGER LL, GOLD RH, BASSETT LW: Shoulder instability: Evaluation with MR imaging. *Radiology* 168:695–697, 1988.

53. GARNEAU RA, RENFREW DL, MOORE TE, ELKHOURY GY, NEPOLA JV, LEMKE JH: Glenoid labrum: Evaluation with MR imaging. *Radiology* 179:519–522, 1991.

54. NEUMAN CH, PETERSEN SA, JANKE AH: MR imaging of the labral-capsular complex: Normal variations. *AJR* 157:1015–1021, 1991.

55. McCAULEY TR, POPE CF, JOKL P: Normal and abnormal glenoid labrum: Assessment with multiplanar gradient-echo MR imaging. *Radiology* 183:35–37, 1992.

56. DAVIS SJ, TERESI LM, BRADLEY WG, RESSLER JA, ETO RT: Effect of arm rotation on MR imaging of the rotator cuff. *Radiology* 181:265–268, 1991.

57. KAPLAN PA, BRYANS KC, DAVICK JP, OTTE M, STINSON WW, DUSSAULT RG: MR imaging of the normal shoulder: Variants and pitfalls. *Radiology* 184:519–524, 1992.

58. NEUMANN CH, HOLT RG, STEINBACH LS, JAHNKE AH, PETERSEN SA: MR imaging of the shoulder: Appearance of the supraspinatus tendon in asymptomatic volunteers. *AJR* 158:1281–1287, 1992.

59. LIOU JTS, WILSON AJ, TOTTY WG, BROWN JJ: The normal shoulder: Common variations that simulate pathologic conditions at MR imaging. *Radiology* 186:435–441, 1993.

60. KJELLIN I, HO CP, CERVILLA V, HAGHIGHI P, KERR R, VANGNESS CT, FRIEDMAN RJ, TRUDELL D, RESNICK D: Alterations in the supraspinatus tendon at MR imaging: Correlation with histopathologic findings in cadavers. *Radiology* 181:837–841, 1991.

61. ZLATKIN MB, IANNOTTI JP, ROBERTS MC, ESTERHAI JL, DALINKA MK, KRESSEL HY, SCHWARTZ JS, LENKINSKI RE: Rotator cuff tears: Diagnostic performance of MR imaging. *Radiology* 172:223–229, 1989.

62. FARLEY TE, NEUMANN CH, STEINBACH LS, JAHNKE AJ, PETERSEN SS: Full-thickness tears of the rotator cuff of the shoulder: Diagnosis with MR imaging. *AJR* 158:347–351, 1992.

63. WORKMAN TL, BURKHAD TK, RESNICK D, GOFF WB, BALSARA ZN, DAVIS DJ, LAPOINT JM: Hill-Sachs lesions: Comparison of detection with MR imaging, radiography, and arthroscopy. *Radiology* 185:847–852, 1992.

64. ERICKSON SJ, FITZGERALD SW, QUINN SF, CARRERA GF, BLACK KP, LAWSON TL: Long bicipital tendon of the shoulder: Normal anatomy and pathologic findings on MR imaging. *AJR* 158:1091–1096, 1992.

65. CERVILLA V, SCHWEITZER ME, HO C, MOTTA A, KERR R, RESNICK D: Medial dislocation of the biceps brachii tendon: Appearance at MR imaging. *Radiology* 180:523–526, 1991.

66. PATTEN RM: Tears of the anterior portion of the rotator cuff (the subscapularis tendon): MR imaging findings. *AJR* 162:351–354, 1994.

67. FLANNIGAN B, KURSUNOGLU-BRAHME S, SNYDER S, KARZEL R, PIZZO WD, RESNICK D: MR arthrography of the shoulder: Comparison with conventional MR imaging. *AJR* 155:829–832, 1990.

68. HODLER J, KURSUNOGLU-BRAHME J, SNYDER SJ, CERVILLA V, KARZEL RP, SCHWEITZER ME, FLANNIGAN BD, RESNICK D: Rotator cuff disease: Assessment with MR arthrography versus standard MR imaging in 36 patients with arthroscopic confirmation. *Radiology* 182:431–436, 1992.

69. PALMER WE, BROWN JH, ROSENTHAL DI: Rotator cuff: Evaluation with fat-suppressed MR arthrography. *Radiology* 188:683–687, 1993.

11 POSTOPERATIVE IMAGING OF THE SHOULDER

Kyle C. Bryans
Leyla H. Alparslan
Barbara N. Weissman

Shoulder joint function depends on both stability and motion. The shoulder provides movement in three planes: flexion-extension, abduction-adduction, and internal and external rotation. Unlike the ball-and-socket hip joint, the shoulder lacks a deep bony socket to provide inherent stability. Even with its fibrocartilaginous labrum, the glenoid is too shallow to provide complete stability. In addition, the surface area of the humeral head is three times that of the glenoid, which is unlike the relationship at the hip articulation. As a result of this unstable bony configuration, the major stabilizer of the shoulder is the surrounding soft tissue.[1] Damage to the joint from instability or from fracture, rotator cuff tear or impingement, or arthritis may necessitate surgical intervention. In this chapter we review some of the surgical procedures and their imaging correlates so that postoperative complications may reliably be identified.

JOINT REPLACEMENT (ARTHROPLASTY)

Arthroplasty is defined as "plastic surgery of a joint or joints; the formation of movable joints."[2] Although removal of the articular end of a bone without replacing it (resection arthroplasty) was often performed in the early history of shoulder surgery (the 1930s and 1940s), it is rarely used today. The procedure affords pain relief, but only a minimally functional joint results.[1,3] Joint fusion, on the other hand, eliminates motion, and though pain may be resolved, it is also not a preferred method of treatment. Most often, replacement of the humeral side of the shoulder joint (hemiarthroplasty) or of both sides of the joint (total shoulder arthroplasty) is the preferred treatment for patients with pain from severe articular damage. At the Brigham and Women's Hospital, total shoulder replacement is performed considerably less often than total hip or total knee replacement; the ratio of total shoulder to total knee arthroplasty, for example, is approximately 1:7.

The principal indication for total shoulder arthroplasty is persistent and increasing pain, often as a consequence of rheumatoid arthritis or osteoarthritis. Hemiarthroplasty is most often utilized to treat sequelae of osteonecrosis or posttraumatic arthritis, whereas total shoulder replacement is performed more frequently when both sides of the joint are damaged, as in patients with rheumatoid arthritis. Total joint arthroplasty is performed more often than hemiarthroplasty. For example, in a series of 804 shoulder arthroplasties by Neer, 639 replacements were total joint arthroplasties and 165 hemiarthroplasties.[4] Satisfactory pain relief and functional improvement can be achieved in 82 to 93 percent of patients treated with either operative procedure.[5]

Major Types of Total Shoulder Prostheses

Nonconstrained prostheses resurface the joint. They have little built-in support and require an intact rotator cuff to maintain joint stability.[6] The Neer II prostheses are nonconstrained. The Neer humeral component has a radius of curvature similar to that of a normal humerus. The Neer glenoid component has a matching radius of curvature and a keel for anchoring the component into the scapular neck. The glenoid component is available with a high-density polyethylene articular surface, with or without metal backing. The metal-backed design is intended to decrease stresses at the bone-cement interface and to provide for porous coating for bone ingrowth fixation. As in the hip, metal backing is thought to decrease the incidence of loosening (Figs. 11-1, 11-2).

Semiconstrained prostheses provide more stability at the glenohumeral articulation, usually by incorporating a more constrained glenoid component. Nonconstrained prostheses can be made semiconstrained by substituting a glenoid component with a superior hood or lip for the conventional glenoid component.[7]

Constrained prostheses are used when the rotator cuff is deficient as a consequence of large rotator cuff tears

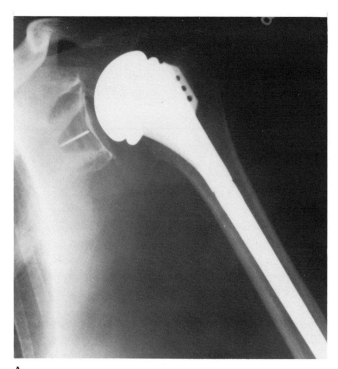

A

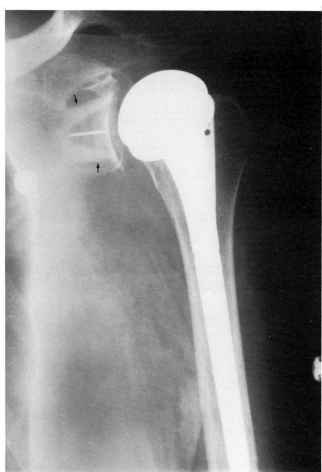

B

Figure 11-1 Uncomplicated total shoulder replacement. **A.** The external rotation view shows the components in profile. There is a non–metal-backed glenoid component and bone-ingrowth humeral component. **B.** The posterior oblique view shows the non–metal-backed glenoid component in profile. The glenoid cement-bone interface (*arrows*) is seen well.

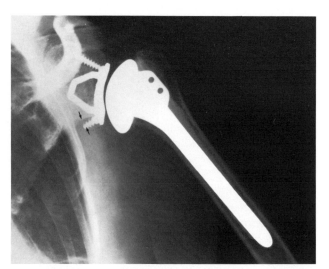

Figure 11-2 Normal left total shoulder prosthesis. There has been total shoulder replacement with a cemented humeral component and a bone-ingrowth glenoid component. One of the screws holding the glenoid component is noted to be in the inferior soft tissues rather than in bone (*arrows*).

or degeneration, excessive scarring from severe injury, previous multiple operations, or radiation therapy to the shoulder girdle.[8] A constrained prosthesis provides a fixed articulation via a linked ball-and-socket joint that allows rotation but prevents translation of the humeral component with relation to the glenoid one. The Michael Reese prosthesis is typical of such devices.[7]

The *bipolar shoulder prosthesis* is a variation of the nonconstrained total shoulder implant. It provides ball and socket interposed between humerus and glenoid. The prosthetic cup moves within the glenoid, and the ball of the humeral component articulates with a polyethylene bearing within the cup. The outer surface of the cup articulates with both the glenoid fossa and the coracoacromial arch, thus providing motion at two sites. (Fig. 11-3).[9]

Hemiarthroplasty usually involves replacement of the humeral side of the joint with a metal component.[6] In the absence of glenoid incongruity or synovitis, humeral hemiarthroplasty can provide pain relief similar to that

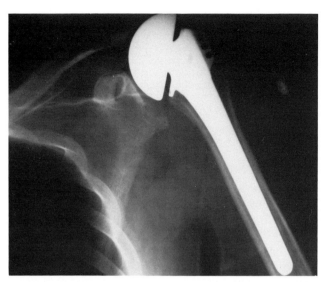

Figure 11-3 Bipolar prosthesis. The bipolar prosthesis articulates with the distal end of the clavicle and the superior aspect of the glenoid.

after total shoulder arthroplasty. It is used, for example, for humeral head fractures, osteoarthritis, and osteonecrosis.[5] In patients with large defects in the rotator cuff, a polyethylene spacer may also be inserted between the acromion process and the humeral component. The spacer is sutured to the coracoacromial ligament.[10]

IMAGING FOLLOWING JOINT REPLACEMENT

Radiographic Examination

An immediate postoperative radiographic examination is important not only to document the component's position and early complications, but to establish a baseline for evaluating the patient's subsequent course. Radiographs are usually obtained immediately after surgery and at 2 weeks, 1 to 2 months, and then annually. Additional radiographs can be made at other times as indicated.

Follow-up radiographs at the Brigham and Women's Hospital consist of an anteroposterior (AP) view of the shoulder with internal rotation of the humerus and a 40° posterior oblique radiograph with external rotation of the humerus. Scapular Y views and/or an axillary radiograph may be added if necessary (Fig. 11-4). As always, successful documentation of subtle radiographic changes demands good technique and careful positioning. The posterior oblique view is often the most informative. This position allows the prosthetic articular surfaces and the glenoid component to be seen in profile while external rotation of the arm allows the normally retroverted hu-

meral component to be viewed in profile. If the radiographic positioning is appropriate, normal appearances in this view virtually exclude dislocation. This projection also allows good visualization of the glenoid prosthesis–cement and cement–bone interfaces, which often cannot be seen well on ordinary AP radiographs because of the obliquity of the glenoid component.

NORMAL RADIOGRAPHIC APPEARANCES AFTER SHOULDER ARTHROPLASTY

Humeral Component

The inferior aspect of the humeral component is at the same level as the inferior edge of the glenoid component. The humeral component is placed so that the edge of the prosthesis is parallel to the cut surface of the neck and the mesh holes are seated in cancellous bone.[11]

In shoulder arthroplasty, the recommended retroversion of the humeral head is 20° to 40°.[12] Correct retroversion of the humeral component is important since it affects the external rotation of the joint and decreased external rotation may be a cause of postoperative pain. Humeral component retroversion explains the observation that radiographs taken with the humerus rotated externally often show the humeral component in profile. The retroversion of the humeral component can be directly measured on the Mukherjee-Sivaya view (Fig. 11-5).[50] Since this view usually is not available, Frich and Moller determined retroversion from the AP projection of the shoulder obtained with the forearm in 35° internal rotation. In this view, retroversion of the prosthetic humeral head can be determined by the formula $d = \cos^{-1}(tg\, p/tg\, a)$, where d is the true angle of retroversion, a the apparent retroversion angle on the internal rotation view, and p the angle between the head and stem of the prosthesis (50° for the Neer prosthesis). For simplification, the measurement may be compared to a table of calculated values. In addition, an estimate of the retroversion angle can be made by subtracting 40° from mea-

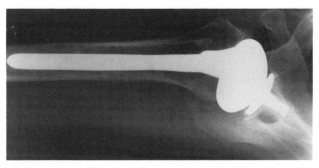

Figure 11-4 Axillary view of a normal total shoulder replacement. This is a total shoulder prosthesis with a metal-backed glenoid component. There is no evidence of subluxation. This is a normal position on an axillary view.

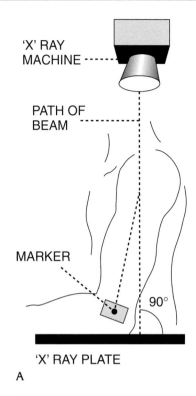

'X' RAY
MACHINE

PATH OF
BEAM

MARKER

90°

'X' RAY PLATE

A

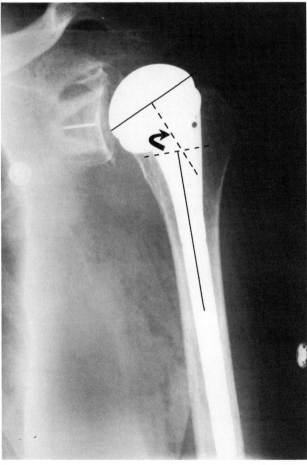

B

Figure 11-5 **A.** The Mukherjee-Sivaya view for determining retroversion. (Redrawn with permission from Saha AK: Dynamic stability of the glenohumeral joint. *Acta Orthop Scand* 42:491–505, 1971.) **B.** Determination of humeral retroversion measurement should be performed on a view with the forearm in 35° of internal rotation. Solid lines indicate the diameter of the humeral head and long axis of the humeral stem of the prothesis. Dashed lines indicate their respective perpendiculars. Subtracting 40° from the angle (*curved arrow*) provides an estimate of the angle of retroversion. (Redrawn with permission from Frich LH, Moller BN: Retroversion of the humeral prosthesis in shoulder arthroplasty. *J Arthroplasty* 4:277–280, 1989.)

sured angle *a*. For all but extreme measurements, the error of this estimation is no more than 5°.[13,14]

Glenoid Component

The glenoid component may be difficult to see when non–metal-backed components are used. A small wire marker indicates its position and should be identified in all cases so that the position of the glenoid component can be ascertained. The high-density polyethylene is slightly lucent in comparison to the adjacent soft tissues. The facing angle of the glenoid component is the angle between the longitudinal axis of the glenoid or the glenoid component and the medial border of the scapula; these are expected to be parallel.[15]

Arthrography

After shoulder arthroplasty, arthrography and aspiration are most often performed to identify infection, confirm loosening of either component, or identify dissociation of the glenoid component. Several difficulties have been noted. Needle placement may be more difficult in the postoperative patient if the needle has to be inserted through a fibrotic pseudocapsule. The shoulder aspiration may also be less reliable when performed on patients with suspected infected prostheses than it is in patients who have no history of surgery. Loculated fluid collections may need to be individually aspirated if fluid obtained from the joint itself does not yield a positive culture. Finally, the arthrographic evaluation for component loosening in patients with painful shoulder arthroplasty may also be unreliable. As noted by Goldman, false negative studies result if loosening occurs at the distal end of the humeral stem or if the interface is filled with granulation tissue and contrast material cannot reach the affected area.[16] Bonutti and coworkers reported that only two of the five arthrograms performed in patients with known glenoid loosening accurately depicted any changes.[17]

Computed Tomography

Beam-hardening artifact has traditionally limited the interpretation of scans in which metallic prostheses are present. Computed tomography (CT), however, has recently been shown to be useful in evaluating loosening of humeral components in resurfacing arthroplasties. Bone resorption inside the metallic cup can be detected by means of new algorithms using high-frequency filters for image reconstruction. In a report by Egund and co-workers, CT reconstruction was performed with the high-frequency filter and viewing of the image at a window level of 200 to 600 and a window width of 4000 to 6000. This decreased the beam-hardening artifact produced by the high-contrast metal component when using a medium-frequency filter, and it became possible to evaluate both the skeletal structures and cement protrusions inside the cup.[18] This technique holds promise for evaluating other types of arthroplasties as well.

COMPLICATIONS OF JOINT REPLACEMENT

Fractures

Periprosthetic fractures of the humerus can occur as a direct complication of arthroplasty or postoperatively. Aggressive humeral reaming or impaction intraoperatively in osteopenic patients may be responsible for the fracture. Postoperative fractures usually follow trauma to the shoulder. Boyd and coworkers reported seven postoperative fractures in a series of 436 shoulder arthroplasties.[19] When a fracture occurs, either intraoperatively or postoperatively, it is slow to heal and may need open reduction and internal fixation (Figs. 11-6, 11-7).[20]

Infection

Infection is a rare complication of shoulder arthroplasty—prevalence approximately 0.4 percent for the Neer design and 2.2 percent for constrained designs.[21] Infections of prosthetic joints arise either as a direct result of wound contamination at surgery or as a secondary effect of sepsis from another focus such as the urinary tract, skin, or teeth. Radiographic evaluation of a suspected infected arthroplasty is useful but findings are nonspecific in most cases. Even in the presence of known infection, the radiograph may show no abnormality. Infection may be suggested on radiographs by the presence of bone destruction, periosteal reaction, or the development of lucent lines of 2 mm or more in width at the bone-cement interface without adjacent sclerosis.[11]

Instability

Instability after shoulder arthroplasty can be classified according to the direction of subluxation of the humeral head on the glenoid. The subluxation can be superior, anterior, posterior, or inferior. The incidence of instabil-

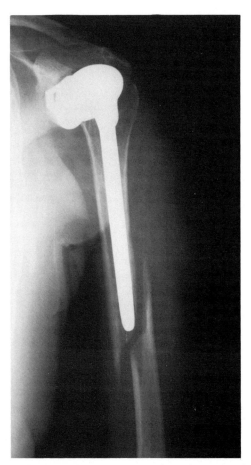

Figure 11-6 Humeral fracture after total shoulder arthroplasty. An AP view of the shoulder shows a total shoulder prosthesis. A posttraumatic fracture of the humerus occurred near the distal tip of the humeral component. There is no evidence of component loosening.

ity ranges from zero to 18.2 percent in nonconstrained implants and, paradoxically, from 6 to 16.7 percent in constrained ones. Dislocation is the major form of instability with constrained implants. Subluxation is more frequently associated with nonconstrained prostheses.[22]

SUPERIOR INSTABILITY

Superior displacement of the humeral head with relation to the glenoid is the most common direction of instability. The causes of postoperative superior migration, which seem to be multiple, include (1) an irreparable rotator cuff tear, (2) an increase in the glenoid facing angle, (3) placement of the humeral component in a "proud" position (higher than the underlying bone), (4) release of the coracoacromial ligament, (5) muscle imbalance between a thin, poorly functioning rotator cuff and a strong deltoid, (6) preoperative proximal migration, and (7) cuff tear arthropathy (Fig. 11-8).

On standard AP radiographs, proximal migration of the humeral head can be evaluated by measuring progressive displacement of the inferior edge of the humeral

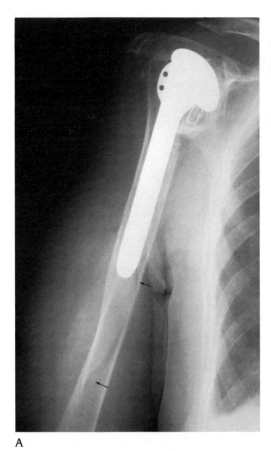

A

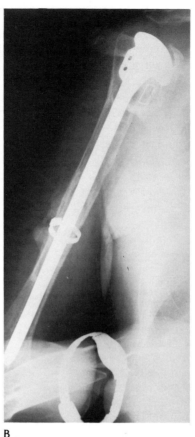

B

Figure 11-7 Humeral fracture. **A.** The AP view shows a total shoulder prosthesis with cemented glenoid and press-fit humeral components. There is upward subluxation of the humeral component. A subtle fracture is seen near the tip of the prosthesis (*arrows*). **B.** The humeral component has been revised with insertion of a long-stem prosthesis and an additional cerclage band for stabilization of the fracture. Heavy callus is noted.

component with relation to the inferior aspect of the glenoid or decreasing distance between the undersurface of the acromion and the humeral prosthesis. Boyd and colleagues have reported proximal migration in 22 percent of patients with 131 Neer prostheses.[23]

INFERIOR INSTABILITY

Inferior subluxation may be seen immediately after shoulder arthroplasty. This is thought to be caused by muscle weakness, or possibly the loss of negative intraarticular pressure (presumably owing to joint effusion or hemorrhage). Persistent inferior instability is most often a consequence of inadequate restoration of humeral length during the replacement. This technical error is most common when hemiarthroplasty is performed after a fracture of the proximal humerus.[22]

ANTERIOR AND POSTERIOR INSTABILITY

Anterior or posterior instability after shoulder arthroplasty is generally caused by soft tissue imbalance or component malposition. As in unoperated shoulders, anterior instability is more common. Moeckel and coworkers found examples of seven anterior and three posterior subluxations in a series of 236 total shoulder arthroplasties.[24] Anterior instability most often results from disrup-

tion of the repaired subscapularis muscle and capsule whereas posterior instability is usually the result of excessive retroversion of either the humeral or the glenoid component (Figs. 11-9, 11-10).

Fracture and Dissociation of Components

FRACTURE

Prostheses with a constrained articulation are more prone to traumatic complications. Mechanical failure usually appears as a humeral neck fracture of the prosthesis. Eight broken and two bent prosthetic humeral necks were reported by Post's group in a series of 24 constrained total shoulder prostheses.[25] Fatigue fracture of the screws fixing the glenoid component occurred twice in a series of 21 patients with porous-coated total shoulder replacements (Fig. 11-11).[26]

DISSOCIATION

Mechanical dissociation of a snap-fit glenoid liner from the metal backing has been reported. Displacement of the radiopaque glenoid marker or the radiolucent plastic liner itself can be detected on radiographs.[27]

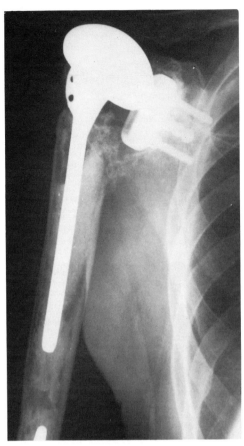

Figure 11-8 Cemented shoulder prosthesis with superior subluxation of the humeral head. This patient with severe rheumatoid arthritis underwent total shoulder replacement. There is striking upward subluxation of the humeral head with relation to the glenoid component. There is marked bone loss from the acromion process, probably from previous surgery.

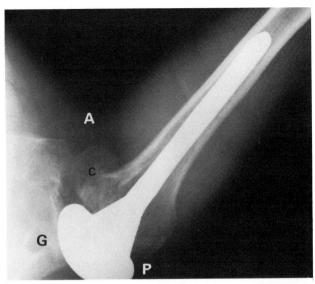

Figure 11-10 Posterior subluxation after hemiarthroplasty. The axillary view shows posterior subluxation of the humeral component with relation to the glenoid (G). There has been erosion of the posterior aspect of the glenoid. (Key: A, anterior; P, posterior; C, coracoid process.)

Loosening

Component loosening is the most common cause of failure after total shoulder arthroplasty. Of the 766 cases of nonconstrained total shoulder arthroplasty contained in the literature (follow-up 20 to 120 months) only 25 cases (3.6 percent) of glenoid loosening have been reported.[28] Another series described a 2.8 percent prevalence of glenoid component loosening and a 1.1 percent prevalence of humeral component loosening (Fig. 11-12).[17] The reported incidence of partial or complete radiolucent lines on postoperative radiographs ranges

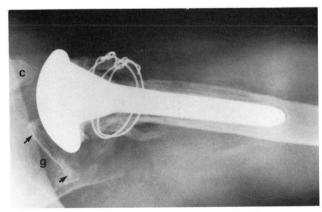

Figure 11-9 Hemiarthroplasty with anterior subluxation and humeral component loosening. Axillary view shows a cemented humeral component with a 2-mm cement-bone lucent zone, suggesting loosening. A healing proximal humeral fracture is held by cerclage wires. Anterior subluxation of the humeral component with relation to the glenoid (g and *arrows*) is noted. The coracoid process (c) indicates the anterior aspect of the shoulder.

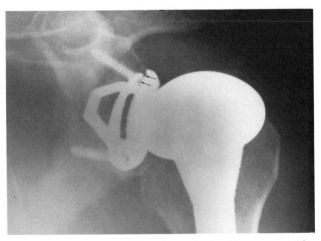

Figure 11-11 Fracture of bone-ingrowth glenoid component. The bone-ingrowth glenoid component is held by two screws. A fracture is noted through the metal backing (*arrows*) in the region of the screw hole.

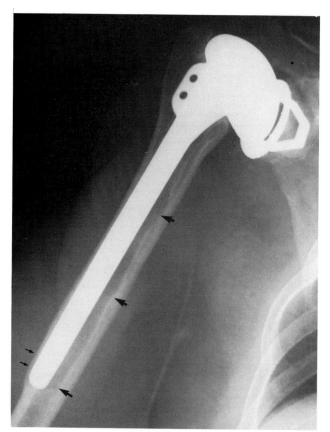

Figure 11-12 Loose humeral component. This is a total shoulder prosthesis with a cemented glenoid component and a press-fit humeral component. The large humeral lucent zone (*large arrows*) and the thinning of the lateral cortex (*small arrows*) attest to the loosening.

from 30 percent to 93 percent. Rotator cuff tears and upward subluxation of the humeral head predispose to glenoid component loosening (Fig. 11-13).[28,29]

Constrained prostheses are more susceptible to loosening because of the powerful forces generated across the glenohumeral articulation (the point at which the components are coupled). Because of this, the rates of component breakage and loosening may be high. The risk of traumatic complications is increased because subluxation, which may provide a "safety valve" in nonconstrained prostheses, cannot occur when a constrained prosthesis is used. Stresses that would be dissipated by subluxation are, therefore, redirected to adjacent tissues and structures.[1] Prevalence rates of loosening as high as 25 percent for a cemented, constrained prosthesis have been reported.[26] Evaluation of total shoulder arthroplasty for component loosening can be difficult. As in other joints, radiographic evidence of loosening does not always correlate with clinical component failure. Definite loosening is usually associated with one or more of the following radiographic findings: (1) a complete radiolucent line of 2 mm or more at the bone-cement interface, (2) fracture of the cement mantle, (3) any radiolucent line at the implant-cement interface, (4) component

migration on serial radiographs (Fig. 11-14).[5] The arthrographic evaluation of loosening is helpful only when the findings are positive.

Glenoid Changes Following Hemiarthroplasty

In hemiarthroplasty the prosthetic humeral head may cause progressive glenoid cartilage wear owing to prolonged metal-on-cartilage articulation. On radiographs, sclerosis or erosive changes indicate such wear. These changes typically are delayed because of the non–weight-bearing status of the shoulder. Clayton and coworkers reported two cases of glenoid erosion in a series of 14 hemiarthroplasties.[10]

Heterotopic New Bone Formation

Ectopic bone formation usually appears 2 to 3 months after surgery and becomes stable 10 to 12 months after surgery. Six percent of 98 shoulder prostheses in one series demonstrated heterotopic bone formation.[11]

IMPINGEMENT AND ROTATOR CUFF REPAIR

Shoulder impingement and rotator cuff tears are periarticular disorders that may require surgical intervention. Some authors report 95 percent of rotator cuff disease to be caused by compression of the cuff by the overlying acromion (Fig. 11-15); the other 5 percent are due to anterior or multidirectional instability with secondary impingement.[30,31] The soft tissue abnormalities that may result from impingement include (1) complete rotator

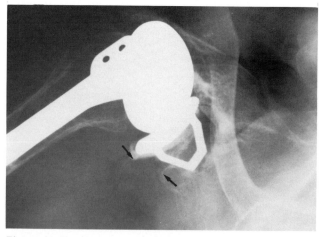

Figure 11-13 Separation of the glenoid component from underlying bone. There is a cemented glenoid component. A wide gap is present between the inferior aspect of the glenoid cement and the bony glenoid (*arrows*). Presumably this represents loosening, though no earlier radiographs are available to document the component's previous position.

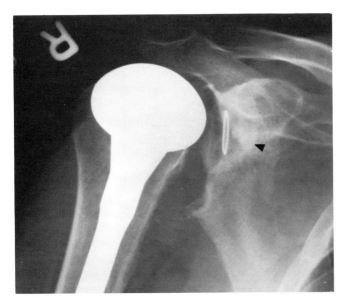

A

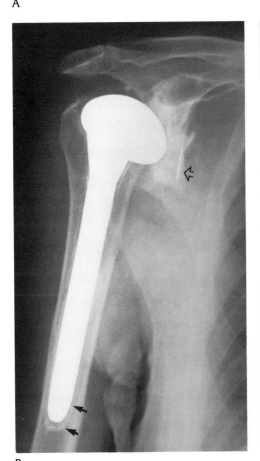

B

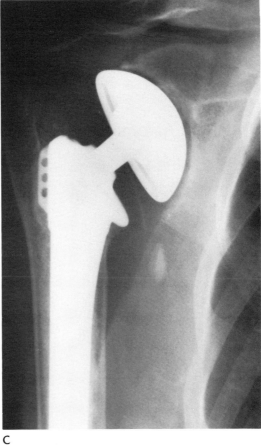

C

Figure 11-14 Loosening of glenoid and humeral components. **A.** Examination shortly after total shoulder replacement, with the arm in internal rotation, shows the glenoid prosthesis to have been inserted high in the glenoid (*arrowhead*). There is, however, no definite loosening. **B.** Follow-up examination 5 years later shows inferior displacement of the glenoid component (*open arrow*). A 1- to 2-mm lucency is noted about the humeral component, suggesting loosening (*arrows*). **C.** At the time of revision, both components were proven to be loose. A bipolar prosthesis was inserted, which articulates largely with the glenoid.

cuff tears, (2) partial tears involving either the articular or bursal side of the cuff, (3) thickening of the subacromial bursa, and (4) fraying of the acromial portion of the coracoacromial ligament. Os acromiale, Type II (curved) or more commonly Type III (hooked) acromial variants, or osteophytes of the inferior acromion or acromioclavicular joint predispose to impingement (Fig. 11-16). Conservative management, consisting of rest, medication, and physical therapy, is the first line of treatment for acromioclavicular arthritis, and for partial, and sometimes complete, rotator cuff tears. For tears that are unresponsive to nonoperative treatment, the surgical options

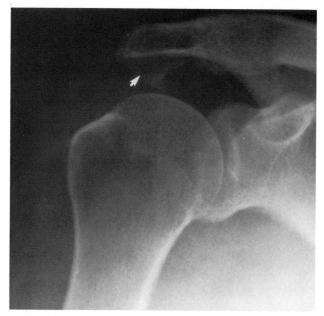

Figure 11-15 Impingement with acromial osteophyte. There are large osteophytes arising from the anterior inferior aspect of the acromion (*arrow*). The acromioclavicular joint is not clearly seen but appears to have hypertrophic changes as well.

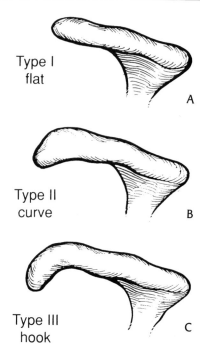

Figure 11-16 Types of acromion processes. **A.** Type I, the flat acromion process. **B.** Type II, the curved acromion process. **C.** Type III, the hooked acromion process. (Redrawn with permission from Rockwood CA, Lyons FR: Shoulder impingement syndrome: Diagnosis, radiographic evaluation and treatment with a modified Neer acromioplasty. *J Bone Joint Surg* 75A:409–424, 1993.)

are usually either open or arthroscopic subacromial decompression, with or without simultaneous cuff repair.[31]

Acromioplasty and Acromionectomy

The goals of surgery are to decompress the subacromial space by reducing both bony and soft tissue sources of compression. This may involve anterior acromionectomy, acromioplasty (which involves shaving the anterior inferior portion of the acromion), or incision of the coracoacromial ligament. An older procedure, lateral acromionectomy, removed the lateral (but not the anteroinferior) portion of the acromion. This was later shown to weaken the origin of the deltoid muscle and to effect no change in impingement symptoms; therefore, it is no longer performed.[32,33] The classic Neer acromioplasty emphasizes osteotome removal of the anteroinferior prominence of the acromion. Rockwood and colleagues studied these postoperative patients retrospectively and found that many went on to reoperation. At the second look, so much of the anterior aspect of the acromion remained that it extended beyond the anterior border of the clavicle and caused impingement with arm flexion. After the removal of the remaining anterior portion, impingement was relieved. They then developed a two-step procedure, consisting initially of removal of the anterior prominence of the acromion (acromionectomy), followed by shaving of its anteroinferior portion (acromioplasty). The resected acromion should not protrude beyond the clavicle (Fig. 11-17).[34] Simultaneously, the inferior aspect of the acromioclavicular joint and the

rotator cuff tendons are inspected for tears. Any osteophytes on the undersurface of the acromioclavicular joint are resected. In addition, varying portions of the distal clavicle may be removed as well.[33] Rotator cuff lesions are repaired if necessary.[4] An additional acromial variant (os acromiale) is seen in as many as 2 percent of operated shoulders and is associated with degenerative change, impingement, and sometimes rotator cuff tear.[35,36] If small, this ossicle may be resected, and the deltoid reattached to the raw acromial edge; if it is large, bone grafting and more extensive surgery may be required (Fig. 11-18).

Rotator Cuff Repair

As in acromioplasty, rotator cuff repair may be performed as an open procedure or arthroscopically. Arthroscopic evaluation and treatment of rotator cuff tears has gained acceptance among orthopedic surgeons because conventional physical examination and preoperative imaging techniques may fail to provide definitive diagnosis to guide treatment.[37,38] At arthroscopy, a suture marker is placed within a small full-thickness or significant inferior surface partial tear to permit identification of the corresponding cuff area on the bursal surface. The remaining cuff tissue is palpated from both the articular and the bursal side to assess its thickness and quality. Then, rotator cuff debridement of the frayed and ragged edges is

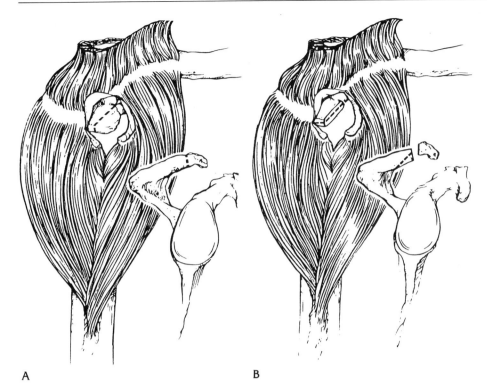

Figure 11-17 Two-step acromioplasty. **A.** The anterior acromion is resected. **B.** The anterior inferior acromion is shaved. (Redrawn with permission from Rockwood CA, Lyons FR: Shoulder impingement syndrome: Diagnosis, radiographic evaluation and treatment with a modified Neer acromioplasty. *J Bone Joint Surg* 75A:409–424, 1993.)

A   B

performed. Additional procedures that may be performed include (1) arthroscopic suture repair of flap tears involving tendon, synovium, and capsule delaminated from the undersurface of the cuff; (2) fixation of small rotator cuff tears to the humerus using suture anchors (Fig. 11-19); (3) mini–open rotator cuff repair for larger lesions; and (4) arthroscopic debridement and decompression alone for massive tears. The repair is often performed in conjunction with acromioplasty or acromionectomy if there are signs of impingement.[37]

Some patients with massive rotator cuff tears and additional loss of glenohumeral joint surface require hemiarthroplasty. These patients may not be candidates for primary rotator cuff repair owing to poor quality of the remaining tendons and secondary findings of chronic cuff tear arthropathy. They are not candidates for total shoulder replacement because of the destruction of the rotator cuff and the fixed upward subluxation of the

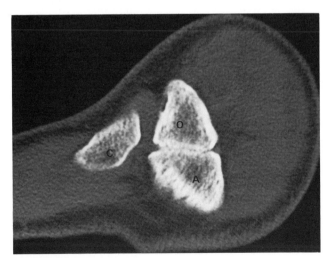

Figure 11-18 Os acromiale. The CT image through the acromioclavicular joint shows the separate ossification center (O) for the anterior acromion (os acromiale). The clavicle (C) and acromion (A) are also indicated.

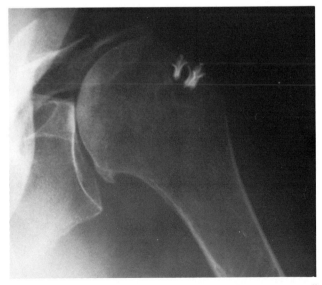

Figure 11-19 Rotator cuff repair. The findings of chronic rotator cuff tear include upward subluxation of the humeral head and secondary osteoarthritis of the glenohumeral joint. Attempted rotator cuff repair is evidenced by two Mytec anchors in the humerus. An acromioclavicular joint osteophyte removal was also performed to relieve impingement.

humeral head. A prerequisite for the hemiarthroplasty is an intact coracoacromial arch, which provides secondary stabilization of the prosthesis. In hemiarthroplasty, as opposed to a primary rotator cuff repair, acromioplasty is not performed in order to preserve this arch.[39]

Repair of Instability

Shoulder instability can be a difficult diagnosis to make, both clinically and radiologically. Bony abnormalities often accompany dislocation or subluxation, and they may provide a clue to the diagnosis. Defects such as a notch in the posterolateral humeral head (the Hill-Sachs lesion) or a fracture of the inferior glenoid or tear of the glenoid labrum (Bankart lesion) occur in anterior dislocation, and a similar compression fracture of the anteromedial humerus (the trough line) occurs in posterior dislocation. In addition, recurrent dislocation may cause joint capsular laxity that necessitates surgical repair. The anterior soft tissue mechanism of the shoulder consists of the glenoid labrum, the anterior capsule, the synovial lining and its recesses, and the subscapularis muscle and tendon. The posterior mechanism, in turn, is made up of the posterior capsule, the labrum, the synovial membrane, and the supraspinatus, infraspinatus, and teres minor muscles and tendons.[15] Recurrent anterior subluxation or dislocation involves the disruption of these complexes, especially detachment of the glenohumeral ligament–labrum complex.

In fact, it has been shown that the key stabilizer that prevents anterior subluxation of the humeral head is the anterior inferior glenohumeral ligament (AIGHL), which is attached to the glenoid neck by the anterior labrum.[40] The main focus of surgical correction of recurrent anterior instability is to repair or reconstruct the AIGHL, as well as the labrum tear. Posterior instability and multidirectional instability are less common than anterior instability, and less is known about the important anatomy of the posterior restraints. Again, the surgical choices are open or arthroscopic repair. The "themes" shared by the many named repairs include tightening of the shoulder capsule, repair of the glenoid labrum–AIGHL complex, and muscle or tendon transfer. Some of the more common procedures include (1) Putti-Platt, which uses staples to shorten and reinforce the joint capsule and subscapularis muscle; (2) Bankart which involves the reattachment of the capsule and labrum to the glenoid rim and often is performed in addition to the Putti-Platt to further increase stability; (3) Magnuson-Stack, which transfers the insertion of the subscapularis muscle from the lesser to the greater tuberosity; and (4) the modified Bristow or anterior bone block operation, consisting of transferring the coracoid process and its conjoined tendon attachment (coracobrachialis and short head of the biceps muscles) to the anterior rim of the glenoid. The bone block impedes anterior dislocation, and the conjoined tendon reinforces the joint capsule. Staple capsulorrhaphy consists of placing one to three staples into the glenoid labrum, AIGHL, and scapular neck to tighten the anterior joint capsule without detaching, shortening, or transplanting muscles. Each staple is positioned away from the glenoid articular surface, and the tines of each staple should not disrupt the articular surface or enter the joint.[41–43]

Postoperative Evaluation of Acromioplasty, Rotator Cuff Repair, and Instability

RADIOGRAPHY

Imaging techniques available for the postoperative assessment of acromioplasty, rotator cuff tears and impingement, and instability repair include the standard radiographic views of the shoulder (an anteroposterior view in internal rotation, a 40° posterior oblique view in external rotation, an axillary view, a tangential scapular Y view). In addition, a supraspinatus outlet or arch view may be added to the usual shoulder series to show the acromial shape and thickness to best advantage (aspects of acromial anatomy that may be partially obscured on the other views).[44] Although this view is important to obtain preoperatively, in failed repairs, postoperative radiographs may show continued prominence of the acromial undersurface or anterior portion, which may not have been adequately removed. The major difference between the scapular "Y" view and the supraspinatus outlet view is that, for the latter, the x-ray beam is tilted 5° to 10° caudad.[34] This may also show the flattened shape of the postoperative acromion in a successful repair (Fig. 11-20).

The sutures used in rotator cuff repair are usually nonopaque and are not visible on standard radiographs. In instability repair, however, there is usually visible metallic hardware (Fig. 11-21). The modified Bristow procedure, for example, may be identified radiographically by screw fixation of the coracoid process to the inferior glenoid rim.[41] In staple capsulorrhaphy, the staple(s) should not be seen to penetrate the glenoid cavity. Comparison of successive radiographs is important to evaluate possible complications such as migration, loosening, or fracture of the hardware. A change in position may indicate loss of the tethering effect and possibly failure of the procedure. Infection is not usually demonstrable on radiographs, but it is rare, occurring in only one of 149 staple capsulorrhaphies reported by Detrisac and coworkers.[42] Research efforts are under way to develop biodegradable fixation devices to reduce the potential complications associated with the hardware in use today.[43]

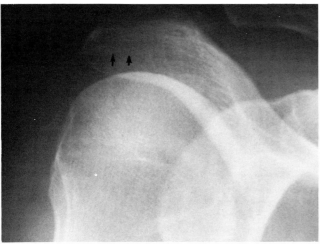
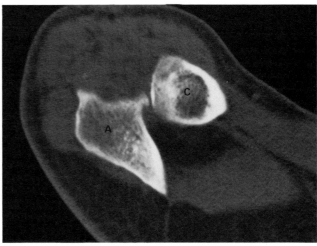

A   B

Figure 11-20   Anterior acromioplasty. **A.** The AP internal rotation view of the operative right shoulder shows absence of the inferior cortex of the anterior acromion (*arrows*) consequent to anterior acromioplasty. A portion of the cortex at the acromioclavicular joint remains visible. **B.** Axial CT image through the acromioclavicular joint more clearly shows that the anterior portion of the acromion (A) has been resected. This includes the majority of the acromioclavicular joint. (Key: C, clavicle.)

COMPUTED TOMOGRAPHY AND ARTHROGRAPHY

In addition to radiography, imaging with CT in conjunction with arthrography may provide better evaluation of postoperative bony and soft tissue anatomy. Although arthrography of the shoulder remains a "gold standard" for evaluation of rotator cuff abnormalities preoperatively, it is controversial as a postoperative examination for rotator cuff repair evaluation. Calvert and associates

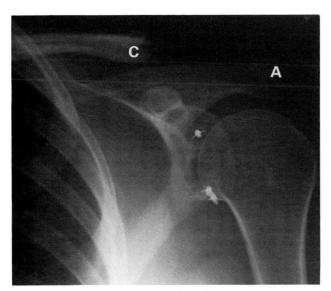

Figure 11-21   Status after acromioclavicular joint resection, anterior acromionectomy, and capsular repair. The AP view shows postoperative changes in the anterior glenoid with sclerosis and lucency. Three capsular fixation anchors are noted. The distal clavicle (C) has been resected. The inferior border of the anterior acromion (A) is not clearly seen consequent to the resection.

studied double-contrast arthrography in 20 patients more than 2 years after operative repair of rotator cuff tears. Eighteen showed persistent cuff defects and yet had complete pain relief and full shoulder elevation. These results suggest that a "watertight" closure is not essential for a functional result, and that arthrography may not be helpful in investigating failed cuff repair.[45] Either single-contrast or double-contrast technique may be used, but the double-contrast approach is often preferred because of decreased patient discomfort after arthrography and the ability to demonstrate the size of the tear and the quality of its edges. Either 10 to 12 ml of 60% meglumine diatrizoate positive contrast medium or 3 to 4 ml of contrast plus 10 ml of room air is injected intraarticularly under fluoroscopic guidance. The presence of contrast or air in the tendon indicates a partial tear, whereas a full-thickness tear is documented by contrast, air, or both, entering the subacromial-subdeltoid bursa. Partial tears that occur on the bursal side of the tendons will be missed by arthrography using glenohumeral injection. The presence of loose bodies and adhesive capsulitis may also be assessed by arthrography.[46] Metallic clips or sutures do not hinder the postoperative interpretation of arthrograms or radiographs.

Shoulder arthrography may also be performed in conjunction with CT to evaluate the status of the repaired rotator cuff, the status of the glenohumeral joint and secondary degenerative changes (if any) and the glenoid labrum. At the Brigham and Women's Hospital, 2-mm thick slices at 2-mm increment axial images are first obtained from the level of the acromioclavicular joint to the inferior glenoid. The affected shoulder is elevated slightly to minimize artifact from the thorax and opposite

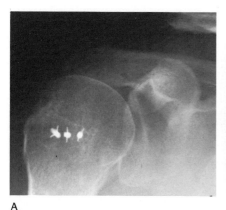

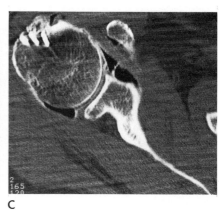

A   B   C

Figure 11-22 Rotator cuff repair, acromioclavicular joint resection, and acromioplasty. **A.** Internal rotation view shows the metal anchors in the humerus from repair of the supraspinatus tendon. The changes of anterior acromioplasty and acromioclavicular joint resection are faintly visible. **B.** The postarthrogram CT better demonstrates resection of the distal clavicle (C) and anteromedial acromion process (A) with small fragments of bone remaining. **C.** A more distal CT image shows the fixation anchors at the insertion of the supraspinatus tendon.

shoulder, and the arm is put in mild external rotation to afford the best evaluation of the labrum. It is noteworthy that Pennes and coworkers suggest internal rotation for evaluation of the anterior labrum and external rotation for studying the posterior labrum.[47] Computer-reconstructed sagittal and coronal oblique images are then obtained. With this protocol, the postoperative bony anatomy of the acromion, humerus, and scapula can be further assessed, and the soft tissues such as the rotator cuff tendons, the glenoid labrum, and the tendon of the long head of the biceps muscle may be evaluated. The relationship of the humeral head to the acromion and glenoid is also better assessed than on routine radiographs. Although there may be some artifact from postoperative metallic clips or staples, these may be assessed for migration, fracture, or possible malposition. The use of high-frequency filters may help to eliminate some of the artifact and allow better interpretation of the images (Figs. 11-22, 11-22C).

MAGNETIC RESONANCE IMAGING

MRI provides a good preoperative evaluation of the painful shoulder, but postoperative imaging presents special difficulties because of the anatomic changes produced

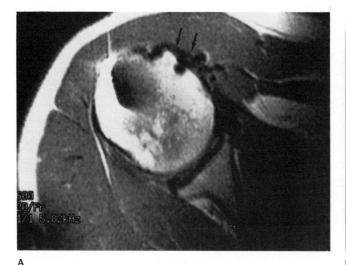
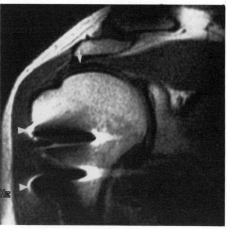

A   B

Figure 11-23 Subscapularis repair. **A.** Axial T1-weighted (TR 600 msec, TE 20 msec) MR image shows suture artifact (*arrows*) within the insertion of the subscapularis tendon. **B.** Coronal oblique T1-weighted (TR 500 msec, TE 20 msec) image shows an intact supraspinatus tendon (*arrow*). This is well seen despite the metal artifacts from a staple in the proximal humerus (*arrowheads*).

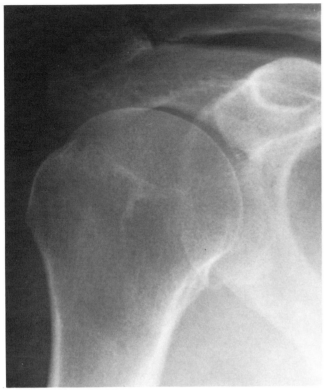

A

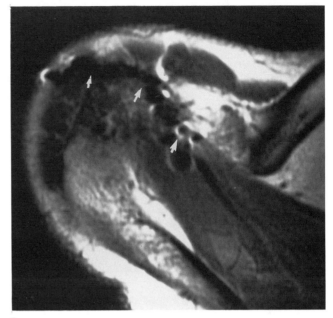

B

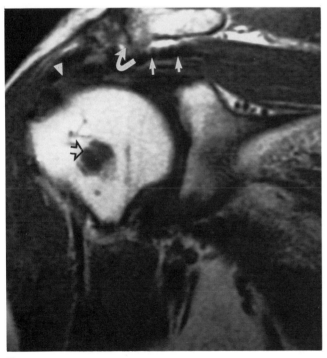

C

Figure 11-24   Repair of partial rotator cuff tear. **A.** An AP radiograph of the shoulder shows no abnormality and no metallic densities in the region of the rotator cuff. **B.** Axial T1-weighted (TR 500 msec, TE 20 msec) MR image shows the susceptibility artifact (*arrows*) in the distal supraspinatus tendon consistent with sutures from the previous rotator cuff repair. **C.** Coronal oblique T1-weighted (TR 500 msec, TE 20 msec) image of the operated right shoulder shows areas of low signal consistent with suture artifact from previous surgery (*arrows*). There is increased signal in the supraspinatus tendon (*arrowhead*). A cyst is incidentally noted in the humeral head (*open arrow*). There are hypertrophic changes at the acromioclavicular joint (*curved arrow*). The patient previously had undergone acromioplasty. *(Continued on p. 350.)*

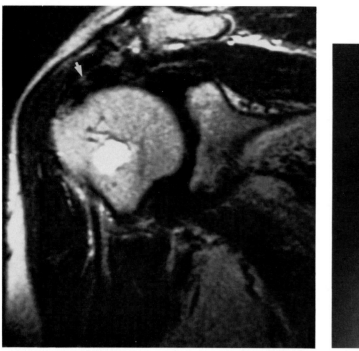

D

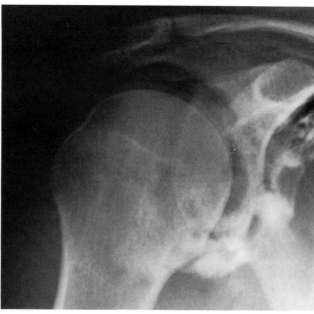

E

Figure 11-24   (continued) **D.** Coronal oblique T2-weighted fast spin-echo images (TR 4500 msec, TE 90 msec) show the irregularity of the supraspinatus tendon with intermediate signal (*arrow*). Definite brightening of the signal on T2 would be more suggestive of a "retear." **E.** Subsequent arthrography showed no "retear" of the rotator cuff.

by surgery and the presence of ferromagnetic clips or sutures, which distort the MR signal. The changes of acromioplasty, however, are easily recognized by the smooth margins of the anteroinferior portion of the acromion and its lateral taper. Additional complications may be seen, such as avascular necrosis of the humeral head, dislocation of the biceps tendon, residual acromioclavicular joint disease, or glenoid labral abnormalities. The rotator cuff tendons themselves are difficult to evaluate postoperatively using MRI, owing to signal changes produced by the surgery that can mimic partial- or full-thickness tears (Figs. 11-23 and 11-24).[48,49]

Conclusion

Postoperative imaging of the shoulder is a challenging task that should be tailored to the individual patient and to the type of operative intervention. Often, a combination of imaging modalities may provide the best evaluation, as each individual technique has advantages and limitations. Standard radiographs plus additional tailored views, arthrography, CT, and MRI all may play a role in the assessment of the shoulder after surgery.

References

1. JOHNSON RL: Total shoulder arthroplasty. *Orthop Nursing* 12:14, 1993.
2. DORLAND'S MEDICAL DICTIONARY, 27th ed, Philadelphia, Saunders, 1988.
3. TILLMANN K, BRAATZ D, RUTHER W, BACKER J: Osteotomy and resection arthroplasty of the shoulder, in Friedman RJ, (ed): *Arthroplasty of the Shoulder*, New York, Thieme, 1994, pp 126–133.
4. NEER CS II: Die Schulterarthroplastik Heute. *Orthopade* 20:320, 1991.
5. BOYD AD, THORNHILL TS: Glenoid resurfacing in shoulder arthroplasty, in Friedman RJ (ed): *Total Shoulder Arthroplasty*, New York, Thieme, 1994, pp 305–316.
6. COONEY WP: Total joint arthroplasty. Introduction to the upper extremity. *Mayo Clin Proc* 54:495, 1979.
7. THORNHILL TS, BARRET WP: Total shoulder arthroplasty, in Rowe CR (ed): *The Shoulder*, New York, Livingstone, 1988, pp 481–505.
8. POST M, HASKELL SS, JABLON M: Total shoulder replacement with a constrained prosthesis. *J Bone Joint Surg* 62A:327, 1980.
9. SWANSON FB: The bipolar shoulder implant: A clinical study. *Orthop Trans* 10:216, 1986.
10. CLAYTON ML, FERLIC DC, JEFFERS PD: Prosthetic arthroplasties of the shoulder. *Clin Orthop* 164:184, 1982.
11. ALIABADI P, WEISSMAN BN, THORNHILL TS, NIKPOOR N, SOSMAN JL: Evaluation of a nonconstrained total shoulder prosthesis. *AJR* 151:1169, 1988.
12. OVESEN J, NIELSEN S: Prosthesis position in shoulder arthroplasty. *Acta Orthop Scand* 56:330, 1985.
13. FRICH LH, MOLLER B: Retroversion of the humeral prosthesis in shoulder arthroplasty. *J Arthroplasty* 4:277, 1989.
14. ALIABADI P, WEISSMAN BN: Radiology of total shoulder arthroplasty, in Friedman RJ (ed): *Total Shoulder Arthroplasty*, New York, Thieme, 1994, pp 53–69.
15. WEISSMAN BN, SLEDGE CB: *Orthopedic Radiology*, Philadelphia, Saunders, 1986, pp 215–278.
16. GOLDMAN A: *Shoulder Arthrography*, Boston, Little, Brown, 1982, pp 164–66.
17. BONUTTI PM, HAWKINS RJ, SADDEMI S: Arthroscopic assessment of glenoid component loosening after total shoulder arthroplasty. *J Arthroscop Rel Surg* 9:272, 1993.
18. EGUND N, JONSSON E, LIDGREN, L, KELLY I, PETTERSSON H: Computed tomography of humeral head cup arthroplasties. A preliminary report. *Acta Radiol* 28:71, 1987.
19. BOYD AD, THORNHILL TS, BARNES C L: Fractures adjacent to humeral prostheses. *J Bone Joint Surg* 74A:1498, 1992.
20. BONUTTI PM, HAWKINS RJ: Fracture of the humeral shaft associated with total replacement arthroplasty of the shoulder. *J Bone Joint Surg* 74A:617, 1992.
21. COFIELD RH: The shoulder results and complications, in

Morrey BF (ed): *Joint Replacement Arthroplasty*, New York, Churchill-Livingstone, 1991, pp 437–453.
22. MOECKEL BH, WARREN RF, DINES DM, ALTCHEK DW: The unstable shoulder arthroplasty, in Friedman RJ (ed): *Total Shoulder Arthroplasty*, New York, Thieme, 1994, pp 254–263.
23. BOYD AD, ALIABADI P, THORNHILL TS: Postoperative proximal migration in total shoulder arthroplasty. Incidence and significance. *J Arthroplasty* 6:31, 1991.
24. MOECKEL BH, ALTCHEK DW, WARREN RF, WICKIEWICZ TL, DINES DM: Instability of the shoulder after arthroplasty. *J Bone Joint Surg* 75A:492, 1993.
25. POST M, JABLON M: Constrained total shoulder arthroplasty. Long-term follow-up observations. *Clin Orthop* 173:109, 1983.
26. McELWAIN JP, ENGLISH E: The early results of porous-coated total shoulder arthroplasty. *Clin Orthop* 218:217, 1987.
27. DRIESSNACK RP, FERLIC DC, WIEDEL JD: Dissociation of the glenoid component in the Macnab/English total shoulder arthroplasty. *J Arthroplasty* 5:15 1990.
28. FRANKLIN JL, BARRETT WP, JACKINS SE, MATSEN FA: Glenoid loosening in total shoulder arthroplasty. *J Arthroplasty* 1:39, 1988.
29. COFIELD RH: Total shoulder arthroplasty with the Neer prosthesis. *J Bone Joint Surg* 66A:899, 1984.
30. JOBE FW, KVITNE RS: Shoulder pain in the overhand or throwing athlete: The relationship of anterior instability and rotator cuff impingement. *Orthop Rev* 18:963, 1989.
31. ESCH JC: Arthroscopic subacromial decompression and postoperative management. *Orthop Clin North Am* 24:161, 1993.
32. BIGLIANI LU, CORDASCO FA, McILVEEN SJ, MUSSO ES: Operative treatment of failed repairs of the rotator cuff. *J Bone Joint Surg* 74A:1505, 1992.
33. NEER CS II: Anterior acromioplasty for the chronic impingement syndrome in the shoulder. *J Bone Joint Surg* 54A:41, 1972.
34. ROCKWOOD CA, LYONS FR: Shoulder impingement syndrome: Diagnosis, radiographic evaluation and treatment with a modified Neer acromioplasty. *J Bone Joint Surg* 75A:409, 1993.
35. EDELSON JG, TAITZ C: Anatomy of the coracoacromial arch. *J Bone Joint Surg* 74B:589, 1992.
36. POST M: Complications of rotator cuff surgery. *Clin Orthop* 254:97, 1990.
37. SNYDER SJ: Evaluation and treatment of the rotator cuff. *Orthop Clin North Am* 24:173, 1993.
38. NEVIASER RJ: Ruptures of the rotator cuff. *Orthop Clin North Am* 18:387, 1987.
39. ARNTZ CT, JACKINS S, MATSEN FA III: Prosthetic replace-

ment of the shoulder for the treatment of defects in the rotator cuff and the surface of the glenohumeral joint. *J Bone Joint Surg* 75A:485, 1993.

40. McINTYRE LF, CASPARI RB: The rationale and the technique for arthroscopic reconstruction of anterior shoulder instability using multiple sutures. *Orthop Clin North Am* 24:55, 1993.

41. WOLF EM: Arthroscopic capsulabral repair using suture anchors. *Orthop Clin North Am* 24:59, 1993.

42. DETRISAC DA, JOHNSON LL: Arthroscopic shoulder capsulorrhaphy using metal staples. *Orthop Clin North Am* 24:71, 1993.

43. YAHIRO MA, MATTHEWS LS: Arthroscopic stabilization procedures for recurrent anterior shoulder instability. *Orthop Rev* 18:1161, 1989.

44. ENGEBRETSON L, CRAIG EV: Radiologic features of shoulder instability. *Clin Orthop* 291:29, 1993.

45. CALVERT PT, PACKER NP, STOKER DJ, BAYLEY JI, KESSEL L: Arthrography of the shoulder after operative repair of the torn rotator cuff. *J Bone Joint Surg* 68B:147, 1986.

46. GOLDMAN AB: Double contrast shoulder arthrography, in Freiberger RH, Kaye JJ (eds): *Arthrography*, Norwalk, CT. Appleton-Century-Crofts, 1979, pp. 168–188.

47. PENNES D, JONSSON K, BUCKWALTER K, BRAUNSTEIN E, BLASIER R, WOJTYS E: Computed arthrotomography of the shoulder. *AJR* 153:1017, 1989.

48. SHANNON M, TENINO P: *MRI of the Shoulder. Clinical Situations and Management*, New York, Thieme, 1992, pp 72–75.

49. SEEGER LL: Magnetic resonance imaging of the shoulder. *Clin Orthop* 244:48, 1989.

12 ENDOCRINE AND METABOLIC DISORDERS OF THE SHOULDER: IMAGING APPEARANCES AND DIAGNOSES

Dennis J. Stoker

It is perhaps impertinent if not misleading to suggest that, in the presence of such mainly generalized diseases as those covered in this chapter, the imaging of the shoulder plays a major part in diagnosis. It should be remembered that, however imperfectly, the shoulder girdle is examined radiographically more than the pelvic girdle and the shoulder joint is the joint of the limbs most frequently included in a radiograph. This, at first seemingly preposterous, statement depends for its validity on the inclusion of some part of the shoulder girdle on every chest radiograph. A chest radiograph is often used as part of the investigatory process in generalized and, as yet undiagnosed, conditions, and the bones of the shoulder girdle may be the osseous structures that are best demonstrated, as many of the ribs and much of the spine are obscured by the intrathoracic structures. Although not presented in an ideal fashion, most or all of the clavicle and some portion of the scapula and humeral head are seen on each side.

The scapula is probably of least value in assessment of bony structures, because only the glenoid process is seen with any clarity. However, the clavicle provides a valuable indicator of the general state of the bony cortex, and the humeral head does the same service for medullary bone.

Of course, it follows that if we need to see the structure of the shoulder accurately we must examine it specifically, and this is dealt with earlier in this book. Nevertheless, it merits repeating that what is sometimes called Grashey's view is the standard view of the shoulder, as it is a true frontal or anteroposterior (AP) projection of the shoulder joint; it has been used at my hospital as the standard view for perhaps 50 years. The projection of the shoulder for which the patient is not rotated and which has sometimes been described as an AP view, is AP not to the shoulder but to the trunk and is a special projection for which I have yet to find a use.

OSTEOPENIA

As a term, *osteopenia* is useful because it denotes reduction in the normal radiographic density of bone without stipulating the cause. Localized osteopenia can be due to direct action of disease, to disuse, or to a combination of the two. When it is generalized it is due to one of "the big three" of metabolic bone disease, osteoporosis, osteomalacia, and hyperparathyroidism, or less commonly to another diffuse disease of bone usually associated with infiltration or deposition of noncalcified material.

Osteoporosis

Osteoporosis of the shoulder, with no other visible bony abnormality, is commonplace as a consequence of reduced use. This is because so many of the painful afflictions and injuries of the shoulder originate in the soft tissues, for example, rupture of the rotator cuff and pericapsulitis. Periarticular osteoporosis therefore may be the only abnormality to be seen on the plain film and, of course, it serves to indicate to some degree the duration of the patient's painful symptoms. One notable anatomic feature of the head of the humerus is that it is mainly composed of medullary spongy bone; the cortex is only a thin peripheral shell. As a consequence of this, destructive medullary lesions such as lytic carcinomatous metastases are not readily demonstrated. The converse is also true, as it is in the region of the greater trochanter of the femur: lytic lesions may be suspected on the basis of the plain radiograph when none are there. The combination of such normal changes or those of disuse alone with overlying calcification in the soft tissue may, together with a mach effect, cause the radiologist to assume the presence of a lytic lesion with central calcification.[1] The determination of the presence of significant osteo-

353

penia from the radiograph alone is well-recognized as an inaccurate and often fruitless exercise. The same conclusion does not apply to localized or periarticular osteopenia because the density of the bone can be compared with that of adjoining bones, making the patient, in effect, his or her own control. Chronic osteoporosis in the past was characterized by coarsening of the trabecular pattern as a consequence of loss of the secondary, rather than the primary, trabeculae. When the patient returns to a less negative calcium balance, the body cannot reform the secondary trabeculae, as they have disappeared for good, so the osteoblastic process lays down new bone on the remaining primary trabeculae, making them more prominent. The process is demonstrated even more strikingly when treatment with fluoride is given.

Most patients with generalized osteoporosis caused by a combination of increasing age, decreased hormone production, and reduced physical activity show the changes in the shoulder girdle as well as elsewhere. The physician's interest in the shoulder is limited by the strong calls for attention from weight-bearing parts of the body where structural collapse of the bone leads to disability (e.g., spine and femoral neck). Even in the upper limb, falls of older women tend to produce Colles' fracture at the wrist, although surgical fractures of the humerus are not uncommon in post-menopausal and senile osteoporosis.

Osteomalacia and Rickets

Deficiency of vitamin D leads to osteopenia, so in adults this mechanism has to be distinguished from osteoporosis. This is often difficult—in early cases, impossible—without biochemical assistance. Nevertheless, in an adult patient younger than 50 years, significant measurable reduction in the cortical thickness of the clavicles is likely to be due to osteomalacia, as, of course, generalized osteoporosis is uncommon in this age group. In osteomalacia, the trabeculae tend to persist but are less well-defined, so that the medulla shows a rather indistinct pattern. Because of its structure and large medullary volume, this change can probably be seen as well in the humeral head as anywhere in the body. The radiographic diagnosis of osteomalacia cannot really be established without the identification of Looser's zones (or pseudofractures). These cortical defects are often, but not always, short defects in the cortex, the lytic lesion being several millimeters wide; occasionally they extend farther, and they are always at risk of being converted into true fractures by subsequent trauma. It is likely that they represent microfractures that everyone sustains in their everyday activity but that in persons with osteomalacia fail to heal. Many but not all of the preferred sites for Looser's zones are similar to those of stress fractures,

notably the ischiopubic rami and proximal femoral shafts. It was once thought that the relatively frequent occurrence of Looser's zones on the axillary border of the scapular blade (Fig. 12-1) was not mimicked by stress trauma, but we now know that stress fractures occur at this site, particularly in manual workers who spend much of their time working with their arms raised above the head. In rickets (osteomalacia of childhood) the changes are mainly seen in the growing metaphysis, where the shortage of vitamin D has its most profound and most immediate effect. When a child with rickets who has been walking reverts to crawling because of the discomfort at the metaphyses on each side of the knee, and probably also because of associated myopathy, the wrists and the shoulders become weight-bearing articulations. Growth at these metaphyses is of course greater than that at the elbow. Most emphasis has been placed on the wrists because they are more visible and swelling and tenderness are clearly identifiable. Nevertheless, the characteristic undermineralization of the metaphyses and fraying of their margins are observable at the shoulders also.

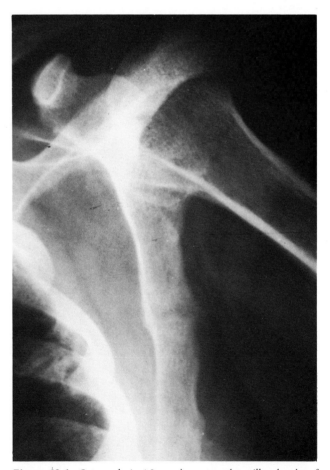

Figure 12-1 Osteomalacia. A Looser's zone on the axillary border of the scapula establishes the diagnosis. This overweight Indian woman managed to maintain her vitamin D intake when she came to the northern hemisphere until she started weight reduction and excluded fats from her diet.

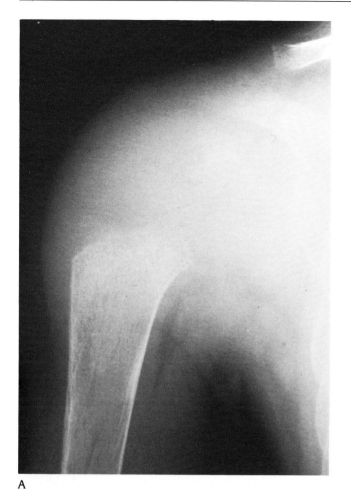

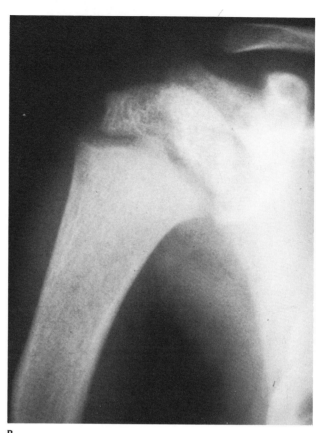

A

B

Figure 12-2 Familial hypophosphatemic rickets. **A.** In this form of vitamin D–resistant rickets, severe retardation of ossification has prevented the centers for the proximal end of the humerus and the glenoid process from appearing. The ragged appearance of the humeral metaphysis is characteristic of rickets. **B.** At a later age, ossification of the humeral epiphysis has occurred. Changes of rickets are still evident, though they have been limited by large doses of vitamin D. In general, treatment is aimed at causing the radiographic appearance to return *almost* to normal. In this way overdose of the vitamin can best be avoided.

The cause of the deficiency cannot generally be determined from the radiologic evidence alone, although evidence of chronic changes and enthesopathy may suggest a vitamin D–resistant mechanism such as familial hypophosphatemia (Fig. 12-2).

Hyperparathyroidism

Affection of the shoulder in this disorder often makes the diagnosis of hyperparathyroidism highly suggestive, but it is unlikely to indicate that the overproduction of parathyroid hormone is either primary or secondary, so the two types are considered together here. The radiologic features of hyperparathyroidism relate to much increased turnover of bone with accelerated osteoblastic, and predominantly osteoclastic, activity. This results in resorption of the trabeculae everywhere, but it is partic-

ularly evident radiologically in the thinner parts of the body such as the hands, for imaging of which high-definition film and screen combinations are employed. Nevertheless, such resorption can be demonstrated in the shoulder girdle, and particularly at the outer end of the clavicle (Fig. 12-3), which, as we have discussed, is often provided as a bonus on every chest film. When a region of osteitis fibrosa (the bony change of hyperparathyroidism) becomes particularly intense or is accompanied by hemorrhage or necrosis, a region of intense resorption called a *brown tumor* is formed. This may be at a distance from the other resorptive changes of the disease, so that such a space-occupying destructive lesion seems to be arising in relatively normal bone (Fig. 12-4). In these circumstances care must be exercised to avoid mistaking the brown tumor for a primary or secondary neoplasm of bone. Clearly, this is achieved by

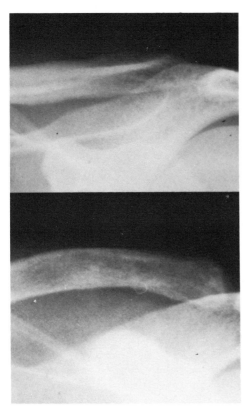

Figure 12-3   The clavicle in hyperparathyroidism. A normal clavicle (*above*) and (*below*) an age-matched clavicle in a patient with hyperparathyroidism. The cortex is reduced in thickness, and it is ill-defined. The bone shows generalized osteopenia, and the outer end of the clavicle is eroded.

looking at the whole patient, undertaking more than local imaging, and therefore by suspecting the diagnosis ensuring that appropriate biochemical studies are made to confirm the disease.

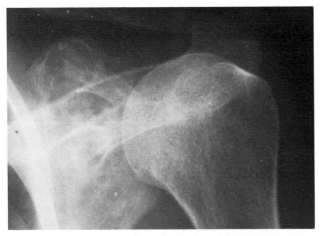

Figure 12-4   Brown tumor in secondary hyperparathyroidism. Deep to the main processes of the scapula, a destructive lesion is expanding the bone. A brown tumor is a region of intense osteitis fibrosa, and the osteoclastic lesion has to be differentiated from neoplasia, both radiographically and histopathologically.

THYROID DISEASE

Hypothyroidism: Cretinism and Myxedema

The effects of thyroid hormone deficiency depend on the age of the person affected. With cretinism (severe hypothyroidism beginning in infancy) the whole growth and maturation of the baby, including that of the skeleton, is retarded. Blood flow through the bones is reduced, and diminished metabolic activity reduces both the formation and resorption of bone. There is some evidence to suggest that the skeleton requires for development a more constant supply of thyroxine than do many other tissues. This is important, as, if skeletal changes are recognized promptly, it may not be too late to prevent irreversible mental retardation. Delay in skeletal maturation may be evident in the epiphyses of the shoulder girdle, but the established standards for the wrist and hand are used, as they are readily available and reasonably reliable. Symmetric maldevelopment is clearly evident in the proximal end of the humerus, where multicentric ossification may be seen in the two major epiphyses (Fig. 12-5). With growth, the bones tend sub-

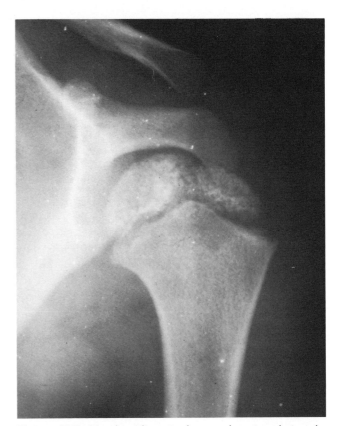

Figure 12-5   Hypothyroidism. Inadequate thyroxine during the growing period has led in this child to multicentric ossification of the humeral head, which now appears stippled. Such developmental change is characteristic of the disorder but is also seen in other epiphyseal disorders such as multiple epiphyseal dysplasia.

sequently to be small and abnormally modeled. In both children and adults the diagnosis of hypothyroidism is occasionally missed because it is never considered. Rarely, a child or adult who proves to be an undiagnosed cretin is found in an institution for the mentally retarded; the diagnosis has usually been some mental disorder or skeletal dysplasia. Naturally, a full skeletal survey is necessary to establish the correct diagnosis. Disorders such as multiple epiphyseal dysplasia, which may fall into the differential diagnosis, cannot be diagnosed on the basis of radiographs of a single region; delay in ossification is generally present but of relatively slight degree. In multiple epiphyseal dysplasia mental development is normal and stature is generally reduced moderately.

In myxedema (adult hypothyroidism) musculoskeletal symptoms are infrequent and nonspecific, consisting of aches in the muscles and joints and occasional joint effusions. There are no specific radiographic features.

Hyperthyroidism

The only radiographically demonstrable effect of thyroxine excess on the adult skeleton is osteopenia. In the immature skeleton, premature ossification of epiphyses occurs.

PITUITARY DISORDERS

Acromegaly and Gigantism

Both acromegaly and gigantism result from overproduction of growth hormone, the first after and the latter before fusion of the epiphyses, so that as an adult the patient with gigantism has the changes of acromegaly superimposed on an already overgrown skeleton. Changes at the shoulder are rarely as striking as, for example, in the hands. Nevertheless, the overgrowth of articular cartilage makes the joint space appear wider than normal and appositional new bone is laid down. If the diagnosis is not made clinically and relatively early, the patient may present with degenerative arthritis affecting the shoulder. As this is not a common site for "idiopathic" osteoarthritis the radiologist should always be alert to seek a predisposing cause, of which acromegaly is but one (Fig. 12-6). Similar changes may be found in the acromioclavicular joints.

Hypercorticosteroidism

Primary and iatrogenic Cushing's syndrome is an important cause of osteoporosis which in the appendicular skeleton has no features to distinguish it from other more common causes in middle-aged women. The other major complication of excessive circulating corticosteroids is

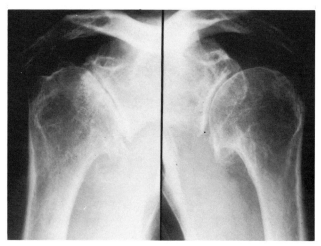

Figure 12-6 Acromegaly. This woman presented for radiographic examination of her painful shoulders. Surprisingly, acromegaly had been suspected only recently by her family doctor, probably because he had known her for years and accepted her appearance as normal. It is important to seek an explanation for degenerative articular changes such as those shown here when they affect a non–weight-bearing joint and there is no history of trauma.

osteonecrosis, and though the hip has always been a more important site for this, the shoulder may also be affected. Again, the radiographic features are no different from those induced by other causes of osteonecrosis, though it is well-recognized that the effects of corticosteroids are greater in bones whose proportion of trabecular to cortical bone is highest. This is the case in the vertebrae, the femoral neck, and the distal radius, but also in the humeral head. Structural collapse may be expected following osteonecrosis in the porotic subchondral bone with subsequent fracture (Fig. 12-7).

In theory, the production of pseudocallus occurs in all regions following compression fracture, but in practice I have not found this to be a useful sign outside the spine. The term *steroid arthropathy* has been applied when, following administration of systemic or intraarticular corticosteroids, an accelerated destructive process affects the articular surfaces with extensive erosion of the subchondral bone on both sides of the joint.

A major complication of hypercorticosteroidism is skeletal infarction, perhaps most common in the hip. The shoulder is by no means immune, and the characteristics of both medullary and subchondral infarction of bone do not differ from the appearance in other disorders associated with such complications. Subchondral infarction may be silent or associated with pain in the shoulder joint. Magnetic resonance imaging (MRI) is the most sensitive method of demonstrating the condition at an early stage, as plain film changes require 6 to 8 weeks to become evident and in the case of central medullary infarction identification of slight sclerosis during the revascularization process requires impeccable radiographic technique. If the process progresses, the subar-

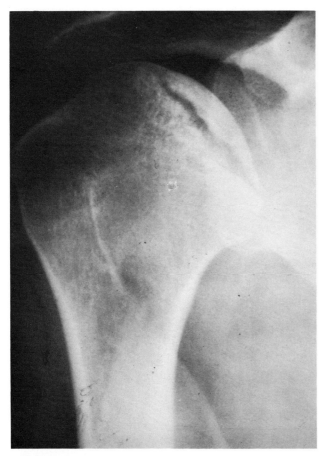

Figure 12-7 Cushing's syndrome. Hyperadrenocorticism in this 58-year-old woman led to progressive pain in her hip, which was shown to be due to osteonecrosis secondary to intraarticular injections of steroids over a period of 7 months. Similar changes in the humeral head were not associated with any symptoms, though osteonecrosis has been associated with subchondral fracture and dissection of the fragment. The sequence of events is rare if not unique.

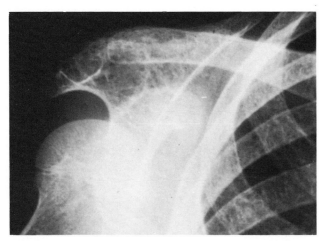

Figure 12-8 Beta thalassemia. Thin cortices and trabeculation of the medulla of all the bones shown are characteristic of this chronic hemolytic anemia. Note also the loss of the normal modeling of the clavicle as a consequence of the increased hematopoietic activity.

ticular segmental necrosis is complicated by fracture and a characteristic lucent line. The episode may progress to dissection and loose body formation (see Fig. 12-7).

Patients receiving steroid therapy have a higher incidence of infection, and there may be delay in diagnosis because of the relatively asymptomatic presentation. The radiologist has to be alert to recognize early infections of the bones or joints so that treatment can be instituted before irreparable damage has occurred. Early recognition of both osteonecrosis and infection is assisted by the use of bone scintigraphy or MRI, but the diagnosis has to be suspected before such imaging methods are likely to be used.

HEMATOLOGIC DISORDERS

The Hemoglobinopathies

THALASSEMIA

Thalassemia results from the production of too few alpha or beta globin chains, so that the first problem is congenital anemia, severe in the homozygous variety of the disease, less severe in the mixed thalassemic hemoglobinopathies, and least severe in heterozygotes who only carry the trait. Because of the need to combat the anemia, compensatory marrow hyperplasia results in relative expansion of the bone marrow at the expense of the cortex. The cortex becomes thinned, and the marrow expansion causes reduction of normal bony modeling with a more cylindrical shape to the long bones (Fig. 12-8), as in other marrow infiltrations such as Gaucher's disease. Occasionally marrow spreads to the subperiosteal regions, producing, through Sharpey's fibers, a brush border or hair-on-end appearance.

SICKLE CELL DISEASE

The anemia of sickle cell disease is less severe than that in thalassemia major, as there is not an absolute deficiency of hemoglobin production but only production of abnormal hemoglobin with a reduced life span. Changes of osteopenia and modeling defects, which relate to increased total mass of the hematopoietic marrow, are therefore seen less frequently than in thalassemia. The main clinical problem relates to the propensity for the blood corpuscles to sickle and sludge, mainly in the venous circulation, causing infarction in the bones (Fig. 12-9) and elsewhere. Secondary infection is common, resulting in osteomyelitis and septic arthritis. Changes in the shoulder girdle characteristically affect the medulla of the proximal humerus (Fig. 12-10) and the subchondral cortex and medulla of the humeral head (Fig. 12-11). Damage to the subchondral bone may lead to pre-

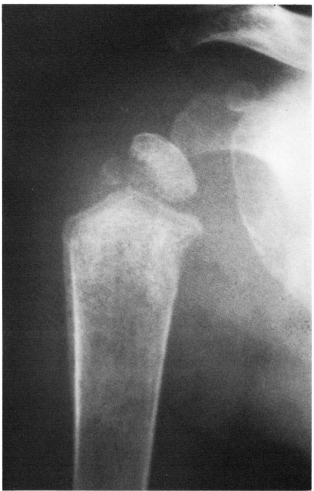

Figure 12-9 Effects of infarction in a child with sickle cell disease. Interference with growth at the humeral metaphysis has resulted in a zone of more normal bone separated from the sclerosis of medullary infarction. Note the continuity of this zone with the periosteal new bone formation on the lateral aspect of the proximal part of the shaft. On this single film it is difficult to determine whether the incident has affected the ossification of the two centers for the proximal end of the humerus. The notch on the medial aspect of the humeral metaphysis is probably a normal variant at this age.

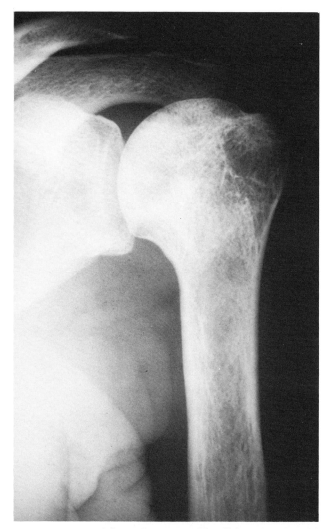

Figure 12-10 Medullary infarction in sickle cell disease. In this adult patient characteristic changes of osteonecrosis have produced sclerotic changes in the head and especially the subchondral bone. No fracture or collapse has supervened. The striation of the diaphyseal cortex and diminution of the corticomedullary differentiation are more likely to be due to disuse osteoporosis than to the hemoglobinopathy itself.

mature osteoarthrosis (Fig. 12-12). Changes on plain radiography, scintigraphy, computed tomography (CT), and MRI reflect those seen in osteonecrosis of other causes and the stage of evolution at which the process is at the time of imaging.

HEMOPHILIA

The brunt of articular bleeding in hemophilia seems to fall on hinge joints such as the knee, ankle, and elbow. Gross destruction does not appear to be common in the shoulder. Nevertheless, bleeding occurs in the shoulder joint from time to time in uncontrolled hemophiliacs, leading to disuse osteoporosis. If the bleeding is recurrent, pannus forms and undermines the articular carti-

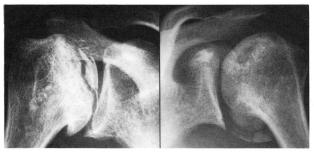

Figure 12-11 Sickle cell disease. This 41-year-old black American woman complained of generalized and prolonged articular pain and discomfort, mainly affecting the shoulder. A total arthroplasty of the right hip had been performed some years earlier. Evidence of disintegration of the humeral heads is shown consequent to osteonecrosis of the subarticular bone.

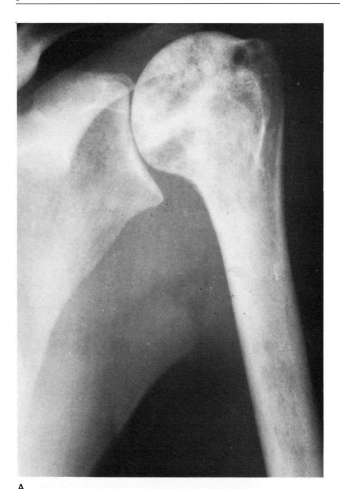

A

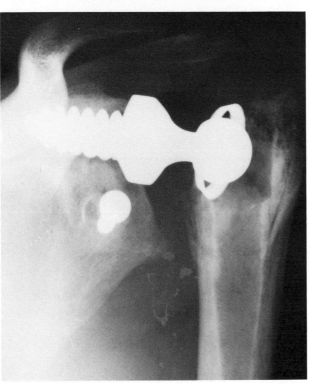

B

Figure 12-12 Sickle cell disease. **A.** In another patient, more extensive change is shown with the reduction in depth of articular cartilage. The patient was experiencing considerable pain by this time. **B.** A total shoulder arthroplasty (Kessel) has been performed.

lage, progressing to premature osteoarthritis (Fig. 12-13), which is indistinguishable radiologically from that of other causes.

Myeloid Metaplasia

A chronic myeloproliferative process, myeloid metaplasia is characterized by anemia, splenomegaly, immature blood cells in the circulation, and a variable degree of fibrosis in the bone marrow. Depending on the host response, the marrow fibrosis causes reactive sclerosis in the medulla that is demonstrable radiologically (Fig. 12-14). The sclerosis tends to affect the axial skeleton and, therefore, may be well-represented in the proximal

Figure 12-13 Secondary degenerative changes of hemophilia. Subluxation with loss of congruity is probably secondary to effusion. Osteophytes and subarticular cyst formation are also present in this young man whose first intraarticular bleed occurred before age 2 years. The shoulder is not one of the joints commonly affected in this way by hemophilia.

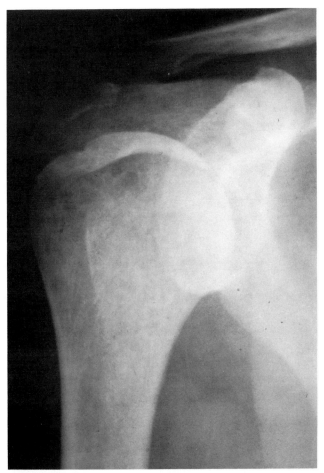

Figure 12-14 Myelosclerosis. The medulla shows increased sclerosis together with patchy lucencies as reaction to fibrosis within the marrow cavity.

end of the humerus. Sclerosis may be diffuse and relatively imperceptible in the first instance, but a coarse trabecular pattern is also encountered. A tendency exists for sclerosis to increase with time. Periosteal reaction may arise on the shafts of the long bones and could be due to secondary hemorrhage associated with thrombocytopenia.

MARROW DISORDERS: STORAGE DISEASES

Gaucher's Disease

This relatively common autosomal-recessive disorder was first described in 1882 by Phillipe Gaucher. It principally affects people of Jewish heritage, especially the European Ashkenazi Jews. As a result of an enzyme defect, excessive amounts of glucocerebrosides accumulate in the liver, spleen, and bone marrow, within the pathognomonic Gaucher cells. The first effect on bone dem-

onstrated in the skeletal radiograph is production of osteopenia as the bony trabeculae are resorbed; later, actual focal destruction may take place (Fig. 12-15). Finally, the packing of the marrow with Gaucher cells causes osteonecrosis (Fig. 12-16). In the growing skeleton the overgrowth of the marrow mass at the expense of the cortex causes defects in modeling such as the Erlenmeyer flask deformity of the distal femur. Such changes are less apparent at the proximal end of the humerus than in the distal end of the femur.

POISONS AND OTHER TOXIC EFFECTS

Lead Poisoning

Long-term absorption of lead by the growing skeleton has its major effect on the metaphyseal region of maximal growth. Though in the upper limb such changes are

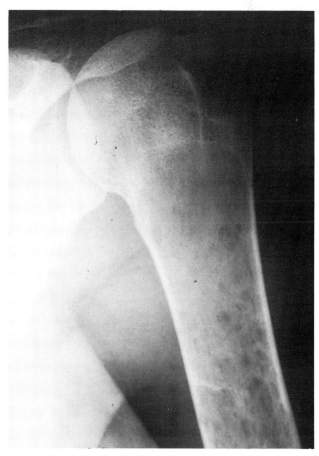

Figure 12-15 Gaucher's disease. Although changes are present in the humeral shaft, they are not specific. Slight widening of the proximal shaft is associated with an area of loss of normal trabecular pattern and featureless "ground-glass" sclerosis, probably a result of medullary infarction. At least some of the associated patchy lysis is due to osteoporosis.

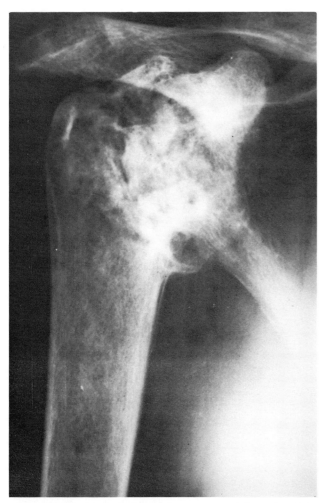

Figure 12-16 Gaucher's disease. Osteonecrosis of almost the whole of the humeral head has been complicated by central sclerosis and peripheral structural collapse. Periosteal reaction is present on the medial aspect of the surgical neck of the humerus.

Fluorosis

Globally, the most common form of skeletal poisoning, fluorosis occurs endemically in those parts of the world where the amount of fluorine in the drinking water is abnormally great. Other less common causes include industrial contamination and ingestion or inhalation of material containing fluorine. Relatively rare in childhood unless the fluorine content of the water is extremely high (> 15 ppm), the changes in the shoulder girdle are generally those of nonspecific bony sclerosis. Irregular formation of appositional new bone at tendinous attachments may be present (Fig. 12-18), and, of course, on a chest radiograph fringing of the inferior margins of the ribs may be apparent. The condition may also be encountered following inappropriate use of sodium fluoride in the treatment of post-menopausal osteoporosis.

Intoxication by Vitamin A and Its Analogues

Hypervitaminosis A was previously the result of well-intentioned self-medication and the theory that if small

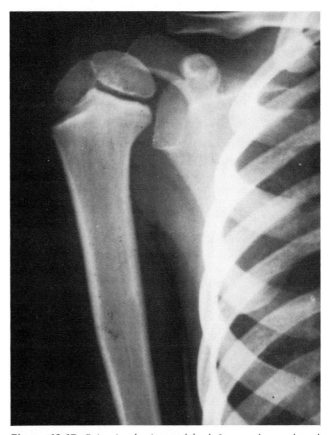

Figure 12-17 Poisoning by ingested lead. Increased metaphyseal sclerosis has occurred in this child as a reaction to incorporation of lead into the growing osteoid. Distinction from sclerosis of the normal growing metaphysis can be difficult, and it would be unwise to conclude abnormality without inspecting several metaphyseal regions.

more evident in the distal ends of the forearm bones, the proximal end of the humerus is also growing rapidly, and the changes may be evident on the chest radiographs of a child who is failing to thrive (Fig. 12-17). The metaphyses become abnormally sclerotic in proportion to the amount of lead absorbed. Intermittent absorption can lead to parallel sclerotic bands with intervening bone of normal density. The metaphyseal changes are not mediated directly by the lead, which is present in minute amounts, but by sclerosis reactive to its presence. Modeling defects are not usually apparent in the humerus, but they may be seen in the femur. Differential diagnosis includes the normal metaphyseal sclerosis of childhood, healed metaphyseal disease such as occurs in rickets and leukemia, and, of course, poisoning by other heavy metals. Such toxic effects, caused by ingestion of bismuth, mercury, or phosphorus, are nowadays excessively rare.

the changes to radiotherapy alone. Revascularization following radiation necrosis results in a diffuse increase in bone density with patchy areas of radiolucency (Fig. 12-19). The relatively minor changes disguise the significant effect on collagen and, through it, the strength of the bone. Pathologic fractures are a well-recognized complication. It is important to distinguish radiation osteitis from radiation-induced sarcoma.

ENZYME DISORDERS

Alkaptonuria (Ochronosis)

Ochronosis is a rare autosomal-recessive disease of amino acid metabolism that is due to deficiency of the enzyme homogentisic acid oxidase. It may be asymptomatic, but generally premature arthritis affects the spine, followed by the knees, shoulders, and hips. The common etiological feature is the early disappearance of articular cartilage as a consequence of its breakdown following deposition within it of homogentisic acid. Calcification

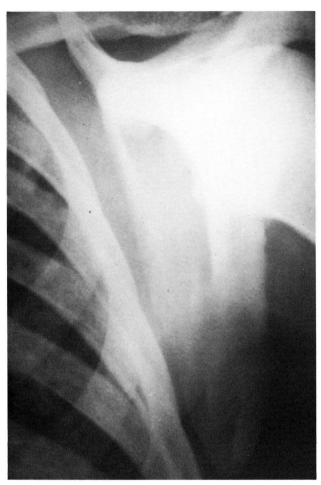

Figure 12-18 Fluorosis. The two typical features of fluorosis, bony sclerosis and irregular periosteal new bone formation, are shown here to affect the scapula particularly.

amounts of vitamin supplements are a good thing then more must be even better. Nowadays the introduction of retinoic acid derivatives as treatment for certain dermatologic disorders is a more likely cause of toxic effects of the same nature. Often vitamin A–intoxicated children present with failure to thrive as well as splaying and cupping of the metaphyses. Classically, the skeletal abnormalities consist of periosteal reactions and cortical thickening. In retinoid toxicity it is unlikely for the shoulder girdle to show major changes, as hyperostosis is generally most prominent in the axial skeleton.

Radiation Necrosis

The application of ionizing radiation to bone results in damage or destruction of the cellular elements of the bone marrow. The threshold dose for such effects is on the order of 3000 c Gy. Often osteopenia is the only detectable change, and, as the region may have been the site of preexisting osteoporosis, it is difficult to attribute

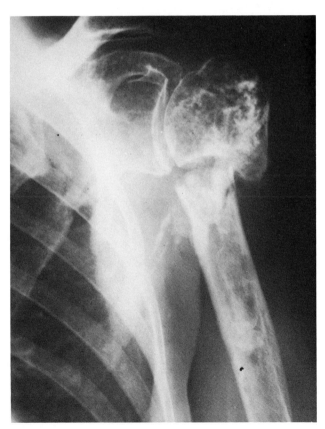

Figure 12-19 Postradiation necrosis. The effect of a large dose of radiotherapy to the axillary lymph nodes in this woman has been to cause radiation osteitis with medullary necrosis and a pathologic fracture of the surgical neck of the humerus. Dystrophic calcification is evident in the soft tissues.

develops relatively infrequently in the articular cartilage before it is destroyed. Radiologically, the articular cartilage space becomes narrowed, osteophytes and subchondral cysts form, and there is sclerotic eburnation of the underlying bone (Fig. 12-20), features shared by severe osteoarthrosis.

Homocystinuria

In this rare disorder of autosomal-recessive inheritance, the abnormality lies in the accumulation of homocystine in the blood and tissues, owing to a deficiency of the enzyme cystathionine synthetase. The disorder bears a passing resemblance to Marfan's syndrome in the 20 percent or so who exhibit arachnodactyly. In childhood about one-third have scoliosis, usually of mild degree. Osteopenia is common but is generally evident only in the axial skeleton, where the vertebral bodies tend to be

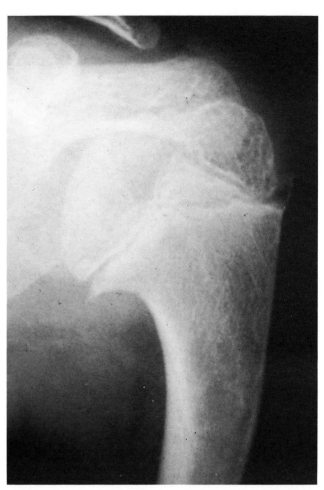

Figure 12-21 Homocystinuria. An enlarged epiphysis and a wide metaphysis are demonstrated. In this patient, some asymmetry of growth has led to a varus deformity and lateral bowing of the humeral shaft.

biconcave. In the upper limb enlargement of the humeral head, humerus varus (Fig. 12-21), a widened distal end of the ulna, and enlargement of the capitate and hamate have all been described.

Hypophosphatasia

The result of a deficiency of alkaline phosphatase, hypophosphatemia is generally classified as one of the metaphyseal chondrodysplasias. Three or four forms have been described according to the patient's age at presentation: neonate, infant, child, and adult. The differential diagnosis of the radiologic features of the severe neonatal form, consisting of gross undermineralization of the skeleton (Fig. 12-22), includes osteogenesis imperfecta and causes of short-limbed dwarfism. In later childhood, changes at the metaphyses of the limb bones mimic almost exactly those of severe rickets, although islands of incompletely ossified cartilage and osteoid may be incorporated into the diametaphysis, which does not

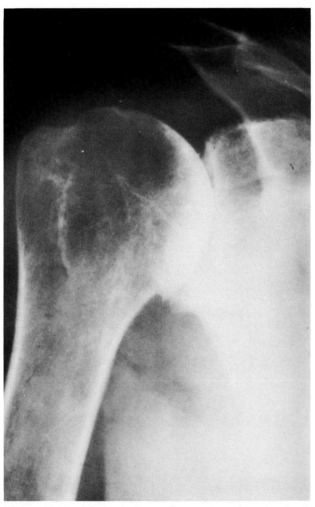

Figure 12-20 Ochronosis. Severe degenerative arthritis has developed as a consequence of loss of the articular cartilage following deposition of pigment in its deeper layers. The radiographic diagnosis cannot be made without, in addition, finding the characteristic degenerative changes in the intervertebral discs.

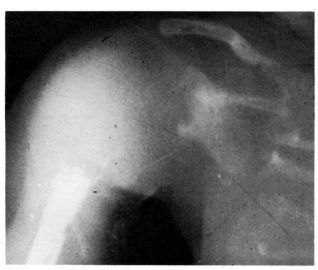

Figure 12-22 Hypophosphatasia. Gross undermineralization of the humeral metaphysis resembles severe rachitic changes. In addition, defects are evident in the cortex of both the humerus and the clavicle.

occur in rickets. The diagnosis is established biochemically from the low level of alkaline phosphatase in the blood and excessive amounts of phosphoethanolamine in the urine.

OTHER METABOLIC DISORDERS

Calcium Pyrophosphate Crystal Deposition

Calcium pyrophosphate crystal deposition is essentially a disorder of unknown origin, despite the wealth of papers on the subject. Chondrocalcinosis itself is an age-related phenomenon and often is asymptomatic and unsuspected in many middle-aged and elderly subjects. The development of acute or chronic arthralgia in a relatively small number of affected patients is attributed to the intermittent shedding of crystals into the synovial space and may be associated with a supervening chronic arthropathy. Although, as in many other arthritides involvement of the knees and hips is common, the shoulder and acromioclavicular joints are affected to a proportionately greater extent than in osteoarthritis not associated with chondrocalcinosis. Rarely, shedding of the crystals into the joints or bursae is associated with persistent mineralization of the synovial lining (Fig. 12-23).

Gout

Although primarily a joint disease, the metabolic element of gout, a disorder of uric acid metabolism, renders it a subject to discuss briefly here. As more than 80 percent of those who suffer acute attacks of gout have the great toe involved (even if other joints are also affected) di-

agnosis based on involvement of the synovial joints of the shoulder girdle is rare indeed. In fact, the involvement of proximal joints in any of the limbs is most uncommon, so that in the upper limb involvement of the hand, wrist, or elbow is predominant.

Mastocytosis

Mast cells occur in normal skin in small numbers, but in mastocytosis they are more numerous, causing a variety of clinical syndromes as a result. Systemic mastocytosis, in which the bones are affected, affects only a minority of persons who have cutaneous mastocytosis. It is most common in middle age but has been observed in early childhood. Multiple systems are affected, usually including skin involvement either by urticaria pigmentosa or more diffuse infiltrative involvement. Skeletal lesions may be present in as many as three-quarters of the patients and are often asymptomatic. For workers in the orthopedic field, however, the classical dermal presentations are seen less frequently, and it is often possible to come across a patient with bone involvement, symptomatic or asymptomatic, who has no other overt indication of systemic mastocytosis. The common radiologic pattern is some degree of medullary sclerosis of either a diffuse or finely nodular pattern. This pattern may vary with mixed lytic and sclerotic elements (Fig. 12-24), and rarely the bone involvement may simply show as generalized osteopenia.

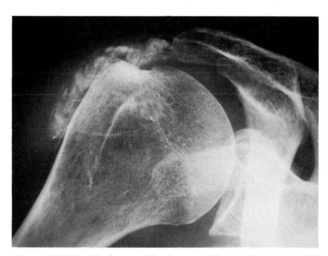

Figure 12-23 Calcification of subacromial bursa. This 53-year-old woman had had discomfort in her right shoulder for 5 years, but it became worse in the preceding 8 months. The radiograph shows outlining of the subdeltoid bursa by massive calcification. On exploration, the wall of the bursa was edematous and lined by some 20 plaques of chalky material. The underlying rotator cuff tendon was intact. As most calcification in the shoulder lies in relation to some tendinous elements of the rotator cuff, the etiology of the calcification here is unclear. Certainly, calcific deposits may rupture into the bursa, causing acute pain; these disseminations, however, tend to produce inflammation, and absorption of the calcium salts usually occurs.

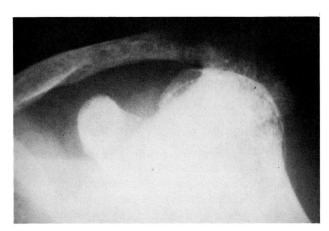

Figure 12-24 Mastocytosis. Both the clavicle and the acromion are affected. Loss of corticomedullary differentiation is associated with an abnormal mixed sclerotic and lytic pattern that constitutes a reaction to the mastocytic reaction in the marrow.

Amyloidosis

The accumulation of amyloid in the tissues is either primary, when in a proportion of patients it may precede the development of myelomatosis, or secondary, when it complicates certain chronic diseases, notably rheumatoid arthritis. Involvement of the skeleton often is associated with pain and thickening around joints—the hands, shoulders, and hips most commonly. As a result of either the primary disorder or the amyloid deposition, periarticular osteopenia is common. Discrete radiolucent defects are observed, particularly in the pelvis, shoulder, hands, and ribs. Deposition of amyloid in the soft tissues causes periarticular masses to be identified radiologically. Such a change around the shoulder has been referred to as the *shoulder pad sign.* The intraosseous deposits result in subchondral erosion and pseudotumor formation. They are quite a common cause of the subchondral destruction in arthritis mutilans of rheumatoid arthritis.

Patients on long-term hemodialysis for chronic renal failure are prone to develop amyloidosis, and the shoulder is the joint most often affected, being involved in one-third of patients.[2] More than one joint is involved in 40 percent of the patients. The frequency of the symptoms is proportional to the duration of dialysis, and such symptoms are almost universal after dialysis exceeding 20 years. Symptoms arise earlier in older patients. Radiologic changes are late to appear but sometimes are severe, with marked destructive changes of the humeral head and glenoid fossa.

Hepatolenticular Degeneration (Wilson's Disease)

As Wilson's disease is a generalized disorder due to a congenital disturbance of copper metabolism, it is best

mentioned here, though the skeletal element of the disorder generally presents as a polyarthropathy. Wilson's disease is inherited as an autosomal-recessive trait, and often the neurologic signs and symptoms of tremor, muscle rigidity, and dysarthria, together with changes in affect, are evident in adolescence, although patients may first be affected at an older age. Radiologically, there is generalized osteopenia due to a combination of osteomalacia (or rickets) and osteoporosis due to the renal tubular disease.

Radiologic changes in the joints consist of a subtle irregularity of the surface of the subchondral bone, progressing in about half the patients to a characteristic fine-fringed border. More destructive changes may occur, but they are most commonly seen in the joints of the lower limbs, wrists, and hands. Ultimately, when destruction of articular cartilage supervenes, apart from their distribution, these changes cannot be distinguished from those of other forms of degenerative joint disease.

Unless the articular picture is itself pathognomonic, the diagnosis is generally suspected by correlation of the disorder in three systems and is confirmed by the demonstration of the Kayser-Fleischer ring caused by deposition of copper pigment around the cornea. Final confirmation is achieved by the demonstration of high copper levels in the tissues and the decrease of ceruloplasmin, the copper-binding protein, to about 10 percent of its normal value.

Hemochromatosis

In hemochromatosis, a chronic disorder of iron metabolism, the osteoarticular effects are due to the deposition of hemosiderin in the soft tissues. The disease may be primary, an autosomal-recessive disease exhibited usually by homozygotes, or in older patients it can be due to iron overload of chronic anemia and multiple transfusions of whole blood. Cirrhosis of the liver and diabetes mellitus are probably inevitable without control of iron metabolism; the pigmentation of the skin caused by hemosiderin deposition accounts for the descriptive term *bronzed diabetes.*

The earliest signs on the skeletal radiography relate to a nonspecific arthropathy with periarticular swelling and osteoporosis. Changes are most often seen early in the joints of the hands, especially the second and third carpometacarpal joints. Involvement of the hips, shoulders, and other large joints tends to be delayed. Chondrocalcinosis, a common feature, affects at least half the patients, and it often heralds the progressive destruction of the affected joints. Crystal deposition also affects fibrocartilage such as the intraarticular disc of the acromioclavicular joint. An additional characteristic feature of the arthropathy is the relatively early formation of small subchondral cysts. The changes are, however, very similar to those observed in calcium pyrophosphate dihydrate

(CPPD) deposition disease and ultimately lead to end-stage degenerative arthritis (Fig. 12-25).

SOME CONGENITAL OSTEOCHONDRODYSPLASIAS

The diagnosis of these disorders cannot and must not be made on the basis of regional radiographs; a full skeletal survey is always required as well as a good history of clinical milestones and defects in other systems. Nevertheless, the shoulder girdle often reflects the general pattern of the dysplasia. In the growing child any deformity in modeling is usually associated with retardation of ossification, and this combination differentiates the disorder from a pure retardation of growth and ossification such as one might expect with thyroxine deficiency.

Achondroplasia

In achondroplasia, the commonest of the nonlethal short-limbed bone dysplasias, rhizomelic shortening of the

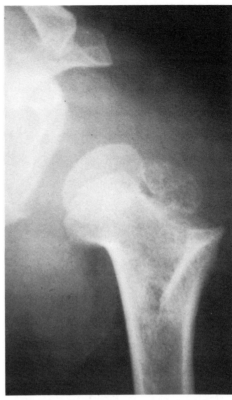

Figure 12-26 Achondroplasia. The effects of restriction of diaphyseal growth result in relative broadening of the proximal end of the humerus, which almost resembles the proximal femur.

limbs is evident. Although the ends of the long bones, such as the proximal end of the humerus, appear enlarged, they are normal in size and just seem to be big because of the shortened diaphysis. Delayed ossification is observed at the ends of the long bones with sometimes a scooped-out metaphysis filled with abnormal uncalcified cartilage (Fig. 12-26).

Cleidocranial Dysplasia

Although associated with widespread skeletal anomalies, cleidocranial dysplasia gains its name from the cardinal features of hypoplastic clavicles and defective ossification of the membranous bone of the calvaria. In the mildest of cases, failure of modeling of the clavicles may be all that is seen radiologically. More often, a part of each clavicle is absent (Fig. 12-27). Complete absence of both clavicles has been reported. The anomaly is sometimes asymmetric and confusion with earlier fracture and resorption must be avoided. The diagnosis is confirmed by the presence of wormian bones and other skeletal anomalies.

Multiple Epiphyseal Dysplasia

The diagnosis of multiple epiphyseal dysplasia, as the diagnosis of most dysplasias, depends on demonstration of the defect in ossification at multiple sites. It must be

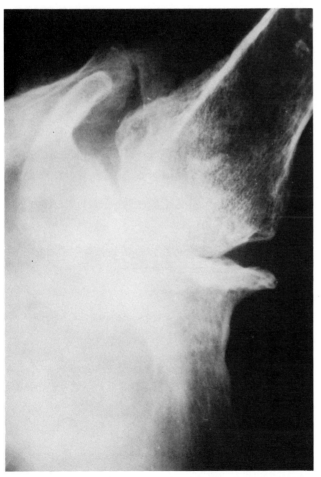

Figure 12-25 Hemochromatosis. The changes are those of premature osteoarthritis. Although there are no diagnostic features of hemochromatosis, osteoarthritis is relatively rare in the shoulder, and specific causative factors should always be suspected and excluded.

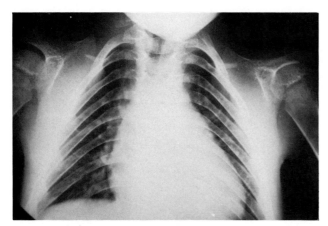

Figure 12-27 Cleidocranial dysplasia. Neither clavicle has developed except for a hypoplastic element of each middle third. Although clavicular abnormality is characteristic of this disorder, the extent of the abnormality varies and is not always symmetric.

rare for the shoulder to be the presenting joint, as this privilege is usually accorded the weight-bearing joints of the lower limb, especially the hips and knees, where symptoms occur earlier as a result of weight-bearing.

When the humeral head is significantly affected it generally becomes rather flattened, losing its hemispheric contour and the clear distinction from the tuberosities through a well-defined anatomic neck (Fig. 12-28). In assessment of the shoulders of 50 patients with multiple epiphyseal dysplasia, Ingram found bilateral symptoms in one-third.[3] Two distinct clinicoradiologic groups were found: (1) those with hypoplastic "hatchet head" humeri, who had had minimal glenohumeral movement since an early age and developed painful symptoms in the fifth or sixth decade of life, and (2) those with relatively minor developmental epiphyseal abnormalities who nevertheless developed pain in the shoulders from osteoarthritis at a mean age of 55 years.

SOME OTHER CONGENITAL DISORDERS

Congenital Indifference to Pain

In this rare condition, almost as soon as the child begins to crawl and walk, the parents notice that painful stimuli fail to produce a normal response. The child may severely damage or burn the fingers unless care is taken to protect him or her from injury. Later on, fractures are frequently incurred, and the only clinical indication is deformity or swelling. The main dangers are these:

1. Gross or multiple fractures, sometimes as a consequence of bravado such as jumping from heights.
2. Stress fractures and especially metaphyseal fracture separations simulating nonaccidental injury.

3. Neuropathic response of joints or fractured long bones (Fig. 12-29).
4. Osteomyelitis and other forms of unappreciated sepsis such as suppurative arthritis or severe dental sepsis.

Enchondromatosis (Ollier's Disease)

The abnormality of enchondromatosis relates to the production of masses of hypertrophic cartilage arising initially in the metaphyseal regions but with growth causing deformity in the diametaphyses. Bulbous expansion may demonstrate some similarity to diaphyseal aclasia, but unlike that dysplasia, no hereditary basis exists. The lesions tend to be monomelic and are particularly florid where growth is maximal, as at the proximal end of the humerus (Fig. 12-30).

Fibrodysplasia Ossificans Progressiva

Although this inherited disorder (autosomal-dominant with frequent sporadic mutations) is classified with the congenital diseases, its disabling features stem from the production of soft tissue swellings, which progress to ossification. It might therefore be considered a disorder

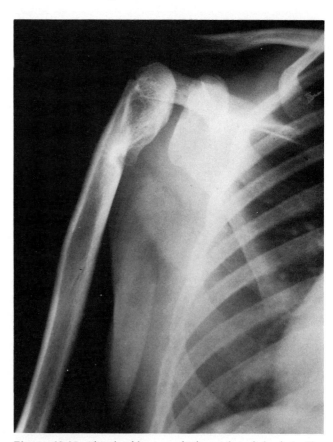

Figure 12-28 The shoulder in multiple epiphyseal dysplasia. The development of the head and proximal shaft of the humerus is grossly abnormal, so that the humeral head is hypoplastic and lacks normal articular congruity with the glenoid fossa. The diagnosis can be substantiated only by demonstrating sequelae of epiphyseal dysplasia in other joints.

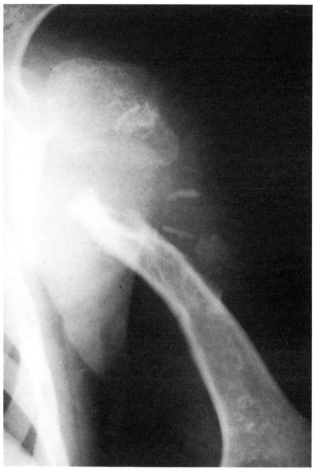

Figure 12-29 Congenital indifference to pain. In this rare congenital disorder the sufferer may injure himself severely without being aware of the trauma. This child sustained a fracture of the surgical neck of the humerus which progressed to nonunion, probably because he continued to use the arm almost normally.

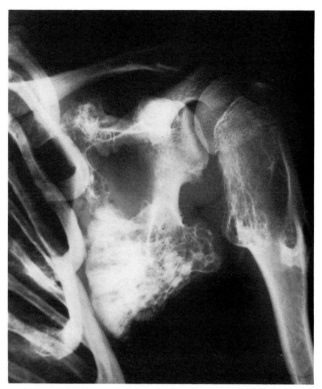

Figure 12-30 The shoulder in enchondromatosis. Multiple enchondromatous lesions with elements resembling cartilage-capped exostoses have produced considerable deformity of the proximal humerus and scapula with secondary effects on the rib cage.

of bone formation; however, the short first metacarpals and other digital abnormalities, coupled with a significant incidence of mandibular condylar dysplasia and possibly mild dysplasia of other joints, suggest that it is more than a simple disorder of bone metabolism.

In terms of the shoulder girdle, there does not seem to be any direct involvement. The presence of soft tissue ossification is extremely common on the surface of the thorax, and osseous struts often stretch across the axilla to reach the proximal humerus (Fig. 12-31).

GRANULOMATOUS DISORDERS

Langerhans' Cell Histiocytosis (Histiocytosis X)

Histiocytosis X, which in many ways resembles an infection but for which no causative agent has yet been found, has been somewhat arbitrarily divided into three clinicoradiologic syndromes: Letterer-Siwe disease, Hand-

Schüller-Christian disease, and eosinophilic granuloma. The latter, consisting of single or scanty skeletal lesions, is the only syndrome likely to be encountered that is confined to the shoulder girdle. The disease begins as well-differentiated lytic lesions involving cortex and medulla. Spontaneous healing leads to periosteal reaction

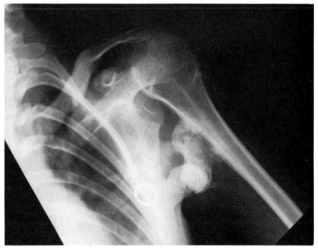

Figure 12-31 Fibrodysplasia ossificans progressiva. A bar of bone extends from the thorax to the humeral shaft, where it has initiated a periosteal reaction. Synostosis followed, making the shoulder the site of extraarticular ankylosis.

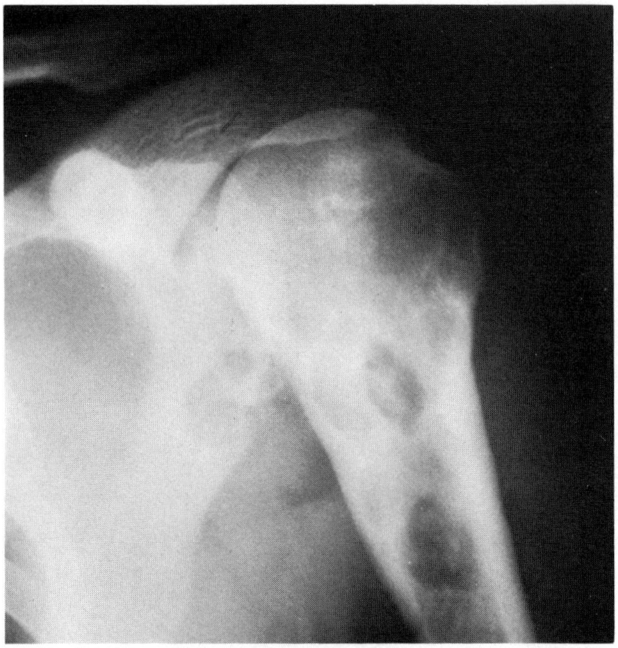

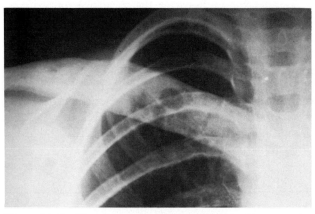

Figure 12-32 Histiocytosis of the humerus. A collection of destructive lesions is present in the proximal shaft. Reactive sclerosis has been initiated, and at several locations endosteal scalloping has occurred. With this healing lesion the main element in the differential diagnosis is pyogenic osteomyelitis. However, solitary lesions of Langerhans' cell histiocytosis at an earlier stage may mimic a benign neoplasm or even a malignant one.

and reactive endosteal sclerosis (Fig. 12-32). The larger lesions may show central reossification at the same time that the process is occurring at the edges of the granuloma.

Differential diagnosis includes infection, neoplasms, and lymphoma. Although not all these lesions take up bone-seeking radionuclides, bone scintigraphy is worth undertaking in attempting to demonstrate another focus. CT and MRI tend to rule out major soft tissue masses.

Chronic Granulomatous Disease of Childhood

Although chronic granulomatous disease is infectious, the unusual host response can lead to misdiagnosis of a metabolic disorder or a multicentric neoplasm. The pathogen tends to be some catalase-positive organism, a common one such as *Staphylococcus aureus* or *Escherichia coli* or a less common one like *Serratia marcescens* or *Candida*. These pathogens are engulfed by neutrophil leukocytes, which are unable to destroy them and release toxins that initiate a low-grade granulomatous process. The intracellular location of the organisms gives some protection from the action of systemically administered antibiotics. Most infections are of the skin, lungs, and lymph nodes; osteoarticular infections are found only in about 25 percent of affected patients.

A variety of groups of the disorder are described. The original group affected, which gave the disease an undeservedly poor prognosis, was in male infants who showed X-linked recessive inheritance. Involvement in later childhood and adolescence tends to produce low-grade inflammatory skeletal lesions, often multiple, metaphyseal, and relatively symmetric ones. Septic arthritis is rarely encountered in these patients. The low-grade indolent nature of the infection often produces only minor discomfort and minimal constitutional disturbance.

Radiologically, though we are dealing here with the skeletal system, it is important to identify other sites of infection in the chest, skin, and lymph nodes. Skeletal lesions tend to be sclerotic and associated with formation of a variable amount of periosteal new bone. (Fig. 12-33). Trephine biopsy by the radiologist is worth undertaking, but it must be remembered that the changes are produced by relatively small numbers of organisms deep in the bone. The problem should be explained to the microbiologist so that every effort is made to culture the organism. To this end the laboratory should be provided with a core of bone for culture and not just the washings that are left after the major part of the biopsy specimen has been sent to the histopathologist.

MISCELLANEOUS DISORDERS

Infantile Cortical Hyperostosis

Described in 1945 by Caffey and Silverman,[4] many cases of infantile cortical hyperostosis were described during the following three decades. It then almost disappeared, but nowadays sporadic cases are again being encoun-

Figure 12-33 Chronic granulomatous disease. This girl presented at age 8 years with radiographic evidence of chronic sclerosing osteomyelitis of the distal humerus. Subsequently, she developed evidence of osteomyelitis at all four metaphyses adjoining the knee joints and the clavicle, as shown here. The features are those of chronic recurrent osteomyelitis, and the patient and her twin sister, who was similarly affected, were shown to have the "lazy leukocyte syndrome." Such immune deficiency disorders have to be considered in all cases of multiple and symmetric osteomyelitis of childhood.

tered. Diffuse cortical hyperostosis develops in the first 6 weeks of life in a febrile, irritable infant. Characteristically the mandible and ribs are affected, but both the clavicle and the scapula (Fig. 12-34) may be, simulating, in the involvement of a single bone, osteomyelitis or even a primary neoplasm. Diagnosis depends on considering the possibility of the disease, finding multiple lesions, and the fact that the other disorders mentioned in the differential diagnosis are extremely rare in the first few months of life.

Paget's Disease

A disease of unknown origin, Paget's shows a regional pattern yet no familial trait, so the evidence that it is due to a slow virus is strong. The disease affects middle-aged and elderly adults, particularly in northern Europe, the northeastern United States, and Australia. A strong preponderance of males is affected.

Radiologically, lytic and progressively sclerotic phases are found. No part of the skeleton is spared, but the pelvis and proximal femurs, spine, and skull are all particularly prone to the disease. Involvement of the shoulder girdle (Fig. 12-35) seems to be rather less frequent

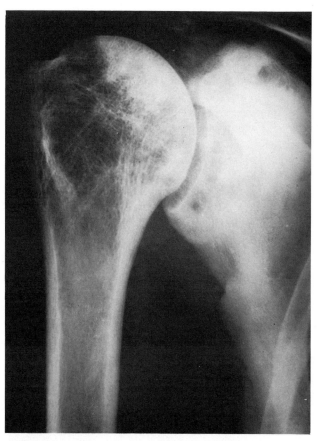

Figure 12-35 Paget's disease. The disease is involving both sides of the glenohumeral joint. In the humeral head some sclerotic change affects the subchondral bone, and there is coarsening of the trabeculae of the medulla. The glenoid process, however, shows dense sclerosis, and some enlargement of the scapula and its processes has occurred.

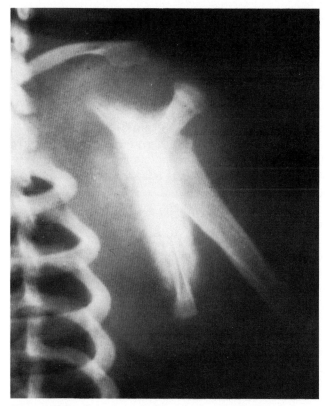

Figure 12-34 Infantile cortical hyperostosis (Caffey-Silverman disease). This 2-month-old infant developed a painful swelling of the left scapula and was at the same time feverish and irritable. Abundant periosteal new bone formation affects the whole of the blade of the scapula. Similar hyperostosis was found to affect the mandible and several ribs shortly afterward, establishing the diagnosis.

than involvement of the pelvic girdle. In its most characteristic appearance, the radiologic diagnosis is not difficult and biopsy is not necessary. On the other hand, a solitary lesion of the sclerotic form of the disease showing little or no expansion of the bone in a patient suspected of having metastatic carcinoma can erode the radiologist's confidence in the diagnosis and prompt a demand for biopsy.

Fibrogenesis Imperfecta Ossium

An extremely rare disorder, fibrogenesis imperfecta ossium was first described by Baker and Turnbull in 1950.[5] It suggested a defect in the formation of collagen apparently confined to lamellar bone. Most patients are between age 50 and 70 years, and a pathologic fracture is a frequent cause for presentation, though skeletal pain without fracture is common as well. Radiologically the appearance is characteristic and can be seen in the shoulder girdle on a plain AP chest radiograph, though the changes in the pelvic girdle are often more striking. The contour of the bone is not altered, but trabeculae are reduced in number and thickened, producing a coarse "fishnet" appearance (Fig. 12-36). Periosteal reaction may occur with appositional new bone forming at tendinous insertions.

The general histopathologist provided with a decalcified section may have difficulty making any diagnosis. With a nondecalcified section, the diagnosis of osteomalacia may seem likely. It is only when the specimen is examined with the polarizing microscope and following staining for reticulin that the collagen fibers are shown to be abnormal and deficient, lacking the normal birefringency. Since the original description, patients with the disease have been shown to have a monoclonal gammopathy, which in certain cases has responded to treatment with melphalan resulting in temporary restoration of normal bone architecture.[6]

Tumoral Calcinosis

A rare disorder of soft tissue, tumoral calcinosis is characterized by the deposition of calcific masses, mainly in

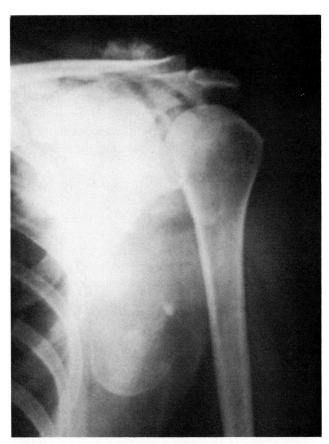

Figure 12-37 Tumoral calcinosis. Periarticular calcification is shown. That in the lower part of the axilla shows a curvilinear element to its lower border, possibly indicating calcified debris within a semicystic space. Such changes are found not infrequently, and nowadays can best be demonstrated with CT and MRI.

the extracapsular region of joints. The groin and axilla (Fig. 12-37) are particularly favored. Most of the early cases were reported from southern Africa or New Guinea, and black patients still predominate. Initially painless, the masses may cause symptoms by pressing on adjoining structures, and ulceration with sinus formation may supervene.

Individual masses tend to be enclosed in a fibrous capsule. The tissue is multicystic, each cystic space holding creamy fluid containing calcific material. The cystic nature of the lesion can often be demonstrated by CT or MRI, enabling the diagnosis to be made before surgery. Otherwise the diagnosis has to be made by excluding other conditions associated with soft tissue deposition of calcium salts. Biochemically, hyperphosphatemia is often found, but the serum calcium, alkaline phosphatase, and parathyroid hormone levels are all normal.

Dermatomyositis

A generalized disease mainly of adult women, dermatomyositis has its main effect on skeletal muscle, producing inflammation initially and later atrophic aseptic myositis.

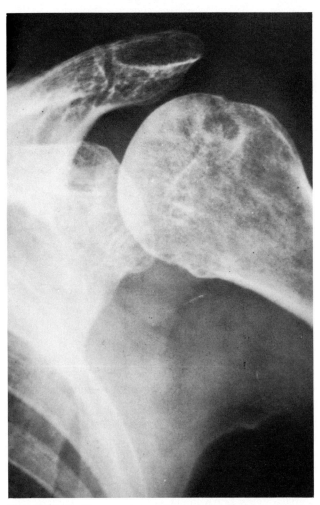

Figure 12-36 Fibrogenesis imperfecta ossium. The shape and cortices of the bones of the shoulder girdle are normal, but the medulla shows gross coarsening of its trabecular pattern.

Necrosis follows, and with it dystrophic calcification due to deposition of hydroxyapatite crystals within the affected muscle groups (Fig. 12-38). Despite the fact that juvenile patients with the disease account for only about 15 percent of cases, 40 to 60 percent of this age group show calcification as compared with some 5 percent of adults. Radiography contributes little to diagnosis of the disease, as, by their very nature, the radiographic changes are evident only in the later stages.

Fibrous Dysplasia

Fibrous dysplasia, a disorder of unknown origin, can be monostotic, pauciostotic, or polyostotic. The polyostotic

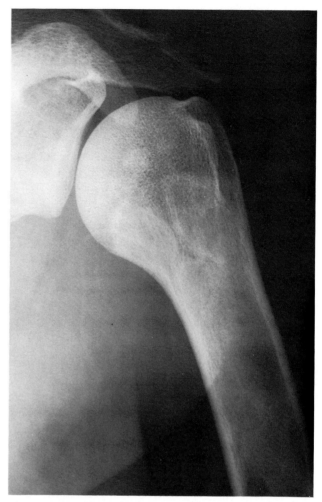

Figure 12-39   Fibrous dysplasia. Although this patient suffered from the polyostotic form of the disease, the changes in the humerus resemble the milder type of monostotic involvement, with no distortion of the bone and medullary sclerosis of the "ground-glass" type.

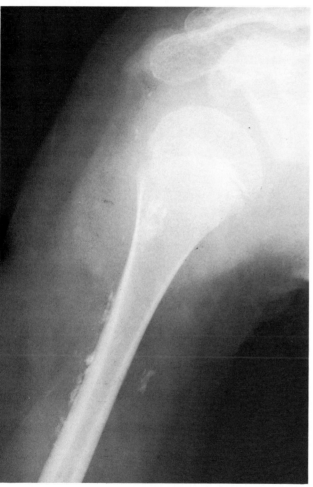

Figure 12-38   Dermatomyositis. The bones are normal though some muscle wasting has occurred. Calcification is present in the soft tissues, and some periosteal new bone formation has occurred on the shaft of the humerus.

variety differs from the other two in its widespread involvement of the skeleton and its occasional association with certain endocrine disorders. Monostotic fibrous dysplasia affecting the shoulder girdle is relatively uncommon, and even in the polyostotic disease a lower limb and its girdle is more commonly affected than an upper limb. Lesions of polyostotic disease, though frequently bilateral, are not symmetric, and one side generally is more extensively affected. Involvement varies from gross deformity to textural change in the medulla, in which case the individual lesions resemble those of the monostotic variety of the disorder (Fig. 12-39).

References

1. BOULIS ZF, DICK R: The greater tuberosity of the humerus: An area for misdiagnosis. *Australas Radiol* 26:267–268, 1982.

2. KURER MHJ, BAILLOD RA, MADGWICK JCA: Musculoskeletal manifestations of amyloidosis: A review of 83 patients on haemodialysis for at least 10 years. *J Bone Joint Surg* 73B:271–276, 1991.

3. INGRAM RR: The shoulder in multiple epiphyseal dysplasia. *J Bone Joint Surg* 73B:277–279, 1991.

4. CAFFEY J, SILVERMAN WA: Infantile cortical hyperostosis: Preliminary report on a new syndrome. *AJR* 54:1, 1945.

5. BAKER SL, TURNBULL HM: Two cases of a hitherto undescribed disease characterised by a gross defect in the collagen of the bone matrix. *J Pathol Bacteriol* 62:132–133, 1950.

6. STAMP TCB, BYERS PD, ALI SY, ET AL.: Fibrogenesis imperfecta ossium; remission with melphalan. Lancet *i*:582–583, 1985.

13 RHEUMATIC DISORDERS OF THE SHOULDER: IMAGING PRINCIPLES

Serge Sintzoff
Serge Sintzoff II

Rheumatic diseases are a wide spectrum of disorders ranging from the common soft tissue rheumatic syndromes to uncommon life-threatening connective tissue diseases such as polyarteritis nodosa.[1] Many of the diseases present with similar features, so it can be difficult to make an accurate diagnosis in the early stages and a high index of suspicion is required, as the glenohumeral joint is deep in tissue. In its general meaning, the term *arthritis* indicates an abnormality of the joint that reflects a degenerative, inflammatory, infectious, or metabolic process, each of which belongs to the corresponding group of arthritic disorders, including the connective tissue arthropathies such as systemic lupus erythematosus and scleroderma.

GLENOHUMERAL JOINT OSTEOARTHRITIS

The glenohumeral joint may be affected by almost any form of arthritis, but shoulder manifestations are rarely the dominant feature of the disease. Monoarticular processes do occur occasionally; probably the most common is osteoarthritis secondary to degeneration of the rotator cuff. Neurotrophic and infectious arthritis are relatively frequent.

Primary osteoarthritis of the glenohumeral joint, in the absence of an underlying or associated cause, is rare. The typical radiographic findings are asymmetric narrowing of the joint space, subchondral sclerosis of bone, and marginal spur formation, commonly on the inferior aspect of the glenoid, and the medial and inferior margins of the humeral head. At times the spurs arising from the humeral head can be quite large.

Before accepting the diagnosis of primary osteoarthritis of the glenohumeral joint, one should rule out calcium pyrophosphate deposition disease (CPPD). Degenerative or osteoarthritic changes in the glenohumeral joint are more commonly secondary to some preexisting condition, particularly previous trauma (Fig. 13-1) and, less commonly, avascular necrosis of the humeral head (Figs. 13-2, 13-3) or disturbances of epiphyseal growth due to juvenile rheumatoid arthritis or congenital malformation syndromes. A common underlying cause of secondary osteoarthritis is deterioration and disruption of the rotator cuff, which results in characteristic superior displacement of the humeral head with respect to the glenoid cavity, narrowing—and, on occasion, obliterating—the space between the humeral head and the acromion. The lower surface of the acromion becomes concave. Subchondral sclerosis of the opposing margins occurs with occasional subchondral cyst formation (Fig. 13-4). Other causes of secondary osteoarthritis are ochronosis, acromegaly, and hemophilia.

IMPINGEMENT SYNDROME AND ROTATOR CUFF PATHOLOGY

Impingement syndrome is a relatively common condition in which the soft tissues constituting the subacromial space (i.e., supraspinatus tendon, biceps tendon, and subacromial bursa) are chronically entrapped between the humeral head and the acromion. Bone excrescences extending from the anterior portion of the acromion or the acromioclavicular joint (Fig. 13-5) or in the coracoacromial ligament itself may contribute to the impingement syndrome (Fig. 13-6, page 379). Inflammation and subsequent degeneration of soft tissues result and may progress to complete disruption of the rotator cuff. Neer has identified three progressive pathologic stages of impingement and has stated that 95 percent of rotator cuff tears result from the impingement syndrome. Stage I consists of edema and hemorrhage in the tendon and is potentially reversible with conservative treatment. In Stage II, thickening and fibrosis of the subacromial soft tissues occur, and treatment, including acromioplasty and bursectomy, is controversial (see Fig. 13-6). Stage III represents complete rotator cuff tears, biceps tendon

375

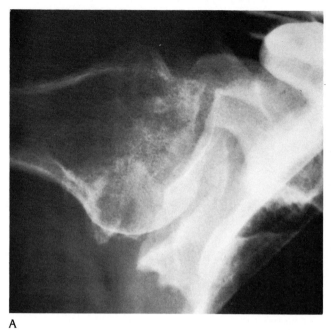

A

B

Figure 13-1 **A.** and **B.** Glenohumeral osteoarthritis following fracture of the humeral head and glenoid process.

rupture, and osseous abnormalities (Figs. 13-7, 13-8, page 380). Repetitive activities such as swimming or pitching predispose to overuse of the arm and result in chronic subacromial loading, and ultimately rotator cuff injury. Additionally, there is a zone of relative avascularity within the supraspinatus tendon just proximal to its insertion on the greater tuberosity that also predisposes to the development of tendinitis with overuse. Early and correct diagnosis of the impingement syndrome may allow proper intervention and direct appropriate therapy before complete disability results.

As the impingement syndrome is a continuous pathologic process, both clinical symptoms and magnetic resonance imaging (MRI) findings vary from mild tendinitis to complete tendon rupture. Careful analysis of osseous and soft-tissue components must be undertaken to assess accurately the progressive changes associated with this syndrome. Bone findings include excrescences arising from the inferior margin of the acromion or acromioclavicular joint as well as hypertrophy of the acromioclavicular joint (Fig. 13-9, page 381) and depression of the acromion with respect to the clavicle. These bony abnormalities result in depression of the supraspinatus tendon and may also cause secondary changes in the greater tuberosity as with abduction of the arm

the humeral head makes contact with these structures. Cystic and sclerotic changes can occur in the greater tuberosity and appear as foci of low-signal on all MRI sequences, of low signal in T1-weighted sequences (bone sclerosis), and high signal in T2-weighted ones (cysts) (Fig. 13-10, page 381).

With continued entrapment of the subacromial bursa and supraspinatus tendon, changes occur in these structures. These are manifested on MRI as thickening of the subacromial bursa, thinning of the supraspinatus tendon, and abnormally increased signal within the tendon that is indicative of tendinitis. Further damage to the supraspinatus tendon is manifested as partial or small full-thickness tears (Figs. 13-11, 13-12, page 382). Findings characteristic of full-thickness rotator cuff tears as seen by MRI include fluid within the subacromial bursa (bright on T2-weighted images), increased signal within the supraspinatus tendon on T2-weighted images (consistent with fluid within a tear) (Figs. 13-13, 13-14, page 382), and loss of the normal signal of the fat plane that surrounds the subacromial-subdeltoid bursa. Musculotendinous retraction at the margins of the tear also may be demonstrated, and an effusion may be detected within the glenohumeral joint.

Partial-thickness tears involve only the upper or lower

surface of the rotator cuff tendons. MRI allows detection of these tears, though sometimes they may be mistaken for full-thickness tears. Distinguishing between upper and lower partial tears is difficult; assessing secondary signs (fluid within the subacromial bursa and loss of the peribursal fat plane) as well as primary signs (abnormal signal within the tendon and disruption of the tendon) may help in making this distinction. Many authors have demonstrated the accuracy of MRI in the identification of the full spectrum of rotator cuff disease. Most recently, Zlatkin and colleagues found MRI to be more sensitive and specific than arthrography in diagnosing rotator cuff tears.

INFLAMMATORY ARTHRITIS

Rheumatoid Arthritis

Rheumatoid arthritis is a generalized inflammatory disease that affects many systems of the body but that pre-

sents through involvement of synovial tissues, producing an inflammatory arthritis that is frequently both destructive and progressive. The cause is unknown. A variety of infectious agents (diphtheroid organisms, mycoplasmas, viruses) have been considered, but so far without proof. The disease is often regarded as an autoimmune phenomenon because of the frequent presence of circulating antibodies to normal immunoglobulins, referred to as *rheumatoid factor*. An increased incidence of HLA antigens of the DR4 type in patients with rheumatoid arthritis may indicate an inherited defect of immune regulation.[2] Rheumatoid arthritis is a common condition, but it varies much in severity and rate of progression. It occurs in the range of 1 to 2 percent of the population in the United States, so at least 4,000,000 patients are affected by this disease. Under age 60, women are more often affected than men by a ratio of 3 to 1. After age 60 the sex distribution is about equal. Male patients tend to have a better outcome, and the rate of spontaneous remission is proportionately higher in males.[3]

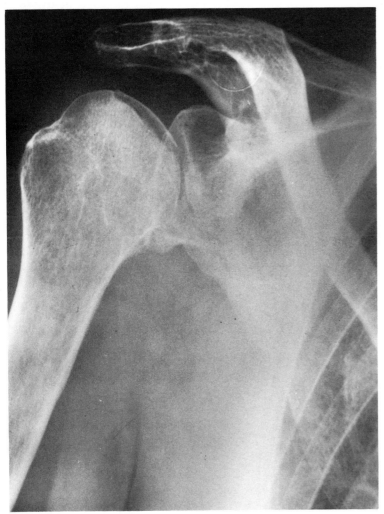

A

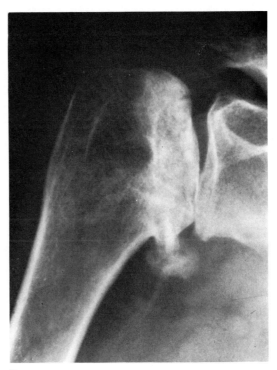

B

Figure 13-2 **A.** and **B.** Glenohumeral osteoarthritis secondary to avascular necrosis.

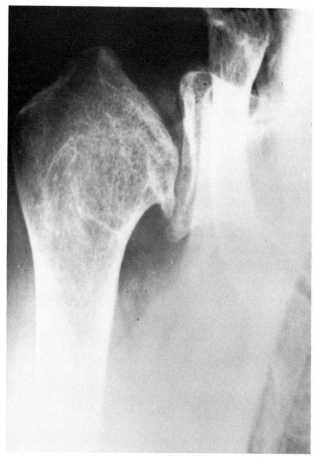

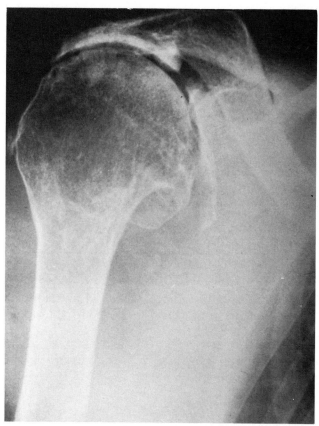

Figure 13-4 Glenohumeral osteoarthritis following long-standing tear of the rotator cuff. The subacromial space is narrowed.

Figure 13-3 Glenohumeral osteoarthritis secondary to avascular necrosis. (Stage IV.)

Figure 13-5 Impingement syndrome. An osseous excrescence arises from the acromioclavicular joint.

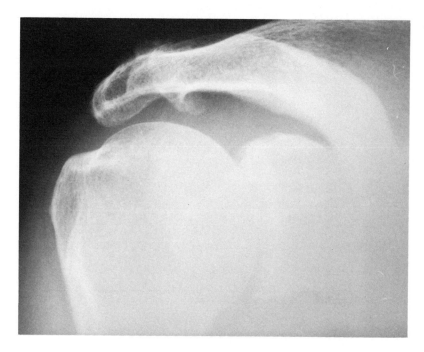

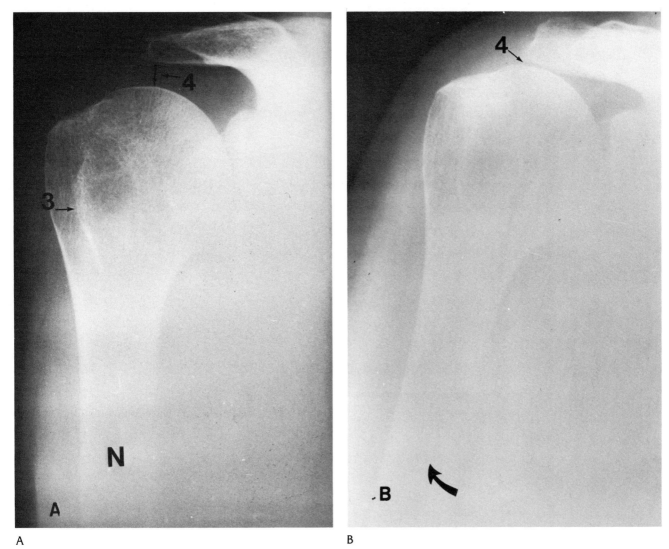

A   B

Figure 13-6 A. Acromioplasty following Neer (N). Greater tuberosity (*arrow*); lesser tuberosity (3); subacromial space in neutral position (4). **B.** Leclercq's test. Abduction below 20 degrees against force (*curved black arrows*). Loss of the subacromial space (*arrow* and 4) indicates complete supraspinatus tendon tear.

Some patients are affected so mildly that, if medical advice is sought at all, it is sought only late in life because of secondary degenerative joint disease. At the other end of the spectrum, the disease may be acute and progressive, particularly in the relatively rare forms recognized in children and adolescents (Still's disease).

CLINICAL PRESENTATION

The majority of cases of rheumatoid arthritis have a slow, insidious onset; symptoms develop over several months.[4] Middle-aged women are predominantly affected. Early in the course of the disease the joints develop pain, tenderness, swelling, and stiffness, often with mild, transient pyrexia. Associated subacromial bursitis can result in prominent soft tissue swelling. Acute exacerbation of clinical symptoms is related to synovial rupture of the joint.

The erythrocyte sedimentation rate is elevated, and serologic tests for rheumatoid disease are usually positive when the disease is polyarticular. As a rule, the younger the patient, the more aggressive is the disease. Later stages may be marked by joint deformities, even ankylosis, although secondary degenerative changes are a common outcome. Atrophy of bones, muscles, and skin may occur.

In the acromioclavicular joint, rheumatoid involvement is manifested as pain, tenderness to direct palpation, and local soft tissue swelling. In the coracoclavicular region, the pathogenesis of erosion along the undersurface of the distal part of the clavicle, usually 2 to 4 mm from the distal end, is unclear.[5] Probably, it is due to inflammation.[6]

RADIOGRAPHIC-PATHOLOGIC CORRELATION

The initial joint abnormality in rheumatoid arthritis is an inflammatory change in the synovial tissue. In the normal

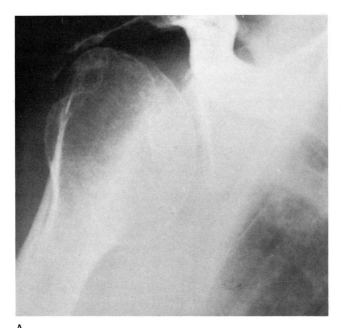
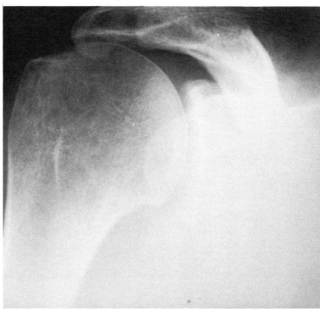

A   B

Figure 13-7 **A.** and **B.** Stage III. Complete rotator cuff tear produces loss of the subacromial space.

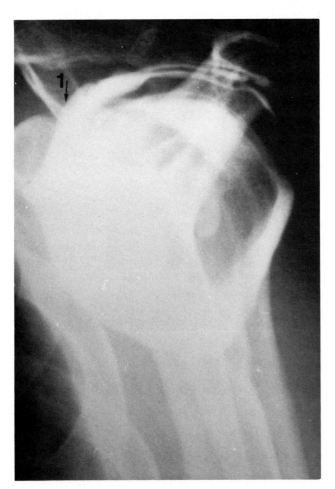

Figure 13-8 Arthrography demonstrates a complete supraspinatus tendon tear in the sagittal plane (*arrow*). The initial point of the tear is indicated (*1* and *arrow*).

joint, synovium secretes a lubricating and nutrient fluid that is rich in hyaluronic acid. Inflammation in joints involved by rheumatoid arthritis is characterized by infiltration with lymphocytes, macrophages, and neutrophils, producing proliferation of the highly vascular connective tissue in the synovium. The thickened synovial tissue spreads over the articular joint surfaces as pannus and fills the synovial cavity.[7]

Both cell-mediated and humeral immunity are involved in the pathogenesis of rheumatoid arthritis. Synovial lymphocytes synthesize immunoglobin, including anti–immunoglobulin G (IgG), the rheumatoid factor. Lymphokines secreted by synovial T cells attack and activate monocyte-macrophages. The activated monocyte-macrophages then secrete proteases and collegenases that destroy the articular cartilage. Other mediators of rheumatoid arthritis include leukotrienes, superoxides, and prostaglandins. The synovium invades bone to produce the erosions that initially are seen at the margins of the joint, where cartilage is absent (bare areas). It progresses to destroy cartilage and bone and damage joint capsule, ligaments, and tendons.

Progressive involvement of the tendon of the rotator cuff leads to cranial displacement of the humeral head, narrowing of the subacromial space, secondary acromiohumeral osteoarthritis with sclerosis, cyst formation, and loss of the normal convex shape of the lower aspect of the acromion. It is a possible cause of late secondary glenohumeral arthritis.

The radiographic pattern includes periarticular osteoporosis due to hyperemia and loss of the subdeltoid fat plane, which is an indirect sign of soft tissue swelling.

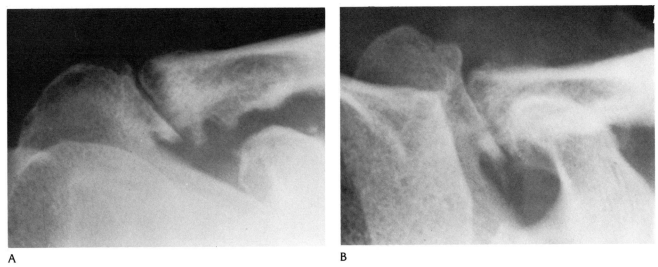

Figure 13-9 **A.** and **B.** Impingement syndrome associated with acromioclavicular joint hypertrophy.

Diffuse loss of articular space appears on plain film; focal synovial lesions appear only on MRI. Marginal erosion, generally in the superolateral aspect of the humeral head in the vicinity of the greater tuberosity, appears in the first 2 years in 90 percent of patients (Figs. 13-15, 13-16).[6] Particularly characteristic are superficial irregularities, deep erosive changes, and cystic erosive changes on the superolateral aspect adjacent to the greater tuberosity[5] that are different from Hill-Sachs compression fracture but similar to the marginal erosions of other synovial processes such as ankylosing spondylitis (Fig. 13-17). Progressive destruction of the chondral surface of the glenoid cavity and humeral head leads to deformities of the articular surface (Fig. 13-18) and to diffuse

loss of joint space, which may be accompanied by subchondral cystic lesions, osteophytes, and sclerosis (Fig. 13-19, page 385).[5] Deep erosion on the medial aspect of the surgical neck is related to abnormal pressure from the adjacent glenoid margin (Fig. 13-20, page 385).[5] The long biceps tendon produces sudden acute pain or a chronic pattern of pain caused by a soft tissue mass on the upper aspect of the tendon, with retraction of the distal segment.

IMAGING TECHNIQUES

Plain films: loss of the subdeltoid fat plane in early phase; osteoporosis, erosion. *Ultrasonography:* effusion in the subacromial bursa and the glenohumeral joint. Partial or

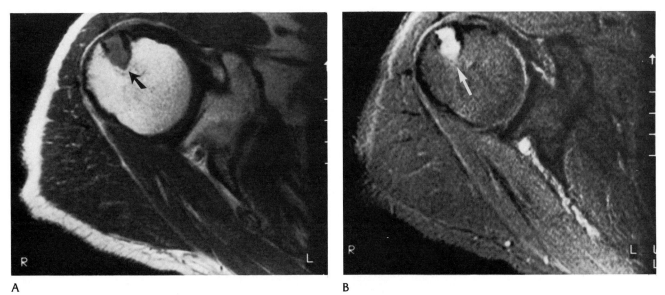

Figure 13-10 Impingement syndrome. A cystic area is visible in the greater tuberosity. **A.** Low signal intensity on T1-weighted MR image. **B.** High signal intensity on T2-weighted image.

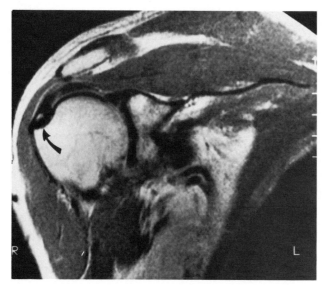

Figure 13-11 Partial inferior tear of supraspinatus tendon (*arrow*) on T1-weighted MR image.

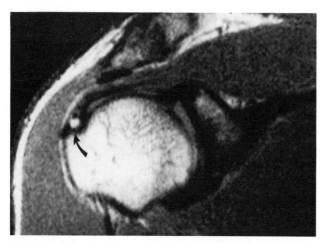

Figure 13-12 Partial tear of the supraspinatus tendon (*arrow*) on T1-weighted MR image. Impingement of musculotendinous junction by subacromial spur.

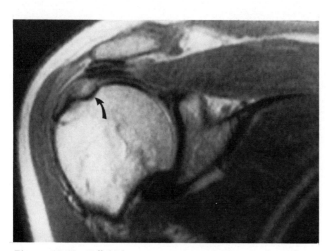

Figure 13-13 Full-thickness supraspinatus tendon tear (*arrow*).

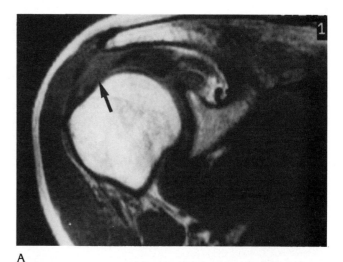

A

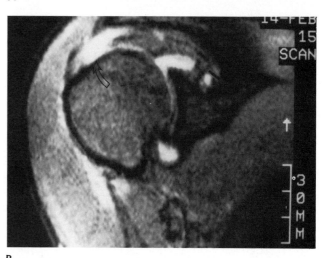

B

Figure 13-14 Full-thickness supraspinatus tendon tear (*arrows*) on **A,** T1-weighted and, **B,** T2-weighted MR images.

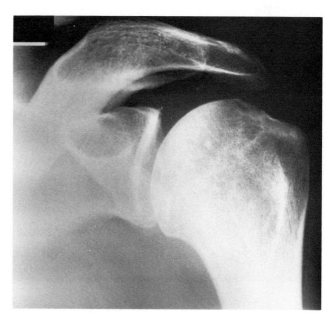

Figure 13-15 Marginal erosion in front of the greater tuberosity.

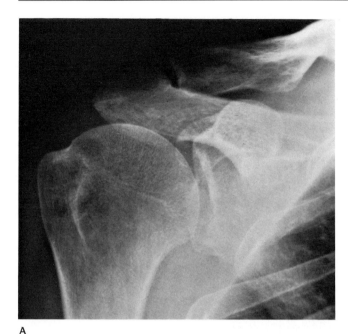

A

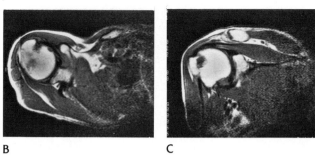

B   C

Figure 13-16 Rheumatoid arthritis. A small erosion is demonstrated with MRI. **A.** On an AP film a small erosion of the greater tuberosity is visible. **B.** Two erosions are demonstrated by a T1-weighted MR image in the axial plane. **C.** In the coronal oblique plane the same erosions are demonstrated on a T1-weighted image.

total tear outside the acromial arch. *Arthrography:* partial inferior or complete rotator cuff tear, synovial cyst and sinus tracts, and synovial changes during treatment. *Scintigraphy:* a sensitive method for evaluating disease activity. Technetium pertechnetate and technetium phosphate scans outline joint inflammation, which may antedate clinical activity, and can be used to monitor therapy. *Computed tomography* (CT): is not required to assess the distribution and extent of joint involvement in rheumatoid arthritis; MRI is the technique of choice.

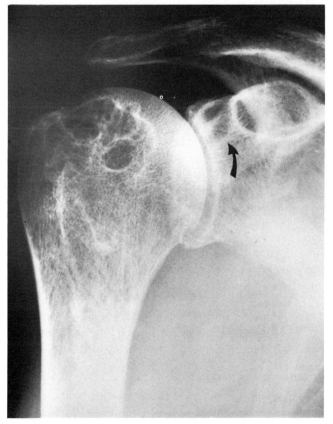

A

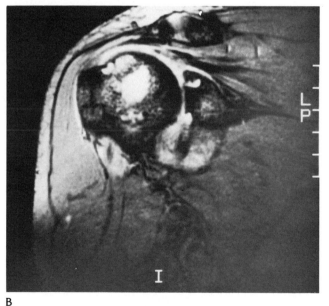

B

Figure 13-17 **A.** On a plain film, deep cystic erosion is visible adjacent to the greater tuberosity and in the glenoid process. **B.** T2-weighted MR image.

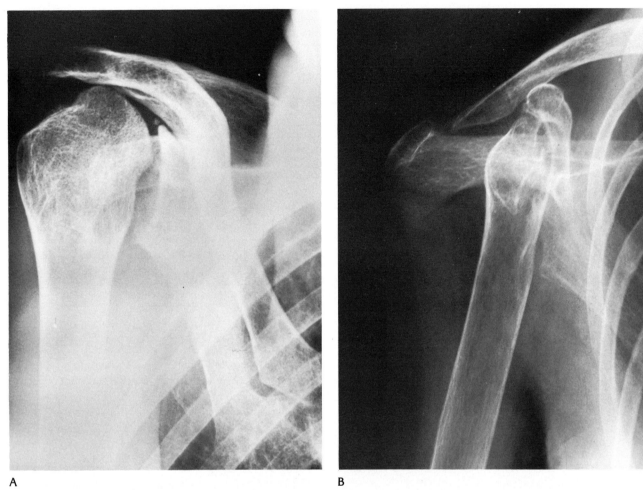

A   B

Figure 13-18   **A.** and **B.** Rheumatoid arthritis. Progressive deformities are visible on the articular surface.

Rheumatoid Variants

ANKYLOSING SPONDYLITIS

The estimated prevalence of ankylosing spondylitis is approximately 0.1 percent in the population at large but higher among blacks.[8] The reported ratio of the disease in men versus women varies from 4 to 1 to 10 to 1, as it is more subtle and difficult to diagnose in female patients. Young adult males are particularly affected. The HLA B27 incidence is 90 percent. With the exception of the hip, the glenohumeral joint is the most frequently affected periarticular site in patients with long-standing ankylosing spondylitis.[8] The changes involving the glenohumeral and the acromioclavicular joints and the upper aspect of the coracoclavicular attachment, which are more commonly bilateral, may occur without involvement of any other appendicular site, simulating rheumatoid arthritis (osteoporosis, diffuse joint space loss, margin erosion in the superolateral aspect of the humeral head, rotator cuff tear) (Figs. 13-21, 13-22).

In contrast to the synovial lesions of rheumatoid ar-

thritis, those of ankylosing spondylitis are less destructive. Severe involvement of the capsules, tendons, and ligaments ultimately leads to both bone production and ankylosis in some instances with intact joints.[9] Histologic examination during active bone erosion reveals a subacute inflammation of the soft tissue and the bone followed by replacement of the joint structures by granulation tissue. Eventually the granulation tissue becomes fibrotic, and metaplastic cartilage and bone form.[10]

Capsular ossification appears to be the primary event. It may then be followed by enchondral ossification and conversion of articular cartilage to bone as a result of disease.

More specific are destruction of the entire outer aspect of the humerus, *the hatchet sign*,[8] and proliferative alteration accompanying the erosion of the clavicle that is a clue to accurate diagnosis (see Fig. 13-21).

PSORIATIC ARTHRITIS

Dermatologic manifestations of psoriasis may be encountered in as many as 4 percent of the population.[11]

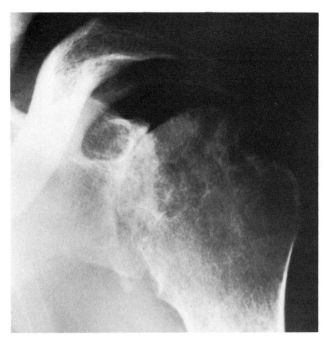

Figure 13-19 Rheumatoid arthritis, late stage. Diffuse loss of glenohumeral space with cystic lesions, osteophytes, and sclerosis are evident.

Articular manifestations are relatively uncommon, their estimated prevalence in the range of 2 to 6 percent.[12]

HLA B27 is present in half these patients. The absence of serologically detectable rheumatoid factor is important, as the clinical manifestations mimic rheumatoid arthritis, with the same pain and stiffness.

Psoriatic arthritis differs from rheumatoid arthritis by its asymmetric or unilateral distribution and from Reiter's syndrome, which predominantly involves the lower extremities. Psoriatic arthritis combines many radiographic features of rheumatoid arthritis, in which synovial inflammation predominates, and ankylosing spondylitis, in which ligamentous inflammation predominates (Fig. 13-22). Thus, although the early manifestations of psoriatic arthritis may be restricted to synovium-lined joints, the inflammatory process eventually involves both synovium and ligaments in at least a quarter of all patients.[13]

Bilateral asymmetric shoulder involvement may occur. Soft tissue swelling is succeeded by marginal erosions, and ultimately surface erosions. The subchondral bone tends to undergo destruction in a uniform manner over the entire articular surface.[14] As in the hands and feet, the erosions are ill-defined and are frequently associated

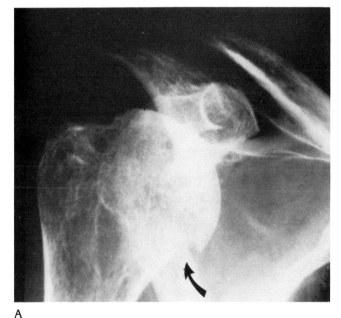

A

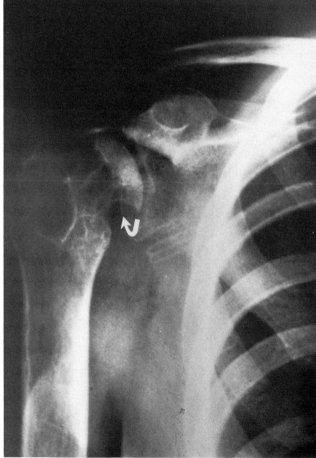

B

Figure 13-20 Erosion on the medial aspect of the surgical neck of the humerus. **A.** Cystic erosion (*arrow*) is visible adjacent to the greater tuberosity. **B.** Deep cystic erosions (*arrow*).

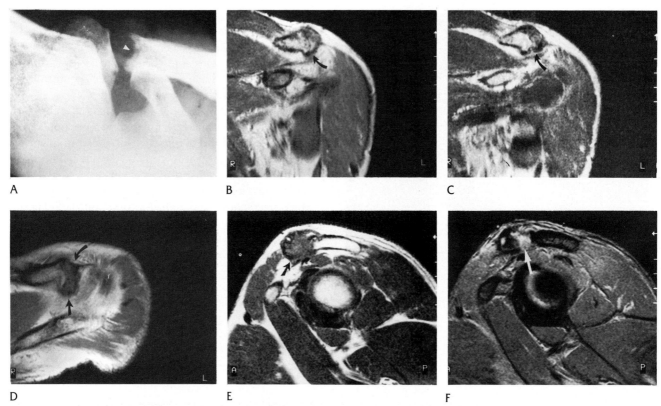

Figure 13-21   Ankylosing spondylitis of the acromioclavicular joint. **A.** On plain film, erosion (*white arrow head*) and bone production simulate rheumatoid arthritis. **B.** MRI, coronal oblique plane, T1-weighted image, erosions and granulation tissue (*black arrow*). **C.** MRI coronal oblique plane T2-weighted image, erosions and granulation tissue (*black arrow*). **D.** Axial plane T1-weighted MR image, granulation tissue (*black curved arrows*). **E.** Sagittal plane T1-weighted image, granulation tissue and effusion (*black arrow*). **F.** Sagittal plane T2-weighted image, articular effusion (*white arrow*).

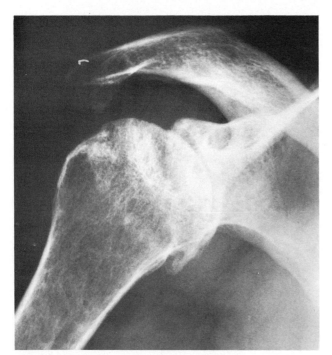

Figure 13-22   Late-stage ankylosing spondylitis simulating rheumatoid arthritis except for less prominent osteoporosis. Diffuse glenohumeral joint space loss, diffuse sclerosis surrounding cystic lesions, and marginal osteophytes are evident.

with exuberant periosteal new bone formation. Osteoporosis may be mild or absent.

The articular symptoms may be acute or insidious. Subcutaneous nodules are not evident. Additional clinical manifestations may include fatigue, fever, and ocular symptoms such as conjunctivitis, iritis, and scleritis. The changes that affect the joints' synovial membranes are comparable to those observed in rheumatoid arthritis. Significant abnormalities of the hip and shoulder are relatively uncommon, and there are fewer changes in the small joints of the hands and feet.

The radiographic presentation varies from minor degrees of osseous erosion to extensive osteolysis with adjacent bone eburnation (Fig. 13-23).[15]

As in the other seronegative spondyloarthropathies, proliferation is a striking feature of psoriatic arthritis, as is periostitis in the metaphyses and diaphyses.

REITER'S SYNDROME

Reiter's is a rare syndrome, a classic triad of arthritis, nonspecific urethritis, and conjunctivitis. It has long been regarded as a venereal disease of young men. It appears likely that the disease may be transmitted in association with either epidemic dysentery or sexual intercourse.[16]

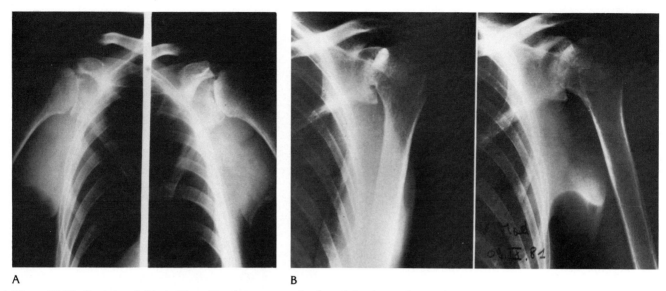

Figure 13-23 Psoriatic arthritis. **A.** Bilateral involvement, complete loss of glenohumeral space, osseous erosions, and bone eburnation are evident. **B.** Osseous proliferation of the inferior glenoid margin is present.

It is the major connective tissue disease reported to date in patients with acquired immunodeficiency syndrome (AIDS) and AIDS-related complex (ARC).[17] Eye involvement, however, often is lacking, and urethritis may be replaced by inflammatory conditions of the bowel such as ulcerative colitis or Crohn's disease.

Reiter's disease, similar to psoriatic arthritis, manifests a strong association with the histocompatibility antigen HLA B27 in three-quarters of patients. It differs from ankylosing spondylitis in its more classic involvement of the peripheral joints. Reiter's syndrome tends selectively to involve the lower limbs, particularly the feet, whereas psoriatic arthritis tends to affect the joints of the upper limbs as extensively as those of the lower limbs.[18] Many similarities exist between Reiter's disease and psoriatic arthritis. In both cases osteoporosis is usually minimal or absent; periosteal new bone is often fluffy and irregular and is especially common at bony prominences, and there are tendinous calcifications and ossification.[19] Histologic study of affected synovium reveals an appearance similar to that of rheumatoid arthritis.

ENTEROPATHIC ARTHRITIS

Musculoskeletal manifestations are frequently associated with disorders of the gastrointestinal system. Peripheral joint arthralgias and arthritis accompany ulcerative colitis, Crohn's disease, and Whipple's disease. Radiographic features are minimal and not specific. Intestinal bypass surgery and intestinal infections related to *Salmonella, Shigella,* or *Yersinia* species can lead to polyarthritis. In biliary cirrhosis arthritis is associated with xanthomas. Pancreatic disorders may manifest themselves as subcutaneous nodules, skin lesions, and polyarthritis (probably related to fat necrosis), epiphyseal and diametaphyseal

infarction, and skeletal metastases. The radiographic features of inflammatory bowel disease are identical to the changes of classic ankylosing spondylitis.

CONNECTIVE TISSUE ARTHROPATHIES

Systemic Lupus Erythematosus

Systemic lupus erythematosus is a relatively common connective tissue disorder characterized by involvement of multiple organ systems. Though the cause remains unknown, a variety of precipitating events appear to be involved, including genetic and infectious factors. The clinical presentation is variable, being related to the distribution and the extent of alterations in the skin and in the musculoskeletal, neural, renal, and cardiopulmonary systems.[20]

Musculoskeletal abnormalities include myositis (30 to 50 percent of patients), symmetric polyarthritis, joint effusion, and synovial inflammation, though the latter two findings are less common than in rheumatoid arthritis. Radiographic features of uncomplicated synovitis in systemic lupus erythematosus simulate rheumatoid arthritis (soft tissue swelling and periarticular osteoporosis). The difference is that the lytic periarticular lesions do not resemble the marginal erosions of rheumatoid arthritis. Generally, the joint space is not narrowed.

It is difficult to relate spontaneous tendon weakening and rupture to systemic lupus erythematosus, since all patients receive steroids. Osteonecrosis has been associated with Raynaud's phenomenon and other signs of vasculitis and with physical activity. The pathogenesis is unclear but it may be related to the duration, total dose, or initial dose of corticosteroids.[21] The radiographic and pathologic features of osteonecrosis are not specific to systemic lupus erythematosus.

The occasional occurrence of bone necrosis in unusual sites such as the shoulder should suggest systemic lupus erythematosus as a possible diagnosis (Fig. 13-24). Several patterns of soft tissue calcification are described: (1) juxtaarticular diffuse linear, striking or nodular, and (2) single or multiple deposits of various sizes, which usually are located in the soft tissue or, more rarely, in the joint capsule.

Progressive Systemic Sclerosis (Scleroderma)

Scleroderma leads to characteristic musculoskeletal abnormalities owing to involvement of skin, subcutaneous tissue, muscles, bones, and joints. Many of the clinical manifestations are radiographically illustrated by soft tissue atrophy calcification, and bone resorption. Diffuse subcutaneous calcification with widespread periarticular and intraarticular calcification occur, along with bone resorption in the clavicle, acromion, and humerus. Synovial calcification may be apparent in tendon sheaths and bursae.[22] Abnormalities of the synovial membrane consist of inflammatory changes similar to those of early rheumatoid arthritis.

Dermatomyositis and Polymyositis

These disorders of unknown cause are characterized by inflammation and degenerative changes in muscle. A variety of clinical patterns affects both children and adults.[23] The radiographic findings—soft tissue edema, atrophy, contracture, calcification, and possibly articular erosion and subluxation—resemble those of other collagen diseases, including scleroderma and systemic lupus erythematosus. The most characteristic and frequent soft tissue calcification occurs in children. The extent of calcification increases with the severity of the disease. The appearance and distribution of subcutaneous calcifications simulate the punctate and curvilinear deposits of scleroderma (Fig. 13-25).

CRYSTAL-INDUCED DISEASES

Gouty Arthritis (Monosodium Urate Crystal Deposition Disease)

Idiopathic gout is a disorder of purine metabolism characterized by hyperuricemia in which crystals of sodium urate are deposited in a variety of tissues, particularly the joints. It affects some 10 to 20 males for every female, usually persons older than 40 years, and has no ethnic

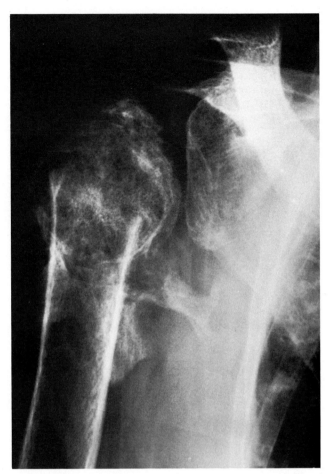

Figure 13-24   Systemic lupus erythematosus produces humeral head necrosis and juxtaarticular soft tissue calcifications.

predilection[24] except for inhabitants of the Mariana Islands and the Maori of New Zealand.[25]

Secondary hyperuricemia, sometimes with symptoms of gout, may be associated with a variety of other diseases, including some rare hereditary disorders (glycogen storage disease, Lesch-Nyhan syndrome), myeloproliferative disorders (particularly leukemia), certain endocrine disorders, or treatment with diuretics, salicylates, and pyrazinamide.

Radiographic changes are not common in the glenohumeral or acromioclavicular joints but when observed, they include soft tissue swelling and typical gouty tophi, well-circumscribed and rounded osteolytic areas occur near, but often remote from, articular surfaces at nonsynovial areas, in contrast to rheumatoid arthritis. Calcification of tophi, which is unusual, appears as irregular or cloudlike dense areas. The joint space is remarkably well-preserved until late in the course of articular disease with extensive cartilaginous and osseous destruction. In advanced disease the extensive erosion of bone produces severe arthritis that may be mistaken radiographically for rheumatoid or psoriatic arthritis.

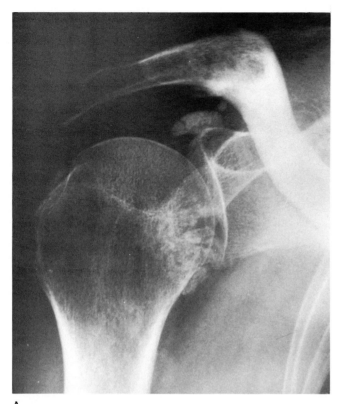

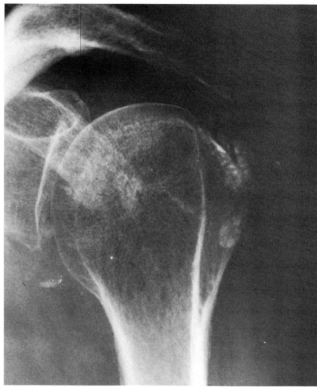

A   B

Figure 13-25 **A.** and **B.** Dermatomyositis. The appearance and distribution of calcifications mimic other collagen diseases, including scleroderma and systemic lupus erythematosus.

Loss of bone density is not characteristic. This is helpful in differentiating the condition from rheumatoid arthritis. Gouty erosions produced by tophaceous deposits may be intraarticular. The overhanging edge is a frequent identifying feature because of its sharply defined, punched-out appearance, elevated bony margins that extend into the soft tissue,[26] and the normal appearance of the uninvolved bone and cartilage. Acromioclavicular involvement produces irregular splaying of the distal end of the clavicle.[27]

Calcium Pyrophosphate Dihydrate Crystal Deposition Disease

Calcium pyrophosphate dihydrate crystal deposition disease results from the presence of calcium pyrophosphate dihydrate (CPPD) crystals in joint tissues. The sex distribution is equal. Most patients are middle-aged to older. *Chondrocalcinosis* is the asymptomatic presentation. The symptomatic form is called *pseudogout.*

Chondrocalcinosis is characterized by the presence of calcium salts in the hyaline and fibrocartilage of one or more joints. Synovial, capsular, tendinous, and soft tissue calcifications may also be associated. The calcium compounds involved include CPPD, dicalcium phosphate dihydrate, and calcium hydroxyapatite. CPPD deposition

disease is a general term used to describe disorders characterized by the presence of CPPD crystals in or around joints. *Pseudogout* is used to describe the acute or chronic inflammatory synovitis induced by the presence of CPPD crystals in the joint. Cartilage calcification may or may not be radiographically detectable. Pyrophosphate arthropathy, also due to the deposition of CPPD crystals, typically is associated with characteristic features that permit it to be differentiated from degenerative joint disease not associated with CPPD deposition. Calcium pyrophosphate arthropathy refers to CPPD crystal deposition disease affecting the joints and causing structural damage in the articular cartilage.

In an effort to explain the relationship between chondrocalcinosis, calcium pyrophosphate arthropathy, and the pseudogout syndrome, Resnick has proposed that the terms be integrated under the heading *CPPD crystal deposition disease.*[28]

Chondrocalcinosis is a condition in which calcification of the hyaline (articular) cartilage or fibrocartilage occurs. It may be seen in other conditions as well, such as gout, rheumatoid arthritis, hyperparathyroidism, hemochromatosis, hepatolenticular degeneration (Wilson's disease), systemic lupus erythematosus, ochronosis, acromegaly, hemophilia, and degenerative joint disease secondary to trauma or infection. In the absence of chondrocalcinosis,

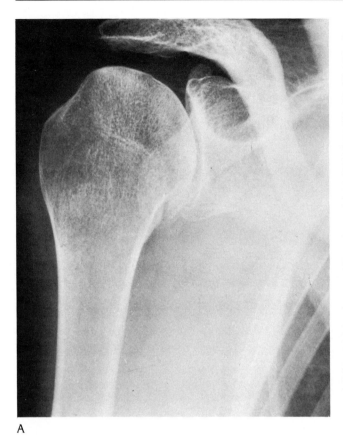

A

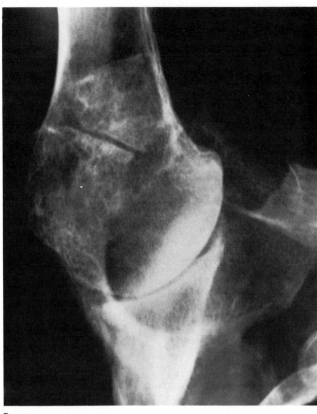

B

Figure 13-26 Chondrocalcinosis. **A.** Glenohumeral joint space narrowing with subchondral sclerosis and pyrophosphate layer in the hyaline cartilage. **B.** In the late stage extensive subchondral eburnation is visible.

CPPD deposition disease can be suspected if the features of pyrophosphate arthropathy are present.[28,29]

Resnick and coworkers distinguish this arthropathy from degenerative joint disease not associated with CPPD by these features: the unusual articular distribution, in which both weight-bearing (knees, hips) and non–weight-bearing (wrist, elbow, shoulder) joints are affected; a predilection for radiocarpal, patello-femoral, and talocalcaneal joint involvement; the unusual intraarticular distribution; large subchondral cyst formation; occasional rapidly progressive destructive arthritis; and variable osteophyte formation.

RADIOGRAPHIC FEATURES

Chondrocalcinosis characteristically involves the hyaline cartilage and is seen as a fine, dense line parallel to the contour of the humeral head. Calcification may also occur in the joint capsule, tendons, bursae (supraspinatus as well as the subacromial bursa), and ligaments. In tendons, calcifications appear thin and linear and may extend some distance from the osseous margin. They simulate the findings of idiopathic calcific tendinitis related to calcium hydroxyapatite crystal deposition but may be more extensive. Rotator cuff tears are common. The joint involvement produces asymmetric narrowing

with subchondral sclerosis as well as chondrocalcinosis (Fig. 13-26).

Advanced destructive erosive arthropathy of the shoulder resembling that of the hip may occur in the later stage. The features include extensive and rapid subchondral bone collapse and fragmentation producing single or multiple intraarticular osseous bodies similar to those of neuroarthropathy (Fig. 13-27).

In general, the arthritis associated with CPPD resembles osteoarthritis, though the cysts are generally more numerous, more widespread, and larger. They are also frequently associated with more disruption, collapse, and fragmentation of subchondral bone. The pyrophosphate crystals are deposited initially in hyaline and fibrocartilage. The condition may result from an inherent metabolic defect, trauma, or most probably a combination of both.[30]

When the crystals are released into the synovial fluid they produce an acute inflammatory arthritis (pseudogout) similar to that seen in association with the release of monosodium urate crystals into the joint. Possibly as a result of trauma, the crystals may also be released into the subchondral bone, where they may cause destruction by a similar mechanism.

Extensive deposits of calcium pyrophosphate crystals

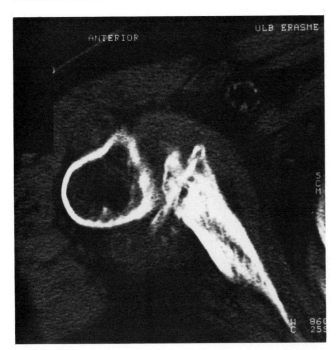

Figure 13-27 Chondrocalcinosis. CT shows subchondral osseous collapse and fragmentation.

can be seen in the joint cartilage on autopsy without evidence of arthritis. If a patient is to develop arthritis, there probably needs to be some other predisposing factor, such as trauma.[31]

Calcium Hydroxyapatite Crystal Deposition Disease

Hydroxyapatite crystal deposition can lead to periarticular accumulation, observed most frequently in the shoulder although similar features may be apparent in other joints. Recurrent painful periarticular deposits in tendons and soft tissues have been described by a variety of terms, such as *peritendinitis calcarea, calcareus tendinitis and bursitis, periarthritis calcarea, calcific tendinitis, peritendinitis, bursitis,* and *hydroxyapatite rheumatism.*[32]

The disease affects both men and women and is common between ages 40 and 70 years. Pain in the shoulder is far more commonly caused by tendinitis and bursitis than by osteoarthritis of the glenohumeral joint.

Radiopaque deposits may be asymptomatic. Manual workers are affected more often than sedentary ones. Acute symptoms include pain, tenderness on pressure, local edema or swelling, restricted active and passive motion, and mild fever.

Granular inclusion of calcium hydroxyapatite in fibrous connective tissue may be associated with necrosis, loss of fibrous structure, and surrounding inflammatory changes. The inclusions are milky or cheesy in consistency and inspissated or chalklike.[32]

RADIOGRAPHIC FEATURES

The radiographic features depend on the site of involvement. Deposits are initially thin, cloudlike, and ill-defined. They subsequently become denser, homogeneous, and more sharply defined. Calcifications may be found within the subacromial space or in various tendons around the shoulder.

Calcific tendinitis or bursitis is usually a monoarticular process, although multiple joints may be involved. Calcium hydroxyapatite deposits remain stable or are extruded from the tendon into a surrounding bursa and ultimately may be resorbed. Deposits in the subacromial bursa appear as cloudlike, amorphous calcification beneath the acromion. The morphology of intratendinous hydroxyapatite crystal is initially linear and hazy, then cloudlike and amorphous.

The supraspinatus tendon is the most frequent site of calcification, particularly the tendinous insertion on the upper margin of the greater tuberosity (Figs. 13-28, 13-29). The calcification is seen in profile on external rotation and remains in profile on internal rotation. Hydroxyapatite deposits in the infraspinatus tendon project better on the internal rotation view of the rotator cuff at the posterosuperior aspect of the humeral head.[33] Teres minor tendon deposits project over the posteroinferior aspect of the humeral head on the same view. Calcification in the subscapularis tendon (inserting on the lesser tuberosity) is projected medial to the humerus on the internal rotation view (Fig. 13-30). Bicipital tendon calcification usually appears on the superior aspect of the glenoid fossa, which does not move with external or internal rotation. Deposits in the short head of this tendon project adjacent to the coracoid tip, and are also seen along the humeral shaft.

Intraarticular Crystal Deposition (Milwaukee Shoulder Syndrome)

This recently encountered syndrome of elderly persons results from intraarticular hydroxyapatite crystal accumulation and leads to loss of joint space, destruction of bone, subchondral sclerosis, intraosseous debris, and joint disorganization with deformity. An associated complete, massive tear of the rotator cuff produces proximal migration of the humeral head, eroding the anterior portion of the acromion, clavicle, glenoid cavity, and coracoid process. This lesion, termed *cuff arthropathy,* is not specific for hydroxyapatite crystal deposition; the initial alteration is tendon disruption.

Analysis of joint fluid reveals hydroxyapatite crystals within microspheroids as well as two enzymes, collagenase and neutral protease. Prominent joint effusions may extend into the subdeltoid bursa causing soft tissue enlargement of the shoulder. Periarticular calcification has not been a constant feature. Without periarticular calcification, distinction of Milwaukee shoulder syndrome

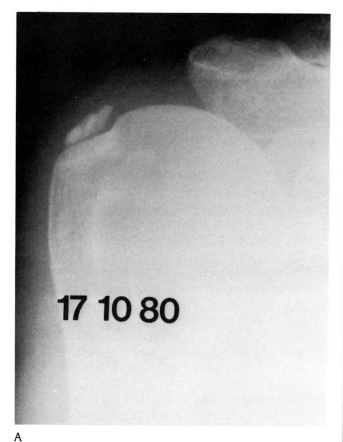

A

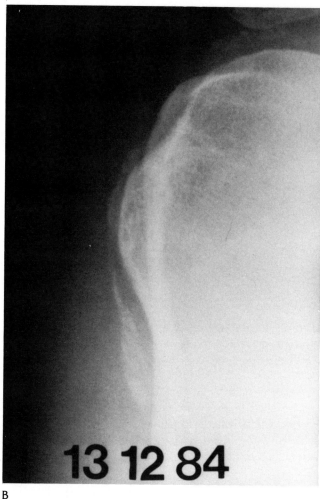

B

Figure 13-28 **A.** Hydroxyapatite deposit in the supraspinatus tendon over the greater tuberosity. **B.** Four years later it has migrated into the subacromial-subdeltoid bursa.

from pyrophosphate arthropathy depends on demonstrating hydroxyapatite crystals in the joint.

ADHESIVE CAPSULITIS

Adhesive capsulitis is characterized by mechanical retriction with associated pain at the extremes of motion in any direction. Although the etiology has not been established, it is thought that any condition causing dependency of the shoulder over an extended period can lead to capsular contracture. Voluntary immobilization, hemiplegia, cervical radiculitis, coronary artery disease, cervical herpes zoster, distal injury to an extremity necessitating dependent immobilization of the arm, mastectomy, shoulder or chest wall surgery requiring prolonged immobilization, and shoulder tendinitis are some of the predisposing conditions.

Reeves[34] distinguished between adhesive capsulitis (frozen shoulder) and posttraumatic stiff shoulder based on cause, joint capacity at arthrography, response to manipulation under anesthesia, and the effect of joint distention under pressure injection. The frozen shoulder

had no history of trauma and a joint capacity at arthrography of 3 ml or less. Manipulation to break up the adhesions is performed by Dussault (Fig. 13-31).[35]

MISCELLANEOUS DISEASES OF UNKNOWN ORIGIN

Primary Synovial Osteochondromatosis

This process of unknown cause affects the synovial lining of articulations, tendon sheaths, and bursae. Chondrometaplasia of the synovial tissue is responsible for the formation of intraarticular osteochondral bodies. It is difficult to differentiate this condition from pigmented villonodular synovitis. It is a progressive, chronic, monoarticular disease that appears in the third, fourth, or fifth decade, without any clear genetic transmission.

The articular type affects the knees and the hips; the tendinous type, the hands and feet. The cartilaginous elements may be fragmented, detached, or reattached to

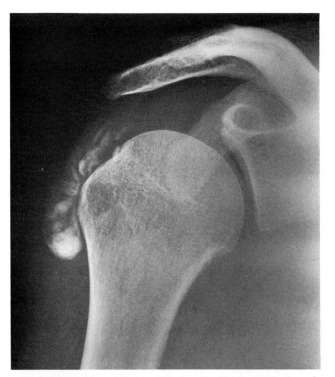

Figure 13-29 Fragmentation of hydroxyapatite deposit in the sub-acromial-subdeltoid bursa.

the synovial membrane or they may penetrate the capsule and enter the periarticular soft tissues, causing infrequent chondral or osteochondral erosions (Fig. 13-32). A radiographic triad determines the diagnosis: (1) Small spotted calcifications are visible in the juxtaarticular soft tissues, underlining the labrum. In the advanced stage of the disease osteochondral fragments are not specific. (2) Pressure defects may be visible on intracapsular cortices, as in pigmented villonodular synovitis. (3) There is no associated injury, osteonecrosis, or impingement. In 35 percent of cases the calcifications in the soft tissues are absent or insufficient to diagnose the disease. The nodules with water density appear as soft tissue hypertrophy in or around the articulation. The uncalcified lesions are an indication for computed arthrotomography, where they present as filling defects outlined by contrast.

The technique shows the intraarticular localization of the nodules, bone erosions, capsular reaction, or, eventually, adhesive capsulitis.

Pigmented Villonodular Synovitis

Pigmented villonodular synovitis is an unexplained, proliferative disorder of the synovial membrane. It is mono-

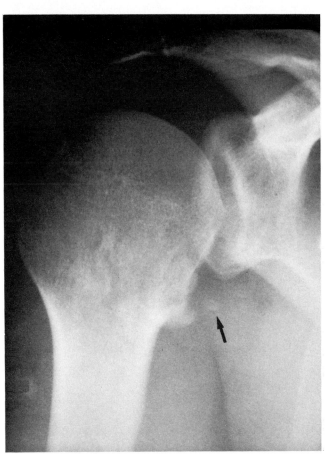

A

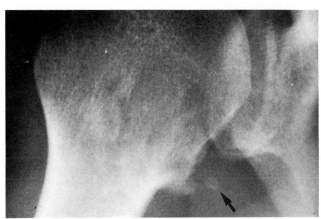

B

Figure 13-30 **A.** and **B.** Hydroxyapatite deposits in the subscapularis tendon adjacent to the lesser tuberosity (*arrows*).

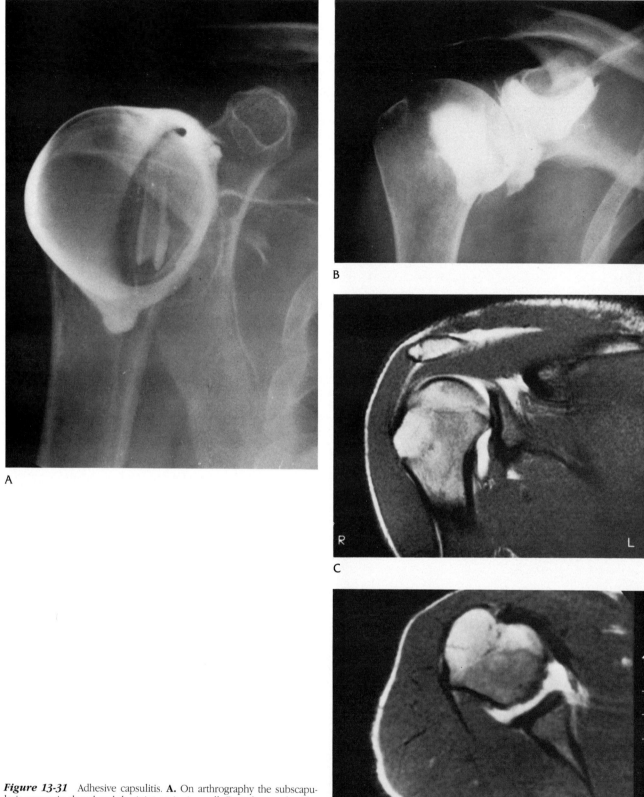

Figure 13-31 Adhesive capsulitis. **A.** On arthrography the subscapularis recess is closed and the joint cavity is small. **B.** Arthrography. The entire joint capsule is small and restricted. The biceps tendon sheath does not fill. **C.** Arthro-MRI in the coronal oblique plane, T1-weighted image. **D.** Arthro-MRI in the axial plane on T1-weighted image shows small joint cavity.

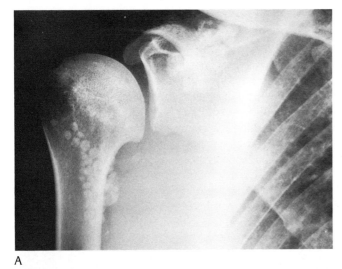

A

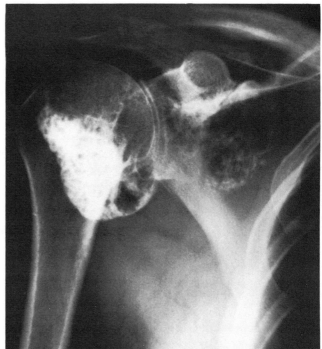

B

C

Figure 13-32 Primary synovial osteochondromatosis. **A.** Plain film. **B, C.** Arthrography. **D, E.** Arthro-CT.

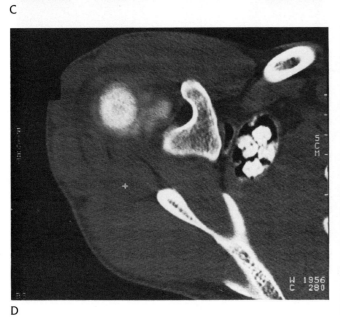

D

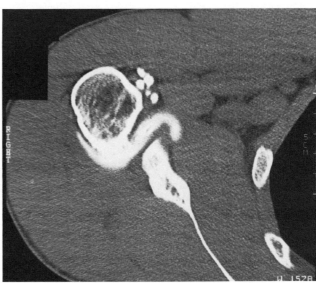

E

articular and usually affects the whole synovial lining. Localized types are rare. The cause remains controversial; however, four prevalent theories exist: (1) an error of lipid metabolism, (2) a response to blood or a blood product, (3) an inflammatory reaction to an unknown nontraumatic agent, (4) and a benign neoplasm, of synovial, vascular, or fibrohistiocytic origin.[36] These conceptions explain the variety of terms: we speak of *xanthoma, xanthogranuloma, fibroxanthoma, chronic hemorrhagic villous synovitis, fibrohemangiomatous tumor with giant-cells, fibrohemosideric sarcoma, benign synovioma,* and *villous arthritis*.[36]

The pigmented villonodular synovitis is often accompanied by hemorrhagic spilling, suggesting a vascular cause, which differentiates it from the simple villonodular type, which is perhaps a reaction to a true neoplastic process. Radiographically, villonodular synovitis appears as a nodular mass of soft tissue. It is frequently associated with paraarticular bone erosions. These have sclerotic margins and occur by pressure from direct extension. Calcifications are rare, hemosiderin deposits induce a subtle increase in density (see Fig. 13-33). The synovial hypertrophy can extend from the joint capsule into the neighboring tendons and bursae. Osteocartilaginous abnormalities, which appear in approximately half of the joints,[36,37] include multiple subchondral cysts, pressure erosions on intracapsular cortices, and gradual joint space narrowing.

The subchondral cysts are usually multiple and clearly defined, with a sclerotic rim. They occur on the non–weight-bearing surfaces or at some distance from the articular surface. A solitary cyst is found more frequently with a focal tendon lesion than in diffuse articular lesions. In the final stage, joint space narrowing can occur. It is more frequent in the tight joint capsule of the hip. Osteophytosis is rare. There is no juxtaarticular osteopenia. CT without contrast material shows density changes due to hemosiderin deposition in the soft tissues.

Arthro-CT studies the distribution of the synovial changes and their extension into adjacent tendons and bursae. The radiographic diagnosis is directed by the prevailing signs on the plain films, soft tissue swelling,

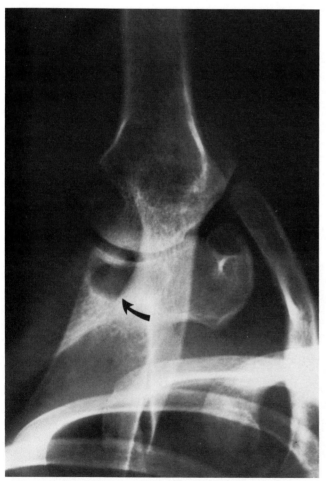

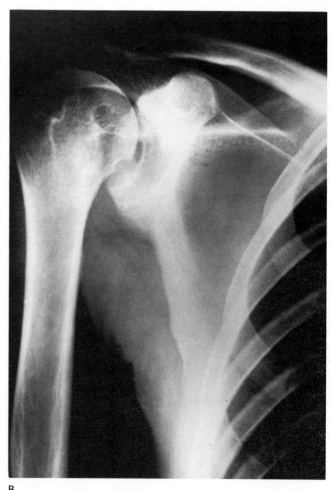

A

B

Figure 13-33 Pigmented villonodular synovitis. **A.** Axillary view shows subchondral cyst (*black arrow*).
B. Subchondral cyst and pressure erosions are evident.

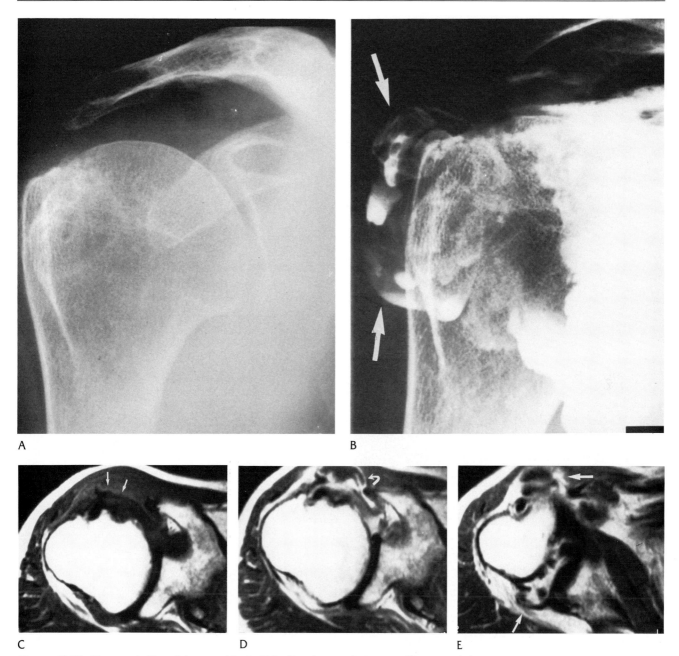

Figure 13-34 Pigmented villonodular synovitis. **A.** Plain film shows soft tissue swelling around the greater tuberosity and small erosions. **B.** Arthrography demonstrates enlargement of the joint cavity outside the greater tuberosity (*white arrows*) with synovial proliferation. **C.** MRI, axial plane, T1-weighted image shows enlargement of the joint cavity behind the greater and the lesser tuberosity (*white arrows*). **D.** MRI, axial T1-weighted image after injection of gadolinium-DTPA. Low signal intensities surrounded by high signal intensities in articular pouch in front of the greater tuberosity (*curved white arrow*) are consistent with hemosiderin and fat. **E.** MRI, axial T1-weighted image after gadolinium-DTPA injection shows areas of low signal intensity within the joint cavity (*white arrows*).

multiple subchondral cysts, and relative preservation of the joint space.

MRI is potentially diagnostic of pigmented villonodular synovitis, owing to the presence of hemosiderin and fat within abnormal tissue.[38] Areas with high fat content have high signal intensity. The study should be specific for pigmented villonodular synovitis if it demonstrates a multinodular intraarticular lesion with patchy areas that have the characteristics of fat and hemosiderin; however, both false negative and false positive results can occur. These substances may not be present in sufficient concentrations to change the signal intensity of synovial tissue. The high signal intensity of fat can overshadow the low signal intensity of hemosiderin (Fig. 13-34).

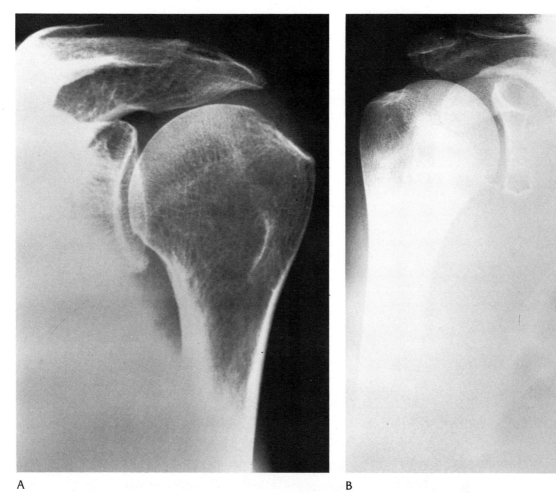

A   B

Figure 13-35 Amyloidosis. **A.** Nodular swelling of the soft tissue over the greater tuberosity without erosion. **B.** The greater tuberosity demonstrates a large erosion and osteoporosis.

DIFFERENTIAL DIAGNOSIS

When there is isolated soft tissue swelling, the differential diagnosis of pigmented villonodular synovitis includes synovioma, synovial hemangioma, and lipoma arborescens. With multiple subchondral cysts, it includes osteoarthritis, tuberculosis, amyloidosis, synovial chondromatosis, and hemophilia.[37]

The cysts of pigmented villonodular synovitis occur on all surfaces (weight-bearing and non–weight-bearing) and can occur at some distance from the joint space. Severe juxtaarticular osteoporosis founded in tuberculous arthritis is not typical of pigmented villonodular synovitis. In cases associated with a single large cyst, this arthropathy becomes part of the differential diagnosis of epiphyseal tumors.

Amyloidosis

Amyloidosis is a systemic disease characterized by an organic infiltration of eosinophilic matter made of protein fibrils enclosed in a mucopolysaccharide matrix. The articular changes accompany the primary or the secondary type.

Amyloid arthropathy is more frequent in the fifth and sixth decades, especially in the upper limbs (shoulder, wrist). The clinical signs include not only arthralgia but also sudden swelling of the periarticular soft tissues.

Amyloid arthropathy is characterized by nodular swelling of the soft tissues and juxtaarticular osteoporosis, which allow distinction from hyperuricemia.

The radiographic abnormalities may be similar to those of rheumatoid arthritis, although the joint space may be preserved. Characteristically, the periarticular erosions are large and rather sharply defined by surrounding sclerosis (Fig. 13-35).

Multicentric Reticulohistiocytosis

Multicentric reticulohistiocytosis is a rare disorder in which polyarthritis usually precedes the onset of nodular cutaneous eruptions, a fact that emphasizes the importance of early roentgenographic recognition. The predominant sites of involvement are the interphalangeal joints of the hands. The synovium lining the glenohumeral joint is rarely involved, but when it is arthritis mutilans may result. The erosions are strikingly symmetric and well-circumscribed and accompanying osteoporosis is disproportionately mild.[39]

References

1. MONGEY AB, HESS EV: Advances in rheumatology. *Radiol Clin North Am* 26:1157–1164, 1988.
2. SISSONS HA, MURRAY RO, KEMP HBS: *Orthopaedic Diagnosis, Clinical, Radiological and Pathological Coordinates.* Springer-Verlag, Berlin Heidelberg, 1984, pp 154–162.
3. RENNER WR, WEINSTEIN AS: Arthritis and other arthropathies. *Radiol Clin North Am* 26:1185–1193, 1988.
4. JACOBY RK, JAYSON MI, COSH JA: Onset, early stages and prognosis of rheumatoid arthritis. *Br Med J* 2:96–100, 1973.
5. RESNICK D, NIWAYAMA G: *Rheumatoid Arthritis in Glenohumeral Joint. Bone and Joint Imaging.* Philadelphia, Saunders, 1989, pp 268–270.
6. SINTZOFF S: *Imagerie de l'Épaule.* Paris, Masson, 1992, p 20.
7. RENNER WR, WEINSTEIN AS: Arthritis and other arthropathies. *Radiol Clin North Am* 26:1186, 1988.
8. RESNICK D, NIWAYAMA G: *Ankylosing Spondylitis in Glenohumeral Bone and Joint Imaging.* Philadelphia, Saunders, 1989, p 311.
9. BALE J: Enthesopathy of rheumatoid ankylosing spondylitis. *Ann Rheum Dis* 30:213, 1971.
10. GOLD RH, BASSET LW, SEEGERS LL: The other arthritides. *Radiol Clin North Am* 26:1198, 1988.
11. SISSONS HA, MURRAY RO, KEMP HBS: *Orthopaedic Diagnosis, Clinical Radiological and Pathological Coordinates.* Springer-Verlag, Berlin Heidelberg, 1984, p 167.
12. RESNICK D: *Reiter's Syndrome in Bone and Joint Imaging.* Philadelphia, Saunders, 1989, p 329.
13. GOLD RH, BASSET LW, SEEGER LL: The other arthritis. *Radiol Clin North Am* 26:1202, 1988.
14. GOLD RH, BASSET LW, SEEGER LL: The other arthritis. *Radiol Clin North Am* 26:1204, 1988.
15. RESNICK R, NIWAYAMA G: *Diagnosis of Bone and Joint Disorders,* 2d ed, Philadelphia, Saunders, 1988, pp 1178–1179.
16. RESNICK D: *Ankylosing Spondylitis in Bone and Joint Imaging.* Philadelphia, Saunders, 1989, p 329.
17. MONGEY AB, HESS EV: Advances in rheumatology. *Radiol Clin North Am* 26:1158, 1988.
18. GOLD RH, BASSET LW, SEEGER LL: The other arthritis. *Radiol Clin North Am* 26:1207, 1988.
19. MASON RM, MURRAY RS, OATES JK, ET AL.: Comparative radiologic study of Reiter's disease, rheumatoid arthritis and ankylosing spondylitis. *J Bone Joint Surg* 41B:137, 1959.
20. RESNICK D: *Systemic Lupus Erythematosus in Bone and Joint Imaging.* Philadelphia, Saunders, 1989, p 347.
21. RESNICK D: *Systemic Lupus Erythematosus in Bone and Joint Imaging.* Philadelphia, Saunders, 1989, pp 349–350.
22. RESNICK D: *Scleroderma (Progressive Systemic Sclerosis) in Bone and Joint Imaging.* Philadelphia, Saunders, 1989, p 358.
23. RESNICK D: *Dermatomyositis and Polyomyositis in Bone and Joint Imaging.* Philadelphia, Saunders, 1989, p 361.
24. SISSONS HA, MURRAY RO, KEMPS HBS: *Orthopaedic Diagnosis, Clinical Radiological and Pathological Coordinates.* Springer-Verlag, Berlin Heidelberg, 1984, p 270.
25. RESNICK D, NIWAYAMA G: *Monosodium Urate Deposition Disease (Gout) in Bone and Joint Imaging.* Philadelphia, Saunders, 1989, p 461.
26. MARTEL W: The overhanging edge of bone: A roentgenologic manifestation of gout. *Radiology* 91:755, 1968.
27. RESNICK D, NIWAYAMA G: *Monosodium Urate Deposition Disease (Gout) in Bone and Joint Imaging.* Philadelphia, Saunders, 1989, p 469.
28. RESNICK D, NIWAYAMA G: Calcium pyrophosphate dihydrate (CPPD) crystal deposition disease. *In* Resnick D, Niwayama G: *Diagnosis of Bone and Joint Disorders,* 2d ed, Philadelphia, Saunders, 1988, p 1672.
29. RESNICK D, NIWAYAMA G, GOERGEN TG, ET AL.: Clinical, radiographic and pathologic abnormalities in calcium py-

rophosphate dihydrate deposition disease (CPPD): Pseudogout. *Radiology* 122:1, 1977.

30. MARKEL SF, HART WR: Arthropathy in calcium pyrophosphate dihydrate crystal deposition disease. *Arch Pathol Lab
Med* 106:529, 1982.

31. BULLOUGH P, MANJULA B: The differential diagnosis of
geodes. Arthritis and other arthropathies. *Radiol Clin North
Am* 26:1180, 1988.

32. RESNICK D: *Calcium Hydroxyapatite Crystal Deposition
Disease in Bone and Joint Imaging*. Philadelphia, Saunders,
1989, p. 497.

33. SINTZOFF S: *Imagerie de l'Épaule*. Paris, Masson, 1992,
p 31.

34. REEVES B: Arthrographic changes in frozen and post-traumatic stiff shoulders. *Proc R Soc Med* 59:827–830, 1966.

35. DUSSAULT RG, SINTZOFF S: Technique et résultats de l'arthrographie de l'épaule. *Feuil Radiol* 27:303–315, 1987.

36. GOLDMAN AB, DICARLO EF: Pigmented villonodular synovitis. Diagnosis and differential diagnosis. *Radiol Clin
North Am* 26:1327–1347, 1988.

37. DOWART RH, GENANT HK, JOHNSON WH, ET AL.: Pigmented villonodular synovitis of synovial joints: Clinical,
pathological and radiologic features. *AJR* 143:877–885,
1984.

38. KOTTAL RA, VOGLER JB III, MATAMOROS A, ET AL.: Pigmented villonodular synovitis: A report of MR imaging in
two cases. *Radiology* 163:551–553, 1987.

39. GOLD RH, BASSET LW, SEEGER LL: The other arthritis.
Radiol Clin North Am 26:1211, 1988.

14 | IMAGING OF NEUROMUSCULAR DISEASE OF THE SHOULDER

Robert R. Brown
Alain Chevrot
David J. Sartoris

Neuromuscular disease has been under radiographic study since 1928 (Hulten, cited by DiChiro[1]). Most effort has been directed to evaluation of the lower extremity musculature, as clinical findings are usually less pronounced in the upper limbs. Initially, plain radiographs were utilized to provide details of disease progression and severity. Paralysis and disuse lead to osteopenia and decreased density of the soft tissues owing to soft tissue atrophy and fatty infiltration. Ultrasonography was described as an asset to the evaluation of primary skeletal muscle diseases, where fat and fibrous infiltration of the muscle bundles correlated with increased echogenicity. Reproducibility was poor, as there was no standard gain setting. This method for analysis was therefore limited.[2] Dock and coworkers studied leg musculature with a high-frequency transducer in patients with muscular dystrophy and noted they had a significantly larger number of perimysial septa than control subjects. Their study, however, showed no significant difference in alterations of the biceps brachii muscles.[3] Although ultrasound is preferred to ionizing radiation for pediatric studies, computed tomography (CT) has also been employed to follow the course of neuromuscular disease: lower attenuation of muscle corresponds to fatty infiltration. Selective muscle preservation has been reported with CT. Magnetic resonance imaging (MRI) more clearly illustrates the tissue contrast between the fat plane and the muscle bundle. Currently, neuromuscular disease, which is typically a relentlessly progressive process, can be accurately monitored using MRI.[4]

MUSCULAR DYSTROPHY

Fascioscapulohumeral muscular dystrophy has an autosomal-dominant mode of inheritance, affecting both sexes with equal frequency. It usually presents in adolescence as characteristic weakening of the shoulder girdle musculature. The "winged" scapulae are apparent clinically, as is muscle involvement in the trunk, pelvis, legs, and face (Fig. 14-1).

Duchenne's muscular dystrophy involves the proximal muscle groups, especially the shoulders and hips, in boys usually younger than 5 years. It is a condition with an X-linked mode of inheritance. Most changes in musculature have been described for the lower extremity—large calf muscles, pes planus, equinovarus, and hip contractures. Cardiopulmonary disease is the usual cause of death, typically in the third decade of life.

Other forms of muscular dystrophy are well known, affecting various different muscle groups. Limb girdle muscular dystrophy may involve the shoulder, but primarily involves the pelvic girdle. Myotonic dystrophy principally involves the hands, sternocleidomastoid muscles, and face. Arthrogryposis multiplex congenita is a rare congenital syndrome of contractures and deformities of multiple joints (Fig. 14-2). Diagnosis can be made with ultrasound in the second trimester of pregnancy.[5]

CONNECTIVE TISSUE DISEASE

Connective tissue disorders can present clinically as a generalized neuropathic condition, with muscle weakness and arthritis. Overlap syndromes are suggested when patients present clinically with more than one collagen vascular disease (Fig. 14-3). Patients with positive extractable nuclear antigen and scleroderma clinically have a mixed connective tissue disease. Scleroderma in the shoulder may lead to fibrinous deposits on the surface of tendon sheaths and fascia, leading to crepitus in the subscapular region. The most characteristic abnormality is proximal muscle weakness.

Polymyositis and dermatomyositis are conditions of unknown cause that result in acute or subacute degeneration of striated muscle with a variable degree of inflammation. Skin involvement is present in dermatomyositis, but both diseases can result in soft tissue and articular manifestations. Usually, no radiographic abnormalities are associated with articular symptoms. Soft tissue changes are more prominent in the proximal musculature, and the extent of muscle calcification appears

401

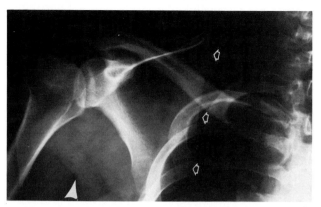

Figure 14-1 Fascioscapular muscular dystrophy. Frontal radiograph demonstrates winged scapula (*arrows*) and decreased radiodensity of musculature (*arrowhead*), indicative of fatty infiltration and atrophy.

to increase with the severity of the disease (Fig. 14-4). Technetium pyrophosphate and similar agents may accumulate in the abnormal muscle involved (Fig. 14-3). Within the last few years, MRI has been utilized to evaluate the extent and severity of myositis. It has been reported that areas of inflammation correlate with increased signal intensity on T2-weighted and short-tau-inversion recovery (STIR) images.[6] It has been suggested that this feature may be useful for directed biopsy during diagnostic intervention and that spectroscopy may also be of value in assessing the patient's clinical status.[7]

NEUROARTHROPATHY

The neuropathic joint is a common sequela to disease or dissociation of both upper and lower motor neurons. The pathogenesis of neuropathic articular disease is currently believed to involve repetitive trauma to an insensitive joint with relaxed ligaments. Cumulative injury leads to progressive degeneration and disorganization of

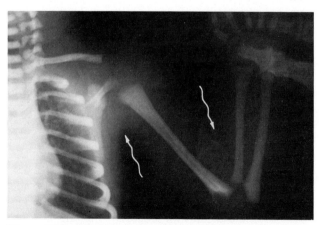

Figure 14-2 Arthrogryposis multiplex congenita. The shoulder and elbow in this newborn infant are fixed in position owing to flexion contractures (*arrows*). Subluxations (not present in this case) may also be a feature of this condition.

the joint. A different radiographic appearance has been described for upper and lower motor neuron lesions, the former resulting in a productive arthritis and the latter in a predominantly destructive process. The different articular changes may be due to selective damage of sympathetic neurons regulating the vascular reflex responsible for osteoclastic bone resorption in peripheral lesions.

Documented cases of central lesions causing neuroarthropathy are extensive and include syringomyelia (Fig. 14-5), tabes dorsalis, spinal cord injury, meningomyelocele, congenital insensitivity to pain, multiple sclerosis, familial dysautonomia (Riley-Day syndrome), Charcot-Marie-Tooth disease, and hepatic encephalopathy (Fig. 14-6). Bismuth intoxication with encephalopathy has also been suggested to cause neuropathic changes (Fig. 14-7).[8] Additional conditions that can lead to neuropathic changes in the shoulder include trauma, intraarticular injection of steroids, diabetes mellitus (Fig. 14-8), alcoholism, amyloidosis, and infection (see Fig. 14-1).

The most common cause of a neuropathic joint in the upper extremity is syringomyelia, first described in 1927 (Fig. 14-5).[9] Posttraumatic syringomyelia may also lead to the development of a Charcot joint.[10] Although syringomyelia may contribute to the degenerative disease in the spine, there is no relationship between the development of spondylotic degeneration and progression of lower motor neuron lesions in the arms.[11] The neuropathic process in peripheral joints progresses independently. MRI can be useful in detecting early disease (Fig. 14-9), whereas arthrography, with or without CT, may demonstrate capsular alterations and synovial cysts (Figs. 14-10, 14-11).

OSTEOPOROSIS

Profound osteoporosis accompanies immobilization, disuse, or paralysis. It can affect the entire skeleton or a portion of it, depending on its cause. Bone atrophy secondary to muscle paralysis due to conditions of the central nervous system, spinal cord, or peripheral nerves may be similar in imaging appearance. "Spontaneous" fracture may result from bone atrophy. *Transient osteoporosis* also can be seen to involve the head of the humerus. Diagnosis is supported by local "radiographic osteopenia" (Fig. 14-12). Bone scintigraphy,[12] MRI, and CT are the usual tools. The role of neurovascular imbalance is discussed.[13]

The *reflex sympathetic dystrophy syndrome* has been observed in as many as 25 percent of hemiplegic patients and is also associated with quadriplegia. Men and women are affected with approximately equal frequency, and unilateral abnormalities predominate. Scintigraphy using bone-seeking radiopharmaceutical agents shows increased radionuclide activity in periarticular regions.

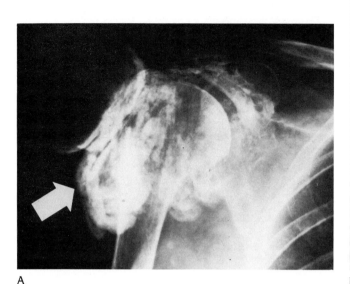

A

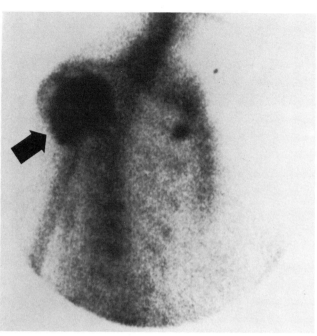

B

Figure 14-3 Dermatomyositis-scleroderma overlap syndrome. **A.** Exuberant soft tissue calcification (*arrow*) is present surrounding the right shoulder; this is calcinosis of collagen vascular disease. **B.** Radionuclide bone scan (RAO positioning) shows soft tissue uptake of radiopharmaceutical in the region (*arrow*).

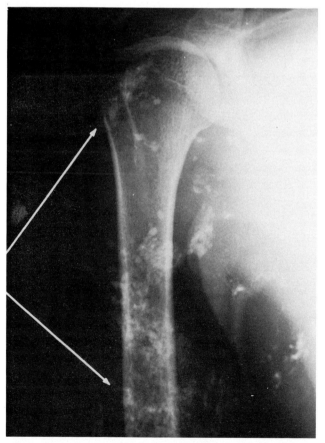

Figure 14-4 Mixed connective tissue disease. In this patient with polymyositis-dermatomyositis, prominent soft tissue calcification (*arrows*) is present surrounding the shoulder and humerus, representing idiopathic calcinosis of collagen vascular disease.

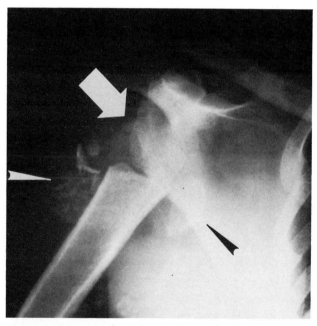

Figure 14-5 Neuroarthropathy in syringomyelia. One month after a normal radiograph, marked destruction of the humeral head (*arrow*) with osseous fragmentation within the joint (*arrowheads*) is evident.

Soft Tissue, Muscle Atrophy

Soft tissue atrophy with muscle wasting and fatty infiltration accompanies most neuromuscular disorders and can be detected on CT or MRI. In Duchenne's muscular dystrophy and congenital myotonia, however, the actual bulk of the musculature is increased. In the former con-

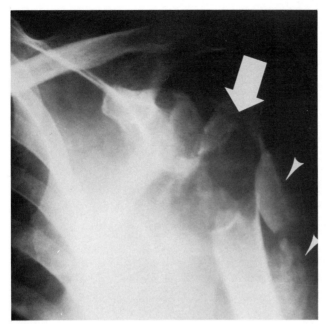

Figure 14-6 Encephalopathy and development of Charcot joint. Frontal radiograph of a patient with a portacaval shunt and hepatic encephalopathy who sustained a comminuted fracture of the humeral head 6 weeks earlier. The humeral head is destroyed (*arrow*), and multiple ossific fragments are present (*arrowheads*), extending laterally along the shaft of the proximal humerus.

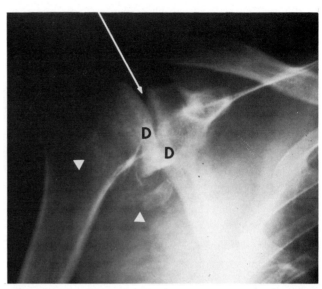

Figure 14-8 Diabetic neuroarthropathy in a 60-year-old. Frontal radiograph demonstrates glenohumeral joint space narrowing (*arrow*) with multiple ossific fragments within the joint space (*arrowheads*). Increased density (D) of the humeral head and glenoid is apparent.

dition, fatty infiltration of muscle is evident. In the musculature of the appendicular skeleton, neural diseases are generally manifested as initial atrophy of the muscle

and a subsequent decrease in radiodensity; primary muscle disorders are characterized by decreased radiodensity followed by atrophy. A decrease in attenuation values on the CT display indicates the presence of intramuscular fat cells. In some specific situations, muscle hypertrophy occurs alone or in combination with atrophy. Lipo-

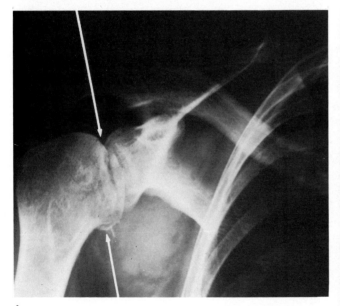

A

Figure 14-7 Bismuth-related neuroarthropathy. Plain film, **A,** and tomogram, **B,** illustrate early neuropathic changes with osteonecrosis of the humeral head (*arrows*) secondary to bismuth encephalopathy.

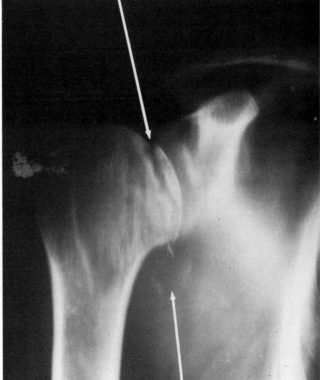

B

atrophic diabetes is characterized by generalized atrophy of adipose tissue, resulting in apparent muscle hypertrophy (Fig. 14-13). Secondary changes in bone shape can appear, owing to microtrauma attributable to the sensory deficit, and physeal abnormalities are reminiscent of those seen in neuroarthropathy (Fig. 14-14).

HETEROTOPIC OSSIFICATION

Heterotopic new bone formation is a well-documented complication of central nervous system and spinal cord disorders. It has often been reported in association with paraplegia secondary to spinal cord trauma, observed in 20 to 60 percent of cases. More rarely, heterotopic ossification is evident following acute anoxia, head injury, cerebrovascular accident, encephalomyelitis, poliomyelitis, multiple sclerosis, neoplastic disease, and tetanus. It occurs in both flaccid and spastic forms of paralysis and is more common and severe in young men. In general, ossification appears 2 to 6 months after the injury.[14] It has been evident as early as 19 days after trauma. Single or multiple sites may be affected, unilaterally or bilaterally. The areas most typically involved are the hip, the knee, and the shoulder; less commonly, the elbow and the small joints of the hand and the foot are altered. Though ossification is almost always seen in a paralyzed limb or limbs, this association is not constant.

The clinical manifestations are variable. Many patients have no symptoms or signs except those of the primary neurologic disorder. Others develop pain, swelling, and restricted joint motion, findings that simulate acute arthritis. In some, synovitis occurring before ossification is radiographically apparent.[15]

Aspiration of articular contents may reveal clear yellow or serosanguineous synovial fluid with a meager number of erythrocytes or leukocytes. Additional laboratory findings may be unrewarding, though elevation of the serum alkaline phosphatase level has been observed.

Radiographic examination delineates initially ill-defined periarticular radiodense areas that do not contain recognizable trabeculae (Fig. 14-15). The collections enlarge, merge with the underlying bone in the form of an irregular excrescence, and demonstrate trabecular architecture (Fig. 14-16). Eventually, complete periarticular osseous bridging may result, associated with significant or total loss of joint motion (Figs. 14-16, 14-17). In some instances ossification develops at a distance from a joint, and eventually it merges with the subjacent bone, forming a peculiar exostosis (Fig. 14-18). Exceptionally, spontaneous regression of heterotopic ossification is observed. Scintigraphic examination may also be used to determine the evolution of this process and the maturity of the heterotopic ossification.[16]

Histologically, the maturing heterotopic ossification consists of essentially normal bone with haversian canals, osteoblasts, blood vessels, and marrow. Heterotopic ossification of soft tissues is not confined to patients with neuromuscular disease. Burns, mechanical trauma, and venous stasis (varicosities) can lead to similar changes. In addition, a progressive form of ossification of unknown cause, myositis (fibrodysplasia) ossificans progressiva, is also recognized.

Joint Capsule Abnormalities

Fibrosis in the joint capsule, especially about the glenohumeral joint, may explain the association of adhesive capsulitis and neurologic injury, particularly hemiparesis. It may also account for the common occurrence of shoulder pain in patients with hemiplegia, though other con-

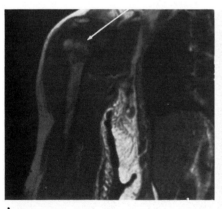
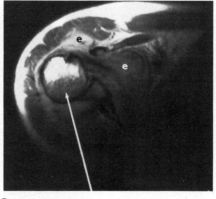
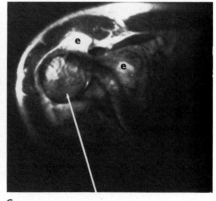

A   B   C

Figure 14-9 Acute neuroarthropathy in syringomyelia. MR images including, **A,** coronal T1 (TR 300 msec/TE 10 msec), **B,** transaxial proton-density (TR 2000 msec/TE 30 msec), and **C,** transaxial T2-weighted (TR 2000 msec/TE 80 msec) sequences illustrate an intact humeral head and glenohumeral joint space. The humeral head and neck show patchy signal loss (*arrows*) on all images, a finding consistent with bone sclerosis. A large joint effusion (e) is documented on the transaxial images.

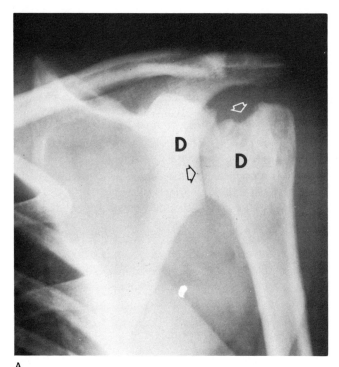

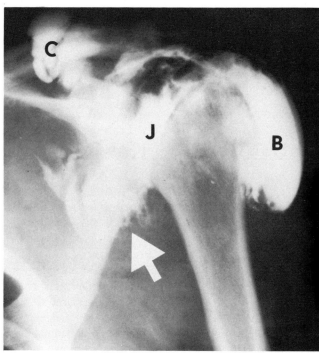

A

B

Figure 14-10 Arthrography in neuropathic joint disease. **A.** Preliminary film demonstrates erosion (*arrows*) and increased density (D) of the humeral head and glenoid. **B.** Following contrast administration there is opacification of an enlarged glenohumeral joint space (J) with filling of the subacromial-subdeltoid bursa (B), there is irregularity of the capsule inferiorly (*arrow*), and a dissecting synovial cyst (C) is present.

ditions such as the reflex sympathetic dystrophy syndrome and humeral subluxation may be contributory, as may rotator cuff disruption. Arthrography documents the restricted capacity of the articular cavity and irregularity of the contrast material consistent with the presence of

fibrosis in the joint itself or its normal extensions (such as the bicipital tendon sheath) (Fig. 14-19).

The *drooping shoulder,* inferior subluxation of the humeral head with respect to the glenoid region of the scapula, is a documented manifestation of paralysis. It should be differentiated from true dislocations of the glenohumeral joints because no surgical manipulation is required.

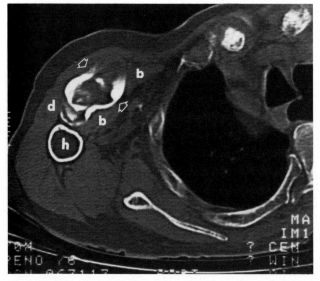

Figure 14-11 Syringomyelia with neuroarthropathy and synovial cyst. CT following intraarticular administration of contrast demonstrates anterior and inferior dissection of a cyst (*arrows*) located between the biceps (b), deltoid (d), and humerus (h).

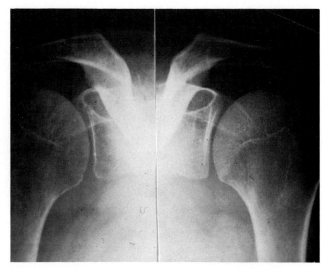

Figure 14-12 Transient osteoporosis of the right shoulder.

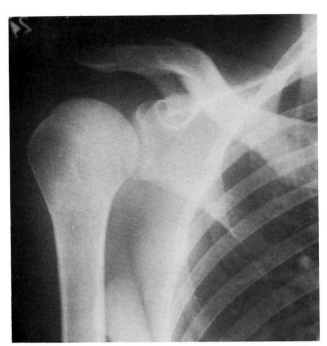

Figure 14-13 Lipoatrophic diabetes. Frontal radiograph of the shoulder demonstrates loss of subcutaneous and intermuscular fat in this patient with insulin-resistant diabetes. The bones are normal, as is the glenohumeral joint space.

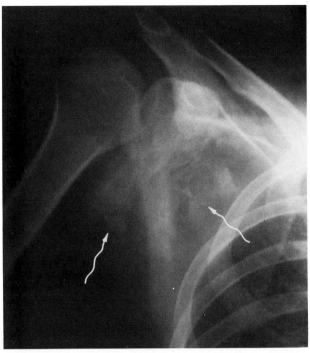

Figure 14-15 Heterotopic ossification in a quadriplegic. Frontal radiograph of the shoulder demonstrates immature bone formation (*arrows*) in the soft tissues. This condition is a common sequela of central nervous system trauma and neurologic deficit.

The drooping shoulder, which also occurs in hemophilia and following capsular injury, has been observed in more than 50 percent of hemiplegic patients. It increases in frequency with more severe paralysis, occurs ipsilateral to the neurologic deficit, is associated with poor arm function, and is evident when the patient is sitting or standing. It is produced by loss of muscle tone leading to stretching of the supportive musculature and capsule by the weight of the dependent, flaccid upper extremity.[17] Inferior subluxation of the humeral head may appear within weeks following flaccid paralysis of any cause, including brachial plexus involvement by a pulmonary neoplasm (Pancoast's tumor).

An early radiographic sign of inferior displacement of the humerus is abduction of the humeral head caused by impingement by the glenoid labrum, which acts as a fulcrum, with a V-shaped interosseous space; as the humerus continues to migrate caudally, this space is transformed into a diffusely widened articular cavity. Subsequently, more obvious subluxation is evident (Figs. 14-18, 14-20). Accurate radiographic diagnosis is facilitated if the patient is examined in the upright position.

Suprascapular Nerve

Entrapment of the suprascapular nerve most commonly occurs as it traverses the suprascapular notch. This nerve,

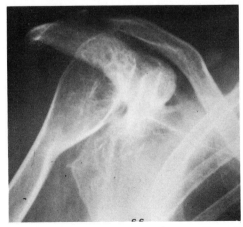

Figure 14-14 Bone shape change secondary to poliomyelitis.

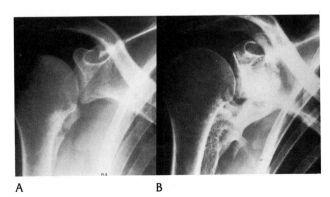

A   B

Figure 14-16 Heterotopic ossification in a case of poliomyelitis. Evolution between **A** and **B.**

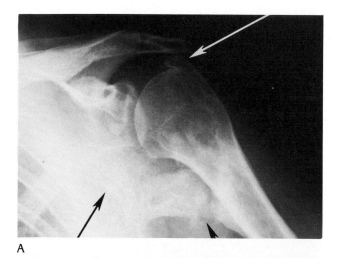

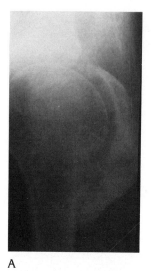

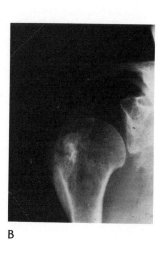

A

B

Figure 14-18   Heterotopic ossification, **A,** and drooping shoulder, **B.**

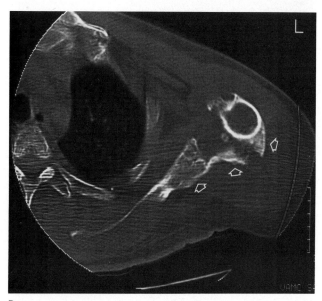

B

Figure 14-17   Mature heterotopic ossification. **A.** Marked ossification (*arrows*) around the shoulder is noted in this patient with a remote history of head trauma. **B.** CT image demonstrates bridging of ossification between the scapula and proximal humerus (*arrows*).

which contains motor and sensory fibers, arises from the upper trunk of the brachial plexus, runs deep to the trapezius and omohyoid muscles, and enters the supraspinous fossa through the suprascapular notch, passing below the superior transverse scapular ligament. Potential causes of suprascapular nerve entrapment include a scapular fracture or glenohumeral joint dislocation, occupational or recreational stress (as in weightlifting), ganglia, tumors, developmental anomalies of the notch, and any condition that leads to traction on the nerve, allowing it to be compressed by the osseous or ligamentous edges of the foramen (Table 14-1). The major clinical findings, which may be unilateral or bilateral, are

Table 14-1   Nerve Entrapment Syndromes

NERVE	CLINICAL FEATURES	CAUSES
Suprascapular	Shoulder pain	Scapular fracture, glenohumeral joint dislocation, ganglion, tumor
Axillary	Quadrilateral space syndrome	
Brachial plexus	Neck and shoulder (thoracic outlet syndrome, scalenus anticus syndrome)	Fracture, dislocation, tumor, infection, surgery, injection, cervical rib

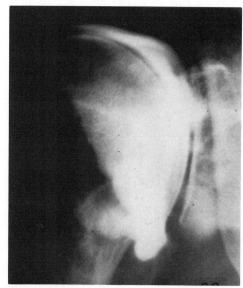

Figure 14-19   Fibrosis of the joint capsule (reduction of the joint capacity).

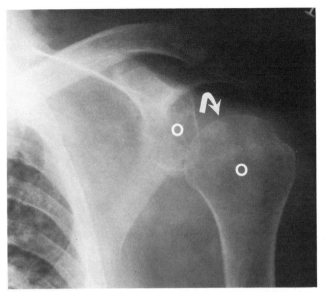

Figure 14-20 Brachial plexus injury in adulthood. Radiography demonstrates drooping shoulder (pseudosubluxation, *arrow*) with patchy disuse osteoporosis (o).

shoulder pain and weakness and atrophy of the supraspinatus and infraspinatus muscles plus limited external rotation and abduction of the humerus (Fig. 14-21).[18–22]

Axillary Nerve

Shoulder pain due to compression of the axillary nerve by fibrous bands in the quadrilateral space has been

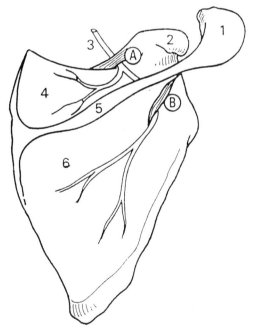

Figure 14-21 Anatomy of the suprascapular nerve. (Key: 1, acromion process; 2, coracoid process; 3, subscapular nerve; 4, supraspinous fossa; 5, spinal process; 6, infraspinous fossa; A, B, two sites of nerve entrapment.)

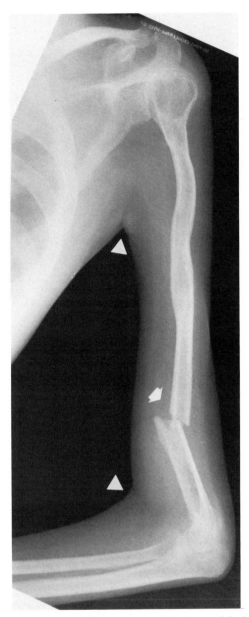

Figure 14-22 Brachial plexus injury at birth. In an adult, the bony structures are hypoplastic and gracile with an undulating humeral contour, suggestive of multiple old healed fractures. An acute fracture is evident in the distal humerus (*arrow*) along with diffuse muscle atrophy and flexion contractures (*arrowheads*).

termed the *quadrilateral space syndrome*. Selective atrophy of the teres minor muscle is very suggestive of the quadrilateral space syndrome. That could be demonstrated by MRI.[23]

Brachial Plexus Neuropathies

Tumors, infections, trauma, surgical and diagnostic procedures, and injections can involve all or some of the branches of the brachial plexus, leading to thoracic out-

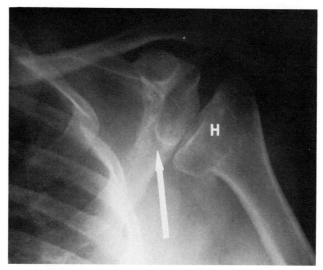

Figure 14-23 Developmental dysplasia of the shoulder. Deformity of the humeral head (H) and hypoplasia of the glenoid neck (*arrow*) are evident, secondary to incongruity of the joint in utero.

let, scalenus anticus, costoclavicular, and other syndromes. Anatomic variations such as a cervical rib may contribute to these neuropathies. Symptoms and signs vary according to the precise site of involvement, and CT is helpful in delineating the nature of the lesion.[24,25] Radiographic findings depend on the age of the patient at the time of the insult (Figs. 14-20, 14-22).

MISCELLANEOUS CONDITIONS

In utero neuromuscular dysfunction may underlie developmental dysplasia of the glenohumeral joint, a condition resulting from incongruity between the humeral head and the glenoid fossa during growth. Radiographically, this disorder is manifested by hypoplasia of the glenoid neck with variable degrees of humeral head deformity (Fig. 14-23) along with a tendency toward instability.

References

1. DiCHIRO G, NELSON KG: Soft tissue radiography of extremities in neuromuscular disease with histological correlations. *Acta Radiol (Diagn)* 3:65–88, 1965.
2. LAMMINEN A, JAASKELAINEN J, ET AL.: High frequency ultrasonography of skeletal muscle in children with neuromuscular disease. *J Ultrasound Med* 7:505–509, 1988.
3. DOCK W, HAPPACK W, GRABENWOGER R, TOIFL K, BITTNER R, FRUBER H: Neuromuscular disease—evaluation with high frequency sonography. *Radiology* 177:825–828, 1990.
4. LIU GC, JONG YJ, CHIANG CH, JAW TS: Duchenne muscular dystrophy: MR grading system with functional correlation. *Radiology* 186:475–480, 1993.
5. GORCZYCA DP, McGAHAN JP, LINDFORD KK, ELLIS WG, GRIX A: Arthrogryposis multiplex congenita: Prenatal ultrasonographic diagnosis. *J Clin Ultrasound* 17:40–44, 1989.
6. FRASER DD, FRANK JA, DALAKAS MC: Inflammatory myopathies: MR imaging and spectroscopy. *Radiology* 179:341–344, 1991.
7. PARK JH, VANSANT JP, KUMAN NG, GIBBS SJ, CURVIN MS, PRICE RR, PARTAIN CL, JAMES AE: Dermatomyositis: Correlative MR imaging and MR spectroscopy for quantitative characterization of inflammatory disease. *Radiology* 177:473–479, 1990.
8. MABILLE JP, GAUDET M, CHARPIN JF: Osteonecrose de la tete humerale au cours de l'encephalopathie bismuthique. *Ann Radiol* 23:515–517, 1980.
9. GARVEY SL, GLASS RL: Tabetic spinal osteoarthropathy. *Radiology* 8:133–139, 1927.
10. KOLAWALE T, BANNA M, HAWASS N, KHAN F, RAHMAN N: Neuropathic arthropathy as a complication of post-traumatic syringomyelia. *Br J Radiol* 60:702–704, 1987.
11. YU YL, MOSELEY IF: Syringomyelia and cervical spondylosis: A clinicoradiological investigation. *Neuroradiology* 29:143–151, 1987.
12. GREYSON ND, TEPPERMAN PS: Three-phase bone studies in hemiplegia with reflex sympathetic dystrophy and the effect of disuse. *J Nucl Med* 25:423–429, 1984.
13. SHUMACKER HB JR: A personal overview of causalgia and other reflex dystrophies. *Ann Surg* 201:278–279, 1985.
14. DAUD O, SETT P, BURR RG, SILVER JR: The relationship of heterotopic ossification to passive movements in paraplegic patients. *Disabil Rehabil* 15:114–118, 1993.
15. KUN EW, BARR WG: Heterotopic ossification presenting as acute arthritis. *J Rheumatol* 19:994–996, 1992.
16. KIM SW, WU SY, KIM RC: Computerized quantitative radionuclide assessment of heterotopic ossification in spinal cord injury patients. *Paraplegia* 30:803–807, 1992.

17. ENDO C, FUKUOKA M, KURODA Y, TSURUTA T: A case of flexion myelopathy with thoracic outlet syndrome. *Rinsho Shinkeigaku* 33:347–350, 1993.

18. FRITZ RC, HELMS CA, STEINBACH LS, GENANT HK: Suprascapular nerve entrapment: Evaluation with MR imaging. *Radiology* 182:437–444, 1992.

19. CALLAHAN JD, SCULLY TB, SHAPIRO SA, WORTH RM: Suprascapular nerve entrapment: A series of 27 cases [comments]. *J Neurosurg* 75:893–896, 1001, 1991.

20. ALON M, WEISS S, FISHEL B, DEKEL S: Bilateral suprascapular nerve entrapment syndrome due to an anomalous transverse scapular ligament. *Clin Orthop* 234:31–33, 1988.

21. POST M, MAYER J: Suprascapular nerve entrapment. Diagnosis and treatment. *Clin Orthop* 223:126–136, 1987.

22. HADLEY MN, SONNTAG VK, PITTMAN HW: Suprascapular nerve entrapment: A summary of seven cases. *J Neurosurg* 64:843–848, 1986.

23. LINKER CS, HELMS CA, FRITZ RC: Quadrilateral space syndrome: Findings at MR imaging. *Radiology* 188:675–676, 1993.

24. ALNOT JY: Traumatic brachial plexus palsy in the adult: Retro and infraclavicular lesions. *Clin Orthop* 237:9–16, 1988.

25. TRAVLOS J, GOLDBERG I, BOOME RS: Brachial plexus lesions associated with dislocated shoulders. *J Bone Joint Surg* 72:68–71, 1990.

Suggested Reading

RESNICK D, NIWAYAMA G: *Diagnosis of Bone and Joint Disorders,* 2d ed, Philadelphia, Saunders, 1988, pp 3115–3187.

MISCELLANEOUS CONDITIONS OF THE SHOULDER: IMAGING PRINCIPLES

Mark D. Murphey

Numerous miscellaneous conditions can affect the shoulder and surrounding structures. Pathologic abnormalities discussed in this chapter include the drooping shoulder, suprascapular and quadrilateral nerve impingement syndrome, posttraumatic osteolysis, myositis ossificans, pigmented villonodular synovitis (PVNS), synovial chondromatosis, amyloid, causes of periarticular calcification about the shoulder, fibrous dysplasia, Paget disease. All of these conditions can be a cause of shoulder pain; however, findings from clinical assessment are often nonspecific and radiologic evaluation is usually necessary to allow differentiation. Conventional radiographs are the first imaging study for these abnormalities, but additional studies, particularly computed tomography (CT) and magnetic resonance imaging (MRI), are also very useful for further evaluation.

DROOPING SHOULDER

In the presence of a joint effusion or owing to muscle laxity the proximal humerus can appear to be in a position of inferior subluxation in relation to the glenoid fossa. This loss of muscle tone may be the result of a neural injury typically involving the brachial plexus.[1-3] Stretching of the muscular support of the glenohumeral joint and capsular detachment can also follow trauma.[4,5] An anteroposterior radiograph reveals the inferior position of the humeral head (Fig. 15-1). It is important to recognize that this condition represents only pseudosubluxation: axillary projection radiograph demonstrates normal alignment. The abnormal inferior position of the humeral head may be apparent only on upright projections in cases due to neuromuscular injury. Treatment need not be directed to the glenohumeral alignment because this will return to normal over several weeks when the joint effusion or muscle laxity resolves. As a cause of drooping shoulder, joint effusion is often related to trauma and humeral neck fractures, though any intraarticular fluid collection can be associated with the

pseudosubluxation. MR imaging or sonography can be used to confirm joint effusion, though the underlying cause may not be apparent.

SUPRASCAPULAR NERVE ENTRAPMENT AND QUADRILATERAL SPACE SYNDROME

The suprascapular nerve originates from the upper trunks of the brachial plexus (fourth, fifth, and sixth cervical nerve roots) and consists of motor and sensory components. The nerve enters the supraspinatus fossa through the suprascapular notch and then extends into the infraspinatus fossa through the spinoglenoid notch. The nerve supplies the supraspinatus muscle via branches that arise within the supraspinatus fossa and supplies the infraspinatus muscle from branches arising within the infraspinatus fossa.[6] Sensory branches from the glenohumeral and acromioclavicular joints are derived from the nerve in the supraspinatus fossa. Entrapment of the suprascapular nerve can be a result of trauma (humeral and scapular fractures, penetrating injury, and anterior shoulder dislocation), masses (particularly ganglion cysts), and a thickened transverse scapular ligament.[7-15] In addition, entrapment can occur at the suprascapular notch and spinoglenoid notch secondary to a sling effect.[16] Symptoms are nonspecific shoulder pain and muscle atrophy. Early diagnosis and treatment are important to improve the chances of return of motor function. MRI may be helpful in the assessment of these patients. Muscle atrophy from nerve entrapment is seen as decreased muscle size and increased striations of fat (high intensity on T1-weighted images, intermediate intensity on T2-weighted images).[6] MRI is better than CT at detecting muscle atrophy because of improved soft tissue contrast. CT changes of muscle atrophy are primarily decreased muscle size; increased fat deposition is difficult to identify. The distribution of muscle atrophy

413

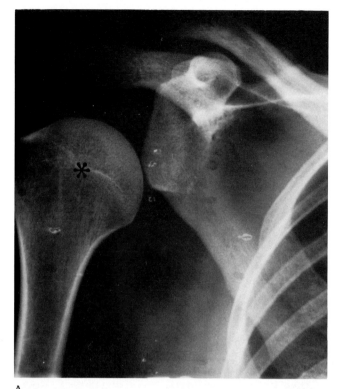

A

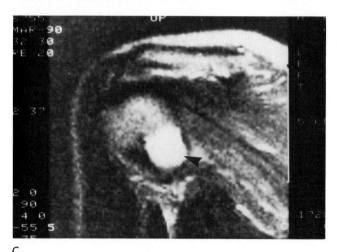

C

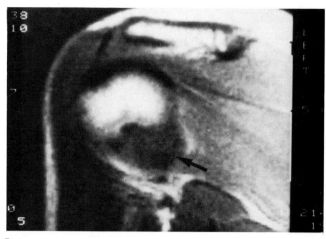

B

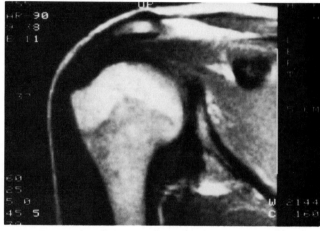

D

Figure 15-1 A 34-year-old woman had brachial plexus injury and drooping shoulder. Anteroposterior upright shoulder radiograph, **A**, shows the humeral head (*) inferior in position relative to the glenoid. Coronal T1-weighted MRI, **B**, shows a joint effusion in the axillary recess which is low intensity (*arrow*) and becomes bright (*arrowhead*) on the coronal T2-weighted image, **C**. Coronal T1-weighted MRI, **D**, more anteriorly shows normal glenohumeral alignment. Electromyography showed shoulder nerve palsy.

(Fig. 15-2) can be used to determine if entrapment is occurring proximal to the supraspinatus fossa (supraspinatus and infraspinatus muscle atrophy) or distally in the infraspinatus fossa or spinoglenoid notch (infraspinatus muscle atrophy only). In addition, localized masses can be identified as the cause of impingement. Ganglion cysts are particularly prone to be associated with suprascapular nerve entrapment as reported by Fritz and colleagues.[6,12] MRI of ganglion cysts shows low to intermediate intensity on T1-weighting and very high signal intensity on T2-weighting. These masses are homogeneous in signal intensity and are well-defined. Axial and coronal MR images appear to be most helpful in evaluating suprascapular entrapment syndrome.[6] When no evi-

dence of mass is seen on MRI, nerve entrapment in either the suprascapular or the spinoglenoid notch is likely, depending on the distribution of muscle atrophy.[16] Entrapment in the spinoglenoid notch is more likely in men because of normal developmental variations that predispose to impingement.

The quadrilateral space syndrome is caused by compression of the axillary nerve by fibrous bands in the quadrilateral space.[17,18] Patients complain of nonspecific posterior shoulder pain that gets worse with abduction and external rotation, and paresthesia of the lateral shoulder and upper posterior arm.[19,20] The quadrilateral space is bounded by the humeral neck laterally, triceps muscle medially, teres major muscle inferiorly, and teres minor muscle superiorly.[19,20] MRI can provide a non-invasive method of evaluating axillary nerve compression, and, specifically, the resultant atrophy of the teres minor or deltoid muscle.[21,22] Just as with suprascapular entrapment, muscle atrophy is seen as increased fat deposition and decreased size of the involved muscle. Sagittal oblique and axial MR images are best to evaluate the quadrilateral space syndrome.[21]

POSTTRAUMATIC OSTEOLYSIS OF THE CLAVICLE

Resorption of the distal clavicle can follow a single episode of trauma or repetitive microtrauma such as weightlifters sustain.[23–25] Osteolysis of the distal clavicle may be manifested as early as 2 to 3 weeks after the traumatic event or as late as several years.[26] Patient symptoms include pain, crepitus, swelling, and limited range of motion.

Radiographs initially reveal irregularity and ill definition of the cortical margins of the distal clavicle (Fig. 15-3). Soft tissue swelling may also be present. The lytic phase may persist for 12 to 18 months in patients who remain active and is associated with progressive resorption of the distal 0.5 to 3.0 cm of the clavicle.[27–32] The acromion may be involved by similar though less extensive resorption.[28] The reparative phase follows this period of osteolysis with reconstitution of the resorbed bone and cortex. Areas of sclerosis may be seen in the reparative phase on radiographs (see Fig. 15-3). Reparative changes occur over 4 to 6 months and may not

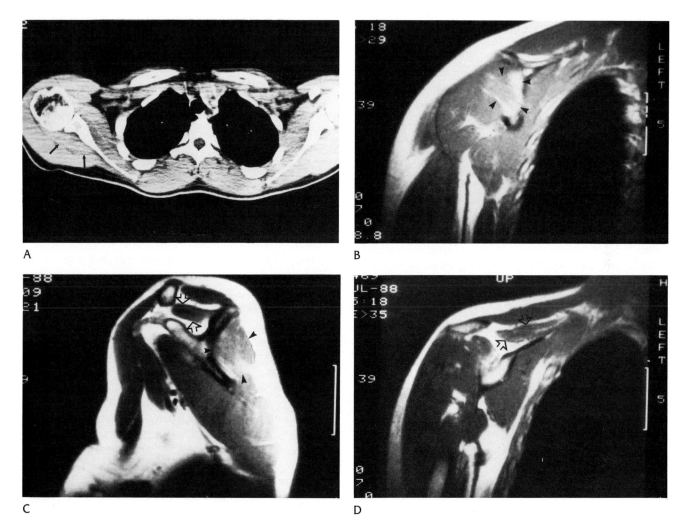

A

B

C

D

Figure 15-2 A 22-year-old woman complained of muscle atrophy about the shoulder and pain. Radiographs were normal (not shown). CT scan, **A,** shows decreased size of the right infraspinatus muscle (*arrows*) as compared with the contralateral side. T1-weighted MRI in the coronal, **B,** and sagittal planes, **C,** shows increased fat deposition from atrophy of the infraspinatus muscle (*arrowheads*). Supraspinatus muscle is normal (*open arrows*) on sagittal image and more anterior coronal T1-weighted MRI, **D.** T2-weighted MRI (not shown) revealed no mass or increased intensity in the involved muscle. At surgery, entrapment of the suprascapular nerve in the spinoglenoid notch was found, which accounts for the distribution of muscle atrophy.

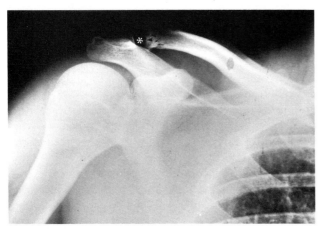

Figure 15-3 A 19-year-old male weightlifter had a painful acromio-clavicular (AC) joint for 6 months. Anteroposterior radiograph of the shoulder in internal rotation shows osseous resorption (*arrowheads*) of the distal clavicle, resulting in widening of the AC joint (*). There is evidence of early repair with mild sclerosis (*arrows*) about the areas of resorption in this patient with posttraumatic osteolysis of the clavicle. The acromion is preserved.

completely restore the bone resorption, leading to persistent widening of the acromioclavicular joint.[27–32] The differential diagnosis of distal clavicular resorption in addition to posttraumatic osteolysis includes infection, rheumatoid and other inflammatory arthritides, gout, scleroderma and other collagen vascular diseases, septic arthritis, and hyperparathyroidism.[27]

Other imaging modalities also reveal abnormalities in posttraumatic osteolysis. Bone scan shows intense increased activity in both the lytic and reparative phases.[27–32] CT can also demonstrate the osseous resorption and soft tissue material replacing these regions.[24] On T1-weighted images MRI shows marrow replacement of the distal clavicle by tissue of heterogeneous intensity, predominantly similar to muscle.[33] There is marked and relatively homogeneous hyperintensity on T2-weighted MR images.[33] Various theories about the pathogenesis of this abnormality that have been advanced include autonomic dysfunction, hyperemia, and posttraumatic synovial reaction. MRI characteristics, while nonspecific, would support synovial hyperplasia with a villous and vascular proliferation, as suggested by Levine and coworkers.[32,33] In their study, this type of synovial tissue was found pathologically and osseous healing followed synovectomy.[32]

MYOSITIS OSSIFICANS (HETEROTOPIC BONE FORMATION)

Myositis ossificans is a nonneoplastic reactive formation of heterotopic bone that is usually a sequela of trauma.[34,35] Heterotopic bone formation can also be associated with burns, paraplegia, and central nervous system injury.[36,37] While the lower extremity is most frequently involved, not uncommonly the shoulder and surrounding soft tissues are affected.[36,37] The distinctive pattern of ossification diagnostic of myositis ossificans may take weeks to months to develop, and a history of trauma may not be apparent in 25 to 40 percent of patients.[38–41] These factors often lead to misdiagnosis of a neoplastic process (Fig. 15-4).

Initially, radiographs show only soft tissue swelling and edema, and the shoulder is usually significantly painful in this early stage (see Fig. 15-4A). Clinically, the lesion then becomes more definable as a soft tissue mass; it may be less painful and often gradually shrinks. Calcification can usually be recognized on radiographs by 2 to 6 weeks in young adults and adolescents, the age group typically affected.[37–42] This mineralization begins peripherally with a mature ossific shell of cortical bone and more immature trabecular bone centrally which is well developed by 2 to 3 months. This zonal pattern of maturation seen on radiographs reflects the pathologic process. Histologically there is immature proliferating osteoid centrally (fibroblastic and myofibroblastic tissue) and more mature osteoid tissue peripherally.[43] Evaluation of biopsy material in earlier stages may be very confusing and suggests soft tissue osteosarcoma unless this zonal phenomenon is recognized. The radiologist or orthopedic surgeon who obtains a biopsy must tell the pathologist which portion of tissue is superficial and which deep when myositis ossificans is a consideration. This allows the pathologist to analyze the histologic characteristics and diagnose heterotopic bone formation.

Bone scans reveal markedly increased uptake on both dynamic and static images within the area of myositis ossificans (see Fig. 15-4B). As maturation occurs with development of a well-defined cortex and medullary canal the activity on bone scan decreases, ultimately becoming equivalent to that in other osseous structures. CT is often the most useful modality for evaluating and diagnosing heterotopic bone formation.[44,45] CT can detect the initial characteristic peripheral calcification at an earlier stage than can radiographs (Fig. 15-4G). This is because of improved contrast resolution and lack of overlying osseous structures that may obscure this early mineralization on radiographs. Maturation is seen on CT as further development of a cortical rim with trabecular bone centrally that is often of fat-type attenuation, representing yellow marrow. Before calcification is seen, CT may show only an ill-defined soft tissue mass of higher attenuation than that of adjacent muscle. In these cases a follow-up scan in 2 to 4 weeks is diagnostic, as peripheral calcification develops.[44,45] Additional nonspecific CT findings are prominent inflammation and edema within muscle, skin thickening, and soft tissue stranding in the subcutaneous tissue.

MRI of heterotopic ossification, particularly in the earlier stages, is often very suggestive of an aggressive neo-

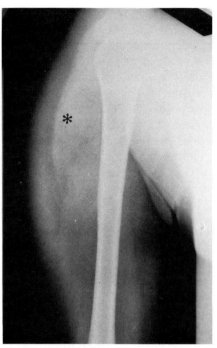

A

Figure 15-4 A 29-year-old woman had shoulder pain after playing slot machines. The patient denied history of other trauma and subsequently developed a soft tissue mass that grew. Radiograph, **A**, 1 month after symptoms began shows only vague soft tissue fullness lateral to the upper humerus (*). Bone scan, **B**, reveals marked increased activity in this region. Digital subtraction angiogram, **C**, shows marked hypervascular mass (*curved arrow*). Axial, **D**, T1-weighted MRI reveals only mild distortion of fascial plane (*small arrowheads*) in the region of the mass. Coronal, **E**, and axial, **F**, T2-weighted MRI reveals a hyperintense mass (*large arrows*) anteriorly with infiltration margins (*small arrows*) that involves both muscle and subcutaneous fat. Axial CT, **G**, performed 2 weeks before the MR study shows earliest findings of peripheral calcification (*large arrowheads*) diagnostic of myositis ossificans, as well as inflammation in the subcutaneous tissue (*open arrow*). The mass is seen better on MRI than on CT.

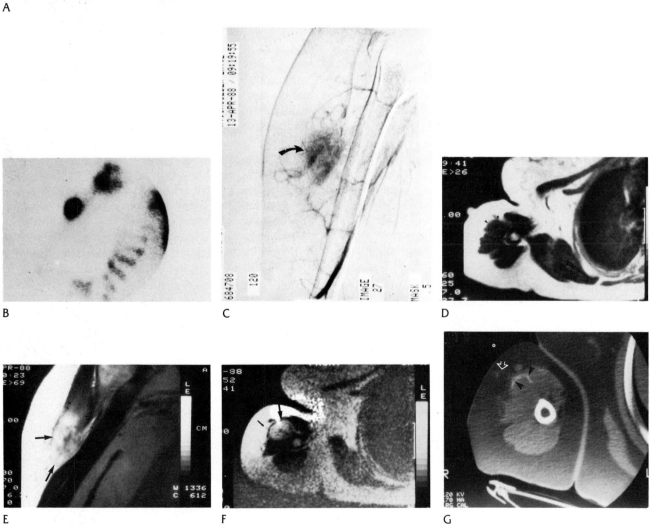

B

C

D

E

F

G

plasm.[37,38,46] Because of this, in my opinion CT is preferable to MRI for evaluation of myositis ossificans; however, several subtle MRI changes should suggest heterotopic bone formation. These are important to recognize because MRI is often the initial radiologic modality used to evaluate any soft tissue abnormality.

The MRI appearance depends on the maturity of the areas of myositis ossificans. In the early to intermediate stage the central area of heterotopic bone formation is generally of low to intermediate intensity, similar to that of muscle on T1-weighted images.[37,38] High signal intensity and fluid-fluids levels related to hemorrhage may rarely be present.[47] The lesion may be recognized only on short TR/TE MR images by its mass effect and disruption of muscle texture (see Fig. 15-4D). On T2-weighted MR images there is heterogeneous high signal intensity (see Fig. 15-4E, F), most prominent centrally within the focus of myositis ossificans owing to myxoid histologic components.[37,38,46] A subtle peripheral rim of lower signal intensity should be sought, as this is the earliest MRI finding of peripheral mineralization characteristic of heterotopic ossification.[37,38,46] Unfortunately, this finding may be obscured by marked associated inflammation and edema on long TR/TE MR images, which are often mistaken for the infiltrating margins of an aggressive neoplasm (see Fig. 15-4E, F). The mass is largest on T2-weighted MR images because of this edema. In the late stages of myositis ossificans with maturation, MRI features are a cortex peripherally (low signal on all pulse sequences) and fat signal centrally. De Smet and coworkers described two cases of heterotopic bone formation with low signal intensity on T2-weighted MR images in the late stages.[46] This appearance likely corresponds to an increased degree of cortical (as opposed to trabecular) bone on review of their cases. Areas of myositis ossificans show enhancement on CT or MRI after intravenous contrast because of increased vascularity (Fig. 15-4C).[48]

Myositis ossificans typically involves deep muscle tissue; however, subcutaneous localization can be seen in as many as 25 percent of cases.[37] Because of its location, heterotopic ossification may restrict nearby joint motion, be deforming, or affect muscle or tendon function and require surgical removal. Resection should not be performed until after maturation has occurred, and in some instances surgery may be delayed for 15 to 20 months.[40] Surgical removal before this time may result in recurrence "with a vengeance." Radiologic evaluation of maturation can be helpful, and generally the identification of largely yellow marrow centrally suggests that the lesion can safely be surgically removed. This determination can be performed with radiography (trabecular bone centrally), bone scan (activity similar to other osseous structures), bone marrow scan (activity within myositis), CT (fat attenuation centrally), or MRI (yellow marrow signal centrally).

PIGMENTED VILLONODULAR SYNOVITIS

PVNS is a proliferative disorder of the synovium. The synovial hypertrophy may be villous, nodular, or villonodular, and some degree of hemosiderin deposition is associated with the synovium. PVNS is almost invariably a monoarticular disease, with an incidence of 2 to 11 per million and no gender predilection.[49–54] PVNS typically affects persons in the second through the fifth decades of life. There are two forms of PVNS, localized and diffuse. The localized form represents 75 percent of cases, typically affects the tendons about the fingers, and is also called *giant cell tumor of tendon sheath* (GCTTS).[55–57] This form of PVNS can also involve the tenosynovial tissues around the shoulder. The diffuse form of PVNS frequently involves larger joints and is most common in the knee and hip. The shoulder is relatively uncommonly affected by this disease. The pathogenesis of PVNS is unknown but there are many theories, including neoplasia, disorder of lipid metabolism, and repetitive trauma, but the most widely supported possible cause is an inflammatory process.

PVNS of the shoulder joint is less likely to produce radiographic changes than is hip involvement. This is because the shoulder is a relatively distensible joint with numerous associated bursae into which synovial hypertrophy can extend. This makes extrinsic erosion of the osseous structures on both sides of the shoulder less common on radiographs, though this finding is reported in 15 to 50 percent of all cases of PVNS[50] (Fig. 15-5A, B).[50] Other radiographic signs usually are not present. Extrinsic erosions are often better seen on CT or MRI because of improved contrast resolution, elimination of overlying osseous structures, and multiplanar imaging capability. Nodular synovial masses are seen on CT and MRI, and an associated effusion is present in almost 80 percent of cases.[49–51] The effusion if aspirated is a xanthochromic to brownish-stained, bloody fluid. The nodular synovial masses may be of higher attenuation than muscle on CT because of hemosiderin deposition.[58,59] There is also diffuse soft tissue thickening about the shoulder, and fluid collections are often seen in the subscapular bursa, in the axillary recess, and about the bicipital tendon. Arthrography or CT following injection of contrast into the joint shows nodular filling defects and synovial thickening.[58,59]

MRI is the modality of choice for evaluating the diffuse form of PVNS because the findings are usually characteristic.[49,51–54] Nodular synovial excrescences and diffuse thickening are well demonstrated on MRI. Low signal intensity is a prominent feature on all MR pulse sequences (Fig. 15-5C, D). There is heterogeneous signal intensity on T2-weighted images, owing to the high signal intensity of associated joint effusion. These pockets of

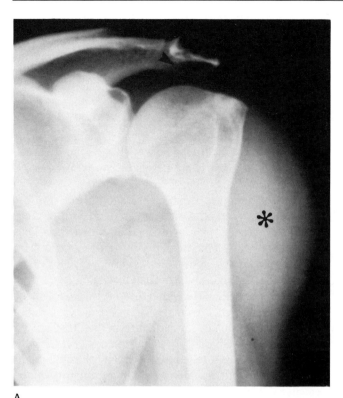

A

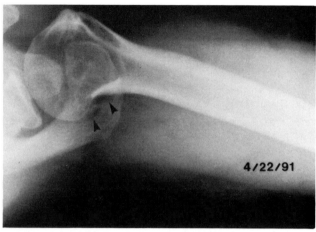

Figure 15-5 A 40-year-old woman experienced increasing shoulder pain and swelling. Anteroposterior, **A,** and axillary, **B,** radiographs of the shoulder show erosions of the acromion and greater tuberosity regions (*large arrowheads*) with a soft tissue mass (*) laterally. T2-weighted MRI in the axial, **C,** and coronal, **D,** planes reveal the mass to have large components of low intensity (*small arrowheads*) owing to hemosiderin deposition in this case of PVNS. Focal areas of fluid (*arrow*) are also present, particularly prominent on the coronal image in the bicipital tendon sheath (*open arrow*).

B

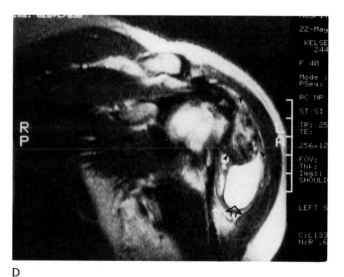

C

D

synovial fluid are usually surrounded by low-intensity hemosiderin-laden synovial tissue. The hypointensity of the synovial tissue in PVNS is a result of the unpaired electrons of iron in the ferric state (Fe^{+3}) interacting with adjacent water molecules and shortening the T2 relaxation time.[60] These effects are accentuated on high–field strength MR units because the T2 relaxation time is proportional to the square of the magnetic field as described by Gomori and coworkers.[60] The synovial pro-

liferation is hypervascular and is enhanced on angiography and on CT or MRI after intravenous contrast injection.[49–59]

The localized form of PVNS can involve tenosynovial tissues about the shoulder. The extent of hemosiderin deposition is more variable than in the diffuse form of PVNS.[55–57] This may result in MRI and CT demonstrating only a nonspecific soft tissue mass. MRI may show only a mass with low to intermediate intensity on T1 weighting and high signal intensity on T2 weighting. However, MRI is often more distinctive in GCTTS, as reported recently by Jelinek and colleagues, with prominent areas of low signal intensity on all pulse sequences owing to hemosiderin, identical to the changes in the diffuse form of PVNS.[57] This finding in a mass located adjacent to or involving a tendon about the shoulder is very suggestive of GCTTS.

Synovectomy is usually the initial treatment for the diffuse form of PVNS[50]; however, because of the difficulty in performing a truly complete synovectomy, recurrences are common. Difficulty in resecting all the synovial tissue is further complicated by the numerous bursal extensions that occur when PVNS involves the shoulder. In the diffuse form of PVNS, recurrence is estimated to occur in 40 to 50 percent of cases, whereas GCTTS has a lower rate of 10 to 14 percent.[49–57] MRI and CT are important for detecting the frequent recurrences in follow-up of patients with PVNS. The radiologic appearance of recurrent disease is identical on MRI and CT to the previously described characteristics of PVNS before therapy. Adjuvant treatment methods for recurrent disease include external radiation therapy and injection of beta-emitting agents into the joint, producing a nonsurgical synovectomy. Yttrium 90 and dysprosium 165 attached to radiocolloid are beta-emitting materials most recently used.[50]

SYNOVIAL CHONDROMATOSIS

Synovial chondromatosis is a disease caused by cartilage metaplasia within the synovial membrane.[61,62] The etiology is unknown; purported causes include neoplastic, inflammatory, and traumatic processes. The disease is twice as frequent in men, almost invariably is monoarticular, and usually involves patients between age 20 and 50 years.[63–68] Clinical symptoms are usually mechanical—joint pain (often of long duration), joint locking, and reduced range of motion. The disease most frequently involves the knee and hip; however, the shoulder is not uncommonly affected.[63–72]

Pathologically there is synovial hyperplasia with nodules of cartilage metaplasia measuring 2 to 3 cm.[61,62,71] These frondlike excrescences frequently become detached to lie free in the joint as intraarticular bodies of relatively uniform size (several millimeters to centimeters). The cartilage fragments, nourished from the synovial fluid, may grow or they may reattach to the synovial lining, where they may enlarge or be resorbed. Endochondral ossification can occur within the cartilage fragments, and then the term *synovial osteochondromatosis* is appropriate. Numerous bursae and tendon structures are present about the shoulder, and this tissue can be involved primarily in an identical process without joint changes that is called *tenosynovial chondromatosis*.[63,71]

The most distinguishing radiographic manifestation of synovial chondromatosis is calcification of the cartilage fragments (Fig. 15-6A). This is seen in 75 to 90 percent of cases on radiographs or CT and often has a typical ringlike appearance distinctive of chondroid tissue.[62,63,68] In my experience CT is the optimal radiologic modality for detecting, characterizing, and localizing these calcifications about the shoulder. Small chondroid bodies may be solidly calcified, whereas larger fragments may undergo ossification with a cortical rim and trabecular bone centrally on CT and radiographs (Fig. 15-6A, B). The central area on CT exhibits fat attenuation, owing to the presence of yellow marrow. A central dot of chondroid calcification may give a target appearance (Figs. 15-6B, 6C). Noncalcified areas of synovial metaplasia appear as thickening about the shoulder on CT with an attenuation similar to or less than that of muscle.

Findings on MRI of the mineralized cartilage fragments vary, depending on the degree of chondroid calcification or ossification. Small intraarticular bodies that are entirely calcified exhibit low signal intensity on all pulse sequences and are better seen by CT or radiography. Larger chondroid fragments with a peripheral ring of calcification show low to intermediate intensity on T1-weighted MR images, and on long-TR images the central region becomes high in signal intensity.[64,65,68] Central calcification may give a target appearance on MRI (Fig. 15-6D, E). Ossified intraarticular bodies demonstrate low signal intensity on all MR pulse sequences in the periphery (corresponding to cortical bone) and fat signal intensity centrally (owing to yellow marrow). Noncalcified areas of synovial thickening with chondroid metaplasia appear as low to intermediate intensity on T1-weighted MR images and very high intensity on T2-weighted images.[64] This appearance on long-TR/TE images is caused by hyaline cartilage, which is composed of 75 to 80 percent water (Fig. 15-6F).[64,65,72] Low–signal intensity fibrous septations may be present within the areas of synovial thickening. Thus, the MRI characteristics of synovial chondromatosis are exactly opposite those of PVNS on T2 weighting, with high–signal intensity tissue peripherally and low-signal calcified intraarticular bodies centrally.

CT, radiography, and MRI may show extrinsic erosions and changes of secondary osteoarthritis with synovial chondromatosis about the shoulder (see Fig. 15-6).[70] This is not a frequent finding in the shoulder, owing to the relatively large volume of the shoulder articulation. Joint effusion may also be detected by CT or MRI in association with synovial chondromatosis.

Arthrography or CT after injection of contrast medium into the joint demonstrates multiple filling defects in the joint and nodular synovial thickening similar to PVNS. There is less enhancement of the synovial thickening after intravenous injection of contrast on CT or MRI (or

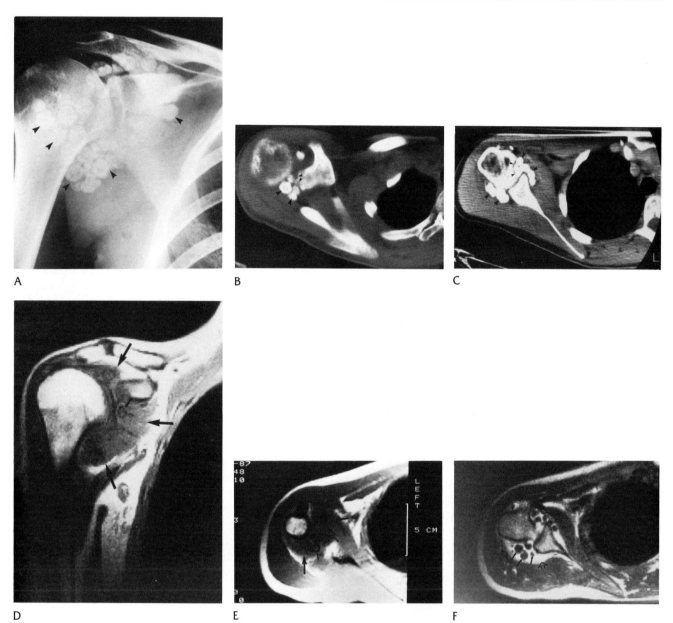

Figure 15-6 A 19-year-old woman had shoulder discomfort and limitation of motion. Anteroposterior radiograph, **A,** shows multiple circular calcifications (*large arrowheads*), several of which have central foci of mineralization as well. CT scans with bone, **B,** and soft tissue, **C,** windows show the multiple calcifications (*large arrowheads*), several with the "target" appearance. Pressure erosions on the glenoid and humerus are seen (*small arrowheads*), as is mild soft tissue thickening (*), representing noncalcified synovial metaplasia. Coronal, **D,** and axial, **E,** T1-weighted MRI reveal extensive thickening of the shoulder joint (*large arrows*). Calcifications are seen as regions with a rim of low intensity peripherally, representing cortical bone. A target appearance is created by yellow marrow and central chondroid (*small arrows*) in many of the osteochondral fragments. On axial T2-weighted MRI, **F,** synovial metaplasia becomes high intensity (*open arrows*) and also involves the bicipital tendon sheath, whereas the areas of calcification (*small arrows*) remain low intensity. These findings are typical of synovial osteochondromatosis, which was proven at surgery.

staining with angiography) because tissue is less hypervascular in synovial chondromatosis than in PVNS. Multiple osteochondral bodies may also occur as a result of previous involvement of the glenohumeral joint by infection, trauma, or arthritis. Associated changes about the

joint should be recognized on radiographs to distinguish this process of secondary synovial chondromatosis from the primary variety. The intraarticular bodies in secondary synovial chondromatosis may demonstrate multiple rings of calcification or ossification, creating a laminated appearance on radiography or CT.[61,62,72] This is a result of growth and is not usually seen in primary synovial chondromatosis. Malignant degeneration of synovial chondromatosis to chondrosarcoma is rare.[68] Osseous invasion or destruction about a glenohumeral joint chronically involved by synovial chondromatosis should suggest this possibility.

AMYLOIDOSIS

Amyloid deposition—both within osseous structures and in tenosynovial tissues of large and small joints—is being reported with increasing frequency.[73–79] It is more common with secondary amyloidosis associated with multiple myeloma (5 to 10 percent of patients) or chronic inflammatory diseases. A unique form of secondary amyloidosis caused by deposition of beta-2-microglobulin is now common in patients with chronic renal failure who receive hemodialysis.[73–77] In a group of 88 patients who had hemodialysis for longer than 4 years, Camacho and colleagues reported an incidence of amyloidosis of 35 percent.[75] While the hip is often described as the large articulation most frequently involved, the distribution of the patients in the study of Camacho and coworkers showed that the prevalence was highest about the shoulder; 71 percent of changes occurred in the glenohumeral joint.[75]

Radiographs and CT reveal punched-out eccentric lytic lesions on both sides of the glenohumeral joint, with predominant involvement of the humeral head. Extrinsic erosions from synovial involvement by amyloid can also be seen. These osseous lesions frequently demonstrate a sclerotic margin on CT or radiography because of their indolent growth.[73–75] Synovial infiltration by amyloid is seen on CT or MRI as diffuse thickening about the glenohumeral joint (Fig. 15-7). The synovial thickening on CT is similar in attenuation to surrounding muscle and is difficult to identify.[75,77] MRI shows the synovial amyloid deposition and associated osseous erosions with marrow replacement as low to intermediate signal intensity on T1-weighting and little change in signal intensity on long-TR/TE images (see Fig. 15-7).[75,77] This interesting T2-weighted MRI appearance is probably due to the fibrillar collagen-like composition of amyloid.[76] Small fluid collections also are often seen as high–signal intensity foci on long-TR/TE images with intraarticular amyloid deposition (see Fig. 15-7).[75,77] The amyloid-laden synovial tissue may enhance on CT and MRI after intravenous injection of contrast medium. Amyloid involvement of the synovium has a similar appearance to PVNS on CT and MRI; however, polyarticular involvement of both shoulders and other joints is typical of amyloid rather than PVNS.

TUMORAL CALCINOSIS

Tumoral calcinosis is an unusual disorder characterized by large periarticular masses composed of calcium hydroxyapatite. The shoulder is one of the most frequent sites of calcified masses in this condition.[80] Patients with this disease are usually young (in the first or second decade of life), frequently are black, and have several joints involved (average three per patient).[80] The cause of tumoral calcinosis is likely an inborn error of phosphorus metabolism.[81–83] Clinically, the masses grow slowly and are often polyarticular and painless, without limitation of motion because initially they are usually located extraarticularly in bursae about the joint.

Radiographs typically reveal a large lobulated calcific mass about the shoulder with radiolucent fibrous septations (Fig. 15-8).[80,84,85] The calcium is often pasty, and milk of calcium with fluid-fluid levels, may be seen on upright radiographs or CT images.[86] These calcified masses can cause the overlying skin to ulcerate and lead to sinus tracts with superimposed infection. In addition, adjacent bone erosion, periosteal reaction, and a calcific osteomyelitis can be associated with tumoral calcinosis.[80] On CT the calcific osteomyelitis is seen as increased attenuation in the marrow space. On MRI it appears as marrow replacement on T1 weighting and as nonspecific increased marrow signal on T2 weighting.[80] These unusual marrow changes are likely caused by calcium hydroxyapatite deposition in the marrow space, and usually occur in the humeral diaphysis. Skeletal scintigraphy is very accurate for detecting and localizing the different sites of involvement because intense increased uptake is seen.[87] Bone scanning may also be useful for following the effects of phosphate depletion therapy in these patients.[88] The differential diagnosis of multifocal periarticular calcifications includes secondary hyperparathyroidism, milk-alkali syndrome, and collagen vascular diseases.

FIBROUS DYSPLASIA

Fibrous dysplasia is a developmental anomaly in which medullary bone is replaced by a fibroosseous tissue. The process is monostotic in 70 to 85 percent of cases and polyostotic in 15 to 30 percent.[89–92] Monostotic fibrous dysplasia involves the humerus in 5 percent of cases.[89–92] Polyostotic fibrous dysplasia also not infrequently involves the proximal humerus. Patients usually present in the first two decades, though monostotic disease may be asymptomatic. Endocrine abnormalities that can occur with fibrous dysplasia include precocious puberty, hyperthyroidism, acromegaly, diabetes mellitus, Cushing's syndrome, and hyperparathyroidism.[89–93]

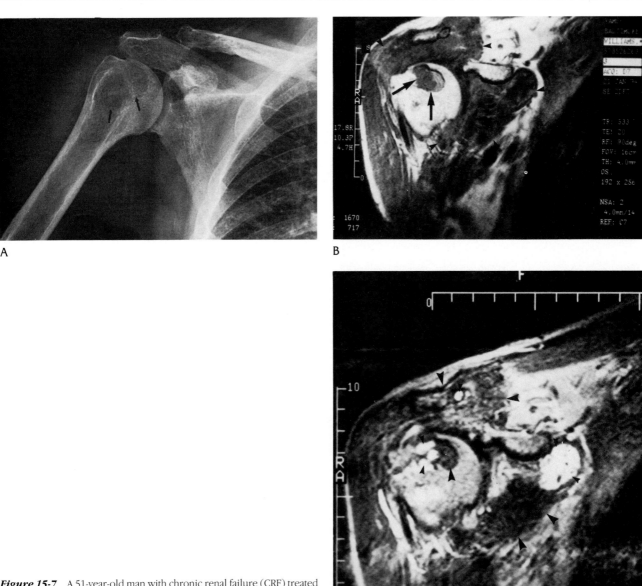

A

B

C

Figure 15-7 A 51-year-old man with chronic renal failure (CRF) treated with hemodialysis for 22 years. Radiograph of the shoulder, **A,** shows vague lucency in the humeral head (*small arrows*) and changes from CRF, with abnormal trabecular pattern and distal clavicle resorption. Coronal T1-weighted MRI, **B,** shows marked thickening of the soft tissues about the shoulder (*large arrowheads*), which is similar in intensity to muscle. This extends both superiorly into the acromioclavicular joint and medially. There is also a large focal area of marrow replacement (*large arrows*) in the humeral head. Coronal T2-weighted MRI, **C,** reveals that most of the soft tissue thickening remains predominantly low intensity (*large arrowheads*), with focal areas of fluid collections (*small arrowheads*). The patient had multiple complaints from amyloid (beta-2-microglobulin) deposition, including his shoulder symptoms and bilateral carpal tunnel syndrome.

Radiographs reveal replacement of the normal trabecular bone that characteristically gives a ground-glass appearance, with cortical thinning caused by endosteal scalloping (Fig. 15-9A). There may be surrounding sclerosis and areas of trabeculation within the lesion that may create a multilocular appearance. The expansion weakens the bone, and in the humerus this can lead to lateral bowing and fracture (see Fig. 15-9A). On CT the normal marrow is replaced by higher-attenuation fibrous tissue in the humeral shaft.[94-96] Endosteal scalloping and ex-

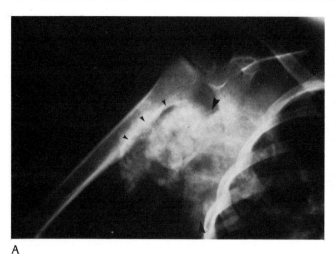

A

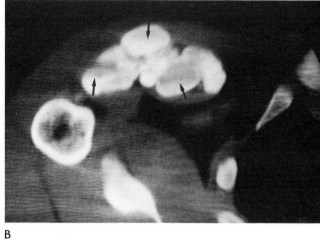

B

Figure 15-8 A 2-year-old boy with shoulder swelling. Radiograph of the shoulder, **A,** shows large calcified mass (*large arrowheads*) with radiolucent septations. Extrinsic erosion of the adjacent humerus is also seen (*small arrowheads*). Bone scan (not shown) revealed marked uptake of radionuclide in this region. CT scan, **B,** shows fluid-fluid levels (*arrows*) within the calcifications. At surgical resection, a pasty material was found, representing tumoral calcinosis.

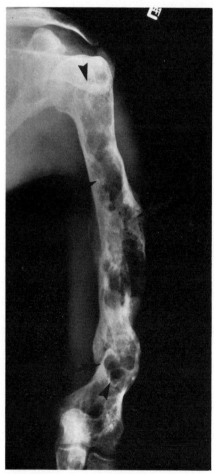

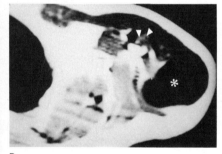

B

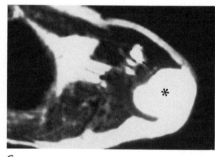

C

Figure 15-9 A 29-year-old man was known to have polyostotic fibrous dysplasia. Humerus radiograph, **A,** shows extensive changes of polyostotic fibrous dysplasia with bone expansion and endosteal scalloping in the humerus and scapula (*large arrowheads*). Several sites of fracture with lateral bowing are seen in the middle and lower humeral shaft (*large arrows*). Axial T1-weighted MRI, **B,** reveals marrow replacement and expansion (*small arrowheads*) of the upper humeral metaphysis with a large posterior mass (*) of low signal intensity. Axial T2-weighted MRI, **C,** shows high intensity in both the area of humeral involvement by fibrous dysplasia (*small arrows*) and the fluid-filled mass posteriorly (*), which represented a myxoma in this patient with Mazabraud's syndrome.

A

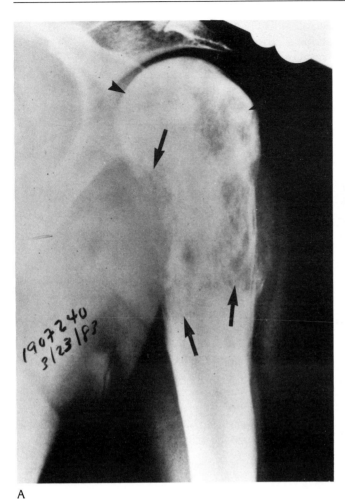

A

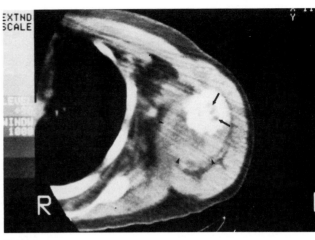

B

Figure 15-10 A 50-year-old man who had long-standing Paget disease and felt a new pain in the shoulder. Anteroposterior shoulder radiograph, **A,** shows changes of Paget disease with trabecular thickening, sclerosis, and bone expansion (*large arrowheads*). Aggressive lytic lesion with cortical destruction is present in the humeral metaphysis (*large arrows*). This lytic focus was not present on radiographs 10 years earlier (not shown). CT scan, **B,** shows a soft tissue mass (*small arrowheads*) posteriorly and increased attenuation in the marrow space (*small arrows*) from Paget disease and malignant degeneration to osteosarcoma.

pansile remodeling are also detected. Bone scans generally demonstrate markedly increased activity in osseous structures involved by fibrous dysplasia.[96,97]

MRI of fibrous dysplasia produces variable findings. There is marrow replacement on T1-weighted images. T2-weighted images exhibit high signal intensity (higher intensity than fat signal) in 64 percent of cases, intermediate intensity (similar to fat) in 18 percent of cases, and low signal intensity (similar to muscle) in 18 percent of cases (Fig. 15-9B, C).[89,98,99] Long-axis MRI (sagittal or coronal) is useful to evaluate the extent of marrow involvement in the humerus. Signal intensity is usually homogeneous; however, fluid-fluid levels from hemorrhage have been described in fibrous dysplasia on MR images.[47]

Malignant degeneration of fibrous dysplasia to osteosarcoma, fibrosarcoma or malignant fibrous histiocytoma, and chondrosarcoma is a rare complication.[89,99–101] It can occur with monostotic or polyostotic disease and in one third of patients is associated with a history of radiation.[89] Radiography, CT, or MRI shows new areas of aggressive bone destruction and soft tissue mass. Intramuscular myxoma (Mazabraud's syndrome) is also as-

sociated with fibrous dysplasia and frequently is multifocal (see Fig. 15-9B, C). These lesions have a cystic appearance on CT or MRI and are usually in the vicinity of the osseous lesions.[89,102,103]

PAGET DISEASE

Paget disease is a common disorder affecting 3 percent of persons older than 40 years and 10 percent of those over 80.[104–108] The pathogenesis is unknown, though many investigators believe that an inflammatory cause is likely. The most frequent sites of involvement are the pelvis, skull, and vertebrae; however the shoulder, particularly the proximal humerus, is also commonly affected.

Radiographs reveal lytic, blastic, or mixed lesions that usually begin from the subchondral region, extending into the metadiaphysis (Fig. 15-10A). Lytic lesions often have a wedge shape at their metadiaphyseal margin. Involvement frequently leads to bone expansion, with cortical and trabecular thickening (see Fig. 15-10A). CT shows similar findings, with replacement of yellow marrow in the proximal humerus by a mixture of osseous thickening and intervening soft tissue (corresponding histologically to fibrovascular tissue).[104–109] Bone scans demonstrate intense activity in regions of involvement by Paget disease.[104,105]

On MRI Paget disease is variable in appearance.[110–114] In uncomplicated cases a relatively normal marrow pattern is usually present. Low-intensity thickened trabeculae are usually seen interrupting the normal yellow marrow. Foci of marrow replacement on T1-weighted MR images that become high signal on long-TR/TE images may also be seen, representing fibrovascular tissue.

Complications of Paget disease that are not infrequent and involve the proximal humerus include fracture, bowing, secondary osteoarthritis, and neoplasms.[104] Fractures are often incomplete initially and usually occur on the convex lateral portion of the humeral shaft. Accelerated osteoarthritis of the glenohumeral articulation is the result of osseous expansion that alters the mechanics of the joint. Sarcomatous degeneration is the most feared complication of Paget disease. In a series by Moore and coworkers the proximal humerus was the second most frequent site of malignant degeneration, surpassed only by the femur.[115] Neoplasms are most commonly osteosarcomas (prevalence 50 to 60 percent), followed by fibrosarcomas or malignant fibrous histiocytomas (20 to 25 percent), chondrosarcomas (10 percent), or rarely giant cell tumor (2 percent).[104,115–120] The radiographic finding most suggestive of malignant degeneration is a new area of bone destruction (Fig. 15-10B). CT and MRI often demonstrate an associated soft tissue mass, confirming malignant degeneration (see 15-10B). MRI can be used to evaluate Paget disease when a secondary neoplasm is suspected. Preservation of normal marrow signal essentially excludes neoplastic involvement. Masslike areas of marrow replacement and associated soft tissue mass strongly suggest malignant degeneration.[112,113,115]

CONCLUSION

Shoulder pain is a frequent clinical complaint; however, physical examination is often unrewarding for distinguishing among the variety of underlying causes of shoulder discomfort. Radiologic studies are thus important for evaluating these patients. In general, radiographs should be the initial imaging study. Additional radiologic studies, particularly CT and MRI, are often useful for further investigation. I have described and illustrated many miscellaneous conditions that involve the shoulder, and the various imaging modalities best used to assess them. Knowledge of these radiologic findings is important for diagnosis, and ultimately to guide our clinical colleagues in patient management.

References

1. RESNICK D, GEORGEN TG, NIWAYAMA G: Physical injury, in Resnick D, Niwayama G (eds): *Diagnosis of Bone and Joint Disorders,* 2d ed, Philadelphia, Saunders, 1988, pp 2835–2840.

2. COTTON F: Subluxation of the shoulder downward. *Boston Med Surg J* 185:403–404, 1921.

3. HAMMOND R: Relaxation of the shoulder following bone injury. *J Bone Joint Surg* 5:712–720, 1923.

4. LASKIN RS, SCHREIBER S: Inferior subluxation of the humeral head: The drooping shoulder. *Radiology* 98:586–587, 1971.

5. LEV-TOAFF AS, KARASICK D, RAO VM: "Drooping shoulder"—nontraumatic causes of glenohumeral subluxation. *Skel Radiol* 12:34–38, 1984.

6. FRITZ RC, HELMS CA, STEINBACH LS, GENANT HK: Suprascapular nerve entrapment: Evaluation with MR imaging. *Radiology* 182:437–444, 1992.

7. HADLEY MN, SONNTAG VKH, PITTMAN HW: Suprascapular nerve entrapment. *J Neurosurg* 64:843–848, 1986.

8. CLEIN LJ: Suprascapular entrapment neuropathy. *J Neurosurg* 43:337–342, 1975.

9. GANZHORN RW, HOCKER JT, HOROWITZ M, SWITZER H: Suprascapular nerve entrapment. *J Bone Surg* 63A:492–494, 1981.

10. HIRAYAMA T, TAKEMITSU Y: Compression of the suprascapular nerve by a ganglion at the suprascapular notch. *Clin Orthop* 155:95–96, 1981.

11. SARNO JB: Suprascapular nerve entrapment. *Surg Neurol* 20:493–497, 1983.

12. YOON TN, GRABOIS M, GUILLEN M: Suprascapular nerve

injury following trauma to the shoulder. *J Trauma* 21:652–655, 1981.

13. ZOLTAN JD: Injury to the suprascapular nerve associated with anterior dislocation of the shoulder. *J Trauma* 19:203–206, 1979.

14. STEIMAN I: Painless infraspinatus atrophy due to suprascapular nerve entrapment. *Arch Phys Med Rehabil* 69:641–643, 1988.

15. DREZ D JR: Suprascapular neuropathy in differential diagnosis of rotator cuff injuries. *Am J Sports Med* 4:43–45, 1976.

16. AIELLO I, SERRA G, TRAINA GC, TUGNOLI V: Entrapment of the suprascapular nerve at the spinoglenoid notch. *Ann Neurol* 12:314–316, 1982.

17. CAHILL BR, PALMER RE: Quadrilateral space syndrome. *J Hand Surg* 8:65–69, 1983.

18. McKOWEN HC, VOORHIES RM: Axillary nerve entrapment in the quadrilateral space: Case report. *J Neurosurg* 66:932–934, 1987.

19. FRANCEL TJ, DELLON AL, COMPBELL JN: Quadrilateral space syndrome: Diagnosis and operative decompression technique. *Plast Reconstr Surg* 87:911–916, 1991.

20. REDLER MR, RULAND LJ III, McCUE FC III: Quadrilateral space syndrome in a throwing athlete. *Am J Sports Med* 14:511–513, 1986.

21. LINKER CS, HELMS CA, FRITZ RC: Quadrilateral space syndrome: Findings at MR imaging. *Radiology* 188:675–676, 1993.

22. CORMIER PJ, MATALON TAS, WOLIN PM: Quadrilateral space syndrome: A rare cause of shoulder pain. *Radiology* 167:797–798, 1988.

23. KAPLAN PA, RESNICK D: Stress-induced osteolysis of the clavicle. *Radiology* 158:139–140, 1986.

24. CAHILL BR: Osteolysis of the distal part of the clavicle in male athletes. *Am J Bone Joint Surg* 64:1053–1058, 1982.

25. SEYMOUR EQ: Osteolysis of the clavicular tip associated with repeated minor trauma to the shoulder. *Radiology* 123:56, 1977.

26. NORFRAY JF: Bone resorption of the distal clavicle. *JAMA* 241:1933–1934, 1979.

27. RESNICK D, NIWAYAMA G: *Diagnosis of Bone and Joint Disorders,* 2d ed, Philadelphia, Saunders, 1988, pp 4143–4146.

28. MADSEN B: Osteolysis of the acromial end of the clavicle following trauma. *Br J Radiol* 36:822–828, 1963.

29. SMART MJ: Traumatic osteolysis of the distal end of the clavicles. *J Can Assoc Radiol* 23:264–266, 1972.

30. MURPHY OB, BELLAMY R, WHEELER W, BROWER TD: Post-traumatic osteolysis of the distal clavicle. *Clin Orthop* 109:108–114, 1975.

31. QUINN SF, GLASS TA: Post-traumatic osteolysis of the clavicle. *South Med J* 76:307–308, 1983.

32. LEVINE AH, PAIS MJ, SCHWARTZ EE: Posttraumatic osteolysis of the distal clavicle with emphasis on early radiologic changes. *AJR* 127:781–784, 1976.

33. ERICKSON SJ, KNEELAND JB, KOMOROWSKI RA, KNUDSON GJ, CARRERA GF: Post-traumatic osteolysis of the clavicle: MR features. *J Comput Assist Tomogr* 14:835–837, 1990.

34. ACKERMAN LV: Extra-osseous localized non-neoplastic

bone and cartilage formation (so-called myositis ossificans). *J Bone Joint Surg* 40A:279–298, 1958.

35. SPJUT HJ, DORFMAN HD, FECHNER RE, ACKERMAN LV: Tumors of bone and cartilage, in Firminger HI (ed) *Atlas of Tumor Pathology,* fasc 5, 2nd ser., Washington, DC, Armed Forces Institute of Pathology, 1971, pp 412–428.

36. HANNAH SL, MAGILL HL, BROOKS MT, BURTON EM, BOULDEN TF, SEIDEL FG: Cases of the day: Pediatric. *RadioGraphics* 10:945–949, 1990.

37. KRANSDORF MJ, MEIS JM, JELINEK JS: Myositis ossificans: MR appearance with radiologic-pathologic correlation. *AJR* 157:1243–1248, 1991.

38. NUOVO MA, NORMAN A, CHUMAS J, ACKERMAN LV: Myositis ossificans: with atypical clinical, radiographic, or pathologic findings: A review of 23 cases *Skel Radiol* 21:87–101, 1992.

39. OGILVIE-HARRIS DJ, FORNASIER VL: Pseudomalignant myositis ossificans: heterotopic new-bone formation without a history of trauma. *J Bone Joint Surg* 62A:1274–1283, 1980.

40. ANGERVALL L, STENER B, STENER I, AHREN C: Pseudomalignant osseous tumor of soft tissue: A clinical, radiological, and pathological study of five cases. *J Bone Joint Surg* 51B:654–663, 1969.

41. PATTERSON DC: Myositis ossificans circumscripta: Report of 4 cases without history of trauma. *J Bone Joint Surg* 52B:296–301, 1970.

42. GOLDMAN AB: Myositis ossificans circumscripta: A benign lesion with a malignant differential diagnosis. *AJR* 126:32–40, 1976.

43. JOHNSON LC: Histogenesis of myositis ossificans. *Am J Pathol* 24:681–682, 1948.

44. AMENDOLA MA, GLAZER GM, AGHA FP, FRANCIS IR, WEATHERBEE L, MARTEL W: Myositis ossificans circumscripta: Computed tomographic diagnosis. *Radiology* 149:775–779, 1983.

45. ZEANAH WR, HUDSON TM: Myositis ossificans: Radiologic evaluation of two cases with diagnostic computed tomograms. *Clin Orthop* 168:187–192, 1982.

46. DE SMET AA, NORRIS MA, FISHER DR: Magnetic resonance imaging of myositis ossificans: Analysis of seven cases. *Skel Radiol* 21:503–507, 1992.

47. TSAI JC, DALINKA MK, FALLON MD, ZLATKIN MB, KRESSEL HY: Fluid-fluid level: A nonspecific finding in tumors of bone and soft tissue. *Radiology* 175:779–782, 1990.

48. YAGHMAI I: Myositis ossificans: Diagnostic value of arteriography. *AJR* 128:811–816, 1977.

49. SPRITZER CE, DALINKA MK, KRESSEL HY: Magnetic resonance imaging of pigmented villonodular synovitis: A report of two cases. *Skel Radiol* 16:316–319, 1987.

50. FLANDRY F, HUGHSTON JC: Current concepts review pigmented villonodular synovitis. *J Bone Joint Surg* 69A:942–949, 1987.

51. JELINEK JS, KRANSDORF MJ, UTZ JA, ET AL.: Imaging of pigmented villonodular synovitis with emphasis on MR imaging. *AJR* 152:337–342, 1989.

52. KOTTAL RA, VOGLER JB, MATAMOROS A, ALEXANDER AH, COOKSON JL: Pigmented villonodular synovitis: A report of MR imaging in two cases. *Radiology* 163:551–553, 1987.

53. GOLDMAN AB, DiCARLO EF: Pigmented villonodular sy-

novitis: Diagnosis and differential diagnosis. *Radiol Clin North Am* 26:1327–1347, 1988.

54. DORWART RH, GENANT HK, JOHNSTON WH, MORRIS JM. Pigmented villonodular synovitis of synovial joints: Clinical, pathologic, and radiologic features. *AJR* 143:877–885, 1984.

55. BALSARA AN, STAINKEN BF, MARTINEZ AJ: MR image of localized giant cell tumor of the tendon sheath involving the knee. *J Comput Assist Tomogr* 13:159–162, 1989.

56. KARASICK D, KARASICK S: Giant cell tumor of tendon sheath: Spectrum of radiologic findings. *Skel Radiol* 21:219–224, 1992.

57. JELINEK JS, KRANSDORF MJ, SHMOOKLER BM, ABOU-LAFIA AA, MALAWER MM: Giant cell tumor of the tendon sheath: MR findings in nine cases. *AJR* 162:919–922, 1994.

58. BUTT YP, HARDY G, OSTLERE SJ: Pigmented villonodular synovitis of the knee: Computed tomographic appearances. *Skel Radiol* 19:191–196, 1990.

59. DARRASON R: Role of arteriography and x-ray computed tomography in the current evaluation of pigmented villonodular synovitis. *J Radiol* 69:645–650, 1988.

60. GOMORI JM, GROSSMAN RJ, GOLDBERG HI, ET AL.: Intracranial hematomas: Imaging by high field magnetic resonance. *Radiology* 157:87–93, 1985.

61. JAFFE HL: Synovial chondromatosis and other articular tumors, in Jaffe HL (ed) *Tumors and Tumorous Conditions of the Bones and Joints,* Philadelphia, Lea & Febiger, 1958, pp 566–567.

62. MILGRAM JW: Synovial osteochondromatosis. A histopathological study of thirty cases. *Am J Bone Joint Surg* 59:792–801, 1977.

63. KARLIN CA, DE SMET AA, NEFF J, LIN F, HORTON W, WERTZBERGER JJ: The variable manifestations of extraarticular synovial chondromatosis. *AJR* 137:731–735, 1981.

64. BURNSTEIN MI, FISHER DR, YANDOW DR, HAFEZ GR, DE SMET AA: Case Report 502. *Skeletal Radiol* 17:458–461, 1988.

65. HERZOG S, MAFEE M: Synovial chondromatosis of the TMJ: MR and CT findings. *AJNR* 11:742–745, 1990.

66. LIU S-K, MOROFF S: Case report 733. *Skel Radiol* 22:50–54, 1993.

67. BAIRD RA, SCHOBERT WE, PAIS MJ, ET AL.: Radiographic identification of loose bodies in the traumatized hip joint. *Radiology* 145:661–665, 1982.

68. KRANSDORF MJ, MEIS JM: From the archives of the AFIP: Extraskeletal osseous and cartilaginous tumors of the extremities. *RadioGraphics* 13:853–886, 1993.

69. SZYPRYT P, TWINING P, PRESTON BJ, HOWELL CJ: Synovial chondromatosis of the hip joint presenting as a pathological fracture. *Br J Radiol* 59:399–401, 1986.

70. NORMAN A, STEINER GC: Bone erosion in synovial chondromatosis. *Radiology* 161:749–752, 1986.

71. MILGRAM JW: Synovial osteochondromatosis. A histopathological study of thirty cases. *J Bone Joint Surg* 59A:792–801, 1977.

72. VILLACIN AB, BRIGHAM LN, BULLOUGH PG: Primary and secondary synovial chondrometaplasia. Histopathologic and clinicoradiologic differences. *Hum Pathol* 10:439–451, 1979.

73. ROSS LV, ROSS GJ, MESGARZADEH M, EDMONDS PR, BONAKDARPOUR A: Hemodialysis-related amyloidomas of bone. *Radiology* 178:263–265, 1991.

74. GIELEN JL, VAN HOLSBECCK MT, HAUGLUSTAINE D, ET AL.: Growing bone cysts in long-term hemodialysis. *Skel Radiol* 19:43–49, 1990.

75. CAMACHO CR, ET AL.: Radiological findings of amyloid arthropathy in long-term haemodialysis. *Eur Radiol* 2–4:305, 1992.

76. CASEY TT, STONE WJ, DiRAIMONDO CR, ET AL.: Tumoral amyloidosis of bone of beta-2-microglobulin origin in association with long term hemodialysis: A new type of amyloid disease. *Hum Pathol* 17:731–738, 1986.

77. COBBY MJ, ADLER RS, SWARTZ R, MARTEL W: Dialysis-related amyloid arthropathy: MR findings in four patients. *AJR* 157:1023–1027, 1991.

78. ATHANASOU NA, ET AL.: Joint and systemic distribution of dialysis amyloid (ab). *Radiology* 181:616, 1991.

79. BARDIN T, KUNTZ D, ZINGRAFF J, VOISON MC, ZELMAR A, LANSAMA J: Synovial amyloidosis in patients undergoing long-term hemodialysis. *Arthritis Rheum* 28:1052–1058, 1985.

80. MARTINEZ S, VOGLER JB III, HARRELSON JM, LYLES KW: Imaging of tumor calcinosis: New observations. *Radiology* 174:215–222, 1990.

81. LYLES KW, HALSEY DL, FRIEDMAN NE, LOBAUGH G: Correlations of serum concentrations of 1,25-dihydroxyvitamin D, phosphorus, and parathyroid hormone in tumoral calcinosis. *J Clin Endocrinol Metab* 67:88–92, 1988.

82. ZERWEKH JE, SANDERS LA, TOWNSEND J, ET AL.: Tumoral calcinosis: Evidence for concurrent defects in renal tubular phosphorus transport and in 1α, 25-dihydroxycholecalciferol synthesis. *Calcif Tissue Int* 32:1–6, 1980.

83. MITNICK PD, GOLDFARB S, SLATOPOLSKY E, ET AL.: Calcium and phosphate metabolism in tumoral calcinosis. *Ann Intern Med* 92:482–487, 1980.

84. BISHOP AF, DESTOUET JM, MURPHY WA: Tumoral calcinosis: Case report and review. *Skel Radiol* 8:269–274, 1982.

85. BARTON DE, CAPTAIN MC, REEVES RJ: Tumoral calcinosis: Report of 3 cases and review. *AJR* 86:351–358, 1961.

86. GORDON LF, ARGER PH, DALINKA MK, ET AL.: Computed tomography in soft tissue calcification layering. *J Comput Assist Tomogr* 8:71–73, 1984.

87. LEICHT E, BERBERICH R, LAUFFENBURGER T, ET AL.: Tumoral calcinosis: Accumulation of bone-seeking tracers in the calcium deposits. *Eur J Nucl Med* 4:419–421, 1979.

88. MANASTER BJ, ANDERSON TM: Tumoral calcinosis: Serial images to monitor successful dietary therapy. *Skel Radiol* 8:123–125, 1982.

89. KRANSDORF MJ, MOSER RP JR, GILKEY FW: Fibrous dysplasia. *RadioGraphics* 10:519–537, 1990.

90. HUDSON TM: Benign fibro-osseous lesions, in Hudson TM (ed): *Radiologic-Pathologic Correlation of Musculoskeletal Lesions,* Baltimore, Williams & Wilkins, 1987, pp 312–340.

91. WILNER D: Fibrous dysplasia of bone, in Wilner D (ed): *Radiology of Bone Tumors and Allied Disorders,* Philadelphia, Saunders, 1982, pp 1443–1580.

92. MIRRA JM, GOLD RH: Fibrous dysplasia, in Mirra JM, Piero P, Gold RH: *Bone Tumors,* Philadelphia, Lea & Febiger, 1989, pp 191–226.

93. ALBRIGHT F, BUTLER AM, HAMPTON AO, SMITH P: Syndrome characterized by osteitis fibrosa disseminata, areas of pigmentation, and endocrine dysfunction, with precocious puberty in females. *N Engl J Med* 216:727–746, 1937.

94. DAFFNER RH, KIRKS DR, GEHWEILER JA, HEASTON DK: Computed tomography of fibrous dysplasia. *AJR* 139:943–948, 1982.

95. DROLSHAGEN LF, REYNOLDS WA, MARCUS NW: Fibrocartilaginous dysplasia of bone. *Radiology* 156:32, 1985.

96. HIGASHI T, IGUCHI M, SHIMURA A, KRUGLIK GD: Computed tomography and bone scintigraphy in polyostotic fibrous dysplasia. *Oral Surg* 50:580–583, 1980.

97. JOHNS WD, GUPTA SM, KAYANI N: Scintigraphic evaluation of polyostotic fibrous dysplasia. Clin Nucl Med 12:627–631, 1987.

98. UTZ JA, KRANSDORF MJ, JELINEK JS, MOSER RP, BERREY BH: MR appearance of fibrous dysplasia. *J Comput Assist Tomogr* 13:845–851, 1989.

99. HARMS SE, GREENWAY G: Musculoskeletal system, in Stark DD, Bradley WG (eds): *Magnetic Resonance Imaging,* St. Louis, Mosby, 1988, pp 1323–1433.

100. SCHWARTZ DT, ALPERT M: The malignant transformation of fibrous dysplasia. *Am J Med Sci* 247:1–20, 1964.

101. DE SMET AA, TRAVERS H, NEFF JR: Chondrosarcoma occurring in a patient with polyostotic fibrous dysplasia. *Skel Radiol* 7:197–201, 1981.

102. SUNDARAM M, McDONALD DJ, MERENDA G: Intramuscular myxoma: A rare but important association with fibrous dysplasia of bone. *AJR* 153:107–108, 1989.

103. WIRTH WA, LEAVITT D, ENZINGER FM: Multiple intramuscular myxomas: Another extraskeletal manifestation of fibrous dysplasia. *Cancer* 27:321–340, 1971.

104. RESNICK D, NIWAYAMA G: Paget's disease, in Resnick D, Niwayama G (eds): *Diagnosis of Bone and Joint Disorders,* 2d ed, Philadelphia, Saunders, 1987, pp 2127–2170.

105. DALINKA MK, ARONCHICK JM, HADDAD JG: Paget's disease. *Orthop Clin North Am* 4:3–19, 1983.

106. SINGER FR: *Paget's Disease of Bone,* New York, Plenum, 1977, pp 44–48.

107. MIRRA JM: Pathogenesis of Paget's disease based on viral etiology. *Clin Orthop* 217:162–170, 1987.

108. MERKOW RL, LANE JM: Paget's disease of bone. *Orthop Clin North Am* 21:171–189, 1990.

109. ZLATKIN MB, LANDER PH, HADJIPAVLOU AG, LEVINE JS: Paget disease of the spine: CT with clinical correlation. *Radiology* 160:155–159, 1986.

110. KELLY JK, DENIER JE, WILNER HI, ET AL.: MR imaging of lytic changes in Paget disease of the calvarium. J Comput Assist Tomogr 13:27–29, 1989.

111. TJON-A-THAM RTO, BLOEM JL, FALKE THM, ET AL.: Magnetic resonance imaging in Paget disease of the skull. *AJNR* 6:879–881, 1985.

112. ROBERTS MC, KRESSEL HY, FALLON MD, ZLATKIN MB, DALINKA MK: Paget disease: MR findings. *Radiology* 173:341–345, 1989.

113. KAUFMANN GA, SUNDARAM M, McDONALD DJ: Magnetic resonance imaging in symptomatic Paget's disease. *Skel Radiol* 20:413–418, 1991.

114. SOM PM, HERMANN G, SACHER M, ET AL.: Paget disease of the calvaria and facial bones with an osteosarcoma of the maxilla: CT and MR findings. *J Comput Assist Tomogr* 11:887–890, 1987.

115. MOORE TE, KING AR, KATHOL MH, ET AL: Sarcoma in Paget disease of bone: Clinical, radiologic, and pathologic features in 22 cases. *AJR* 156:1199–1203, 1991.

116. PRICE CHG, GOLDIE W: Paget's sarcoma of bone: A study of eighty cases from the Bristol and the Leeds Bone Tumour Registries. *Br J Bone Joint Surg* 51-B:205–224, 1969.

117. SMITH J, BOTET JF, YEH SDJ: Bone sarcomas in Paget disease: A study of 85 patients. *Radiology* 152:583–590, 1984.

118. HAIBACH H, FARRELL C, DITTRICH FJ: Neoplasms arising in Paget's disease of bone: A study of 82 cases. *Am J Clin Pathol* 83:594–600, 1985.

119. WICK MR, SLEGAL GP, UNNI KK, McLEOD RA, GREDITZER HG III: Sarcomas of bone complicating osteitis deformans (Paget's disease): Fifty years' experience. *Am J Surg Pathol* 5:47–59, 1981.

120. SCHAJOWICZ F, ARAUJO ES, BERENSTEIN M: Sarcoma complicating Paget's disease of bone: A clinicopathological study of 62 cases. *J Bone Joint Surg* 65-B:299–307, 1983.

16 IMAGING OF THE SHOULDER: A SURGICAL PERSPECTIVE

Joseph P. Iannotti

In this chapter, I discuss the pathologic findings assessed by imaging studies that are important prognostic factors in the surgical management of common shoulder disorders. I will define how and why these anatomic findings influence the surgical management of rotator cuff disease, glenohumeral instability, glenohumeral arthritis, and proximal humeral fractures.

ROTATOR CUFF DISEASE

Disorders of the rotator cuff and coracoacromial arch are a broad spectrum of disease that include rotator cuff tendinitis, calcific and degenerative tendinopathy, partial- and full-thickness rotator cuff tears, and cuff tear arthropathy. The anatomic findings associated with this broad spectrum of rotator cuff disease are quite varied and often are well visualized on various imaging studies. The pathologic changes of the coracoacromial arch, which are important in the surgical management of rotator cuff disease, include the shape, size, and orientation of the acromion and associated acromial spurs, the presence of os acromiale, and the presence and severity of acromioclavicular joint arthritis. Anatomic factors that are important in surgical management of rotator cuff tears include the degree of tendon degeneration, the size and location of the rotator cuff tear, the degree of tendon retraction, and muscle atrophy. Degenerative partial and complete tears of the long head of the biceps tendon and secondary degenerative changes of the glenohumeral joint often are associated with chronic rotator cuff tears, and these are also important prognostic factors for surgical management.

Clinical symptoms associated with rotator cuff disease are defined by the impingement syndrome. Impingement syndrome is defined as pain in the region of the rotator cuff and coracoacromial arch that is exacerbated by the impingement signs and relieved by performing the impingement test. Although many etiologic factors are associated with the impingement syndrome, only some are associated with true narrowing of the subacromial space (supraspinatus outlet). Surgical decompression of the subacromial space or resection of the distal clavicle when the impingement syndrome is refractory to nonoperative measures is reserved for patients who clearly demonstrate the anatomic findings of significant mechanical subacromial narrowing or significant degenerative acromioclavicular joint disease. For these patients the reported result of surgical intervention is good to excellent in 85% to 90% of cases.[1-4] Plain radiography remains a useful primary imaging modality for assessing acromial morphology, the presence of acromioclavicular disease, and the degree of supraspinatus outlet narrowing.[5-7] Assessment of the coracoacromial arch by plain radiography should include the supraspinatus outlet view (Fig. 16-1), the coronal plane anteroposterior (AP) 30° caudad tilt view (Rockwood's tilt view; Fig. 16-2), and the coronal plane AP 15° to 30° cephalic tilt view (Zanca's view; Fig. 16-3). The supraspinatus outlet view defines the morphology of the undersurface of the acromion, the size of the acromial spur, and the degree of supraspinatus outlet narrowing (see Fig. 16-1). The coronal plane AP 30° caudad tilt view (Rockwood's tilt view) demonstrates how much bone extends anterior to the anterior border of the clavicle, and represents the anterior and inferior extension of the acromial spur (see Fig. 16-2). The coronal plane cephalic tilt view (Zanca's view) is most valuable for defining the degree of degenerative changes in the acromioclavicular joint. These views should be considered standard and routine films in all patients who have clinical findings consistent with rotator cuff disease. The morphology of the coracoacromial arch and the degree of supraspinatus outlet narrowing can also be assessed by magnetic resonance imaging (MRI) utilizing the 30° oblique views in the sagittal and the coronal plane (Figs. 16-4, 16-5). MRI in these planes can define acromial morphology, the size of the acromial spur, the degree of subacromial and acromioclavicular joint impingement, and the degree of acromioclavicular joint arthritis.

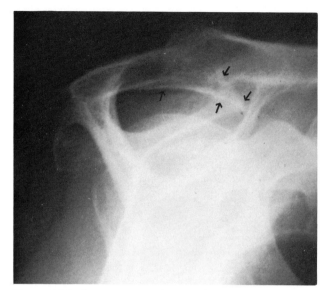

Figure 16-1 Supraspinatus outlet view demonstrates a large subacromial spur (*arrows*).

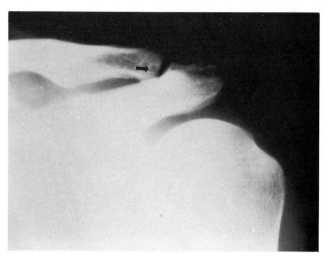

Figure 16-3 Zanca's view demonstrates a degenerative cyst at the distal end of the clavicle (*arrow*).

Os acromiale results from failure of fusion of the centers of ossification formed within the acromion. Though many patients with os acromiale may be asymptomatic, there is a greater prevalence of full-thickness rotator cuff tears in this population.[8,9] The ununited acromial fragment may be mobile and have a significant caudad tilt and associated fibrocartilaginous tissue formation on the undersurface of the acromion. Each of these features can result in supraspinatus outlet narrowing and associated full-thickness rotator cuff tears. The presence of os acromiale can easily be seen with plain radiographs, particularly the axillary view. MRI utilizing the 30° oblique sag-

ittal plane is ideal for evaluating acromial morphology, the presence and location of the os acromiale, and the degree of fibrocartilaginous tissue formation (Fig. 16-6).

The presence of significant rotator cuff tendon degeneration, partial-thickness rotator cuff tear, or full-thickness rotator cuff tear, and associated clinical symptoms of impingement syndrome can alter the patient's treatment and prognosis. Patients with an intact rotator cuff and insignificant subacromial outlet impingement have the best chance of having their pain relieved and achieving functional recovery with nonoperative man-

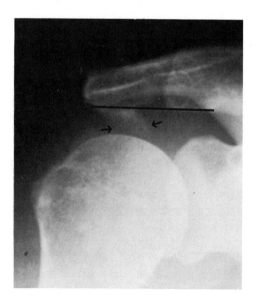

Figure 16-2 Rockwood's tilt view demonstrates an acromial spur (*arrows*) extending anterior to the anterior border of the clavicle (*black line*).

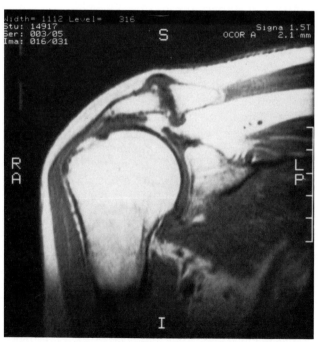

Figure 16-4 MRI 30° oblique plane, 14-cm field of view, TR-1000 TE-13 demonstrates significant hypertrophic degenerative changes of the acromioclavicular joint with subacromial impingement.

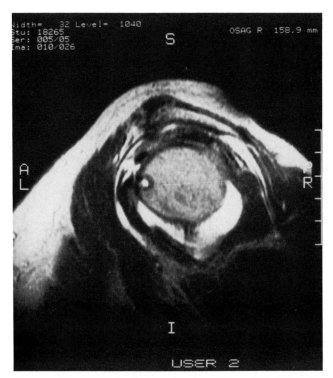

Figure 16-5 MRI 30° sagittal oblique plane 14-cm field of view, TR-2500 TE-70 demonstrates a large, full-thickness rotator cuff tear, a hooked anterior acromion, and a large joint effusion.

agement. For patients with significant subacromial outlet narrowing in association with a large partial-thickness or full-thickness rotator cuff tear, nonoperative management is less likely to be successful, though many of these patients are initially treated with nonoperative measures. In patients with rotator cuff tears, the size, location, degree of tendon retraction, and degree of muscle atrophy can influence what type of surgery is performed as well as the prognosis for postoperative recovery. The size of the rotator cuff tear, measured in the AP and mediolateral dimensions and expressed in square centimeters, has been shown to be the most significant determinant in overall postoperative shoulder scores and postoperative shoulder strength.[10] Rotator cuff tears greater than 18 cm^2 are statistically correlated with a higher incidence of moderate or severe supraspinatus and infraspinatus muscle atrophy, fair or poor quality tendon tissue, and presence of chronic rupture of the long head of the biceps tendon. These larger cuff tears are also associated with more difficult surgical repair, as defined by difficulty of tendon mobilization, and with decreased postoperative shoulder strength.[10] Preoperative assessment of these anatomic findings is important and useful in predicting the outcome of surgical intervention and preoperative patient counseling. Cuff tear size can be estimated clinically by the degree of shoulder weakness and periscapular atrophy and by the presence of rupture of the long head of the biceps tendon. Cephalad migration of

the humeral head, when visualized by plain radiography or MRI, is an indicator of a massive rotator cuff tear that is chronic in nature.

Although arthrography has been shown to be very accurate in determining the presence of full-thickness rotator cuff tears, it has not been as useful in determining their size.[11] The presence of contrast material in the subacromial space and acromioclavicular joint (geyser sign) has been associated with massive long-standing rotator cuff tears.[12] Ultrasonography and MRI have been utilized to determine rotator cuff tear size and rupture of the long head of the biceps tendon.[13–16] MRI has also demonstrated its accuracy in determining the degree of tendon retraction, degree of supraspinatus and infraspinatus muscle atrophy, and the presence of degenerative changes of the glenohumeral joint consistent with cuff tear arthropathy (Fig. 16-7). The size and location of the rotator cuff tear can also influence what type of surgery is performed. Patients with an intact rotator cuff or a partial-thickness tear, in association with significant subacromial outlet narrowing, can be treated by arthroscopic subacromial decompression, with or without debridement of the degenerative cuff tissue.[2,3] Recent reports have demonstrated the ability to repair, by arthroscopic techniques, small full-thickness rotator cuff tears.[17] After arthroscopic surgery patients with these specific anatomic findings enjoy more rapid postoperative rehabilitation and an end result equal to that of open surgery. The vast majority of patients with clinically significant large or massive rotator cuff tears should be treated by open acromioplasty and rotator cuff repair. In

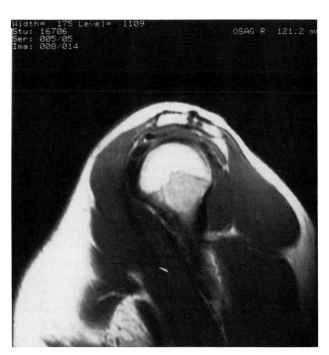

Figure 16-6 A 30° sagittal oblique MRI, 16-cm field of view, TR-800 TE-20, demonstrates an os acromiale.

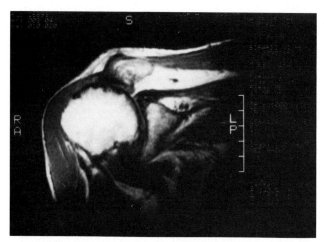

Figure 16-7   A 30° coronal oblique MRI, 16-cm field of view, TR-1000 TE-20, demonstrates cuff tear arthropathy characterized by subchondral collapse and cephalad migration of the humeral head which articulates with the coracoacromial arch. A massive full-thickness cuff tear with retraction to the glenoid margin and associated marked muscle atrophy are evident.

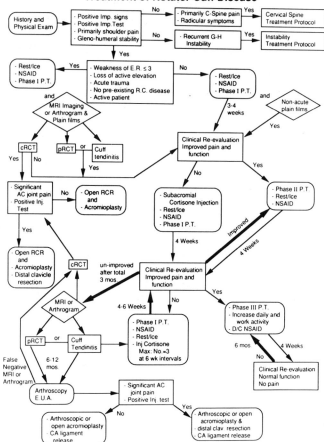

Figure 16-8   University of Pennsylvania algorithm for evaluation and treatment of rotator cuff disease.

the vast majority of these patients, open repair can be accomplished. In some patients with chronic massive rotator cuff tears involving the subscapularis, supraspinatus, and infraspinatus tendons with retraction of the tendon edge to the glenoid margin, rotator cuff repair by primary means may not be feasible. If these findings are noted preoperatively, alternative surgical options can be considered, such as the use of tendon transfers for rotator cuff reconstruction. For patients with large chronic rotator cuff tears associated with significant glenohumeral arthritis, hemiarthroplasty and an attempt at rotator cuff repair or reconstruction is indicated.

It has been routine practice for our shoulder service to initially evaluate all patients with chronic rotator cuff disease by clinical history, physical examination, and the use of local anesthetic impingement (injection) tests to the subacromial space and/or the acromioclavicular joint. All patients initially obtain plain radiographs, including an AP view in the scapular plane, and axillary supraspinatus outlet, Zanca's, and Rockwood's tilt views. In patients who have had long-standing symptoms which were initiated without significant high-velocity trauma and have maintained Grade 3 or greater external rotation strength, initial nonoperative treatment options are instituted and scheduling of advanced imaging studies is postponed. If, then, nonoperative measures fail, or for patients who initially present with acute high-velocity trauma and significant rotator cuff weakness, MRI is scheduled to evaluate the integrity of the rotator cuff. The evaluation and treatment algorithm for rotator cuff disease shown in Figure 16-8 has been useful and standard policy at our shoulder service at the University of Pennsylvania.

In summary, patients with clinically significant rotator cuff disease should undergo imaging studies to evaluate the coracoacromial arch. The arch should be evaluated for supraspinatus outlet narrowing, acromioclavicular joint disease, and os acromiale. Imaging of the rotator cuff should evaluate rotator cuff integrity, the degree of tendon degeneration, and the presence of partial- and full-thickness rotator cuff tears. Rotator cuff tears should be assessed for location, size, degree of tendon retraction, and muscle atrophy. Significant degenerative changes of the glenohumeral joint and rupture of the long head of the biceps tendon should be evaluated as associated findings in chronic large and massive rotator cuff tears. Each of these anatomic findings significantly influences both nonoperative and surgical management of rotator cuff disease. These anatomic findings are also important prognostic factors for functional outcome and results of treatment.

GLENOHUMERAL INSTABILITY

Glenohumeral instability is defined clinically as pathologic translation of the humeral head which results in

pain and fun[...]
nohumeral in[...]
symptoms and r[...]
translation. There[...]
of normal humer[...]
nosis of glenohume[...]
based on clinical c[...]
dysfunction secondary[...]
matics, which in turn re[...]
tion. The spectrum of cli[...]
ics is quite varied. Abno[...]
can result from injuries o[...]
mal glenohumeral motion c[...]
control of the patient. Volunt[...]
tion can be secondary to psyc[...]
these phenomena are associa[...]
metric muscle contraction. T[...]
ognized by clinical criteria, [...]
untary instability show no pa[...]
studies. Involuntary instabili[...]
or atraumatic. Involuntary tr[...]
unilateral, involves a specific [...]
sults in significant pain, and [...]
traumatic lesions of the glenoh[...]
glenoid rim, or humeral head. T[...]
avulsion, Bankart lesions, gle[...]
Sachs lesions has been r[...]
patients with traumati[...]
voluntary atraum[...] ex-
perience subluxa[...] ulder.
This type of insta[...] with
generalized ligame[...] der involvement.[21,22] Atrau[...] es not
involve acute injury, but it can in[...] overuse
of the shoulder that stretches the anterio[...] sular tissues. True traumatic lesions such as glenoid rim fractures, Bankart lesions, and Hill-Sachs lesions are uncommon in this group of patients.[23] The direction of
instability can be characterized as anterior, inferior, posterior, or multidirectional, but in the vast majority of
cases it is anterior and unidirectional. Most cases of atraumatic instability are also anterior unidirectional, but
many are multidirectional, having a significant inferior
or posterior component. Defining the nature of the instability with respect to voluntary or involuntary patterns,
traumatic or atraumatic type, and the directionality of the
instability is based principally on a careful history and
physical examination. Although this classification of instability is clinically useful, it is understood that there is
overlap between these groups. Small subsets of patients
have traumatic inferior instability without a significant
Bankart's lesion or multidirectional instability of the
shoulder associated with capsular and labral tears. Diagnostic imaging is useful and important in documenting
the location and pattern of anatomic abnormalities which

may be associated with the clinical diagnosis of gleno-
[...]ral instability.
[...]ment and prognosis for patients with gleno-
[...]ity often depend on the type of instability
[...]esence of anatomic anomalies. Patients
[...]raumatic unidirectional or multidirec-
[...]e often successfully treated by non-
[...], which include strengthening of the
[...], and scapular musculature. The over-
[...]nonoperative measures in this patient
[...]% to 90%.[23] Patients whose symptoms
[...]nonoperative measures are best treated
[...]lar shift procedures.[21,22] Patients with in-
[...]umatic unidirectional instability of the
[...]ssociation with glenoid rim fracture or la-
[...]have little chance of success with nonoper-
[...]s, particularly younger individuals who par-
[...]rhead-throwing or contact sports.[23] For the
[...]of patients with clinically significant symp-
[...]intervention for capsular repair, by either
[...]r open techniques, provides good to ex-
[...]ts.[19,20,24] Utilization of diagnostic imaging,
[...]n clinical evaluation, allows accurate classifica-
[...]the instability pattern, which is important for
[...]sis and treatment.
[...]n radiography can be useful in the evaluation of
patients with clinically significant glenohumeral instability. Most patients with atraumatic instability have normal
radiographs. Occasionally, patients with atraumatic instability demonstrate glenoid hypoplasia or abnormalities
in glenoid version (Fig. 16-9). Axial computed tomography (CT) is quite helpful in these cases in determining
the degree of glenoid abnormality (Figs. 16-10, 16-11).
Patients with traumatic anterior instability can demonstrate calcification within the soft tissues of the anteroinferior glenoid rim, best seen on the axillary West Point
or apical oblique views (Figs. 16-12, 16-13). Posterosu-

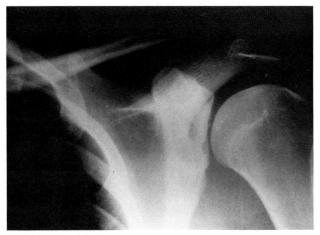

Figure 16-9 AP radiograph demonstrates glenoid hypoplasia.

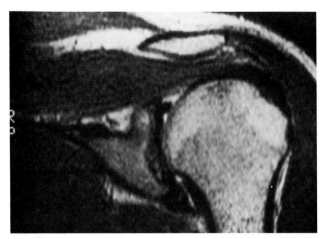

Figure 16-10 Coronal plane MRI demonstrates glenoid hypoplasia.

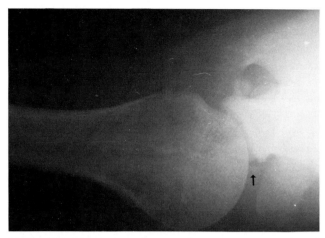

Figure 16-12 West Point axillary view demonstrates anterior glenoid rim calcification (*black arrow*).

perior humeral head defects (Hill-Sachs lesions) can be seen on the AP internal rotation view or Stryker notch view (Figs. 16-14, 16-15). CT arthrography and MRI are also quite useful in patients with traumatic anterior instability for demonstrating rim fractures and capsular or labral avulsion (Bankart lesions; Figs. 16-16, 16-17, 16-18). Although the incidences of capsular and labral tears and humeral head fractures are low in traumatic posterior instability, MRI and CT can be diagnostic for these lesions (Fig. 16-19). It is the practice of the shoulder service at the University of Pennsylvania initially to perform clinical evaluation, including history and physical examination. Based on this clinical evaluation, lesions are categorized as either voluntary or involuntary. Within the involuntary group, they are further categorized as traumatic or atraumatic, depending on the nature of the initial symptoms and the mechanism of injury. Instability is further categorized with respect to direction—anterior, posterior, or multidirectional. Initial imaging studies include plane-of-the-scapula AP views in internal and external rotation, West Point axillary, Garth's, and Stryker notch views. Initial treatment is based on clinical evaluation and assessment of these views. If patients have atraumatic instability, a nonoperative strengthening rehabilitation program is initiated. Patients with traumatic recurrent instability, in whom nonoperative measures have failed and who demonstrate traumatic anatomic lesions on plain radiographs (i.e., glenoid rim fracture, soft tissue calcification, or Hill-Sachs lesion) without glenoid dysplasia, should undergo surgical intervention using Bankart repair without further diagnostic imaging. Patients who have chronic shoulder pain and a suspected but unconfirmed clinical diagnosis of glenohumeral instability of either the traumatic or atraumatic type with normal radiographs should undergo MRI, followed by examination under anesthesia and arthroscopic evaluation. Based on findings of the clinical examination, MRI, examination under anesthesia, and arthroscopy, the instability pattern would then be accurately classified and

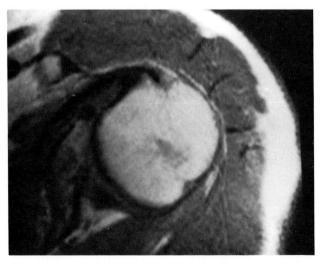

Figure 16-11 Axial MRI demonstrates glenoid hypoplasia.

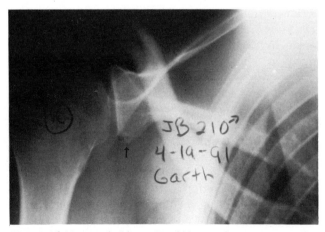

Figure 16-13 Apical oblique (Garth's) view demonstrates anterior glenoid calcification.

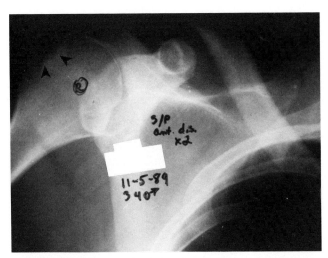

Figure 16-14 AP internal rotation view demonstrates Hill-Sachs lesion (*black arrowheads*).

nonoperative or surgical management undertaken according to the evaluation and treatment algorithm shown in Figure 16-20.

In summary, glenohumeral instability is a clinical diagnosis based on pain and dysfunction that are due to

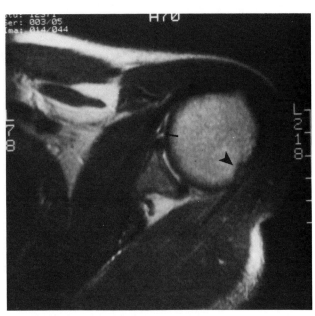

Figure 16-16 Axial MRI shows anterior labral tear (*black arrow*) and small Hill-Sachs lesion (*black arrowhead*).

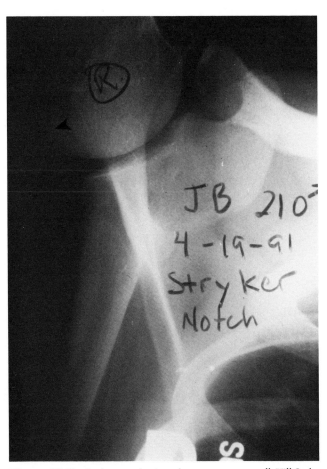

Figure 16-15 Stryker notch view demonstrates a small Hill-Sachs lesion (*black arrowhead*).

abnormal humeral translation. The associated lesions exhibit much variability. Utilizing a simple clinical classification of instability patterns, diagnostic imaging is useful for evaluating the anatomic lesions associated with humeral head impaction fractures, glenoid rim fractures, capsular and labral avulsions, and developmental abnormalities of the glenoid. The use of diagnostic imaging in conjunction with clinical diagnosis is important for accurate classification of the instability pattern and formulation of nonoperative and surgical treatment.

GLENOHUMERAL ARTHRITIS

Many conditions affect the osteoarticular surfaces of the glenohumeral joint, resulting in pain and joint dysfunction: osteoarthrosis, posttraumatic arthritis secondary to acute fracture, osteoarticular injury secondary to acute blunt trauma or repetitive overuse trauma (as seen in lifters of heavy weights), or weight-bearing in the shoulders of paraplegic patients.[25–27] Arthritis may result from repetitive glenohumeral dislocations and instability or postcapsulorrhaphy arthropathy secondary to excessive shortening of the anterior capsule.[28,29] Collagen vascular diseases and autoimmune diseases can affect the shoulder, resulting in synovitis, pannus formation, and damage to the periarticular soft tissues, rotator cuff, and osteoarticular surfaces. Osteonecrosis from a variety of causes commonly affects the shoulder, as well as many other joints. Arthropathy associated with long-standing rotator cuff disease or with crystalline arthropathy is specific and unique to the shoulder joint.[30,31] Miscellaneous and un-

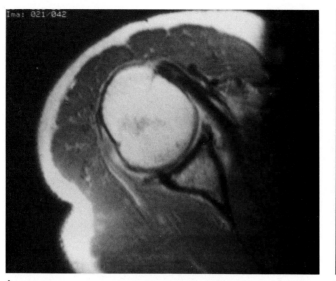

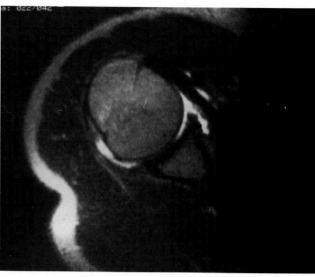

A   B

Figure 16-17 **A,** T1- and, **B,** T2-weighted axial MRI in the midaxial plane demonstrate Type II capsular insertion and absence of the anterior glenoid labrum consistent with a traumatic anterior Bankart lesion.

common causes of glenohumeral arthropathy include pigmented villonodular synovitis, ochronosis, acromegaly, and Gaucher's disease. The broad spectrum of diseases that affect the glenohumeral articulation will result in a wide and varied array of anatomic findings. Defining the differences and unique characteristics of each of these diseases is accomplished in Chapter 13. In this section, I discuss the common clinical factors and anatomic features which influence surgical decision making and management.

Patients undergoing surgical evaluation for end-stage osteoarticular disease from any cause have severe pain that is refractory to nonoperative measures. Preoperative assessment of their clinical status evaluates their general

health and medical condition. The function of both upper extremities, as it relates to their shoulders and other joints of the upper extremities, is important to clinical management, particularly in patients who have a polyarticular disease such as rheumatoid arthritis. Use of the upper extremities for weight bearing during ambulation and the need to use ambulation aids may significantly influence the timing of surgical procedures for patients

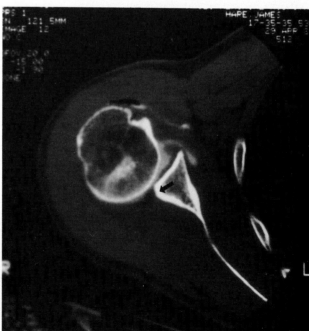

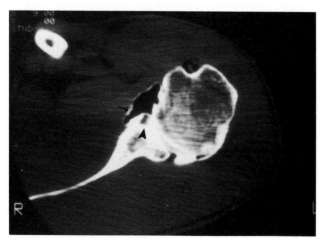

Figure 16-18 CT arthrogram demonstrates an anterior glenoid rim fracture (*black arrowhead*) and capsular Bankart lesion (*black arrow*).

Figure 16-19 Axial CT arthrogram demonstrates posterior humeral head subluxation and posterior glenoid rim fracture (*arrow*).

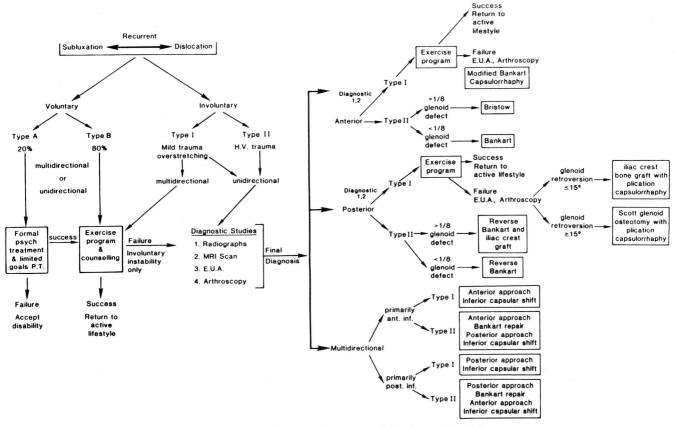

Figure 16-20   University of Pennsylvania algorithm for evaluation and treatment of glenohumeral instability.

with polyarticular disease and may also influence postoperative rehabilitation and long-term success of an upper extremity prosthetic reconstruction. Each of these issues is important for clinical decision making and is not significantly influenced by the anatomic findings demonstrated by shoulder imaging.

Each of the diseases that affect the glenohumeral joint has some effect on the soft tissue and osseous anatomy. The degree of capsular integrity, capsular contracture, rotator cuff integrity and function, and osteoarticular deformity vary among the different types of arthritis. These factors significantly influence the type of surgical procedure, choice of prosthetic reconstruction, and the results of surgical intervention. The integrity of the rotator cuff significantly influences the functional results of prosthetic reconstruction with respect to active range of motion and strength. Patients with large rotator cuff tears, particularly irreparable ones, have weak shoulder function following prosthetic reconstruction.[25,26] Weakness is particularly noted on attempted elevation of the arm above shoulder level. Patients with irreparable large rotator cuff tears continue to demonstrate cephalad migration of the humerus postoperatively, which in turn leads to a higher incidence of glenoid loosening; so, for these patients hemiarthroplasty is preferred.[32] The incidence

of rotator cuff deficiency is high in patients with rheumatoid arthritis, crystalline arthropathy, and cuff tear arthropathy. The incidence of full-thickness rotator cuff tears is very low in association with osteoarthritis, osteonecrosis, and posttraumatic arthritis. The integrity of the rotator cuff can be assessed, as previously described, using clinical examination and imaging studies. When the clinical examination findings suggest an intact rotator cuff and radiographic studies demonstrate osteoarthritis, osteonecrosis, or posttraumatic arthritis, formal imaging of the rotator cuff usually is unnecessary. In these cases, if a rotator cuff tear is present, it is generally small and can easily be diagnosed and repaired at the time of surgery. Surgical management is not significantly altered in these patients by the preoperative diagnosis of a small full-thickness rotator cuff tear. In patients with the diagnosis of rheumatoid arthritis, cuff tear arthropathy, crystalline arthropathy, or other primary synovial disease, MRI is useful for evaluating both the degree of osteoarticular disease and the integrity of the rotator cuff (Fig. 16-21).

The degree of glenoid erosion is important for preoperative planning. The amount of glenoid erosion is quite variable among the common osteoarticular diseases, being most severe in long-standing osteoarthritis

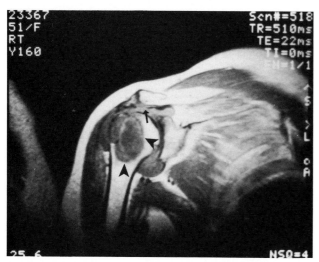

Figure 16-21 Coronal oblique MRI of a patient with rheumatoid arthritis showing full-thickness rotator cuff tear (*black arrow*) and large synovial erosion of the humeral head (*arrowheads*).

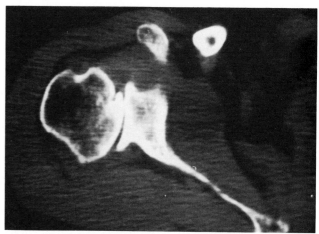

Figure 16-23 Axial CT demonstrates posterior glenoid erosion and posterior humeral head subluxation with osteoarthritis.

associated with asymmetric anterior capsular tightness. Most commonly it is seen in the posterior aspect of the glenoid. Central and superior erosion is commonly seen in patients with cuff tear arthropathy and rheumatoid arthritis, and anterior or posterior glenoid erosion is seen with unreduced long-term dislocation of the shoulder. The degree of glenoid erosion and of bone loss are best evaluated by axillary views of the shoulder, axial CT, or axial MRI (Figs. 16-22, 16-23). Severe glenoid deficiency may require alteration in the surgical approach, asymmetric glenoid reaming, or use of a custom glenoid component or a bone graft. If severe enough, it may result in inability to use a glenoid prosthetic component. Humeral deformity, tuberosity malunion, and the bone stock of the proximal humeral shaft are particularly important variables in prosthetic treatment of posttraumatic

arthritis secondary to malunited fractures and in revision total shoulder arthroplasty. CT arthrography with three-dimensional reconstruction (Fig. 16-24) and long cassette plain radiographs are particularly useful for evaluating the humeral shaft (Fig. 16-25).

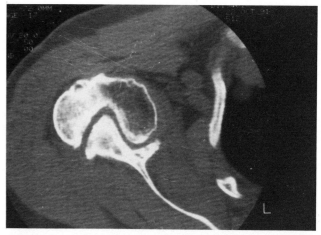

A

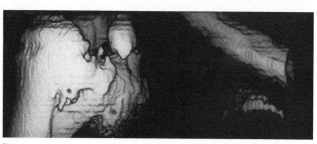

B

Figure 16-24 **A,** Two- and, **B,** three-dimensional CT demonstrate malunion of a nonreduced four-part fracture and anterior dislocation of the humeral head. The humeral head is dislocated in a subcoracoid location with an osseous bridge to the remaining portion of the humeral shaft.

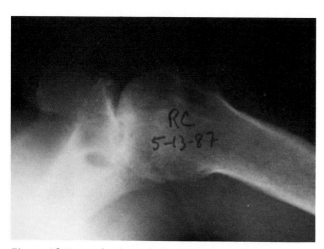

Figure 16-22 Axial radiograph demonstrates posterior glenoid erosion and posterior humeral head subluxation.

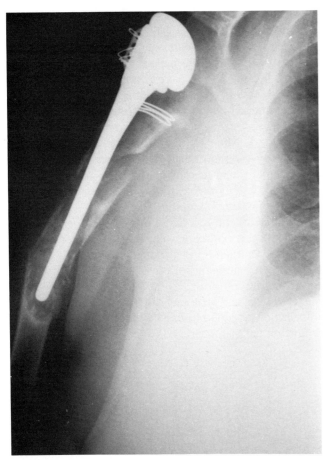

Figure 16-25   Massive osteolysis in a patient who underwent hemiarthroplasty. The osteolysis is secondary to metallic corrosion resulting from the use of a titanium stem and stainless steel wires (dissimilar metals produce corrosion).

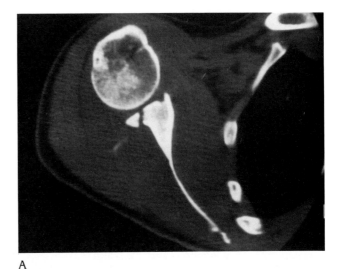

A

B

Figure 16-27   **A,** Two-dimensional and, **B,** three-dimensional CT of glenoid and scapular body fracture.

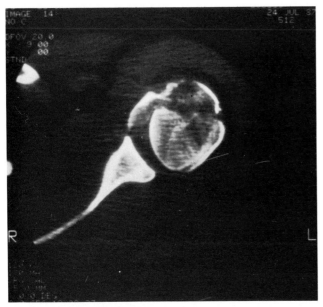

Figure 16-26   Axial CT demonstrates humeral head split and proximal humeral head fracture.

PROXIMAL HUMERAL FRACTURES

The most commonly used classification for proximal humeral fractures describes four segments of the proximal humerus.[33,34] These segments include the metaphyseal-diaphyseal shaft, the greater tuberosity, the lesser tuberosity, and the articular surface of the humeral head. This classification describes these four segments as being discrete parts when they are displaced more than 1 cm or angulated more than 45° from their normal anatomic position. When the amount of displacement and angulation are greater than or equal to these values, the fracture fragment is considered unstable, and in many cases is associated with a defect in the rotator cuff mechanism. These proximal humeral fracture fragments may be associated with dislocation of the humeral head from the glenoid fossa—a proximal humeral fracture-dislocation. High-grade displaced fractures and fracture-dislocations may be associated with neurovascular injury, most commonly to the axillary and musculocutaneous nerves. The factors which influence surgical management and the functional results following surgery depend on several clinical and anatomic features of the fracture pattern. The clinical factors that influence surgical decisions relate to the age, activity level, and general medical health of the patient. The anatomic features which influence treatment and results are the degree of comminution, fracture of the articular surface (head-split fracture), degree of osteopenia, degree of displacement of the fracture fragments, preexisting rotator cuff disease, or glenohumeral arthritis. Most high-grade displaced and angulated three- and four-part fractures are treated by surgical intervention. The results of surgery are influenced by achieving an anatomic reduction, stable internal fixation, early mobilization, and rehabilitation. If these goals are attained, the functional result is better than that of nonoperative treatment.

Diagnostic imaging of proximal humeral fractures requires radiographs to be obtained in three orthogonal planes. This is generally accomplished by obtaining an AP and a lateral view in the plane of the scapula and an axillary view. In the setting of acute trauma an axillary view can be obtained with only 20° to 30° of abduction of the shoulder with the patient in the supine position. In most patients the fracture pattern can be clearly defined with routine radiographic imaging and appropriate surgical intervention can be determined. When articular involvement of the glenoid fossa or humeral head is suspected, or when routine radiographs are difficult to interpret, two-dimensional CT is indicated (Fig. 16-26). Three-dimensional reconstruction can be helpful for complex fractures involving the glenoid fossa, scapular body, and proximal humerus (Fig. 16-27).

In summary, the most common clinical problems affecting the glenohumeral joint include rotator cuff disease, glenohumeral instability, glenohumeral arthritis, and proximal humeral fractures. A rational approach to the management of these problems depends on an accurate clinical and anatomic diagnosis that integrates the information obtained from a careful history, physical examination, and appropriate imaging studies.

References

1. NEER CS II: Anterior acromioplasty for the chronic impingement syndrome in the shoulder: A preliminary report. *J Bone Joint Surg* 54A:41–50, 1972.
2. ELLMAN H: Arthroscopic subacromial decompression: Analysis of one to three year results. *Arthroscopy* 3:173–181, 1987.
3. GARTSMAN GM: Arthroscopic acromioplasty for lesions of the rotator cuff. *J Bone Joint Surg* 72A:169–180, 1990.
4. HAWKINS RJ, KENNEDY JC: Impingement syndrome in athletes. *Am J Sports Med* 8:151–158, 1980.
5. ROCKWOOD CA, LYONS FR: Shoulder impingement syndrome: Diagnosis, radiographic evaluation and treatment with a modified Neer acromioplasty. *J Bone Joint Surg* 75A:409–424, 1993.
6. ZANCA P: Shoulder pain: Involvement of the acromioclavicular joint: Analysis of 1,000 cases. *AJR* 112:493–506, 1971.
7. MORRISON DS, BIGLIANI LU: The clinical significance of variations in acromial morphology. *Orthop Trans* 11:234, 1987.
8. BIGLIANI LU, NORRIS TR, FISCHER J, ET AL.: The relationship between the unfused acromial epiphysis and subacromial impingement lesions. *Orthop Trans* 7:138, 1983.
9. NEER CS II: Unfused acromial epiphysis in impingement and cuff tears. Presented at the 45th Annual Meeting of the American Academy of Orthopaedic Surgeons, Dallas, Feb 21–23, 1978.
10. IANNOTTI JP, BERNOT M, KUHLMAN J, KELLEY M: Prospective evaluation of rotator cuff repair. *J Shoulder Elbow Surg* 2:S9, 1993.
11. HATTRUP SJ COFIELD RH, BERQUIST TH, McGOUGH PF, HOFFMEYER PJ: Shoulder arthrography for determination of size of rotator cuff tears. *J Shoulder Elbow Surg* 1:98–105, 1992.
12. CRAIG EV: The geyser sign and torn rotator cuff: Clinical significance and pathomechanics. *Clin Orthop* 191:213–215, 1984.
13. MACK LA, MATSEN FA III, KILCOYNE RF, ET AL.: US evaluation of the rotator cuff. *Radiology* 157:205–209, 1985.

14. MIDDLETON WD, REINUS WR, TOTTY WG, ET AL.: Ultrasonographic evaluation of the rotator cuff and biceps tendon. *J Bone Joint Surg* 68A:440–450, 1986.

15. IANNOTTI JP, ZLATKIN MB, ESTERHAI JL, ET AL.: Magnetic resonance imaging of the shoulder: Sensitivity, specificity, and predictive value. *J Bone Joint Surg* 73A:17–29, 1991.

16. ZLATKIN MB, IANNOTTI JP, ROBERTS MC, ET AL.: Rotator cuff tears: Diagnostic performance of MR imaging. *Radiology* 172:223–229, 1989.

17. PALETTA GA, WARNER JP, ALTCHEK DW, O'BRIEN SJ, WICKIEWICZ TL, WARREN RF: Arthroscopic rotator cuff repair: Evaluation of results and a comparison of techniques. Trans. AAOS 60th Annual Meeting, San Francisco, p 205, 1993.

18. HARRYMAN DT, SIDLES JA, HARRIS SL, MATSEN FA: Laxity of the normal glenohumeral joint: A quantitative in vivo assessment. *J Shoulder Elbow Surg* 1:66–76, 1992.

19. ROWE CR, PATEL D, SOUTHMAYD WW: The Bankart procedure, a long-term end-result study. *J Bone Joint Surg* 60A:1–16, 1978.

20. ROWE, CR: Prognosis in dislocations of the shoulder. *J Bone Joint Surg* 38A:957–977, 1956.

21. NEER CS II, FOSTER CR: Inferior capsular shift for involuntary inferior and multidirectional instability of the shoulder. A preliminary report. *J Bone Joint Surg* 62A:897–907, 1980.

22. COOPER RA, BREMS JJ: The inferior capsular shift procedure for multidirectional instability of the shoulder. *J Bone Joint Surg* 74A:1516–1529, 1992.

23. BURKHEAD WZ, ROCKWOOD CA: Treatment of instability of the shoulder with an exercise program. *J Bone Joint Surg* 74A:890–896, 1992.

24. CASPARI, RB: Arthroscopic reconstruction for anterior shoulder instability. *Techniques Orthop* 3:59–66, 1988.

25. NEER CS II, WATSON KC, STANTON FJ: Recent experience in total shoulder replacement. *J Bone Joint Surg* 64A:319–337, 1982.

26. COFIELD RH: Total shoulder arthroplasty with the Neer prosthesis. *J Bone Joint Surg* 66A:899–906, 1984.

27. BAYLEY JC, COCHRAN TP, SLEDGE CB: The weight bearing shoulder: The impingement syndrome in paraplegia. *J Bone Joint Surg* 169A:676–679, 1987.

28. O'DRISCOLL SW, EVANS DC: Long term results of staple capsulorrhaphy for anterior instability of the shoulder. *J Bone Joint Surg* 75A:249–258, 1993.

29. HAWKINS RJ, ANGELO RL: Glenohumeral osteoarthrosis. A late complication of the Putti-Platt repair. *J Bone Joint Surg* 72A:1193–1197, 1990.

30. NEER CS II, CRAIG EV, FUKUDA H: Cuff tear arthropathy. *J Bone Joint Surg* 65A:1232–1244, 1983.

31. HALVERSON PB, CHEUNG HS, McCARTY DJ, GRANCIS J, MANDEL N: "Milwaukee shoulder"—Association of microspheroids containing hydroxyapatite crystals, active collagenase and neutral protease with rotator cuff defects. *Arthritis Rheum* 24:474–483, 1981.

32. FRANKLIN JL, BARRETT WP, JACKINS SE, MATSEN FA III: Glenoid loosening in total shoulder arthroplasty. *J Arthroplasty* 3:39–46, 1988.

33. NEER CS: Displaced proximal humerus fractures. Part I. Classification and evaluation. *J Bone Joint Surg* 52A:1077–1089, 1970.

34. NEER CS: Displaced proximal humeral fractures. Treatment of three-part and four-part displacement. *J Bone Joint Surg* 52:1090–1103, 1970.

INDEX

Page numbers followed by *t* and *f* indicate tables and figures.

A

Abscess
  Brodie, 178
    magnetic resonance imaging, 185
  cortical, 259*f*
    magnetic resonance imaging, 185, 186*f*
  in musculoskeletal infection, percutaneous drainage, 112, 113*f*
  soft-tissue, 177
    computed tomography, 181–182
    magnetic resonance imaging, 185
  subperiosteal, 176–177
Achondroplasia, 367, 367*f*
Ackerman needle, 109
Acquired immunodeficiency syndrome
  and musculoskeletal infection, 177–178
  and Reiter syndrome, 386–387
Acromegaly, 357, 357*f*
Acromial spur(s), 317, 318*f*
Acromioclavicular joint, 50, 51*f*
  abnormalities, 147
  degenerative changes, with impingement, 318–319
  dislocation or subluxation, 7, 266*f*–267*f*, 275*f*, 275–276, 276*f*
    congenital, 147
  normal planar MR anatomy, oblique coronal plane, 54–56, 55*f*
  plain radiography, technical aspects, 3*f*, 4–8, 7*f*–8*f*, 8*t*
  separation, 266*f*–267*f*, 275*f*, 275–276
    grade 1, 7
    grade 2, 7
    grade 3, 7, 8*f*, 266*f*
    plain film radiography, 7–8, 8*f*
    positioning of arms simulating, 129*f*
  variable configurations, 125, 133*f*
Acromiohumeral distance, 318
Acromion, 49*f*

developmental variants, 145
hooked (type III), 14, 14*f*, 59, 59*f*
shape
  and impingement, 316
  variations, 316, 316*f*
unfused apophysis, versus fracture, 266, 267*f*
Acromionectomy, 344
Acromion process, 50
  low-lying, 59, 60*f*
  magnetic resonance imaging, anatomic variations and pitfalls, 59*f*, 59–60, 60*f*
  normal planar MR anatomy
    oblique coronal plane, 54–56, 55*f*
    oblique sagittal plane, 56*f*, 56–57
  ossification centers, 144–145
    plain radiography, 117, 118*f*–119*f*
  plain film radiography, 3*f*–5*f*
  types of, 342–343, 344*f*
Acromioplasty, 344, 345*f*, 379*f*, 433–434
  postoperative evaluation, 346–350
Adamantinoma (angioblastoma), 220
Adhesive capsulitis, 392, 394*f*. *See also* Frozen shoulder
  arthrography, 25*f*, 25–26
  scintigraphic techniques with, 95–98, 96*f*
  treatment, 26, 105–108
  ultrasound in, 69–70
Aggressive fibromatosis, 228, 233–234, 235*f*
Albers-Schonberg disease (osteopetrosis), 166–167
Alcoholism, neuroarthropathy due to, 402
Alkaline phosphatase deficiency, 364–365
Alkaptonuria, 363–364
AMBRI syndrome, with shoulder dislocations, 292
Amyloidosis, 366, 398, 398*f*, 422, 423*f*
  computed tomography in, 422, 423*f*

magnetic resonance imaging in, 422, 423*f*
  neuroarthropathy due to, 402
Anatomy, of shoulder joint
  and biomechanics of shoulder stabilizers, 285–288
  computed tomography, 36–43
  magnetic resonance imaging, 48*t*, 48–52, 49*f*–52*f*
    normal planar, 52–57, 53*f*, 55*f*–57*f*
    variations and pitfalls, 57–62
  muscular, 51–52, 52*f*
  radiographic, 15–18, 16*f*–18*f*
  regional, 15
  and soft tissue injury, 285
  variants, 117
Anemia. *See also* Sickle cell disease; Thalassemia
Aneurysmal bone cyst. *See* Bone cyst, aneurysmal
Angioblastoma, 220
Angiography. *See also* MR angiography
  with hemangioma, 230
Angiosarcoma, 219, 219*f*
  multifocal, 219
  solitary, 219
Ankylosing spondylitis, 384, 386*f*
  epidemiology, 384
Anterior capsule, 49–50. *See also* Capsulolabral complex
  attachments, 137*f*–139*f*, 138–139
    magnetic resonance imaging, 137*f*–139*f*, 138–139
    computed tomography and arthrography, 33, 34*f*, 35, 139
Anterior instability, arthrography, 27, 27*f*
Anterior interval pitfall, 135
Anterior oblique view, 2, 5*f*
Anteroposterior view(s), 1, 3*f*, 7, 353, 413, 414*f*
  in external rotation, 16, 16*f*
  with glenohumeral instability, 435*f*, 436, 437*f*

Anteroposterior view(s) *(Cont.)*
in internal rotation, 16, 17*f*
in osseous trauma, 263–264
with soft tissue injury, 317, 318*f*
with weight-bearing stress, 7
Apatite deposition disease, in rotator cuff, aspiration of, 103–105, 104*f*–105*f*, 106*t*, 106*f*
Apical oblique projection, 3–4, 6*f*
Aplastic anemia, 253
Appliances, orthopedic, fluoroscopic evaluation of, 14–15
Apprehension syndrome, 307
Arachnodactyly, 364
Arthritis. *See also* Osteoarthritis; Rheumatoid arthritis; Septic arthritis
aseptic, scintigraphic techniques for, 82
with biliary cirrhosis, 387
in calcium pyrophosphate dihydrate crystal deposition disease, 390
definition, 375
enteropathic, 387
glenohumeral, imaging, surgical perspective, 437–440, 440*f*–441*f*
gonococcal, 177
gouty, 388–389
inflammatory, 377–387
in ochronosis, 364, 364*f*
psoriatic, 384–386, 387*f*
scintigraphic techniques with, 90–99, 94*f*–98*f*
ultrasound in, 67, 67*f*, 69, 69*f*
villous, 396
Arthrography. *See also* Computed arthrotomography; MR-arthrography
abnormal, 22–28
of adhesive capsulitis, 25*f*, 25–26, 394*f*
of anterior instability, 27, 27*f*
comparison with other modalities, 71–73
complications of, 20–22
contrast material for, 19
contrast reactions in, 21–22
double-contrast, 18, 20
advantages of, 28–29
normal, 15, 22, 22*f*
of shoulder dislocations, 27–28
of infections, 181
in neuroarthropathic joint disease, 402, 406*f*
of normal anatomy, 18, 19*f*
of osteochondral body, 26, 26*f*
of osteochondromatosis, 26, 26*f*
postoperative, after joint replacement, 338
of primary synovial osteochondromatosis, 395*f*
in rheumatoid arthritis, 26*f*, 26–27, 383

of rotator cuff tears, 433
complete, 22–24, 23*f*–24*f*
partial, 24–25, 25*f*
single-contrast, 18–20
of soft tissue injury, 319–321, 320*f*
technical aspects, 15–28
technique, 18–22, 21*f*
Arthrogryposis multiplex congenita, 149, 401, 402*f*
Arthroplasty. *See also* Joint replacement; Prostheses
definition, 335
resection, definition, 335
total shoulder
definition, 335
indications for, 335
Arthroscopy, SLAP lesion, 309, 309*t*, 322, 323*f*
Arthrotomography, double-contrast, 28*f*, 28–29
Articulations
atypical, 122–123, 132*f*–133*f*
variable, 122–123, 132*f*–133*f*
Aspiration, in infection, 181
Atelosteogenesis, 150–151
radiographic abnormalities on shoulder, 150–151
radiographic findings in, 150–151
Avascular necrosis
of humeral head, in sickle cell disease, 252*f*
osteoarthritis of glenohumeral joint with, 375, 376*f*–377*f*
Axillary artery injury
with anterior shoulder dislocation, 278
with fractures of proximal humerus, 273
Axillary nerve
entrapment, 408*t*, 409, 414–415
injury, with fractures of proximal humerus, 273
Axillary view, 1, 3*f*, 4
in osseous trauma, 263
with soft tissue injury, 317
Axillary Y view, 17, 17*f*

B

Bankart lesion, 26*f*, 27, 41*f*, 42, 278, 293, 295, 300*f*, 303*f*, 322*f*, 346, 436, 438*f*
double-contrast arthrography, 28
with false-negative MR examination, 304, 307*f*
instability and, 289
MR arthrography, 329–331, 331*f*
osseous, 289, 298*f*, 305*f*
plain film radiography, 2, 26*f*, 27
Benign fibrous histiocytoma, 209

Benign neonatal hemangiomatosis, 231
Benign synovioma, 396
Beta-2 microglobulin deposition, in hemodialysis patient, 422, 423*f*
Biceps muscle, 49*f*, 52, 52*f*
long head, 49*f*, 52, 52*f*
short head, 49*f*, 52, 52*f*
Biceps tendon (bicipital tendon), 52
abnormalities
arthrography, 27, 27*f*
magnetic resonance imaging, 328
computed tomography, 34*f*, 39–41, 40*f*
dislocation
magnetic resonance imaging, 328
medial, 322, 322*f*
ultrasound of, 70
long head, 41, 48–49, 49*f*, 52
dislocation, arthrography, 27
embryology, 15
normal planar MR anatomy
axial plane, 52–54, 53*f*
oblique coronal plane, 54–56, 55*f*
oblique sagittal plane, 56*f*, 56–57, 57*f*
sheath, fluid in, magnetic resonance imaging, 136, 136*f*
Bicipital groove, 48, 52
deep, artifacts due to, 131*f*
normal variants, 148
Bicipital groove projection, 4, 6*f*, 18, 18*f*
Biliary cirrhosis, arthritis with, 387
Bismuth toxicity, neuroarthropathy in, 402, 404*f*
Bladder cancer, scintigraphic techniques with, 88–89
Blood pool imaging, 75. *See also* Scintigraphy
in osteomyelitis, 81, 82*f*
Blue rubber bleb nevus syndrome, 231, 232*f*
magnetic resonance imaging in, 231, 232*f*
Bone
defects, 121
lymphomas of, 215–216, 216*f*
pyogenic infection, percutaneous biopsy, indications for, 108
trabecular pattern simulating disease, 119, 124*f*
tuberculosis, percutaneous biopsy, indications for, 108
tumorlike lesions of, 216–218. *See also* Bone cyst, aneurysmal; Bone cyst, unicameral (simple); Eosinophilic granuloma
Bone compartment, radionuclides for, 94–95
Bone cyst

aneurysmal, 217, 218*f*
  prevalence, 193
  scintigraphic techniques with, 85
scintigraphic techniques with, 85
unicameral (simple), 216*f*, 216–217
  scintigraphic techniques with, 85,
    86*f*
Bone-forming tumor(s), 203–208. *See
  also* Osteoblastoma; Osteoid osteoma; Osteosarcoma
Bone marrow
  blood supply to, 241
  computed tomography, 244, 245*f*–246*f*
  conversion
    failure of, 249
    in humerus, 148
  conversion to fat, with age, 242–243
  disorders, 361
    imaging, 241–261
  edema, 253–256, 259*f*
  fibrosis, in myeloid metaplasia, 360,
    361*f*
  hematopoietic, 241–242
  imaging, 243–249
    technical aspects, 77–78, 78*f*
  infiltration, 253, 253*f*–258*f*
  innervation, 241
  ischemia, 256
  magnetic resonance imaging, 244–
    249, 247*f*–250*f*
  microanatomy, 241–242
  myeloid depletion, 249–253, 252*f*
  normal, 241–243
  physiology, 241–242
  plain film radiography, 243
  reconversion to red marrow, 242–
    243, 249
  red, 241–242
  scans (scintigraphy), 243*f*, 243–244
  yellow, 242
Bone scan(s) (scintigraphy)
  analysis, 76–77
  cold spots, 75
  hot spots, 75
  hyperemic phenomenon on, 76
  indications for, 76
  interpretation, 76–77, 77*f*
  mechanism of localization, 75–76
  in myositis ossificans, 416, 417*f*
  pediatric, technique and analysis, 76–
    77, 77*f*
  photopenia, 75
  technical aspects, 75
  technique, 76–77
  three-phase, 75
    in noninfectious processes, 183
  in trauma, 78–79, 79*f*
Bone trephine needles, 109
Bone tumor(s), 193–226. *See also* spe-
  cific tumor

benign, scintigraphic techniques with,
  84–87
cartilage-forming, 194–203
chemotherapy, posttreatment imaging,
  220–221
fibrous, 208–211
  benign, 208–210
  malignant, 210–211
  percutaneous biopsy, 108
  primary malignant, scintigraphic tech-
    niques with, 87–88, 88*f*–89*f*
  round cell, 213–216
  vascular, 218–220
Brachial plexus
  avulsion
    complete, 282
    incomplete, 282
  injury, 414*f*
    with fractures of proximal hu-
      merus, 273
    obstetric, 147, 147*f*
  neuropathies, 408*t*, 409–410
Breast cancer
  metastases, 193, 194*f*
  scintigraphic techniques with, 88–89,
    91*f*, 93*f*
Brisement procedure, 26
Brodie abscess, 178
  magnetic resonance imaging, 185
Bronzed diabetes, 366
Brown tumor, in hyperparathyroidism,
  355, 356*f*
Bursitis
  calcareus, 391
  ultrasound in, 66–70, 69*f*–70*f*

C

Caffey-Silverman disease (infantile cortical hyperostosis), 370–371, 371*f*
Calcareus tendinitis and bursitis, 391
Calcification(s)
  in dermatomyositis, 372–373, 373*f*
  of subacromial bursa, 365, 365*f*
  ultrasound with, 69, 70*f*
Calcific bursitis, 391
Calcific tendinitis, 391
Calcium hydroxyapatite crystal deposition disease, radiographic features,
  391, 392*f*–393*f*
Calcium pyrophosphate crystal deposition, 365, 365*f*, 375
Calcium pyrophosphate dihydrate crystal deposition disease, 390–391
  radiographic features, 390*f*, 390–391,
    391*f*
Candida, in chronic granulomatous disease, 370
Capsular constraint mechanism, 286–
  288

Capsular stripping
  anterior, 304, 306*f*
  posterior, 304, 306*f*
Capsule. *See also* Anterior capsule; Posterior capsule
  abnormalities, 405–407
  fibrosis in, 405–407, 408*f*
Capsulolabral complex. *See also* Anterior capsule; Glenoid labrum; Posterior capsule
  magnetic resonance imaging
    anatomic variations and pitfalls, 60–
      62, 60*f*–62*f*
    normal anatomy, axial plane, 52–54,
      53*f*
Cardiomelic syndrome (Holt-Oram syndrome), 156–157
Carpomelic dysplasia, 151–152
  radiographic findings in, 151–152
    in shoulder, 151*f*, 151–152
Catheter(s), for abscess drainage, 112
Cat scratch disease, in HIV-positive patient, 177
Cellulitis, 177
  computed tomography, 181
  imaging evaluation, 179–181
  scintigraphic techniques for, 82
Ceruloplasmin, 366
Cervical cancer, scintigraphic techniques
  with, 88–89
Cervical rib, 410
Cervical spine, scintigraphic techniques
  for, 91, 94*f*
Charcot joint, development, 402, 404*f*–
  405*f*
Charcot-Marie-Tooth disease, neuroar-
  thropathy in, 402
Chemotherapy, posttreatment imaging,
  220–221
Child abuse, evaluation of, 78–79
CHILD syndrome, 152
  radiographic findings in, 152
    in shoulder, 152
Chondroblastoma, 198–200
Chondrocalcinosis, 365–366
  associated conditions, 389–390
  in calcium pyrophosphate dihydrate
    crystal deposition disease, 389–
    390, 390*f*–391*f*
Chondrodysplasia punctata, 152
  Conradi-Hünermann type, 152
  radiographic findings in, in shoulder,
    152, 153*f*
  rhizomelic type, 152
Chondroma, periosteal, 197–198
Chondromyxoid fibroma, 200
Chondrosarcoma, 200–203, 200*f*–203*f*
  central, 200
  clear cell, 202–203
  dedifferentiated, 202

Chondrosarcoma *(Cont.)*
  extraskeletal, 200
  histology, 200
  in Paget disease, 426
  periosteal, 197–198, 201–202, 203*f*
  peripheral, 200
  prevalence, 193
  primary (de novo), 200
  secondary, 200
Chronic granulomatous disease of
    childhood, 370, 370*f*
Chronic hemorrhagic villous synovitis,
    396
Cinefluoroscopy, 13
Clavicle
  anomalies, 142–144
  aplasia and hypoplasia, 143, 143*t*
  broad or thickened, 143–144, 144*t*
    conditions associated with, 143,
        144*t*
  congenital pseudarthrosis, 142, 142*f*
  distal
    ligamentous anatomy, 265–266,
        266*f*
    posttraumatic osteolysis, 276, 276*f*,
        415–416, 416*f*
  duplication, 143
  epiphyses, 141, 142*f*
  fetal, in assessment of gestational age,
      141
  fractures, 264–266, 264*f*–266*f*
    at birth, 263, 264*f*
  growth and development, 141, 142*f*
  hooked, 142–143, 143*t*
  in hyperparathyroidism, 355, 356*f*
  medial end, bifid, 133, 134*f*
  metastatic disease in, 193, 194*f*
  neoplasms in, 193, 194*f*
  nontraumatic lesions, types, 194
  normal planar MR anatomy
    oblique coronal plane, 54–56, 55*f*
    oblique sagittal plane, 56*f*, 56–57
  normal variants, 141, 142*f*
  nutrient canal of, 121, 125*f*, 141, 142*f*
  ossification centers, 141
    plain radiography, 119, 123*f*
  plain film radiography, 6*f*
  plasma cell osteomyelitis, 243*f*
  straight/long, 143, 143*t*
  vascular or neural channels simulat-
      ing lesions, 121, 125*f*
Clear cell chondrosarcoma, 202–203
Cleidocranial dysplasia, 142, 152–154,
    367, 368*f*
  clavicular absence or hypoplasia with,
      143
  radiographic findings in, 152–154
    in shoulder, 152–153, 153*f*–154*f*
Computed arthrotomography (arthro-
    CT), 33, 34*f*–35*f*

  of capsule, 139
  of glenohumeral ligaments, 139, 139*f*
  of labrum, 139, 139*f*
  normal variants and artifacts, 139
  of partial rotator cuff tears, 37*f*, 37–
      38, 38*f*
  of pigmented villonodular synovitis,
      396–397
  of posterior capsule, 33, 34*f*, 35
  of primary synovial osteochondroma-
      tosis, 393, 395*f*
  of rotator cuff tears, 37*f*, 37–38, 38*f*,
      321, 321*f*
  of shoulder instability, 296–300, 298*t*,
      299*f*–301*f*
  of soft tissue injury, 321–323, 321*f*–
      323*f*
  of subscapularis bursa, 139, 139*f*
  of synovial chondromatosis, 420–422
  technique, 33–35
Computed tomography
  in amyloidosis, 422, 423*f*
  anatomy, 36–43
  of biceps tendon (bicipital tendon),
      34*f*, 39–41, 40*f*
  of bone marrow, 244, 245*f*–246*f*
  in cellulitis, 181
  closed (fused) physeal line on, 135,
      135*f*, 139*f*
  of coracoacromial arch, 37
  of coracoid process, 34*f*
  external rotation axial view, 34*f*, 35
  of fractures, 264
  of glenohumeral instability, 40*f*–42*f*,
      42–43
  of glenohumeral joint instability, 435,
      436*f*
  of glenohumeral ligaments, 33, 34*f*–
      35*f*, 39–41, 40*f*, 296
  of glenoid fossa, 39–43
  of Hill-Sachs deformity, 296, 299*f*
  of humeral head, 34*f*, 36
  humeral pseudocyst on, 134, 135*f*
  in impingement syndrome, 37
  internal rotation axial view, 35, 35*f*
  after joint replacement, 338–339
  of labral attachments, 38*f*, 40*f*–41*f*,
      41–42
  of labrum, 34*f*–35*f*, 39*f*, 39–43
  of lipomas, 228, 228*f*
  in myositis ossificans, 416, 417*f*
  in neuromuscular disease, 401
  normal variants and artifacts, 134–
      135
  in osteomyelitis, 181–182
  of pigmented villonodular synovitis,
      418–420
  postoperative
    of acromioplasty, rotator cuff repair,

    and instability repair, 347–348,
        348*f*
    after joint replacement, 338–339
  of proximal humeral fractures, 441*f*,
      442
  in rheumatoid arthritis, 383
  of rotator cuff, 34*f*, 36–39, 36*f*–39*f*
  of rotator cuff avulsion, 38, 39*f*
  of rotator cuff tears, 36, 37*f*
    horizontal, 38, 39*f*
    multiplanar reformation, 37*f*–39*f*,
        38–39
  in septic arthritis, 182, 182*f*
  of shoulder instability, 295*f*, 296–300,
      298*f*–299*f*
  of SLAP lesion, 41*f*
  of soft-tissue abscess, 181–182
  of soft tissue neoplasms, 227–228
  of subscapularis tendon, 34*f*
  of synovial chondromatosis, 420–422
  zebra stripe artifacts on, 134, 135*f*
Computed tomography and arthrogra-
    phy. *See* Computed arthrotomogra-
    phy
Condensing osteitis, scintigraphic tech-
    niques with, 86–87
Congenital disorders, 141–174
Congenital myotonia, 403–404
Congenital pseudarthrosis, clavicle, 142,
    142*f*
Connective tissue arthropathies, 387–
    388
Connective tissue disease, 401–402, 403*f*
Conoid tubercle, 141
Conventional radiography. *See also* Plain
    film radiography
  technical aspects, 1–11
Conventional tomography
  applications of, 9
  of infections, 181
  technical aspects, 9, 10*f*
Coracoacromial arch, 50
  computed tomography, 37
  magnetic resonance imaging, 431,
      432*f*–433*f*
  pathology, 431
  radiographic evaluation, 431, 432*f*,
      434
Coracoacromial ligament, 50
  normal planar MR anatomy
    oblique coronal plane, 54–56, 55*f*
    oblique sagittal plane, 57*f*
Coracobrachialis muscle, 36*f*, 52, 52*f*
  normal planar MR anatomy, oblique
      sagittal plane, 56*f*, 56–57
Coracoclavicular bar, 147
Coracoclavicular joint, 122, 132*f*, 147
Coracoclavicular ligament
  abnormalities, 147
  attachment, 121, 127*f*

calcification, 125, 133f
normal planar MR anatomy, oblique coronal plane, 54–56, 55f
Coracohumeral ligament, 49f, 50, 50f
normal planar MR anatomy
oblique coronal plane, 54–56, 55f
oblique sagittal plane, 57f
Coracoid fracture, 266f, 266–267, 267f
Coracoid process, 50
computed tomography, 34f
developmental variants, 145
normal planar MR anatomy
axial plane, 52–54, 53f
oblique coronal plane, 54–56, 55f
oblique sagittal plane, 56f, 56–57
ossification centers, 144
plain radiography, 117, 118f
plain film radiography, 3f–6f
Coronal plane anteroposterior 30° caudad tilt view, 431, 432f, 434
Coronal plane anteroposterior 15° to 30° cephalic tilt view, 431, 432f, 434
Cortical abscess, 259f
CPPD. See Calcium pyrophosphate crystal deposition
Craig needle, 109
Cretinism, 356–357
Critical zone, 25, 316, 326
focal increased signal at, on magnetic resonance imaging, 57f, 57–58, 135, 135f
Crohn disease, 387
Cryptococcus neoformans infection, in HIV-positive patient, 177
Crystal-induced disease, 388–392
CTA. See Computed arthrotomography
Cuff arthropathy, 391
Cushing syndrome, 357, 358f

D

DCSA. See Arthrography, double-contrast
Dead arm syndrome, 307
Dedifferentiated chondrosarcoma, 202
Deltoid muscle, 36, 36f, 49f, 51, 52f
insertions, on humerus, 121, 128f
normal planar MR anatomy
axial plane, 52–54, 53f
oblique coronal plane, 54–56, 55f
oblique sagittal plane, 56f, 56–57
ultrasound, 65–66, 66f–68f
Dermatomyositis, 372–373, 373f, 388, 389f, 401
Dermatomyositis-scleroderma overlap syndrome, 401, 403f
Desmoplastic fibroma, 209
Developmental disorders, 141–174
Developmental dysplasia, of shoulder, 410, 410f
Diabetes mellitus

lipoatrophic, 405, 407f
neuroarthropathy in, 402, 404f
Diaphyseal aclasis (multiple cartilaginous exostoses), 85, 87f, 162, 163f
Diaphyseal dysplasia, 154
clavicular abnormalities with, 144
radiographic findings in, 154, 154f
Diastrophic dysplasia, 155
radiographic findings in, 155, 155f
Didiee projection, 2
with glenohumeral instability, 295
Diffuse idiopathic skeletal hyperostosis, scintigraphic techniques with, 98–99
Diffuse neonatal hemangiomatosis, 231, 232f
Dirkum disease, 228
Dislocation(s), 274–282
acromioclavicular joint, 7, 147, 266f–267f, 275f, 275–276, 276f
glenohumeral joint, 435
congenital, 149
shoulder, 276–281
AMBRI syndrome with, 292
anterior, 270f, 272f, 277–278, 278f, 290, 294f
axillary, 290, 291f
chronic, 291–292
congenital, 149
imaging, 293–295, 293f–295f
inferior, 277f, 277, 279
positioning of arms simulating, 129f–130f
posterior, 279–281, 280f–281f, 291, 291f, 295f
recurrence, 292
superior, 279, 279f, 291
TUBS syndrome with, 292
sternoclavicular joint, 9, 10f, 274f, 274–275
Double-density sign, 85
Drooping shoulder, 406–407, 408f, 413, 414f
Duchenne muscular dystrophy, 401, 403–404
Dysplasia epiphysealis multiplex (multiple epiphyseal dysplasia), 163–165, 357, 367–368, 368f

E

Effusion(s), 413, 414f
Elderly, infection in, 175
Embryology, glenohumeral joint, 15
Enchondroma, 195–197, 197f–199f
scintigraphic techniques with, 86
Enchondromatosis, 162–163, 164f, 368, 369f
Endocrinopathies, 353–374
with fibrous dysplasia, 422

Endometrial cancer, scintigraphic techniques with, 88–89
Engelmann-Camurati disease. See Diaphyseal dysplasia
Enteropathic arthritis, 387
Enzyme disorder(s), 363–365. See also specific disorder
Eosinophilic granuloma, 217–218, 219f, 250f, 369–370
marrow infiltration in, 253, 257f–258f
prevalence, 193
scintigraphic techniques with, 85
Erb's palsy, 147, 147f
lateral clavicular hook with, 147
Erdheim-Chester disease, marrow infiltration in, 253, 256f
Erlenmeyer flask deformity, 361
Escherichia coli, in chronic granulomatous disease, 370
Ewing's sarcoma, 213–214, 214f
prevalence, 193
prognostic features, 214
scintigraphic techniques with, 87–88, 89f
treatment, 214

F

Fallen fragment sign, 216f, 217
Familial dysautonomia, neuroarthropathy in, 402
Familial hypophosphatemia, rickets in, 355, 355f
Fibrodysplasia ossificans progressiva, 155–156, 368–369, 369f
radiographic findings in, 155–156, 156f
Fibrogenesis imperfecta ossium, 371–372, 372f
Fibrohemangiomatous tumor with giant cells, 396
Fibrohemosideric sarcoma, 396
Fibroma(s), nonossifying, 208–209
scintigraphic techniques with, 85
Fibromatosis, aggressive, 228, 233–234, 235f
Fibrosarcoma, 236
of bone, 210–211, 211f
in Paget disease, 426
Fibrosis, in joint capsule, 405–407, 408f
Fibrous cortical defect, 208–209, 209f
Fibrous dysplasia, 209–210, 210f, 373, 373f, 422–425, 424f
magnetic resonance imaging, 424f, 425
malignant degeneration, 425
monostotic, 209, 373, 422
pauciostotic, 373
polyostotic, 209–210, 373, 422, 424f
scintigraphic techniques with, 86

Fibrous histiocytoma
 benign, 209
 malignant. *See* Malignant fibrous histiocytoma
Fibroxanthoma, 208–209, 396
First and second branchial arch syndrome (Goldenhar syndrome), 156
Fluoroscopy
 physics, 13
 technical aspects, 13–15
 uses, 13–15, 14*f*
Fluorosis, 362, 363*f*
Foreign bodies, in soft tissue, fluoroscopic evaluation of, 15
Fracture(s)
 clavicle, 264–266, 264*f*–266*f*
  at birth, 263, 264*f*
  computed tomography, 264
  in congenital indifference to pain,
   368, 369*f*
 coracoid, 266*f*, 266–267, 267*f*
 glenoid and scapular body, 441*f*, 442
 glenoid neck, 267, 268*f*
 glenoid rim, 436, 438*f*
  anterior inferior, 267, 268*f*
  posterior, 267, 269*f*
 humeral
  greater tuberosity, 270, 270*f*, 278
   ultrasound of, 70
  surgical neck, 270, 270*f*
 humeral head, 278, 278*f*
  head-splitting, 271, 273*f*
  impression or compression of articular surface, 271–273, 272*f*
 after joint replacement, 339, 339*f*–
  340*f*
 of joint replacement components,
  340, 341*f*
 lateral clavicular hook with, 143
 nonunion. *See* Nonunion
 versus nutrient canal of clavicle,
  125*f*
 versus os acromiale, 145
 osteoporotic, 354
 pathologic
  bone scan with, 79
  of hemangioendothelioma, 219,
   219*f*
  in non-Hodgkin's lymphoma, 216,
   216*f*
  scintigraphic techniques with, 85,
   86*f*
  of simple bone cyst, 216*f*, 217
 proximal humeral. *See* Proximal humerus, fractures
 scapular, 266–268, 266*f*–269*f*, 441*f*,
  442
 with shoulder dislocations, 294–295
 traumatic, bone scan with, 79, 79*f*
 versus vascular channels, 125*f*

Frontal view, for plain film radiography
  of acromioclavicular joint, 4, 7*f*
Frozen shoulder. *See also* Adhesive capsulitis
 with fractures of proximal humerus,
  273
 hydraulic distension with steroids and
  motion exercise program
  results, 107–108
  technique, 107, 107*f*
 management, 105–108

G

Gadolinium enhancement, in evaluation
  of soft tissue neoplasms, 236
Gadopentate dimeglumine (Magnevist),
  instillation for MR-arthrography,
  47–48
Gallium-67 labeled leukocytes
 in evaluation of nonunion, 80, 80*f*
 in osteomyelitis, 82–84
 in shoulder infections, 82–84, 182
 technical aspects, 77
Ganglion cysts, 414
Garth view, with glenohumeral instability, 436*f*, 436
Gastrointestinal tumors, scintigraphic
  techniques with, 88–89
Gaucher's disease, 361, 361*f*–362*f*
 marrow infiltration in, 253, 258*f*
Geyser sign, 23, 24*f*, 433
Giant cell tumor(s), 211–213, 212*f*–213*f*
 in Paget disease, 426
 prevalence, 193
 scintigraphic techniques with, 87, 87*f*
 of tendon sheath, 418
Gigantism, 357
Glenohumeral joint
 anatomy, 15, 48, 49*f*
 arthritis, imaging, surgical perspective, 437–440, 440*f*–441*f*
 biomechanics, 434–435
 capsule, 49*f*, 49–50, 50*f*. *See also* Anterior capsule; Posterior capsule
 developmental dysplasia, 410, 410*f*
 dislocations, 435
  congenital, 149
 embryology, 15
 gas in (vacuum phenomenon), 133,
  134*f*
 instability
  atraumatic, 435
  computed tomography, 40*f*–42*f*, 42–
   43, 435, 436*f*
  evaluation and treatment, algorithm
   for, 436–437, 439*f*
  imaging, surgical perspective, 434–
   437, 435*f*–439*f*

 magnetic resonance imaging, 436,
  437*f*–438*f*
 plain film radiography, 435, 435*f*
 prognosis for, 435
 traumatic, 435
 treatment, 435
 voluntary versus involuntary, 435
 kinematics, 285, 435
 muscles of, 48, 48*t*
 normal planar MR anatomy
  axial plane, 52–54, 53*f*
  oblique coronal plane, 54–56, 55*f*
  oblique sagittal plane, 56*f*, 56–57
 osteoarthritis, 375, 376*f*–378*f*
 plain radiography, technical aspects,
  1–4, 2*f*–6*f*, 6*t*
 stabilizers, 15, 285, 315
 synovial membrane, percutaneous biopsy, 110–112
  complications, 111–112
  indications for, 110–111
  results, 111
  technique, 111, 112*f*
Glenohumeral ligament(s)
 anatomy, 49*f*, 49–50, 50*f*, 286–287,
  287*f*
 anterior inferior, 346
 computed arthrotomography, 139,
  139*f*
 computed tomography, 33, 34*f*–35*f*,
  39–41, 40*f*, 296
 magnetic resonance imaging, 302*f*, 303
  anatomic variations and pitfalls, 61–
   62, 61*f*–62*f*
 normal planar MR anatomy
  axial plane, 52–54, 53*f*
  oblique sagittal plane, 57*f*
 restraint mechanisms, 287–288
Glenoid, 49*f*
 calcification, 436, 436*f*
 changes after hemiarthroplasty, 342
 dentate, 148
 erosion, in arthritis, 439–440, 440*f*–
  441*f*
 hypoplasia, 148, 436, 436*f*
 ossification centers, 144, 148
  plain radiography, 117, 120*f*–121*f*
 plain film radiography, 6*f*
Glenoid and scapular body fracture(s),
  441*f*, 442
Glenoid cavity, plain film radiography,
  3*f*–4*f*
Glenoid fossa, 15, 48–49, 49*f*
 abnormalities, 148, 148*t*
 computed tomography, 39–43
 ring apophysis, 117, 119*f*, 144
 shallow, conditions associated with,
  148, 148*t*
Glenoid labrum, 49*f*, 50. *See also* Capsulolabral complex

abnormalities, 302–303, 303*f*
 in stable shoulder, 308*f*, 308–309
anatomy, 285–286
anterior avulsion, 307*f*
attachments, functional significance, 38*f*, 40*f*–41*f*, 41–42
avulsion, 303, 303*f*
computed arthrotomography, 139, 139*f*
computed tomography, 33, 34*f*–35*f*, 39*f*, 39–43
deficiency, 39, 39*f*
embryology, 15
imaging, with SLAP lesion, 41*f*, 42, 309*t*, 309–310
magnetic resonance imaging, 300–306, 305*f*
 anatomic variations and pitfalls, 60–62, 60*f*–62*f*
 increased signal intensity in normal persons, 62, 62*f*
 undercutting on, 136–138, 137*f*–138*f*
normal, 301–302, 302*f*
normal planar MR anatomy
 axial plane, 52–54, 53*f*
 oblique coronal plane, 54–56, 55*f*
 oblique sagittal plane, 56*f*, 56–57
pseudotears, magnetic resonance imaging, 136–138, 137*f*–139*f*
shapes, magnetic resonance imaging, 137*f*–139*f*, 138
tears, 39, 40*f*–41*f*, 41–42, 297–300, 303*f*, 303, 308–309, 322*f*
 magnetic resonance imaging, 327–328, 328*f*
 MR arthrography, 331*f*, 331–332
 variants simulating, 136–138, 137*f*–139*f*
Glenoid neck fracture, 267, 268*f*
Glenoid rim fracture, 436, 438*f*
 anterior inferior, 267, 268*f*
 posterior, 267, 269*f*
Goldenhar syndrome, 156
Goltz syndrome, 156
Gorham syndrome (massive osteolysis), 166
Gout, 365, 388–389
Gouty arthritis, 388–389
Grafts, scintigraphic techniques with, 80
Gram-negative organisms, septic arthritis caused by, 177
Granulomatous disorder(s), 369–370
Grashey view, 353
 in osseous trauma, 263–264, 267, 268*f*–269*f*, 270, 270*f*, 280*f*, 280–281
Growth recovery lines of Harris, 150

H

Haemophilus influenzae, septic arthritis caused by, 177
Hand-Schüller-Christian disease, 217, 369
Hatchet sign, 384
Head trauma, heterotopic ossification (heterotopic new bone formation) after, 405, 408*f*
Heinig view, of sternoclavicular joint, 9
Hemangioendothelioma, 219, 219*f*
Hemangioma(s), 218–219, 230–231
 capillary, 219, 230
 cavernous, 219, 228, 230
 large-vessel, 230
 magnetic resonance imaging of, 230–231, 231*f*
 scintigraphic techniques with, 86
 skeletal muscle, 230
Hemangiomatosis, neonatal
 benign, 231
 diffuse, 231, 232*f*
Hemangiopericytoma, 220
Hemangiosarcoma, 219, 219*f*
Hematologic disorder(s), 358–361. *See also specific disorder*
Hematoma, subacute, versus lipoma, 229
Hematopoiesis, 241
Hemiarthroplasty, 336–337
 definition, 335
 glenoid changes after, 342
 indications for, 335
 osteolysis after, 441*f*
Hemiplegia, joint capsule abnormalities with, 405–407
Hemochromatosis, 366–367, 367*f*
Hemoglobinopathy, 358–360. *See also specific disorder*
Hemophilia, 359–360, 360*f*
Hemosiderin deposition, in pigmented villonodular synovitis, 418, 419*f*
Hepatic encephalopathy, neuroarthropathy in, 402, 404*f*
Hepatolenticular degeneration, 366
Hereditary multiple osteochondromatosis, 195
Hermodsson tangential projection, 2
Heterotopic ossification (heterotopic new bone formation, myositis ossificans), 405, 407*f*–408*f*, 416–418, 417*f*
 after arthroplasty, 342
 progressive, 405
 spontaneous regression, 405
Hill-Sachs deformity, 26*f*, 27, 346, 436, 437*f*
 with anterior shoulder dislocation, 277

computed tomography, 296, 299*f*
 detection, 293, 295, 297*f*–298*f*, 300–302, 302*f*
 double-contrast arthrography, 28
 instability and, 288–289
 plain film radiography, 2, 4, 26*f*, 27
 ultrasound, 70
Histiocytosis X (Langerhans' cell histiocytosis), 217, 369–370, 370*f*
Hobbs view, of sternoclavicular joint, 8, 9*f*
Hodgkin's disease
 of bone, 215–216
 scintigraphic techniques with, 89
Holt-Oram syndrome, 149, 156–157
Homocystinuria, 364, 364*f*
Human immunodeficiency virus infection, and musculoskeletal infection, 177–178
Humeral head, 48
 absence of, 149, 149*f*
 articular surface, impression or compression fracture, 271–273, 272*f*
 computed tomography, 34*f*, 36
 fracture, 278, 278*f*
  head-splitting, 271, 273*f*
 lytic lesion, biopsy under fluoroscopic guidance, 110, 111*f*
 normal planar MR anatomy, axial plane, 52–54, 53*f*
 ossification centers, 148
 plain radiography, 119, 123*f*
 osteonecrosis, with fractures of proximal humerus, 273
 plain film radiography, 3*f*–6*f*
 ultrasound, 67*f*–68*f*
Humeral notches, 121, 126*f*
Humeral pseudocyst, 119, 124*f*
 on computed tomography, 134, 135*f*
Humeral subluxation, 406–407, 413. *See also Drooping shoulder*
Humeral translation, 434–435
Humerus. *See also Proximal humerus*
 absence of, 149, 149*f*
 anatomic neck of, 48
 anatomy, 268
 anomalies, 149–150
 defects, notches, and foramens, 121, 126*f*
 greater tuberosity, 48
  degenerative changes with impingement, 318
  fracture, 270, 270*f*, 278
  ultrasound of, 70
 fracture-dislocation, 296*f*
 ossification, 148
 plain film radiography, 2*f*
 radiolucency, 119, 124*f*
 growth and development, 148
 growth recovery lines of Harris, 150

Humerus *(Cont.)*
  lesser tuberosity, 48
    ossification, 148
    plain film radiography, 2*f*
  muscle attachments, 49
  normal variants, 148–149
  supratubercular ridge of Meyer, 149
  surgical neck, 49
    fracture, 270, 270*f*
  transverse lines of Park, 150
Humerus varus, 149, 161, 161*f*
Hurler's syndrome, 161–162, 162*f*
  clavicular abnormalities with, 143
Hydraulic distension with steroids and
    motion exercise program, for fro-
    zen shoulder
  results, 107–108
  technique, 107, 107*f*
Hydroxyapatite rheumatism, 391
Hypercorticosteroidism, 357–358, 358*f*
Hyperparathyroidism, 355–356, 356*f*
Hyperphosphatasia, 157, 157*f*
Hyperthyroidism, 357
Hyperuricemia, 388
Hypervitaminosis A, 362–363
Hypophosphatasia, 157–158, 364–365,
    365*f*
  adult, 157–158
  childhood, 157–158
  humeral abnormalities in, 150, 151*f*
  infantile, 157–158
Hypophosphatemia, familial, rickets in,
    355, 355*f*
Hypothyroidism, 356*f*, 356–357

I

I-cell disease, 159–161, 161*f*
Immunodeficiency, and infection, 175
Impingement syndrome, 315–316, 316*f*,
    431
  classification of, 14
  computed tomography in, 37
  fluoroscopic evaluation in, 14, 14*f*
  magnetic resonance imaging, 376,
    381*f*–382*f*
  nonoutlet, 14
  outlet, 14
  plain film radiography, 317
  and rotator cuff pathology, 342–344,
    344*f*, 375–377, 378*f*–382*f*
  stages, 315–316, 375–376, 380*f*
  surgical management, 431
  ultrasound, 66–70, 69*f*
Incisura scapulae, 144
Indium-111 labeled leukocytes
  in evaluation of nonunion, 80
  in osteomyelitis, 82–84

in shoulder infections, 82–84, 182–
    183
  technical aspects, 77
Infantile cortical hyperostosis, 370–371,
    371*f*
Infarction, skeletal
  with hypercorticosteroidism, 357
  with sickle cell anemia, 358, 359*f*
Infection(s), 175–191. *See also specific
    infection*
  arthrography, 181
  aspiration in, 181
  in chronic granulomatous disease,
    370
  clinical features, 177–178
  computed tomography, 179*f*, 181–182,
    182*f*
  conventional tomography, 181
  with hypercorticosteroidism, 358
  imaging evaluation, 178–187
  after joint replacement, 339
  magnetic resonance imaging, 184–
    186, 186*f*
  neuroarthropathy due to, 402
  pathophysiology, 175–177
  plain film radiography, 176*f*, 178–181,
    179*f*–180*f*
  pyogenic, bone, percutaneous biopsy,
    108
  scintigraphy, 180*f*, 182–184
  after shoulder replacement, 187
  sinography, 181
  ultrasonographic diagnosis of, 186–
    187
Inflammatory arthritis, 377–387
Inflammatory bowel disease, 387
Inflammatory site compartment, radio-
    nuclides for, 94–95
Infrascapular bone, 145, 145*f*
Infraspinatus muscle and tendon, 36,
    36*f*, 51, 52*f*
  normal planar MR anatomy
    axial plane, 52–54, 53*f*
    oblique coronal plane, 54–56, 55*f*
    oblique sagittal plane, 56*f*, 56–57
Injection drug use, and infection, 175
Insertion(s), prominent, 121–122, 127*f*–
    128*f*
Instability, 285–313. *See also* Anterior in-
    stability; Dislocation(s); Glenohu-
    meral joint, instability
  anterior, after joint replacement, 340,
    341*f*
  and Bankart lesion, 289
  classification, 290–292
  computed arthrotomography, 296–
    300, 298*t*, 299*f*–301*f*
  computed tomography, 295*f*, 296–300,
    298*f*–299*f*
  degree, 292

direction, 290–291
  etiology, 290
  frequency, 291–292
  functional, 285
  and Hill-Sachs lesion, 288–289
  imaging, principles, 293–306
  inferior, after joint replacement, 340
  after joint replacement, 339–340, 341*f*
  magnetic resonance imaging, 300–
    306, 302*t*, 302*f*–307*f*
  MR arthrography, 305–306, 307*f*
  occult, 307–308
  pathologic changes related to, 288–
    290
  plain film radiography, 291*f*, 293*f*–
    295*f*, 293–295, 296*f*–298*f*
  posterior, after joint replacement,
    340, 341*f*
  repair, 346
    postoperative evaluation, 346–350
  and rotator cuff injury, 289–290
  superior, after joint replacement,
    339–340, 341*f*
  in throwing athletes, 310
Interventional procedures, technical as-
    pects, 103–115
Intraarticular crystal deposition, 391–
    392
Involucrum, 176

J

Jamshidi trephine needle, 109
Joint capsule. *See* Capsule
Joint effusion, in septic arthritis, 185–
    186
Joint replacement, 335–337. *See also*
    Prostheses
  complications of, 339–342
  components
    dissociation, 340
    fracture, 340, 341*f*
    loosening, 341–342, 342*f*–343*f*
  computed tomography after, 338–339
  fracture after, 339, 339*f*–340*f*
  glenoid component, normal appear-
    ances, 338
  heterotopic new bone formation af-
    ter, 342
  humeral component, normal appear-
    ances, 337–338, 338*f*
  imaging after, 337–339
  infection after, 339
  instability after, 339–340
  normal appearances after, 337–338
  postoperative arthrography, 338
  postoperative radiographic examina-
    tion, 337, 337*f*
Juvenile Paget disease (hyperphosphata-
    sia), 157, 157*f*

K

Kaposi's sarcoma, 236
Kayser-Fleischer ring, 366

L

Lanceolate deformity, 142
Langerhans' cell histiocytosis, 217, 369–
370, 370f
Laredo-Bard needle, 109
Lateral clavicular hook, 142–143
syndromes associated with, 143, 143t,
146–147
Latissimus dorsi muscle, 52, 52f
normal planar MR anatomy, oblique
coronal plane, 54–56, 55f
Lazy leukocyte syndrome, 370f
Lead poisoning, 361–362
Leclercq test, 379f
Leiomyoma(s), 228
Letterer-Siwe disease, 217, 369
Leukemia(s)
marrow infiltration in, 253, 253f
scintigraphic techniques with, 89
Leukocyte scanning, in shoulder infections, 182–184
Ligaments. See also Coracoacromial ligament; Coracoclavicular ligament;
Coracohumeral ligament; Glenohumeral ligament(s)
of shoulder joint, 15
Lipoatrophic diabetes, 405, 407f
Lipoblastoma, 229
Lipoblastomatosis, 229
Lipoma(s), 220
computed tomography of, 228, 228f
encapsulated, 228–229
infiltrating muscular, 229, 230f
intracortical, 220
intramuscular, 228, 228f
intraosseous, 220, 220f, 247f–248f
magnetic resonance imaging of, 228–
229, 229f
parosteal, 220
simple, 228f, 228–229, 229f
subcutaneous, 228, 229f
Lipomatosis, 228
Liposarcoma(s)
versus infiltrating intramuscular lipoma, 229
magnetic resonance imaging, 232–
233, 234f
malignant, 232–233, 234f
myxoid, 232
pleomorphic, 232
round cell, 232
well-differentiated, 232
Loose bodies, fluoroscopic evaluation
of, 14, 14f

Looser zones, 354, 354f
Lordotic view, of sternoclavicular joint,
8, 9f
Lung cancer, scintigraphic techniques
with, 88–89, 93f .
Luxatio erecta, 277, 277f, 279, 291, 292f
Lymphedema, scintigraphic techniques
with, 89, 93f
Lymphoma(s)
of bone, 215–216, 216f
marrow infiltration in, 253, 254f
scintigraphic techniques with, 89, 92f
in soft tissue, 236

M

Maffucci syndrome, 162–163
Magic angle effect, 58, 135, 326
Magnetic resonance imaging. See also
MR-arthrography
of acromion process, anatomic variations and pitfalls, 59f, 59–60, 60f
in amyloidosis, 422, 423f
anatomy, 48t, 48–52, 49f–52f
axial plane, 52–54, 53f
normal planar, 52–57, 53f, 55f–57f
oblique coronal plane, 54–56, 55f
oblique sagittal plane, 56–57, 56f–
57f
variations and pitfalls, 57–62
of anterior capsular attachments,
137f–139f, 138–139
of biceps tendon abnormalities, 328
of biceps tendon dislocation, 328
in blue rubber bleb nevus syndrome,
231, 232f
of bone marrow, 244–249, 247f–250f
of Brodie abscess, 185
of capsulolabral complex
anatomic variations and pitfalls, 60–
62, 60f–62f
normal anatomy, axial plane, 52–54,
53f
chemical shift
for marrow assessment, 249
of soft tissue neoplasms, 227
comparison with other modalities,
72–73
contrast-enhanced
dynamic, for posttreatment imaging
after chemotherapy, 221
of soft tissue neoplasms, 227, 236
subtraction, for posttreatment imaging after chemotherapy, 221
conventional spin-echo, 45
of coracoacromial arch, 431, 432f–
433f
fast spin-echo, 45–46
of soft tissue neoplasms, 227

fat-suppression, 46
of fibrous dysplasia, 424f, 425
FLASH (fast low-angle shot) image,
post-chemotherapy evaluation
with, 221
of fluid in biceps tendon sheath, 136,
136f
focal increased signal at critical zone
on, 57f, 57–58, 135, 135f
focal obliteration of subacromial-subdeltoid fat plane, 136, 136f
of glenohumeral joint instability, 436,
437f–438f
of glenohumeral ligaments, 302f,
303
anatomic variations and pitfalls, 61–
62, 61f–62f
of glenoid labrum, 300–306, 305f
anatomic variations and pitfalls, 60–
62, 60f–62f
increased signal intensity in normal
persons, 62, 62f
of glenoid labrum pseudotears, 136–
138, 137f–139f
of glenoid labrum shapes, 137f–139f,
138
of glenoid labrum tears, 327–328,
328f
glenoid labrum undercutting on,
136–138, 137f–138f
gradient-echo, 46
of soft tissue neoplasms, 227
of hemangiomas, 230–231, 231f
imaging planes, 46–47
axial, 46, 47f
anatomy, 52–54, 53f
oblique coronal, 46–47, 47f
anatomy, 54–56, 55f
oblique sagittal, 47, 47f
anatomy, 56–57, 56f–57f
of impingement syndrome, 376, 381f–
382f
of infection, 184–186, 186f
of lipomas, 228–229, 229f
of liposarcomas, 232–233, 234f
in myositis ossificans, 416–418, 417f
in neuroarthropathic joint disease,
402, 405f
in neuromuscular disease, 401
normal variants and artifacts in, 135–
139
in osteomyelitis, 184–186
patient positioning for, 46
of pigmented villonodular synovitis,
397, 397f, 418–420, 419f
postoperative, of acromioplasty, rotator cuff repair, and instability repair, 348–350, 348f–350f
pulse sequences, 45–46
in pyomyositis, 185

Magnetic resonance imaging *(Cont.)*
of rheumatoid arthritis, 439–440
of rotator cuff, 57*f*, 57–59, 58*f*, 325, 326*f*
axial plane, 52–54, 53*f*
of rotator cuff tears, 326–327, 326*f*–327*f*, 376–377, 433, 434*f*
in septic arthritis, 184–186
short-tau inversion recovery (STIR) images
for marrow assessment, 248
in myositis, 402
in shoulder infections, 184
of soft tissue neoplasms, 227
of shoulder instability, 300–306, 302*t*, 302*f*–307*f*
of soft-tissue abscess, 185
of soft tissue injury, 325–328, 326*f*–328*f*
of soft tissue neoplasms, 227–239
coil selection, 227
gadolinium enhancement in, 227, 236
imaging plane, 227
patient positioning, 227
sequence selection, 227
spin-echo
for posttreatment imaging after chemotherapy, 221
of soft tissue neoplasms, 227
of subacromial pseudospur, 135–136, 136*f*
of subacromial-subdeltoid bursa, anatomic variations and pitfalls, 59
of subchondral infarction, 357
of supraspinatus musculotendinous junction, anatomic variations and pitfalls, 57*f*–58*f*, 58–59
of supraspinatus tendon
anatomic variations and pitfalls, 57*f*, 57–59, 58*f*
focal increased signal at critical zone, 135, 135*f*
varied appearances, 135, 135*f*
of synovial chondromatosis, 420, 421*f*
technical aspects, 45–64
technique, 45–48
Maladie de Toulouse-Lautrec (pycnodysostosis), 168
Malformation syndrome(s), lateral clavicular hook with, 143
Malignant fibrous histiocytoma, 234–235, 236*f*
of bone, 210, 211*f*
in Paget disease, 426
Mandibuloacral dysplasia, 158, 158*f*
Mannosidosis, 158, 159*f*
Marble bone disease (osteopetrosis), 166–167
Marfan syndrome, 364

Massive osteolysis, 166
Mastocytosis, 365, 366*f*
marrow infiltration in, 253, 256*f*
Mazabraud syndrome, 424*f*, 425
McCune-Albright syndrome, 209
MED. *See* Multiple epiphyseal dysplasia
Melanoma, scintigraphic techniques with, 89, 92*f*
Melnick-Needles syndrome (osteodysplasty), 165
Meningomyelocele, neuroarthropathy in, 402
Metabolic disorder(s), 353–374
Metaphyseal chondrodysplasia
Jansen type, 158–159, 160*f*
Schmid type, 150, 150*f*
Metaphyseal fibrous defect, 208–209
Metastatic disease, in soft tissue, 236
Metastatic musculoskeletal disease
scintigraphic techniques with, 88–89, 90*f*–93*f*
therapy, 89–90
Metatropic dysplasia, 159, 161*f*
Milwaukee shoulder syndrome, 391–392
percutaneous biopsy of glenohumeral joint in, 110–111, 112*f*
Monosodium urate crystal deposition disease (gouty arthritis), 388–389
Morquio syndrome, 161–162
MR angiography, 230
MR-arthrography, 47–48, 48*f*
of adhesive capsulitis, 394*f*
advantages and disadvantages of, 47
of Bankart lesion, 329–331, 331*f*
contrast techniques, 47, 328–329
gadopentate dimeglumine instillation for, 47–48
image sequence used in, 48
of normal rotator cuff, 328–329
normal variants and artifacts, 139
saline instillation for, 47–48, 305–306, 307*f*
of shoulder instability, 305–306, 307*f*
of soft tissue injury, 328*f*–331*f*, 328–332
of superior labrum tears, 331*f*, 331–332
technique, 19–20
Mucolipidoses, 159–161, 161*f*
Mucopolysaccharidoses, 161–162, 162*f*
clavicular abnormalities with, 143
Mukherjee-Sivaya view, 337, 338*f*
Multicentric reticulohistiocytosis, 398–399
Multiple cartilaginous exostoses, 85, 87*f*, 162, 163*f*
Multiple enchondromatosis, 162–163, 164*f*, 368, 369*f*
Multiple epiphyseal dysplasia, 163–165, 357, 367–368, 368*f*
Multiple myeloma, 214–215, 215*f*

marrow infiltration in, 253, 255*f*
scintigraphic techniques with, 89, 92*f*
Multiple osteocartilaginous exostosis syndrome, 85, 87*f*
Multiple sclerosis, neuroarthropathy in, 402
Muscle abnormalities, with Sprengel deformity, 146
Muscle atrophy, 403–405
with suprascapular nerve entrapment, 413–414, 415*f*
Muscular anatomy, of shoulder, 51–52, 52*f*
Muscular dystrophy, 401, 402*f*
Duchenne, 401, 403–404
fascioscapulohumeral, 401, 402*f*
limb girdle, 401
Musculoskeletal infection, abscess in, percutaneous drainage, 112, 113*f*
Musculoskeletal lesions, percutaneous biopsy, 108–110
anesthesia, 110
hand drill use, 109
hospitalization, 110
indications for, 108
instruments, 110
needles, 108–110
preoperative assessment, 110
radiologic guidance, choice of modality, 108, 109*f*
technique of approach, 110, 111*f*
Myeloid depletion, 249–253, 252*f*
Myeloid metaplasia, 360–361, 361*f*
Myelosclerosis, in myeloid metaplasia, 360, 361*f*
Myositis ossificans, 416–418, 417*f*
magnetic resonance imaging in, 416–418, 417*f*
scintigraphic techniques with, 85
Myositis ossificans progressiva, 405. *See also* Fibrodysplasia ossificans progressiva
Myotonic dystrophy, 401
Myxedema, 356–357
Myxoma, 234, 424*f*, 425

N

Needle aspiration biopsy, 108
Needle aspiration of tendinous calcific deposits, 103–105, 104*f*–105*f*, 106*t*, 106*f*
Needles, bone trephine, 109
Neer II prostheses, 335
Neisseria asteroides infection, in HIV-positive patient, 177
Nerve entrapment syndromes, 408*t*
Nerve injury, with anterior shoulder dislocation, 278

Nerve sheath neoplasms, 231
Neural channel(s), simulating disease, 121, 125f
Neuroarthropathic joint disease, magnetic resonance imaging in, 402, 405f
Neuroarthropathy, 402, 403f–406f
Neurofibroma(s), 228, 231–232
    plexiform, 231–232, 233f
Neurofibromatosis, 231
Neuromuscular disease, 401–411. *See also specific disease*
    magnetic resonance imaging in, 401
Non-Hodgkin's lymphoma
    of bone, 215–216, 216f
    marrow infiltration in, 253, 254f
Nonunion
    atrophic, 80
    reactive, 80
    scintigraphic techniques in, 80, 80f
Noonan syndrome, 165
Nuclear medicine
    mechanism of localization, 75–76
    technical aspects, 75

O

Oblique view, of sternoclavicular joint, 8, 8f
Ochronosis, 363–364, 364f
Oculoauriculovertebral dysplasia (Goldenhar syndrome), 156
Ollier disease (enchondromatosis), 162–163, 164f, 195, 200, 368, 369f
Omovertebral bone, 146f, 146–147
Opportunistic infections, musculoskeletal, 177–178
Os acromiale, 117, 119f, 145, 343–344, 345f, 432, 433f
    versus fracture, 145
Os coracosternale vestigiale, 145
Os infracoracoideum, 145
Os infrascapulare, 145, 145f
Osseous bodies, intracapsular, 14, 14f
Osseous trauma, 263–284. *See also* Dislocation(s); Fracture(s)
    radiographic examination of, 263–264
Ossification centers, 141, 144
    accessory, 144
    persistent, 144
    plain radiography, 117–119
Os subclaviculare, 143
Osteitis fibrosa, 355
Osteoarthritis
    of glenohumeral joint, 375, 376f–378f
        with avascular necrosis, 375, 376f–377f
        posttraumatic, 375, 376f
        primary, 375
        with rotator cuff tear, 375, 377f
    in hemophilia, 360

scintigraphic techniques with, 98f, 98–99
Osteoarthrosis, with sickle cell anemia, 359, 360f
Osteoblastoma, 204–205
    aggressive, 204
    malignant, 204
Osteochondral bodies, 14, 14f
    arthrography of, 26, 26f
    ultrasound of, 71f
Osteochondritis dissecans, 249f
Osteochondrodysplasia(s), congenital, 367–368
Osteochondroma, 194–195, 196f
    prevalence, 193
    scintigraphic techniques with, 85, 87f
Osteochondromatosis
    arthrography, 26, 26f
    primary synovial, 392–393, 395f
    synovial, 420
Osteodysplasty, 165
Osteogenesis imperfecta, 165–166, 166f
    clavicular abnormalities with, 143–144
    lateral clavicular hook with, 143
Osteogenic sarcoma, prevalence, 193
Osteoid osteoma, 203–204, 204f
    nidus removal
        with radiofrequency electrodes, 113
        through bone trephination, 114
    percutaneous removal, under CT guidance, 113–114
        results, 114
        technique, 113–114
    scintigraphic techniques with, 85
Osteolysis
    idiopathic, 166
    massive, 166
    posttraumatic, of distal clavicle, 276, 276f, 415–416, 416f
Osteolytic bone lesion(s), percutaneous biopsy, instruments, 110
Osteomalacia, 354, 354f
Osteomyelitis
    chronic, 177–178
        computed tomography, 182
    clinical features, 177
    computed tomography, 181–182
    due to direct extension, 175–176
    hematogenous, 175
    imaging evaluation, 176f, 178–187, 179f
    magnetic resonance imaging, 184–186
    pathophysiology, 175–177
    periosteal new bone formation in, 176, 176f
    postoperative, 175–176
    scintigraphic techniques with, 81–84, 82f–84f, 95–98, 98f, 182–184
    site of involvement, 176
    staphylococcal, 175–176, 176f

subacute, 177–178
    magnetic resonance imaging, 185
    ultrasonographic diagnosis of, 186–187
Osteonecrosis, 250f, 256, 257f
    with fractures of proximal humerus, 273
    with steroid excess, 357, 358f
Osteopenia, 353–356
    definition, 353
    localized, 353–354
    periarticular, 353–354
Osteopetrosis, 166–167
Osteophyte, subacromial, 316
Osteoporosis, 353–354, 402, 406f
    in infection, 179, 179f–180f
    transient, 402, 406f
Osteosarcoma, 205–208, 205f–208f
    high grade surface, 208
    multicentric (multifocal), 206–207
    in Paget disease, 208, 208f, 426
    parosteal, 206
    periosteal, 198, 205–206, 207f
    radiation-induced, 208, 208f
    scintigraphic techniques with, 87–88, 88f
    small cell, 205
    telangiectatic, 205

P

Paget disease, 371, 371f, 425f, 425–426
    complications, 426
    malignant degeneration, 425f, 426
    osteosarcoma in, 208, 208f, 426
    sarcomatous transformation, 207–208
    scintigraphic techniques with, 87, 88f
Pain, congenital insensitivity to, 368, 369f
    neuroarthropathy in, 402
Pancoast tumor, 407
Pancreatic disorder(s), 387
Pannus, inflammatory, in septic arthritis, 177
Patient positioning
    for magnetic resonance imaging, 46
    radiographic appearances affected by, 122, 129f–131f
Pectoralis major muscle, normal planar MR anatomy, axial plane, 52–54, 53f
Pectoralis minor muscle, 36f
    normal planar MR anatomy, axial plane, 52–54, 53f
Pectus carinatum, 162
Pectus excavatum, 162
Periarthritis calcarea, 391
Periosteal chondroma, 197–198
Periosteal chondrosarcoma, 197–198, 201–202, 203f
Periosteal new bone formation, in osteomyelitis, 176, 176f

Periosteal osteosarcoma, 198, 205–206, 207f
Periostitis
    versus deltoid muscle insertion, 128f
    positioning of arms simulating, 130f
    projections simulating, 131f
Peripheral nerve neoplasms, 231–232, 233f
Peritendinitis, 391
Peritendinitis calcarea, 391
Phlebolith, with hemangioma, 219, 230, 231f
Photopenia, on bone scans, 75
Physeal line, closed (fused), on computed tomography, 135, 135f, 139f
Pigmented villonodular synovitis, 393–398, 396f–397f, 418–420, 419f
    differential diagnosis, 398
    diffuse, 418–420, 419f
    localized, 418–420
    magnetic resonance imaging of, 397, 397f, 418–420, 419f
Pituitary disorder(s), 357–358. See also specific disorder
Plain film radiography
    of acromioclavicular joint, technical aspects, 3f, 4–8, 7f–8f, 8t
    of acromioclavicular joint separation, 7–8, 8f
    of acromion process, 3f–5f
        ossification centers, 117, 118f–119f
    of Bankart lesion, 26f, 27
    of bone marrow, 243
    of clavicle, 6f
        medial end, ossification centers, 119, 123f
    of coracoid process, 3f–6f
        ossification centers, 117, 118f
    of glenohumeral joint, technical aspects, 1–4, 2f–6f, 6t
    of glenohumeral joint instability, 435, 435f
    of glenoid, 6f
        ossification centers, 117, 120f–121f
    of glenoid cavity, 3f–4f
    of greater tuberosity of humerus, 2f
    of Hill-Sachs deformity, 2, 4, 26f, 27
    of humeral head, 3f–6f
        ossification centers, 119, 123f
    in impingement syndrome, 317
    of infections, 176f, 178–181, 179f–180f
    of inferior angle of scapula, ossification centers, 117, 122f
    of lesser tuberosity of humerus, 2f
    normal variants and artifacts on, 117–133
    of ossification centers, 117–119
    overlap on, 122
    postoperative, of acromioplasty, rotator cuff repair, and instability repair, 346, 347f

of primary synovial osteochondromatosis, 395f
    projections, variants, 122, 129f–131f
    in rheumatoid arthritis, 26f, 26–27, 381
    of shoulder instability, 291f, 293f–295f, 293–295, 296f–298f
    of soft tissue injury, 317–319, 318f–319f
    of sternoclavicular joint, technical aspects, 8f, 8–9, 9f
    technical aspects, 1–9
Plasma cell osteomyelitis, of clavicle, 243f
Plasmacytoma
    marrow infiltration in, 253, 255f
    scintigraphic techniques with, 92f
    of shoulder girdle, 246f
Pleural effusion, scintigraphic techniques with, 89, 93f
Plexiform neurofibroma, 231–232, 233f
Pneumoarthropathy, in septic arthritis, 179
POEMS syndrome, 215
Poison(s), 361–363
Poland syndrome, 167
Poliomyelitis, heterotopic ossification (heterotopic new bone formation) in, 405, 407f
Polymyositis, 388, 401
Polyneuropathy, organomegaly, endocrinopathy, M protein, and skin changes (POEMS) syndrome, 215
Positive rim sign, 280
Posterior capsule, 49–50. See also Capsulolabral complex
    computed tomography and arthrography, 33, 34f, 35
    restraint mechanisms, 287–288
Posterior oblique view, 4
Postoperative imaging, 335–352
    ultrasonography in, 70
Posttraumatic osteolysis, of distal clavicle, 276, 276f, 415–416, 416f
Primary synovial osteochondromatosis, 392–393, 395f
Progeria, 167–168
Progressive systemic sclerosis, 388
Prostate cancer
    metastatic, marrow infiltration in, 253, 255f
    scintigraphic techniques with, 88–89, 90f
Prostheses, shoulder
    bipolar, 336, 337f
    constrained, 335–336
    nonconstrained, 335, 336f
    semiconstrained, 335
    types of, 335–337
Proximal humerus
    epiphysis, fractures, 273–274

fracture-dislocation, 271, 272f, 296f
fractures, 268–273, 269f–273f
    classification, 270–271
    complications, 273
    computed tomography, 441f, 442
    displaced, 271
    epiphyseal, 273–274
    four-part, 270–271, 271f–272f
    imaging, surgical perspective, 441f, 441–442
    one-part, 269f, 270, 270f
    osteonecrosis with, 273
    three-part, 270, 271f
    two-part, 270, 270f
    metaphysis
        growth abnormalities, conditions associated with, 150, 151t
        mineralization, 149–150, 150f
        staphylococcal osteomyelitis, 245f
Pseudoarticulations, 122–123, 132f–133f
Pseudocallus, 357
Pseudogout, 389–391
Pseudomonas aeruginosa infection, 175
Pseudosubluxation, 286, 286f, 413
Psoriatic arthritis, 384–386, 387f
Pycnodysostosis, 168
Pyogenic infection(s), bone, percutaneous biopsy, indications for, 108
Pyomyositis
    in HIV-positive patient, 177–178
    magnetic resonance imaging, 185

Q

Quadrilateral space syndrome, 409, 413–415
Quadriplegia, heterotopic ossification (heterotopic new bone formation) in, 405, 407f

R

Rachitic rosary, 158
Radiation necrosis, 363, 363f
    scintigraphic techniques with, 90
Radiolucency, normal areas of, 119, 124f
Radionuclide angiograms, 75
Radionuclides, applications of, 93–95
Reflex sympathetic dystrophy, 402, 406
    scintigraphic techniques with, 80–81, 81f
Reiter syndrome, 386–387
Renal cell carcinoma, scintigraphic techniques with, 89, 91f
Renal failure, chronic, and hemodialysis, amyloidosis with, 422, 423f
Reticular cells, 242
Retinoic acid derivatives, toxicity, 363
Reverse Hill-Sachs lesion, 293, 295f

Rhabdomyosarcoma, 236
Rheumatic disorder(s), 375–400
Rheumatoid arthritis, 377–383
  arthrography, 26f, 26–27, 383
  clinical features, 379
  computed tomography, 383
  epidemiology, 377
  imaging techniques, 381–383
  magnetic resonance imaging, 439–440
  plain film radiography, 26f, 26–27, 381
  radiographic-pathologic correlation, 379–381, 382f–385f
  scintigraphic techniques with, 91, 93, 94f–95f, 95–98, 98f, 383
  ultrasound in, 67, 67f, 381–382
Rheumatoid factor, 377, 380
Rheumatoid variants, 384–387
Rhomboid fossa, 122, 127f, 141, 142f
Rickets, 354–355, 355f
  in familial hypophosphatemia, 355, 355f
  humeral abnormalities in, 150, 151f
  versus hypophosphatasia, 364–365
Riley-Day syndrome, neuroarthropathy in, 402
Rim sign, 293
Ring-MacLean Sump, 112
Rockwood tilt view, 431, 432f, 434. See also Coronal plane anteroposterior 30° caudad tilt view
Rotator cuff, 51
  anatomy, 15
    magnetic resonance imaging, axial plane, 52–54, 53f
  avulsion, computed tomography, 38, 39f
  computed tomography, 34f, 36–39, 36f–39f
  injury
    and impingement syndrome, 342–344, 375–377, 378f–382f
    instability and, 289–290
  magnetic resonance imaging
    anatomic variations and pitfalls, 57f, 57–59, 58f
    focal or generalized increased signal intensity, 57f, 57–59, 58f
    normal anatomy, 325, 326f
    axial plane, 52–54, 53f
  muscles, 315
  normal, MR arthrography, 328, 328f
  pathology
    evaluation and treatment, algorithm for, 434, 434f
    imaging, surgical perspective, 431–434, 432f–434f
    and impingement syndrome, 431. See also Impingement syndrome
  repair, 342–344, 432–434
  postoperative evaluation, 346–350
  techniques, 344–346, 345f
  tear arthropathy, 431
    magnetic resonance imaging, 433, 434f
  tears, 316, 380f, 431
    associated pathology, 431
    complete, 342–343
      arthrography, 22–24, 23f–24f, 433
      computed arthrotomography, 321, 321f
      computed tomography, 36, 37f
        multiplanar reformation, 37f–39f, 38–39
    frequency of, 65
    horizontal, computed tomography, 38, 39f
    imaging
      comparison of modalities, 71–73
      preferred modalities, 65
    magnetic resonance imaging, 326–327, 326f–327f, 376–377, 433
    management, 343–344
    MR arthrography, 329f, 329–331, 330f
    osteoarthritis of glenohumeral joint with, 375, 377f
    partial, 343
      arthrography, 20, 21f, 24–25, 25f
      computed arthrotomography, 37f, 37–38, 38f
      ultrasound, 66–70, 67t, 67f–68f, 323–325, 433
  tendinitis, 431
  tendinous calcium deposits, aspiration, 103–105
    clinical evaluation for, 103
    indications for, 103
    radiologic evaluation for, 103
    results, 105
    selection criteria for, 103
    technique, 103–104, 104f–106f, 106t
  ultrasound, 323–325, 324f
    comparison with other modalities, 71–73
    misinterpretation, 70
    technique, 65–66
Round cell tumors of bone, 213–216. See also Ewing's sarcoma; Lymphoma(s), of bone; Multiple myeloma

S

Salmonella
  infection, in HIV-positive patient, 177
  osteomyelitis caused by, 175
Sarcoma(s). See also Angiosarcoma; Chondrosarcoma; Ewing's sarcoma; Osteosarcoma
  fibrohemosideric, 396
  Kaposi's, 236
  osteogenic, prevalence, 193
  synovial, 228, 236
Scapula
  anomalies, 145–148
  articulations with ribs, 122, 132f
  congenital absence, 148
  congenital undescended. See Sprengel deformity
  defects, notches, and foramens, 121, 126f
  duplication, 147–148
  fractures, 266–268, 266f–269f, 441f, 442
  growth and development, 144
  inferior angle of, ossification centers, plain radiography, 117, 122f
  neoplasms in, 193, 194f
  normal excrescences from, 121, 128f
  normal variants, 144–145
  ossification centers, 117, 122f, 144
  Sprengel deformity, 145–147, 146f
  swallowtail malformation, 144
  vascular or neural channels simulating lesions, 121, 125f
  wing of, radiolucency, 119, 124f
Scapula alta, in Noonan syndrome, 165
Scapular foramens, 121, 126f
Scapular spine, normal planar MR anatomy
  axial plane, 52–54, 53f
  oblique coronal plane, 54–56, 55f
Scapular Y view, 2, 5f, 293, 293f
  in osseous trauma, 263, 267, 267f, 281
  with soft tissue injury, 317
Scapuloiliac dysostosis, 168
Scapulothoracic dissociation, 281–282, 282f
Schwannoma, 231–232
  malignant, 231–232
Scintigraphy. See also Bone scan(s) (scintigraphy)
  with adhesive capsulitis, 95–98, 96f
  with arthritis, 90–99, 94f–98f
  with bladder cancer, 88–89
  with bone cyst, 85, 86f
  bone marrow, 243f, 243–244
  with bone tumors
    benign, 84–87
    primary malignant, 87–88, 88f–89f
  with breast cancer, 88–89, 91f, 93f
  for cellulitis, 82
  with cervical cancer, 88–89
  of cervical spine, 91, 94f
  with condensing osteitis, 86–87
  with diffuse idiopathic skeletal hyperostosis, 98–99
  with enchondroma, 86
  with endometrial cancer, 88–89
  with eosinophilic granuloma, 85

Scintigraphy *(Cont.)*
  with Ewing's sarcoma, 87–88, 89f
  with fibrous dysplasia, 86
  with gastrointestinal tumors, 88–89
  with giant cell tumor, 87, 87f
  with grafts, 80
  with hemangioma, 86
  with Hodgkin's disease, 89
  of infection, 180f, 182–184
  with leukemia, 89
  with lung cancer, 88–89, 93f
  with lymphedema, 89, 93f
  with lymphoma, 89, 92f
  with melanoma, 89, 92f
  with metastatic musculoskeletal dis-
      ease, 88–89, 90f–93f
  with multiple myeloma, 89, 92f
  with myositis ossificans, 85
  with nonossifying fibroma, 85
  in nonunion, 80, 80f
  with osteoarthritis, 98f, 98–99
  with osteochondroma, 85, 87f
  with osteoid osteoma, 85
  with osteomyelitis, 81–84, 82f–84f,
      95–98, 98f, 182–184
  with osteosarcoma, 87–88, 88f
  with Paget disease, 87, 88f
  with pathologic fracture, 85, 86f
  with plasmacytoma, 92f
  with pleural effusion, 89, 93f
  with prostate cancer, 88–89, 90f
  with radiation necrosis, 90
  with reflex sympathetic dystrophy,
      80–81, 81f
  of rheumatoid arthritis, 91, 93, 94f–
      95f, 95–98, 98f, 383
  in septic arthritis, 180f, 183
  with septic arthritis, 95–98, 98f, 180f,
      183
  with synovitis, 95–98, 95f–98f
  with systemic lupus erythematosus,
      91
  technical aspects, 75–102
  thallium-201, serial, for posttreatment
      imaging after chemotherapy,
      220–221
  in trauma, 78–79, 79f
Scleroderma (progressive systemic scle-
    rosis), 388, 401, 403f
Scoliosis, 364
Seizure(s), and posterior shoulder dis-
    location, 280
Septic arthritis, 175
  clinical features, 177
  computed tomography, 182, 182f, 182,
      182f
  imaging evaluation, 178–187, 179f–
      180f
  magnetic resonance imaging, 184–186
  pathophysiology, 177

scintigraphic techniques with, 95–98,
    98f, 180f, 183
  ultrasound in, 69, 69f
Serratia marcescens, in chronic granu-
    lomatous disease, 370
Shoulder dislocation(s), 276–281
  AMBRI syndrome with, 292
  anterior, 270f, 272f, 277–278, 278f,
      290, 294f
  arthrographic evaluation, 27f, 27–28
  axillary, 290, 291f
  chronic, 291–292
  congenital, 149
  fractures with, 294–295
  imaging, 293–295, 293f–295f
  inferior, 277, 277f
  intrathoracic, 290
  positioning of arms simulating, 129f–
      130f
  posterior, 291, 291f, 295f
      subacromial, 291
      subglenoid, 291
      subspinous, 291
  recurrence, 292
  subclavicular, 290
  subcoracoid, 290, 290f
  subglenoid, 290, 291f
  superior, 279, 279f, 291
  TUBS syndrome with, 292
Shoulder girdle, plasmacytoma, 246f
Shoulder-hand syndrome
  bone scanning in, 80–81, 81f
  scintigraphic techniques with, 97f
Shoulder pad sign, 366
Shoulder pain, 413, 426
Shoulder pathology, ultrasonography,
    66–70, 67t, 67f–70f
Shoulder replacement
  indications for, 187
  infection after, 187
Sickle cell disease, 358–359, 359f–360f
  avascular necrosis of humeral head
      in, 252f
  skeletal infarction in, 358, 359f
Single photon emission computed to-
    mography, 75
  technique, 76
Sinography, of infections, 181
SLAP lesion, 42, 309–310, 322, 323f
  arthroscopic classification, 309, 309t
  computed tomography, 41f
Small cell osteosarcoma, 205
Soft tissue
  abscess, 177
      computed tomography, 181–182
      magnetic resonance imaging, 185
  atrophy, 403–405
  foreign bodies in, fluoroscopic evalu-
      ation of, 15
  infection, pathophysiology, 177

injury, 315–334
  anatomical considerations, 285
  arthrography, 319–321, 320f
  computed arthrography (arthro-
      CT), 321–323, 321f–323f
  definition, 315
  functional considerations, 285
  imaging, 316–317
  magnetic resonance imaging, 325–
      328, 326f–328f
  MR arthrography, 328f–331f, 328–
      332
  plain film radiography, 317–319,
      318f–319f
  ultrasonography, 323–325, 324f
neoplasms
  benign, 228–232
      versus malignant, differential di-
          agnosis, 228, 228t
  computed tomography, 227–228
  magnetic resonance imaging
      coil selection, 227
      gadolinium enhancement in, 227,
          236
      imaging plane, 227
      patient positioning, 227
      sequence selection, 227
      technique, 227
  nonneoplastic processes that simu-
      late, 228, 228t
  with nonspecific appearances, 233–
      236
  posttreatment evaluation, 237
      spectroscopy in, 237
  with specific appearances, 228–233
ossification, in fibrodysplasia ossifi-
    cans progressiva, 369, 369f
percutaneous biopsy, instruments,
    110
Spectroscopy
  in myositis, 402
  in posttreatment evaluation of soft tis-
      sue neoplasms, 237
Spinal cord injury, neuroarthropathy in,
    402
Spondylohumerofemoral hypoplasia
    (atelosteogenesis), 150
Sprengel deformity, 145–147, 146f
  lateral clavicular hook with, 146
Stability, mechanisms of, 285–290
Stable shoulder, lateral abnormalities in,
    308–309
Staphylococcus aureus
  in chronic granulomatous disease,
      370
  infection, in HIV-positive patient,
      177
  osteomyelitis caused by, 175
Sternoclavicular joint
  dislocation, 9, 10f, 274f, 274–275

plain radiography, technical aspects, 8f, 8–9, 9f
Sternum, plain film radiography, lateral projection of, 9
Steroid arthropathy, 357
Steroid injection, neuroarthropathy due to, 402
Stress fracture, bone scan with, 79
Stryker notch view, 3–4, 6f
    with glenohumeral instability, 295, 298f, 436, 437f
Subacromial bursa
    calcification, 365, 365f
    embryology, 15
Subacromial pseudospur, magnetic resonance imaging, 135–136, 136f
Subacromial spur(s), 317–318
Subacromial-subdeltoid bursa (space), 36–37, 37f, 50, 51f
    bursitis, ultrasound of, 67, 67f
    fluid in, ultrasound of, 66, 67f, 69f
    hydroxyapatite deposition in, 391, 393f
    magnetic resonance imaging, anatomic variations and pitfalls, 59
Subacromial-subdeltoid fat plane, magnetic resonance imaging, focal obliteration of, 136, 136f
Subdeltoid bursa, 49f
    embryology, 15
    fluid in, ultrasound, 66, 67f
Subdeltoid bursitis, ultrasound, 66–70, 69f–70f
Subdeltoid fat, ultrasound, 65–66, 66f, 69f
Subscapularis bursa, 36–37, 51
    computed tomography and arthrography, 139, 139f
    embryology, 15
Subscapularis muscle, 36, 36f, 49f, 51, 52f
    normal planar MR anatomy
        axial plane, 52–54, 53f
        oblique coronal plane, 54–56, 55f
        oblique sagittal plane, 56f, 56–57
Subscapularis recess, 15, 35f
Subscapularis tendon, 36f, 36, 51
    computed tomography, 34f
    hydroxyapatite deposition in, 391, 393f
    normal planar MR anatomy, oblique sagittal plane, 56f, 56–57
Supraclavicular nerve, middle, canal of, 121, 125f, 141, 142f
Suprapsinatus muscle, 51, 52f
Suprapsinatus tendon, 51
Suprascapular nerve, 51
    anatomy, 409f
    entrapment, 407–409, 408t, 413–415, 415f

Supraspinatus muscle, 36f, 36–37
    normal planar MR anatomy
        axial plane, 52–54, 53f
        oblique coronal plane, 54–56, 55f
        oblique sagittal plane, 56f, 56–57
Supraspinatus musculotendinous junction, magnetic resonance imaging, anatomic variations and pitfalls, 57f–58f, 58–59
Supraspinatus outlet, radiographic evaluation, 431, 432f
Supraspinatus outlet view, 431, 432f, 434
    with soft tissue injury, 317, 318f
Supraspinatus tendon, 36f, 36–37
    hydroxyapatite deposition in, 391, 392f
    magnetic resonance imaging
        anatomic variations and pitfalls, 57f, 57–59, 58f
        focal increased signal at critical zone, 135, 135f
        varied appearances, 135, 135f
    normal planar MR anatomy, oblique sagittal plane, 56f, 56–57
    tear, 380f, 382f
    ultrasound, 65–66, 66f
Supratubercular ridge of Meyer, of humerus, 149
Surgical perspective, in shoulder imaging, 431–443
Swallowtail malformation, of scapula, 144
Synovial chondromatosis, 420–422, 421f
    computed tomography of, 420–422
Synovial osteochondromatosis, 420
Synovial sarcoma, 228, 236
Synovitis, scintigraphic techniques with, 95–98, 95f–98f
Syringomyelia, neuroarthropathy due to, 402, 403f, 405f–406f
Systemic lupus erythematosus, 387–388, 388f
    scintigraphic techniques with, 91
Systemic mastocytosis, marrow infiltration in, 253, 256f

T

Tabes dorsalis, neuroarthropathy in, 402
TAR syndrome. See Thrombocytopenia–absent radius syndrome
Technetium 99m-hydroxyethylidene diphosphonate, 75
Technetium 99m-hydroxymethylene diphosphonate, 75
Technetium 99m-MDP bone scans, in shoulder infections, 182–183
Technetium 99m-methylene diphosphonate, 75

Telangiectatic osteosarcoma, 205
Tendinitis, calcareus, 391
Tendinopathy, 326
Tendinosis, 326
Tenosynovial chondromatosis, 420
Teres major muscle, 36f, 49f, 51, 52f
    normal planar MR anatomy
        oblique coronal plane, 54–56, 55f
        oblique sagittal plane, 56f, 56–57
Teres minor muscle, 36, 36f, 51, 52f
    normal planar MR anatomy, oblique sagittal plane, 56f, 56–57
Teres minor tendon, 36, 36f
Thalassemia, 358, 358f
    with marrow hyperplasia, 251f
Thallium-201 scintigraphy, serial, for posttreatment imaging after chemotherapy, 220–221
Thrombocytopenia–absent radius syndrome, 168f, 168–169
    lateral clavicular hook with, 143
Throwing athletes
    shoulder instability in, 310
    subclinical shoulder subluxations in, 292
Thyroid disorder(s), 356–357
Tomography. See Computed tomography; Conventional tomography
Toxin(s), 361–363
Transverse lines of Park, 150
Trap door fragment, 217
Trapezius muscle, normal planar MR anatomy, oblique coronal plane, 54–56, 55f
Trapezoid line, 141
Trauma. See also Soft tissue, injury
    marrow edema in, 256
    neuroarthropathy due to, 402
    osseous, 263–284. See also Dislocation(s); Fracture(s)
    scintigraphic techniques in, 78–79, 79f
    ultrasound in, 70
Trauma series, 293
Trephine biopsy, 108
Triceps muscle, 52, 52f
    normal planar MR anatomy, oblique sagittal plane, 56f, 56–57
Trisomy 18, 169, 169f
Trough line, 281, 281f, 293, 346
Tru-Cut needle, 109–110
Tuberculosis
    bone, percutaneous biopsy, indications for, 108
    in HIV-positive patient, musculoskeletal manifestations, 178
    musculoskeletal abscess in, percutaneous drainage of, 112–113, 113f
TUBS syndrome, with shoulder dislocations, 292

...moral calcinosis, 372, 372f, 422, 424f
...urner syndrome, 165

U

Ulcerative colitis, 387
Ultrasonography
    in adhesive capsulitis, 69–70
    in arthritis, 67, 67f, 69, 69f
    of biceps tendon (bicipital tendon)
        dislocation, 70
    in bursitis, 66–70, 69f–70f
    with calcifications, 69, 70f
    comparison to other modalities, 71–
        73
    of deltoid muscle, 65–66, 66f–68f
    of fluid
        in subacromial-subdeltoid bursa,
            66, 67f, 69f
        in subdeltoid bursa, 66, 67f
    of fracture of greater tuberosity of
        humerus, 70
    of Hill-Sachs deformity, 70
    of humeral head, 67f–68f
    in impingement syndrome, 66–70, 69f
    of infection, 186–187
    in neuromuscular disease, 401
    of osteochondral bodies, 71f
    in osteomyelitis, 186–187
    of postoperative shoulder, 70
    in rheumatoid arthritis, 67, 67f, 381–
        382
    of rotator cuff, 323–325, 324f
        comparison with other modalities,
            71–73

    misinterpretation, 70
    technique, 65–66
    of rotator cuff tears, 66–70, 67t, 67f–
        68f, 323–325, 433
    in septic arthritis, 69, 69f
    of shoulder pathology, 66–70, 67t,
        67f–70f
    of soft tissue injury, 323–325, 324f
    of subacromial-subdeltoid bursitis, 67,
        67f
    in subdeltoid bursitis, 66–70, 69f–70f
    of subdeltoid fat, 65–66, 66f, 69f
    of supraspinatus tendon, 65–66, 66f
    technical aspects, 65–74
    technique, 65–66
    in trauma, 70

V

Vacuum phenomenon, 133, 134f
van Sonnenberg Sump, 112
Vascular channel(s), simulating disease,
    121, 125f
Vascular compartment, radionuclides
    for, 94–95
Vascular tumor(s), 218–220. *See also* An-
    gioblastoma; Angiosarcoma; He-
    mangioendothelioma; Hemangi-
    oma(s); Hemangiopericytoma;
    Hemangiosarcoma
Videofluoroscopy, 13
Villous arthritis, 396
Vitamin A toxicity, 362–363
Vitamin D deficiency, 354

W

Weight-bearing view(s), 7
West Point view, 1–2, 4f, 4, 5f
    with glenohumeral instability, 295,
        436f, 436
Whipple disease, 387
White blood cell scans, in shoulder in-
    fections, 182–184
Wilson disease (hepatolenticular degen-
    eration), 366
Wormian bones, 367

X

Xanthogranuloma, 396
Xanthoma, 396

Y

Yunis-Varón syndrome, 169

Z

Zanca view, 431, 432f, 434. *See also* Co-
    ronal plane anteroposterior 15° to
    30° cephalic tilt view
Zebra stripe artifacts, on computed to-
    mography, 134, 135f